## The Cambridge Handbook of Successful Aging

Recent studies show that more people than ever before are reaching old age in better health and enjoying that health for a longer time. This *Handbook* outlines the latest discoveries in the study of aging from biomedicine, psychology, and socio-demography. It treats the study of aging as a multidisciplinary scientific subject, since it requires the interplay of broad disciplines, while offering high motivation, positive attitudes, and behaviors for aging well and lifestyle changes that will help people to stay healthier across life span and in old age. Written by leading scholars from various academic disciplines, the chapters delve into the most topical aspects of aging today – including biological mechanisms of aging, aging with health, active and productive aging, aging with satisfaction, aging with respect, and aging with dignity. Aimed at health professionals as well as general readers, the *Cambridge Handbook* offers a new, positive approach to later life.

ROCÍO FERNÁNDEZ-BALLESTEROS is Emeritus Professor in the Department of Psychobiology and Health at the University of Madrid. She has been researching and promoting healthy and active aging since 1980. Throughout her career she has served as a consultant to UNESCO, the United Nations, the World Health Organization, and the European Union.

ATHANASE BENETOS is Professor of Geriatric Medicine and Biology of Aging at the University of Lorraine. He has published more than 360 papers in peer-reviewed international scientific journals and participated in several scientific books. He is the President Elect of the European Geriatric Medicine Society (EUGMS).

JEAN-MARIE ROBINE is the Research Director at INSERM, the French National Institute of Health and Medical Research. He is also a professor at the advanced school École pratique des hautes études (EPHE) in Paris. Since its creation in 1989, he has also been the coordinator of the International Network on Health Expectancy (REVES).

# The Cambridge Handbook of Successful Aging

Edited by

**Rocío Fernández-Ballesteros**
Autonoma University of Madrid

**Athanase Benetos**
Université de Lorraine and Institut national de la santé et de la
recherche médicale (INSERM) Nancy

**Jean-Marie Robine**
INSERM

# CAMBRIDGE
## UNIVERSITY PRESS

University Printing House, Cambridge CB2 8BS, United Kingdom

One Liberty Plaza, 20th Floor, New York, NY 10006, USA

477 Williamstown Road, Port Melbourne, VIC 3207, Australia

314–321, 3rd Floor, Plot 3, Splendor Forum, Jasola District Centre,
New Delhi – 110025, India

79 Anson Road, #06-04/06, Singapore 079906

Cambridge University Press is part of the University of Cambridge.

It furthers the University's mission by disseminating knowledge in the pursuit of
education, learning, and research at the highest international levels of excellence.

www.cambridge.org
Information on this title: www.cambridge.org/9781107162259
DOI: 10.1017/9781316677018

First published 2019

Printed in the United States of America by Sheridan Books, Inc.

*A catalogue record for this publication is available from the British Library.*

*Library of Congress Cataloging-in-Publication Data*
Names: Fernandez Ballesteros, Rocio, editor. | Benetos, Athanase, editor. |
    Robine, Jean-Marie, editor.
Title: The Cambridge handbook of successful aging / edited by Rocio
    Fernandez-Ballesteros, Athanase Benetos, Jean-Marie Robine.
Description: New York, NY : Cambridge University Press, 2018. | Includes
    bibliographical references and index.
Identifiers: LCCN 2018010111 | ISBN 9781107162259 (hardback : alk. paper)
Subjects: | MESH: Healthy Aging | Aging | Geriatrics | Aged
Classification: LCC RA564.8 | NLM WT 104 | DDC 613/.0438—dc23
LC record available at https://lccn.loc.gov/2018010111

ISBN 978-1-107-16225-9 Hardback
ISBN 978-1-316-61474-7 Paperback

# Contents

# Figures

# Tables

# Contributors

TONI C. ANTONUCCI, University of Michigan, USA

LIA ARAÚJO, Center for Health Technologies and Services Research, Portugal

MAGNUS BÄCK, Karolinska University Hospital, Sweden and University of Lorraine, France

JUERGEN M. BAUER, University of Heidelberg, Germany

ATHANASE BENETOS, University of Lorraine and the French National Institute of Health and Medical Research (INSERM), France

KATHERINE E. BERCOVITZ, Harvard University, USA

CHRISTELLE BOULANGER, University of Liège, Belgium

MARÍA DOLORES CALERO, Mind, Brain, and Behavior Research Center, University of Granada, Spain

MARÍAGIOVANNA CAPRARA, National Distance Education University (UNED), Spain

MATTEO CESARI, University of Toulouse, France

SHEUNG-TAK CHENG, Rey Juan Carlos University, Spain

KAARE CHRISTENSEN, University of Southern Denmark, Denmark

ALAN A. COHEN, University of Sherbrooke, Canada

MÓNICA DE LA FUENTE, Complutense University of Madrid, Spain

REBECCA DIEKMANN, Carl von Ossietzky University Oldenburg, Germany

GILLES DUPUIS, University of Sherbrooke, Canada

CLAIRE FALANDRY, University of Lyon, Hospices Civils de Lyon, France

ROCÍO FERNÁNDEZ-BALLESTEROS, Autonoma University of Madrid, Spain

BERTRAND FOUGÈRE, University of Toulouse, France

ALEXANDRA M. FREUND, University of Zurich, Switzerland

TAMÀS FULOP, University of Sherbrooke, Canada

DANIEL GILLAIN, University Hospital of Liège, Belgium

LAURA N. GITLIN, Drexel University, USA

KATSUIKU HIROKAWA, Tokyo Medical and Dental University, Japan

RUTH KATZ, University of Haifa, Israel

KIYOKA KINUGAWA, Sorbonne University, France

ANDREAS KRUSE, University of Heidelberg, Germany

UTE KUNZMANN, University of Leipzig, Germany

ELLEN J. LANGER, Harvard University, USA

ANIS LARBI, Singapore Immunology Network (SIgN), Biopolis, Agency for Science Technology and Research (A*STAR), Singapore

CATHERINE LE GALÈS, Paris Descartes University, France

RUNE LINDAHL-JACOBSEN, University of Southern Denmark, Denmark

ANDRÉS LOSADA, Rey Juan Carlos University, Spain

ARIELA LOWENSTEIN, University of Haifa, Israel

MARÍA DE LA LUZ MARTÍNEZ-MALDONADO, National Autonomous University of Mexico, Mexico

SOPHIE MARIEN, Université catholique de Louvain, Belgium

MARÍA MÁRQUEZ-GONZÁLEZ, Autonoma University of Madrid, Spain

VÍCTOR MANUEL MENDOZA-NÚÑEZ, National Autonomous University of Mexico, Mexico

NEYDA MA. MENDOZA-RUVALCABA, University of Guadalajara CUTONALA, Mexico

MARÍA ÁNGELES MOLINA, Francisco de Vitoria University, Spain

CHRISTELLE NGNOUMEN, Harvard University, USA

JANA NIKITIN, University of Basel, Switzerland

CONSTANÇA PAÚL, University of Porto, Portugal

STANY PERKISAS, University of Antwerp, Belgium

JEAN PETERMANS, University of Liège and University Hospital of Liège, Belgium

MIRKO PETROVIC, Ghent University, Belgium

SÉBASTIEN PICCARD, University of Liège, Belgium

OSCAR RIBEIRO, University of Aveiro and CINTESIS - Center for Health Technology and Services Research, Portugal

JEAN-MARIE ROBINE, French National Institute of Health and Medical Research (INSERM) and École pratique des hautes études (EPHE), France

MARCOS ALONSO RODRÍGUEZ, European University of Madrid, Spain

MICHEL E. SAFAR, Descartes University and APHP, France

MARTA SANTACREU, European University of Madrid, Spain

ERIC SCHMITT, University of Heidelberg, Germany

HAROLD SMULYAN, State University of New York, USA

ANNEMIE SOMERS, Ghent University Hospital, Belgium

ANNE SPINEWINE, Université catholique de Louvain, Belgium

TIMO E. STRANDBERG, University of Helsinki and Helsinki University Hospital, University of Oulu, Finland

SIMON TOUPANCE, French National Institute of Health and Medical Research (INSERM) and University of Lorraine, France

AVIAD TUR-SINAI, Max Stern Yezreel Academic College, Israel

MARGE UNT, Tallinn University, Estonia

MAURITS VANDEWOUDE, University of Antwerp, Belgium

HANS-WERNER WAHL, University of Heidelberg, Germany

ALAN WALKER, University of Sheffield, UK

NOAH J. WEBSTER, University of Michigan, USA

JACEK M. WITKOWSKI, Medical University of Gdansk, Poland

AZGHAR ZAIDI, University of Southampton, UK

# Introduction

Some Traits about This Handbook of Successful Aging

Rocío Fernández-Ballesteros, Jean-Marie Robine, and Athanase Benetos

The study of aging is considered to be a multidisciplinary scientific subject because it involves the concurrence of three broad scientific fields: biomedicine, psychology, and socio-demography (among others). Individual aging is a non-linear process expressed in a given contextual environment, the long process of aging being the product of multiple transactions between the organism, his/her individual behaviors, and environmental conditions. Thus, a problematic issue is that across life, when we study a cross-sectional marker of aging (i.e., age) it is particularly difficult to disentangle the bio-psycho-socio-environmental bases of particular aging condition; in other words, these disciplines are transversal to the life-long process of aging (Baars, 2010).

Furthermore, aging is necessarily subject to influences which are contextually multi-level (e.g., from family to society as a whole) and multi-systemic, that is, expressed from micro (e.g., the cell) to macro level (e.g., the most abstract human expression). In other words, at the individual level it is possible to examine complex behaviors from the cell to the organism, while at a contextual level, we can investigate from the social group to society.

Throughout the history of the three groups of disciplines, aging has been linked to a "deficit paradigm," which sees aging in terms of functional decline, impairment, illness, and loss of social ties and social roles. As described in Chapter 1, recent decades have seen a shift in the study of aging, focusing not only on its dynamic aspects (such as wisdom or resilience), but also emphasizing that throughout the process of aging there is not only decline in some functions, but also growth and improvement in certain others.

This paradigmatic perspective has emerged from scientific results at both micro and macro levels – from the individual to the population. As pointed out by Gould (1977, 1981), although from a genetic perspective human beings do not differ from our Neolithic ancestors, our species has developed the most sophisticated products from art to technology and in communications. Phylogenies developing over millennia are consolidated through ontogenesis; in his/her first years every newborn manages to capitalize on previous human beings' experiences, developing the most sophisticated capacities accumulated over centuries.

This new paradigm, which in lay vocabulary can be called "aging well," has been expressed in different constructs: *healthy*, *successful*, *optimal*, *productive*, and *active* aging. This paradigmatic shift occurred because the history of human development is driven by social and environmental improvements of life conditions, thus giving rise to the title of this handbook. It is interesting to note that the shift to a more positive view of aging concerns all of our disciplines, even if it has taken different routes in our different domains, which will be clearly illustrated in this handbook (e.g., Martin et al., 2015). For instance, aging variability as a key aspect or plasticity as a general characteristic of human beings are investigated by biology, psychology, and social sciences. For similar reasons, demographers are moving from the study of mortality at the population level to the study of the distribution of individual life spans and, at the same time, psychologists are considering both human behaviors and psychological traits as determinants for longevity (Batty et al., 2007).

This handbook deals with this positive approach toward aging and examines and assesses the various ways of aging with some valuable outputs at least for some people and some segments of society: aging with health, aging with well-being, aging with autonomy, and being a respected and valuable social group.

## About This Handbook

### Part I: Biomedical Aspects

This handbook aims to present some of the biomedical concepts and approaches that have shown their interest in aging populations. The biomedical part of this book is composed of 12 chapters, written by international opinion leaders in their scientific domains.

The first three chapters of this part deal with some major biological mechanisms of the aging process: the connection between cellular senescence and age-related diseases (Chapter 4); the relationship between inflamm-aging and immunosenescence (Chapter 5); and the role of telomere dynamics in age-related diseases (Chapter 6) represent mechanistic concepts that have been largely developed these last years. Chapter 7 develops the "Gene-Lifestyle Interactions in Longevity" which is a major issue in the understanding of the respective roles of genetic and environmental factors in the aging process, whereas Chapter 8 deals with a major issue of the successful aging, the plasticity of the brain, and the cognitive functions in older adults. Chapter 9 describes the "arterial stiffness and blood pressure changes" which are typical expressions of the arterial aging and contribute to the development of cardiovascular and non-cardiovascular age-related diseases. Chapter 10 discusses the possibilities for preventing frailty, which has recently become a major aspect of preventive geriatrics; the effects of physical activity (Chapter 11) and of nutrition on cognition (Chapter 12) and on muscle function (Chapter 13) provide documented information about the influence of lifestyle in slowing down the age-related functional alterations and diseases. Chapter 14 deals with the growing thematic of the contribution of gerontechnologies on successful aging. Finally, Chapter 15 develops one of the major medical and public health issues in the older adults: the optimization of drug therapy.

The aim of the biomedical part of this handbook is not the exhaustive coverage of the biomedical aspects of the aging process. Our objective is to show that the aging process and its functional consequences are the result of multiple conditions and mechanisms, and that the actions to increase the probability for successful aging go through a comprehensive assessment and a holistic approach of the older individual.

## Part II: Psychosocial Factors

As has been discussed in Chapter 1 (see Table 1.2), the important components of successful aging, both as *outcomes* and as *predictors* or *determinants*, are behavioral (e.g., activity, lifestyles), psychological (e.g., life satisfaction, socio-emotional selectivity), or psychosocial (e.g., social productivity, optimizing opportunities) conditions. Therefore, this part contains the most relevant of those psychosocial conditions for successful aging. In this section, 14 chapters written by experts from several countries in the world are integrated.

As emphasized at the very beginning of Chapter 2, it is difficult to disentangle the bio-psycho-social dimensions of aging; thus, the first and second chapters of this part deal with the *bio-psycho-social bridge* (Chapter 16) and the psycho-neuroimmune system in successful aging with the adaptive mechanisms of the successful aging process (Chapter 17).

The central chapters of this section deal with the most general behavioral and psychological aspects of successful aging; thus, Chapter 18 deals with behavioral health.

Regarding cognition, Chapter 19 is devoted to environmental enrichment and training across life optimizing and/or compensating cognitive functioning, and, linking cognition and personality, Chapter 20 deals with "Wisdom: The Royal Road to Personality Growth."

Chapters 21–23 are devoted to affect and control as important ingredients of successful aging; thus, Chapter 21 deals with *emotions and successful aging*; Chapter 22 is devoted to the exercise of control, entitled "Personal Control and Successful Aging"; and Chapter 23 exposes the coping mechanisms through successful aging.

Although most of the definitions of successful aging do not take into consideration non-scientific aspects, this has been highly criticized; thus, Chapter 24 is devoted to successful aging, spirituality, and sense of transcendence.

Chapters 25 and 26 are devoted to psychosocial components of successful aging.

Before dealing with more practical and applied matters, it has been considered that the very old is an important issue for successful aging; thus, we are dealing with this subject in Chapter 27.

The final portion of this part is devoted to the promotion of successful aging at the individual level in Chapter 28, promoting active aging through psychosocial *programs* and at the community level in Chapter 29, promoting successful aging in the community.

## Part III: Socio-Demographic Issues

The socio-demographic part of this book is composed of four chapters, also written by international opinion leaders in their domains.

The first three chapters discuss the concept of active and healthy aging. While the concept of "successful aging" is older, more American, and dealing more with individual issues and behaviors, the concept of "active and healthy aging" is more European and more public policy-oriented. Chapter 30 defines and introduces the potential of active aging. In particular, it lists many kinds of barriers preventing active aging that can be removed. Chapter 31 illustrates the key role of the environment to maintain or improve well-being while aging. As listed in Chapter 30, many policies can facilitate active aging, in particular, environmental policies. Chapter 31, introducing the field of environmental gerontology, presents in details the two dimensions of the environment that which can be hardly separated, the physical and the social dimensions. Chapter 32 presents a monitoring framework aiming to support policies that can improve active aging in four domains: employment and labor force participation, voluntary activities, such as caring for others and political participation, living conditions, such as financial security and physical safety, and the capacity for aging well. It is of interest to note that if three domains concern the actual experience of active aging, the fourth domain concerns the coming years through the capacity to actively age.

Finally, Chapter 33 underlines new challenges that "successful aging" and "active aging" are facing as models and shared objectives. These concepts have been largely developed in the 1980s and 1990s in relation to the existing models of health, disability, and quality of life. Since that time, new models have been developed and have gained in social importance. Chapter 33 introduces the concept of capabilities and defines it by comparison with the concepts of International Classification of Functioning (ICF), the concepts of quality of life and the concepts of life satisfaction. Is this approach through capabilities compatible with our approach of successful and active aging?

These chapters, like the handbook as a whole, illustrate the different challenges that models of successful aging have encountered since their first proposal with the accumulation of new knowledge in the different disciplines involved and, to begin, better understanding of the biological mechanisms that accompany the life course, the roles of environmental factors in the broad sense, the new possibilities for responding to and managing the medical problems associated with this same life course, and all the social and psychosocial transformations that have crossed our societies during the last 30 years. No doubt that the future imposes at least as important challenges on these models in the coming decades.

## References

Baars, J. (2010). Philosophy of Aging, Time, and Finitude. T. R. Cole, R. Ray and R. Kastenbaum (Eds.), *A Guide to Humanistic Studies in Aging* (pp. 105–20). Baltimore, MD: Johns Hopkins University Press.

Batty, G. D., Deary, I. J. and Gottfredson, L. S. (2007). Premorbid (early life) IQ and later mortality risk: systematic review. *Ann. Epidemiology* 17, 278–88.

Gould, R. L. (1977). *Ontogeny and Phylogeny*. Cambridge, MA: Harvard University Press.

   (1981). *The Mismeasure of Man*. New York: Norton.

Martin P., Kelly N., Kahana B. et al. (2015). Defining successful aging: a tangible or elusive concept? *The Gerontologist* 55, 14–25.

# 1 The Concept of Successful Aging and Related Terms

Rocío Fernández-Ballesteros

## Antecedents

In the history of human thought there have been two traditions in the study of aging: a positive view arising from Platonic thinking and a negative perspective as a result of an Aristotelian heritage. When, at the beginning of the twentieth century, the multidisciplinary field of gerontology began, the two most important consolidated social theories of aging developed by social gerontologists were "disengagement" and "activity" theories; the former positing that aging is the process of unavoidable separation between individual and society, while the activity theory states that a human being's life is directly related to his/her degree of social interaction and level of activity. Authors agree that during many decades of the century, gerontology, perhaps due to the influence of geriatrics, has been interested more in pathological aging than in other aspects or conditions of aging. As Johnson and Mutchler (2014) emphasize, it was during the final decades of the century when a new *positive gerontology* emerged considering successful aging to be an important key concept in this new vision of aging.

But it must be remembered that these two views or, perhaps better, two sides of aging, have an objective basis, given that aging is a natural lifelong process, associated with illness, which unavoidably terminates with death and dying. Making this process longer and healthier, more positive, optimal, active, or successful could be considered a key issue at individual and population level from a scientific and socio-political perspective.

From a scientific point of view, this new paradigm in gerontology is based on the results from large longitudinal studies on aging, initiated at about the middle of the past century (e.g. Baltimore Longitudinal Study of Aging in United States began in 1958 and Bonn Gerontological Longitudinal Study of Aging started in 1965, initiated by James Birren and Hans Thomae, respectively, two pioneers in the study of aging). These and other studies yielded extremely high variability in the way people aged, showing different profiles in all the multidimensions assessed throughout the process of aging. Based both on this variability and the profiles discovered, the results support John W. Rowe and Robert L. Khan in their seminal paper published in *Science* in 1987, in which they distinguish between pathological aging on the one hand, and normal and

This study was supported by the ICESEN (PSI2014-P) research project of the Spanish Ministry of Economy and Innovation. State Secretary of Science and Innovation.

successful aging as non-pathological states on the other, justifying this classification "with the purpose to counteract the longstanding tendency of gerontology to emphasize only the distinction between the pathologic and non-pathologic, that is, between older people with diseases or disabilities and those suffering from neither" (p. 433). Finally, this view has been empirically supported by the MacArthur Foundation Research Network on Successful Aging.

This view is not only supported by longitudinal studies of aging but also by biomedical, demographic, and epidemiological professionals who share the same positive assumptions. Among them, at the very beginning of positive gerontology we must place James Fries (see Fries, 1980). Based on the evolution of survival curves and their differences by age, the starting point of chronic disease and the plasticity and potential (reserve, Lerner) of human beings, Dr. Fries predicted a society in which "aging well," that is, the active and vital years during a life span would increase, the onset of morbidity would be postponed, and the total amount of lifetime disability would decrease. Very importantly, at the heart of his vision is an emphasis on improvements in preventive medicine and the untapped potential of health promotion and prevention.

Nowadays, Christensen et al. (2009) consider that in those countries with *good practices*, aging has been postponed by ten years and the human life span ceiling is unknown. Thus, along the same lines of other gerontologists, a positive view of aging is also urged.

Finally, given a globally aging society, it must be remembered that the most important threat is not aging *per se* but rather what it represents at societal and at individual levels because pathological aging is highly expensive to society and/or to individuals, and because of the stereotypical over-generalizations of pathological aging. Thus, the promotion of successful aging is without doubt the most important public policy because, at the same time, it is one of the ways of preventing pathological aging and disability.

## The Meaning of Successful Aging

From a semantic point of view, the word "successful" is an adjective with a variety of following synonyms in *Webster's Thesaurus and Dictionary* (1990): prosperous, fortunate, lucky, victorious, triumphant, auspicious, happy, unbeaten, favorable, strong, propitious, advantageous, encouraging, contented, satisfied, thriving, flourishing, and wealthy, among others. But, as Baltes and Carstensen (1996) have emphasized, any utilitarian conceptualization of success refers to favorable attainments without considering the process of reaching these positive outcomes, which depend on the individual's efforts in, and therefore on his/her behavior and actions. Thus, success refers to the attainment of personal goals of all types, ranging from the maintenance of physical functioning and good health to other psychosocial outcomes (p. 400). In sum, "successful" could be considered a cross-culturally and highly positive value. But the first issue to consider is that this positive adjective is attributed to the word "aging."

From a grammatical point of view, aging is the *gerund* of the verb *age*, referring to the human/life process bringing stability and change, growth and decline across a life span (e.g., Baltes, 1987). Moreover, aging is also considered as a *noun*, the external signs of aging as a process of change in the properties of material occurring over a period of time, either spontaneously or deliberately. Finally, aging is also an *adjective*, describing the process of growing old, with broadly negative synonyms such as decrepit, tired, fossilized, broken-down, debilitated, enfeebled, and exhausted, among others (see *Merriam-Webster's Thesaurus and Dictionary*). In sum, although the process of aging (as verb or noun) is scientifically tested as a process with broad inter-individual variability yielding heterogeneous trajectories, aging has a mainly negative meaning. If "successful" is interpreted as "no aging," then "successful aging" could be considered an oxymoron.

An oxymoron is a rhetorical device that paradoxical or contradictory adjacent words, in our case juxtaposing positive (successful) and negative (aging) terms (Torres & Hammarstrom, 2009). The concept "successful aging" involves a noun (that is the process of aging) and an adjective (successful); Baltes and Carstensen (1996: p. 400) alluded to the fact that "some critics argue that successful aging is an oxymoron only when 'successful aging' means not aging at all ... however a conceptualization of successful aging founded on denial is ultimately an untenable position." This argument implies that aging is radically negative, but this is not in agreement with data from two different perspectives: (1) the process of aging can carry positive outcomes such as a lower frequency of negative affect, higher affect balance, global understanding, etc., and (2) when research considers not only negative but also positive stereotypes, older adults can be characterized with positive labels (such as "friendly"). Therefore, in our opinion, the juxtaposition of successful-positive and aging-negative is a *subtle* one because aging implies both growth and decline throughout a life span. Thus, both negative and positive events are associated with aging to a greater or lesser probability; similarly, when considering cultural views and stereotypes, aging has not have a totally negative connotation when not only negative views but also positive evaluative images are introduced. In sum, successful aging could be considered only a *subtle oxymoron*.

## Semantic Network of Successful Aging

Successful aging belongs to a set of conceptual labels that emerged during the last decades of the twentieth century characterizing the so-called new paradigm in gerontology: successful, healthy, optimal, active, productive are positive labels characterizing "aging well" as a common or pop verbal expression.

Table 1.1 shows the evolution (1996–2015) of these labels in three scientific databases (MEDLINE, PsycINFO, and SocioFile) by searching in keywords and abstracts. The evolution over 20 years has been exponential, with the exception of "optimal aging." The most-used term is "healthy aging" followed by "successful aging."

Table 1.1 *Successful aging and related terms in scientific databases (1996–2015)*

| MEDLINE, PsycINFO, SocioFile | 1996–2000 | 2001–5 | 2006–10 | 2011–15 | Total |
|---|---|---|---|---|---|
| **Successful** | 110 | 260 | 466 | 611 | 1,447 |
| **Active** | 12 | 34 | 86 | 207 | 339 |
| **Healthy** | 81 | 268 | 708 | 1,466 | 2,523 |
| **Optimal** | 10 | 12 | 29 | 57 | 108 |
| **Productive** | 6 | 12 | 37 | 60 | 115 |
| **Total** | 219 | 586 | 1,326 | 2,401 | 4,532 |

The first consideration must be whether the term is developed from a *population* or an *individual* perspective; for example, "active aging" emerged from the World Health Organization (WHO, 2002) attempts to overcome "healthy aging" as a population term (see Table 1.3). It is defined as a process that includes outcomes such as "health" and "participation," as well as determinants of active aging such as "security." This mixture of dependent and independent variables in the definition of a concept seems to be rooted in the purpose of such a definition, that is, the promotion of policies at a population level. Conversely, from an individual perspective, "successful aging" is defined through three domain outcomes (health and functionality, physical and cognitive competence, and life involvement; see Table 1.3), and it has been criticized because it does not consider intersecting social issues (Katz & Calasanti, 2016).

Moreover, the second relevant factor focuses on the *multidimensionality* of the components included. Carver and Buchanan (2016) examine in *Ovid Medline* to what extent successful aging articles are reduced to non-biomedical components. In this search they rejected 37 (48 percent), which, although dealing with successful aging, they exclusively refer to phenotype/genotype, physiological process, a particular disease, or a single component. This is in line with the core contents of the European Innovation Partnership of Active and Healthy Aging (EIP AHA) set up by the European Union.[1] All action groups are devoted to biomedical conditions and the key concept is not active aging, but frailty. Finally, WHO defined the key term "active aging" in 2002, transformed it 13 years later into "healthy aging" (Table 1.3), and reduced it to *biomedical components* (see Table 1.2; WHO, 2015; Fernández-Ballesteros, 2017).

The third issue refers to whether these terms are synonymous. Martin et al. (2015) tried to establish an *equivalence* between "successful aging" and others such as "healthy aging," "active aging," or "productive aging" – all of which are technical terms integrating bio-psycho-social domains, while trying to specify with technical/scientific terms the simple and pop concept of *aging well*.

---

1 See https://ec.europa.eu/eip/ageing/home_en

Table 1.2 *Summary of successful aging (and related terms) outcomes and predictors or determinants (modified from Fernández-Ballesteros, 2008)*

| Component | Outcomes | Predictors or determinants |
|---|---|---|
| **Biomedical** | ✔ Longevity<br>✔ Biological health<br>✔ Cardiovascular and pulmonary functioning<br>✔ Mental health<br>✔ Functional abilities<br>✔ Physical strength<br>✔ Vital capacity<br>✔ Absence of disability<br>✔ Autonomy | ✔ Long-life ancestors<br>✔ Maximizing health across life span<br>✔ Socioeconomic conditions<br>✔ Social/health services<br>✔ Environmental conditions |
| **Psychological** | ✔ Subjective health<br>✔ Activity<br>✔ Competence (motor and cognitive)<br>✔ Mental and physical positive functioning<br>✔ Life and social engagement<br>✔ Behave according to own values and beliefs<br>✔ Coping<br>✔ Purpose in life<br>✔ Personal growth<br>✔ Psychological well-being<br>✔ Life satisfaction<br>✔ Perceived quality of life<br>✔ Adaptation capabilities<br>✔ Mature defense mechanism<br>✔ Family relationships<br>✔ Affective states<br>✔ Meaning in life<br>✔ Maintenance of valued activities and relationships | ✔ Selective Optimization with Compensation (SOC)<br>✔ Development and maintenance of primary control<br>✔ Socio-emotional selectivity<br>✔ Adaptive process developing capacities for solving difficulties and minimizing the effects of deficits<br>✔ Coping strategies across life cycle<br>✔ Behavioral lifestyles |
| **Social** | ✔ Social productivity<br>✔ Social networks<br>✔ Material security<br>✔ Environmental mastery | ✔ Optimizing opportunities for security<br>✔ Education |

Table 1.3 *Technical definitions of successful aging and related terms (modified and updated from Fernández-Ballesteros, 2008)*

Neugarten (1972): antecedent of a positive view of aging as multidimensional, considering *personality* as a central determinant for aging well.

Riff (1982, *successful aging*): feeling well based in positive or ideal functioning related to developmental work over the life course.

Guralnik and Kaplan (1989, *healthy aging*): low chronic disease, high level of physical functioning.

Rowe and Khan (1987, 1997, *successful aging*): "low probability of disease and (disease related) disability, high physical and mental functioning, and active engagement with life."

Fries (1989, *aging well*): "independence, healthy lifestyles, to be active, to be enthusiastic, to have a good image of one's self, and to be individual."

Baltes and Baltes (1990, *successful aging*): "length of life, biological health, mental health, cognitive efficacy, social competence and productivity, personal control, and life satisfaction." Perhaps most important has been the Baltes and Baltes's process theory of promoting gains and preventing losses through Selective Optimization with Compensation (SOC). Empirical evidence supports SOC as a theory of successful aging (see: Freund and Baltes, 2007).

Vaillant and Vaillant (1990, *successful aging*): "physical health, mental health, and life satisfaction."

Baltes and Carstensen (1996, *successful aging*): "life satisfaction and subjective well-being, perceived social support, and involvement in life; physical health, functional abilities, and lifestyle; bio-physical conditions, such as strength or vital capacity; and social conditions, such as social network or education."

O'Really and Caro (1995, *productive aging*): "describes an array of activities through which older people contribute to society ... the extent of current productive activities among older people and the barriers to more extensive productive activity."

Schulz and Heckhausen (1996, *successful aging*): "Cardiovascular and pulmonary functioning, absence of disability, cognitive and intellectual performance, primary control and achievements in physical and artistic domains."

Yoon (1996, *successful aging*): physical health, personal income and financial stability, family dynamics and cohesiveness; social support networks, meaning of life, optimal cognitive functioning, personal control, prevention for depression; coping strategies, mastery bereavement, self-justification mechanism of negative life outcomes.

Reed et al. (1998, *healthy aging*): surviving late life free of major life-threatening illness and maintaining physical and mental ability.

WHO (2002, *active aging*): "The process of optimizing opportunities for health, participation, and security in order to enhance well-being and quality of life as people age ..."

(*cont.*)

Table 1.3 (*cont.*)

Haveman-Nies et al. (2003, *healthy aging*): "… Maintenance of health at old age (being alive and remaining independent)."

Fernández-Ballesteros and others (2008, 2013, *active aging*, *aging well*): "the life course adaptation process for arriving to an optimal functioning and health, psychological (optimal physical and cognitive functioning and emotional-motivational regulation) and social participation in old age … four domains are included for this way of aging: health maintenance and ADL preservation, physical and cognitive fitness, positive affect and control, and social participation and engagement."

WHO (2015, *healthy aging*): "the process of developing and maintaining the functional ability … [which] comprises the health related attributes that enable people to be and to do what they have reason to value" (p. 41).

ILC (2015, *active aging*): "the process of optimizing opportunities for health, life-long learning, participation, and security to enhance quality of life as people age."

The fourth and final issue, already mentioned earlier, is related to the type of conceptualization involved; thus, most definitions involved *outcomes*, in other words, the operational definition of the term proposed (e.g., physical and/or mental health, functionality, satisfaction or well-being, participation); some posit determinants or predictors of these outcomes (physical exercise, diet, etc.), while others consider the *process* across a life span promoting aging well, such as the Baltes and Baltes's (1990) theoretical development of "Selective Optimization with Compensation," which posited these mechanisms as avenues for achieving successful aging. This confusion can be checked by comparing Tables 1.2 and 1.3.

In order to examine the extent of equivalence between successful aging and the others, let us review several sources of information:

(1) The outcomes and predictors arising from cross-sectional and longitudinal studies in this field
(2) Conceptual definitions proposed by authors dealing with aging well, that is, successful aging and related terms
(3) The construction of the meaning of those terms
(4) Testing hypotheses about the semantic network of aging well through Structural Equation Modeling (SEM) with data from two different studies and several data sources.

## Most Frequent Outcomes and Predictors/Determinants Used in Cross-Sectional and Longitudinal Studies in the Field

Peel et al. (2005) and Depp and Jeste (2006) reviewed most of the cross-sectional and longitudinal studies involving successful and related terms by searching for the outcomes specified and the predictors or determinants posited.

Table 1.2 shows these outcomes classified by the bio-psycho-social components taken into consideration in these studies as well as their assumed predictors or determinants.

In sum, there is a high degree of heterogeneity in the bio-psycho-social domains introduced in the studies reviewed by Peel et al. (2005) and Depp and Jeste (2006), the majority being psychological components. Nevertheless, it must be emphasized that the complexity or simplicity of these classifying factors is also diverse and it cannot be concluded that psychology is the most important component for successful aging. Yet, it is highly important that there is a clear distinction between outcomes and predictors/determinants, which are much more evident in research with dependent and independent variables which will not be the case, as we will see, in authors' definitions.

## Conceptual Definitions of Successful Aging and Related Terms Proposed by Authors

Table 1.3 shows the most well-known authors' updated definitions of aging well, such as successful, healthy, active, and productive aging as defined by the authors (most of them reviewed by Fernández-Ballesteros, 2008). Each definition is composed of one or more criteria, which can be classified following a set of domains.

A classification of target terms (successful, healthy, active, or productive aging) by criteria (coded 19) is present in each definition. A summary of this analysis is the following: (1) healthy aging (4 definitions) is consistently defined by two criteria: health/illness and functionality; successful aging (7 definitions) is defined from 4 to 11 criteria; active aging (3 definitions) is defined by 3 to 8 criteria; and finally, productive aging (1 definition) is defined by 3 criteria. (2) These 19 criteria were classified into 4 domains: *Health (or Illness) and Functionality*, *Physical and Cognitive Functioning*, *Positive Affect* (e.g., life satisfaction) *and Control* (e.g., self-control, coping with stress), and *Participation and Engagement* (e.g., social support network). Only two criteria were not classified in any of these four domains.

In sum, almost all criteria used by the authors who defined our target terms about aging well seem to be embedded in these four domains.

## Common Problematic Issues

Taking into consideration definitions emerging from both research studies and theory-based arguments provided by authors, we can outline the most common flaws and problematic issues found.

(1) First of all, mention must be made of the *criticisms* received by *successful aging*, as conceptualized by Rowe and Khan (2015). Martinson and Berrig-de (2015) analyzed and synthesized the range of critiques received through a systematic review of journal article abstracts published on 1987–2013 in

*Social Gerontology* (*n* = 453); only 67 met the criteria of presenting a critique of successful aging models as a key component of the article. Authors classified these critiques into four categories: (1) The *Add and Stir* suggested an expansion of successful aging criteria; (2) The *Missing Voices* category advocated adding older adults' subjective meanings of successful aging to established objective measures; (3) The *Hard Hitting* critiques call for an embrace of diversity, avoiding stigma and discrimination, and intervene at structural contexts of aging; and (4) The *New Frames and Names* classifies alternative ideal models, often grounded in Eastern philosophies. In sum, authors concluded that since successful aging is a normative model and by definition exclusionary, greater reflexivity about the use of "successful aging" and other normative models is suggested.

(2) The second issue refers to the position of Martin et al. (2015) regarding the lack of *equivalence* between "successful aging" and other terms such as "healthy aging," "active aging," or "productive aging." If we examine Table 1.3 carefully, successful aging and active aging can be differentiated clearly from healthy and productive aging. Thus, *successful aging* and *active aging* both contain multiple dimensions (Rowe & Khan, 1997, 1998; WHO, 2002) but definitions regarding *healthy aging* usually refer only to health and functionality (Guralnik & Kaplan, 1989; Haveman-Nies et al., 2003; Reed et al., 1998; WHO, 2015). Similarly, *productive aging* mainly emphasizes economic productivity. Therefore, it can be stated that multidimensionality is the only characteristic for successful and active aging. Next section describes our evaluation based on SEM of a semantic network positing the non-equivalence of the definitions reviewed here, but considers an overlap among domains, at least for successful and active aging conceptualizations (see also Figure 1.2).

(3) Another differential characteristic in the definitions of successful aging refers to the *nature of the domains*. Some authors include objective conditions such as physical health and physical performance, cognitive fitness, and social participation (e.g., Rowe & Khan, 1997, 1998), while others only take into consideration subjective conditions such as life satisfaction, positive affects, and coping with stress (e.g., Baltes & Carstensen, 1996; Riff, 1982; Vaillant & Vaillant, 1990). As Pruchno et al. (2010) and Fernández-Ballesteros (2011) emphasized and claimed after performing empirical research, successful aging must be considered as a multidimensional construct having both objective and subjective dimensions, providing greater clarity, helping in the development of promotion programs, and taking into consideration more reliable prevalence.

(4) The final problematic issue regarding definitions of successful aging and related terms emerges from the *confusion about dependent* (outcomes) and *independent* (predictors or determinants) components. One of the first critiques of Rowe and Khan's "successful aging" concept came from Riley et al. (1998: p. 151) stating: "We believe that their model remains seriously incomplete: Although it elaborates the potentials for individual success, it

fails to develop adequately the social structural opportunities necessary for realizing success." This is a confusion between *outcomes* (*individual success*), or *dependent variables*, and what Rowe and Khan termed as, "*social structure opportunities*," which are *independent variables*. Of course, any type of aging is dependent on the interactions between a person's behaviors and psychological characteristics in the social context over a life span, along the lines of Bandura's socio-cognitive theory. But if a type of aging is going to be described, the observable conditions in the individual are the way *to operationalize* it. In fact, when *active aging* is defined by "*health, participation, and security*," *while health* and *participation* are *outcomes* of *active aging*, then security is an external social condition and must therefore be considered an environmental and independent variable for active aging.

In sum, beyond the criticisms received by Rowe and Khan's definition published in *The Gerontologists Special Issue* (2015), any study supporting a definition related with aging well, in order to fulfill certain standards, should meet three essential conditions: be multidimensional, be assessed multi-domain/multi-method, and take into consideration both objectives and subjective conditions.

## Testing This Semantic Network

Two strategies have been used in order to test the semantic network of aging well: the review of literature based on the ATLAS.ti and a Confirmatory Factor Analysis through SEM on the basis of two distinct databases from two cross-sectional studies.

## Construction of the Meaning of Successful Aging and Related Terms

Fernández-Mayoralas et al. (2014) developed a study through ATLAS.ti, which is a sophisticated tool to arrange, reassemble, and manage written or verbal materials in systematic ways. The authors conducted a systematic search for "active, healthy, productive, successful ageing/aging, older adults/elderly" in the following databases: (a) English databases: PubMed, WOK, Scopus, Sociological Abstracts, and PsycINFO (1/1/1997 to 6/30/2012); (b) Spanish databases (from Spain and Latin America): Portal, "Mayores/Envejecimiento," Scielo, Clacso, Redalyc, Cepal, Latindex, and Dialnet (1982–2012). In both cases, the search referred to: title, summary, keywords, and qualitative analysis; (c) 1,436 references were managed through the EndNote (v5) program limited to book, edited book, book chapter, journal article, reports, and theses.

Figure 1.1 shows the word clouds yielded by ATLAS.ti, where the following can be found: (a) the most-used terms defining the population group (older, adults, elderly, etc.) as well as the process (aging, ageing) and (b) in any type of analysis, there are interactions among the four constructs examined (successful, active, healthy, productive).

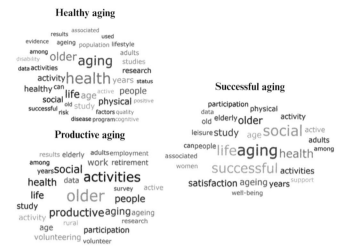

**Figure 1.1.** *Word clouds yielded by ATLAS.ti for active, healthy, productive, and successful aging*

## Testing Hypotheses about the Semantic Network of Aging Well through SEM with Data from Two Different Studies

Fernández-Ballesteros et al. (2013) used SEM to analyze the model of four domains of aging well through two studies with different samples (self-report data about the implicit concept of "aging well" from several cultures on four continents) and a diversity of multi-content, multi-methods (subjective and objective) administered in a cross-sectional study with a sample of older Spaniards. The hypothesis is that this set of verbal levels regarding aging well supports the existence of a semantic network in which there is no equivalence between verbal levels but an overlap among domains included, at least for the successful and active aging concepts.

Thus, after a review of the more extended definitions of aging well shown in Table 1.3 (such as healthy, successful, active, and productive aging well) the *four-domains model* (see Fernandez-Ballesteros, 2008) is shown in Figure 1.2: health and functioning, physical and cognitive competences, positive affect and control, and social participation and engagement. Aging well, as the common and pop term, is embedded in a semantic network of a set of *technical terms* used as modifiers of "aging" (such as *healthy, successful, active, productive*), sharing a cross-culturally positive value but positing that not all the technical terms are equivalent.

Figure 1.2 shows not only the four domains but also the four technical concepts implied. As can be observed, *healthy aging* is defined by only one domain: health and functionality, while *successful aging* is defined by the four domains, if the definition by Baltes and Baltes or Baltes and Carstensen are considered, or only three domains using Rowe and Khan's definition (health and functioning, physical and cognitive competences, and social participation and engagement) but not including positive affect and control. *Active aging* as defined by WHO (2001) considers three domains (health, positive affect, and participation)

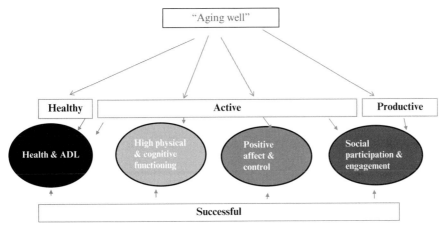

**Figure 1.2.** *Four domains model of aging well*
Modified from Fernandez-Ballesteros (2008) and Fernandez-Ballesteros et al. (2013)

because it does not include physical and cognitive functioning, and finally, *productive aging* refers only to one domain, that is social participation and engagement.

This four-factor model was our theoretical basic model and was tested through Confirmatory Factor Analysis. Thus, SEM was performed with LISREL 8.8 (Jöreskog & Sorbom, 2006) using unweighted least squares (ULS) estimation and polychoric correlations because of the ordinal nature of our data. Base data from two studies were examined:

(1) *Lay concept study* (Fernández-Ballesteros et al., 2008): The research question in this study was: "What are the central characteristics of aging well across older adults, across ages, and across cultures?" The 20-item Questionnaire "Your Ideas About Growing Older" developed by Phelan et al. (2004), was administered to a sample of US Caucasians ($N = 2,581$) and Japanese ($N = 1,985$) citizens, and also by Matsubayashi et al. (2006) in Japan ($N = 5,207$). It was then administered ($N = 1,189$ individuals; 58 percent women; mean age = 68, range = 50–100) across seven Latin American countries (Brazil, Chile, Colombia, Cuba, Ecuador, Mexico, and Uruguay) and three European countries (Greece, Portugal, and Spain). Minor differences were found among countries and among ages. In sum, 75 percent of each sample considered that the most important conditions for aging well were the following: *remaining in good health until death, feeling satisfied with life, having friends and family, adjusting to changes related to aging, being able to take care of oneself,* and *remaining free of chronic diseases (including mental).* Thus, the four-domain model seems to be supported for older lay persons for aging well.

(2) We tested the four-factor model using the same procedure, with the ELEA (Estudio Longitudinal sobre Envejecimiento Activo) database, a multi-methods, multi-contents, multi-nature protocol containing 412 objective

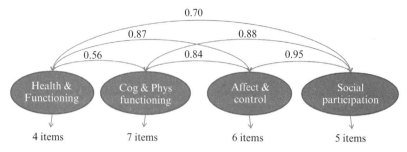

RMSEA = 0.095; TLI = 1.01; SRMR = 0.072; Chi-square = 2243.91, gl = 203, $p < 0.005$; AIC = 2343.91

(a)

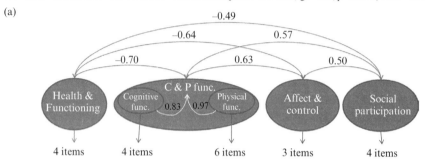

(b)    RMSEA = 0.058; SRMR = 0.086; Chi-Square = 459.65, df = 182, $P$-value = 0.00000

**Figure 1.3.** *Structural Equations Modeling of four-domain model of aging well: (a) from lay conceptualizations (N = 1,189) and (b) from ELEA PROJECT multi-method data base (N = 458)*
Fernandez-Ballesteros et al., 2013

and subjective variables assessing 23 bio-psycho-social domains through multi-methods based on the EXCELSA study and protocol involving seven European countries (Fernández-Ballesteros et al., 2004, 2011; Fernández-Ballesteros, 2011). Thus, our theoretical model was tested through the ELEA Spanish sample: $N = 458$ participants: 63.8 percent women; mean age = 66.47; range = 55–75.

Figure 1.3 shows graphical representations corresponding to both Study 1 and Study 2 of our four-domain model of aging well and the mathematical fit of this model testing the multidimensionality of successful and active aging across the lay concepts of people from three continents and considering multi-method/multi-contents study of successful aging. Also, at the same time, it can be emphasized that taking into consideration only health and functionality (such in the last definition of WHO, 2015) without social participation could be considered a reduction of aging well.

Regarding successful aging, our testing model considers Health and Functionality, Physical and Cognitive Fitness, and Social Participation and Engagement but introduces a fourth domain not included by Rowe and Khan in their proposal: affect and control comprising positive mood, life satisfaction, life control, and self-efficacy for aging.

Our analysis testing the semantic network through a four-domain model supports the construct validity of the separated domains involving a variety of criteria present in some of the definitions of *healthy, successful, active*, or *productive aging*. The first domain loaded by health and functionality, also tests a separate domain of *healthy aging* as defined by Guralnik and Kaplan (1989), Yoon (1996), Reed et al. (1998), and WHO (2015). With respect to successful aging definitions, these were confirmed by Baltes and Baltes (1990) and Baltes and Carstensen (1996), as well as by the three domains present in Rowe and Khan (1987, 1997). Along the same lines, our results confirm the four-domain model of *active aging* (Fernández-Ballesteros, 2002, 2008), but with only two components of the original definition proposed by WHO (2002), health and participation. Nevertheless, as a limitation to our study, it should be emphasized that several criteria present in some of the reviewed definitions, such as security or spirituality, were not assessed in either of the two studies introduced in the SEM, and could therefore not be tested.

## Conclusions

First of all, it can be concluded that healthy aging is not an equivalent concept to successful, active, or even productive aging. While *healthy aging* is not a multidisciplinary concept – it seems to be reduced to biomedical aspects – both *successful* and *active* aging concepts are multidimensional, including also, health and functionality. Nevertheless, it must be emphasized that, although there is high consensus in the definition of healthy aging, this consensus is in opposition to the multidisciplinary definition of health emerging from the WHO Constitution: "state of complete physical, mental, and social well-being and not merely the absence of disease or infirmity."

Second, although there is little consensus about what successful aging is, all definitions show a variety of components which can be classified in four domains: health and functionality, physical and cognitive fitness, positive affect and control, and social participation and engagement. These four domains have been confirmed through SEM.

Third, *active aging* (WHO, 2002) is the most recent construct, and is losing relevance since WHO (2015) is returning to *healthy aging*, and the political network developed by the European Union is moving to other biomedical concepts such as frailty. And, finally, the presence of *productive aging* is merely testimonial in this field.

In sum, returning to the antecedents of positive gerontology, successful aging seems to be a technical term fulfilling the objectives described by Rowe and Khan in 1987, by Fries in 1980, or by WHO in 2002. This positive view has had important consequences: the introduction all around the world of public policy for the promotion of successful aging supported by the *Madrid-Second International Plan of Action on Ageing* (United Nations, 2002) and *Active Ageing: A Policy Framework* (WHO, 2002).

Without doubt, given certain limitations, the concept of successful aging, under different terms, is at the core of the global movement of an aging society hoping and demanding to age successfully, which requires individual's commitment to this goal.

## References

Baltes, P. B. (1987). Theoretical propositions of life-span developmental psychology: on the dynamic between growth and decline. *Developmental Psychology*, 23, 611–26.

Baltes, P. B., Baltes, M. M. (1990). Psychological perspectives on successful aging: the model of selective optimization with compensation. In P. B. Baltes & M. M. Baltes (Eds.), *Successful Aging: Perspectives from the Behavioral Sciences* (pp. 1–34). Cambridge: Cambridge University Press.

Baltes, M. M., Carstensen, L. (1996). The process of successful aging. *Ageing & Society*, 16, 397–422.

Carver, L. F., Buchanan, D. (2016). Successful aging: considering non-biomedical constructs. *Clinical Intervention in Aging*, 11, 1523–630.

Christensen, K., Doblhammer, G., Rau, R., Vaupel, J. W. (2009). Ageing populations: the challenges ahead. *Lancet*, 374, 9696, 1196–208. doi: 10.1016/S0140-6736(09)61460-4.

Depp, C. A., Jeste, D. V. (2006). Definitions and predictors of successful aging: a comprehensive review of larger quantitative studies. *American Journal Geriatric Psychiatry*, 14, 6–20.

Fernández-Ballesteros, R. (2008). *Active Aging: Contribution of Psychology*. Göttingen, Germany: Hogrefe.

(2011). Positive aging: objective, subjective and combined outcomes. *E-Journal of Applied Psychology*, 7, 22–30.

(2017). Active versus healthy aging: a step backwards? *Open Access Journal of Gerontology & Geriatric Medicine*, 1(2): 555558. doi: 10.19080/OAJGGM.2017.01.555558002

Fernández-Ballesteros, R., Zamarron, M. D., Rudinger, G., et al. (2004). Assessing competence: the European survey on aging protocol. *Gerontology*, 50, 330–47.

Fernández-Ballesteros, R., García, L. F., Abarca, D., et al. (2008). Lay concept of aging well: cross-cultural comparisons. *Journal American Geriatric Society*, 56, 950–2.

Fernández-Ballesteros, R., Zamarron, M. D., López, M. D., et al. (2011). Successful aging: criteria and predictors. *Psychology in Spain*, 15, 330–347.

Fernández-Ballesteros, R., Molina, M. A., Schettini, R., Santacreu, M. (2013). The semantic network of aging well. In J. M. Robine, C. Jagger, & E. M. Crimmins (Eds.), *Healthy Longevity: Annual Review of Gerontology and Geriatrics* (p. 33). New York, NY: Springer.

Fernández-Mayoralas, G., Rojo-Pérez, F., Prieto-Flores, M. E., et al. (2014). *Revisión conceptual del envejecimiento activo en el contexto de otras formas de vejez. Cambio demográfico y socio territorial en un contexto de crisis.* Sevilla: AGE.

Freund, A. M., Baltes, P. B. (2007). Toward a theory of successful aging: selection, optimization and compensation. In R. Fernández-Ballesteros (Ed.), *GeroPsychology: An European Perspective for an Aging World* (pp. 239–44). Göttingen: Hogrefe & Huber.

Fries J. F. (1980). Aging, natural death, and the compression of morbidity. *New England Journal of Medicine*, 303, 130–5.

Fries, J. F. (1989). *Aging Well*. Reading, MA: Addison-Wesley Pub.

Guralnik J. M., Kaplan, G. A. (1989). Predictors of healthy aging: prospective evidence from the Alameda County study. *American Journal of Public Health*, 79, 703–8.

Haveman-Nies, A., De Groot, L. C., Van Staveren, W. A. (2003). Dietary quality, life styles factors and healthy aging in Europe: the SENECA study. *Age and Aging*, 32, 427–34.

ILC (2015). *Active Ageing: A Policy Framework in Response to Longevity Revolution*. Rio de Janeiro: Institute of Longevity Center.

Johnson, K. J., Mutchler J. E. (2014). The emergence of a positive gerontology: from disengagement to social involvement. *Gerontologist*, 54 (1), 93–100. doi: 10.1093/geront/gnt099

Jöreskog, K. G., Sörbom, D. (2006). LISREL 8.80 for Winsows (Computer Software). Lincolnwood, IL: Scientific Software International.

Katz S., Calasanti, T. (2015). Critical perspectives on successful aging: does it "appeal more than it illuminates"? *The Gerontologist*, 55, 26–33. doi:10.1093/geront/gnu027

Katz, S., Calasanti, T. (2016). Critical perspective on successful aging: does it "appeal more than it illuminates." *The Gerontologist*, 56(6), 1093–101.

Martin, P., Kelly, N., Kahana, B., et al. (2015). Defining successful aging: a tangible or elusive concept? *The Gerontologist*, 55, 1–14.

Martinson, M., Berridge, C. (2015). Successful aging and its discontents: a systematic review of the social gerontology literature *Gerontologist*, 55(1), 58–69.

Matsubayashi, K., Ishine, M., Wada, T., Okumiya, K. (2006). Older adults' views of "successful aging": comparison of older Japanese and Americans. *Journal of the American Geriatrics Society*, 54(1), 184–7.

Neugarten, B. (1972). Personality and the aging process. *The Gerontologist*, 12(1, Pt. 1), 9–15. doi:http://dx.doi.org/10.1093/geront/12.1_Part_1.9

O'Reilly, P., Caro, F. G. (1995). Productive aging: an overview of literature. *Journal of Aging & Social Policy*, 4(2), 39–71.

Peel, N. M., McClure, R. J., Bartlett, H. P. (2005). Behavioral determinants of health aging. *American Journal of Prevention Medicine*, 28, 298–304.

Phelan, E. A., Anderson, L. A., Lacroix, A.-Z., Larson, E. B. (2004). Older adults' views of "successful aging" – how do they compare with researchers' definitions? *Journal of American Geriatric Society*, 52, 211–16.

Pruchno, R. A., Wilson-Genderso, M., Rose, M. (2010). Successful aging: early influences and C contemporary characteristics. *Gerontologist*, 50(6), 821–33.

Reed, D. M., Foley, D. J., White, L. R. et al. (1998). Predictors of healthy aging in men with high life expectancies. *American Journal of Public Health*, 88, 463–1467.

Riff, C. D. (1982). Beyond Ponce de león and life satisfaction: new directions in quest of successful aging. *International Journal Behavioral Development*, 12, 35–55.

Riley (1998). Letter to editor. *The Gerontologist*, 38(2), 151.

Rowe, J. W., Kahn, R. L. (1987). Human aging: usual and successful. *Science*, 237, 143–9. doi:10.1126/science.3299702

(1997). Successful aging. *The Gerontologist*, 37, 433–40. doi:10.1093/geront/37.4.433.

(1998). *Successful Aging*. New York, NY: Pantheon Books.

Rowe, J. W., Kahn, R. L. (2015). Successful aging: conceptual expansions for the 21st century. *The Journals of Gerontology Series B*, 70(4) 593–6, https://doi.org/10.1093/geronb/gbv025

Schulz, R. Keckhausen, J. (1996). A life model of successful aging. *American Psychologist*, 51, 702–14.

Torres, S., Hammarstrom, G. (2009). Successful aging as an oxymoron: older people – with and without home-help care – talk about what aging well means to them. *International Journal of Ageing and Later Life*, 4(1), 23–54.

United Nation. (2002). *Madrid-International Plan of Action on Ageing*. New York, NY: United Nation.

Vaillant, G. E., Vaillant, C. O. (1990). Natural history of male psychological health: XII. A 45-year study of predictors of successful aging at age of 65. *American Journal of Psychiatry*, 147, 31–7.

WHO. (2001). *Health and Aging: A Discussion Paper*. Geneva: World Health Organization.

(2002). *Active Aging: A Policy Framework*. Geneva: World Health Organization.

(2015). *Health and Aging Reports*. Geneva: World Health Organization.

Yoon, G. (1996). Psychological factors of successful aging. *Australian Journal of Aging*, 15, 69–72.

# 2  The Biomedical Bases of Successful Aging

Athanase Benetos

In France, life expectancy has increased by 33 years in the twentieth century. It should be noted that, globally, life expectancy at birth corresponds to the average age of death in a given area and time period. This increase is essentially not only due to the drastic decline in infant mortality, but also due to the eradication of a number of infectious diseases. Indeed, the disappearance of these causes of early mortality has led to dramatic effects in terms of average age of death, thus explaining its considerable increase, especially during the first half of the twentieth century, an unprecedented fact in the history of mankind.

Hence, we have "gained" more than 10 years since 1960 and, contrary to certain predictions, life expectancy continues to grow steadily by about 1 to 2 months per year. However, these developments in the second half of the twentieth century are less important than those which occurred in the first half, and correspond to the period when medicine and societies began facing chronic diseases related to age (e.g., heart failure, dementia, stroke, several types of cancers). This trend continued on and, unsurprisingly, the result was a greater number of individuals living to be 80, 90, and 100 years old. All of these do not necessarily mean that we have altered the barriers of the human race in terms of maximum longevity – at least not radically. Nonagenarians and centenarians have existed throughout the centuries, even though, for reasons stated above, their numbers were very low.

Is the record for maximum longevity currently changing dramatically? Will the record of Ms. Jeanne-Louise Calment (122 years and 164 days), established 20 years ago in August 1997, be exceeded at some point in the near future? According to current data, this milestone will not be surpassed until at least the end of 2023, since the oldest living person as of today (June 2018), Ms Chiyo Miyako born on May 2, 1901 in Japan. Still, this hypothesis is very weak, since the probability that Ms Chiyo Miyako will be alive at the end of 2023 is less than 1 percent. Thus, for at least 25 years, the record Jeanne-Louise Calment established in 1997 will not be broken.

## Is There a Genuine Potential for Preventing Functional Decline, Thereby Increasing the Probability of Successful Aging?

Over the last 40 years, the population over 80 years of age has expanded substantially. Whereas this segment of the population represented 3.8 percent of Europe's total population in 2006, it is expected to reach 9.5 percent in 2050, an increase of approximately 130 percent (Health at a glance 2009). Currently, mean life expectancy for a person of 80 years living in a European country is approximately 9 years compared to approximately 6 years in the 1970s, corresponding to an increase of 50 percent. This new and unexpected demographic transition is analyzed today as an adult longevity revolution (Robine 2016). The steadily increasing number of individuals over 80 years of age has led to a growing population prone to multimorbidity, frailty, polypharmacy, and partial or complete loss of autonomy. During the last few decades, the question of prevention of these aging-related alterations has become one of our foremost biomedical, social, and societal issues (Berrut et al., 2013; Ferrucci et al., 2004; Studenski et al., 2011). How can we preserve our cognitive and physical functions until a very advanced age? Can we fight against major age-related diseases and syndromes such as dementia, depression, heart failure, sarcopenia, osteoporosis, falls, and sensorial disorders? Can we preserve the interaction between social environment and older people, which is one of the bases of successful aging? These questions are at the heart of an intense debate among clinicians, researchers, and public authorities alike – who face the problems of aging and their medical, social, and economic consequences on a collective basis.

## To Go Further, Can Biomedical Progress Alter the Limits of Human Maximum Longevity and Stop the Aging Process?

The fantasy of immortality has always been part of human history and of the collective imagination. Magic potions, concoctions, and cocktails have long been proposed to fight off aging and prolong life. Can the tremendous advances in biology and biotechnologies make these dreams reality? Every day we are bombarded by "scientific and biomedical revolutions" that boast the miraculous effects of a new diet, a molecule, a new genetic manipulation, or a new method for achieving the objective of eternal youth. The annual market for new molecules able to cleanse the body of accumulated lesions that ultimately cause aging and death represents billions of euros and dollars with only a few clicks on a computer. Defining biological age with accuracy, and proposing methods for stopping or even regressing it has become increasingly popular.

Many "scientists" create false but very lucrative antiaging industry by offering easy solutions to very complex questions. We can here mention a number of examples of such simplistic and false "solutions" based on real situations. For example, it is known that oxidative stress and free radicals are involved in cellular and tissue aging. There is a large antiaging industry proposing that antioxidants will correct these deficiencies and prevent alterations and pathologies related to aging. However, the controlled clinical studies discarded this hypothesis by showing the absence of any long-term benefits of the pills containing antioxidants substances (Krause and Roupas, 2015; Pincemail et al., 2014). Similar negative results have been obtained when clinical trials tested the antiaging effects of hormonal supplementation. Actually, as we age there is a hormonal decline, especially with regard to estrogen in all women (menopause), testosterone in a large proportion of men (andropause), and growth hormone in a large proportion of the elderly population (somatopause). Although these deficits are associated with several manifestations of aging, hormonal supplementation is unable to slow down the aging process, indicating that hormonal deficits may be only one component, or just an epiphenomenon, of the organic aging process, and not the causal mechanism of the aging process (Heutling and Lehnert, 2008; Sansone et al., 2017).

There are several other such examples of false "antiaging" therapies and interventions. How do we distinguish between true advances in science and fantasy, deception and quackery? While not easy, first we must always require scientific proof and tangible effects, rather than the sole conviction of one person, however important he or she may be. One also has to realize that aging is not a disease that can be cured with a medication or by modifying the function of a gene; the aging process is in fact a very complex lifelong process with strong influences from biological, medical, and social factors, and interactions between our genetic background and the environment.

One thing is certain: if the fountain of youth were ever discovered, and especially if it were up for sale (in truth, anything can be sold, even fresh air), there would be dozens of studies conducted to confirm its effects. In an era where information travels at vertiginous speeds, and in unlimited quantity, such good news would certainly be heard instantly.

There is, however, "real" good news about the biomedical aspects of successful aging. Indeed, in these last years, a large amount of biological and clinical data has been accumulated, allowing for a better understanding of the biological bases of the aging process and the implementation of actions contributing to the maintenance of function and the prevention of frailty.

Thus, at the biological level, several major hallmarks of aging have been identified. In this respect, well-known scientists proposed that genomic instability, telomere dynamics, epigenetic alterations, loss of proteostasis, deregulated nutrient-sensing, mitochondrial dysfunction, cellular senescence, stem-cell exhaustion, and altered intercellular communication could be considered as the main hallmarks of the aging process, which suggests that intervention could modulate these mechanisms (López-Otín et al., 2013, 2016).

At the clinical level, these last years have been marked by a considerable knowledge about the loss of function and frailty concepts (Berrut et al., 2013; Ferrucci et al., 2004; Fried et al., 2001; Studenski et al., 2011). More than 15 years ago, Fried et al. (2001) defined frailty as "a biological syndrome of decreased reserve and resistance to stressors, resulting from cumulative declines across multiple physiologic systems and causing vulnerability to adverse outcomes." Although chronological age is a major determinant of the loss of function and frailty, several other somatic, psychological, environmental, and social factors influence this process. We now know that the prevention of frailty and the maintenance of functional capacities require a comprehensive assessment of the different functions leading to the implementation of specific preventive actions.

This holistic approach, including multidimensional assessment and a combination of preventive strategies such as physical activities, nutritional interventions, cognitive exercises, social interventions, better use of medication, as well as the implementation of new technologies for living assistance, can prevent age-related diseases, functional decline, and loss of autonomy, while promoting successful aging.

## References

Berrut G., Andrieu S., Araujo de Carvalho I., et al. Promoting access to innovation for frail old persons. IAGG (International Association of Gerontology and Geriatrics), WHO (World Health Organization) and SFGG (Societe Francaise de Geriatrie et de Gerontologie) Workshop – Athens January 20–21, 2012. *J Nutr Health Aging*. 2013;17:688–93.

Ferrucci L., Guralnik J. M., Studenski S., et al. Interventions on Frailty Working Group. Designing randomized, controlled trials aimed at preventing or delaying functional decline and disability in frail, older persons: a consensus report. *J Am Geriatr Soc*. 2004;52:625–34.

Fried L. P., Tangen C. M., Walston J., et al. Frailty in older adults: Evidence for a phenotype. *J Gerontol A Biol Sci Med Sci*. 2001;56:146–56.

Health at a glance 2009 – OECD indicators: www.google.com/url?sa=t&rct=j&q=&esrc= s&source=web&cd=1&ved=0CCIQFjAA&url=http%3A%2F%2Fwww.oecd .org%2Fhealth%2Fhealth- systems%2F44117530.pdf&ei=DvK7VN7SJMX kasibgrAI&usg=AFQjCNHKC9qNe87Gdi-BIi_VTS0dfWpigg&bvm=bv .83829542,d.d2s&cad=rja). Last accessed on June 2018.

Heutling D., Lehnert H. Hormone therapy and anti-aging: Is there an indication? *Internist (Berl)*. 2008;49:572–9.

Krause D., Roupas P. Effect of vitamin intake on cognitive decline in older adults: Evaluation of the evidence. *J Nutr Health Aging*. 2015;19:745–53.

López-Otín C., Blasco M. A., Partridge L., Serrano M., Kroemer G. The hallmarks of aging. *Cell*. 2013;153:1194–217.

López-Otín C., Galluzzi L., Freije J. M., Madeo F., Kroemer G. Metabolic control of longevity. *Cell*. 2016;166:802–21.

Pincemail J., Ricour C., Defraigne J. O., Petermans J. Oxidative stress, antioxidants and the ageing process. *Rev Med Liege*. 2014;69:270–5.

Robine J.-M. La révolution de la longévité des adultes. *Gerontologie et Société*. 2016;39:21–40.

Sansone A., Sansone M., Lenzi A., Romanelli F. Testosterone replacement therapy: The emperor's new clothes. *Rejuvenation Res*. 2017;20:9–14.

Studenski S., Perera S., Patelet K., et al. Gait speed and survival in older adults. *JAMA*. 2011;305:50–8.

# 3  Successful Aging and the Longevity Revolution

Jean-Marie Robine

This handbook shows that the models and concepts of "successful aging" emerged during the 1970s (Fernandez-Ballesteros, Chap 1). A key date is surely the 1987 publication by Rowe and Kahn of "Human Aging: Usual versus Successful" in *Science*. At the time, the limits to human longevity was thought to be nearby. The reference paper is an article published by James Fries in the *New England Journal of Medicine* in 1980. James Fries thought that human longevity was limited to an average of 85 years. He believed that it was possible, through the adoption of good health practices, to push back the age of onset of chronic diseases and thus virtually eliminate all mortality before the age of 70 years. Like most biologists at that time, he also believed that the longevity of man depended entirely on genes and that, without modification of this genetic endowment, maximum longevity was limited to 100 years. For him, there had always been centenarians, few in number, since the Neolithic period, and there would always be as many in the future, i.e., in very small numbers.

In other words, for James Fries, advances in medicine and the gradual reduction of modifiable risk factors would, in combination with biological limitations to human longevity, lead to a very high concentration of individual lifetimes, centered on 85 years (i.e., between the ages of 70 and 100 years) with more than two-thirds of the deaths occurring between the ages of 80 and 90 years. This vision of the demographic future made it possible to predict a fantastic compression of morbidity and disability, concentrated on a few years at the end of life (Fries, 1980). This vision, described as optimistic, was widely shared by the scientific community of the time. Examples include the biologist Leonard Hayflick, who considered in 1981 that if we were able to eliminate aging-related loss without changing the biological clock itself, "the result would be a society whose members would live full, physically vigorous, youthful lives until death claimed them at the stroke of midnight on their one-hundredth birthday" (Hayflick, 1981). It is in this context that Rowe and Kahn very clearly proposed their model of successful aging: "a revolutionary increase in life span has already occurred [i.e., the rectangularisation of the survival curve]. A corresponding increase in health span, the maintenance of full function as nearly as possible to the end of life, should be the next gerontological goal. The focus on successful aging urges that goal for researchers, practitioners, and for older men and women themselves" (Rowe and Kahn, 1987).

## The Continuing Increase in Life Expectancy

The vision of the future, as proposed by Fries, assumed a halt, or at least a strong slowdown, in the increase in life expectancy observed since the end of World War II in the most developed countries. This is the scenario chosen in the 1980s and 1990s by the national statistical institutes for their demographic projections. But this scenario has never occurred (Oeppen and Vaupel, 2002). Life expectancy continues to increase on average by 3 months per year (1 in every 4 years) in countries with the highest life expectancy (Christensen at al., 2009). Paul and Margret Baltes noted an unexpected number of very old people as early as 1990 (Baltes and Baltes, 1990). The term, oldest-old, emerged to distinguish elderly people aged 65 years and more, aged 80 or 85 years and more. In the mid-1990s, scientific literature started to report a decrease in mortality among the oldest-old people. In several countries, women's life expectancy reached and exceeded the value of 85 years, considered by many as a limit value that would never be reached. According to the Human Mortality Database, Japan reached the value of 85 years in 2002, Spain in 2010, and France in 2013. All these observations strongly question Fries's view of the future of mortality and longevity, but paradoxically, they had little impact on the development of successful and active aging models.

Henceforth, the main debate concerns the continuation of the increase in life expectancy, when will it stop and at what level? The debate is lively as evidenced by the latest exchanges in *Nature* (Dong et al., 2016, with five brief communications in 2017). Simply put, there are experts in the field who think that biological constraints are very strong and that survival beyond the age of reproduction is somehow artificial or heroic. For this group of scientists, the increase in life expectancy must slow down or stop. There are a second group of experts who believe, on the contrary, that the progress to come is such that the increase in life expectancy should accelerate and attain values unimaginable today. Finally, there are another group of scientists who think that the increase in life expectancy could continue for a long time, but without retaining specific hypotheses concerning a slowdown, or, on the contrary, an acceleration.

Today it is widely acknowledged that the reduction in mortality and the increase in life expectancy depend on many factors. These include exposure to a multitude of risk factors such as air pollution throughout the life cycle and lifestyle habits such as diets, medical treatments, and surgery. In all these areas, much progress is expected and all could contribute to fuelling the future decline in mortality, as they have already fueled the decline in mortality observed since World War II. Current debates on the limits of human longevity include central values such as life expectancy at birth, as well as extreme values, such as those of maximum ages reported at death.

## The Rectangularization of the Survival Curve

James Fries's vision of the future relies heavily on the rectangularization model of the survival curve originally proposed by Alex Comfort in 1964 (Comfort, 1964). Comfort observed that the more a country is developed, the more its survival curve seems rectangular. Fries will reinforce or even force this rectangularization by deciding, without any scientific or empirical justification, that each survival curve will stop at 100 years with the death of the last survivor of each cohort. A modern study of the mechanisms of the apparent rectangularization of survival curves has shown that it is first due to the drop in infant mortality, which somehow "horizontalizes" the survival curve for several years. The rest is largely due to the fixed point introduced by Fries at the age of 100 years (Cheung et al., 2005). It is important to understand a fundamental difference between infant mortality, premature mortality, and mortality among the elderly. If infant mortality and premature mortality can be reduced or eliminated, then the mortality of the elderly will not be reduced or eliminated as a matter of course. This mortality can only be postponed because no one will become immortal. The difference is fundamental. Reducing infant mortality or premature mortality does not affect the longevity of the human species. The only consequence is that more individuals reach the fullness of adulthood – old age – but without changing its duration. Reducing mortality at the higher ages is actually postponing deaths. Elderly people do not die less, but they die later and this directly impacts the longevity of the human species. In this regard, it is interesting to note that when we began to observe a decrease in mortality at the higher ages, it was not understood that this meant that our species began to live longer, to change its longevity (Robine, 2016).

Since the work of Wilhem Lexis (1878), demographers distinguish three kinds of mortality: infant mortality, which affects children under the age of 1, premature mortality which, as the name suggests, prematurely interrupts a life course, and the mortality of elderly people, i.e., the mortality of those who did not die prematurely. The fight against infant and juvenile mortality was the main concern of the twentieth century and the fight against premature mortality, which still affects certain segments of the population, remains one of the primary objectives of current public health programs, but the fight against the mortality of elderly has never been a health objective. Described as "normal" by Lexis, elderly mortality is considered inevitable by all health actors, until recently. Its decrease has occurred inadvertently and its primary consequence, namely to change the longevity parameters of our species, continues to surprise us.

## The Revolution of Adult Longevity

The life table of demographers generally provides three statistical series: the age-specific probability of dying (or how many die from each age), the probability to survive at each anniversary (or how many survive at each age), and the life expectancy at each age (or how many years remain to be lived from each age). Demographers often provide the corresponding distribution of deaths by age. However, if the first three series are widely discussed and commented upon and give rise to different debates on, for example, the existence of a plateau of mortality at the highest ages, the fourth series has largely been ignored. It is there for technical reasons, to allow the calculation of the other three series. Its name is indicative of its interest. It is the distribution of ages at death. Now, from a simple change of view, it becomes the distribution of lifetimes. It is, by far, the richest information of the table. It first provides information on the most frequent life span, which is significantly higher than life expectancy at birth, and then it provides information on the shape of the distribution of individual life spans, their dispersion, and extreme values. For countries, such as Japan and France, which have time series, the distribution of lifetimes clearly illustrates the revolution of adult longevity (Figure 3.1), at least since the end of World War II, but no one was observing these series until very recently.

The drivers of the adult longevity revolution have certainly more to do with the general improvement of living conditions (food, hygiene, and safety) than with particular medical progress. Better fed adults are more resistant to diseases in general; less exposed to health risks and insecurity, they live longer. The emergence of this revolution during a historical period blurred by the world economic crisis of the 1930s and by World War II makes precise dating difficult (Robine and Cheung, 2008). It is illustrated in Figure 3.1, with French survival data dating back to 1816 for the oldest.

The first two distributions, life spans observed under the mortality conditions of 1816 and 1900, are not very different from the distribution described by Lexis in 1878. In both distributions, 1816 and 1900, more than 80 years apart, there is a very high concentration of deaths during the first years of life, especially in the first year, illustrating the importance of infant and child mortality throughout the nineteenth century. The premature mortality of young adults creates a kind of plateau between the ages of 20 and 50 years, similar in appearance to men and women, although the causes are very different. Then, we can clearly see the number of deaths rising from the age of 50 to reach a maximum of between 70 and 75 years, the modal age or the most frequent age at death, before going down again. No more deaths will be observed around 100 years. It is remarkable to note that the distributions of 1816 and 1900 appear to be almost superimposable. Nothing seems to have changed, or very little, throughout the nineteenth century. The presence of the plateau of premature mortality before the age of 50 years prevents a view of the whole distribution of elderly mortality. But one can easily imagine a bell-shape distribution – the famous normal curve of Adolphe Quételet (1835, 1848). Thus, if we distribute symmetrically, before the modal age at death (the life spans observed between the mode and the age of 100 years) we can quite easily visualize this "normal" or "natural" distribution of lifetimes, suggesting that the first deaths associated with aging occurred a little bit after the age of 40 years. (See Horiuchi et al., 2013, for more information on the modal age at death.)

Under these conditions, the twentieth century was logically mobilized to combat the mortality of children and young adults. The third distribution of Figure 3.1, the life spans observed under the mortality conditions of 1980, when Fries published his article, shows how much success has been achieved: infant mortality and premature mortality virtually disappeared by 1980. But this distribution also shows an unexpected phenomenon, namely the shift toward higher ages of all adult life spans. Thus, the most common age at death is now 80 years

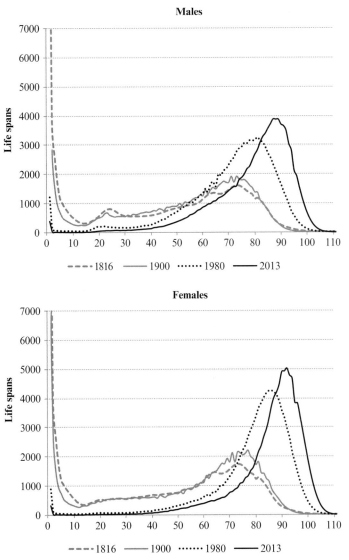

**Figure 3.1.** *Distribution of the individual life spans, under the mortality conditions observed in France in 1816, 1900, 1980, and 2013, by sex (for 100,000 at birth)*
*Source:* Human Mortality Database

for men and 85 years for women. The distribution of life spans under the most recent mortality conditions confirms this unexpected evolution. Indeed, under the conditions of 2013, the most common age at death is 86 years for men and 91 years for women. These developments constitute a real revolution: the revolution of adult longevity. It explains the dynamics of the emergence of the very old populations, like that of centenarians. If a vertical line is drawn in Figure 3.1 at a high age, for example at the age of 90 years, it can be seen that we move from a very small number in 1816 or 1900 to a very large number in 1980, and an even larger number in 2013. Thus, under the mortality conditions of 1900, less than 1 percent of women reached the age of 90 and died beyond that age. Under the mortality conditions observed in 2013, 42 percent of women reached the age of 90 and died beyond. For now, there is no sign that we are approaching any limit that would put an end to this revolution of longevity.

Compared to the "ideal" survival curve of James Fries, presented in 1980 as a limit survival curve that would never be reached, four important points can be noted for the distribution of female life spans, corresponding to the mortality conditions observed in France in 2013: (1) there are many more survivors at higher ages, for example at age 90 or age 100, than in the ideal curve; (2) the last survivors are observed at the age of 115 years, not 100 years as predicted by the model of rectangularization of the survival curve; (3) there are far fewer women dying at the modal age at death, about 5 percent, rather than the 10 percent predicted by the model; but, on the other hand, (4) there are far fewer survivors at the age of 70 than in the ideal curve. In other words, the extent of the empirical life spans observed in 2013 are greater by 15 years. The modal age at death was higher than expected but individual lives are more dispersed around the central lifetime, with more women than expected dying before the modal age and many more women dying later than the modal age, at the age of 95 or 100 years.

When an imaginary vertical line is drawn in Figure 3.1 at the age of 100, the result is usually an exponential increase in the number of centenarians, from a few individuals to several tens of thousands in a few decades, as is the case for France and the United Kingdom (Price, 2010; Blanpain and Buisson, 2016), which leads to the next question.

## Are Centenarians a Model of Successful Aging?

Scientific teams, who are dedicated to their study, ask this question regularly. For some, the mere fact of surviving up to 100 years is proof of successful aging. For others, reaching 100 years of age is not enough to say that aging is successful. At the centenarian level, aging is no longer a public health objective, but an individual objective. The team of the New England Centenarian Study is the first team that has proposed a typology with three categories among centenarians: escapers, delayers, and survivors (Evert et al., 2003). Escapers are individuals who attain the age of 100 years without the diagnosis of common age-associated illnesses. Delayers are individuals who delay the onset of age-associated illnesses until at least the age of 80 years, and survivors are individuals who have a diagnosis of an age-associated illness prior to the age of 80. Evert and her coauthors observed 32 percent of escapers among males and 15 percent among females. But the sample of the New England Centenarian Study is not a representative sample of centenarians, but rather a convenient sample. On the basis of a representative and almost exhaustive sample, a Danish study considers that almost all centenarians carry one or more degenerative diseases (Andersen-Ranberg et al., 2001). They are survivors and delayers according to the typology of Evert and colleagues, but they cannot be considered as a model of successful aging in the sense of Rowe and Kahn (Rowe and Kahn, 1987, 2015). Two large studies, a Japanese study and an Italian study, specifically looked at whether the centenarians in their study met the criteria of successful aging (Motta et al., 2005; Gondo et al., 2006). Bringing together a significant number of centenarians, the two studies aimed to be representative of the centenarian people. In both cases, almost all centenarians did not meet the criteria of successful aging. In the Japanese study, centenarians who did not have visual and hearing problems, were independent for the basic activities of daily life, and had good cognitive functions represented less than 2 percent of the sample. In the Italian study, 20 percent of the centenarians were in "good health" according to the criteria of the study but no one maintained social or productive activities. It is clear that the majority of the centenarians in the studies did not meet the criteria for successful aging. This raises two questions: are centenarians a group who have failed at aging well or is the criteria of successful aging not appropriated to the very old, like nonagenarians and centenarians?

## The Variability of End-of-Life Trajectories

In addition to the now well-established variability of life spans, several recent studies have illustrated the variability of end-of-life trajectories. Thus, in their study published in 2010, Gill and his colleagues identified five distinct trajectories of disability in the last year of life that are significant in terms of public health among individuals who die beyond the age of 70 years (Gill et al., 2010). A first group of people, representing 17 percent of end-of-life trajectories, died suddenly without reporting any disability in the year before their death. A second group, representing 19.8 percent of end-of-life trajectories, died after an episode of catastrophic disability in the last two months of their life. A third group, representing 17.5 percent of end-of-life trajectories, died after a long episode of accelerated disability over the last 9 months of their life. A fourth group, representing 23.8 percent of end-of-life trajectories, died after a progressive increase in their disability, already present one year before death. A fifth and last group, representing 21.9 percent of end-of-life trajectories, died after at least one year of severe disability. It is interesting to note that the first group died, on average, at 82.8 years, the second at 82.1 years, the third at 83.6 years, the fourth at 85.7 years, and the fifth at 86.8 years. There is an obvious positive correlation between the age at death and the number of months spent with severe disability in the last year of life. It is also interesting to note that cancer and sudden death led to death on average at 81.9 and 82.5 years, respectively, and that advanced dementia and frailty led to death on average at 87.3 and 85.7 years, respectively.

34    JEAN-MARIE ROBINE

## Trade-Off and Dynamic Approach

These five end-of-life trajectories, such as the existence of contradictory results between Denmark and Japan, where the former slowly accumulates centenarians in its population compared with the latter (Robine et al., 2010), suggest that the longer one lives, the more difficult it is to meet the criteria of successful aging. Indeed, in Denmark, nonagenarians and centenarians appear to have better functional performances over time (Engberg et al., 2008; Christensen et al., 2013; Rasmussen et al., 2017), whereas the reverse was observed in Japan (Suzuki et al., 1995; Gondo personal communication).

Studies on disability-free life expectancy suggest a similar result. The continuing increase in life expectancy is best accompanied by a parallel increase in disability-free life expectancy, as the number of years lived with disability does not decline over time. In general, there is a smaller increase in disability-free life expectancy than in total life expectancy. Which means that at the current population level, scenarios of expansion of disability (Gruenberg, 1977; Kramer, 1980) are more frequent than scenarios of compression of disability (Jagger and Robine, 2011).

Awareness of the variability of life spans and the variability of end-of-life trajectories should allow us to develop a more dynamic vision of successful aging (Robine and Michel, 2004), otherwise every advance in terms of longevity will be paid by an apparent decline in terms of successful aging. Instead of opposing, longevity and successful aging should complement each other. Setting different goals in terms of successful aging for each age group (the 65s, the 70s, etc.) would be tantamount to denying the variability of health conditions for a given age, and paradoxically, would lead us back to a negative view of aging. We must therefore have a conceptual framework, allowing for the integration of concepts and measures, which respects both the variability of states and durations as the unlimited possibility of improvement in the future. This is theoretically possible with the calculations of health expectancy, along with the traditional calculations of life expectancy (LE) at birth, which today makes it possible to measure the average gains in longevity. Thus, a series of health expectancies (LE without chronic diseases, LE without disability, LE with good social participation, etc.), corresponding to the main criteria of successful or active aging, could be calculated to ensure that longevity gains, whatever they are, are also accompanied on average by gains according to the criteria of successful or active aging. The study of the distribution of lifetimes according to the same criteria (sometimes referred to as health spans) should make it possible to see whether the revolution of longevity has been accompanied or not by a revolution of successful or active aging, always postponing to higher ages the comorbidities, the frailty, the lack of social participation, and the loss of autonomy experienced by the elderly at the age of 70 or 80 years in the 1980s or 1990s.

In 1980, the year James Fries published his demographic vision of the future, there were 913 centenarians in Japan and life expectancy at birth was 78.8 years for women. In 2016, there were 65,692 centenarians in Japan, 72 times more, and in 2014, the last available year, life expectancy reached 86.8 years for women, 8 years more than in 1980. If the Japanese people live longer under the present conditions than under the conditions of 1980, then to find out if they are getting older better it would be necessary to compare the specific health expectancies, indicative of successful aging, over the same period. Studies currently available in Japan on health expectancies (Yong and Saito, 2009; Seko et al., 2012; Health Japan 21, 2014) show that LE without limitation in daily activities (i.e., without dependency and loss of autonomy) increased between 2001 and 2013 but at a slower rate than the total increase in life expectancy at birth. This result illustrates the complexity of the current transitions. Under the current conditions, Japanese people live on average longer without dependency, indicating an improvement in active aging, but on another hand, they live longer with some loss of autonomy and with care needs, especially after the age of 85 years, which can be misunderstood as a failure of successful aging.

## References

Andersen-Ranberg, K., Schroll, M., and Jeune, B. (2001). Healthy centenarians do not exist, but autonomous centenarians do: A population-based study of morbidity among Danish centenarians. *Journal of the American Geriatrics Society*, 49, 900–8.

Baltes P. B. and Baltes M. M. (1990). Psychological perspectives on successful aging: The model of selective optimization with compensation. In P. B. Baltes & M. M. Baltes (Eds.), *Successful Aging: Perspectives from the Behavioral Science* (pp. 1–34). New York: Cambridge University Press.

Blanpain N. and Buisson G. (2016). 21 000 centenaires en 2016 en France, 270 000 en 2070? *INSEE Première, 1620*. www.insee.fr/fr/accueil [Accessed on January 15, 2017].

Cheung S. L. K., Robine J.-M., Tu, E. J. C., and Caselli, G. (2005). Three dimensions of the survival curve: Horizontalization, verticalization, and longevity extension. *Demography*, 42 (2), 243–58.

Christensen K., Doblhammer G., Rau R., and Vaupel J. W. (2009). Ageing populations: The challenges ahead. *Lancet* 374: 1196–208.

Christensen K., Thinggaard M., Oksuzyan A., et al. (2013). Physical and cognitive functioning of people older than 90 years: A comparison of two Danish cohorts born 10 years apart. *Lancet*, 382, 1507–13.

Comfort A. (1964). *Ageing, the Biology of Senescence* (2nd edn.). London, England: Routledge & Kegan Paul.

Dong X., Milholland B., and Vijg S. (2016). Evidence for a limit to human lifespan. *Nature* 538: 257–9; doi: 10.1038/nature19793 With 5 brief communications in *Nature* **546** (29 June 2017) by Brown N. L. J., Albers C. J., & Ritchie S. J., Hughes B. G., & Hekimi S., Rozing M. P., Kirkwood T. B. L. & Westendorp R. G. J., Lenart A., & Vaupel J. W., de Beer J., Bardoutsos A., & Janssen F.

Engberg H., Christensen K., Andersen-Ranberg K., Vaupel J. W., and Jeune B. (2008). Improving activities of daily living in Danish Centenarians – But only in women: A comparative study of two birth cohorts born in 1895 and 1905. *Journal of Gerontology: Medical Sciences*, 63A (11), 1186–92.

Evert J., Lawler E., Bogan H., and Perls T. (2003). Morbidity profiles of centenarians: Survivors, delayers, and escapers. *Journal of Gerontology: Medical Sciences* 58A (3), 232–7.

Fries J. F. (1980). Aging, natural death, and the compression of morbidity. *The New England Journal of Medicine*, 303 (3): 130–5.

Gill T. M., Gahbauer E. A., Han L., and Allore H. G. (2010). Trajectories of disability in the last year of life. *The New England Journal of Medicine*, 362, 1173–80.

Gondo Y., Hirose N., Arai Y., et al. (2006). Functional status of centenarians in Tokyo, Japan: Developing better phenotypes of exceptional longevity. *The Journals of Gerontology Series A: Biological Sciences and Medical Sciences*, 61 (3), 305–10.

Gruenberg E. M. (1977). The failures of success. *The Milbank Memorial Fund Quarterly. Health and Society*, 55, 3–24.

Hayflick L. (1981). Prospects for human extension by genetic manipulation. In D. Danon, N. W. Shock, and M. Marois (dir.), *Aging: Challenge to Science and Society* (Vol. 1, pp. 162–79). New York, NY: Oxford University Press.

Health Japan 21 (2014). Report on Health Japan 21 Committee Meeting [In Japanese]. www.mhlw.go.jp/file/05-Shingikai-10601000-Daijinkanboukouseikagakuka-Kouseikagakuka/sinntyoku.pdf

Horiuchi S., Ouellette N., Cheung S. L., and Robine J.-M. (2013). Modal age at death: Lifespan indicator in the era of longevity extension. *Vienna Yearbook of Population Research*, 11, 37–69.

Jagger C. and Robine J.-M. (2011). Healthy life expectancy. In R. G. Rogers & E. M. Crimmins (Eds.), *International Handbook of Adult Mortality. International Handbooks of Population* (Vol. 2, pp. 551–68). Dordrecht, Heidelberg, London, and New York: Springer.

Kramer M. (1980). The rising pandemic of mental disorders and associated chronic diseases and disabilities. *Acta Psychiatrica Scandinavica* 62 (Suppl 285):382–97.

Lexis W. (1878). Sur la Durée Normale de la Vie Humaine et sur la Théorie de la Stabilité des Rapports Statistiques [On the normal duration of human life and the stability theory of statistical reports]. *Annales de Démographie Internationale*, 2 (5), 447–60.

Motta, M., Bennata, E., Malaguarnera, M., and Motta, I. (2005). Italian multicenter study on centenarians (IMUSCE). Successful aging in centenarians: Myths and reality. *Archives of Gerontology and Geriatrics*, 40, 241–51.

Oeppen J. and Vaupel J. W. (2002). Broken limits to life expectancy. *Science* 296, 1029–31.

Price E. (2010). Number of future centenarians. Récupéré sur le site du Gouvernement anglais, Department for Work and Pensions (DWP): www.gov.uk/government/uploads/systeNumber of future centenariansm/uploads/attachment_data/file/223229/Centenarians.pdf

Quételet A. (1848). *Du système social et des lois qui le régissent* [On the social system and the laws that govern it]. Paris, France: Guillaumin.

Quételet S. (1835). *Sur l'homme et le développement de ses facultés, essai d'une physique sociale* [A treatise on man and the development of his faculties, 1842]. Paris, France: Bachelier (Nouvelle édition publiée en 1991, Paris, France: Fayard).

Rasmussen S. H., Andersen-Ranberg K., Thinggaard M., et al. (2017) Cohort profile: The 1895, 1905, 1910 and 1915 Danish Birth Cohort Studies – Secular trends in the health and functioning of the very old. *International Journal of Epidemiology*, 46 (6), 1746–46j.

Robine J.-M. (2016). La révolution de la longévité des adultes [The revolution of adult longevity]. *Gérontologie et société*, 38 (151), 23–40.

Robine J.-M. and Cheung S. L. K. (2008). Nouvelles observations sur la longévité humaine [New facts in the human longevity]. *Revue Economique*, 59 (5), 941–54.

Robine J. M., Cheung S. L. K., Saito Y., et al. (2010). Centenarians today: New insights on selection from the 5-COOP study. *Current Gerontology and Geriatrics Research*, 2010, Article ID 120354, 9 pages. doi:10.1155/2010/120354

Robine J.-M. and Michel, J.-P. (2004). Looking forward to a general theory on population aging. *Journals of Gerontology Series A, Biological Sciences and Medical Sciences*, 59A (6), 590–7.

Rowe J. W. and Kahn R. L. (1987). Human aging: Usual versus successful. *Science*, 237, 143–9.

(2015). Editorial: Successful aging 2.0: Conceptual expansions for the 21st century. *Journals of Gerontology, Series B: Psychological Sciences and Social Sciences*, 70 (4), 593–6.

Seko R., Hashimoto S., Kawado M., et al. (2012). Trends in life expectancy with care needs based on long-term care insurance data in Japan. *Journal of Epidemiology* 22 (3), 238–243.

Suzuki M., Akisaka M., Ashitomi I., Higa K., and Nozaki H. (1995). Chronological study concerning ADL among Okinawan centenarians. *Nippon Ronen Igakkai Zasshi (Japanese Journal of Geriatrics)*, 32, 416–23.

Yong, V. and Saito, Y. (2009). Trends in healthy life expectancy in Japan: 1986–2004. *Demographic Research*, 20, 467–94.

PART I

# Biomedical Aspects

# 4  The Connection between Cellular Senescence and Age-Related Diseases

Claire Falandry

## Introduction

Accumulating time is associated in all molecules by the accumulation of events of small magnitude that may be interpreted as hallmarks of aging. Such hallmarks have been used phylogenetically by the most basic unicellular eukaryotes – like *Saccharomyces cerevisiae* – to differentiate young cells from old ones (Aguilaniu et al., 2003). In multicellular organisms, tissue homeostasis is allowed by the limited reproductive capacity of somatic cells and the highly regulated switching of cell division. However, if apoptosis is the leading pathway to eliminate old cells in some tissues, many cell types (e.g., fibroblasts, keratinocytes, melanocytes, monocytes, and epithelial cells) develop *in vitro*, as well as *in vivo*, a stereotyped response called cellular senescence in response to various stimuli. This review will focus on delineating the shared characteristics – but also the differential triggers and specificities – of cellular senescence(s), as well as their proposed relationships with age-related diseases. Indeed, despite being blocked in a post-mitotic (quiescent) state, senescent cells are metabolically active and develop cell-autonomous (intrinsic) and non-cell-autonomous (extrinsic) properties, particularly through a specific secretome that contributes to their autocrine and paracrine properties, and are proposed to participate in age-associated phenotypes.

## Why Do Somatic Cells Have to Senesce?

In all organisms, metabolism and exogenous radiations (e.g., UV, X, $\gamma$) induce reactive compounds that are at the basis of many theories of aging developed in the 1950s under the terms of the mutation accumulation theory (Medawar, 1952), the free radical theory (Harman, 1956), or the oxidative stress theory. These mutations affect DNA as well as proteins, compromising both the genome and epigenome integrity of those organisms, which have developed proofreading mechanisms. At the genome level, DNA-damage sensors will induce a DNA-damage response (DDR) and a correction of mutated sequence will occur, according to the corresponding DNA counterpart or by different recombination pathways. At the epigenome level, histone acetylation, methylation, and methylation of CpG are tightly regulated during replication in order to maintain specific sequences of an active (euchromatic) or silent (heterochromatic) state. However, such proofreading mechanisms are expansive in energy and higher eukaryotes have developed differential levels of accuracy for those mechanisms in cells with different fates: (1) as germinal cells have to transmit a preserved genome to the lineage, a high level of accuracy is maintained, and any defective cell is eliminated; on the contrary, (2) somatic cells responding to the wear-and-tear theory – or the disposable soma theory (Kirkwood and Holliday, 1979) – of aging, maintain a low level of accuracy and are limited in their division capacity. Hayflick was the first to demonstrate, in 1961, that primary cell lines have a limited capacity of division – around 40 cycles – leading to an irreversible growth arrest (Hayflick and Moorhead, 1961). Later studies showed that telomere shortening is the molecular support of this mitotic clock, and that this state of permanent cycle arrest corresponds to replicative senescence.

## How to Define Cell Senescence(s)?

During replicative senescence, cells display several phenotypic modifications in addition to a post-mitotic (quiescent) state that have been subsequently defined as the shared hallmarks of cell senescence: among other characteristics, the cells develop modifications in their shape, becoming enlarged and heterogeneous in their metabolism, in which they are characterized by an enhanced protein synthesis (mediated by PI3K-mTor pathway activation), lipogenesis, glycogenesis (mediated by GSK3), and the pathognomonic accumulation of SA-β-Gal (senescence-associated-β-galactosidase), as well as a specific secretome with autocrine and paracrine properties, known as the SASP (senescence-associated secretion profile). At the molecular level, the changes are induced by the induction of cyclin-dependent kinase inhibitors such as p16ink4a or p21, significant chromatin and nuclear remodeling, which leads some cells to the apparition of specific heterochromatic foci called SAHF (senescence-associated heterochromatic foci), and changes in the transcriptional program of the cell.

## How Is Senescence Activated?

Replicative senescence is activated in response to an excess attrition of the telomere. In somatic cells, a part of telomeric DNA is lost during each round of replication because of the end replication problem. Telomeric chromatin is an assembly of telomeric DNA and specific proteins, known as the Shelterin complex. The obligatory lengthening of telomeric DNA induces a disassembly of this complex and may lead to the unfolding of telomeric sequences, inducing a permanent activation of the DNA-damage response cascade and finally to senescence.

In addition to replicative senescence, many other conditions can induce premature senescence, all characterized by the activation of p16ink4a. Among these are oncogene-induced senescence (OIS), oxidative stress, radiation-induced stress, and therapy-induced stress. During such a so-called irreversible senescence, p16ink4a is activated in response to sustained DNA-damage, leading to the phosphorylation of Rb protein and to cell cycle arrest.

## What Are the Phenotypic Changes Induced by Senescence?

During senescence, the cell is not only blocked in a G0/G1 quiescent state, but also in refractory to apoptosis. A senescent cell displays an enlarged shape and very particular secretion properties, called the senescent messaging secretome (SMS) or the senescent-associated secreting phenotype (SASP). The lysosomal activity is highly activated, explaining the characteristic expression of β-galactosidase. Such phenotypic changes induce both intrinsic (cell-autonomous) and extrinsic (non-cell-autonomous) properties in patterns of aging:

— *At the cell-autonomous level*, as senescent cells stop to proliferate but are refractory to apoptosis, they may accumulate in tissues with a high turnover rate and be exposed to pro-oncogenic conditions. Senescence appears in this context to display tumor-protection properties (Campisi, 2001; Prieur and Peeper, 2008; Collado and Serrano, 2010). Thus, senescent cells were shown to accumulate in both UV-exposed skin (in the periphery of pre-malignant regions) and HPV-infested cervixes. At the same time, senescence causes clonal restriction of somatic tissues with a high turnover. Therefore, as senescent cells have no more proliferation ability, they contribute to the progressive exhaustion of such tissues, thus illustrating the antagonist pleiotropy theory of aging, that such anti-cancer properties, however beneficial in younger ages, may display the detrimental characteristics of aging (Williams, 1957). In the hematopoietic system, such characteristics may lead to some loss of heterogeneity, ultimately leading, for example, to myelodysplasia. Lately, the accumulation of senescent cells appears to have pro-oncogenic properties – as these cells are refractory to apoptosis, they are more prone than normal cells to develop immortality and oncologic features in response to an additional mutational event (Gosselin et al., 2009).

— *At the non-cell-autonomous level*, the SASP includes growth factors, cytokines, extracellular matrix, and degradative enzymes able to alter the tissue micro-environment, affect proliferative properties of nearby cells, and are proposed to affect more remote cells through endocrine pathways. As for cell-autonomous properties of senescent cells, the SASP has a dual role during cancer development (Mitri and Alimonti, 2016). In one hand, it prevents carcinogenesis, by the activation of innate immunity and immune clearance of senescent cells (Xue et al., 2007; Krizhanovsky et al., 2008; Kang et al., 2011), and by event-inducing senescence in neighboring healthy cells (Hubackova et al., 2012; Acosta et al., 2013; Hoare and Narita, 2013). In the other hand, it favors the transformation of precancerous cells (Krtolica et al., 2001), and the epithelial-mesenchymal transition of tumor cells (Coppé et al., 2008). This secretory phenotype is not unique, but may be regulated by lateral induction, since NOTCH1 was recently shown to promote a TGFβ-dependent secretome and to inhibit pro-inflammatory cytokines, thus favoring adaptive immunity (Hoare et al., 2016). If the ability of senescent cells to develop paracrine as well as endocrine properties is speculated to play a major role in the phenotypic characteristics of aging, and in particular in its associated chronic inflammatory state, also called inflamm-aging, then this link has not been demonstrated *in vivo*. Moreover, Campisi et al. speculate that the SASP could be related to the continuous activation of the DNA-damage response pathway and not specific to senescence itself (Campisi et al., 2011).

## What Are the Relationships between Senescence and the Longevity Pathways?

With the discovery of genetic mutations able to extend life span, and conserved in small invertebrates (*Caenorhabditis elegans*) to mammalians, the idea arose that aging and senescence could be downregulated, thus both slowing the rate of intrinsic aging and preventing age-related degenerative diseases. These longevity pathways imply the regulation of metabolism, germinal cells, and mitochondrial activity. According to the metabolic pathway, food excess induces the activation of insulin, insulin growth factor 1 (IGF-1), and target of rapamycin (TOR, mammalian target of rapamycin (mTOR) in mammals) pathways, whereas food restriction activates AMP-activated protein kinase and sirtuins. In several laboratory models, caloric restriction (CR) without malnutrition, pharmaceutical inhibition of TOR, and the reduction in functional mutations in the insulin/IGF-1 signaling pathway promoted longevity. Longevity pathways may be considered as applications of the hyperfunction theory of aging – aging as the result of a quasi-program induced by the overstimulation of physiological processes after adult development (Blagosklonny, 2010, 2012), explaining many age-related diseases linked to an overload in tissue function, the proliferation of vascular smooth muscle cell (VSCM), leading to atherogenesis and ultimately to atherosclerosis and hyperactivity of osteoclast leading to osteoporosis (see next paragraph). Accumulating evidence has demonstrated several interconnections between senescence regulation pathways and longevity pathways (Xu et al., 2014). In particular, two conserved TOR complexes (TORC) have been identified as TORC1 and TORC2, each with different functions. TORC1 regulates nutrient signaling and growth regulation. In higher organisms, TORC1 is activated by insulin and IGF1, and in turn, inhibits three important pathways: mitochondrial metabolism, autophagy, and protein translation, finally leading to cellular senescence (Xu et al., 2014). Thus, pharmaceutical inhibition of TORC1 by rapamycin analogs prevents cellular senescence.

## What Are the Relationships between Senescence and Age-Related Diseases?

According to Campisi et al., age-related diseases should be segregated into two broad categories: the diseases related to a loss of function and the diseases related to a gain of function. Into the first category should fall sarcopenia, macular degeneration, osteoporosis, and some neurodegenerative diseases, while hyperplasia and atherosclerosis should fall into the second category (Campisi et al., 2011). Evidence accumulated *in vitro* proposes a link between age-associated phenotypes and the consequences of cell-autonomous and non-cell-autonomous functions of senescent cells through alterations of their microenvironment.

### Osteoporosis

Osteoporosis is the consequence of an aberrant balance of bone remodeling between resorption by osteoclasts and formation by osteoblasts. Osteoclasts derive from bone marrow cells (BMC) and osteoblasts from mesenchymal stem cells (MSCs), also called bone marrow stromal cells (BMSC). During the aging process, this imbalance implies both dysfunctional osteoblasts, as well as an activation in excess of osteoclasts. MSCs from elderly patients display characteristics of senescent cells, like B-Gal staining, short telomeres (Baxter et al., 2004; Zhou et al., 2008), and a decreased ability to differentiate into the osteoblastic lineage. As MSCs from patients suffering from osteoporosis display a higher level of p16ink4a and p21 expression than MSCs from healthy individuals, senescence is considered to contribute physiopathologically to the disease (Benisch et al., 2012). In telomerase dysfunction (terc−/−) mice, an accelerated aging phenotype is observed, illustrated by a premature bone loss starting at 3 months of age. In those mice, MSCs and osteoprogenitors, which normally give rise to osteoblasts, show intrinsic defects in proliferation and osteogenic differentiation. Those cells display a high level of DNA-damage and senescence-associated β-galactosidase. At the same time, a sustained expression of pro-inflammatory genes contribute to a high level of osteoclast activity (Kassem and Marie, 2011; Saeed et al., 2011). A similar phenotype is observed in progeroid syndrome ERCC1-XPF–deficient mice (Chen et al., 2013), as well as in p53 overexpressing ones (Tyner et al., 2002). The activation of the SASP leads to an NF-κB-dependent enhanced secretion of inflammatory cytokines such as interleukin-6 (IL-6), tumor necrosis factor α (TNFα), and receptor activator of NF-κB ligand (RANKL), with pro-osteoclastogenic properties (Chen et al., 2013). On the contrary, telomerase overexpression leads to enhanced MSCs differentiation in osteoblasts *in vitro* and to increased bone formation *in vivo* (Shi et al., 2002; Yudoh and Nishioka, 2004).

### Neurodegenerative Diseases

Neurodegenerative diseases are characterized by a high level of neuroinflammation, a phenotype proposed to be partly dependent on senescent astrocytes.

With *in vitro*, astrocytes are highly sensitive to senescence, characterized by the expression of p16ink4a and matrix metalloproteinase-1 (MMP-1). While with *in vivo*, an increased expression of these two genes has been demonstrated both in the aging brain and during Alzheimer's disease (Bhat et al., 2012). More globally, astrocytes seem to recapitulate characteristics of senescence (Bitto et al., 2010) and SASP (Salminen et al., 2011).

During Alzheimer's disease brain atrophy is accompanied by two biochemical hallmarks: extracellular β-amyloid peptide deposits and intracellular accumulation of phosphorylated tau. Activated microglial cells, which represent a specific subspecies of macrophages, accumulate at the periphery of amyloid plaques both in humans and in mice (Akiyama et al., 2000; Perry et al., 2010), and display a pro-inflammatory profile, which leads to neuronal and synaptic damage (Schott and Revesz, 2013).

## Atherosclerosis

Two phenomena contribute to cardiovascular risk at the arterial wall level: the atherogenesis – mainly due to a sustained proliferation of VSMC, and the atherosclerosis, in which inflammation plays a major role. In injured arteries, cells of the vascular system display a decreased proliferation potential, an increased risk of death, telomere shortening, and DNA-damage. Among the physiopathological pathways contributing to such a chronic arterial injury, telomere shortening in VSCMs and ECs, and senescence activation seem to play a major role (Minamino and Komuro, 2007). An accumulation of senescent cells – characterized by a B-Gal staining and elevated levels of p53, p16, and p14 expression – was demonstrated, both in endothelial cells and in VSMCs (Minamino et al., 2002). Such an accumulation is correlated to cardiovascular risk and located in injured arteries, and not in normal ones. During aging, the expression of TERT is decreased (Hsiao et al., 1997; Minamino et al., 2001), contributing to the decreased proliferation of VSCMs and ECs. At this stage, the rupture of a vulnerable plaque overhanging a necrotic core induces the morbidity of cardiovascular diseases. This phenomenon has recently been attributed to the activation of senescence in the VSMC, in response to a p53-dependent degradation of TRF2, a protein of the Shelterin complex (Wang et al., 2015). Such dysfunctional telomeres induce the activation of a DNA-damage response, contributing to the pro-inflammatory state and to plaque instability. In parallel, senescent ECs display a decreased basal activity of nitrite oxide synthase (eNOS) (Matsushita et al., 2001; Minamino et al., 2002), as well as a decreased induction in response to injury, leading to the accumulation of reactive oxygen species. Oxidative stress may also be chronically induced by chemical oxidants like oxidized low-density lipoprotein (LDL) in the context of hypercholesterolemia (Maier et al., 1996) or glycated type I collagen in the context of diabetes (Chen et al., 2002). Such an accumulation of oxidative stress contributes to the pro-inflammatory phenotype, characterized by increased levels of thromboxane A2, endothelin-1, plasminogen activator inhibitor 1 (PAI-1), ICAM-1, inflammatory cytokine (IL1, IL6, IL8), matrix remodeling proteins (elastase,

MMP), and the decreased levels of prostacyclin (Minamino and Komuro, 2007). In turn, chronically maintaining high levels of DNA-damage, reducing telomerase activity, and activating senescence creates a vicious circle. Moreover, senescence is associated with a decreased secretion of Sirtuin 1 (SIRT1), an NAD+/-dependent deacetylase considered to be an anti-aging molecule induced during CR, giving an illustration of the connection between metabolic pathways and senescence. SIRT1 is currently considered as a future therapeutic target to prevent cardiovascular diseases (Chen et al., 2016; Kitada et al., 2016).

## Type 2 Diabetes

Insulin resistance plays a major role during pathogenesis of type 2 diabetes (T2D), inducing the initially functional expansion of islets β-cells. A chronic inflammation of those cells (insulitis), partly related to pro-inflammatory cytokines secreted by fat tissues, contributes to insulin deficiency. A growing piece of evidence has linked this pro-inflammatory phenotype to the accumulation of senescent cells in adipose tissues (Minamino and Komuro, 2007; Markowski et al., 2013), and notably white adipose tissue (WAT) – a phenomenon amplified in progeroid models (Minamino and Komuro, 2007) and reduced in the context of GH-deficiency, known to protect against T2D (Stout et al., 2014). As mentioned earlier, the accumulation of glycated adjuncts contributes to the accumulation of ROS and the chronic pro-inflammatory phenotype to diabetes-related complications.

## Cataract

Cataract is characterized by the modifications of the characteristics and functions of the lens, leading to more compact and less refractive properties, pigment deposits, and reduced accommodation capacity (Asbell et al., 2005). Lens fibers are constituted by lens epithelial cells (LECs) that are highly sensitive to oxidative stress (Babizhayev et al., 2011). During aging, cataractogenesis is triggered by LECs's telomere attrition, leading to senescence. LECs from elderly patients, as well as from BubR1 progeroid mice (Baker et al., 2006), display reduced proliferation, high SA-β-Gal activity, and a high expression of p16ink4a, p19Arf, and p21. On the contrary, p21 overexpression is sufficient to drive cataractogenesis (Baker et al., 2013).

## Respiratory Diseases

Senescence and autophagy dysfunction appear as drivers of two degenerative respiratory diseases (Kuwano et al., 2016):

– During *chronic obstructive pulmonary disease* (COPD), cell senescence is at the crossroads between aging and chronic inflammation, mediated by environmental pollutants (and particularly cigarette smoke) and driving chronic oxidative stress. Chronic inflammation (either in response to environ-mental stress or SASP-driven) is a mediator of chronic bronchitis, leading to tissue remodeling, immune cells recruitment (macrophages, neutrophils, and T cells), and maintenance of cell senescence (Tsuji et al., 2010). Senescence of pulmonary cells progenitors – called Clara-cells – impairs cell proliferation and tissue repair, participating in the destruction of pulmonary alveoli and emphysema (Aoshiba and Nagai, 2009). In addition, such a pro-inflammatory micro-environment may lead to circulating senescent T cells, in turn, contrib-uting to chronic inflammation maintenance (Lambers et al., 2009).

- In *idiopathic pulmonary fibrosis* (IPF), replicative senescence is proposed to play a major role, since shorter telomere are found in blood leukocytes and alveolar epithelial cells from patients with IPF (Minagawa et al., 2011). In this disease, ac-celerated epithelial cell senescence is associated with an epithelial-mesenchymal transition and a myofibroblast differentiation, contributing to fibrosis. The association of IPF with either telomere syndrome features (skin, liver, and/or hematological abnormalities) or a familial history of interstitial lung disease is more frequent in the presence of TERT/TERC mutations (Borie et al., 2016).

## Cancer

Cancer may finally be considered as an archetype of an age-related disease, based on the exponential increase of its incidence in older age. As developed earlier, cell senescence may be interpreted as a barrier to cancer development but acts both in tumor prevention and tumor promotion, at the cell-autonomous as well as at the non-cell-autonomous levels, interacting with precancerous cells, their micro-environment, and the immune system, as well as with (tumor) stem cells (Falandry et al., 2014).

## Conclusion – Perspectives

If senescence may be considered as the price to pay for cancer preven-tion in somatic cells, then the pro-inflammatory and tissue remodeling properties of SASP, demonstrated *in vitro*, will play a major role in intrinsic aging and age-related pathologies (Campisi, 2005). More recently, an experimental model leading to the *in vivo* clearance of p16ink4a was shown to increase life span and delay the development of age-related diseases, demonstrating the validity of such a hypothesis in an *in vivo* model (Baker et al., 2011). The regulation of cellular senescence and its relationships with longevity pathways give rise to therapeutic perspectives, leading to the idea that both intrinsic aging and age-related degenerative diseases, including cancer, may be prevented. Among these, one may consider not only the influence of pharmaceutical strategies, as it is currently evaluated in clinical studies with rapamycin analogs or SIRT1 activators, but also the beneficial impacts of healthier lifestyles.

## References

Acosta J. C., Banito A., Wuestefeld T., et al. A complex secretory program orchestrated by the inflammasome controls paracrine senescence. *Nat Cell Biol.* août 2013;15(8):978–90.

Aguilaniu H., Gustafsson L., Rigoulet M., and Nyström T. Asymmetric inheritance of oxidatively damaged proteins during cytokinesis. *Science.* 14 mars 2003; 299(5613):1751–3.

Akiyama H., Barger S., Barnum S., et al. Inflammation and Alzheimer's disease. *Neurobiol Aging.* 1 mai 2000;21(3):383–421.

Aoshiba K., Nagai A. Senescence hypothesis for the pathogenetic mechanism of chronic obstructive pulmonary disease. *Proc Am Thorac Soc.* 1 déc 2009;6(7):596–601.

Asbell P. A., Dualan I., Mindel J., et al. Age-related cataract. *The Lancet.* 12 févr 2005;365(9459):599–609.

Babizhayev M. A., Vishnyakova K. S., Yegorov Y. E. Telomere-dependent senescent phenotype of lens epithelial cells as a biological marker of aging and cataractogenesis: the role of oxidative stress intensity and specific mechanism of phospholipid hydroperoxide toxicity in lens and aqueous. *Fundam Clin Pharmacol.* 1 avr 2011;25(2):139–62.

Baker D. J., Jeganathan K. B., Malureanu L., et al. Early aging-associated phenotypes in Bub3/Rae1 haplo insufficient mice. *J Cell Biol.* 13 févr 2006;172(4):529–40.

Baker D. J., Weaver R. L., van Deursen J. M. p21 both attenuates and drives senescence and aging in BubR1 progeroid mice. *Cell Rep.* 25 avr 2013;3(4):1164–74.

Baker D. J., Wijshake T., Tchkonia T., et al. Clearance of p16Ink4a-positive senescent cells delays ageing-associated disorders. *Nature.* 2 nov 2011;479(7372):232–6.

Baxter M. A., Wynn R. F., Jowitt S. N., et al. Study of telomere length reveals rapid aging of human marrow stromal cells following in vitro expansion. *Stem Cells.* 1 sept 2004;22(5):675–82.

Benisch P., Schilling T., Klein-Hitpass L., et al. The transcriptional profile of mesenchymal stem cell populations in primary osteoporosis is distinct and shows overexpression of osteogenic inhibitors. *PLoS ONE.* 24 sept 2012;7(9):e45142.

Bhat R., Crowe E. P., Bitto A., et al. Astrocyte senescence as a component of Alzheimer's disease. *PLoS ONE.* 12 sept 2012;7(9):e45069.

Bitto A., Sell C., Crowe E., et al. Stress-induced senescence in human and rodent astrocytes. *Exp Cell Res.* 15 oct 2010;316(17):2961–8.

Blagosklonny M. V. Revisiting the antagonistic pleiotropy theory of aging: TOR-driven program and quasi-program. *Cell Cycle.* 15 août 2010;9(16):3171–6.

Answering the ultimate question What is the Proximal Cause of Aging? *Aging.* 30 déc 2012;4(12):861–77.

Borie R., Tabèze L., Thabut G., et al. Prevalence and characteristics of TERT and TERC mutations in suspected genetic pulmonary fibrosis. *Eur Respir J.* 1 déc 2016;48(6):1721–31.

Campisi J. Senescent cells, tumor suppression, and organismal aging: good citizens, bad neighbors. *Cell.* 25 févr 2005;120(4):513–22.

Cellular senescence as a tumor-suppressor mechanism. *Trends Cell Biol.* 1 nov 2001;11(11):S27–31.

Campisi J., Andersen J. K., Kapahi P., Melov S. Cellular senescence: a link between cancer and age-related degenerative disease? *Semin Cancer Biol.* déc 2011;21(6):354–9.

Chen H.-Z., Wang F., Gao P., et al. Age-associated Sirtuin 1 reduction in vascular smooth muscle links vascular senescence and inflammation to abdominal aortic aneurysm novelty and significance. *Circ Res.* 28 oct 2016;119(10):1076–88.

Chen J., Brodsky S. V., Goligorsky D. M., et al. Glycated collagen I induces premature senescence-like phenotypic changes in endothelial cells. *Circ Res.* 28 juin 2002;90(12):1290–8.

Chen Q., Liu K., Robinson A. R., et al. DNA damage drives accelerated bone aging via an NF-κB-dependent mechanism. *J Bone Miner Res.* 1 mai 2013;28(5):1214–28.

Collado M., Serrano M. Senescence in tumours: evidence from mice and humans. *Nat Rev Cancer.* janv 2010;10(1):51–7.

Coppé J.-P., Patil C. K., Rodier F., et al. Senescence-associated secretory phenotypes reveal cell-nonautonomous functions of oncogenic RAS and the p53 tumor suppressor. *PLoS Biol.* déc 2008;6(12):e301.

Falandry C., Bonnefoy M., Freyer G., Gilson E. Biology of cancer and aging: a complex association with cellular senescence. *J Clin Oncol.* 20 août 2014;32(24):2604–10.

Gosselin K., Martien S., Pourtier A., et al. Senescence-associated oxidative DNA damage promotes the generation of neoplastic cells. *Cancer Res.* 15 oct 2009;69(20):7917–25.

Harman D. Aging: a theory based on free radical and radiation chemistry. *Journal of Gerontology.* juill 1956;11(3):298–300.

Hayflick L., Moorhead P. S. The serial cultivation of human diploid cell strains. *Exp Cell Res.* 1961;25:585–621.

Hoare M., Ito Y., Kang T.-W., et al. NOTCH1 mediates a switch between two distinct secretomes during senescence. *Nat Cell Biol.* sept 2016;18(9):979–92.

Hoare M., Narita M. Transmitting senescence to the cell neighbourhood. *Nat Cell Biol.* août 2013;15(8):887–9.

Hsiao R., Sharma H. W., Ramakrishnan S., Keith E., Narayanan R. Telomerase activity in normal human endothelial cells. *Anticancer Res.* avr 1997;17(2A):827–32.

Hubackova S., Krejcikova K., Bartek J., Hodny Z. IL1- and TGFβ-Nox4 signaling, oxidative stress and DNA damage response are shared features of replicative, oncogene-induced, and drug-induced paracrine "Bystander senescence." *Aging.* 30 déc 2012;4(12):932–51.

Kang T.-W., Yevsa T., Woller N., et al. Senescence surveillance of pre-malignant hepatocytes limits liver cancer development. *Nature.* 24 nov 2011;479(7374):547–51.

Kassem M., Marie P. J. Senescence-associated intrinsic mechanisms of osteoblast dysfunctions. *Aging Cell.* 1 avr 2011;10(2):191–7.

Kirkwood T. B., Holliday R. The evolution of ageing and longevity. *Proc R Soc Lond B Biol Sci.* 21 sept 1979;205(1161):531–46.

Kitada M., Ogura Y., Koya D. The protective role of Sirt1 in vascular tissue: its relationship to vascular aging and atherosclerosis. *Aging.* 15 oct 2016;8(10):2290–307.

Krizhanovsky V., Yon M., Dickins R. A., et al. Senescence of activated stellate cells limits liver fibrosis. *Cell.* 22 août 2008;134(4):657–67.

Krtolica A., Parrinello S., Lockett S., Desprez P.-Y., Campisi J. Senescent fibroblasts promote epithelial cell growth and tumorigenesis: a link between cancer and aging. *Proc Natl Acad Sci.* 10 sept 2001;98(21):12072–7.

Kuwano K., Araya J., Hara H., et al. Cellular senescence and autophagy in the pathogenesis of chronic obstructive pulmonary disease (COPD) and idiopathic pulmonary fibrosis (IPF). *Respir Investig.* 1 nov 2016;54(6):397–406.

Lambers C., Hacker S., Posch M., et al. T cell senescence and contraction of T cell repertoire diversity in patients with chronic obstructive pulmonary disease. *Clin Exp Immunol.* 1 mars 2009;155(3):466–75.

Maier J. A. M., Barenghi L., Bradamante S., Pagani F. Induction of human endothelial cell growth by mildly oxidized low density lipoprotein. *Atherosclerosis.* 1 juin 1996;123(1):115–21.

Markowski D. N., Thies H. W., Gottlieb A., et al. HMGA2 expression in white adipose tissue linking cellular senescence with diabetes. *Genes Nutr.* 1 sept 2013;8(5):449–56.

Matsushita H., Chang E., Glassford A. J., et al. eNOS activity is reduced in senescent human endothelial cells. *Circ Res.* 26 oct 2001;89(9):793–8.

Medawar P. B. *Unsolved Problems of Biology.* London: H.K. Lewis; 1952.

Minagawa S., Araya J., Numata T., et al. Accelerated epithelial cell senescence in IPF and the inhibitory role of SIRT6 in TGF-β-induced senescence of human bronchial epithelial cells. *Am J Physiol – Lung Cell Mol Physiol.* 1 mars 2011;300(3):L391–401.

Minamino T., Komuro I. Vascular cell senescence. *Circ Res.* 5 janv 2007;100(1):15–26.

Minamino T., Mitsialis S. A., Kourembanas S. Hypoxia extends the life span of vascular smooth muscle cells through telomerase activation. *Mol Cell Biol.* mai 2001;21(10):3336–42.

Minamino T., Miyauchi H., Yoshida T., et al. Endothelial cell senescence in human atherosclerosis. *Circulation.* 2 avr 2002;105(13):1541–4.

Mitri D. D., Alimonti A. Non-cell-autonomous regulation of cellular senescence in cancer. *Trends Cell Biol.* 1 mars 2016;26(3):215–26.

Perry V. H., Nicoll J. A. R., Holmes C. Microglia in neurodegenerative disease. *Nat Rev Neurol.* avr 2010;6(4):193–201.

Prieur A., Peeper D. S. Cellular senescence in vivo: a barrier to tumorigenesis. *Curr Opin Cell Biol.* avr 2008;20(2):150–5.

Saeed H., Abdallah B. M., Ditzel N., et al. Telomerase-deficient mice exhibit bone loss owing to defects in osteoblasts and increased osteoclastogenesis by inflammatory microenvironment. *J Bone Miner Res.* 1 juill 2011;26(7): 1494–505.

Salminen A., Ojala J., Kaarniranta K., et al. Astrocytes in the aging brain express characteristics of senescence-associated secretory phenotype. *Eur J Neurosci.* 1 juill 2011;34(1):3–11.

Schott J. M., Revesz T. Inflammation in Alzheimer's disease: insights from immunotherapy. *Brain.* 1 sept 2013;136(9):2654–6.

Shi S., Gronthos S., Chen S., et al. Bone formation by human postnatal bone marrow stromal stem cells is enhanced by telomerase expression. *Nat Biotechnol.* juin 2002;20(6):587–91.

Stout M. B., Tchkonia T., Pirtskhalava T., et al. Growth hormone action predicts age-related white adipose tissue dysfunction and senescent cell burden in mice. *Aging.* 20 juill 2014;6(7):575–86.

Tsuji T., Aoshiba K., Nagai A. Alveolar cell senescence exacerbates pulmonary inflammation in patients with chronic obstructive pulmonary disease. *Respir Int Rev Thorac Dis.* 2010;80(1):59–70.

Tyner S. D., Venkatachalam S., Choi J., et al. p53 mutant mice that display early ageing-associated phenotypes. *Nature.* 3 janv 2002;415(6867):45–53.

Wang J., Uryga A. K., Reinhold J., et al. Vascular smooth muscle cell senescence promotes atherosclerosis and features of plaque vulnerability: clinical perspective. *Circulation*. 17 nov 2015;132(20):1909–19.

Williams G. C. Pleiotropy, natural selection, and the evolution of senescence. *Evolution*. 1957;11:398–411.

Xu S., Cai Y., Wei Y., et al. mTOR signaling from cellular senescence to organismal aging. *Aging Dis*. 4 nov 2014;5(4):263–73.

Xue W., Zender L., Miething C., et al. Senescence and tumour clearance is triggered by p53 restoration in murine liver carcinomas. *Nature*. 8 févr 2007;445(7128): 656–60.

Yudoh K., Nishioka K. Telomerized presenescent osteoblasts prevent bone mass loss in vivo. *Gene Ther*. 1 avr 2004;11(11):909–15.

Zhou S., Greenberger J. S., Epperly M. W., et al. Age-related intrinsic changes in human bone-marrow-derived mesenchymal stem cells and their differentiation to osteoblasts. *Aging Cell*. 1 juin 2008;7(3):335–43.

# 5  From Inflamm-Aging to Immunosenescence

Tamàs Fulop, Jacek M. Witkowski, Alan A. Cohen, Gilles Dupuis, Katsuiku Hirokawa, and Anis Larbi

## Introduction

Aging, crudely defined as the period in life when bodily functions became progressively less-than-perfect, eventually precipitating the inevitable end, has always fascinated human beings, who have sought for multiple "fountains of eternal youth life" – i.e., the reversion of aging effects. Even now, despite decades of scientific efforts to understand it and despite huge progress, we are far from understanding the essence of aging and so it remains "mysterious" (Lipsky and King, 2015). Recently, the understanding of the aging processes of various systems of the organism, including the immune system, made significant steps forward (Cohen et al., 2015). The paradigm that the immune response is adversely altered with aging, leading to various clinical consequences, exists from the earliest studies on coping with the effects of aging on immunity performed decades ago and drives our conceptualization on the assessment of these changes (Effros, 2004). Conceptually, the study of the immune system aging emerged from the necessity to better understand why elderly people are more susceptible to various diseases such as infections (Bandaranayake and Shaw, 2016). With better understanding of the cellular and molecular basis of the immune response in various living organisms including humans, the age-related changes in the immune reactivity have been also better unraveled (Le Saux S1, 2012; Müller et al., 2013). Thus, the study of the immune response in aged organisms describing its deleterious alterations occurring with aging led to the concept of *immunosenescence* (Pawelec et al., 2005; Pawelec, 2014). However, the changes observed especially in the adaptive immune system did not explain all aspects of the observed clinical consequences (Cannizzo et al., 2011). Thus, in an attempt to capture the age-related immune changes more widely, and from a different point of view, a new concept emerged, and was called *inflamm-aging* (Franceschi et al., 2000; Salvioli et al., 2013). The inflamm-aging concept gained popularity very quickly as it is an observable and measurable way to conceptualize the

This work was partly supported by grants from the Canadian Institutes of Health Research (No. 106634 and No. 106701), the University of Sherbrooke, and the Research Center on Aging; Polish Ministry of Science and Higher Education statutory grant 02-0058/07/262 to JMW; Agency for Science Technology and Research (A*STAR) to AL. AAC is supported by a New Investigator Salary Award from the Canadian Institutes of Health Research and is a member of the Fonds de recherche du Quebec-Santé-supported Centre de recherche sur le vieillissement and Centre de recherche du CHUS.

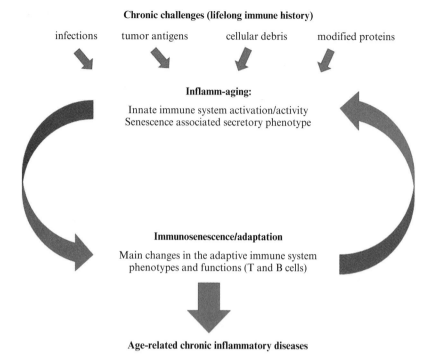

**Figure 5.1.** *The vicious circle between inflamm-aging and immunosenescence/ adaptation*

The life long immune history is inducing a constant activation of the innate immune system which will produce pro-inflammatory mediators, which concomitantly with the direct antigenic challenges induce the well-known changes in the adaptive immune response. Inversely, the changed adaptive response will contribute to the persistent stimulation of the Inflammaging process by the lack of elimination of chronic aggressions. Ultimately, these changes lead to the development and progression of the age-related chronic inflammatory diseases.

aging-associated immune changes and because it could be directly related to the pathological changes in the elderly. Recent progress in the understanding of immune changes that come with aging attempts to merge these two concepts. The final result suggests that both reflect the same process, but differentially – either in the innate immune system (inflamm-aging) or in the adaptive immune system (immunosenescence) (Figure 5.1). It is difficult at this stage to determine which one is predominant, if there is any hierarchy between the two, but we can put forward the idea that the inflamm-aging is somehow occurring earlier or at least in parallel to immunosenescence (Fulop et al., 2014).

## What Is Inflamm-Aging and What Does It Mean?

Claudio Franceschi stated already in 2000 that aging is accompanied by a low-grade inflammation and coined the term inflamm-aging to describe this phenomenon (Cannizzo et al., 2011). The current understanding of the inflamm-aging process is that levels of some very common pro-inflammatory mediators in biological material are increased with aging. These mediators include pro-inflammatory cytokines, chemokines, and free radicals (Fulop et al., 2015). These substances are mainly (although not exclusively) secreted by the cells of the innate immune system. The recent discovery of so-called senescent cells accumulating in many tissues with aging and displaying the senescence-associated secretory phenotype (SASP), indicates a likelihood that every cell type in an aging organism may contribute to this secretion (Byun et al., 2015; Herranz et al., 2015; Lasry and Ben-Neriah, 2015; Chandrasekaran et al., 2017).

Inflammation is a very common phenomenon, which is vital for life as the first line of protection against pathogen challenge (Arulselvan et al., 2016). This means that during a lifetime, the immune system is under constant pressure to combat all types of aggressions that physiologically result in the resolution of the harm caused by the aggression. These aggressions are causing the activation of the innate immune system first, and the adaptive immune system consequently (Fortin et al., 2008). Consistently, aging of the immune system reflects the immune history occurring during the whole life. Physiologically, inflammation is short (acute) and relatively tightly controlled in order to avoid excessive damage to the organism by agents participating in the elimination of pathogens. The activation of the immune system is resolved by the phenomenon of apoptosis and the establishment of immune memory.

If the pathogen or other challenge persists, then the immune system has no means to return to the basic level. When the inflammatory process cannot be resolved, a chronic inflammatory state occurs. The maintenance of chronic inflammation is costly for the organism and diverts the immune system from fighting against new challenges and reduces its ability to continuously perform the surveillance of the ever-occurring viral reactivations. Thus, the term inflamm-aging refers to a state that is chronic and unregulated (Fougère et al., 2017).

Numerous agents induce this chronic antigenic stimulation. The most commonly accepted ones are the chronic infections, including viral and bacterial (van Baarle et al., 2005; Marandu et al., 2015). The best-known viral infection inducing inflamm-aging is the cytomegalovirus (CMV) (Pawelec et al., 2009; Solana et al., 2012). However, its effect is mainly on the adaptive immune system (especially on the CD8+ T cells). It is conceivable that the detrimental changes observed in the adaptive immune system, due to these constant stimulations, favor the "hypertrophy" (or hyperactivity) of the innate immune system and cause chronic imbalance. Other challenges are represented by the constant production of waste products such as the advanced glycation end products (AGE), by the oxidatively modified proteins and lipids such as oxLDL, by the glycation-induced protein modification such as the Maillard reaction, or by cancerous cells.

What is the molecular mechanism of inflamm-aging? The common endpoint is the production of pro-inflammatory molecules such as cytokines, chemokines, and reactive oxygen species (ROS). The agents mentioned above would stimulate the cells of the innate immune system such as natural killer (NK) cells, monocytes/macrophages, and neutrophils to react to the challenges. The first step is the stimulation by a ligand (a pathogen- or damage-associated (danger) molecular pattern, PAMP, and DAMP, respectively) of the innate receptors, which will all converge to induce the activation of the transcription factor NFκB to translocate to the nucleus and stimulate pro-inflammatory molecules' genes such as TNFα or IL-6 (Kaufmann and Dorhoi, 2016; Rivera et al., 2016). The many pathways converging on NFκB activation occur through the Toll-like receptors (TLRs), the Rig-like, and the NOD receptors, initiating a signal transduction resulting in NFκB activation (Satoh and Akira, 2016). The role of inflammasome (also being a consequence of triggering of the above-mentioned receptors) resulting in IL-1β, IL-18, and IL-33 production is also important in low-grade inflammation (Jha et al., 2017). The common endpoint is the production of multiple species of pro-inflammatory molecules such as cytokines, chemokines, and ROS. Presently, some scientists call this phenomenon an oxy-inflamm-aging, to stress the role of ROS in the process (Bauer and Fuente Mde, 2016).

All these chronic stimulations are maintaining a state of basal activation of the NK cells, monocytes/macrophages, and neutrophils with aging (Smallwood et al., 2011). This means that these cells are manifesting a sustained activity in the elderly, detectable as an increased production of pro-inflammatory mediators in the absence of specific stimulants (at the quiescent state). The signaling pathways (such as the PI3K, STAT, and MAPKs) in these cells are all in a state of increased phosphorylation, reflecting an activated state (Pinti et al., 2016). The NFκB transcription factor is also in a state of increased activation in the absence of specific stimulant. This basic state of innate immune system activation has many consequences for the aging organism (Ponnappan and Ponnappan, 2011).

## What Are the Consequences of This Basal Activation State?

Many functional changes were demonstrated in both parts of the immune response with aging. In the innate immune part many functions of the NK cells, monocytes/macrophages, dendritic cells (DCs), and neutrophils were found to be altered (Solana et al., 2012; Montgomery and Shaw, 2015). In the **NK** cells there are decreased cytotoxic, secretory, and proliferative capacities under specific challenges (Gabrielli et al., 2016). They also change their phenotype by acquiring senescent-type markers, as well as inhibitory receptors (Pera et al., 2015). The **monocytes/macrophages** show altered functioning by decreasing their chemotaxis, phagocytosis, and killing functions (Albright et al., 2016). In the meantime, the proportion of monocyte subpopulations is also shifted toward the inflammatory subtypes, such as the intermediate subpopulation (Seidler et al., 2010). The **neutrophils** – the first cells to arrive at the site of an aggression – have also shown altered functions with aging such as chemotaxis, free radical production, and intra- and extracellular killing of bacteria (Xia et al., 2016). The **DCs** present an altered antigen presentation to CD4+ T cells. As all these functions necessitate an intact receptor functioning, it was shown that the signaling pathways elicited by the above-mentioned receptor families and ultimately leading to these functions in the innate immune cells are also altered in aging (Qian et al., 2011; Magrone and Jirillo, 2014). By means of their functions these cells play an essential role in the immune response against various challenges such as infections, cancer development, and autoimmune phenomena. Thus, with the decrease (or alteration) of their functions, they may contribute to the numerous diseases occurring in an age-dependent manner (Fulop et al., 2004; Solana et al., 2012).

Under specific challenges these innate cells are unable to perform adequately in an aging organism, which raises the question of whether or not a sustained basal activation state is a contributing factor (Fulop et al., 2016). As these cells are already stimulated, the effect of a further stimulation (by a pathogen) seems altered. However, we should consider two important and different appreciations. When we study these functions in the elderly, we compare them constantly to the young subjects and this way we see a decrease in many measurable parameters. However, we do not know whether this decrease has deleterious consequences, because we do not know what an aging immune system needs for its protective functioning in the physiologic milieu of an aging body. As not all elderly present fatal infections or cancer each time they are challenged by a pathogen or oncogenic mutation, the functioning of the innate part of the immune system is still adequate for the circumstances. This suggests also another approach, which is to consider basal activation as a *necessary* state for the adequate functioning of the innate immune system with aging, even if it is not at the level of the young. Thus, it could be that, evolutionarily, the activation of the innate immune system with aging is necessary for it to adequately function, even if parameters of this function seem to be lower than those measured in young subjects.

## What Could Be the Molecular Mechanism of This Sustained Activation?

The question is why the innate immune cells are in a state of sustained activation in aging. One hypothesis is that they represent a sort of trained innate memory state. This concept is rather new and was first seen after a specific stimulation, such as with the bacilli Calmette-Guérin (BCG). Even 3 months after the challenge, the innate cells (monocyte/macrophages) were able to sustain a certain "memory" of the infection and react in the absence of BCG (Kleinnijenhuis et al., 2012). This has led to the concept that the innate immune system has a certain "memory," which was not foreseen from the previous paradigm of the immune system functioning. This would mean that even the innate immune system is remembering a previous contact with the pathogen and can react more quickly to similar aggressions.

In the frame of the aging innate immune system, we can also suggest that it has a *sustained trained immune "memory,"* which is leading to the maintained activation state, even in the absence of the specific challenge. This memory is likely due to a shift in the epigenetic landscape (epigenome) of the innate cells and fueled by an energetic shift inside of these cells. We do not have formal proof for the contribution of these phenomena to the basic activation of the innate immune cells, but this seems strongly probable. If this would be the case, then the epigenome and pathways involved in energy production, use, and conservation inside the immune cells could be perfect targets for immune modulation in the elderly.

Besides being able to demonstrate the trained memory as the definitive cause of this phenomenon, recent experiments showed that basal activation of aging innate immune cells is important for their functioning. Modulation of the basal activation state, either on the inhibitory feedback side or directly on the activation of the signaling molecules, was applied. The modulation of the inhibitory feedback, such as SHP-1, led to increased ROS production in neutrophils of elderly. On the other hand, the decreased activation of PI3K in neutrophils of elderly at the basal state led to increased chemotaxis. However, these modulations were made *in vitro*, so we do not know what the impact would be of such modulation in an aging organism *in vivo*.

Inflamm-aging has a Janus face; on the one hand contributing to a low inflammatory status by decreasing the innate immune response efficacy, and on the other hand, inducing an "ever ready" state to react more rapidly to successive aggressions during the aging of the organism.

## How the Inflamm-Aging Is Participating to Immunosenescence?

As the immune system is composed from an innate and adaptive part, we should also consider now the adaptive immune response with aging. The immunosenescence concept originally mainly applied to the aging-associated changes in the adaptive immune system, considered to be the most important and the driving force for the age-related immune alterations. Thus, immunosenescence means an alteration, mainly in the aging adaptive immune system, leading to various diseases such as infections, cancers or, autoimmune diseases (Fulop et al., 2013; Fülöp et al., 2016; Weinberger, 2017). The main changes in the aging adaptive immune system occur in the T-cell compartment (Tu and Rao, 2016; Weyand and Goronzy, 2016). There is an increase in the memory CD8+ T cells, which were originally considered relatively non-functional (Weltevrede et al., 2016). These cells are characterized by the loss of naïve T-cell surface markers such as CD28, CD27, and the emergence of new senescent markers such as KLRG1. The corollary of this increase was the decrease of naïve T cells with aging due to thymic involution (Appay et al., 2011; Pawelec, 2012). We know now that thymic involution is important for the decrease in the naïve T cells, but a different phenomenon called the homeostatic proliferation emerged to replace them, to some extent (Qi et al., 2014). Of course, this cannot really replace all of them but may help to attenuate the physiological effects. Moreover, the recently discovered stem cell-like memory T cells may also participate in incomplete replenishment of the naïve compartment (Ahmed et al., 2016).

It was found that the increase of memory T cells, as well as later that of B cells, may be due, in the phenomenon of inflamm-aging, to the continuous chronic antigenic stimulation. From the panoply of potential stimulating agents the role of CMV emerged above all (Pawelec et al., 2012; Söderberg-Nauclér et al., 2016). This virus is characterized by the constant reactivation in the presence of the decrease in immune surveillance. So the body throughout life devotes a huge part of its immune resources to contain this specific infection. Consequently, the immune space is filled with the CMV-specific memory $CD8^+$ T cells. They were first considered as inactive, but recently they have been considered as metabolically active and participating in the phenomenon of inflamm-aging by their senescent phenotype (SASP). Thus, chronic antigenic stimulation leads both to the phenomenon of inflamm-aging and the increase of senescent T-cell numbers.

Another consequence of chronic stimulation is the phenomenon of exhaustion, which occurs also with aging, as in any case of chronic stimulation and is manifested by the emergence of the inhibitory receptors such as the PD-1 and CTLA-4, as well as many others (Wherry and Kurachi, 2015; Catakovic et al., 2017). These cells may be modulated to become functional again in the aging organism, as well as in the young ones (Henson et al., 2015).

The other cell types of the adaptive immune system are also suffering from aging but to various extents. Thus, the $CD4^+$ T-cell population is also undergoing similar changes to the $CD8^+$ T cells, but to a different extent (Larbi and Fulop, 2014). The regulatory T-cell (Treg) population is also increasing with aging, as well as the proinflammatory Th17 subpopulation (Holcar et al., 2015). Finally, the B-cell compartment is also altered with aging (Leandro, 2013; Frasca et al., 2016).

The functional consequences of these changes manifest collectively in a decreased ability to fight new challenges. Thus, clonal expansion and cytokine production – the specific antibody production – are compromised. This leads to increased infections, cancer, and chronic diseases in the elderly (Fülöp et al., 2016). In the meantime, the inhibitory functions of the adaptive immune response are reinforced.

It can be assumed that inflamm-aging and immunosenescence progress in parallel and form a vicious cycle. Increased production of inflammatory mediators characteristic for inflamm-aging contribute to the decrease in adaptive immune response and eventually to immunosenescence, while the decrease of the adaptive immune response reinforces the stimulation of the innate immune response (as the means to protect organism from infections in the circumstances when adaptive immunity fails), leading to the inflamm-aging. Both processes are important not only as causes of immune changes in the elderly, but also (or even mainly) because of their consequences in the aging organism.

## What Is Inflamm-Aging and Immunosenescence in Evolutionary Perspective?

Considering all these changes in the immune system with aging it can be asked whether and how they really cause the numerous age-related alterations and pathologies attributed to them. Recent observations tend to challenge this view of the immune changes with aging.

A recent paper reporting a very good response to a new herpes zoster vaccine even in very elderly raises the question on the role of immunosenescence and inflamm-aging in the decreased response to vaccination (Lal et al., 2015). This high, protective response to vaccination was elicited mainly due to the addition of different adjuvant to the vaccine; adjuvants work by stimulating the innate immunity, which in turn helps build an adequate adaptive response. Also in a recent paper, inflammation was suggested as a driving force for longevity in super semi-centenarians (Arai et al., 2015). Of course this was not chronic, uncontrolled inflammation, but the well-balanced inflammatory and anti-inflammatory equilibrium. It could be that changes observed during aging only represent an adaptation to the various challenges to maintaining a necessary homeostasis for appropriate functioning in the well-known challenging milieu (containing mostly the cognate pathogens, with the exception of cancer cells generated by semi-random mutations). Under new pressure (i.e., contact with a novel, previously unknown pathogen), the aging immune system can either adapt by using its reserves or be unable to adapt, presenting either a maladaptation manifesting as age-related diseases or a lethal reaction.

In this perspective, it is interesting to evoke the putative role of inflamm-aging in *frailty*. The definition of frailty is already controversial, as two main approaches exist, namely the phenotypical definition of Fried (Fried et al., 2001) and the multiple composite burden (deficit accumulation) of Rockwood (Rockwood et al., 2007). Frailty can be conceptualized from an evolutionary point of view as the decrease of the reserves of aging organs/organism, leading to less efficient responses to stresses and therefore producing deleterious effects, even death (Fulop et al., 2010). It can be said that this is normal (usual) aging, frequently observed at some earlier or later stage, by opposition to successful and the pathological aging (Robert and Fulop, 2014). Independent of its definition, one of the most accepted causes of frailty is inflamm-aging (Wilson et al., 2017), representing the biological threshold between the successful aging process and the pathological process. In this way, it seems a dynamic process that can still be reversed if the underlying causes such as the inflamm-aging are contained, but may also progress through diseases to death, when it becomes uncontrolled and hyperinflammatory, as would be predicted by the trained innate memory process (Fulop et al., 2015). In this perspective, frailty may be considered as a surrogate measure for the biological age, independent of the chronological age, by setting the threshold of inflamm-aging toward health or disease/vulnerability.

## Geroscience, Age-Related Diseases, and Health Span?

Following these considerations, a new concept recently emerged (Franceschi and Garagnani, 2016; Sonntag and Ungvari, 2016), called geroscience, which considers it more rewarding to study and intervene in the aging process to decrease the incidence and prevalence of age-related diseases than to try to decrease these diseases individually. Thus, the conceived interventions would lead to an increased health span and the very late apparition of any age-related diseases. This approach is a very important new way to conceptualize age-related processes, not only for its participation in age-related pathologies, but also for its appreciation of more longitudinally. It is conceivable that not all changes with aging lead to disease and may even be amenable to modulation. As this is a dynamic concept, it should not only decrease the occurrence of diseases, but be able to drive interventions to extend health span concomitantly with the function-span.

## Conclusion

Aging is a complex process and its understanding should lead to the decrease of many age-related diseases. As the immune system is interacting with many other systems in the organism (mainly the neural and the endocrine systems), it is one of the most ubiquitous master systems of an organism. As such, it is orchestrating health when it functions well, and when it is maladapted it leads to disease in the aging organism. Many changes have been described and most were considered deleterious in explaining many age-related diseases. Changes are occurring in the innate and in the adaptive immune parts, but perhaps not to the same extent or with the same consequences. There is an intricate interrelationship among inflamm-aging and immunosenescence, which are somehow identical and in other aspects very different, yet occurring in parallel, influencing each other mutually. Future studies are necessary to elucidate these interactions and raise targets for new interventions that will decrease the deleterious effects of aging, using the beneficial effects for a better health span and function-span in the elderly.

## References

Ahmed R., Roger L., Costa Del Amo P., et al. Human stem cell-like memory T cells are maintained in a state of dynamic flux. *Cell Rep.* 2016 Dec 13;17(11):2811–18.

Albright J. M., Dunn R. C., Shults J. A., et al. Advanced age alters monocyte and macrophage responses. *Antioxid Redox Signal.* 2016 Nov 20;25(15):805–15.

Appay V., Fastenackels S., Katlama C., et al. Old age and anti-cytomegalovirus immunity are associated with altered T-cell reconstitution in HIV-1-infected patients. *AIDS.* 2011;25:1813–22.

Arai Y., Martin-Ruiz C. M., Takayama M., et al. Inflammation, but not telomere length, predicts successful ageing at extreme old age: a longitudinal study of semi-supercentenarians. *EBioMedicine.* 2015 Jul 29;2(10):1549–58.

Arulselvan P., Fard M. T., Tan W. S., et al. Role of antioxidants and natural products in inflammation. *Oxid Med Cell Longev.* 2016;2016:5276130.

van Baarle D., Tsegaye A., Miedema F., Akbar A. Significance of senescence for virus-specific memory T cell responses: rapid ageing during chronic stimulation of the immune system. *Immunol Lett.* 2005;97:19–29.

Bandaranayake T., Shaw A. C. Host resistance and immune aging. *Clin Geriatr Med.* 2016 Aug;32(3):415–32.

Bauer M. E., Fuente Mde L. The role of oxidative and inflammatory stress and persistent viral infections in immunosenescence. *Mech Ageing Dev.* 2016 Sep;158:27–37.

Byun H. O., Lee Y. K., Kim J. M., Yoon G. From cell senescence to age-related diseases: differential mechanisms of action of senescence-associated secretory phenotypes. *BMB Rep.* 2015 Oct;48(10):549–58.

Cannizzo E. S., Clement C. C., Sahu R., Follo C., Santambrogio L. Oxidative stress, inflamm-aging and immunosenescence. *J Proteomics.* 2011 Oct 19;74(11): 2313–23.

Catakovic K., Klieser E., Neureiter D., Geisberger R. T cell exhaustion: from pathophysiological basics to tumor immunotherapy. *Cell Commun Signal.* 2017 Jan 5;15(1):1.

Chandrasekaran A., Idelchik M. D., Melendez J. A. Redox control of senescence and age-related disease. *Redox Biol.* 2017 Apr;11:91–102.

Cohen A. A., Milot E., Li Q., et al. Detection of a novel, integrative aging process suggests complex physiological integration. *PLoS One.* 2015 Mar 11;10(3):e0116489.

Effros R. B. Replicative senescence of CD8 T cells: effect on human ageing. *Exp Gerontol.* 2004 Apr;39(4):517–24.

Fortin C. F., McDonald P. P., Lesur O., Fülöp T., Jr. Aging and neutrophils: there is still much to do. *Rejuvenation Res.* 2008 Oct;11(5):873–82.

Fougère B., Boulanger E., Nourhashémi F., Guyonnet S., Cesari M. Chronic inflammation: accelerator of biological aging. *J Gerontol A Biol Sci Med Sci.* 2017 Sep 1;72(9):1218–25.

Franceschi C., Bonafè M., Valensin S., et al. Inflamm-aging: an evolutionary perspective on immunosenescence. *Ann N Y Acad Sci.* 2000 Jun;908:244–54.

Franceschi C., Garagnani P. Suggestions from geroscience for the genetics of age-related diseases. *PLoS Genet.* 2016 Nov 10;12(11):e1006399.

Frasca D., Diaz A., Romero M., Blomberg B. B. The generation of memory B cells is maintained, but the antibody response is not, in the elderly after repeated influenza immunizations. *Vaccine.* 2016 May 27;34(25):2834–40.

Fried, L. P., Tangen, C. M., Walston, J., et al. Frailty in older adults: evidence for a phenotype. *J Gerontol Ser A Biol Sci Med Sci.* 2001;56:M146–57.

Fulop T., Dupuis G., Baehl S., et al. From inflamm-aging to immune-paralysis: a slippery slope during aging for immune-adaptation. *Biogerontology.* 2016 Feb;17(1):147–57.

Fülöp T., Dupuis G., Witkowski J. M., Larbi A. The role of immunosenescence in the development of age-related diseases. *Rev Invest Clin.* 2016 Mar–Apr;68(2):84–91.

Fulop T., Larbi A., Douziech N., et al. Signal transduction and functional changes in neutrophils with aging. *Aging Cell.* 2004 Aug;3(4):217–26.

Fulop T., Larbi A., Witkowski J. M., et al. Aging, frailty and age-related diseases. *Biogerontology.* 2010 Oct;11(5):547–63.

Fulop T., Larbi A., Witkowski J. M., et al. Immunosenescence and cancer. *Crit Rev Oncog.* 2013;18(6):489–513.

Fulop T., McElhaney J., Pawelec G., et al. Frailty, inflammation and immunosenescence. *Interdiscip Top Gerontol Geriatr.* 2015;41:26–40.

Fulop T., Witkowski J. M., Pawelec G., Cohen A., Larbi A. On the immunological theory of aging. *Interdiscip Top Gerontol.* 2014;39:163–76.

Gabrielli S., Ortolani C., Del Zotto G., et al. The memories of NK cells: innate–adaptive immune intrinsic crosstalk. *J Immunol Res.* 2016;2016:1376595.

Henson S. M., Macaulay R., Riddell N. E., Nunn C. J., Akbar A. N. Blockade of PD-1 or p38 MAP kinase signaling enhances senescent human CD8(+) T-cell proliferation by distinct pathways. *Eur J Immunol.* 2015;45:1441–51.

Herranz N., Gallage S., Mellone M., et al. mTOR regulates MAPKAPK2 translation to control the senescence-associated secretory phenotype. *Nat Cell Biol.* 2015 Sep;17(9):1205–17.

Holcar M., Goropevšek A., Ihan A., Avčin T. Age-related differences in percentages of regulatory and effector T lymphocytes and their subsets in healthy individuals and characteristic STAT1/STAT5 signalling response in helper T lymphocytes. *J Immunol Res.* 2015;2015:352934.

Jha S., Brickey W. J., Ting J. P. Inflammasomes in myeloid cells: warriors within. *Microbiol Spectr.* 2017 Jan;5(1). doi: 10.1128/microbiolspec.MCHD-0049-2016.

Kaufmann S. H., Dorhoi A. Molecular determinants in phagocyte–bacteria interactions. *Immunity.* 2016 Mar 15;44(3):476–91.

Kleinnijenhuis J., Quintin J., Preijers F., et al. Bacille Calmette-Guerin induces NOD2-dependent nonspecific protection from reinfection via epigenetic reprogramming of monocytes. *Proc Natl Acad Sci U S A.* 2012;109:17537–42.

Lal H., Cunningham A. L., Godeaux O., et al. ZOE-50 Study Group. Efficacy of an adjuvanted herpes zoster subunit vaccine in older adults. *N Engl J Med.* 2015 May 28;372(22):2087–96.

Larbi A., Fulop T. From "truly naïve" to "exhausted senescent" T cells: when markers predict functionality. *Cytometry A.* 2014 Jan;85(1):25–35.

Lasry A., Ben-Neriah Y. Senescence-associated inflammatory responses: aging and cancer perspectives. *Trends Immunol.* 2015 Apr;36(4):217–28.

Le Saux S1, Weyand C. M., Goronzy J. J. Mechanisms of immunosenescence: lessons from models of accelerated immune aging. *Ann N Y Acad Sci.* 2012 Jan;1247:69–82.

Leandro M. J. B-cell subpopulations in humans and their differential susceptibility to depletion with anti-CD20 monoclonal antibodies. *Arthritis Res Ther.* 2013;15 (Suppl 1):S3.

Lipsky M. S, King M., Biological theories of aging. *Disease-a-Month.* 61 (2015) 460–66.

Magrone T., Jirillo E. Disorders of innate immunity in human ageing and effects of nutraceutical administration. *Endocr Metab Immune Disord Drug Targets.* 2014;14(4):272–82.

Marandu T. F., Oduro J. D., Borkner L., et al. Immune Protection against virus challenge in aging mice is not affected by latent herpesviral infections. *J Virol.* 2015 Nov;89(22):11715–17.

Montgomery R. R., Shaw A. C. Paradoxical changes in innate immunity in aging: recent progress and new directions. *J Leukoc Biol.* 2015 Dec;98(6):937–43.

Müller L., Fülöp T., Pawelec G. Immunosenescence in vertebrates and invertebrates. *Immun Ageing.* 2013 Apr 2;10(1):12.

Pawelec G. Hallmarks of human "immunosenescence": adaptation or dysregulation? *Immun Ageing.* 2012 Jul 25;9(1):15.

Pawelec G. Immunosenenescence: role of cytomegalovirus. *Exp Gerontol.* 2014 Jun;54:1–5.

Pawelec G., Akbar A., Caruso C., et al. Human immunosenescence: is it infectious? *Immunol Rev.* 2005;205:257–68.

Pawelec G., Derhovanessian E., Larbi A., Strindhall J., Wikby A. Cytomegalovirus and human immunosenescence. *Rev Med Virol.* 2009 Jan;19(1):47–56.

Pawelec G., McElhaney J. E., Aiello A. E. Derhovanessian E: the impact of CMV infection on survival in older humans. *Curr Opin Immunol.* 2012;24:507–11.

Pera A., Campos C., López N., et al. Immunosenescence: implications for response to infection and vaccination in older people. *Maturitas.* 2015 Sep;82(1):50–5.

Pinti M., Appay V., Campisi J., et al. Aging of the immune system: focus on inflammation and vaccination. *Eur J Immunol.* 2016 Oct;46(10):2286–301.

Ponnappan S., Ponnappan U. Aging and immune function: molecular mechanisms to interventions. *Antioxid Redox Signal.* 2011 Apr 15;14(8):1551–85.

Qi Q., Zhang D. W., Weyand C. M., Goronzy J. J. Mechanisms shaping the naïve T cell repertoire in the elderly – thymic involution or peripheral homeostatic proliferation? *Exp Gerontol.* 2014;54:71–4.

Qian, F., Wang, X., Zhang, L., et al. Impaired interferon signaling in dendritic cells from older donors infected in vitro with West Nile virus. *J Infect Dis.* 2011;203:1415–24.

Robert L., Fulop T. Longevity and its regulation: centenarians and beyond. *Interdiscip Top Gerontol.* 2014;39:198–211.

Rockwood, K., Andrew, M., Mitnitski, A. A comparison of two approaches to measuring frailty in elderly people. *J Gerontol Ser A Biol Sci Med Sci.* 2007;62:738–43.

Rivera A., Siracusa M. C., Yap G. S., Gause W. C. Innate cell communication kick-starts pathogen-specific immunity. *Nat Immunol.* 2016 Apr;17(4):356–63.

Salvioli S., Monti D., Lanzarini C., et al. Immune system, cell senescence, aging and longevity – inflamm-aging reappraised. *Curr Pharm Des.* 2013;19(9):1675–9.

Satoh T., Akira S. Toll-like receptor signaling and its inducible proteins. *Microbiol Spectr.* 2016 Dec;4(6). doi: 10.1128/microbiolspec.MCHD-0040-2016.

Seidler S., Zimmermann H. W., Bartneck M., Trautwein C., Tacke F. Age-dependent alterations of monocyte subsets and monocyte-related chemokine pathways in healthy adults. *BMC Immunol.* 2010 Jun 21;11:30.

Smallwood H. S., López-Ferrer D., Squier T. C. Aging enhances the production of reactive oxygen species and bactericidal activity in peritoneal macrophages by upregulating classical activation pathways. *Biochemistry.* 2011 Nov 15;50(45):9911–22.

Söderberg-Nauclér C., Fornara O., Rahbar A. Cytomegalovirus driven immunosenescence – an immune phenotype with or without clinical impact? *Mech Ageing Dev.* 2016 Sep;158:3–13.

Solana R., Tarazona R., Aiello A. E., et al. CMV and immunosenescence: from basics to clinics. *Immun Ageing* 2012;9:23.

Solana R., Tarazona R., Gayoso I., et al. Innate immunosenescence: effect of aging on cells and receptors of the innate immune system in humans. *Semin Immunol.* 2012 Oct;24(5):331–41.

Sonntag W. E., Ungvari Z. GeroScience: understanding the interaction of processes of aging and chronic diseases. *Age (Dordr).* 2016 Dec;38(5–6):377–8.

Tu W., Rao S. Mechanisms underlying T cell immunosenescence: aging and cytomegalovirus infection. *Front Microbiol.* 2016 Dec 27;7:2111.

Weinberger B. Immunosenescence: the importance of considering age in health and disease. *Clin Exp Immunol.* 2017 Jan;187(1):1–3.

Weltevrede M., Eilers R., de Melker H. E., van Baarle D. Cytomegalovirus persistence and T-cell immunosenescence in people aged fifty and older: a systematic review. *Exp Gerontol.* 2016 May;77:87–95.

Weyand C. M., Goronzy J. J. Aging of the immune system: mechanisms and therapeutic targets. *Ann Am Thorac Soc.* 2016 Dec;13(Suppl 5):S422–8.

Wherry E. J., Kurachi M. Molecular and cellular insights into T cell exhaustion. *Nat Rev Immunol.* 2015 Aug;15(8):486–99.

Wilson D., Jackson T., Sapey E., Lord J. M. Frailty and sarcopenia: the potential role of an aged immune system. *Ageing Res Rev.* 2017;36:1–10.

Xia S., Zhang X., Zheng S., et al. An update on inflamm-aging: mechanisms, prevention, and treatment. *J Immunol Res.* 2016;2016:8426874.

# 6 Telomere Dynamics and Aging Related Diseases

Simon Toupance and Athanase Benetos

## The Meaning of Aging

Aging is a complex and multi-factorial process characterized by impaired homeostasis and a declining ability to respond to stress (Fedarko, 2011). From a bio-clinical perspective, aging displays an array of traits, principally frailty, degenerative diseases, and compromised cognition, which individually and more so jointly, may lead to a loss of autonomy and ultimately to demise (Gavrilov and Gavrilova, 2009). While aging is an amorphous entity, longevity is a quantitative trait defined as the expected life span under ideal conditions (Hayflick, 2007). Both aging and longevity are complex traits; they are affected by genetic and environmental factors as well as a stochastic element, which predominantly stems from gene-environment interaction (Luciani et al., 2001). These features largely account for the heterogeneous expressions of aging and the wide variation in longevity across the population. Moreover, the environment has a particular and lasting influence on the aging trajectory during early life (i.e., embryonic, fetal, and early post-natal growth and development), when organismal programing takes place (Metcalfe and Monaghan, 2001, 2003; Entringer et al., 2011; Tzanetakou et al., 2011).

A 2013 review lists nine major hallmarks of aging, including genomic instability, telomere dynamics, epigenetic alterations, loss of proteostasis (primary or causal hallmarks at the molecular level), dysregulated nutrient-sensing, mitochondrial dysfunction, cellular senescence (antagonistic hallmarks at the cellular level), stem cell exhaustion, and altered intercellular communication (integrative hallmarks at the systemic level) (López-Otín et al., 2013). The present chapter focuses on telomere dynamics, its relationship with cellular senescence, and its impact on human aging.

## Telomere Length and Its Link with Cellular Senescence

Telomeres form caps that protect chromosome ends and maintain genomic integrity. They comprise non-coding TTAGGG repeats associated with a family of proteins referred to as the shelterin complex (TRF1, TRF2, POT1, TIN2, TPP1, and Rap1) (Blackburn, 2005; de Lange, 2005). This structure allows cell machinery to differentiate telomeres from double-stranded DNA breaks and prevent end-to-end fusions (Griffith et al., 1999; de Lange, 2009).

Cellular senescence may play a key role in aging since, in principle, it can affect both tissue degeneration and repair, which are dependent on the replicative capacities of cells throughout the somatic cell hierarchy, i.e., the stem cell level at the top and differentiated cells at the bottom (Sharpless and DePinho, 2007; van Deursen, 2014). Senescent differentiated cells display unique features that can enhance organ dysfunction (Coppé et al., 2008; Rodier and Campisi, 2011). Studies in mice have shown that clearing senescent cells has little effect on life span, although it does prolong "heath span" (Baker et al., 2011, 2016; Chang et al., 2016; Hashimoto et al., 2016).

Telomere shortening is due to the "end replication problem" (Harley et al., 1990; Lindsey et al., 1991). With each cell division of somatic cells, the DNA located at the extreme end of the lagging strand is not fully replicated, leading to telomere attrition and ultimately critically short telomeres. At this stage, a signal is relayed to the replicative machinery in order to activate a DNA-damage response, which causes growth arrest known as replicative senescence (Shay et al., 1991; d'Adda di Fagagna et al., 2003). Therefore, all somatic cells have limited cell proliferation capacity, referred to as the Hayflick limit (Hayflick and Moorhead, 1961; Olovnikov, 1973).

Telomerase, a reverse transcriptase consisting of a catalytic subunit (hTERT) and a subunit that includes an RNA template (hTERC), is capable of offsetting telomere attrition by adding TTAGGG sequences at the chromosome ends (Greider and Blackburn, 1985). Telomerase is active in embryonic and germ cells as well as in about 90 percent of primary human tumors, but is largely silent in adult somatic cells (Shay and Wright, 1996, 2001). Since critically short telomeres may impact chromosome integrity, chromatin stability, and cellular replicative capacity, telomere length (TL) is an indicator of both the replicative history and replicative potential of a cell.

Studies in cultured somatic cells have shown that telomeric shortening per cell division is related to the level of oxidative stress (von Zglinicki, 2002; Kurz et al., 2004), while research in certain mouse models has shown a potential role of both oxidative stress (Cattan et al., 2008) and chronic inflammation (Ilmonen et al., 2008) in TL dynamics *in vivo*.

In humans, leukocyte TL (LTL), which is typically measured in an epidemiological setting, decreases with age and has traditionally been regarded as an indicator of biological age (Benetos et al., 2001; Cawthon et al., 2003). However, this concept overlooks the fact that LTL at any age largely reflects LTL at birth, and perhaps during the first two decades of life (Honig et al., 2015) (see chapter: "Regulation of Telomere Length *In Vivo*: Respective Roles of LTL at Birth and Telomere Attrition During Body Growth and Adulthood"). Thus, although TL can be considered as a biomarker of cellular senescence, meaning that it denotes the replicative potential of a cell, it cannot be considered as the clock of biological age since TL is predominantly determined by TL at birth, and much less by telomere attrition.

## Link between Telomere, Longevity, and Aging-Related Diseases

### Telomeres and Longevity: What We Have Learned from Animal Models and Clinical Studies

Mouse models with knockout (KO) of telomerase have been used in the past years to study the role of telomerase in aging and longevity. Common laboratory mouse strains having very long telomeres (30 to 50 kb), with three to five times that of humans (8 to 11 kb), the KO necessitates at least three generations of animals to produce animals with short telomeres (Lee et al., 1998). These animals have a decreased life span and present phenotypes of premature aging in comparison to wild type controls. The phenotypes include hair greying, alopecia, skin lesions, delayed wound healing capabilities, male and female infertility, intestinal and spleen atrophy, and reduced proliferative capacity of bone marrow stem cells (Lee et al., 1998; Rudolph et al., 1999). Interestingly, reintroduction of telomerase in these animals is able to rescue chromosomal instability and prevent premature aging phenotype (Samper et al., 2001; Jaskelioff et al., 2011).

Epidemiological studies have used LTL, which reflects TL in other somatic tissues (Youngren et al., 1998; Daniali et al., 2013), to examine the potential role of TL in health and disease. LTL shortens with age (Baird and Kipling, 2004; Blackburn et al., 2015; Rizvi et al., 2015); in adults, the rate of this shortening amounts to 20 to 35 base pairs (bp) per year (Müezzinler et al., 2013; Steenstrup et al., 2013). A body of research has shown that a long LTL is associated with increased longevity and better survival in the elderly (Bakaysa et al., 2007; Kimura et al., 2008a; Fitzpatrick et al., 2011; Deelen et al., 2014). At present, there is ongoing controversy as to whether there is a natural limit to the human life span (Dong et al., 2016). In principle, in some individuals, LTL could potentially define such a limit (Steenstrup et al., 2017).

### The "Gender Effect"

Women typically have a longer LTL than men (Jeanclos et al., 2000 Benetos et al., 2001; Nawrot et al., 2004). The difference is approximately 200 bp; with age-dependent LTL attrition estimated at 25 to 35 bp/year (Müezzinler et al., 2013; Steenstrup et al., 2013), this sex gap is equivalent to six to eight years of LTL shortening in adults, which is within the range of the gender effect in developed countries (Candore et al., 2006).

The prevailing view, based on cross-sectional data (Bekaert et al., 2007), is that a slower rate of age-dependent LTL attrition in women explains the LTL gender gap. A slower LTL attrition in women, if true, could stem from the effect of estrogen on telomerase, given that an estrogen-response element is present in the promoter of the catalytic subunit of telomerase (Bayne et al., 2007). Thus, estrogen-mediated stimulation of telomerase may attenuate the rate of age-dependent LTL shortening in premenopausal women and thereby partially explain the LTL gender gap. Although telomerase activity is repressed in somatic tissues during extra-uterine life, it is not totally absent from highly proliferative tissues such as the hematopoietic system and skin (Artandi and DePinho, 2010).

However, longitudinal studies have reported conflicting findings. Chen et al. showed that the rate of LTL attrition was slightly slower in premenopausal women than in men (Chen et al., 2011), while subsequent studies suggested that the rate of LTL attrition was not increased in post-menopausal women (Kark et al., 2012; Dalgård et al., 2015). A recent study had shown, however, that the gender gap is already present at birth (Factor-Litvak et al., 2016). Another possible explanation is that the gender gap is established before adulthood. This finding is reinforced by a study in twins, in which female co-twins of opposite sex (OS) displayed LTL that was equivalent to male co-twins, which were shorter than the same sex (SS) female twins (Benetos et al., 2014). This observation could be explained by the testosterone transfer hypothesis (Tapp et al., 2011), which posits that the female co-twin of OS twins may potentially be masculinized *in utero* (Lummaa et al., 2007; Vuoksimaa et al., 2010; Tapp et al., 2011; Ribeiro et al., 2013).

## Genetic Diseases

Rare mutations in *TERT, TERC*, genes encoding proteins of the shelterin complex and other proteins that regulate telomerase may result in critically short telomeres, causing monogenic diseases such as dyskeratosis congenital (Savage et al., 2008; Ballew and Savage, 2013), idiopathic pulmonary fibrosis (Armanios et al., 2007), liver cirrhosis (Calado et al., 2009), aplastic anemia (Fogarty et al., 2003), and Hoyeraal-Hreidarsson syndrome (Glousker et al., 2015). The clinical manifestations of these diseases are highly heterogeneous, although, in general, reflect compromised replicative potential. Patients suffering from these diseases very often present bone marrow failure (Vulliamy et al., 2002; Dokal, 2003; Yamaguchi et al., 2003; Yamaguchi et al., 2005; Savage and Alter, 2008; Armanios and Blackburn, 2012), as well as intestinal villous atrophy and immunodeficiency (Stanley and Armanios, 2015).

Lung diseases are the most common diseases related to mutations in telomerase (*TERT, TERC, DKC1*) and telomere maintenance (*TINF2, RTEL1, PARN*) genes in adults (Stanley and Armanios, 2015); approximately one-third of idiopathic pulmonary fibrosis cases display mutations leading to short telomeres (Armanios, 2012; Alder et al., 2015; Cogan et al., 2015; Stuart et al., 2015). *TERT* mutations are also associated with an increased risk of emphysema (Stanley et al., 2015). Clinical studies indicate that individuals with *TERT* mutations are at high risk for developing emphysema in the presence of tobacco smoking, while the development of pulmonary fibrosis is the predominant disease in non-smokers (Stanley et al., 2015).

## Telomere Length and Cancer

Earlier studies examining the association between LTL and sporadic cancer showed poor concordance, perhaps because of faulty design and methodological shortcomings (Savage et al., 2013). The majority of these studies were retrospective, i.e., LTL was measured in subjects after the development of cancer. Retrospective studies are indeed confounded by the various therapeutic regimens (including chemotherapy and irradiation), which can impact LTL. Moreover, the overwhelming majority of studies used a qPCR-based method to measure LTL, given the high throughput and low cost of this method. However, the qPCR-based method has a high measurement error (Aviv et al., 2011; Lynch et al., 2016) and thus requires a large sample size to offset the error, which was not the case for the majority of these studies.

Recently, large-scale prospective studies have generated more consistent findings showing that a long LTL is associated with increased risk for common cancers. This association was observed more constantly for melanoma (Caini et al., 2015) and cancers of the pancreas (Lynch et al., 2013; Campa et al., 2014), prostate (Julin et al., 2015), and lung (Sanchez-Espiridion et al., 2014; Seow et al., 2014).

## Telomere Length and Degenerative Diseases

Shorter LTL is associated with numerous degenerative diseases linked to aging such as cardiovascular disease (CVD), neurodegenerative disease, and metabolic disorders.

A number of studies have observed associations of LTL with indices of insulin resistance or with type 2 diabetes mellitus (T2DM). The majority of these studies (Adaikalakoteswari et al., 2005; Gardner et al., 2005; Aviv et al., 2006; Demissie et al., 2006; Tentolouris et al., 2007; Al-Attas et al., 2010; Salpea et al., 2010; Ahmad et al., 2012; Monickaraj et al., 2012; Willeit et al., 2014), although not all (Barbieri et al., 2009; Hovatta et al., 2012), found that LTL (or TL length in subsets of leukocytes) was inversely associated with insulin resistance and was shorter in patients with T2DM than in their peers.

Short LTL has also been observed in individuals with neurodegenerative diseases, including dementia (von Zglinicki et al., 2000; Jenkins et al., 2006; Grodstein et al., 2008; Zekry et al., 2010), Alzheimer's disease (Panossian et al., 2003; Thomas et al., 2008; Guan et al., 2012; Hochstrasser et al., 2012; Honig et al., 2012), and Parkinson's disease (Guan et al., 2008; Watfa et al., 2011; Maeda et al., 2012). However, other studies failed to find such associations (Wang et al., 2008; Lukens et al., 2009; Eerola et al., 2010; Schürks et al., 2014). These inconsistent findings may be related to actual biological differences across populations or possibly to the reliance on qPCR-based methodology to measure telomere DNA content, as this method has a high measurement error (Aviv et al., 2011; Lynch et al., 2016) and requires large samples, as stated above.

A large body of research has demonstrated that short LTL is linked to CVD in several of its underlying causes and outcomes. For example, short LTL is associated with higher CV mortality (Cawthon et al., 2003; Rode et al., 2015), hypertension (Demissie et al., 2006; Ma et al., 2015), heart failure (van der Harst et al., 2007), stroke (Ding et al., 2012), arterial stiffness (Jeanclos et al., 2000; Benetos et al., 2001; Nawrot et al., 2010; Wang et al., 2011), arterial calcifications (Mainous et al., 2010; Hunt et al., 2015), valvular calcifications (Kurz et al., 2006), atherosclerosis of the coronary arteries (Samani et al., 2001; Brouilette et al., 2003), endothelial dysfunction (Minamino et al., 2002), and diabetic vascular disease(Testa et al., 2011; Spigoni et al., 2016). With few exceptions (De Meyer et al., 2009; Fernández-Alvira et al., 2016), studies have also shown that individuals with atherosclerosis of the carotid artery have short LTL (Benetos et al., 2004; O'Donnell et al., 2008; Panayiotou et al., 2010; Huzen et al., 2011; Nzietchueng et al., 2011; Chen et al., 2014; Raymond et al., 2016). Two recent systematic reviews and meta-analyses, including several thousand subjects, concluded that short LTL is associated with CVD in several populations, principally due to atherosclerosis (Haycock et al., 2014; D'Mello et al., 2015).

## The Biomarker Hypothesis

Chronic inflammation and oxidative stress are believed to be key determinants in the aging process and most age-related chronic diseases (Ross, 1999; O'Rourke and Hashimoto, 2007; Cai et al., 2012). Chronic inflammation increases the rate of hematopoietic stem cell (HSC) replication, while oxidative stress increases the size of telomere repeats clipped off from chromosome ends with each replication (von Zglinicki, 2002; Houben et al., 2008). Both mechanisms would thereby increase the pace of TL attrition in the hematopoietic system, as expressed in age-dependent LTL shortening. Thus, the conventional paradigm considers LTL as a marker of the chronic burden of oxidative stress and inflammation in adulthood and therefore a marker of the aging process and aging-related diseases (Fyhrquist et al., 2013; Yeh and Wang, 2016). For example, it is assumed that people at high risk of atherosclerosis, a typical aging-related disease, have an accelerated LTL attrition due to the effects of factors that increase the burden of oxidative stress and inflammation on the arteries. A number of studies have emphasized this concept by linking short LTL with these risk factors, including smoking (Valdes et al., 2005; Vasan et al., 2008; Mirabello et al., 2009; Du et al., 2012), sedentary lifestyle (Cherkas et al., 2008; Du et al., 2012), nutritional factors (high fat, low fiber diets) (Kark et al., 2012; Cassidy et al., 2010), and high BMI (Valdes et al., 2005; Nordfjäll et al., 2008; Strandberg et al., 2011; Du et al., 2012).

However, these studies failed to address the following key issue: to what extent can the inter-individual variation in LTL attrition rates during adulthood explain the association of LTL with atherosclerosis and other aging-related diseases (Nilsson et al., 2013)? There is currently an open debate as to whether short TL, as expressed in leukocytes, increases the risk of developing aging-related disease, or whether it is the outcome of mechanisms that bring about these diseases. It is therefore essential to determine what renders LTL short or long during adulthood.

## Regulation of Telomere Length *In Vivo*: Respective Roles of LTL at Birth and Telomere Attrition During Body Growth and Adulthood

At a given age, TL essentially depends on its initial size at birth and subsequent attrition during life (Figure 6.1).

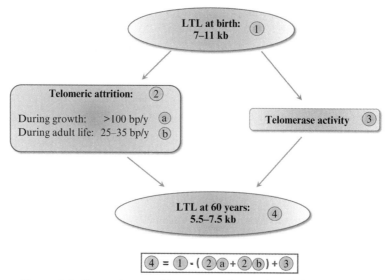

**Figure 6.1.** *Determinants of leucocyte telomere length (LTL) at adult life*
At a given age, LTL (is dependent, depends) on LTL at birth (1) minus the attrition during
extra-uterine life (2). Attrition is much higher during the first years of life (2a >100 bases/year),
subsequently dropping during adult life (2b = 25–35 bases/year). Telomerase activity contributes
very little in most somatic cells.

## Telomere Length at Birth

LTL is approximately 65 percent heritable (Broer et al., 2013; Hjelmborg et al.,
2015a; Honig et al., 2015) and displays a wide inter-individual variation at birth
(range of approximately 4 kb, SD of approximately 0.7 kb) (Factor-Litvak
et al., 2016) that largely holds in young adults (Baker et al., 2016; Hashimoto
et al., 2016) and thereafter (Factor-Litvak et al., 2016). This variation is largely
dependent on genetic factors. Indeed, recent genome-wide association studies
have identified several genes explaining inter-individual variation in LTL in the
general population (Codd et al., 2013). However, several other factors also regulate TL at birth and can contribute to longer TL: increased paternal age (Unryn
et al., 2005; De Meyer et al., 2007; Kimura et al., 2008b; Hjelmborg et al.,
2015b), female sex (Jeanclos et al., 2000; Benetos et al., 2001; Nawrot et al.,
2004), and African ancestry (Hunt et al., 2008; Hansen et al., 2016; Benetos and
Aviv, 2017).

In the human fetuses and newborns, TL is largely equivalent in all somatic
tissues (Butler et al., 1998; Youngren et al., 1998; Okuda et al., 2002). This phenomenon may be due in part to the activity of telomerase, which counteracts
TL shortening resulting from cell replication during early intra-uterine growth.

## Telomere Attrition in Early Life

Telomerase activity is largely repressed in somatic tissues during extra-uterine
life (Seluanov et al., 2007), although it is not totally abolished in somatic stem

and progenitor cells. However, such activity is not sufficient to prevent TL short-ening during replication altogether. Indeed, TL in the various somatic tissues is negatively related to their replicative activity. Notably, LTL, and by extrapola-tion HSC-TL, is shorter than TLs of somatic tissues with low replicative activ-ity. Despite these inter-tissue differences, the available data from human studies indicates strong correlations in TL across somatic tissues, and individuals with long (or short) TL in one tissue also have long (or short) TL in other tissues. This "synchrony" in TL across somatic tissues has been observed not only in humans (Youngren et al., 1998; Daniali et al., 2013), but also in other mammals (Benetos et al., 2011). Epidemiological reports on age-dependent attrition in TL are based primarily on studies of leukocytes. These studies suggest that the rate of age-dependent LTL shortening is high early in life, but decreases during adulthood (Aubert et al., 2012). As a result, HSC-TL shortens by approximately 2–3 kb during the first 20 years of life. This massive TL attrition is largely attrib-uted to the expansion of the HSC and hematopoietic progenitor cell (HPC) pools in tandem with body growth. Thus by the end of the second decade, the difference between LTL and TL in skeletal muscle, a minimally proliferative tis-sue, is about 1.5 kbp. Such a difference is largely associated with the higher pace of replication of HSCs needed to expand the HSC and HPC pools (Morrison and Kimble, 2006) in order to accommodate the tremendous turnover rate of blood cells during growth and development, as well as later in life. It is believed that during this period of high cellular replicative activity and body growth, any factor that can increase the number of cell divisions and/or telomeric attrition per cell division may have a major impact on TL dynamics. Specifically, at the level of HSC, indolent inflammation (due, for instance, to abdominal obesity), and increased oxidative stress (due to nutritional factors) may augment the rate of LTL attrition.

## Telomere Attrition During Adult Life

LTL attrition rate in the course of adult life is estimated at 25–35 bp/year, which translates into a total average shortening of 1.5–2.0 kb in LTL during adult life for an individual reaching the age of 80 years. Based on cross-sectional analy-ses (i.e., studying individuals of different ages on one occasion) several factors have been observed to affect LTL attrition during adulthood, including cigarette smoking (Valdes et al., 2005; Vasan et al., 2008; Mirabello et al., 2009; Du et al., 2012), high body mass index (Valdes et al., 2005; Nordfjäll et al., 2008; Du et al., 2012; Strandberg et al., 2011), a sedentary lifestyle (Cherkas et al., 2008; Du et al., 2012), and nutritional factors (high fat, low fiber diets) (Cassidy et al., 2010; Kark et al., 2012). However, longitudinal studies did not find any relation-ship between LTL attrition rate and the presence of these risk factors in adults (Weischer et al., 2014). While these aforementioned factors might influence the attrition rate to some extent, their relative contribution to overall LTL is rela-tively modest compared to LTL at birth and perhaps inter-individual variation in LTL attrition during early life (2 to 3 kb). Further support for this idea stems from a recent longitudinal study showing that an individual's LTL ranking in relation to his or her peers during adult life is essentially fixed, meaning that having a short or a long LTL is determined prior to adulthood (Benetos et al., 2013).

## New Paradigm: Telomere as a Determinant in Aging Diseases

Given that TL is mainly determined prior to adulthood, in the majority of individuals, short LTL precedes by many years the clinical manifestations of degenerative diseases. This suggests that TL may not be just a passive marker of, but an active determinant in aging-related human diseases.

### The Cancer/Degenerative Disease Trade-Off

Further support for an active role of TL in adult-onset human diseases is provided by recent Mendelian randomization studies, using LTL-associated single nucleotide polymorphism (SNPs). These studies show that alleles associated with short LTL are overrepresented in individuals with clinical manifestations of atherosclerosis (Codd et al., 2013; Scheller Madrid et al., 2016; Haycock et al., 2017), dementia (Zhan et al., 2015; Hägg et al., 2017), type 2 diabetes mellitus (Zee et al., 2011; Saxena et al., 2014; Al Khaldi et al., 2015), and CVD mortality (Burnett-Hartman et al., 2012). These findings exclude reverse causality, i.e., that these diseases heighten LTL attrition. Interestingly, the same LTL-associated alleles are also associated with melanoma (Iles et al., 2014; Haycock et al., 2017), neuroblastoma (Walsh et al., 2016; Haycock et al., 2017), glioma (Walsh et al., 2015; Haycock et al., 2017), and adenocarcinoma of the lung (Machiela et al., 2015; Zhang et al., 2015). The difference between the above associations rests in the directionality of their alleles, such that alleles that increase the risk for degenerative disease, due to short LTL, are associated with diminished risk for melanoma, neuroblastoma, glioma, and adenocarcinoma of the lung. These findings point to a temporal relationship and "directionality" in the associations of TL, as expressed in LTL, with degenerative disease and some cancers (Figure 6.2). That is, short LTL, which is primarily determined early in life, increases the risk for degenerative disease and diminishes the risk for some cancers rather than the other way around. All of the above data also indicate that LTL is a strong determinant of mortality at different ages. From an evolutionary perspective, TL in humans may represent the optimal length to balance degenerative diseases against cancers (Stone et al., 2016).

### Short Telomeres: A Bio-Determinant of Atherosclerotic Cardiovascular Disease

This causal hypothesis is supported by several clinical studies: indeed, the Strong Heart Family Study reported that individuals with shorter telomeres were at higher risk of developing carotid atherosclerosis over a period of 5.5

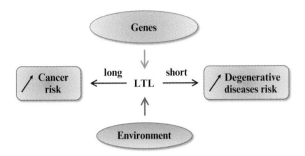

**Figure 6.2.** *The cancer/degenerative disease trade-off*
As expressed in leucocyte TL (LTL), telomere length in somatic tissues is determined by genes and environmental factors. An emerging body of data suggests that telomere length modifies the risks for developing age-related degenerative diseases and major cancers, such that short telomeres increase the risk for degenerative diseases, whereas long telomeres increase the risk for some cancers.

years (Chen et al., 2014), while the Bruneck Study reported that shorter LTL was associated with progression to advanced stages of carotid atherosclerosis over a 5-year period (Willeit et al., 2010). More recently, the ERA study (Toupance et al., 2017) showed that carotid atherosclerosis was not associated with increased LTL attrition rate over a 9.5-year follow-up period, whereas carotid atherosclerosis was associated with short LTL, principally in younger participants. Furthermore, in this latter study, short LTL predicted development of carotid atherosclerosis, as expressed by an increased number of anatomic regions with carotid atherosclerotic plaques (Toupance et al., 2017).

The active role of short TL in atherogenesis may be due to impaired homeostasis of vascular tissues containing cells with short telomeres. Impaired tissue homeostasis is defined by an imbalance between injury and repair, with short telomeres potentially playing a role in both mechanisms.

Short telomeres can lead to cellular senescence (Blasco, 2007), and senescent cells, in turn, are known to alter their secretion pattern, a phenomenon called senescence-associated secretory phenotype (SASP) (Tchkonia et al., 2013; Malaquin et al., 2016). An increased number of senescent vascular smooth muscle cells (Matthews et al., 2006; Wang et al., 2015; Uryga and Bennett, 2016), endothelial cells (Minamino et al., 2002; Raymond et al., 2016), and monocytes (Calvert et al., 2011) are observed in atherosclerotic lesions; these senescent cells contribute to tissue injury through their SASP by promoting inflammation (Calvert et al., 2011; Childs et al., 2016), apoptosis (Bennett et al., 1995), and tissue remodeling (Childs et al., 2016; Lundberg et al., 2016).

Moreover, short telomeres in vascular tissues, as expressed by a shorter LTL (Zhang et al., 2013), may also reflect a compromised repair capacity of precursor cells with short telomeres (Marión and Blasco, 2010; Boonekamp et al., 2013). This is primarily because TL reflects cellular repair capacity, while a short LTL denotes diminished repair reserves (Calado and Young, 2009). The vascular endothelium, where atherosclerosis begins, and the hematopoietic system

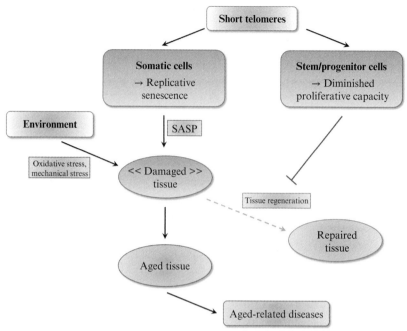

**Figure 6.3.** *Dual role of short telomeres in tissue aging*
Short TL impairs tissue homeostasis by promoting tissue injury and decreasing repair capacity. Short telomeres in somatic cells trigger replicative senescence that contributes to tissue injury through senescence-associated secretory phenotype (SASP) by promoting inflammation, apoptosis and tissue remodeling. Moreover, short telomeres in progenitor and stem cells compromise tissue repair capacity by reducing the proliferative capacities of these cells.

originate from a common embryonic precursor, the hemogenic endothelium, and could be viewed as conjoined elements of a larger system, which has been termed the hemothelium (Aviv, 2012). Various animal models have shown the capacity of bone marrow-derived endothelial progenitor cells (EPCs) to participate in restoring endothelial lining after arterial injury, while strategies that enhance EPC availability may attenuate atherosclerosis progression (Hill et al., 2003). Clinical studies have shown that the circulating numbers of EPCs and their function are compromised in patients with atherosclerosis (Swiers et al., 2010). These data indicate that EPCs are engaged in vascular repair and are putatively able to counteract certain CV risk factors in order to attenuate the progression of atherosclerosis. In this regard, EPC number and/or function decline with age and are dependent on their TLs (Dei Cas et al., 2013; Vemparala et al., 2013). It follows that hematopoietic stem cells (HSCs) with short telomeres give rise to fewer EPCs, which in turn, display diminished replicative potential (Hammadah et al., 2017) and perhaps vascular repair ability.

Shorter TL may thus entail both increased vascular injury by senescent cells and reduced tissue repair capacity by stem cells engaged in tissue repair (Figure 6.3).

## Conclusions

In conclusion, TL, as expressed in LTL, likely represents an active player in successful aging. The link between short TL and degenerative aging diseases is probably established early in life. It is therefore likely that lifestyle and its modification during adulthood exert only a minor influence on TL. It has been suggested that behavioral modifications, including regular exercise, diet, smoking cessation, or weight loss (Ornish et al., 2013; Sjögren et al., 2014; García-Calzón et al., 2016; Rafie et al., 2017), all well as potentially certain drug treatments (e.g. resveratrol (Xia et al., 2008), statins (Spyridopoulos et al., 2004; Saliques et al., 2011), or imidazoledipeptides (Babizhayev et al., 2014) may help individuals with short telomeres in slowing TL attrition or even lengthen telomeres. However, longitudinal studies are often of short duration (<6 months) and their TL measurement techniques (qPCR) do not have the ability to detect expected changes in LTL during a short follow-up (Steenstrup et al., 2013). No doubt, maintaining a healthy lifestyle can reduce one's cardiovascular risk, as well as other disease risk (Arem et al., 2015; Carter et al., 2015; O'Donovan et al., 2017), and hence affect longevity. However, it is very unlikely that these outcomes are principally mediated through mere attenuation of the rate of TL shortening in the hematopoietic system or other somatic tissues (Rode et al., 2014).

CVD-related mortality is the leading cause of death in contemporary humans, particularly after the age of 75 years (Mozaffarian et al., 2016). Cancer is second to CVD as a cause of death. Between ages 65 and 75, cancer mortality is higher than CVD mortality (Driver et al., 2008; Mozaffarian et al., 2016), after which, CVD mortality overtakes cancer mortality. Thus, although mortality from both cancer and CVD increases with age, cancer mortality declines with age, from nearly 40 percent of all deaths between the ages of 50 and 69 years to 4 percent in centenarians (Smith, 1996). While TL is causal in the development of certain cancers and atherosclerotic CVD, individuals with short LTL may display a lower cancer-related death rate prior to the seventh decade, but a higher CVD-related death rate thereafter.

## References

Adaikalakoteswari A., Balasubramanyam M., Mohan V. Telomere shortening occurs in Asian Indian Type 2 diabetic patients. *Diabet Med.* 2005;22(9):1151–6.

Ahmad S., Heraclides A., Sun Q., et al. Telomere length in blood and skeletal muscle in relation to measures of glycaemia and insulinaemia. *Diabet Med.* 2012;29(10):e377–81.

Al Khaldi R., Mojiminiyi O., AlMulla F., Abdella N. Associations of TERC single nucleotide polymorphisms with human leukocyte telomere length and the risk of Type 2 diabetes mellitus. *PloS One.* 2015;10(12):e0145721.

Al-Attas O. S., Al-Daghri N. M., Alokail M. S., et al. Adiposity and insulin resistance correlate with telomere length in middle-aged Arabs: the influence of circulating adiponectin. *Eur J Endocrinol.* 2010;163(4):601–7.

Alder J. K., Stanley S. E., Wagner C. L., Hamilton M., Hanumanthu V. S., Armanios M. Exome sequencing identifies mutant TINF2 in a family with pulmonary fibrosis. *Chest.* 2015;147(5):1361–8.

Arem H., Moore S. C., Patel A., et al. Leisure time physical activity and mortality: a detailed pooled analysis of the dose-response relationship. *JAMA Intern Med.* 2015;175(6):959–67.

Armanios M. Telomerase and idiopathic pulmonary fibrosis. *Mutat Res.* 2012;730 (1–2):52–8.

Armanios M., Blackburn E.H. The telomere syndromes. *Nat Rev Genet.* 2012;13(10):693–704.

Armanios M. Y., Chen J. J.-L., Cogan J. D., et al. Telomerase mutations in families with idiopathic pulmonary fibrosis. *N Engl J Med.* 2007;356(13):1317–26.

Artandi S. E., DePinho R. A. Telomeres and telomerase in cancer. *Carcinogenesis.* 2010;31(1):9–18.

Aubert G., Baerlocher G. M., Vulto I., Poon S. S., Lansdorp P. M. Collapse of telomere homeostasis in hematopoietic cells caused by heterozygous mutations in telomerase genes. *PLoS Genet.* 2012;8(5):e1002696.

Aviv A. Genetics of leukocyte telomere length and its role in atherosclerosis. *Mutat Res.* 2012;730(1–2):68–74.

Aviv A., Hunt S. C., Lin J., Cao X., Kimura M., Blackburn E. Impartial comparative analysis of measurement of leukocyte telomere length/DNA content by Southern blots and qPCR. *Nucleic Acids Res.* 2011;39(20):e134.

Aviv A., Valdes A., Gardner J. P., Swaminathan R., Kimura M., Spector T. D. Menopause modifies the association of leukocyte telomere length with insulin resistance and inflammation. *J Clin Endocrinol Metab.* 2006;91(2):635–40.

Babizhayev M. A., Vishnyakova K. S., Yegorov Y. E. Oxidative damage impact on aging and age-related diseases: drug targeting of telomere attrition and dynamic telomerase activity flirting with imidazole-containing dipeptides. *Recent Pat Drug Deliv Formul.* 2014;8(3):163–92.

Baird D. M., Kipling D. The extent and significance of telomere loss with age. *Ann N Y Acad Sci.* 2004;1019:265–8.

Bakaysa S. L., Mucci L. A., Slagboom P. E., et al. Telomere length predicts survival independent of genetic influences. *Aging Cell.* 2007;6(6):769–74.

Baker D. J., Childs B. G., Durik M., et al. Naturally occurring p16(Ink4a)-positive cells shorten healthy lifespan. *Nature.* 2016;530(7589):184–9.

Baker D. J., Wijshake T., Tchkonia T., et al. Clearance of p16Ink4a-positive senescent cells delays ageing-associated disorders. *Nature.* 2011;479(7372):232–6.

Ballew B. J., Savage S. A. Updates on the biology and management of dyskeratosis congenita and related telomere biology disorders. *Expert Rev Hematol.* 2013;6(3):327–37.

Barbieri M., Paolisso G., Kimura M., et al. Higher circulating levels of IGF-1 are associated with longer leukocyte telomere length in healthy subjects. *Mech Ageing Dev.* 2009;130(11–12):771–6.

Bayne S., Jones M. E. E., Li H., Liu J.-P. Potential roles for estrogen regulation of telomerase activity in aging. *Ann N Y Acad Sci.* 2007;1114:48–55.

Bekaert S., De Meyer T., Rietzschel E. R., et al. Telomere length and cardiovascular risk factors in a middle-aged population free of overt cardiovascular disease. *Aging Cell.* 2007;6(5):639–47.

Benetos A., Aviv A. Ancestry, telomere length, and atherosclerosis risk. *Circ Cardiovasc Genet.* 2017;10(3):e001718.

Benetos A., Dalgård C., Labat C., et al. Sex difference in leukocyte telomere length is ablated in opposite-sex co-twins. *Int J Epidemiol.* 2014;43(6):1799–805.

Benetos A., Gardner J. P., Zureik M., et al. Short telomeres are associated with increased carotid atherosclerosis in hypertensive subjects. *Hypertension.* 2004;43(2):182–5.

Benetos A., Kark J. D., Susser E., et al. Tracking and fixed ranking of leukocyte telomere length across the adult life course. *Aging Cell.* 2013;12(4):615–21.

Benetos A., Kimura M., Labat C., et al. A model of canine leukocyte telomere dynamics. *Aging Cell.* 2011;10(6):991–5.

Benetos A., Okuda K., Lajemi M., et al. Telomere length as an indicator of biological aging: the gender effect and relation with pulse pressure and pulse wave velocity. *Hypertension.* 2001;37(2 Pt 2):381–5.

Bennett M. R., Evan G. I., Schwartz S. M. Apoptosis of human vascular smooth muscle cells derived from normal vessels and coronary atherosclerotic plaques. *J Clin Invest.* 1995;95(5):2266–74.

Blackburn E. H. Telomeres and telomerase: their mechanisms of action and the effects of altering their functions. *FEBS Lett.* 2005;579(4):859–62.

Blackburn E. H., Epel E. S., Lin J. Human telomere biology: a contributory and interactive factor in aging, disease risks, and protection. *Science.* 2015;350(6265): 1193–8.

Blasco M. A. Telomere length, stem cells and aging. *Nat Chem Biol.* 2007;3(10): 640–9.

Boonekamp J. J., Simons M. J. P., Hemerik L., Verhulst S. Telomere length behaves as biomarker of somatic redundancy rather than biological age. *Aging Cell.* 2013;12(2):330–2.

Broer L., Codd V., Nyholt D. R., et al. Meta-analysis of telomere length in 19,713 subjects reveals high heritability, stronger maternal inheritance and a paternal age effect. *Eur J Hum Genet.* 2013;21(10):1163–8.

Brouilette S., Singh R. K., Thompson J. R., Goodall A. H., Samani N. J. White cell telomere length and risk of premature myocardial infarction. *Arterioscler Thromb Vasc Biol.* 2003;23(5):842–6.

Burnett-Hartman A. N., Fitzpatrick A. L., Kronmal R. A., et al. Telomere-associated polymorphisms correlate with cardiovascular disease mortality in Caucasian women: The Cardiovascular Health Study. *Mech Ageing Dev.* 2012;133(5): 275–81.

Butler M. G., Tilburt J., DeVries A., et al. Comparison of chromosome telomere integrity in multiple tissues from subjects at different ages. *Cancer Genet Cytogenet.* 1998;105(2):138–144.

Cai Z., Yan L.-J., Ratka A. Telomere shortening and Alzheimer's disease. *NeuroMolecular Med.* 2012;15(1):25–48.

Caini S., Raimondi S., Johansson H., et al. Telomere length and the risk of cutaneous melanoma and non-melanoma skin cancer: a review of the literature and meta-analysis. *J Dermatol Sci.* 2015;80(3):168–74.

Calado R. T., Young N. S. Telomere diseases. *N Engl J Med.* 2009;361(24):2353–65.

Calado R. T., Regal J. A., Kleiner D. E., et al. A spectrum of severe familial liver disorders associate with telomerase mutations. *PloS One.* 2009;4(11):e7926.

Calvert P. A., Liew T.-V., Gorenne I., et al. Leukocyte telomere length is associated with high-risk plaques on virtual histology intravascular ultrasound and increased proinflammatory activity. *Arterioscler Thromb Vasc Biol.* 2011;31(9): 2157–64.

Campa D., Mergarten B., De Vivo I., et al. Leukocyte telomere length in relation to pancreatic cancer risk: a prospective study. *Cancer Epidemiol Biomark Prev.* 2014;23(11):2447–54.

Candore G., Balistreri C. R., Listì F., et al. Immunogenetics, gender, and longevity. *Ann N Y Acad Sci.* 2006;1089:516–37.

Carter B. D., Abnet C. C., Feskanich D., et al. Smoking and mortality – beyond established causes. *N Engl J Med.* 2015;372(7):631–40.

Cassidy A., De Vivo I., Liu Y., et al. Associations between diet, lifestyle factors, and telomere length in women. *Am J Clin Nutr.* 2010;91(5):1273–80.

Cattan V., Mercier N., Gardner J. P., et al. Chronic oxidative stress induces a tissue-specific reduction in telomere length in CAST/Ei mice. *Free Radic Biol Med.* 2008;44(8):1592–8.

Cawthon R. M., Smith K. R., O'Brien E., Sivatchenko A., Kerber R. A. Association between telomere length in blood and mortality in people aged 60 years or older. *Lancet.* 2003;361(9355):393–5.

Chang J., Wang Y., Shao L., et al. Clearance of senescent cells by ABT263 rejuvenates aged hematopoietic stem cells in mice. *Nat Med.* 2016;22(1):78–83.

Chen S., Lin J., Matsuguchi T., et al. Short leukocyte telomere length predicts incidence and progression of carotid atherosclerosis in American Indians: the Strong Heart Family Study. *Aging.* 2014;6(5):414–27.

Chen W., Kimura M., Kim S., et al. Longitudinal versus cross-sectional evaluations of leukocyte telomere length dynamics: age-dependent telomere shortening is the rule. *J Gerontol A Biol Sci Med Sci.* 2011;66A(3):312–19.

Cherkas L. F., Hunkin J. L., Kato B. S., et al. The association between physical activity in leisure time and leukocyte telomere length. *Arch Intern Med.* 2008;168(2):154–8.

Childs B. G., Baker D. J., Wijshake T., Conover C. A., Campisi J., van Deursen J. M. Senescent intimal foam cells are deleterious at all stages of atherosclerosis. *Science.* 2016;354(6311):472–7.

Codd V., Nelson C. P., Albrecht E., et al. Identification of seven loci affecting mean telomere length and their association with disease. *Nat Genet.* 2013;45(4):422–7, 427e1–2.

Cogan J. D., Kropski J. A., Zhao M., et al. Rare variants in RTEL1 are associated with familial interstitial pneumonia. *Am J Respir Crit Care Med.* 2015;191(6):646–55.

Coppé J.-P., Patil C. K., Rodier F., et al. Senescence-associated secretory phenotypes reveal cell-nonautonomous functions of oncogenic RAS and the p53 tumor suppressor. *PLOS Biol.* 2008;6(12):e301.

d'Adda di Fagagna F., Reaper P. M., Clay-Farrace L., et al. A DNA damage checkpoint response in telomere-initiated senescence. *Nature.* 2003;426(6963):194–8.

D'Mello M. J. J., Ross S. A., Briel M., Anand S. S., Gerstein H., Paré G. Association between shortened leukocyte telomere length and cardiometabolic outcomes: systematic review and meta-analysis. *Circ Cardiovasc Genet.* 2015;8(1):82–90.

Dalgård C., Benetos A., Verhulst S., et al. Leukocyte telomere length dynamics in women and men: menopause vs age effects. *Int J Epidemiol.* 2015;44(5):1688–95.

Daniali L., Benetos A., Susser E., et al. Telomeres shorten at equivalent rates in somatic tissues of adults. *Nat Commun.* 2013;4:1597.

de Lange T. Shelterin: the protein complex that shapes and safeguards human telomeres. *Genes Dev.* 2005;19(18):2100–10.

How telomeres solve the end-protection problem. *Science.* 2009;326(5955):948–52.

De Meyer T., Rietzschel E. R., De Buyzere M. L., et al. Paternal age at birth is an important determinant of offspring telomere length. *Hum Mol Genet.* 2007;16(24):3097–102.

De Meyer T., Rietzschel E. R., De Buyzere M. L., et al. Systemic telomere length and preclinical atherosclerosis: the Asklepios Study. *Eur Heart J.* 2009;30(24):3074–81.

Deelen J., Beekman M., Codd V., et al. Leukocyte telomere length associates with prospective mortality independent of immune-related parameters and known genetic markers. *Int J Epidemiol.* 2014;43(3):878–86.

Dei Cas A., Spigoni V., Franzini L., et al. Lower endothelial progenitor cell number, family history of cardiovascular disease and reduced HDL-cholesterol levels are associated with shorter leukocyte telomere length in healthy young adults. *Nutr Metab Cardiovasc Dis.* 2013;23(3):272–8.

Demissie S., Levy D., Benjamin E. J., et al. Insulin resistance, oxidative stress, hypertension, and leukocyte telomere length in men from the Framingham Heart Study. *Aging Cell.* 2006;5(4):325–30.

Ding H., Chen C., Shaffer J. R., et al. Telomere length and risk of stroke in Chinese. *Stroke.* 2012;43(3):658–63.

Dokal I. Inherited aplastic anaemia. *Hematol J Off J Eur Haematol Assoc.* 2003;4(1):3–9.

Dong X., Milholland B., Vijg J. Evidence for a limit to human lifespan. *Nature.* 2016;538(7624):257–9.

Driver J. A., Djoussé L., Logroscino G., Gaziano J. M., Kurth T. Incidence of cardiovascular disease and cancer in advanced age: prospective cohort study. *BMJ.* 2008;337:a2467.

Du M., Prescott J., Kraft P., et al. Physical activity, sedentary behavior, and leukocyte telomere length in women. *Am J Epidemiol.* 2012;175(5):414–22.

Eerola J., Kananen L., Manninen K., Hellström O., Tienari P. J., Hovatta I. No evidence for shorter leukocyte telomere length in Parkinson's disease patients. *J Gerontol A Biol Sci Med Sci.* 2010;65(11):1181–4.

Entringer S., Epel E. S., Kumsta R., et al. Stress exposure in intrauterine life is associated with shorter telomere length in young adulthood. *Proc Natl Acad Sci U S A.* 2011;108(33):E513–18.

Factor-Litvak P., Susser E., Kezios K., et al. Leukocyte telomere length in newborns: implications for the role of telomeres in human disease. *Pediatrics.* 2016;137(4): e20153927.

Fedarko N. S. The biology of aging and frailty. *Clin Geriatr Med.* 2011;27(1):27–37.

Fernández-Alvira J. M., Fuster V., Dorado B., et al. Short telomere load, telomere length, and subclinical atherosclerosis: The PESA Study. *J Am Coll Cardiol.* 2016;67(21):2467–76.

Fitzpatrick A. L., Kronmal R. A., Kimura M., et al. Leukocyte telomere length and mortality in the Cardiovascular Health Study. *J Gerontol A Biol Sci Med Sci.* 2011;66(4):421–9.

Fogarty P. F., Yamaguchi H., Wiestner A., et al. Late presentation of dyskeratosis congenita as apparently acquired aplastic anaemia due to mutations in telomerase RNA. *Lancet.* 2003;362(9396):1628–30.

Fyhrquist F., Saijonmaa O., Strandberg T. The roles of senescence and telomere shortening in cardiovascular disease. *Nat Rev Cardiol.* 2013;10(5):274–83.

García-Calzón S., Martínez-González M. A., Razquin C., et al. Mediterranean diet and telomere length in high cardiovascular risk subjects from the PREDIMED-NAVARRA study. *Clin Nutr Edinb Scotl.* 2016;35(6):1399–405.

Gardner J. P., Li S., Srinivasan S. R., et al. Rise in insulin resistance is associated with escalated telomere attrition. *Circulation.* 2005;111(17):2171–7.

Gavrilov L. A., Gavrilova N. Interview with Leonid A. Gavrilov, Ph.D.and Natalia Gavrilova, Ph.D. *Rejuvenation Res.* 2009;12(5):371–4.

Glousker G., Touzot F., Revy P., Tzfati Y., Savage S. A. Unraveling the pathogenesis of Hoyeraal-Hreidarsson syndrome, a complex telomere biology disorder. *Br J Haematol.* 2015;170(4):457–71.

Greider C. W., Blackburn E.H. Identification of a specific telomere terminal transferase activity in Tetrahymena extracts. *Cell.* 1985;43(2 Pt 1):405–13.

Griffith J. D., Comeau L., Rosenfield S., et al. Mammalian telomeres end in a large duplex loop. *Cell.* 1999;97(4):503–14.

Grodstein F., van Oijen M., Irizarry M. C., et al. Shorter telomeres may mark early risk of dementia: preliminary analysis of 62 participants from the nurses' health study. *PloS One.* 2008;3(2):e1590.

Guan J. Z., Maeda T., Sugano M., et al. A percentage analysis of the telomere length in Parkinson's disease patients. *J Gerontol A Biol Sci Med Sci.* 2008;63(5):467–73.

Guan J.-Z., Guan W.-P., Maeda T., Makino N. Effect of vitamin E administration on the elevated oxygen stress and the telomeric and subtelomeric status in Alzheimer's disease. *Gerontology.* 2012;58(1):62–9.

Hägg S., Zhan Y., Karlsson R., et al. Short telomere length is associated with impaired cognitive performance in European ancestry cohorts. *Transl Psychiatry.* 2017;7(4):e1100.

Hammadah M., Al Mheid I., Wilmot K., et al. Telomere shortening, regenerative capacity, and cardiovascular outcomes. *Circ Res.* 2017;120(7):1130–8.

Hansen M. E. B., Hunt S. C., Stone R. C., et al. Shorter telomere length in Europeans than in Africans due to polygenetic adaptation. *Hum Mol Genet.* 2016;25(11):2324–30.

Harley C. B., Futcher A. B., Greider C. W. Telomeres shorten during ageing of human fibroblasts. *Nature.* 1990;345(6274):458–60.

Hashimoto M., Asai A., Kawagishi H., et al. Elimination of p19ARF-expressing cells enhances pulmonary function in mice. *JCI Insight.* 2016;1(12):e87732.

Haycock P. C., Burgess S., Nounu A., et al. Association between telomere length and risk of cancer and non-neoplastic diseases: A Mendelian Randomization Study. *JAMA Oncol.* 2017;3(5):636–51.

Haycock P. C., Heydon E. E., Kaptoge S., Butterworth A. S., Thompson A., Willeit P. Leucocyte telomere length and risk of cardiovascular disease: systematic review and meta-analysis. *BMJ.* 2014;349:g4227.

Hayflick L. Biological aging is no longer an unsolved problem. *Ann N Y Acad Sci.* 2007;1100:1–13.

Hayflick L., Moorhead P. S. The serial cultivation of human diploid cell strains. *Exp Cell Res.* 1961;25:585–621.

Hill J. M., Zalos G., Halcox J. P. J., et al. Circulating endothelial progenitor cells, vascular function, and cardiovascular risk. *N Engl J Med.* 2003;348(7):593–600.

Hjelmborg J. B., Dalgård C., Möller S., et al. The heritability of leucocyte telomere length dynamics. *J Med Genet.* 2015a;52(5):297–302.

Hjelmborg J. B., Dalgård C., Mangino M., et al. Paternal age and telomere length in twins: the germ stem cell selection paradigm. *Aging Cell*. 2015b;14(4):701–3.

Hochstrasser T., Marksteiner J., Humpel C. Telomere length is age-dependent and reduced in monocytes of Alzheimer patients. *Exp Gerontol*. 2012;47(2):160–3.

Honig L. S., Kang M. S., Cheng R., et al. Heritability of telomere length in a study of long-lived families. *Neurobiol Aging*. 2015;36(10):2785–90.

Honig L. S., Kang M. S., Schupf N., Lee J. H., Mayeux R. Association of shorter leukocyte telomere repeat length with dementia and mortality. *Arch Neurol*. 2012;69(10):1332–9.

Houben J. M. J., Moonen H. J. J., van Schooten F. J., Hageman G. J. Telomere length assessment: biomarker of chronic oxidative stress? *Free Radic Biol Med*. 2008;44(3):235–46.

Hovatta I., de Mello V. D. F., Kananen L., et al. Leukocyte telomere length in the Finnish Diabetes Prevention Study. *PloS One*. 2012;7(4):e34948.

Hunt S. C., Chen W., Gardner J. P., et al. Leukocyte telomeres are longer in African Americans than in whites: the National Heart, Lung, and Blood Institute Family Heart Study and the Bogalusa Heart Study. *Aging Cell*. 2008;7(4): 451–8.

Hunt S. C., Kimura M., Hopkins P. N., et al. Leukocyte telomere length and coronary artery calcium. *Am J Cardiol*. 2015;116(2):214–18.

Huzen J., Peeters W., de Boer R. A., et al. Circulating leukocyte and carotid atherosclerotic plaque telomere length: interrelation, association with plaque characteristics, and restenosis after endarterectomy. *Arterioscler Thromb Vasc Biol*. 2011;31(5):1219–25.

Iles M. M., Bishop D. T., Taylor J. C., et al. The effect on melanoma risk of genes previously associated with telomere length. *J Natl Cancer Inst*. 2014;106(10):dju267.

Ilmonen P., Kotrschal A., Penn D. J. Telomere attrition due to infection. *PloS One*. 2008;3(5):e2143.

Jaskelioff M., Muller F. L., Paik J.-H., et al. Telomerase reactivation reverses tissue degeneration in aged telomerase-deficient mice. *Nature*. 2011;469(7328): 102–06.

Jeanclos E., Schork N. J., Kyvik K. O., Kimura M., Skurnick J. H., Aviv A. Telomere length inversely correlates with pulse pressure and is highly familial. *Hypertension*. 2000;36(2):195–200.

Jenkins E. C., Velinov M. T., Ye L., et al. Telomere shortening in T lymphocytes of older individuals with Down syndrome and dementia. *Neurobiol Aging*. 2006;27(7):941–5.

Julin B., Shui I., Heaphy C. M., et al. Circulating leukocyte telomere length and risk of overall and aggressive prostate cancer. *Br J Cancer*. 2015;112(4):769–76.

Kark J. D., Goldberger N., Kimura M., Sinnreich R., Aviv A. Energy intake and leukocyte telomere length in young adults. *Am J Clin Nutr*. 2012;95(2):479–87.

Kimura M., Hjelmborg J. V. B., Gardner J. P., et al. Telomere length and mortality: a study of leukocytes in elderly Danish twins. *Am J Epidemiol*. 2008a;167(7): 799–806.

Kimura M., Cherkas L. F., Kato B. S., et al. Offspring's leukocyte telomere length, paternal age, and telomere elongation in sperm. *PLoS Genet*. 2008b;4(2):e37.

Kurz D. J., Kloeckener-Gruissem B., Akhmedov A., et al. Degenerative aortic valve stenosis, but not coronary disease, is associated with shorter telomere length in the elderly. *Arterioscler Thromb Vasc Biol*. 2006;26(6):e114–17.

Kurz D. J., Decary S., Hong Y., Trivier E., Akhmedov A., Erusalimsky J. D. Chronic oxidative stress compromises telomere integrity and accelerates the onset of senescence in human endothelial cells. *J Cell Sci.* 2004;117(Pt 11): 2417–26.

Lee H. W., Blasco M. A., Gottlieb G. J., Horner J. W., Greider C. W., DePinho R. A. Essential role of mouse telomerase in highly proliferative organs. *Nature.* 1998;392(6676):569–74.

Lindsey J., McGill N. I., Lindsey L. A., Green D. K., Cooke H. J. In vivo loss of telomeric repeats with age in humans. *Mutat Res.* 1991;256(1):45–8.

López-Otín C., Blasco M. A., Partridge L., Serrano M., Kroemer G. The hallmarks of aging. *Cell.* 2013;153(6):1194–217.

Luciani F., Valensin S., Vescovini R., et al. A stochastic model for CD8(+)T cell dynamics in human immunosenescence: implications for survival and longevity. *J Theor Biol.* 2001;213(4):587–97.

Lukens J. N., Van Deerlin V., Clark C. M., Xie S. X., Johnson F. B. Comparisons of telomere lengths in peripheral blood and cerebellum in Alzheimer's disease. *Alzheimers Dement.* 2009;5(6):463–9.

Lummaa V., Pettay J. E., Russell A. F. Male twins reduce fitness of female co-twins in humans. *Proc Natl Acad Sci U S A.* 2007;104(26):10915–20.

Lundberg A. K., Jönsson S., Stenmark J., Kristenson M., Jonasson L. Stress-induced release of matrix metalloproteinase-9 in patients with coronary artery disease: the possible influence of cortisol. *Psychoneuroendocrinology.* 2016;73: 117–24.

Lynch S. M., Major J. M., Cawthon R., et al. A prospective analysis of telomere length and pancreatic cancer in the alpha-tocopherol beta-carotene cancer (ATBC) prevention study. *Int J Cancer.* 2013;133(11):2672–80.

Lynch S. M., Peek M. K., Mitra N., et al. Race, ethnicity, psychosocial factors, and telomere length in a multicenter setting. *PloS One.* 2016;11(1):e0146723.

Ma L., Li Y., Wang J. Telomeres and essential hypertension. *Clin Biochem.* 2015;48 (16–17):1195–9.

Machiela M. J., Hsiung C. A., Shu X.-O., et al. Genetic variants associated with longer telomere length are associated with increased lung cancer risk among never-smoking women in Asia: a report from the female lung cancer consortium in Asia. *Int J Cancer.* 2015;137(2):311–19.

Maeda T., Guan J. Z., Koyanagi M., Higuchi Y., Makino N. Aging-associated alteration of telomere length and subtelomeric status in female patients with Parkinson's disease. *J Neurogenet.* 2012;26(2):245–51.

Mainous A. G., Codd V., Diaz V. A., et al. Leukocyte telomere length and coronary artery calcification. *Atherosclerosis.* 2010;210(1):262–7.

Malaquin N., Martinez A., Rodier F. Keeping the senescence secretome under control: Molecular reins on the senescence-associated secretory phenotype. *Exp Gerontol.* 2016;82:39–49.

Marión R. M., Blasco M. A. Telomeres and telomerase in adult stem cells and pluripotent embryonic stem cells. *Adv Exp Med Biol.* 2010;695:118–31.

Matthews C., Gorenne I., Scott S., et al. Vascular smooth muscle cells undergo telomere-based senescence in human atherosclerosis: effects of telomerase and oxidative stress. *Circ Res.* 2006;99(2):156–64.

Metcalfe N. B., Monaghan P. Compensation for a bad start: grow now, pay later? *Trends Ecol Evol.* 2001;16(5):254–60.

Growth versus lifespan: perspectives from evolutionary ecology. *Exp Gerontol.* 2003;38(9):935–40.

Minamino T., Miyauchi H., Yoshida T., Ishida Y., Yoshida H., Komuro I. Endothelial cell senescence in human atherosclerosis: role of telomere in endothelial dysfunction. *Circulation.* 2002;105(13):1541–4.

Mirabello L., Huang W.-Y., Wong J. Y. Y., et al. The association between leukocyte telomere length and cigarette smoking, dietary and physical variables, and risk of prostate cancer. *Aging Cell.* 2009;8(4):405–13.

Monickaraj F., Aravind S., Gokulakrishnan K., et al. Accelerated aging as evidenced by increased telomere shortening and mitochondrial DNA depletion in patients with type 2 diabetes. *Mol Cell Biochem.* 2012;365(1–2):343–50.

Morrison S. J., Kimble J. Asymmetric and symmetric stem-cell divisions in development and cancer. *Nature.* 2006;441(7097):1068–74.

Mozaffarian D., Benjamin E. J., Go A. S., et al. Heart disease and stroke statistics-2016 update: A Report From the American Heart Association. *Circulation.* 2016;133(4):e38–360.

Müezzinler A., Zaineddin A. K., Brenner H. A systematic review of leukocyte telomere length and age in adults. *Ageing Res Rev.* 2013;12(2):509–19.

Nawrot T. S., Staessen J. A., Gardner J. P., Aviv A. Telomere length and possible link to X chromosome. *Lancet.* 2004;363(9408):507–10.

Nawrot T. S., Staessen J. A., Holvoet P., et al. Telomere length and its associations with oxidized-LDL, carotid artery distensibility and smoking. *Front Biosci (Elite Ed).* 2010;2:1164–8.

Nilsson P. M., Tufvesson H., Leosdottir M., Melander O. Telomeres and cardiovascular disease risk: an update 2013. *Transl Res.* 2013;162(6):371–80.

Nordfjäll K., Eliasson M., Stegmayr B., Lundin S., Roos G., Nilsson P. M. Increased abdominal obesity, adverse psychosocial factors and shorter telomere length in subjects reporting early ageing; the MONICA Northern Sweden Study. *Scand J Soc Med.* 2008;36(7):744–52.

Nzietchueng R., Elfarra M., Nloga J., et al. Telomere length in vascular tissues from patients with atherosclerotic disease. *J Nutr Health Aging.* 2011;15(2):153–6.

O'Donnell C. J., Demissie S., Kimura M., et al. Leukocyte telomere length and carotid artery intimal medial thickness: the Framingham Heart Study. *Arterioscler Thromb Vasc Biol.* 2008;28(6):1165–71.

O'Donovan G., Lee I.-M., Hamer M., Stamatakis E. Association of "Weekend Warrior" and other leisure time physical activity patterns with risks for all-cause, cardiovascular disease, and cancer mortality. *JAMA Intern Med.* 2017;177(3):335–42..

O'Rourke M. F., Hashimoto J. Mechanical factors in arterial aging: a clinical perspective. *J Am Coll Cardiol.* 2007;50(1):1–13.

Okuda K, Bardeguez A, Gardner JP, et al. Telomere length in the newborn. *Pediatr Res.* 2002;52(3):377–81.

Olovnikov AM. A theory of marginotomy. The incomplete copying of template margin in enzymic synthesis of polynucleotides and biological significance of the phenomenon. *J Theor Biol.* 1973;41(1):181–90.

Ornish D, Lin J, Chan JM, et al. Effect of comprehensive lifestyle changes on telomerase activity and telomere length in men with biopsy-proven low-risk prostate cancer: 5-year follow-up of a descriptive pilot study. *Lancet Oncol.* 2013;14(11): 1112–20.

Panayiotou A. G., Nicolaides A. N., Griffin M., et al. Leukocyte telomere length is associated with measures of subclinical atherosclerosis. *Atherosclerosis.* 2010;211(1):176–81.

Panossian L. A., Porter V. R., Valenzuela H. F., et al. Telomere shortening in T cells correlates with Alzheimer's disease status. *Neurobiol Aging.* 2003;24(1):77–84.

Rafie N., Golpour Hamedani S., Barak F., Safavi S. M., Miraghajani M. Dietary patterns, food groups and telomere length: a systematic review of current studies. *Eur J Clin Nutr.* 2017;71(2):151–8.

Raymond A. R., Brooksbank R. L., Millen A. M. E., et al. Telomere length, endothelial activation and carotid atherosclerosis in black and white African patients with rheumatoid arthritis. *Clin Exp Rheumatol.* 2016;34(5):864–71.

Ribeiro D. C., Brook A. H., Hughes T. E., Sampson W. J., Townsend G. C. Intrauterine hormone effects on tooth dimensions. *J Dent Res.* 2013;92(5):425–31.

Rizvi S., Raza S. T., Mahdi F. Telomere length variations in aging and age-related diseases. *Curr Aging Sci.* 2015;7(3):161–7.

Rode L., Bojesen S. E., Weischer M., Nordestgaard B. G. High tobacco consumption is causally associated with increased all-cause mortality in a general population sample of 55,568 individuals, but not with short telomeres: a Mendelian randomization study. *Int J Epidemiol.* 2014;43(5):1473–83.

Rode L., Nordestgaard B. G., Bojesen S. E. Peripheral blood leukocyte telomere length and mortality among 64,637 individuals from the general population. *J Natl Cancer Inst.* 2015;107(6):djv074.

Rodier F., Campisi J. Four faces of cellular senescence. *J Cell Biol.* 2011;192(4):547–56.

Ross R. Atherosclerosis is an inflammatory disease. *Am Heart J.* 1999;138 (5, Supplement):S419–S420.

Rudolph K. L., Chang S., Lee H. W., et al. Longevity, stress response, and cancer in aging telomerase-deficient mice. *Cell.* 1999;96(5):701–12.

Saliques S., Teyssier J.-R., Vergely C., et al. Circulating leukocyte telomere length and oxidative stress: a new target for statin therapy. *Atherosclerosis.* 2011;219(2): 753–60.

Salpea K. D., Talmud P. J., Cooper J. A., et al. Association of telomere length with type 2 diabetes, oxidative stress and UCP2 gene variation. *Atherosclerosis.* 2010;209(1):42–50.

Samani N. J., Boultby R., Butler R., Thompson J. R., Goodall A. H. Telomere shortening in atherosclerosis. *Lancet.* 2001;358(9280):472–3.

Samper E., Flores J. M., Blasco M. A. Restoration of telomerase activity rescues chromosomal instability and premature aging in Terc−/− mice with short telomeres. *EMBO Rep.* 2001;2(9):800–7.

Sanchez-Espiridion B., Chen M., Chang J. Y., et al. Telomere length in peripheral blood leukocytes and lung cancer risk: a large case-control study in Caucasians. *Cancer Res.* 2014;74(9):2476–86.

Savage S. A., Alter B. P. The role of telomere biology in bone marrow failure and other disorders. *Mech Ageing Dev.* 2008;129(1–2):35–47.

Savage S. A., Gadalla S. M., Chanock S. J. The long and short of telomeres and cancer association studies. *J Natl Cancer Inst.* 2013;105(7):448–9.

Savage S. A., Giri N., Baerlocher G. M., Orr N., Lansdorp P. M., Alter B. P. TINF2, a component of the shelterin telomere protection complex, is mutated in dyskeratosis congenita. *Am J Hum Genet.* 2008;82(2):501–9.

Saxena R., Bjonnes A., Prescott J., et al. Genome-wide association study identifies variants in Casein Kinase II (CSNK2A2) to be associated with leukocyte telomere length in a Punjabi Sikh Diabetic Cohort. *Circ Cardiovasc Genet.* 2014;7(3):287–95.

Scheller Madrid A., Rode L., Nordestgaard B. G., Bojesen S. E. Short telomere length and ischemic heart disease: observational and genetic studies in 290 022 individuals. *Clin Chem.* 2016;62(8):1140–9.

Schürks M., Buring J., Dushkes R., Gaziano J. M., Zee R. Y. L., Kurth T. Telomere length and Parkinson's disease in men: a nested case-control study. *Eur J Neurol.* 2014;21(1):93–9.

Seluanov A., Chen Z., Hine C., et al. Telomerase activity coevolves with body mass not lifespan. *Aging Cell.* 2007;6(1):45–52.

Seow W. J., Cawthon R. M., Purdue M. P., et al. Telomere length in white blood cell DNA and lung cancer: a pooled analysis of three prospective cohorts. *Cancer Res.* 2014;74(15):4090–8.

Sharpless N. E., DePinho R. A. How stem cells age and why this makes us grow old. *Nat Rev Mol Cell Biol.* 2007;8(9):703–3.

Shay J. W., Wright W. E. Telomerase activity in human cancer. *Curr Opin Oncol.* 1996;8(1):66–71.

Telomeres and telomerase: implications for cancer and aging. *Radiat Res.* 2001;155(1 Pt 2):188–93.

Shay J. W., Wright W. E., Werbin H. Defining the molecular mechanisms of human cell immortalization. *Biochim Biophys Acta.* 1991;1072(1):1–7.

Sjögren P., Fisher R., Kallings L., Svenson U., Roos G., Hellénius M.-L. Stand up for health – avoiding sedentary behaviour might lengthen your telomeres: secondary outcomes from a physical activity RCT in older people. *Br J Sports Med.* 2014;48(19):1407–9.

Smith D. W. Cancer mortality at very old ages. *Cancer.* 1996;77(7):1367–72.

Spigoni V., Aldigeri R., Picconi A., et al. Telomere length is independently associated with subclinical atherosclerosis in subjects with type 2 diabetes: a cross-sectional study. *Acta Diabetol.* 2016;53(4):661–7.

Spyridopoulos I., Haendeler J., Urbich C., et al. Statins enhance migratory capacity by upregulation of the telomere repeat-binding factor TRF2 in endothelial progenitor cells. *Circulation.* 2004;110(19):3136–42.

Stanley S. E., Armanios M. The short and long telomere syndromes: paired paradigms for molecular medicine. *Curr Opin Genet Dev.* 2015;33:1–9.

Stanley S. E., Chen J. J. L., Podlevsky J. D., et al. Telomerase mutations in smokers with severe emphysema. *J Clin Invest.* 2015;125(2):563–70.

Steenstrup T., Hjelmborg J. V. B., Kark J. D., Christensen K., Aviv A. The telomere lengthening conundrum – artifact or biology? *Nucleic Acids Res.* 2013;41(13):e131.

Steenstrup T., Kark J. D., Verhulst S., et al. Telomeres and the natural lifespan limit in humans. *Aging.* 2017;9(4):1130–42.

Stone R. C., Horvath K., Kark J. D., Susser E., Tishkoff S. A., Avi A. Telomere length and the cancer-atherosclerosis trade-off. *PLoS Genet.* 2016;12(7): e1006144.

Strandberg T. E., Saijonmaa O., Tilvis R. S., et al. Association of telomere length in older men with mortality and midlife body mass index and smoking. *J Gerontol A Biol Sci Med Sci*. 2011;66(7):815–20.

Stuart B. D., Choi J., Zaidi S., et al. Exome sequencing links mutations in PARN and RTEL1 with familial pulmonary fibrosis and telomere shortening. *Nat Genet*. 2015;47(5):512–17.

Swiers G., Speck N. A., de Bruijn M. F. T. R. Visualizing blood cell emergence from aortic endothelium. *Cell Stem Cell*. 2010;6(4):289–90.

Tapp A. L., Maybery M. T., Whitehouse A. J. O. Evaluating the twin testosterone transfer hypothesis: a review of the empirical evidence. *Horm Behav*. 2011;60(5):713–22.

Tchkonia T., Zhu Y., van Deursen J., Campisi J., Kirkland J. L. Cellular senescence and the senescent secretory phenotype: therapeutic opportunities. *J Clin Invest*. 2013;123(3):966–72.

Tentolouris N., Nzietchueng R., Cattan V., et al. White blood cells telomere length is shorter in males with type 2 diabetes and microalbuminuria. *Diabetes Care*. 2007;30(11):2909–15.

Testa R., Olivieri F., Sirolla C., et al. Leukocyte telomere length is associated with complications of type 2 diabetes mellitus. *Diabet Med*. 2011;28(11):1388–94.

Thomas P., O' Callaghan N. J., Fenech M. Telomere length in white blood cells, buccal cells and brain tissue and its variation with ageing and Alzheimer's disease. *Mech Ageing Dev*. 2008;129(4):183–90.

Toupance S., Labat C., Temmar M., et al. Short telomeres, but not telomere attrition rates, are associated with carotid atherosclerosis. *Hypertension* 2017;70(2):420–5.

Tzanetakou I. P., Mikhailidis D. P., Perrea D.N. Nutrition during pregnancy and the effect of carbohydrates on the offspring's metabolic profile: in search of the "Perfect Maternal Diet." *Open Cardiovasc Med J*. 2011;5:103–9.

Unryn B. M., Cook L. S., Riabowol K. T. Paternal age is positively linked to telomere length of children. *Aging Cell*. 2005;4(2):97–101.

Uryga A. K., Bennett M. R. Ageing induced vascular smooth muscle cell senescence in atherosclerosis. *J Physiol*. 2016;594(8):2115–24.

Valdes A. M., Andrew T., Gardner J. P., et al. Obesity, cigarette smoking, and telomere length in women. *Lancet*. 2005;366(9486):662–4.

van der Harst P., van der Steege G., de Boer R. A., et al. Telomere length of circulating leukocytes is decreased in patients with chronic heart failure. *J Am Coll Cardiol*. 2007;49(13):1459–64.

van Deursen J. M. The role of senescent cells in ageing. *Nature*. 2014;509(7501):439–46.

Vasan R. S., Demissie S., Kimura M., et al. Association of leukocyte telomere length with circulating biomarkers of the renin-angiotensin-aldosterone system: the Framingham Heart Study. *Circulation*. 2008;117(9):1138–44.

Vemparala K., Roy A., Bahl V. K., et al. Early accelerated senescence of circulating endothelial progenitor cells in premature coronary artery disease patients in a developing country – a case control study. *BMC Cardiovasc Disord*. 2013;13:104.

von Zglinicki T. Oxidative stress shortens telomeres. *Trends Biochem Sci*. 2002;27(7):339–44.

von Zglinicki T., Serra V., Lorenz M., et al. Short telomeres in patients with vascular dementia: an indicator of low antioxidative capacity and a possible risk factor? *Lab Invest*. 2000;80(11):1739–47.

Vulliamy T., Marrone A., Dokal I., Mason P. J. Association between aplastic anaemia and mutations in telomerase RNA. *Lancet.* 2002;359(9324):2168–70.

Vuoksimaa E., Eriksson C. J. P., Pulkkinen L., Rose R. J., Kaprio J. Decreased prevalence of left-handedness among females with male co-twins: evidence suggesting prenatal testosterone transfer in humans? *Psychoneuroendocrinology.* 2010;35(10):1462–72.

Walsh K. M., Codd V., Rice T., et al. Longer genotypically-estimated leukocyte telomere length is associated with increased adult glioma risk. *Oncotarget.* 2015;6(40):42468–77.

Walsh K. M., Whitehead T. P., de Smith A. J., et al. Common genetic variants associated with telomere length confer risk for neuroblastoma and other childhood cancers. *Carcinogenesis.* 2016;37(6):576–82.

Wang H., Chen H., Gao X., et al. Telomere length and risk of Parkinson's disease. *Mov Disord.* 2008;23(2):302–5.

Wang J., Uryga A. K., Reinhold J., et al. Vascular smooth muscle cell senescence promotes atherosclerosis and features of plaque vulnerability. *Circulation.* 2015;132(20):1909–19.

Wang Y.-Y., Chen A.-F., Wang H.-Z., Xie L.-Y., Sui K.-X., Zhang Q.-Y. Association of shorter mean telomere length with large artery stiffness in patients with coronary heart disease. *Aging Male.* 2011;14(1):27–32.

Watfa G., Dragonas C., Brosche T., et al. Study of telomere length and different markers of oxidative stress in patients with Parkinson's disease. *J Nutr Health Aging.* 2011;15(4):277–81.

Weischer M., Bojesen S. E., Nordestgaard B. G. Telomere shortening unrelated to smoking, body weight, physical activity, and alcohol intake: 4,576 general population individuals with repeat measurements 10 years apart. *PLoS Genet.* 2014;10(3):e1004191.

Willeit P., Raschenberger J., Heydon E. E., et al. Leucocyte telomere length and risk of type 2 diabetes mellitus: new prospective cohort study and literature-based meta-analysis. *PloS One.* 2014;9(11):e112483.

Willeit P., Willeit J., Brandstätter A., et al. Cellular aging reflected by leukocyte telomere length predicts advanced atherosclerosis and cardiovascular disease risk. *Arterioscler Thromb Vasc Biol.* 2010;30(8):1649–56.

Xia L., Wang X. X., Hu X. S., et al. Resveratrol reduces endothelial progenitor cells senescence through augmentation of telomerase activity by Akt-dependent mechanisms. *Br J Pharmacol.* 2008;155(3):387–94.

Yamaguchi H., Baerlocher G. M., Lansdorp P. M., et al. Mutations of the human telomerase RNA gene (TERC) in aplastic anemia and myelodysplastic syndrome. *Blood.* 2003;102(3):916–18.

Yamaguchi H., Calado R. T., Ly H., et al. Mutations in TERT, the gene for telomerase reverse transcriptase, in aplastic anemia. *N Engl J Med.* 2005;352(14): 1413–24.

Yeh J.-K., Wang C.-Y. Telomeres and telomerase in cardiovascular diseases. *Genes.* 2016;7(9):E58.

Youngren K., Jeanclos E., Aviv H., et al. Synchrony in telomere length of the human fetus. *Hum Genet.* 1998;102(6):640–3.

Zee R. Y. L., Ridker P. M., Chasman D. I. Genetic variants of 11 telomere-pathway gene loci and the risk of incident type 2 diabetes mellitus: the Women's Genome Health Study. *Atherosclerosis*. 2011;218(1):144–6.

Zekry D., Herrmann F. R., Irminger-Finger I., et al. Telomere length and ApoE polymorphism in mild cognitive impairment, degenerative and vascular dementia. *J Neurol Sci*. 2010;299(1–2):108–11.

Zhan Y., Song C., Karlsson R., et al. Telomere length shortening and Alzheimer disease – A Mendelian Randomization Study. *JAMA Neurol*. 2015;72(10):1202–3.

Zhang C., Doherty J. A., Burgess S., et al. Genetic determinants of telomere length and risk of common cancers: a Mendelian randomization study. *Hum Mol Genet*. 2015;24(18):5356–66.

Zhang W., Chen Y., Wang Y., et al. Short telomere length in blood leucocytes contributes to the presence of atherothrombotic stroke and haemorrhagic stroke and risk of post-stroke death. *Clin Sci*. 2013;125(1):27–36.

# 7 Gene–Lifestyle Interactions in Longevity

Rune Lindahl-Jacobsen and Kaare Christensen

## Introduction

Longevity is often preceded by many years of good health; it therefore allows for an easy operational definition of successful aging (Engberg et al., 2009; Brooks-Wilson, 2013; Christensen and McGue, 2016). Traditionally, two major lines of research have been applied to understand why some people live long and others do not: studies on the genetic components and studies on environmental factors. Environmental studies have been quite successful in identifying factors associated with longevity, whereas only a few consistent results have been found with regard to the genetic component (Schächter et al., 1994; Frisoni et al., 2001; Novelli et al., 2008; Jacobsen et al., 2010; Deelen et al., 2011; McKay et al., 2011; Nebel et al., 2011; Lindahl-Jacobsen et al., 2012; Sebastiani et al., 2012; Beekman et al., 2013; Schupf et al., 2013; Soerensen et al., 2013; Corella and Ordovás, 2014; Garatachea et al., 2014, 2015).

Although a host of environmental and lifestyle factors have been found to be associated with longevity, such as socioeconomic position, education, smoking, body mass index (BMI), and chronic diseases (Martelin et al., 1998; Stevens et al., 1998; Lee et al., 2008; Newman and Murabito, 2013; Levine and Crimmins, 2014; Luo et al., 2015), only a small degree of the variance in longevity is explained by these factors per se. Studies have shown that the gene with the strongest and most consistent association – the Apolipoprotein E (ApoE) gene – explains only approximately 3.5 percent of the variance in life expectancy (Ewbank, 2004). This suggests a more complicated causation for the longevity trait. Possible explanations include the impact of: (1) a high number of common genetic variants, each of which contributes with only very small effects (Finch and Tanzi, 1997; Deelen et al., 2013); (2) rare mutations specific to individuals, families, or populations (Christensen et al., 2006); (3) stochasticity (Kirkwood et al., 2011); (4) differences in selection and frailty across birth cohorts (Vaupel et al., 1979; Nygaard et al., 2014); or (5) gene–gene (Tan et al., 2002), environment–environment (Haveman-Nies et al., 2002; Spencer et al., 2005; Yates et al., 2008), and gene–environment interactions.

In this chapter, we will focus on gene–environment interactions in longevity, using as an example the top candidates for causal factors for longevity within genetic and environmental studies so far, namely ApoE and lifestyle factors.

## The Importance of Studying Longevity and Gene–Environment Interactions

The response to environmental changes at the molecular level is reflected in individual alterations to tissue and organs. Environmental exposure thus results in different phenotypes; results that are also dependent on the genetic background on which the phenotypes occur when mediated through our genes. A classic example of gene–environment interaction is the effect of sunlight exposure on skin cancer risk in light-skinned humans, when compared to darker-skinned individuals (Adami et al., 2009). The genes that code for skin color interact with solar UV radiation to reduce skin cancer risk with increased darkness of the skin (Adami et al., 2009). Another well-known example is phenylketonuria, in which mutations in the phenylalanine hydroxylase gene (PAH) cause an autosomal recessive disorder, with the lack of ability to degrade phenylalanine (Cunningham, 1966). The disease results in severe intellectual disability, other medical disorders and a short life span, if normal diet is consumed (Cunningham, 1966). However, a restricted diet can nullify the effects of the gene; the carriers live a normal life, except for their diet. The case of phenylketonuria is a rare example of how an environmental factor, in this case, diet, can have a huge impact on life span, depending on genotype.

Throughout life, individuals are shaped in a continuous process of gene–environment interaction; genes are activated at different periods of life and modulation of gene actions occurs over the life course and across generations (Kulminski, 2013). If the separate effects of genes and environment on longevity were identified, but their interaction disregarded, this would lead to an erroneous estimation of the degree of longevity that could be explained by genes and environment and their joint effect. This is because it would not take into account the estimation of the actual joint effect (e.g., the joint effect could be attributed incorrectly to either the gene effect or the environmental effect). Understanding the effects of gene–environment interaction on longevity could potentially lead to the identification of new biological pathways of importance for longevity and perhaps, over time, to suggested individualized strategies to increase the chance of a long and healthy life span.

## Gene–Environment Interaction Assessment

Gene–environment interactions are biological effects and their assessment calls for the same carefulness of evaluations as other causal relationships. Confounding factors and systematic bias in gene–environment interaction studies can result in incorrect conclusions, similar to those in other studies of exposures and outcomes. Therefore, it is important to differentiate between actual causal mechanisms and observed associations. A definition of biological interaction is useful in their differentiation. The sufficient-component cause model, defined by Rothman (Rothman, 1976; Rothman et al., 2014), is useful for this purpose

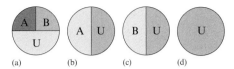

**Figure 7.1.** *Defining biological interaction using the sufficient-component cause model (Rothman, 1976, 2014)*
There are four possible combinations for two known component causes A and B and unknown causes U to cause a trait (e.g. death, disease, pregnancy). The unknown causes may be present or not. For the trait to appear the circle needs to be complete. In diagram (a) both A and B are component causes and therefore interact. Without either of the two the trait in question would not appear. Other unknown causes U may still be a part of the causation as illustrated in a). In (b), (c), and (d) the appearance of the trait in question does not depend on the co-presence of the causes and no interaction is thus present.

(Figure 7.1). The empirical criterion for a biological interaction is a departure from the addition of the risks from each of the interacting factors (Hammond et al., 1979; Rothman et al., 2014). Because the causes illustrated in the sufficient-component cause model are seldom measurable, measures of interaction and the use of statistics for defining their uncertainty are relied upon. Besides this theoretical framework for understanding and defining biological interaction, it is also suggested that the interaction should fulfill one of Hill's important criteria (Hill, 1965) – that is, it should be biologically plausible (Hunter, 2005).

## Measuring Interaction

Measuring interaction generally involves a test for interaction, in a departure from using a statistical model, such as a linear model (departure from additive effects) or a logistic model (departure from multiplicative effects) (Ahlbom and Alfredsson, 2005). In epidemiology, the departure is called effect modification, where the effect of one variable changes over values of some other variable (Rothman et al., 2014). Some statistical models can be transformed into a linear scale, such as in logistic regression models, where the linearity is present on the logarithmic scale but multiplicatively is present on the original scale. If two exposures both have an effect on an outcome, then there must be interaction on one of the scales. Thus, interaction can be present on the original scale and absent on the transformed scale, or vice versa (Rothman, 2012). When searching for interaction, it is therefore recommended to perform interaction analysis on both the additive scale (i.e. scale-dependent interaction where baseline risk varies across the strata) and the multiplicative scale.

One important issue when examining for gene–lifestyle interaction is the need for large sample sizes. The general rule of thumb, for a sample size for the detection of multiplicative interaction in two variables, is four times what is needed for each separate effect (Smith and Day, 1984). Many epidemiological studies are underpowered for even main effects (Hunter, 2005). Gene frequencies and the model used for the analysis (dominant, additive, or recessive gene model) further complicate estimation of sample sizes needed. Attempts have been made to calculate sample sizes[1] needed under different assumptions of gene frequencies and relative risk estimates of interaction. Even when simplified circumstances are assumed, large numbers are needed to detect even moderate effects (Gauderman, 2002). The use of meta-studies with pooled data across studies is therefore generally needed for detection of interaction effects.

## Study Designs for Identification of Gene–Lifestyle Interaction

Inherent to measuring interaction in gene–lifestyle studies is the problem of multiple comparisons, when examining thousands or millions of sequence variants in associations studies (Hunter, 2005). Inclusion of multiple exposures and multiple interactions further complicate the situation. Therefore, it is recommended that, besides using appropriate statistical methods, the observed gene–environment interactions be reproduced in at least two or more studies (Hunter, 2005). Such a procedure can be problematic, however, if the variants are population-specific or if publication bias is present. Publication bias can potentially result in an overrepresentation of false positive findings (Hunter, 2005).

In studies of candidate genes in gene–lifestyle interactions on longevity, any of the standard epidemiological study designs can be used (Thomas, 2010). For the study of gene–lifestyle interactions in common and rare diseases, the use of retrospective designs is often beneficial, because of sample size considerations (Gauderman, 2002). In longevity studies, the case–control design is undesirable because selection of the control group is problematic (i.e., birth-year controls matched to long-lived cases are deceased; otherwise they would be cases). The prospective designs, such as the cohort study design or nested case control studies are favorable, but require time and huge sample sizes (Christensen et al., 2006).

Epidemiological longevity study designs can be applied both in family-based studies and population-based studies (Lawlor and Mishra, 2009). In family-based studies, the inheritance of disease or longevity alleles from parents to pedigrees is studied (Hunter, 2005; Lawlor and Mishra, 2009; Aslibekyan, 2014). In twin studies, the correlation in life span or concordance in longevity between monozygotic and dizygotic twins can be used to partition components of variance between genetic and shared and non-shared environmental factors (Elston et al., 2002; Hunter, 2005; Hjelmborg et al., 2006). Thereby, it is possible to directly estimate specific gene–environment interactions on longevity – albeit on the proviso that information on the environment is present. In population-based study designs, phenotype, lifestyle information, and genotype are obtained from unrelated individuals to examine for the gene–lifestyle interaction (Elston et al., 2002; Hunter, 2005). The possibilities for bias and confounding in these study designs are similar to those in other epidemiological studies (Dempfle et al., 2008; Thomas, 2010).

1 A software program that computes sample size for studies of G × G interaction and for studies of gene–environment (G × E) interaction is freely available at: http://biostats.usc.edu/software.

Since 2005, genome-wide association studies (GWAS) have been used to examine genetic variants, in order to identify association with specific traits, such as diseases or longevity (Klein et al., 2005; Bush and Moore, 2012). The concept involves comparing the frequency of possible risk alleles in individuals with a trait or disease to that of controls without the trait/disease in question (Bush and Moore, 2012). Although GWAS studies have led to the discovery of multiple genes and pathways involved in various complex diseases, they have had limited success in identifying new specific loci linked to longevity, and so far only two genes have consistently been identified – the ApoE and FOXO genes (Zeng et al., 2016). The reason for the low number of genes identified could be the missing integration of environmental factors and their interaction with the genes (Dunn et al., 2015; Zeng et al., 2016). An extension of the GWAS technique is the inclusion of gene–environment interaction analysis – so-called gene–environment-wide interaction studies (GEWIS) (Costello et al., 2013). GEWIS studies have been successful in identifying associations for other complex phenotypes such as diabetes (Hamza et al., 2011; Zheng et al., 2013), depressive symptoms (Dunn et al., 2016), and cancer (Wu et al., 2012; Siegert et al., 2013) that were not revealed in genetic main effect analyses (Manning et al., 2012; Wu et al., 2012; Siegert et al., 2013). GEWIS could be a new study approach for identifying genes that influence longevity under different environmental regimes (Zeng et al., 2016). One strategy would be to integrate the most consistent gene known to be associated with longevity (ApoE gene) in these designs and examine how the various lifestyle factors modulate its effect on longevity. It should be noted, however, that the effect could be altered by external and internal environments that change with age, calendar time, and year of birth, and that these elements could complicate such attempts.

The inherent problem of the requirement of large sample sizes for detection of genes and gene–lifestyle interactions on longevity has led to meta-studies or joint cohort analyses. More recently, there have been examples of meta-studies for detection of the effect of genes on longevity (Newman et al., 2010; Beekman et al., 2013; Ganna et al., 2013; Zeng et al., 2016). The extension into meta-analysis of gene–lifestyle interactions will most probably follow, because studies have been done on gene–lifestyle interactions in relation to specific diseases (Ahmad et al., 2013; Nettleton et al., 2013; Nettleton et al., 2015).

## Known Genetic and Lifestyle Factors Associated with Human Longevity

### Genetic Factors Associated with Human Longevity

Twin studies show that genetic factors are estimated to account for approximately 25 percent of the variation in human life span in Nordic populations born around the beginning of the twentieth century (Hjelmborg et al., 2006). This means that 75 percent of the variation is caused by environmental factors

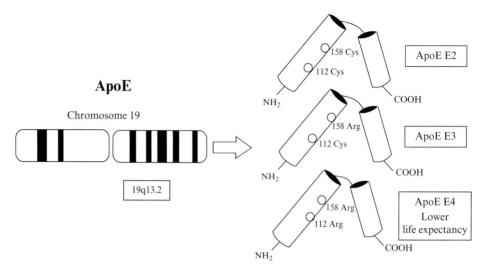

**Figure 7.2.** *The three isoforms of apolipoprotein E*
The ApoE gene codes for a multifunctional protein, apolipoprotein E, that combines with lipids to form lipoproteins. It is situated on chromosome 19 (Mahley et al., 1999). The most important function of lipoproteins is to transport cholesterol and other fats around the body (Mahley et al., 1999; Huang, 2014). ApoE is polymorphic and has three major alleles (Frikke-Schmidt, 2000; Huang, 2014): the ApoE E2, ApoE E3, and ApoE E4 alleles. ApoE E3 is the most frequently found allele, carried by more than half of the general population (Huang, 2014; Raichlen and Alexander, 2014). The three allelic forms differ by only one or two amino acids at positions 112 and 158. However, these differences have an impact on human longevity. For example, the ApoE E4/E3 haplotype could have a four-years shorter life expectancy at age fifteen, when compared to the ApoE E2/E3 haplotype (Figure modified after Ortiz et al., 2015).

and stochasticity. As mentioned, only a few genes to date have been consistently associated with mortality in candidate gene studies and GWAS studies – the most prominent finding being the ApoE gene (Schächter et al., 1994; Frisoni et al., 2001; Novelli et al., 2008; Jacobsen et al., 2010; Deelen et al., 2011; McKay et al., 2011; Nebel et al., 2011; Lindahl-Jacobsen et al., 2012; Sebastiani et al., 2012; Beekman et al., 2013; Schupf et al., 2013; Soerensen et al., 2013; Corella and Ordovás, 2014; Garatachea et al., 2014; Garatachea et al., 2015) (Figure 7.2). Another promising candidate gene is the FOXO gene, which has been associated with longevity in numerous candidate studies (Willcox et al., 2008; Anselmi et al., 2009; Flachsbart et al., 2009; Corella and Ordovás, 2014; Däumer et al., 2014), but which could not be replicated in GWAS studies (Corella and Ordovás, 2014). Most recently, in a large, European meta-analysis of human longevity, the 5q33.3 locus was identified as being associated with survival to beyond 90 years of age, and it has therefore been suggested as the third human longevity locus, alongside ApoE and FOXO (Deelen et al., 2014). However, additional studies are needed to further improve the understanding of the role of the 5q33.3 locus in longevity and survival. It is surprising that only two genes have been associated with longevity, given the extent of the searches in various populations (Atzmon et al., 2006; Salvioli et al., 2006; Rosvall et al., 2009; Jacobsen et al., 2010; Iannitti and Palmieri, 2011; Murabito et al., 2012; Beekman et al., 2013;

Kulminski, 2013; Gentschew et al., 2013; Kulminski et al., 2013, 2014; Morris et al., 2014). As mentioned, one possible reason for the lack of identification of genes associated with longevity could be the missing integration of both the environment and the genes (Brooks-Wilson, 2013; Corella and Ordovás, 2014). The finding of an association of a gene with longevity in one population, but not in another population, could be because of the different internal and external environments involved. An environment can modify the effect of the gene, and the criteria of reproducibility cannot be met without the integration of this environment (Brooks-Wilson, 2013; Corella and Ordovás, 2014).

## Lifestyle Factors Associated with Human Longevity

In older people, lifestyle factors, including smoking (Ruigómez et al., 1995; de Groot et al., 2004; Knoops et al., 2004; Dupre et al., 2008; Yates et al., 2008; Halme et al., 2010; Newson et al., 2010), alcohol intake (Ruigómez et al., 1995; Halme et al., 2010) (Nybo et al., 2003; Yates et al., 2008; Thinggaard et al., 2010), body weight (Nybo et al., 2003; Yates et al., 2008; Thinggaard et al., 2010), and physical activity (Ruigómez et al., 1995; Fried et al., 1998; Knoops et al., 2004; Benetos et al., 2005; Rodriguez-Laso et al., 2007; Yates et al., 2008) are associated with mortality. After the age of 75, lifestyle has an association with survival, but the association decreases with age (Rizzuto et al., 2012). At very old ages, the association with these lifestyle risk factors diminishes (Nybo et al., 2003; Dupre et al., 2008; Hagberg and Samuelsson, 2008; Yates et al., 2008; Gellert et al., 2012; Jacobsen et al., 2010; Rizzuto and Fratiglioni, 2014) or even disappears (Nybo et al., 2003). The principal reason behind the decreasing association with age and of unhealthy lifestyle behavior is believed to be selection (Vaupel et al., 1979). Via selection, the surviving individuals possess compensatory factors for their unhealthy behavior, which protect them (Vaupel et al., 1979; Jacobsen et al., 2010). This explains why the association between smoking and mortality diminishes, and even becomes protective at advanced age, as has been observed, for example, in the Cancer Prevention Study (Burns et al., 1997) in the United States (Figure 7.3). Whereas the single effect of each lifestyle factor seems to diminish with age, the combined effects of unfavorable lifestyles still show effects even at the oldest ages, even though the combined effects decrease with age (Rizzuto et al., 2012; Thinggaard et al., 2016).

## The Influence of the ApoE Gene on Life Span

The differences in life expectancy at age 15 (the mean age at death for survivors to 15) in Denmark for individuals born from 1855 to 1899 by genotype was: 58.7 years for the ApoE E2/E3 haplotype and 54.6 for the E3/E4 haplotype (Ewbank, 2004). In general, the ApoE E2/E3 haplotype has been found to be protective, with a 5–10 percent lower mortality risk than the E3/E3 haplotype (Ewbank, 2007) and a 22–35 percent excess risk associated with the E3/E4 haplotype (Ewbank, 2007). The effect could be modulated by race and ethnicity.

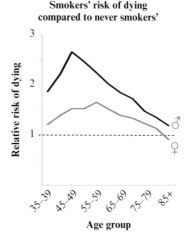

**Figure 7.3.** *Age- and sex-specific risk of dying for smokers*
The risk of dying for smokers first increases and then decreases over age. Smoking can even become protective at very high ages, as is the case for female smokers (Data from The American Cancer Society Cancer Prevention Study).

For example, no excess risk of carrying the ApoE E3/E4 haplotype among African Americans has been observed (Ewbank, 2007), and a lower risk for this haplotype has also been found for Japanese and Koreans, when compared to the risk level in Caucasian populations (Ewbank, 2007).

## ApoE–Age Interaction

Age is the most important risk factor in relation to mortality and longevity (Niccoli and Partridge, 2012). External and internal environments can change throughout a person's life course, and thereby alter the effect of genes and gene variants. A gene that has an unfavorable effect at a younger age can become favorable at an older age – or vice versa (Figure 7.4). Age-related selection effects could dilute the effect of harmful gene effects, or the accumulation of risk factors over age could increase the effect of a genotype. These considerations have been reflected in two hypotheses: (1) the heterogeneity hypothesis (Vaupel et al., 1979; Vaupel, 1988) and (2) causal composite component models (multifactorial threshold models – see Figure 7.1) (Jacobsen et al., 2010; Rothman, 2012; Rothman et al., 2014). According to the heterogeneity hypothesis, the mortality of individuals carrying a "frail" or "risky" genotype in a population will approach that of non-carriers with age because of a selection pressure on carriers (i.e., only the otherwise most robust will survive with a "frail" genotype) (Vaupel et al., 1979; Vaupel, 1988). The implication of this hypothesis is that each individual carries a frailty through his/her entire life (Vaupel et al., 1979; Vaupel, 1988). In the causal composite component models, the continued accumulation of harmful events (components) from the internal and external environment

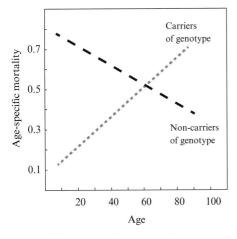

(A) hypothetical example on how a specific genotype may change from being beneficial at younger ages and unfavorable at older ages.

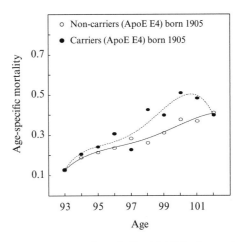

(B) Data from the Danish 1905 cohort and the Longitudinal Study of Centenarians showing age-specific mortality by ApoE E4 status. The curves illustrate that carriers of the ApoE E4 have increased age-specific mortality rates on the additive scale.

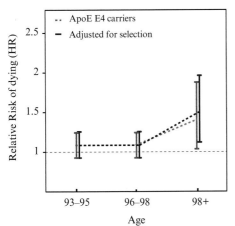

(C) The relative risk of dying by age for ApoE E4 carriers compared to non-carriers when adjusted for dependency status, and incorporation of selection effects. Vertical lines represent 95% confidence intervals. Thus, there is also an interaction with age on the multiplicative scale.

**Figure 7.4.** *Illustrating Gene × Age interaction*

could increase the effects of also carrying a harmful gene (Hjelmborg et al., 2006; Jacobsen et al., 2010; Rothman et al., 2014) (Figure 7.1).

In a previous study, we examined the age-dependency of the ApoE genotype at the highest ages, by following the Danish 1905 birth cohort and the Longitudinal Study of Danish centenarians (Danes born 1895 aged 100 and above) from age 92 to 103 (Jacobsen et al., 2010). We found that the effect of the ApoE gene increased with age (Jacobsen et al., 2010). This is the opposite of what the heterogeneity hypothesis predicts, where the effect of the ApoE genotype on mortality would decline with age (Vaupel et al., 1979). We argue that causal field models (multifactorial threshold models – Figure 7.1) could contribute to this explanation: in a multifactorial threshold model, many single factors with small effect can add up and contribute to a disorder/death, reaching a threshold at which the disorder/death occurs (Jacobsen et al., 2010); for example, a scenario in which an increasing frequency in causes is needed for an event (disease or death) to occur with age, thus leading to the greater influence of a frail genotype (Jacobsen et al., 2010). The multifactorial threshold model allows for competing risks, because an increasing number of sufficient causes can be expected with increasing age (Jacobsen et al., 2010).

## ApoE–Lifestyle Interactions on Longevity

Many studies have examined the interaction effects between ApoE and lifestyles on various morbidities associated with survival and longevity, but few studies have directly examined interaction effects of ApoE genotypes and lifestyles on survival or longevity. One study examined the interaction between the ApoE genotype and BMI and found that a protective effect of the ApoE E2 variant on overall mortality was only present among normal weight individuals (BMI between 18.5 and 25 kg/m$^2$) (Pardo Silva et al., 2008). This effect was, however, further modulated by age, because no protective effect of ApoE E2 was found for any weight categories for people above 80 years of age (Pardo Silva et al., 2008), thus illustrating how genes that have an effect on longevity could be age-specific, because gene and environment interactions at older ages could be different to those at younger ages (Christensen et al., 2006; Pardo Silva et al., 2008).

Direct studies on interactions between the ApoE gene and lifestyle factors on longevity are limited, but a larger number of examples for lifestyle factors are known to influence survival. For example, smoking has been found to interact with the ApoE gene for cognitive function and Alzheimer's disease (Dufouil et al., 2000; Sabia et al., 2010; Ghebranious et al., 2011; Weng et al., 2016). Smoking among ApoE E4 carriers was found to decrease cognitive deterioration, when compared to non-smoking ApoE E4 carriers – thus, surprisingly, showing that the ApoE E4 allele was, in fact, protective (the opposite of its normal effect) (Dufouil et al., 2000). Among ApoE E4 non-carriers, the contrary was found, with an increased risk for cognitive deterioration among smokers (Dufouil et al., 2000). ApoE-smoking interactions have also been found for cardiovascular diseases in some studies, but with the effect of smoking increased among ApoE E4 carriers (Humphries et al., 2001; Pezzini et al., 2004; Talmud et al., 2005). Other studies have found no interaction between smoking and ApoE (Grammer et al., 2013; Holmes et al., 2014).

Diet associated with survival could also interact with the ApoE genotypes. Intake of saturated fat (that increases mortality risk) has been found to modify the risk of cardiovascular heart disease (Corella et al., 2011). If the saturated fat intake was less than 10 percent of the total energy intake, then no significant association was found with cardiovascular heart disease risk. When fat intake was above 10 percent, then carriers of the ApoE E4 had, approximately, a three times increased risk of cardiovascular heart disease, when compared to ApoE E2 carriers (Corella et al., 2011). Another study found that cognitive decline was lower in obese individuals carrying the ApoE E4 allele, when compared to individuals with normal weight (Rajan et al., 2014).

Physical activity could increase longevity and can in late life alter the effect of the ApoE gene, such that the co-presence of ApoE E4 with low physical activity increases the risk for dementia and Alzheimer's disease, compared to the presence of ApoE E4 or low physical activity alone (Luck et al., 2014). This suggests that physical activity in late life may be beneficial for prevention of mental health-related diseases, especially for ApoE E4 carriers (Luck et al., 2014). Similar results have been found for cognitive performance, where physical activity among old-aged individuals that carried the ApoE E4 allele (but not non-carriers) reduced the risk of cognitive decline (Niti et al., 2008; Woodard et al., 2012). Contrary to these results, midlife physical activity was found to have no interacting effect with ApoE (Sabia et al., 2010). Similar results were observed among 65–79-year-old Finns, where no significant interaction was found between ApoE genotype and physical inactivity and risk of dementia (Kivipelto et al., 2008). The difference in results of these studies (Kivipelto et al., 2008; Niti et al., 2008; Sabia et al., 2010; Woodard et al., 2012; Luck et al., 2014) suggests that the age of the studied individuals could alter the effect of the interaction.

Alcohol intake is a well-known risk factor for mortality and has been found to interact with ApoE genotypes on both the additive and multiplicative scale, where ApoE E4 allele carriers drinking alcohol infrequently or frequently had a higher risk of dementia than non-drinkers in the Finnish population (Kivipelto et al., 2008). However, the study did not adjust for smoking habits in the analysis (Kivipelto et al., 2008) and the result could be a result of confounding, because alcohol drinkers tend to smoke more often.

A few studies have examined the combined interaction effects of various lifestyles in combination with ApoE (Kivipelto et al., 2008; Sabia et al., 2010; Strand et al., 2015). The studies used differently aged study populations, making effects over age possible. For example, in a Finnish study, physical activity, alcohol consumption, and fruit and vegetable consumption were found to have no interacting effect with ApoE on cognitive function in midlife – around age 60 (Sabia et al., 2010), whereas a significant interaction was found among 65–79 year olds, together with a combined effect on cognitive function of physical activity, intake of saturated and poly unsaturated fat, and alcohol intake (Kivipelto et al., 2008). Similar results were found in a Norwegian study of people aged 65 and above, where more unhealthy lifestyle risk factors in combination increased dementia-related mortality more among ApoE E4 allele carriers than among non-carriers (Strand et al., 2015). These three studies exemplify the complications of studies that examine interactions between genes and lifestyles on diseases related to longevity where internal and external environments associated with age change the effects of the gene–environment interaction.

## Perspectives

Alternative strategies are required to better understand the mechanisms behind differences in life span among individuals because few candidate genes have been identified in longevity studies. The increasing evidence that the environment interacts with genes to alter their causal effects makes an integration of the environmental factors in the exploration for genes associated with longevity a key component in order to understand the mechanisms of aging. Promising approaches include studies that explore mechanisms of already known candidate gene effects under different environments. GEWIS studies have the potential to identify new genes that under certain environments are associated with longevity and under other environments are not. Meta studies on both approaches might help overcome the need for very large sample sizes. A deeper understanding of the gene–lifestyle interaction on longevity is likely to be a stepping stone toward improved insight into the mechanism underlying successful aging generally.

## References

Adami, H. O., Hunter, D. & Trichopoulos, D. *Textbook of Cancer Epidemiology* (Oxford University Press, New York, 2009).

Ahlbom, A. & Alfredsson, L. Interaction: A word with two meanings creates confusion. *Eur. J. Epidemiol.* 20, 564 (2005).

Ahmad, S., Rukh, G., Varga, T. V., et al. (2013) Gene × physical activity interactions in obesity: Combined analysis of 111,421 individuals of European ancestry. *PLoS Genet.* 9, e1003607 (2013).

Anselmi, C. V., Malovini, A., Roncarati, R., et al. Association of the FOXO3A locus with extreme longevity in a southern Italian centenarian study. *Rejuvenation Res.* 12, 04 (2009).

Aslibekyan, S. Gene-environment interaction in *Cardiovascular Genetics and Genomics in Clinical Practice* (eds. Shah, S. & Arnett, D.) (Demos Medical Publishing, New York, 2014).

Atzmon, G., Rincon, M., Schechter, C. B., et al. Lipoprotein genotype and conserved pathway for exceptional longevity in humans. *PLoS Biol.* 4, 569 (2006).

Beekman, M., Blanché, H., Perola, M., et al. Genome-wide linkage analysis for human longevity: Genetics of Healthy Aging Study. *Aging Cell* 12, 193 (2013).

Benetos, A., Thomas, F., Bean, K. E., Pannier, B. & Guize, L. Role of modifiable risk factors in life expectancy in the elderly. *J. Hypertens.* 23, 18 (2005).

Brooks-Wilson, A. R. Genetics of healthy aging and longevity. *Hum. Genet.* 132, 1323–38 (2013).

Burns, D. M., Lee, L., Shen, L. Z., et al. in *Tobacco Control Monograph series 2* (National Institute Of Health, 1997). at https://pubs.cancer.gov/ncipl/detail.aspx?prodid=M040

Bush, W. S. & Moore, J. H. Chapter 11: Genome-wide association studies. *PLoS Comput. Biol.* 8, e1002822 (2012).

Christensen, K. & McGue, M. Genetics: Healthy ageing, the genome and the environment. *Nat. Rev. Endocrinol.* 12, 30 (2016).

Christensen, K., Johnson, T. E. & Vaupel, J. W. The quest for genetic determinants of human longevity: challenges and insights. *Nat. Rev. Genet.* 7, 48 (2006).

Corella, D. & Ordovás, J. M. Aging and cardiovascular diseases: The role of gene–diet interactions. *Ageing Res. Rev.* 18, 3 (2014).

Corella, D., Portolés, O., Arriola, L., et al. Saturated fat intake and alcohol consumption modulate the association between the APOE polymorphism and risk of future coronary heart disease: A nested case-control study in the Spanish EPIC cohort. *J. Nutr. Biochem.* 22, 494 (2011).

Costello, E. J., Eaves, L., Sullivan, P., et al. Genes, environments, and developmental research: Methods for a multi-site study of early substance abuse. *Twin Res. Hum. Genet.* 16, 55 (2013).

Cunningham, G. C. Phenylketonuria. Early detection, diagnosis and treatment. *Calif. Med.* 105, 1–7 (1966).

Däumer, C., Flachsbart, F., Caliebe, A., et al. Adjustment for smoking does not alter the FOXO3A association with longevity. *Age (Dordr).* 36, 91 (2014).

de Groot, L. C. P. M. G., Verheijden, M. W., de Henauw, S., et al. Lifestyle, nutritional status, health, and mortality in elderly people across Europe: A review of the longitudinal results of the SENECA study. *J. Gerontol. Ser. A Biol. Sci. Med. Sci.* 59, 12284 (2004).

Deelen, J., Beekman, M., Uh, H.-W., et al. Genome-wide association meta-analysis of human longevity identifies a novel locus conferring survival beyond 90 years of age. *Hum. Mol. Genet.* 23, 44432 (2014).

Deelen, J., Beekman, M., Uh, H.-W., et al. Genome-wide association study identifies a single major locus contributing to survival into old age; the APOE locus revisited. *Aging Cell* 10, 68 (2011).

Deelen, J., Beekman, M., Capri, M., Franceschi, C. & Slagboom, P. E. Identifying the genomic determinants of aging and longevity in human population studies: Progress and challenges. *BioEssays* 35, 396 (2013).

Dempfle, A., Scherag, A., Hein, R., et al. Gene–environment interactions for complex traits: Definitions, methodological requirements and challenges. *Eur. J. Hum. Genet.* 16, 11172 (2008).

Dufouil, C., Tzourio, C., Brayne, C., et al. Influence of apolipoprotein E genotype on the risk of cognitive deterioration in moderate drinkers and smokers. *Epidemiology* 11, 284 (2000).

Dunn, E. C., Brown, R. C., Dai, Y., et al. Genetic determinants of depression: Recent findings and future directions. *Harv. Rev. Psychiatry* 23, 1–18 (2015).

Dunn, E. C., Wiste, A., Radmanesh, F., et al. Genome-wide association study (GWAS) and genome-wide by environment interaction study (GWEIS) of depressive symptoms in African American and Hispanic/Latina women. *Depress. Anxiety* 33, 280 (2016).

Dupre, M. E., Liu, G. & Gu, D. Predictors of longevity: Evidence from the oldest old in China. *Am. J. Public Health* 98, 12 (2008).

Elston, R. C., Olson, J. M. & Palmer, L. *Biostatistical Genetics and Genetic Epidemiology* (Wiley, Chichester, United Kingdom, 2002).

Engberg, H., Oksuzyan, A., Jeune, B., Vaupel, J. W. & Christensen, K. Centenarians – A useful model for healthy aging? A 29-year follow-up of hospitalizations among 40,000 Danes born in 1905. *Aging Cell* 8, 2 (2009).

Ewbank, D. C. Differences in the association between apolipoprotein E genotype and mortality across populations. *J. Gerontol. A. Biol. Sci. Med. Sci.* 62, 807 (2007).

The APOE gene and differences in life expectancy in Europe. *J. Gerontol. Ser. A Biol. Sci. Med. Sci.* 59, B16–B20 (2004).

Finch, C. E. & Tanzi, R. E. Genetics of aging. *Science.* 278, 411 (1997).

Flachsbart, F., Caliebe, A., Kleindorp, R., et al. Association of FOXO3A variation with human longevity confirmed in German centenarians. *Proc. Natl. Acad. Sci. U. S. A.* 106, 27 (2009).

Fried, L. P., Kronmal, R. A., Newman, A. B., et al. Risk factors for 5-year mortality in older adults: The Cardiovascular Health Study. *JAMA* 279, 52 (1998).

Frikke-Schmidt, R., Nordestgaard, B. G., Agerholm-Larsen, B., Schnohr, P. & Tybjaerg-Hansen, A. Context-dependent and invariant associations between lipids, lipoproteins, and apolipoproteins and apolipoprotein E genotype. *J. Lipid Res.* 41, 182 (2000).

Frisoni, G. B., Louhija, J., Geroldi, C. & Trabucchi, M. Longevity and the epsilon2 allele of apolipoprotein E: The Finnish Centenarians Study. *J. Gerontol. A. Biol. Sci. Med. Sci.* 56, M75–8 (2001).

Ganna, A., Rivadeneira, F., Hofman, A., et al. Genetic determinants of mortality. Can findings from genome-wide association studies explain variation in human mortality? *Hum. Genet.* 132, 51 (2013).

Garatachea, N., Emanuele, E., Calero, M., et al. ApoE gene and exceptional longevity: Insights from three independent cohorts. *Exp. Gerontol.* 53, 3(2014).

Garatachea, N., Marín, P. J., Santos-Lozano, A., et al. The ApoE gene is related with exceptional longevity: A systematic review and meta-analysis. *Rejuvenation Res.* 18, 3–13 (2015).

Gauderman, W. J. Sample size requirements for matched case-control studies of gene-environment interaction. *Stat. Med.* 21, 35 (2002).

Gellert, C. Schöttker, B., Brenner, H., et al. Smoking and all-cause mortality in older people: systematic review and meta-analysis. *Arch. Intern. Med.* 172, 254 (2012).

Gentschew, L., Flachsbart, F., Kleindorp, R., et al. Polymorphisms in the superoxidase dismutase genes reveal no association with human longevity in Germans: A case-control association study. *Biogerontology* 14, 727 (2013).

Ghebranious, N., Mukesh, B., Giampietro, P. F., et al. A pilot study of gene/gene and gene/environment interactions in Alzheimer disease. *Clin. Med. Res.* 9, 5 (2011).

Grammer, T. B., Hoffmann, M. M., Scharnagl, H., et al. Smoking, apolipoprotein e genotypes, and mortality (the Ludwigshafen RIsk and Cardiovascular Health study). *Eur. Heart J.* 34, 12305 (2013).

Hagberg, B. & Samuelsson, G. Survival after 100 years of age: A multivariate model of exceptional survival in Swedish centenarians. *J. Gerontol. A. Biol. Sci. Med. Sci.* 63, 126 (2008).

Halme, J. T., Seppä, K., Alho, H., et al. Alcohol consumption and all-cause mortality among elderly in Finland. *Drug Alcohol Depend.* 106, 2 (2010).

Hammond, E. C., Selikoff, I. J. & Seidman, H. Asbestos exposure, cigarette smoking and death rates. *Ann. N. Y. Acad. Sci.* 330, 40 (1979).

Hamza, T. H., Chen, H., Hill-Burns, E. M., et al. Genome-wide gene-environment study identifies glutamate receptor gene GRIN2A as a Parkinson's disease modifier gene via interaction with coffee. *PLoS Genet.* 7, e1002237 (2011).

Haveman-Nies, A., Groot, L. (C. ) P. G. M. de, Burema, J., et al. Dietary quality and lifestyle factors in relation to 10-year mortality in older Europeans: The SENECA study. *Am. J. Epidemiol.* 156, 968 (2002).

Hill, A. B. The environment and disease: Association or causation? *Proc. R. Soc. Med.* 58, 200 (1965).

Hjelmborg, J. B., Iachine, I., Skytthe, A., et al. Genetic influence on human lifespan and longevity. *Hum. Genet.* 119, 321 (2006).

Holmes, M. V., Frikke-Schmidt, R., Melis, D., et al. A systematic review and meta-analysis of 130,000 individuals shows smoking does not modify the association of APOE genotype on risk of coronary heart disease. *Atherosclerosis* 237, 5–12 (2014).

Huang, Y. & Mahley, R. W. Apolipoprotein E: Structure and function in lipid metabolism, neurobiology, and Alzheimer's diseases. *Neurobiol. Dis.* 72, 3–12 (2014).

Humphries, S. E., Talmud, P. J., Hawe, E., et al. Apolipoprotein E4 and coronary heart disease in middle-aged men who smoke: A prospective study. *Lancet* 358, 119 (2001).

Hunter, D. J. Gene-environment interactions in human diseases. *Nat. Rev. Genet.* 6, 298 (2005).

Iannitti, T. & Palmieri, B. Inflammation and genetics: An insight in the centenarian model. *Hum. Biol.* 83, 59 (2011).

Jacobsen, R., Martinussen, T., Christiansen, L., et al. Increased effect of the ApoE gene on survival at advanced age in healthy and long-lived Danes: Two nationwide cohort studies. *Aging Cell* 9, 10009 (2010).

Kirkwood, T. B. L., Partridge, L., Murphy, C. T., et al. Systems biology of ageing and longevity. *Philos. Trans. R. Soc. Lond. B. Biol. Sci.* 366, 64 (2011).

Kivipelto, M., Rovio, S., Ngandu, T., et al. Apolipoprotein E epsilon4 magnifies lifestyle risks for dementia: A population-based study. *J. Cell. Mol. Med.* 12, 271 (2008).

Klein, R. J., Zeiss, C., Chew, E. Y., et al. Complement factor H polymorphism in age-related macular degeneration. *Science* 308, 3 (2005).

Knoops, K. T. B, Zeiss, C., Chew, E. Y., et al. Mediterranean diet, lifestyle factors, and 10-year mortality in elderly European men and women: The HALE project. *JAMA* 292, 14 (2004).

Kulminski, A. M. Unraveling genetic origin of aging-related traits: Evolving concepts. *Rejuvenation Res.* 16, 32 (2013).

Kulminski, A. M., Culminskaya, I., Arbeev, K. G., et al. The role of lipid-related genes, aging-related processes, and environment in healthspan. *Aging Cell* 12, 246 (2013).

Kulminski, A. M., Arbeev, K. G., Culminskaya, I., et al. Age, gender, and cancer but not neurodegenerative and cardiovascular diseases strongly modulate systemic effect of the apolipoprotein E4 allele on lifespan. *PLoS Genet.* 10, e1004141 (2014).

Lawlor, D. A. & Mishra, G. D. *Family Matters: Designing, Analysing and Understanding Family based Studies in Life Course Epidemiology*. Oxford University Press, New York (2009). doi:10.1093/acprof:oso/9780199231034.001.0001

Lee, S. J., Go, A. S., Lindquist, K., Bertenthal, D. & Covinsky, K. E. Chronic conditions and mortality among the oldest old. *Am. J. Public Health* 98, 124 (2008).

Levine, M. & Crimmins, E. Not all smokers die young: A model for hidden heterogeneity within the human population. *PLoS One* 9, e87403 (2014).

Lindahl-Jacobsen, R., Tan, Q., Mengel-From, J., et al. Effects of the APOE {varepsilon}2 allele on mortality and cognitive function in the oldest old. *J. Gerontol. A Biol. Sci. Med. Sci.* (2012). doi:10.1093/gerona/gls192

Luck, T., Riedel-Heller, S. G., Luppa, M., et al. Apolipoprotein E epsilon 4 genotype and a physically active lifestyle in late life: Analysis of gene-environment interaction for the risk of dementia and Alzheimer's disease dementia. *Psychol. Med.* 44, 139 (2014).

Luo, Y., Zhang, Z. & Gu, D. Education and mortality among older adults in China. *Soc. Sci. Med.* 127, 12 (2015).

Mahley, R. W., Huang, Y. & Rall Jr., S. C. Pathogenesis of type III hyperlipoproteinemia (dysbetalipoproteinemia). Questions, quandaries, and paradoxes. *J. Lipid Res.* 40, 19949 (1999).

Manning, A. K., Hivert, M.-F., Scott, R. A., et al. A genome-wide approach accounting for body mass index identifies genetic variants influencing fasting glycemic traits and insulin resistance. *Nat. Genet.* 44, 69 (2012).

Martelin, T., Koskinen, S. & Valkonen, T. Sociodemographic mortality differences among the oldest old in Finland. *J. Gerontol. B. Psychol. Sci. Soc. Sci.* 53, S83–90 (1998).

McKay, G. J., Silvestri, G., Chakravarthy, U., et al. Variations in apolipoprotein E frequency with age in a pooled analysis of a large group of older people. *Am. J. Epidemiol.* 173, 134 (2011).

Morris, B. J., Donlon, T. A., He, Q., et al. Association analyses of insulin signaling pathway gene polymorphisms with healthy aging and longevity in Americans of Japanese ancestry. *J. Gerontol. - Ser. A Biol. Sci. Med. Sci.* 69 A, 273 (2014).

Murabito, J. M., Yuan, R. & Lunetta, K. L. The search for longevity and healthy aging genes: Insights from epidemiological studies and samples of long-lived individuals. *J. Gerontol. - Ser. A Biol. Sci. Med. Sci.* 67 A, 479 (2012).

Nebel, A., Kleindorp, R., Caliebe, A., et al. A genome-wide association study confirms APOE as the major gene influencing survival in long-lived individuals. *Mech. Ageing Dev.* 132, 330 (2011).

Nettleton, J. A., Hivert, M.-F., Lemaitre, R. N., et al. Meta-analysis investigating associations between healthy diet and fasting glucose and insulin levels and modification by loci associated with glucose homeostasis in data from 15 cohorts. *Am. J. Epidemiol.* 177, 15 (2013).

Nettleton, J. A., Follis, J. L., Ngwa, J. S., et al. Gene × dietary pattern interactions in obesity: Analysis of up to 68 317 adults of European ancestry. *Hum. Mol. Genet.* 24, 478 (2015).

Newman, A. B. & Murabito, J. M. The epidemiology of longevity and exceptional survival. *Epidemiol. Rev.* 35, 197 (2013).

Newman, A. B., Walter, S., Lunetta, K. L., et al. A meta-analysis of four genome-wide association studies of survival to age 90 years or older: The Cohorts for Heart and Aging Research in Genomic Epidemiology Consortium. *J. Gerontol. A. Biol. Sci. Med. Sci.* 65, 47 (2010).

Newson, R. S., Witteman, J. C. M., Franco, O. H., et al. Predicting survival and morbidity-free survival to very old age. *Age (Dordr).* 32, 54 (2010).

Niccoli, T. & Partridge, L. Ageing as a risk factor for disease. *Current Biol.* 22 (2012).

Niti, M., Yap, K. B., Kua, E. H., Tan, C. H. & Ng, T. P. Physical, social and productive leisure activities, cognitive decline and interaction with APOE-epsilon 4 genotype in Chinese older adults. *Int. Psychogeriatr.* 20, 21 (2008).

Novelli, V., Viviani Anselmi, C., Roncarati, R., et al. Lack of replication of genetic associations with human longevity. *Biogerontology* 9, 2 (2008).

Nybo, H., Petersen, H. C., Gaist, D., et al. Predictors of mortality in 2,249 nonagenarians – The Danish 1905-Cohort Survey. *J. Am. Geriatr. Soc.* 51, 133 (2003).

Nygaard, M., Lindahl-Jacobsen, R., Soerensen, M., et al. Birth cohort differences in the prevalence of longevity-associated variants in APOE and FOXO3A in Danish long-lived individuals. *Exp. Gerontol.* 57 (2014).

Ortiz, G. G., Pacheco-Moisés, F. P., González-Renovato, E. D., et al. Genetic, biochemical and histopathological aspects of familiar Alzheimer's disease in *Alzheimer's Disease – Challenges for the Future* (ed. Inga Zerr) (InTech, London, UK, 2015). doi:10.5772/59809

Pardo Silva, M. C., Janssens, A. C. J. W., Hofman, A., Witteman, J. C. M. & van Duijn, C. M. Apolipoprotein E gene is related to mortality only in normal weight individuals: The Rotterdam Study. *Eur. J. Epidemiol.* 23, 12 (2008).

Pezzini, A., Grassi, M., Del Zotto, E., et al. Synergistic effect of apolipoprotein E polymorphisms and cigarette smoking on risk of ischemic stroke in young adults. *Stroke.* 35, 442 (2004).

Raichlen, D. A. & Alexander, G. E. Exercise, APOE genotype, and the evolution of the human lifespan. *Trends Neurosci.* 37, 255 (2014).

Rajan, K. B., Skarupski, K. A., Rasmussen, H. E. & Evans, D. A. Gene-environment interaction of body mass index and apolipoprotein E ε4 allele on cognitive decline. *Alzheimer Dis. Assoc. Disord.* 28, 10 (2014).

Rizzuto, D. & Fratiglioni, L. Lifestyle factors related to mortality and survival: A mini-review. *Gerontology* 60, 335 (2014).

Rizzuto, D., Orsini, N., Qiu, C., Wang, H.-X. & Fratiglioni, L. Lifestyle, social factors, and survival after age 75: Population based study. *BMJ* 345, e5568 (2012).

Rodriguez-Laso, A., Zunzunegui, M. V. & Otero, A. The effect of social relationships on survival in elderly residents of a Southern European community: A cohort study. *BMC Geriatr.* 7, 19 (2007).

Rosvall, L., Rizzuto, D., Wang, H.-X., et al. APOE-related mortality: Effect of dementia, cardiovascular disease and gender. *Neurobiol. Aging* 30, 15551 (2009).

Rothman, K. J. Causes. *Am. J. Epidemiol.* 104, 52 (1976).

*Epidemiology: An Introduction* (Oxford University Press, New York, 2012).

Rothman, K. J., Greenland, S. & Associate, T. L. L. *Modern Epidemiology*, 3rd Edition. Taylor & Francis Ltd, London, UK (2014).

Ruigómez, A., Alonso, J. & Antó, J. M. Relationship of health behaviours to five-year mortality in an elderly Cohort. *Age Ageing* 24, 119 (1995).

Sabia, S., Kivimaki, M., Kumari, M., Shipley, M. J. & Singh-Manoux, A. Effect of Apolipoprotein E epsilon4 on the association between health behaviors and cognitive function in late midlife. *Mol. Neurodegener.* 5, 23 (2010).

Salvioli, S., Olivieri, F., Marchegiani, F., et al. Genes, ageing and longevity in humans: Problems, advantages and perspectives. *Free Radic. Res.* 40, 13323 (2006).

Schächter, F., Faure-Delanef, L., Guénot, F., et al. Genetic associations with human longevity at the APOE and ACE loci. *Nat. Genet.* 6, 2 (1994).

Schupf, N., Barral, S., Perls, T., et al. Apolipoprotein E and familial longevity. *Neurobiol. Aging* 34, 121 (2013).

Sebastiani, P., Solovieff, N., Dewan, A. T., et al. Genetic signatures of exceptional longevity in humans. *PLoS One* 7, e29848 (2012).

Siegert, S., Hampe, J., Schafmayer, C., et al. Genome-wide investigation of gene-environment interactions in colorectal cancer. *Hum. Genet.* 132, 231 (2013).

Smith, P. G. & Day, N. E. The design of case-control studies: The influence of confounding and interaction effects. *Int. J. Epidemiol.* 13, 365 (1984).

Soerensen, M., Dato, S., Tan, Q., et al. Evidence from case-control and longitudinal studies supports associations of genetic variation in APOE, CETP, and IL6 with human longevity. *Age (Dordr).* 35, 400 (2013).

Spencer, C. A., Jamrozik, K., Norman, P. E. & Lawrence-Brown, M. A simple lifestyle score predicts survival in healthy elderly men. *Prev. Med. (Baltim).* 40, 7 (2005).

Stevens, J., Pamuk, E. R., Williamson, D. F., Thun, M. J., & Wood, J. L. The effect of age on the association between body-mass index and mortality. *N. Engl. J. Med.* 338, 1–7 (1998).

Strand, B. H., Rosness, T. A., Engedal, K., et al. Interaction of apolipoprotein E genotypes, lifestyle factors and future risk of dementia-related mortality: The Cohort of Norway (CONOR). *Dement. Geriatr. Cogn. Disord.* 40, 17 (2015).

Talmud, P. J., P. J., Stephens, J. W., Hawe, E., et al. The significant increase in cardiovascular disease risk in APOE E4 carriers is evident only in men who smoke: Potential relationship between reduced antioxidant status and ApoE4. *Ann. Hum. Genet.* 69, 622 (2005).

Tan, Q., Benedictis, G. De, Ukraintseva, S. V., et al. A centenarian-only approach for assessing gene-gene interaction in human longevity. *Eur. J. Hum. Genet.* 10, 119 (2002).

Thinggaard, M., Jacobsen, R., Jeune, B., Martinussen, T. & Christensen, K. Is the relationship between BMI and mortality increasingly U-shaped with advancing age? A 10-year follow-up of persons aged 70–95 years. *J. Gerontol. A. Biol. Sci. Med. Sci.* 65, 51 (2010).

Thinggaard, M., McGue, M., Jeune, B., et al. Survival prognosis in very old adults. *J. Am. Geriatr. Soc.* 64, 8 (2016).

Thomas, D. Gene–environment-wide association studies: emerging approaches. *Nat. Rev. Genet.* 11, 272 (2010).

Vaupel, J. W. Inherited frailty and longevity. *Demography* 25, 287 (1988).

Vaupel, J. W., Manton, K. G. & Stallard, E. The impact of heterogeneity in individual frailty on the dynamics of mortality. *Demography* 16, 44 (1979).

Weng, P.-H., Chen, J.-H., Chen, T.-F., et al. CHRNA7 polymorphisms and dementia risk: Interactions with apolipoprotein ε4 and cigarette smoking. *Sci. Rep.* 6, 27231 (2016).

Willcox, B. J., Donlon, T. A., He, Q., et al. FOXO3A genotype is strongly associated with human longevity. *Proc. Natl. Acad. Sci. U. S. A.* 105, 1392 (2008).

Woodard, J. L., Sugarman, M. A., Nielson, K. A., et al. Lifestyle and genetic contributions to cognitive decline and hippocampal structure and function in healthy aging. *Curr. Alzheimer Res.* 9, 46 (2012).

Wu, C., Kraft, P., Zhai, K., et al. Genome-wide association analyses of esophageal squamous cell carcinoma in Chinese identify multiple susceptibility loci and gene-environment interactions. *Nat. Genet.* 44, 10097 (2012).

Yates, L. B., Djoussé, L., Kurth, T., Buring, J. E. & Gaziano, J. M. Exceptional longevity in men: modifiable factors associated with survival and function to age 90 years. *Arch. Intern. Med.* 168, 20 (2008).

Zeng, Y., Nie, C., Min, J., et al. Novel loci and pathways significantly associated with longevity. *Sci. Rep.* 6, 21243 (2016).

Zheng, J.-S., Arnett, D. K., Lee, Y.-C., et al. Genome-wide contribution of genotype by environment interaction to variation of diabetes-related traits. *PLoS One* 8, e77442 (2013).

# 8 Plasticity of the Brain and Cognition in Older Adults

Kiyoka Kinugawa

## What Is Brain Plasticity

Brain plasticity refers to the brain's ability to modify its existing cortical structures and functions in response to intrinsic and extrinsic factors, experience, learning, training, stimulation, or injury (Wall et al., 2002; Cai et al., 2014; Li et al., 2017). It is a dynamic process, continuously modified by experience. Any new experience can affect the existing neural networks, circuits, and structures built by neurons and synapses. Brain plasticity is a biological mechanism of the learning brain (Taubert et al., 2010), promoted by structural and functional changes of the brain, supported by neurogenesis (development of new neurons), gliogenesis (generation of new glial cells), synaptic plasticity (changes in the inter-neuronal connections, by strengthening of existing connections or growth of new synapses), and by angiogenesis (creation of new blood vessels in the brain) (Buonomano and Merzenich, 1998; Singh and Abraham, 2017).

Learning dependent brain plasticity is a lifelong developmental process, but there are age-related critical periods for significant cortical reorganization (Buonomano and Merzenich, 1998). What underlies this ability to store and retrieve information is synaptic plasticity: the strengthening or weakening of existing connections between neurons and the formation or removal of synapses. The capacity for synaptic plasticity and, by consequence, for learning and memory is not constant throughout life; it often peaks relatively soon after birth and then typically declines with age, at variable rates. In many animals, plasticity for specific sensory experiences or sensorimotor interactions is greatly enhanced in distinct phases. These critical periods are intensely studied in the mammalian visual system (Trachtenberg, 2015). Neuronal plasticity is particularly intense in the developing brain, but it is not exclusively restricted to that frametime. It is also widespread in the adult brain and is a key feature of many brain regions. The experiments in somatosensory cortex done by Merzenich and colleagues were the first to clearly indicate that cortical representation, and therefore cortical circuitry changes, can occur in the adult brain (Merzenich et al., 1984; Clark et al., 1988; Recanzone et al., 1993).

## Synaptic Strengthening and Weakening

Cellular and molecular processes underlying the plastic remodeling of the "wiring" in brain circuits have been extensively studied. Donald Hebb postulated the central governing rule: "What fires together, wires together." At the synaptic level, Hebbian plasticity refers to increases in synaptic strength between neurons that fire together (Morris, 1949). A change in the synaptic efficacy between two neurons is a substrate for learning and memory. At a higher level of neural reorganization, Hebbian-based learning rules relate to the detection of temporally correlated inputs. Through a multiplicity of synaptic physical changes amplifying connection strength, and by synaptogenesis, this coincident-input-dependent costrengthening of synaptic connections is achieved in a learning context. The magnitude of such changes can be important: as the brain acquires any significant skill or ability, a large amount of synapses in any directly engaged cortical zone (many millions to billions of synapses) is altered in connection strength (Kleim et al., 2002). As we master any skill or ability through experience or progressive learning, these changes in brain circuitry result in specialization of the brain as a master receiver and master controller of all of the inputs and actions.

Nonetheless, these same processes are also driven backward, for other non-behaviorally contributing synapses, in a synaptic weakening and synapse elimination direction for "normalization." By depriving neurons of a major source of their inputs in other experimental models, this "normalization" of collective synaptic input power has been extensively studied. Synaptic strengths are rapidly adjusted to sustain neurons within a narrow electrical potential window that assures their ongoing functional viability (Horng and Sur, 2006; Cooper and Bear, 2012; Feldman, 2012).

Studies of plasticity mechanisms have shown that every brief change cycle involves a synapse-strengthening phase (e.g., strengthening all inputs, whose coordinated actions moment by moment in time are correlated with a positive behavioral outcome), followed by a synapse-weakening phase (e.g., weakening all inputs occurring within a brief, following epoch of time) (Dan and Poo, 2006; Cooper and Bear, 2012). This synapse weakening is like an electrically homeostatic process that contributes to the ongoing weakening of behaviorally nonmeaningful intrinsic activities or inputs, to a normalization of internal or background external/environmental noise.

From another perspective, plasticity processes can be viewed as continuously competitive. Through these two-way plasticity processes, neurons in coupled "mini-columns" are continuously competing with their neighbors, for the domination of neurons on their mutual boundaries. By giving one coupled group the competitive advantage over their neighbors, it is easy to expand their team a thousandfold, or, if they are a competitive loser, then to reduce its "membership" many times other. By these two-way processes, one can easily both refine (for some inputs) and degrade (other inputs) even the most fundamental aspects of representation of visual/auditory/somatosensory inputs in the adult brain (Merzenich et al., 2014).

## Remodeling the Physical Brain by Plasticity

Changing synaptic strengths and synaptogenesis are possible by complex physical change processes resulting from changes in genetic expression of several hundred well-described molecular processes. The physical processes of neurons involve the receiving dendrites and their synaptic spines, the transmitting axons and the elaboration of their terminal arbors, the distribution of collateral axons that richly interconnect neurons within cortical networks, and the processes and cell-to-cell contacts of closely coupled nonneuronal glial cells. These neuronal processes can be plastically altered on a large scale, resulting in changes in cortical thickness, neuropil volumes, cortical area, and subcortical nucleus volumes. Size of specific cell types can shrink or greatly increase and cells can be greatly metabolically reduced or invigorated. The insulating myelin can be thickened – or thinned – under plastic control (de Villers-Sidani et al., 2010; Zhou et al., 2012). Trophic factors, transporters, excitatory, inhibitory, and neuromodulatory neurotransmitters and receptors, controlling operational characteristics of brain systems, or contributing to the regulation of plasticity, are all altered physically, when the brain advances, or retreats, by the action of adult neuroplasticity processes.

## Neurogenesis

In the adult mammalian brain, the vast majority of neuronal precursor cells are terminally differentiated; however, the subgranular zone (located in the dentate gyrus of the hippocampus) and the subventricular zone are brain regions where neurogenesis occurs: new neurons are continually produced (Aimone et al., 2014). In humans, studying neurogenesis is challenging, but there is evidence that hippocampal neurogenesis does occur in humans throughout adulthood and that the number of new cells declines with age (Göritz and Frisén, 2012).

Why is neurogenesis relevant to information processing? New brain cells in the dentate gyrus of the hippocampus are essential for discriminating differences in experiences and sensory inputs (Jessberger and Gage, 2014). Newness is based on this awareness of differences in small details. In their first few days of life, new brain cells, which grow dendrites that reach into the dentate gyrus and axons, are evident. It is during their sixth to eighth week that new neurons are more excitable than mature brain cells (Ge et al., 2007), allowing the plastic response of stimulated adult-born new brain cells, while preserving existing neuronal function. This important period is when the proportion of new brain cells that survive and get integrated (Tashiro et al., 2006) can be influenced by intrinsic and extrinsic factors (Dranovsky et al., 2011). It is also when a plastic response such as survival, integration, memory, or long-term potentiation (cellular based memory) can be provoked by less strong exciting currents. It is during this young and excitable period that new neurons require experiences such as physical activity and learning that includes challenge and newness to become integrated and stable in the dentate gyrus. These new brain cells are also thought to hold associations between time-related experiences that may not be related in content like those that occur during memory flashbacks. Although the many steps between birth and the connectivity including synaptic integration are still awaiting definition, there is largely no difference between mature brain cells and newborn ones by the time new neurons are about eight weeks old (Deshpande et al., 2013). According to Jessberger and Gage, "Current hypotheses suggest that it will depend on both intrinsic and signaling pathways and extrinsic regulators and local network activity" (Jessberger and Gage, 2014).

## Example of Factor Modulating Plasticity: Sleep

Sleep and sleep loss bidirectionally alter structural plasticity, by affecting spine numbers and morphology, which ultimately can affect the functional output of the brain in the term of alertness, information processing, and cognition (Kreutzmann et al., 2015). Experimental data from studies in rodents suggest that sleep deprivation may impact structural plasticity in different ways. At the molecular level, sleep and sleep deprivation bidirectionally alter molecular signaling pathways that regulate synaptic strength and control plasticity-related gene transcription and protein translation. At the cellular level, sleep deprivation alters cellular excitability necessary for inducing synaptic potentiation and accelerates the decay of long-lasting forms of synaptic plasticity (Abel et al., 2013). The synaptic homeostasis hypothesis, one of the current views, suggests that wakefulness promotes synaptic potentiation whereas sleep facilitates synaptic downscaling. On the other hand, several studies have now shown that sleep deprivation can reduce spine density and attenuate synaptic efficacy in the hippocampus (Abel et al., 2013; Kreutzmann et al., 2015; Raven et al., 2018). Moreover, sleep disruption can markedly suppress neurogenesis in the hippocampus, one of the processes underlying brain plasticity, as evoked earlier (Kent and Mistlberger, 2017). Studies on the impact of brief or longer periods of sleep loss on brain plasticity have emphasized that the hippocampus is particularly susceptible to sleep deprivation. Therefore, it is of no surprise that altered hippocampal function is also observed with sleep disorders such as sleep apnea and insomnia (Kreutzmann et al., 2015). These data are the basis for the view that sleep promotes hippocampal structural plasticity critical for memory formation (Raven et al., 2018).

## Aging Effect on Brain Plasticity

### The Brain Is Continuously Plastic

Although these modifications occur in the aging brain, plasticity is not limited to an early childhood epoch – a "critical" or "sensitive" period. Brain remodeling can be induced in a large scale at any age of life, and experience-dependent plasticity of brain and behavior subsists into late adulthood (Swain and Thompson, 1993; Merzenich and DeCharms, 1996; Merzenich, 2001; Weinberger, 2004; Gilbert et al., 2009; Lövdén et al., 2013; Merzenich et al., 2014). Adults respond to a variety of challenges with structural changes in task-relevant brain areas. According to one model (Lövdén et al., 2010a), plastic changes occur by a mismatch between environmental demand and the potential for a plastic response that possesses the organism. There is a distinction between plasticity and flexibility in this model. Whereas flexibility refers to the capacity for variations in behavioral repertoire that do not require reorganization of brain structures and connections, plasticity refers to changes in behavior that do. Mismatches between supply and demand need to be prolonged to overcome the inertia of plasticity and to push the system away from its current dynamic equilibrium (Lindenberger, 2014). With aging, an increasingly large behavioral repertoire is stocked and plastic reorganization of the brain is metabolically costly (Kuzawa et al., 2014; Morrison and Baxter, 2014). The brains of healthy older adults are less likely, and may have less need, to react to environmental challenges with a plastic response than the brains of children. Older adults have a richer model of the world that enables deployment of established behavioral repertoires. Downregulating plasticity during adulthood may favor the emergence of stable social structures, which in turn may facilitate the deployment of plastic potential in the next generation.

The main difference with aging is the way in which the brain regulates plasticity. In the very young brain, almost all inputs continuously engage competitive plasticity processes. In older brains, plasticity is regulated as a function of behavioral context and outcomes.

## Context- and Outcomes-Dependent Release of Neuromodulators in Older Brains

In the perinatal and early-childhood "critical" period, plasticity is always switched on. In the older child and adult brain, changes in the control of the release of neuromodulatory neurotransmitters and in the properties of the receptors in the brain enable the older brain's moment-by-moment control of changes. It is allowed only when the specific contextual conditions triggering plasticity are met, with changes arising "saved" (driving enduring changes in connection strengths) as a function of behavioral outcome (Merzenich et al., 2014). The study by Bergan and colleagues also supports the general notion that, in the adult brain, plasticity depends crucially on attention (and thus shares similarities with learning), whereas purely passive sensory experience is often sufficient to drive plasticity in the critical period (Bergan et al., 2005).

We now have a first-level understanding of the rules that control the release and the actions of the neuromodulators in learning, and of the modulator-specific ways that they nuance brain changes in experience and learning.

Under conditions of focused attention, any stimulus excites acetylcholine (ACh), releasing neurons in the basal nucleus of Meynert (Richardson and DeLong, 1990; Sarter et al., 2001, 2006). In the cortex, Ach inputs positively enable plasticity by selectively amplifying only anticipated inputs ("selectively attended") and by selectively weakening nonanticipated inputs (Sarter et al., 2006; Froemke et al., 2007). Brain plasticity occurs by advantaging inputs strengths for those specific activities that the brain can gain in ability by changing to, and can disadvantage behaviorally the noncontributing inputs that they change from.

For another example of neurotransmitter, noradrenaline (NA) releasing neurons in the locus coeruleus (LC) and in the nucleus accumbens and amygdala, broadly amplify neuronal activity, increasing the general level of excitability (arousal or baseline level of attention) in subcortical and cortical structures in any closely attentive context in stimulus- or goal-seeking, or other motivated states (Aston-Jones and Cohen, 2005; Sara, 2009; Sara and Bouret, 2012). NA is also released to selectively amplify the activities evoked by unexpected/novel input (Aston-Jones et al., 1999), conferring special powers for the representation of new inputs or activities for driving enduring representational change.

Dopamine (DA) releasing neurons in the ventral tegmental area and substantia nigra are highly specific plastic enablers (Bao et al., 2001; Winder et al., 2002; Bao et al., 2003; Lisman et al., 2011). DA is released when the brain receives or first predicts the occurrence of a reward input, or when the brain achieves or first predicts behavioral success (for which it rewards itself) in a learning cycle (Schultz, 2007). With their release, inputs that predict reward are selectively strengthened; competitive inputs uncorrelated with reward prediction arriving in a short postreward epoch are selectively weakened (Ahissar et al., 1992; Bao et al., 2003).

It should be noted that this crucial neuromodulatory system, controlling learning and memory abilities throughout life, is also plastic (Nakamura and Sakaguchi, 1990; Sara and Segal, 1991; Steiner et al., 2006; Smith et al., 2011). Intensive training can significantly improve the strengths, selectivity, and reliability of its actions, in most individuals with neurological or psychiatric impairment or disability.

## Most Plasticity-Induced Changes Are Reversible

Plasticity engages fundamentally reversible neurological change processes. Merzenich et al. have conducted a number of studies that have demonstrated that neuroplasticity follows Hebbian principles: the representations if inputs and actions are competitively sorted on the basis of the temporal distributions of inputs (Merzenich et al., 1993; Merzenich and DeCharms, 1996). To degrade the brain's processing abilities is as easy as it is to strengthen or refine them.

Studies in animals showed that plasticity processes are broadly reversible. In the brains of aged versus young adult animals, it was shown that every functional, anatomical, and chemistry measure differed markedly (de Villers-Sidani et al., 2010; de Villers-Sidani and Merzenich, 2011). The animals had intensive behaviorally training in operant tasks to determine which of these operational characteristics of the brain could be rejuvenated. With training limited in these aged rats to approximately 1 hour/day for about 1 month, all of the degraded operational and physical-chemical characteristics of the aged brain could be substantially, if not completely, restored to a "youthful" state in the aged animals (de Villers-Sidani et al., 2010; de Villers-Sidani and Merzenich, 2011). Given its reversible nature, inversely, plasticity processes can be engaged in a young animal in ways that drive their brains in an increasingly uncorrelated pattern activity, as seen in aged animals. By an environmental exposure strategy, all of the functional and physical characteristics of the auditory brain of young adults animals altered as if the animal had advanced to an "old age" status (Zhou et al., 2012; Kamal et al., 2013).

Because these reversible change processes can drive neural changes in either an advancing or degrading direction, driving the processing and physical characteristics of the brain rapidly "forward" to simulate aging is equivalent to driving the animal backward in age: the physical and functional properties of the brain near the end of life closely correspond to those same characteristics in the brain recorded near the beginning of life (Zhou et al., 2012).

## Age-Related Impairment and Resilience against Neurodegenerative Disease Onset

The average aging brain expresses progressively cognitive deficits in all of its major processing systems in perception, speed of action and fluency, phasic, sustained and divided attention, different aspects of memory, social cognition, and executive, social, and action control (Salthouse, 2000; Salthouse, 2012). There is about an average of one-third of a standard deviation per decade in ability past the age of 30 for men, and beyond the age of about 45 for women. In neurological terms, substantial degradation is recorded in all great representational systems, in representational accuracy, processing speed, local response and system coordination, excitatory and especially inhibitory powers, tracking of rapidly successive inputs, representation of temporal details of inputs (durations, intervals, rhythmic sequences), accurate representations of sequenced inputs, scenes, and scenarios, sustained responses supporting working memory/selective attention/associative memory and prediction, and the more complex "mental" neurological activities supporting executive, social, and motor control, ideation, and thought (Nahum et al., 2013; Merzenich et al., 2014). Decline in all of these processes in aging is contributed by parallel atrophy of the neuromodulatory centers regulating the release of DA, norepinephrine, acetylcholine, serotonin, etc. (Barili et al., 1998; Mufson et al., 2002; Bäckman et al., 2010), which crucially support the plasticity processes that account for both functional maintenance and learning-based remodeling, as evoked earlier.

From a physical view, cognitive aging is based on connectional dis-elaboration and disconnection, de-myelination, reduced blood flow, and neuropil and cortical shrinkage reduction attributable to dendrite, axonal arbor, glial process, and synaptic simplification (Mufson et al., 2002; Lo et al., 2011; Hahn et al., 2013; Jagust, 2013). Many age-related morphological aspects of the brain are documented by postmortem studies, such as reduced size and weight, expansion of cerebral ventricles and sulci, deformation and loss of myelin sheathing, region-specific loss of dendritic arborization and neuronal bodies, rarefication of cerebral vasculature, and reduced synaptic density (Raz and Rodrigue, 2006). Animal models help to identify mechanisms of age-related cognitive decline at the cellular level. In nonhuman primates, the degeneration of thin synaptic spines in dorsolateral prefrontal cortex, as well as synaptic alterations in the dentate gyrus of the hippocampus, contributes to age-related losses in memory (Morrison and Baxter, 2014). Rodent models indicate that normal aging alters excitatory synaptic transmission in hippocampal granule cells and in CA3 and CA1 pyramidal cells (Burke and Barnes, 2010).

Due to this decline, there is a lot of reengagement required to drive the brain broadly in a rejuvenating direction, conferring greater resilience against the onset of cognitive aging and neurodegenerative diseases.

## How to Improve and Enhance Brain Plasticity and Cognition?

### Mechanisms of Successful Cognitive Aging

Cognitive aging is highly individualized, and information based on between-person differences or averages may misrepresent the individual aging process to some degree (Brose et al., 2012; Lindenberger, 2014; Voelkle et al., 2014). Hence, attempts at promoting successful cognitive aging (Rowe and Kahn, 1987) should also be directed toward the physical and social environment of the aging individual. In particular, assistive adaptive technology (Lindenberger et al., 2008) provides individuals with cuing structures that connect properties of the environment to their personal action goals. However, there are both advantages and disadvantages: chronic reliance on technological aids may deplete brain resources through disuse of skills and abilities, undermine motivation, and engender loss of autonomy. Conversely, assistive adaptive technology may foster cognitive maintenance and plasticity by combining support with challenges, thereby enhancing motivation, social participation, and a sense of autonomy, with positive repercussions on cognitive development in old age.

Turning toward aging individuals' brains and behavior, a number of general mechanisms have been linked to more favorable aging trajectories. These mechanisms are not mutually exclusive, and their viability and reciprocal relations remain to be determined. Animal models of individual differences in adult development play an important role in this effort (Freund et al., 2013; Haberman et al., 2013; Morrison and Baxter, 2014).

### Maintenance

As a general observation, older adults with more "youth-like" brain structure and functional brain responses show higher levels of cognitive performance than older adults whose brain structure and function are markedly different from that of younger adults (Lindenberger, 2014). This observation was shown in cross-sectional and longitudinal studies (Persson et al., 2012; Burzynska et al., 2013). Brains with relatively well-preserved anatomy and neurochemistry are more likely to generate functional activation patterns, like younger brains.

An important implication is that cognitive interventions should aim at preserving or, at least partially, restoring youth-like brain physiology.

## Compensation

High levels of cognitive functioning in old age may reflect instances of successful compensation (Lindenberger, 2014). According to one definition, compensation in the context of normal aging refers to structural or functional reorganization of the brain that evolves in response to aging induced decline in brain functioning. Other than maintenance and restoration, compensation does not consist in preserving or reestablishing the function that was lost, but in creating an alternative in response to a loss. Compared with damaging events, such as a stroke, cerebral aging is a process without clear boundaries in space and with no clear onset in time. The gradual loss in functional capacity in normal aging concerns many different brain areas, networks, and neurotransmitter systems. Compensatory reactions to normal aging may evolve differently and arguably less often than compensatory reactions to damaging events. Brain circuitry, potentially capable of compensating for a loss, may itself be particularly vulnerable to normal aging. Compensatory recruitment of the prefrontal cortex may attenuate the adverse effects of aging on other areas of the brain (Grady, 2012), given its pivotal role for the organization of behavior. However, far from being spared by aging, prefrontal areas and associated corticostriatal circuits show early and precipitous age-related decline (Raz et al., 2005). Hence, although the frontal lobes are increasingly needed, they have difficulty counteracting the adverse consequences of brain aging.

## Selection

Younger adults' brains can execute a given task in more than one way. Different brain implementations of a given cognitive function may be differentially vulnerable to aging because some brain areas, circuits, and activation patterns are more resilient than others. More robust brain processing routes and areas with advancing adult age may signal selective survival due to differential robustness, rather than compensatory development of alternate functional activation patterns. Individuals with a larger pool of available processing routes in early adulthood may draw on a greater cognitive reserve (Barulli and Stern, 2013) or functional cerebral spaces that provide protection against the adverse effects of normal and pathological age-related cognitive changes because it offers a greater choice set for selection.

Multimodal longitudinal and experimental evidence is needed to probe the relative importance of maintenance, compensation, and selection as mechanisms of successful cognitive aging.

## Novelty and Challenge: Environmental Stimulation

Animal and human research have shown that environmental stimulation is critical for enhancing and maintaining cognitive function. For novelty, focused attention and challenge are essential components of enhancing cognitive function (Mahncke et al., 2006a; Mahncke et al., 2006b; Houillon et al., 2013). Perceived challenge is associated with enjoyment of the task; it functions as reinforcement for humans.

Even when additional stimulation was not provided until rats were middle-aged, an enriched environment resulted in a fivefold increase in neuronal phenotypes that were associated with "significant improvements in learning parameters, exploratory behavior, and locomotor activity" (Kempermann et al., 2002). In addition, these new and enriching experiences resulted in decreased age dependent degeneration as shown by less accumulation of lipofuscin in the dentate gyrus of the hippocampus. Neuroplastic gains with new and enriched environments are not limited to a brief "critical" period (Malkasian and Diamond, 1971; Uylings et al., 1978).

The timing of enrichment has also been the focus of studies with humans such as the Mayo Clinic Study of Aging (Vemuri et al., 2014), showing that academic and career achievements in the seventy-fifth percentile showed higher levels of cognition with a delay of cognitive impairment of 8.7 years as compared to individuals in the twenty-fifth percentile. This research involved nearly 2000 people without dementia aged 70–89, of whom only 277 had mild cognitive impairment (MCI). Since people, whose intellectual enrichment was focused in midlife also showed significant gains, newness and challenge can be seen as a powerful way to lengthen the "healthy life span."

## Cognitive Training

In the designs of therapeutic training regimes, the Hebbian rule must be considered, to assure that training-driven changes are always in the positive, strengthening, and recovering direction of brain plasticity. The training program designed by Merzenich and colleagues to address these broad issues requires up to 200 hours to complete (dosing is dependent on the depth and breadth of neurological loss), with additional training on a lighter schedule required for many individuals to sustain a safe position over subsequent years (Merzenich et al., 2014). Again, all training is progressive and adaptive, and presented in game-like training formats on computers or other mobile devices. Their goal is to recover neurological representational accuracy, speed, coordination, sequencing, recording (remembering, selectively attending), noise control (distractor suppression), and executive processes in the brain. At the same time, exercises are designed to upregulate, refine, and reinvigorate modulatory control processes controlling learning, memory, attention states, and mood.

An important goal of this training is to increase resilience against the onset of neurodegenerative disease. Because we know the patterns of progression in pathology across a long epoch of time before frank "disease" onset, the preclinical state, we increasingly understand how it relates to progressive changes in brain engagement. This understanding is also richly informed by the many factors that can accelerate the advance to Alzheimer's, Parkinson's, and other neurodegenerative diseases. Positive improvements have been shown to endure for many months to years following training completion (Wolinsky et al., 2006; Wolinsky et al., 2009; Zelinski et al., 2011; Wolinsky et al., 2013).

Another important question is: are adult plastic changes elicited by intervention studies sufficiently large and persistent enough to improve cognitive competence in everyday life? One indicator of practical relevance is transfer of training: Does improvement on trained tasks generalize to untrained tasks that tap into the same cognitive ability or to tasks measuring affiliated cognitive abilities? The experimental design and statistical analysis procedures of most intervention studies to date are not well suited to answer this question (Noack et al., 2014). The most common threat to validity concerns the distinction between task-specific effects and improvements at the ability level. Positive transfer to multiple indicators of a given cognitive ability is a necessary condition for claiming that the intervention has led to improvements at that level. In one extensive intervention study, transfer of training to cognitive abilities was observed, but transfer effects were reduced in scope (Schmiedek et al., 2010) and maintenance (Schmiedek et al., 2014) in older, relative to younger, adults. In both younger and older adults, the intervention was associated with improved white matter integrity in the anterior part of the corpus callosum (Lövdén et al., 2010b) and reduced age-related shrinkage in the cerebellum (Raz et al., 2013). In another study, 4 months of spatial navigation training protected the hippocampus against age-related shrinkage (Lövdén et al., 2012), both in younger and older adults. However, training-related cortical thickening in the left precuneus and paracentral lobule was observed in younger adults alone (Wenger et al., 2012). These results provide some reason to hope that cognitive interventions may ameliorate the course of cognitive aging, but also suggest that plasticity decreases from early to late adulthood.

## Exercise

Physical exercise is an enhancer of brain health and brain plasticity (Cotman and Berchtold, 2002; Ryan and Nolan, 2016). Independent of vascular risk factors, low or no leisure physical activity was associated with greater decline in processing speed and memory across five years as compared to individuals with moderate to intensive physical exercise (Willey et al., 2016). Regarding the effect of exercise on brain plasticity, a cross-sectional study has shown that very fit older adults outperformed those less fit in behavioral and neuroimaging parameters (Colcombe et al., 2004). Better cardiovascular fitness resulted in superior performances on executive functions, suggesting exercise-dependent brain plasticity of the aging brain. By improving physical fitness, plasticity can be strengthened. Exercise induces a cascade of molecular and sub/cellular processes favoring angiogenesis, neurogenesis, synaptogenesis, and increasing synthesis/releasing of brain derived neurotrophic factor BDNF (Deslandes et al., 2009; Coelho et al., 2013). Regular exercise improves many cognitive functions (executive, attention, processing speed, memory, learning) throughout life span (Curlik and Shors, 2013; Dresler et al., 2013). Longitudinal studies suggest that engagement in exercise at young age leads to better cognitive performance at older age. The process seems to follow a dose-response effect. More robust effects are obtained in individuals who have exercised more intensively in their youth (Middleton et al., 2010). Physical exercise prescriptions should to be part of healthcare for successful brain aging (Shaffer, 2016).

## Sleep

As humans spend one-third of their life asleep, sleep must have an evolutionary advantage and be of fundamental importance for proper brain function. As noted earlier, sleep and sleep disruption have an important impact on hippocampal neurogenesis and synaptogenesis. Chronically restricted and disrupted sleep is a serious problem as a result of our modern lifestyle, high workload, shift-work, psychosocial stress, and sleep disorders such as insomnia and sleep apnea. Because sleep is considered to play an essential role in regulating brain synaptic plasticity and neurogenesis: (1) sleep remediation should be a therapeutic target, with the objective of normalizing sleep parameters; (2) understanding the role of sleep in hippocampal shrinkage and malfunction may ultimately provide novel therapeutic approaches to treat brain disorders that are accompanied by sleep disturbances and sleep loss (Raven et al., 2018).

## Pharmacologic Interventions

What makes the study of adult brain plasticity particularly relevant is that understanding its mechanistic detail may help in developing treatments for pathological conditions in humans. The correction of developmentally mis-wired neuronal connections or rehabilitation after stroke or traumatic brain injury depends crucially on the adult brain's capacity for plasticity. Thus, another way of promoting plasticity is to directly interfere with these molecular determinants of plasticity. This approach is frequently taken in another clinically relevant field, the regeneration of injured axons in the central nervous system (CNS). Unlike in the peripheral nervous system, where severed axons can regrow over long distances, long-range regeneration is normally absent in the adult mammalian CNS. The search for molecular factors that prevent the growth of CNS axons and limits adult plasticity has revealed a growing list of candidates, which are now collectively referred to as "brakes on plasticity." The first of these brakes was found in CNS myelin and was named Nogo-A by Schwab and colleagues (Schwab et al., 2000). Blocking Nogo-A with a specific antibody was shown to promote axonal regeneration in the spinal cord of a rat (Schnell and Schwab, 1990). Nogo signaling also has a rapid, negative effect on LTP (Delekate et al., 2011) and influences dendritic and spine structure (Zagrebelsky et al., 2010; Akbik et al., 2013). Thus, Nogo and other myelin associated axonal growth inhibitors are important factors limiting plasticity throughout the adult CNS and interfering with their signaling, which holds the potential for the treatment of spinal cord injury, stroke, and diseases like multiple sclerosis.

Pharmacological intervention aimed at enhancing or maintaining cognitive function has been intensively studied in recent years (Pieramico et al., 2014). As these cognitive enhancer drugs deal with neurotransmitters, it should be underlined that brain plasticity can be driven into either a positive or negative direction (increased excitatory synaptic transmission, reduced synaptic pruning). In this pharmacological domain, brain plasticity-based therapeutics that enhance cognitive function need to be developed.

## Conclusion

By understanding the mechanisms of brain plasticity, age-related cognitive variation and neural systems changes are dynamic and not irreversible processes. Cognitive development in adulthood and old age differs substantially from person to person and is malleable within individuals. Maintaining cognitive abilities into old age and postponing or preventing pathologies leading to a diagnosis of dementia late in life are key aims for science and society. There is a need of nonpharmacological and pharmacological interventions to enhance cognition and brain plasticity in healthy older individuals, as well as delaying cognitive decline in dementia patients.

Regions of the brain that are particularly plastic and provide the substrate for new learning and plasticity, such as the hippocampus, are also particularly vulnerable to risk factors such as stress, sleep disruption, and vascular conditions, which are modifiable. Combining pharmacological and behavioral interventions may reopen "windows of plasticity" in adulthood and old age (Gervain et al., 2013). If the relevant molecular mechanisms are function-specific and can be brought under control, then they may provide a basis for regulating plasticity in adulthood and old age (Takesian and Hensch, 2013).

Dealing with nonpharmacological interventions (e.g., exercise, cognitive training), many unknowns are still present, for example, the intensity, frequency, and duration are still unclear to promote significant, reproducible, and durable effects on cognition. A limiting factor that should not be overlooked is individual variability, needing a more accurate customization of any given set of intervention. In analogy with pharmacogenomics, a "cognitogenomic" approach, in which genetic differences are explored in relation to response to nonpharmacological interventions is necessary (Pieramico et al., 2014).

Jessberger and Gage stated a message of hope and empowerment: "Despite the dramatic reductions in hippocampus-dependent function that accompany advancing age, there is also striking evidence that even the aged brain retains a high level of plasticity" (Jessberger and Gage, 2008). Thus, one promising avenue to reach the goal of successful aging might be to boost and recruit this plasticity, which is the interplay between neural structure, function, and experience, to prevent age-related cognitive decline and age-associated comorbidities. The concept of "brain-plasticity-based" therapeutics, both nonpharmacological and pharmacological, proposed by Merzenich (Merzenich et al., 2014), can be expected to drive fundamental corrections of brain systems and will represent future treatment strategy.

## References

Abel, T., Havekes, R., Saletin, J. M., Walker, M. P. Sleep, plasticity and memory from molecules to whole-brain networks. *Curr Biol.* Elsevier; 2013;23: R774–88. doi:10.1016/j.cub.2013.07.025

Ahissar, E., Vaadia, E., Ahissar, M., et al. Dependence of cortical plasticity on correlated activity of single neurons and on behavioral context. *Science.* 1992;257: 1412–5. Available: http://ncbi.nlm.nih.gov/pubmed/1529342

Aimone, J. B., Li, Y., Lee, S. W., et al. Regulation and function of adult neurogenesis: From genes to cognition. *Physiol Rev.* 2014;94: 991–1026. doi:10.1152/physrev.00004.2014

Akbik, F. V., Bhagat, S. M., Patel, P. R., Cafferty, W. B. J., Strittmatter, S. M. Anatomical plasticity of adult brain is titrated by Nogo receptor 1. *Neuron.* 2013;77: 859–66. doi:10.1016/j.neuron.2012.12.027

Aston-Jones, G., Cohen, J. D. An integrative theory of locus coeruleus-norepinephrine function: Adaptive gain and optimal performance. *Annu Rev Neurosci.* 2005;28: 403–50. doi:10.1146/annurev.neuro.28.061604.135709

Aston-Jones, G., Rajkowski, J., Cohen, J. Role of locus coeruleus in attention and behavioral flexibility. *Biol Psychiatry.* 1999;46: 1309–20. Available: http://ncbi.nlm.nih.gov/pubmed/10560036

Bäckman, L., Lindenberger, U., Li, S.-C., Nyberg, L. Linking cognitive aging to alterations in dopamine neurotransmitter functioning: Recent data and future avenues. *Neurosci Biobehav Rev.* 2010;34: 670–7. doi:10.1016/j.neubiorev.2009.12.008

Bao, S., Chan, V. T., Merzenich, M. M. Cortical remodelling induced by activity of ventral tegmental dopamine neurons. *Nature.* 2001;412: 79–83. doi:10.1038/35083586

Bao, S., Chan, V. T., Zhang, L. I., Merzenich, M. M. Suppression of cortical representation through backward conditioning. *Proc Natl Acad Sci.* 2003;100: 1405–8. doi:10.1073/pnas.0337527100

Barili, P., De Carolis, G., Zaccheo, D., Amenta, F. Sensitivity to ageing of the limbic dopaminergic system: A review. *Mech Ageing Dev.* 1998;106: 57–92. Available: http://ncbi.nlm.nih.gov/pubmed/9883974

Barulli, D., Stern, Y. Efficiency, capacity, compensation, maintenance, plasticity: Emerging concepts in cognitive reserve. *Trends Cog. Sci.* 2013;17(10): 502–9. doi:10.1016/j.tics.2013.08.012

Bergan, J. F., Ro, P., Ro, D., Knudsen, E. I. Hunting increases adaptive auditory map plasticity in adult barn owls. *J Neurosci.* 2005;25: 9816–20. doi:10.1523/JNEUROSCI.2533-05.2005

Brose, A., Schmiedek, F., Lövdén, M., Lindenberger, U. Daily variability in working memory is coupled with negative affect: The role of attention and motivation. *Emotion.* 2012;12: 605–17. doi:10.1037/a0024436

Buonomano, D. V., Merzenich, M. M. Cortical plasticity: From synapses to maps. *Annu Rev Neurosci.* Annual Reviews 4139 El Camino Way, P.O. Box 10139, Palo Alto, CA 94303-0139, USA; 1998;21: 149–86. doi:10.1146/annurev.neuro.21.1.149

Burke, S. N., Barnes, C. A. Senescent synapses and hippocampal circuit dynamics. *Trends Neurosci.* 2010;33: 153–61. doi:10.1016/j.tins.2009.12.003

Burzynska, A. Z., Garrett, D. D., Preuschhof, C., et al. A scaffold for efficiency in the human brain. *J Neurosci.* 2013;33: 17150–9. doi:10.1523/JNEUROSCI.1426-13.2013

Cai, L., Chan, J. S. Y., Yan, J. H., Peng, K. Brain plasticity and motor practice in cognitive aging. *Front Aging Neurosci.* 2014;6: 1–12. doi:10.3389/fnagi.2014.00031

Clark, S. A., Allard, T., Jenkins, W. M., Merzenich, M. M. Receptive fields in the body-surface map in adult cortex defined by temporally correlated inputs. *Nature.* 1988;332: 444–5. doi:10.1038/332444a0

Coelho, F. G. de M., Gobbi, S., Andreatto, C. A. A., et al. Physical exercise modulates peripheral levels of brain-derived neurotrophic factor (BDNF): A systematic review of experimental studies in the elderly. *Arch Gerontol Geriatr.* 2013;56: 10–15. doi:10.1016/j.archger.2012.06.003

Colcombe, S. J., Kramer, A. F., Erickson, K. I., et al. Cardiovascular fitness, cortical plasticity, and aging. *Proc Natl Acad Sci.* 2004;101: 3316–21. doi:10.1073/pnas.0400266101

Cooper, L. N., Bear, M. F. The BCM theory of synapse modification at 30: Interaction of theory with experiment. *Nat Rev Neurosci.* 2012;13: 798–810. doi:10.1038/nrn3353

Cotman, C. W., Berchtold, N. C. Exercise: A behavioral intervention to enhance brain health and plasticity. *Trends Neurosci.* 2002;25: 295–301. doi:10.1016/S0166-2236(02)02143-4

Curlik, D. M, Shors, T. J. Training your brain: Do mental and physical (MAP) training enhance cognition through the process of neurogenesis in the hippocampus? *Neuropharmacology.* 2013;64: 506–14. doi:10.1016/j.neuropharm.2012.07.027

Dan, Y., Poo, M.-M. Spike timing-dependent plasticity: From synapse to perception. *Physiol Rev.* 2006;86: 1033–48. doi:10.1152/physrev.00030.2005

de Villers-Sidani, E., Alzghoul, L., Zhou, X., et al. Recovery of functional and structural age-related changes in the rat primary auditory cortex with operant training. *Proc Natl Acad Sci.* 2010;107: 13900–5. doi:10.1073/pnas.1007885107

de Villers-Sidani, E., Merzenich, M. M. Lifelong plasticity in the rat auditory cortex. *Progress in Brain Research.* 2011;191: 119–31. doi: 10.1016/B978-0-444-53752-2.00009-6

Delekate, A., Zagrebelsky, M., Kramer, S., Schwab, M. E., Korte, M. NogoA restricts synaptic plasticity in the adult hippocampus on a fast time scale. *Proc Natl Acad Sci.* 2011;108: 2569–74. doi:10.1073/pnas.1013322108

Deshpande, A., Bergami, M., Ghanem, A., et al. Retrograde monosynaptic tracing reveals the temporal evolution of inputs onto new neurons in the adult dentate gyrus and olfactory bulb. *Proc Natl Acad Sci U S A.* 2013;110: E1152–61. doi:10.1073/pnas.1218991110

Deslandes, A., Moraes H., Ferreira C., et al. Exercise and mental health: Many reasons to move. *Neuropsychobiology.* 2009;59: 191–8. doi:10.1159/000223730

Dranovsky, A, Picchini, A. M., Moadel, T., et al. Experience dictates stem cell fate in the adult hippocampus. *Neuron.* 2011;70: 908–23. doi:10.1016/j.neuron.2011.05.022

Dresler, M., Sandberg, A., Ohla, K., et al. Non-pharmacological cognitive enhancement. *Neuropharmacology.* 2013;64: 529–43. doi:10.1016/j.neuropharm.2012.07.002

Feldman, D. E. The spike-timing dependence of plasticity. *Neuron.* 2012;75: 556–71. doi:10.1016/j.neuron.2012.08.001

Freund, J., Brandmaier, A. M., Lewejohann, L., et al. Emergence of individuality in genetically identical mice. *Science.* 2013;340(6133): 756–9. doi:10.1126/science.1235294

Froemke, R. C., Merzenich, M. M., Schreiner, C. E. A synaptic memory trace for cortical receptive field plasticity. *Nature.* 2007;450: 425–9. doi:10.1038/nature06289

Ge, S., Yang, C.-H., Hsu, K.-S., Ming, G.-L., Song, H. A critical period for enhanced synaptic plasticity in newly generated neurons of the adult brain. *Neuron.* 2007;54: 559–66. doi:10.1016/j.neuron.2007.05.002

Gervain, J., Vines, B. W., Chen, L. M., et al. Valproate reopens critical-period learning of absolute pitch. *Front Syst Neurosci.* 2013;7. doi:10.3389/fnsys.2013.00102

Gilbert, C. D., Li, W., Piech, V. Perceptual learning and adult cortical plasticity. *J Physiol.* 2009;587: 2743–51. doi:10.1113/jphysiol.2009.171488

Göritz, C., Frisén J. Neural stem cells and neurogenesis in the adult. *Cell Stem Cell.* 2012;10: 657–9. doi:10.1016/j.stem.2012.04.005

Grady, C. The cognitive neuroscience of ageing. *Nat Rev Neurosci.* 2012;13: 491–505. doi:10.1038/nrn3256

Haberman, R. P., Colantuoni, C., Koh, M. T., Gallagher, M. Behaviorally activated mRNA expression profiles produce signatures of learning and enhanced inhibition in aged rats with preserved memory. Ginsberg SD, editor. *PLoS One.* 2013;8: e83674. doi:10.1371/journal.pone.0083674

Hahn, K., Myers, N., Prigarin, S., et al. Selectively and progressively disrupted structural connectivity of functional brain networks in Alzheimer's disease – Revealed by a novel framework to analyze edge distributions of networks detecting disruptions with strong statistical evidence. *Neuroimage.* 2013;81: 96–109. doi:10.1016/j.neuroimage.2013.05.011

Horng, S. H., Sur, M. Visual activity and cortical rewiring: Activity-dependent plasticity of cortical networks. *Prog Brain Res.* 2006;157: 3–11. Available: http://ncbi.nlm.nih.gov/pubmed/17167899

Houillon, A., Lorenz, R. C., Boehmer, W., et al. The effect of novelty on reinforcement learning. *Progress in Brain Research.* 2013;202: 415–39. doi:10.1016/B978-0-444-62604-2.00021-6

Jagust, W. Vulnerable neural systems and the borderland of brain aging and neurodegeneration. *Neuron.* 2013;77: 219–34. doi:10.1016/j.neuron.2013.01.002

Jessberger, S., Gage, F. H. Adult neurogenesis: Bridging the gap between mice and humans. *Trends Cell Biol.* 2014;24: 558–63. doi:10.1016/j.tcb.2014.07.003

Stem-cell-associated structural and functional plasticity in the aging hippocampus. *Psychol Aging.* 2008;23: 684–691. doi:10.1037/a0014188

Kamal, B., Holman C., de Villers-Sidani E. Shaping the aging brain: Role of auditory input patterns in the emergence of auditory cortical impairments. *Front Syst Neurosci.* 2013;7: 52. doi:10.3389/fnsys.2013.00052

Kempermann, G., Gast, D., Gage, F. H. Neuroplasticity in old age: Sustained fivefold induction of hippocampal neurogenesis by long-term environmental enrichment. *Ann Neurol.* 2002;52: 135–43. doi:10.1002/ana.10262

Kent, B. A., Mistlberger, R. E. Sleep and hippocampal neurogenesis: Implications for Alzheimer's disease. *Front Neuroendocrinol.* 2017;45: 35–52. doi:10.1016/j.yfrne.2017.02.004

Kleim, J. A., Barbay, S., Cooper, N. R., et al. Motor learning-dependent synaptogenesis is localized to functionally reorganized motor cortex. *Neurobiol Learn Mem.* 2002;77: 63–77. doi:10.1006/nlme.2000.4004

Kreutzmann, J. C., Havekes, R., Abel, T., Meerlo, P. Sleep deprivation and hippocampal vulnerability: Changes in neuronal plasticity, neurogenesis and cognitive function. *Neuroscience*. 2015;309: 173–90. doi:10.1016/j.neuroscience.2015.04.053

Kuzawa, C. W., Chugani, H. T., Grossman, L. I., et al. Metabolic costs and evolutionary implications of human brain development. *Proc Natl Acad Sci.* 2014;111: 13010–13015. doi:10.1073/pnas.1323099111

Li, S. Spasticity, motor recovery, and neural plasticity after stroke. *Front Neurol. Frontiers Media SA*; 2017;8: 120. doi:10.3389/fneur.2017.00120

Lindenberger, U., Lövdén, M., Schellenbach, M., Li, S.-C., Krüger, A. Psychological principles of successful aging technologies: A mini-review. *Gerontology.* 2008;54: 59–68. doi:10.1159/000116114

Lindenberger, U. Human cognitive aging: Corriger la fortune? *Science.* 2014;346(6209): 572–8. doi:10.1126/science.1254403.

Lisman, J., Grace, A. A., Duzel, E. A neoHebbian framework for episodic memory; role of dopamine-dependent late LTP. *Trends Neurosci.* 2011;34: 536–47. doi:10.1016/j.tins.2011.07.006

Lo, R. Y., Hubbard, A. E., Shaw, L. M., et al. Longitudinal change of biomarkers in cognitive decline. *Arch Neurol.* 2011;68: 1257. doi:10.1001/archneurol.2011.123

Lövdén, M., Bäckman, L., Lindenberger, U., Schaefer, S., Schmiedek, F. A theoretical framework for the study of adult cognitive plasticity. *Psychol Bull.* 2010a;136: 659–76. doi:10.1037/a0020080

Lövdén, M., Bodammer, N. C., Kühn, S., et al. Experience-dependent plasticity of white-matter microstructure extends into old age. *Neuropsychologia.* 2010b;48: 3878–83. doi:10.1016/j.neuropsychologia.2010.08.026

Lövdén, M., Schaefer, S., Noack, H., et al. Spatial navigation training protects the hippocampus against age-related changes during early and late adulthood. *Neurobiol Aging.* 2012;33: 620. e9–620. e22. doi:10.1016/j.neurobiolaging.2011.02.013

Lövdén, M., Wenger, E., Mårtensson, J., Lindenberger, U., Bäckman, L. Structural brain plasticity in adult learning and development. *Neurosci Biobehav Rev.* 2013;37: 2296–310. doi:10.1016/j.neubiorev.2013.02.014

Mahncke, H. W., Bronstone, A., Merzenich, M. M. Brain plasticity and functional losses in the aged: Scientific bases for a novel intervention. *Progress in Brain Research.* 2006a;157:81–109

Mahncke, H. W., Connor, B. B., Appelman, J., et al. Memory enhancement in healthy older adults using a brain plasticity-based training program: A randomized, controlled study. *Proc Natl Acad Sci.* 2006b;103: 12523–8. doi:10.1073/pnas.0605194103

Malkasian, D. R., Diamond, M. C. The effects of environmental manipulation on the morphology of the neonate rat brain. *Int J Neurosci.* 1971;2: 161–9. Available: http://ncbi.nlm.nih.gov/pubmed/5161309

Merzenich, M. M., Vleet, T. M. Van, Nahum, M. Brain plasticity-based therapeutics. *Front Hum Neurosci.* 2014;8: 1–16. doi:10.3389/fnhum.2014.00385

Merzenich, M. M. Cortical plasticity contributing to child development. J. L. McClelland & R. S. Siegler (Eds.), *Carnegie Mellon Symposia on Cognition. Mechanisms of Cognitive Development: Behavioral and Neural Perspectives.* Mahwah, NJ: Lawrence Erlbaum Associates Publishers. 2001. pp. 67–96.

Merzenich, M. M., DeCharms, R. C. Neural representations, experience, and change. In R. R. Llinás & P. S. Churchland (Eds.), *The Mind–Brain Continuum: Sensory Processes.* Cambridge, MA: The MIT Press. 1996. pp. 61–81.

Merzenich, M. M., Nelson, R. J., Stryker, M. P., et al. Somatosensory cortical map changes following digit amputation in adult monkeys. *J Comp Neurol.* 1984;224: 591–605. doi:10.1002/cne.902240408

Merzenich, M. M., Schreiner, C., Jenkins, W., Wang, X. Neural mechanisms underlying temporal integration, segmentation, and input sequence representation: Some implications for the origin of learning disabilities. *Ann N Y Acad Sci.* 1993;682: 1–22. Available: http://ncbi.nlm.nih.gov/pubmed/8323106

Middleton, L. E., Barnes, D. E., Lui, L.-Y., Yaffe, K. Physical activity over the life course and its association with cognitive performance and impairment in old age. *J Am Geriatr Soc.* 2010;58: 1322–6. doi:10.1111/j.1532-5415.2010.02903.x

Morris, R. G. D.O. Hebb: The Organization of Behavior, Wiley: New York; 1949. *Brain Res Bull.* 50: 437. Available: http://ncbi.nlm.nih.gov/pubmed/10643472

Morrison, J. H., Baxter, M. G. Synaptic health. *JAMA Psychiatry.* 2014;71: 835. doi:10.1001/jamapsychiatry.2014.380

Mufson, E. J., Ma, S. Y., Dills, J., et al. Loss of basal forebrain P75(NTR) immunoreactivity in subjects with mild cognitive impairment and Alzheimer's disease. *J Comp Neurol.* 2002;443: 136–53. Available: http://ncbi.nlm.nih.gov/pubmed/11793352

Nahum, M., Lee, H., Merzenich, M. M. Principles of neuroplasticity-based rehabilitation. *Prog Brain Res.* 2013;207: 141–71. doi:10.1016/B978-0-444-63327-9.00009-6

Nakamura, S., Sakaguchi, T. Development and plasticity of the locus coeruleus: A review of recent physiological and pharmacological experimentation. *Prog Neurobiol.* 1990;34: 505–26. Available: http://ncbi.nlm.nih.gov/pubmed/2202018

Noack, H., Lövdén, M., Schmiedek, F. On the validity and generality of transfer effects in cognitive training research. *Psychol Res.* 2014;78: 773–89. doi:10.1007/s00426-014-0564-6

Persson, J., Pudas, S., Lind, J., et al. Longitudinal structure-function correlates in elderly reveal MTL dysfunction with cognitive decline. *Cereb Cortex.* 2012;22: 2297–304. doi:10.1093/cercor/bhr306

Pieramico, V., Esposito, R., Cesinaro, S., Frazzini, V., Sensi, S. L. Effects of non-pharmacological or pharmacological interventions on cognition and brain plasticity of aging individuals. *Front Syst Neurosci.* 2014;8: 153. doi:10.3389/fnsys.2014.00153. eCollection 2014.

Raven, F., Van der Zee, E. A., Meerlo, P., Havekes, R. The role of sleep in regulating structural plasticity and synaptic strength: Implications for memory and cognitive function. *Sleep Med Rev.* 2018;39:3–11. doi: 10.1016/j.smrv.2017.05.002

Raz, N., Rodrigue, K. M. Differential aging of the brain: Patterns, cognitive correlates and modifiers. *Neurosci Biobehav Rev.* 2006;30: 730–48. doi:10.1016/j.neubiorev.2006.07.001

Raz, N., Lindenberger, U., Rodrigue, K. M., et al. Regional brain changes in aging healthy adults: General trends, individual differences and modifiers. *Cereb Cortex.* 2005;15: 1676–89. doi:10.1093/cercor/bhi044

Raz, N., Schmiedek, F., Rodrigue, K. M., et al. Differential brain shrinkage over 6-months shows limited association with cognitive practice. *Brain Cogn.* 2013;82: 171–80. doi:10.1016/j.bandc.2013.04.002

Recanzone, G. H., Schreiner, C. E., Merzenich, M. M. Plasticity in the frequency representation of primary auditory cortex following discrimination training in adult owl monkeys. *J Neurosci.* 1993;13: 87–103. Available: http://ncbi.nlm.nih.gov/pubmed/8423485

Richardson, R. T., DeLong, M. R. Context-dependent responses of primate nucleus basalis neurons in a go/no-go task. *J Neurosci.* 1990;10: 2528–40. Available: http://ncbi.nlm.nih.gov/pubmed/2388078

Rowe, J. W., Kahn, R. L. Human aging: Usual and successful. *Science.* 1987;237: 143–9. Available: http://ncbi.nlm.nih.gov/pubmed/3299702

Ryan, S. M., Nolan, Y. M. Neuroinflammation negatively affects adult hippocampal neurogenesis and cognition: Can exercise compensate? *Neurosci Biobehav Rev.* 2016;61: 121–31. doi:10.1016/j.neubiorev.2015.12.004

Salthouse, T. Consequences of age-related cognitive declines. *Annu Rev Psychol.* 2012;63: 201–26. doi:10.1146/annurev-psych-120710-100328

Salthouse, T. A. Aging and measures of processing speed. *Biol Psychol.* 2000;54: 35–54. Available: http://ncbi.nlm.nih.gov/pubmed/11035219

Sara, S. J. The locus coeruleus and noradrenergic modulation of cognition. *Nat Rev Neurosci.* 2009;10: 211–23. doi:10.1038/nrn2573

Sara, S. J., Bouret, S. Orienting and reorienting: The locus coeruleus mediates cognition through arousal. *Neuron.* 2012;76: 130–41. doi:10.1016/j.neuron.2012.09.011

Sara, S. J., Segal, M. Plasticity of sensory responses of locus coeruleus neurons in the behaving rat: Implications for cognition. *Prog Brain Res.* 1991;88: 571–85. Available: http://ncbi.nlm.nih.gov/pubmed/1813935

Sarter, M., Gehring, W. J., Kozak, R. More attention must be paid: The neurobiology of attentional effort. *Brain Res Rev.* 2006;51: 145–60. doi:10.1016/j.brainresrev.2005.11.002

Sarter, M., Givens, B., Bruno, J. P. The cognitive neuroscience of sustained attention: Where top-down meets bottom-up. *Brain Res Brain Res Rev.* 2001;35(2): 146–60.

Schmiedek, F., Lövdén, M., Lindenberger, U. Hundred days of cognitive training enhance broad cognitive abilities in adulthood: Findings from the COGITO study. *Front Aging Neurosci.* 2010;2: pii: 27. doi:10.3389/fnagi.2010.00027
    Younger adults show long-term effects of cognitive training on broad cognitive abilities over 2 years. *Dev Psychol.* 2014;50: 2304–10. doi:10.1037/a0037388

Schnell, L., Schwab, M. E. Axonal regeneration in the rat spinal cord produced by an antibody against myelin-associated neurite growth inhibitors. *Nature.* 1990;343: 269–72. doi:10.1038/343269a0

Schultz, W. Multiple dopamine functions at different time courses. *Annu Rev Neurosci.* 2007;30: 259–88. doi:10.1146/annurev.neuro.28.061604.135722

Schwab, M. E., Chen, M. S., Huber, A. B., et al. Nogo-A is a myelin-associated neurite outgrowth inhibitor and an antigen for monoclonal antibody IN-1. *Nature.* 2000;403: 434–9. doi:10.1038/35000219

Shaffer, J. Neuroplasticity and clinical practice actice acbrain power for health. *Front Psychol.*. 2016;7: 1118. doi:10.3389/fpsyg.2016.01118

Singh, A., Abraham, W. C. Astrocytes and synaptic plasticity in health and disease. *Exp Brain Res.* Springer Berlin Heidelberg; 2017;235: 1645–55. doi:10.1007/s00221-017-4928-1

Smith, B. A., Goldberg, N. R. S., Meshul, C. K. Effects of treadmill exercise on behavioral recovery and neural changes in the substantia nigra and striatum of the 1-methyl-4-phenyl-1,2,3,6-tetrahydropyridine-lesioned mouse. *Brain Res.* 2011;1386: 70–80. doi:10.1016/j.brainres.2011.02.003

Steiner, B., Winter, C., Hosman, K., et al. Enriched environment induces cellular plasticity in the adult substantia nigra and improves motor behavior function in the 6-OHDA rat model of Parkinson's disease. *Exp Neurol.* 2006;199: 291–300. doi:10.1016/j.expneurol.2005.11.004

Swain, R. A., Thompson, R. F. In search of engrams. *Ann N Y Acad Sci.* 1993;702: 27–39. Available: http://ncbi.nlm.nih.gov/pubmed/8109877

Takesian, A. E., Hensch, T. K. Balancing plasticity/stability across brain development. *Prog Brain Res.* 2013;207: 3–34. doi:10.1016/B978-0-444-63327-9.00001-1

Tashiro, A., Sandler, V. M., Toni, N., Zhao, C., Gage, F. H. NMDA-receptor-mediated, cell-specific integration of new neurons in adult dentate gyrus. *Nature.* 2006;442: 929–33. doi:10.1038/nature05028

Taubert, M., Draganski, B., Anwander, A., et al. Dynamic properties of human brain structure: Learning-related changes in cortical areas and associated fiber connections. *J Neurosci.* 2010;30. Available: http://jneurosci.org/content/30/35/11670.long

Trachtenberg, J. T. Competition, inhibition, and critical periods of cortical plasticity. *Curr Opin Neurobiol.* 2015;35: 44–8. doi:10.1016/j.conb.2015.06.006

Uylings, H. B., Kuypers, K., Diamond, M. C., Veltman, W. A. Effects of differential environments on plasticity of dendrites of cortical pyramidal neurons in adult rats. *Exp Neurol.* 1978;62: 658–77. Available: http://ncbi.nlm.nih.gov/pubmed/750216

Vemuri, P., Lesnick, T. G., Przybelski, S. A., et al. Association of lifetime intellectual enrichment with cognitive decline in the older population. *JAMA Neurol.* 2014;71: 1017. doi:10.1001/jamaneurol.2014.963

Voelkle, M. C., Brose, A., Schmiedek, F., Lindenberger, U. Toward a unified framework for the study of between-person and within-person structures: Building a bridge between two research paradigms. *Multivariate Behav Res.* 2014;49: 193–213. doi:10.1080/00273171.2014.889593

Wall, J., Xu, J., Wang, X. Human brain plasticity: An emerging view of the multiple substrates and mechanisms that cause cortical changes and related sensory dysfunctions after injuries of sensory inputs from the body. *Brain Res Rev.* 2002;39: 181–215. doi:10.1016/S0165-0173(02)00192-3

Weinberger, N. M. Specific long-term memory traces in primary auditory cortex. *Nat Rev Neurosci.* 2004;5: 279–90. doi:10.1038/nrn1366

Wenger, E., Schaefer, S., Noack, H., et al. Cortical thickness changes following spatial navigation training in adulthood and aging. *Neuroimage.* 2012;59: 3389–97. doi:10.1016/j.neuroimage.2011.11.015

Willey, J. Z., Gardener, H., Caunca, M. R., et al. Leisure-time physical activity associates with cognitive decline. *Neurology.* 2016;86: 1897–903. doi:10.1212/WNL.0000000000002582

Winder, D. G., Egli, R. E., Schramm, N. L., Matthews, R. T. Synaptic plasticity in drug reward circuitry. *Curr Mol Med.* 2002;2: 667–76. Available: http://ncbi.nlm.nih.gov/pubmed/12420805

Wolinsky, F. D., Mahncke, H. W., Weg, M. W. V., et al. The ACTIVE cognitive training interventions and the onset of and recovery from suspected clinical depression. *J Gerontol Ser B Psychol Sci Soc Sci.* 2009;64B: 577–85. doi:10.1093/geronb/gbp061

Wolinsky, F. D., Unverzagt, F. W., Smith, D. M., et al. The ACTIVE cognitive training trial and health-related quality of life: Protection that lasts for 5 years.

*J Gerontol A Biol Sci Med Sci.* 2006;61: 1324–9. Available: http://ncbi.nlm.nih.gov/pubmed/17234829

Wolinsky, F. D., Vander Weg, M. W., Howren, M. B., Jones, M. P., Dotson, M. M. A randomized controlled trial of cognitive training using a visual speed of processing intervention in middle aged and older adults. Laks J., editor. *PLoS One.* 2013;8: e61624. doi:10.1371/journal.pone.0061624

Zagrebelsky, M., Schweigreiter, R., Bandtlow, C. E., Schwab, M. E., Korte, M. Nogo-A stabilizes the architecture of hippocampal neurons. *J Neurosci.* 2010;30: 13220–34. doi:10.1523/JNEUROSCI.1044-10.2010

Zelinski, E. M., Spina, L. M., Yaffe, K., et al. Improvement in memory with plasticity-based adaptive cognitive training: Results of the 3-month follow-up. *J Am Geriatr Soc.* 2011;59: 258–65. doi:10.1111/j.1532-5415.2010.03277.x

Zhou, J., Gennatas, E. D., Kramer, J. H., Miller, B. L., Seeley, W. W. Predicting regional neurodegeneration from the healthy brain functional connectome. *Neuron.* 2012;73: 1216–27. doi:10.1016/j.neuron.2012.03.004

# 9 Arterial Stiffness and Blood Pressure during the Aging Process

Athanase Benetos, Magnus Bäck,
Michel E. Safar, and Harold Smulyan

## Introduction

Aging is accompanied by significant structural changes, with a gradual remodeling of the arteries and heart (Lakatta, 2003). This change is characterized by an increase in the size of large arteries and heart cavities, as well as major modifications of the arterial system involving fragmentation and disruption of arterial elastic fibers, increased collagen content, and non-enzymatic glycation of collagen. These structural alterations lead to an increased stiffness of cardiac and arterial walls. Increased stiffness of the aorta and other large arteries, referred to as arteriosclerosis, reduction in vascular distensibility, and the amplification of reflected pressure waves from the periphery to the aorta. Both of these mechanisms contribute to an increase in systolic blood pressure (SBP) and pulse pressure (PP), and a decrease in diastolic blood pressure (DBP) (O'Rourke et al., 2010) (Figure 9.1).

It is important to distinguish arteriosclerosis from atheromatosis (or atherosclerosis), which refers to the development of focal lesions (atheromatous plaques) that protrude into the lumen of the large arteries and lead to occlusive and/or thromboembolic complications. Although these two age-related arterial abnormalities coexist in many subjects, it is important to distinguish them, since they represent different pathophysiological processes, each leading to different complications and necessitating different preventive and therapeutic approaches.

The main purpose of this paper is to summarize the development of arterial stiffness, the main manifestation of vascular aging, and its consequences on blood pressure regulation and age-related diseases. This subject requires a description of, the methods available to evaluate arteriosclerosis, and the major environmental factors and other risk factors that influence the pace of arterial stiffening during the aging process. Finally, this paper takes into account the complex relationships between arterial stiffness, blood pressure (BP) regulation, and common problems in older adults such as frailty, comorbidities, polymedication, and loss of autonomy.

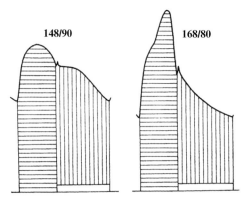

148/90          168/80

**Figure 9.1.** *Arterial aging, stiffness, and blood pressure regulation*
A typical example of the evolution of pulse waveforms recorder in a central artery (carotid)
between the age of 55 (left) and 75 (right). We observe an increase in SBP and a decrease in DBP
especially in proto-diastolic period. Note that Mean BP expressed here as area under the two
curves shows little change during this period.

## Impact of the Development of Arteriosclerosis on Cardiovascular Diseases and Other Age-Related Disease

### From Arterial Aging to the Decompensated Heart

Although large artery stiffening is common with aging, especially in subjects
with chronic hypertension, it is now confirmed that older subjects with higher
arterial stiffness have a significantly higher cardiovascular morbidity and mortality than subjects of the same age with lower arterial stiffness, mainly as a
consequence of increased SBP and PP (Lakatta, 2003; O'Rourke et al., 2010).
High arterial stiffness and the consequent BP modifications, increase left ventricular (LV) afterload, reduce coronary artery perfusion leading to LV remodeling, hypertrophy, and dilatation, and promote ischemic heart disease and
cardiac arrhythmias (Figure 9.2). This abnormal heart-vessel coupling combined with intrinsic aging-related myocardial structural and functional alterations (e.g., cardiac tissue fibrosis and stiffness, valvular calcifications, coronary
and carotid atherosclerosis, and arrhythmias) all contribute to the increasing
cardiovascular (CV) risk with age (Nichols and O'Rourke, 2006). A major risk,
heart failure (HF) (Kane et al., 2011), affects up to 10 percent of older people
(Ambrosy et al., 2014). Interestingly, the dominant type of HF in older people with hypertension and the above-described hemodynamic profiles, presents
with a preserved ejection fraction. It is well known that, despite remarkable
progress in the treatment of HF, with reduced ejection fraction, current evidence for the efficacy of the treatment of HF with preserved ejection fraction
(HFpEF) remains very poor (Braunwald, 2013). This therapeutic failure may
be due to HFpEF being a multisystem disease implicating not only the heart
and the arteries, but also several other systems that also experience age-related

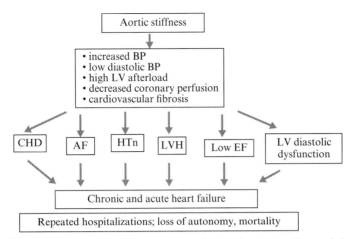

**Figure 9.2.** *Schematic representation of the deleterious effects of the development of arterial stiffness on aging pace and age-related diseases*
BP: blood pressure; LV: Left Ventricle; CHD: coronary heart disease; AF: atrial fibrillation; HTn: Hypertension; LVH: left ventricular hypertrophy; EF: ejection fraction.

alterations and decline. Thus, extra-CV age-related changes, such as sarcopenia, decreased renal function, pulmonary disease, and anemia, increase the susceptibility for decompensation and acute HF in older subjects.

## From Vascular Stiffening and Cognitive Decline

Recently there has been increasing evidence that arterial stiffness is not only a major determinant of cardiovascular morbidity and mortality, but also of cognitive decline and dementia (Valenti and Pantoni, 2014; van Sloten et al., 2015; Satizabal et al., 2016). Cross-sectional (Kearney-Schwartz et al., 2009; Scuteri et al., 2013; Zhong et al., 2014) but also longitudinal studies (Waldstein et al., 2008; Hazzouri et al., 2013; Watfa et al., 2015) have observed in older adults associations between increased arterial stiffness and cognitive impairment of both vascular and neurodegenerative origin, mainly Alzheimer's disease. Although the exact mechanisms for these observations remain unclear, several possible mechanisms have been proposed. It has been shown that arterial stiffness is associated with lesions related to cognitive decline such as silent brain infarct (Saji et al., 2012) and white matter hyperintensities (WMH) (Rabkin, 2012; Singer et al., 2014), and could also activate mechanisms leading to neurodegenerative lesions and the development of Alzheimer's disease (Hughes et al., 2015). Increasing evidence suggests that vascular etiologies – including aortic stiffness and micro-vascular damage – contribute to memory impairment and the pathogenesis of dementia, including Alzheimer's disease. Interventions that reduce aortic stiffness might delay memory decline among older individuals.

## BP and CV Risk during the Aging Process

In the general population, high BP and increased risk of morbidity and mortality are well correlated. This concept has dominated hypertension epidemiology as well as clinical trials, which have shown that in hypertensive subjects, the greater the decrease in systolic BP (SBP of diastolic BP (DBP), the greater the benefits, in terms of cardiovascular morbidity and mortality, are in all ages of both genders (Authors/Task Force et al., 2008). Although this is an appealing message in terms of public health policy, it may be misleading in terms of a pathophysiological explanation and clinical impact. For example, low DBP in young and middle-aged individuals mainly reflects low peripheral resistance and is associated with a lower cardiovascular risk than high DBP. By contrast, over age 65, when increased arterial stiffness is common, low DBP often reflects high arterial stiffness, rather than low peripheral resistance, especially in the presence of high pulse pressure (SBP-DBP) (Franklin et al., 1999; O'Rourke and Frolich, 1999; Benetos et al., 2000). This explains why in older people for a given SBP level, the lower the DBP the higher the cardiovascular risk (Franklin et al., 1999; O'Rourke and Frolich1999; Benetos et al., 2000; Safar and Smulyan, 2004). Therefore, low DBP in the aged is a sign of poor arterial health, and thus a marker of Cardiovascular Disease (CVD) morbidity and mortality. In addition, there is evidence that a very low DBP and high PP (e.g., SBP: 145 mmHg, DBP: 60 mmHg, PP: 85mmHg), as compared to higher DBP levels (e.g., SBP: 145 mmHg; DBP: 90 mmHg, PP: 55mmHg), is not only a marker but also a determinant of CV complications, since low DBP can compromise coronary perfusion and high PP increases cardiac afterload and arterial stress.

Furthermore, a similar inverse relationship with risk has also been observed with SBP in very old frail subjects (Molander et al., 2008; Benetos et al., 2012; Wu et al., 2017). In these people, the available data originates from observational studies that show no relationship, or even an inverse relationship, between systolic BP and morbidity and mortality (Molander et al., 2008; Benetos et al., 2012; Benetos et al., 2015; Benetos et al., 2016; Wu et al., 2017). These inverse relationships are partially related to the fact that several comorbidities in the very old lead to a decrease in SBP, making low SBP a marker of a poor general medical status. In addition, several studies have shown that in these very old, frail patients, the association between low SBP and increased morbidity and mortality was observed mostly in those taking antihypertensive medications (Aparicio et al., 2015; Benetos et al., 2015; Mossello et al., 2015) and less so among those whose BP's were spontaneously low. These results can be related to the failure of homeostatic mechanisms that maintain organ perfusion in the presence of medication-induced BP reduction. These results should lead physicians to less aggressive therapeutic strategies in very old, frail patients when considering anti-hypertensive therapy.

Data obtained in older subjects over the last twenty years has changed the dogma of the relationship between BP and cardiovascular risk, and demonstrates that most important is not the BP value itself, but the reason for its abnormality, the general functional status, and the degree of frailty of the patient.

## Do We Have to Reduce BP in Older Subjects?

In patients between 65 and 80 years old, there is strong evidence from a large number of clinical trials showing the benefits of BP lowering (Authors/Task Force et al., 2013). For these patients, international guidelines recommend that SBP lowering rather than DBP should be the main target of treatment. After the age of 80, there is now substantial evidence, mainly from the HYVET study (Beckett et al., 2008), for the beneficial effect of lowering an elevated SBP with drug treatment. Based on this observation, the 2013 ESC-ESH Guidelines (Authors/Task Force et al., 2013) for the management of arterial hypertension stated that in the elderly (over 80 years old) evidence is limited to individuals with initial SBP of >160 mmHg, whose SBP was reduced to values <150 mmHg. Therefore, this recommendation is evidence-based. More recently, the Systolic Blood Pressure Intervention Trial (SPRINT) (Williamson et al., 2006) showed that even in subjects 75 years and older, CVD outcomes and total mortality were reduced with intensive treatment as compared to the standard therapeutic strategies. However, similar to HYVET, SPRINT was conducted in selected populations that excluded the frailest subjects, those with clinically significant cognitive decline and dementia, those with several CVD and other comorbidities, and patients living in nursing homes. Therefore, the evidence for the beneficial effects of BP lowering after the age of 80 concerns relatively fit people with few comorbidities and the absence of major functional decline. Presently, there is no evidence favoring anti-hypertensive therapy for the most frail – very old subjects with major functional decline and loss of autonomy.

Taken together, the data indicates that a normal BP in younger and middle-age people can describe their arterial status as "good arterial health" in the vast majority of these individuals. In these subjects, complementary studies could add important information on target organ damage and CVD risk, but the simplicity of BP measurements has made this measurement the gold standard. However, as patients get older and exhibit increased arterial stiffness, comorbidities, and frailty, both DBP (after the age of 65–70 years) and SBP (in the very old, frail persons) are misleading. These BP values are strongly influenced by their underlying arterial state, which alters their ability to predict cardiovascular events and are further modified by the above-mentioned conditions. For these patients, direct measurements of arterial stiffness and other parameters of arterial aging (see below) can be a major aid in better assessment of CV risk.

## Noninvasive Methods to Measure Arteriosclerosis: Methodological Aspects and Clinical Interest

From Frederick Akbar Mahomed (Mahomed, 1872; O'Rourke, 1992) to Scipione Riva Rocci (Riva-rocci, 1896) and Nicolai Korotkoff (Korotkoff, 1906), methodological studies of large arteries began in the second part of the twentieth century and have continued to developed. Accurate tonometric recordings at different arterial sites (radial, carotid) and analysis of pressure waves by various algorithms (McEniery et al., 2005) have permitted the calculation of ascending aortic waveforms. In addition to the calculation of central BP, these records provide the means to define the elastic properties of the arterial wall and the timing of reflection waves (McEniery et al., 2005; Nichols and O'Rourke, 2006). Such analyses have allowed for better insight into the cardiovascular system, with more accuracy than the brachial BP measured with conventional cuff sphygmomanometers (O'Rourke and Seward, 2006; Benetos et al., 2011). In addition, such validated noninvasive methods permit the recording of arterial waveforms (O'Rourke and Gallagher, 1996; Avolio et al., 2009) in various arterial segments. Devices to determine the BP curve through analysis software are currently available (Pauca et al., 2001; Salvi et al., 2004) and provide additional significant knowledge about the mechanisms of the aging process within the arterial system.

## Analysis of Pressure Waveforms and Augmentation Index (Aix)

At a given location in the arterial tree, the amplitude of the PP corresponds to the difference between systolic peak and the end of the diastolic phase. BP amplification is defined as the rise of PP from the central aorta to the periphery and is mainly attributed to the elevation of SBP (McEniery et al., 2005; Nichols and O'Rourke, 2006; O'Rourke and Seward, 2006; Avolio et al., 2009) This systolic pressure is the summation of forward and backward (after reflection) BP waves. Propagation of the BP wave from the heart to the periphery occurs at a given pulse wave velocity (PWV). Depending on the PWV and the distance covered, the reflected wave from the periphery adds to the forward BP wave, at various times during the cardiac cycle. In the presence of a normal PWV, the arrival of the reflected waves at the central arteries occurs during diastole and does not contribute to increasing the SBP or PP. By contrast, in the presence of increased aortic PWV and/or arterial lesions that induce proximal (early) reflection sites, backward waves will arrive in the central aorta earlier during the systolic period and will contribute to an increase in central SBP and PP. These reflected waves can be identified and studied when central BP pulses are recorded. It is therefore possible to distinguish the initial anterograde systolic wave from the added reflection wave, called the "augmentation pressure." The ratio of augmentation pressure to PP is the augmentation index (Aix) and represents the percentage of the reflection waves that are part of the total PP amplitude (Nichols and O'Rourke, 2006; Avolio et al., 2009; Namasivayam et al., 2009). Aix increases with age and is higher in women than in men. Several factors, especially heart rate (HR), codetermine this parameter, particularly in the elderly (Segers et al., 2007).

## Pulse Pressure Amplification (PPA)

Pulse Pressure Amplification (PPA) is defined as the elevation of PP from the central aorta toward the periphery and is attributed to the elevation of SBP

(McEniery et al., 2005; Nichols and O'Rourke, 2006; Avolio et al., 2009). In a hydraulic system such as the cardiovascular system, pressure at the periphery (radial artery) is higher than in the center (carotid artery). This finding needs further explanation. In a mechanical hydraulic system, the objective is to minimize the loss of energy as the wave travels from the central part of the system toward the periphery. In the pulsatile cardiovascular system, by contrast, peripheral SBP is higher than central aortic SBP, located adjacent to the heart. Since the aim of the cardiovascular system is to distribute oxygen and nutritional elements to organs and peripheral tissues, it is important to reduce heart work as much as possible, while maintaining the peripheral pressure to support perfusion. Therefore, in the CV system, the ultimate goal is to achieve optimal peripheral perfusion with lowest cardiac effort. The process of amplification satisfies this physiological scheme: the higher the amplification, the lower the central BP, after-load, and cardiac work.

An important aspect of the reduction of the cardiac work/peripheral perfusion relation is heart rate regulation (Nichols and O'Rourke, 2006; O'Rourke and Seward, 2006). A slower heart rate is associated with reduced cardiac work and lower amplification. Indeed, the effects of a slow heart rate on cardiac work may be both positive (reduction in the number of systolic contractions) and negative (reduction of amplification). It is necessary to consider together PPA and HR in the general context when assessing total cardiac work. The reduction or disappearance of aortic-brachial PP amplification has been shown to be a significant predictor of all-cause mortality in end-stage renal disease patients undergoing hemodialysis (Safar et al., 2002). We showed that low PPA from central to peripheral arteries also predicts mortality and CV adverse effects in both middle-aged and very old subjects (Benetos et al., 2010; Benetos et al., 2012). Noteworthy, PPA is little dependent on BP levels (Benetos et al., 2012) and is therefore of importance in very old, frail people with low BP levels due to comorbidities. Several studies have shown that the different classes of anti-hypertensive drugs may impact differently on PPA (Williams et al., 2006). For example, angiotensin converting enzyme inhibitors (ACEI) and/or calcium channel blockers (CCB) have more pronounced effects on arterial elastic properties and peripheral resistance than beta blockade with atenolol, probably due to the HR lowering effect of the latter drug (London et al., 2004).

## Arterial Stiffness Measured by PWV

PWV is the speed with which the pulse wave advances through an arterial segment (Figure 9.3) (Young, 1809; Asmar et al., 1995; Nichols and O'Rourke, 2006). In order to measure PWV, it is necessary to record the pressure (or flow velocity waves) from two arterial segments and determine the distance that separates them. The calculated velocity is inversely proportional to the square root of arterial distensibility. The principle of PWV measurement was initially described in the nineteenth century (Young, 1809; Korteweg, 1878). Acquisition of the waves and calculation of the PWV have been simplified by using various

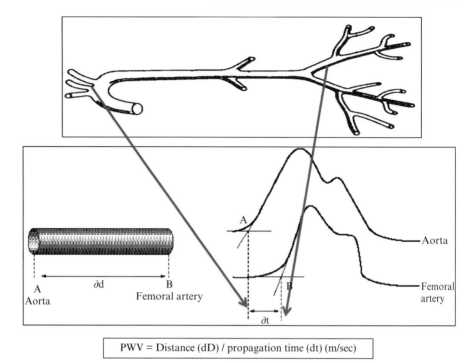

PWV = Distance (dD) / propagation time (dt) (m/sec)

**Figure 9.3.** *Pulse wave velocity (PWV) between carotid and femoral arteries by the use of a noninvasive device*

noninvasive devices and dedicated software (Pauca et al., 2001; Asmar et al., 1995; Asmar et al., 2001; Safar et al., 2006; Alecu et al., 2008; Joly et al., 2009). At the present time, carotid femoral PWV is considered to be the most reliable noninvasive method to evaluate aortic stiffness and assess its associated cardiovascular risk (Laurent et al., 2006).

Interestingly, the observed increase in carotid-femoral PWV with age is not linear, becoming more pronounced after the age of 55 (Benetos et al., 2002). The annual increase in PWV before the age of 50 is approximately 80–100 mm/sec (i.e., an annual increase of less than 1 percent) and rises to an annual increase of more than 150 mm/sec after the age of 60. Aside from age, other hemodynamic and biological parameters (Sehgel et al., 2013) modify the annual increase in PWV (Safar et al., 2006; Henry et al., 2003b). PWV is conventionally measured between the carotid and femoral arteries, and to a lesser extent in peripheral arteries, particularly of the upper and lower limbs (Benetos et al., 2010).

Over the past few years, aortic PWV has been shown to be a more powerful CV risk factor than mean arterial pressure, SBP or PP values (Willum-Hansen et al., 2006). This finding has been demonstrated not only in the general population but also in subgroups of patients, especially among hypertensive and diabetic subjects (Laurent et al., 2001; Laurent et al., 2003), patients with coronary heart disease (Boutouyrie et al., 2002; Mattace-Raso et al., 2006), very old subjects (Meaume et al., 2001), and hemodialysis patients (Blacher and Guerin, 1999; Shoji et al., 2001; Pannier et al., 2005). PWV is also considered as a marker of early atherosclerosis (Oliver and Webb, 2003). Risk assessment by use of the Framingham equations was linearly correlated with the sole measurement of PWV (Blacher et al., 1999a). The recommendations of the European Societies of Hypertension (ESH) and Cardiology (ESC) in 2013 (Authors/Task Force et al., 2013), point out the independent role of PWV in the risk of CV morbidity and mortality, and believe that a PWV >10 m/s should be considered as an abnormally high value associated with increased CV risk. Nevertheless, although arterial stiffness may serve as a useful biomarker to improve CV risk prediction, systematic evaluation of PWV in the general population was not recommended in the 2016 European Guidelines on cardiovascular disease prevention (Piepoli et al., 2016). PWV values according to age, gender, and presence of CV risk factors have been described in various populations (Pries et al., 1996). In addition, other studies have assessed values of PWV in children (Reusz et al., 2010), and very old, frail individuals (>80 years) (Benetos et al., 2010). For the same age and mean arterial pressure, PWV has been shown to be significantly higher in diabetic than in non-diabetic subjects (Smulyan et al., 2016a). Nevertheless, PWV values show a relative dependency on BP levels that can be problematic in very old, frail subjects with several comorbidities.

The Cardio-Ankle-Vascular-Index, CAVI, represents another noninvasive, easy to perform approach for a direct measurement of arterial stiffness (Shirai et al., 2006). CAVI is a function of the stiffness index ($\beta$) and is marginally influenced by BP levels during the CAVI measurements (Smulyan et al., 2016b). The stiffness index ($\beta$) relies on relative changes in arterial diameter ($\Delta D/D$) to the SBP/DBP ratio over a cardiac cycle, according to the equation: $\ln(SBP/DBP) = \beta(\Delta D/D)$ and thus $\beta = (\ln(SBP/DBP))/(\Delta D/D)$. The stiffness Index $\beta$ is the tangent line of the pressure/diameter relationship during the cardiac cycle and reflects the intrinsic elastic properties of the arterial wall (Hayashi et al., 1980). Thus measurements of the CAVI may have value for the measurements of arterial stiffness, especially in older individuals.

Noninvasive arterial measurements including analysis of central and peripheral arterial waveforms and assessment of PWV and CAVI constitute reliable and noninvasive measurements in the study of arterial aging. In very old people, assessment of mechanical elastic properties using methods that are not influenced by BP levels (PPA, CAVI) may be of particular interest.

## Influence of Metabolic Factors, Diet, and Physical Activity on Arterial Stiffness

Although chronological age is a major determinant of increased arterial stiffness, several other factors also influence the early appearance of changes associated with aging.

## Diabetes

The dramatic increase in obesity and associated metabolic disorders has an important impact on arterial health and aging. Diabetes is a major determinant of accelerated arterial aging and increased stiffness (Henry et al., 2003b; Smulyan et al., 2016a). Very old adults with diabetes exhibit a 20 percent increase in arterial stiffness, compared with non-diabetic subjects of the same age (Salvi et al., 2010). Non-enzymatic glycation of arterial collagen may represent a major mechanism of the effects of diabetes across the entire arterial tree, especially in large arteries. Endothelial dysfunction, commonly observed in diabetics, may also contribute to this effect, even if the relationship between endothelial function and arterial stiffness remains poorly understood.

## Obesity and Metabolic Factors

Changes in body composition in men and women occur with aging with exponential loss of lean tissues (Genton et al., 2011). The prevalence of metabolic syndrome (MetS) dramatically increases with age until the age of 60 years (Akbulut et al., 2011). This is observed in both developed (Pannier et al., 2006) and even more frequently in developing countries (Temmar et al., 2007; Temmar et al., 2013). Therefore, MetS has become, at the present time, a pandemic disease with major consequences for public health. Presence of MetS is associated with a greater increase of stiffness during the aging process (Safar et al., 2006).

Obesity raises BP and increases cardiovascular risk, making weight loss in the obese an obvious therapeutic goal. The mechanisms by which weight loss in the obese lowers BP remain obscure, but possible factors include reduction of insulin resistance, sympathetic stimulation, inflammation, angiotensin II, and/or increased arterial stiffness. Studies that investigate weight loss as a means for lowering arterial stiffness are observational in design and face multiple other interpretive difficulties. Weight loss may be intentional or unintentional and life style modifications for diet and exercise are often not faithfully followed, especially over long periods. Age makes a difference. In obese children, weight loss prior to reaching adult life lowers their CV risks to normal (Juonala et al., 2011) and in the adult population, intentional weight loss results in a reduction of all obesity related comorbidities (Rueda-Clausen et al., 2015). However, dietary weight loss among the elderly may be of little benefit (Shea et al., 2011) or even harmful, since it reduces muscle mass (and strength) as well as adipose tissue (Miller and Wolfe, 2008). The evaluation of weight loss in middle-aged subjects has been facilitated by studies in patients undergoing bariatric surgery (Sjöström, 2013), but the effect of weight loss surgery on stiffness remains to be established. Despite these caveats, the results of several studies suggest that dietary weight loss in middle-aged adults may be efficacious in reducing large artery stiffness (Toto-Moukouo et al., 1986; Balkestein et al., 1999; Services, 2005; Barinas-Mitchell et al., 2006; Miyaki et al., 2009). Balkestein et al. (1999) reported that weight loss increased carotid artery distensibility, but that exercise did not result in an additive effect. Dengo et al. (2010) tested the hypothesis that weight loss via hypocaloric diet would reduce arterial stiffness in overweight and obese middle-aged and older adults. In this study, 36 individuals were randomly assigned to a weight loss or a control group. Body weight, body fat, abdominal adiposity, blood pressure, stiffness index, and carotid-femoral PWV were similar in the two groups at baseline. Brachial systolic and diastolic BP declined only in the weight loss group. Aortic stiffness index, largely independent of the BP and carotid-femoral PWV, adjusted for the BP, decreased in the weight loss group but not in the control group. The reduction in carotid-femoral PWV correlated with a reduction in total body and abdominal adiposity. These results, associated with other clinical studies, indicate that weight loss reduces arterial stiffness in overweight/obese middle-aged and older adults, and that the magnitude of these improvements is related to the loss of total and abdominal adiposity (Wildman et al., 2005).

## Effects of Nutrients and Diet Patterns

The effects of individual micro- and macro-nutrients and diet patterns on arterial stiffness have been studied in a number of clinical and epidemiological studies (Sacre et al., 2014). Presently, there is no convincing evidence for a consistent beneficial effect of vitamin supplementation or other micronutrients (Pase et al., 2011). Systematic reviews showed that Vitamin D supplementation was not associated with consistent benefits on arterial stiffness (Upala et al., 2016), whereas supplementation with antioxidant vitamins (Vitamin C, E, A, and beta-carotene) had a small, protective effect (Ashor, 2014). Salt restriction has also been shown to have a favorable effect (Pase et al., 2011; Sacre et al., 2014). High intake of fruits and vegetables in adolescence and young adulthood was also associated with lower aortic stiffness in adulthood (Aatola et al., 2010). Reduced arterial stiffness has been associated with the increasing intake of dairy products (Crichton et al., 2012) and soy isoflavones (Pase et al., 2011). Omega-3 fatty acids may be of particular importance. Observational studies have associated high intake of fish, rich in eicosapentaenoic and docosahexanoic acid, with lower arterial stiffness. Interventional studies evaluating the effects of omega-3 supplementation on arterial stiffness have however generated contradictory results, which is the case also for studies of omega-3 in cardiovascular disease prevention (Piepoli et al., 2016). A recent study however reported that 12 weeks of omega-3 supplementation decreased PWV in older, but not younger subjects (with no effect on BP or arterial wave reflection) (Monahan et al., 2015). The mechanisms of the potential beneficial effects of omega-3 fatty acids on arterial stiffness remain to be established, but could potentially involve the formation of a group of lipid mediators, referred to as resolvins, which are derived from the enzymatic metabolism of omega-3 fatty acids (Bäck and Powell, 2014; Serhan, 2014), and which have gained recent interest as predictors of a beneficial vascular profile (Thul et al., 2017).

Investigating dietary patterns, rather than individual nutrients is of high interest, especially in studies dealing with aging, rather than specific diseases and may better capture synergistic long-term health effects of these patterns. A recent study investigated whether long-term adherence to a Mediterranean dietary during adolescence and early adulthood has an impact on arterial stiffness later in life (van de Laar et al., 2013). This study showed that subjects who better adhered to a Mediterranean dietary pattern throughout 24 years of adolescence and early adulthood had reduced arterial stiffness in later life. Interestingly, these possible beneficial effects were only partially related to the known effects of the Mediterranean diet on classical CV risk factors such as blood pressure and body composition. These results of long-term observational studies should be confirmed in controlled randomized interventional studies.

## Role of Physical Activity

Several studies (Cole et al., 1999; Haskell et al., 2007; Leeper et al., 2007; Sacre et al., 2014) have now shown that increased physical activity is of value in improving the opportunities for healthy aging, especially in subjects at high cardiovascular risk. Despite the salutary reputation of exercise as an overall benefit for CV health, its studied effects on arterial stiffening are few. Several years ago, Cameron and Dart showed in sedentary young adults (Cameron and Dart, 1994) that aerobic exercise improved systemic arterial compliance after a short-term training period (a few weeks). Recently, in the short term (4 weeks), exercise training reduced arterial stiffness but the long-term benefit was difficult to demonstrate (Sacre et al., 2014). Thus far, limited studies on the effects of exercise on the stiffened aorta of aging have failed to show significant effects on aortic properties (Shibata and Levine, 2012). These results argue for exercise-mediated arterial adaptations being predominantly functional rather than structural in origin. However increased physical activity is difficult to maintain over long periods in the elderly, especially in those with other clinical conditions. Furthermore, the noninvasive study of specific vascular territories, such as those related to coronary collateral growth, remains the object of research (Mobius-Winkler et al., 2016).

## Effects of Drug Treatment

In subjects with hypertension, aortic stiffness and wave reflections can be lowered using conventional agents as thiazide diuretics, angiotensin converting enzyme inhibitors (ACEIs), various angiotensin blockers, and calcium channels blockers (CCBs) (Mitchell et al., 2007; Mackenzie et al., 2009; Ait-Oufella et al., 2010; Ong et al., 2011; Shahin et al., 2012). Their primary mode of action is to reduce the total vascular resistance and, by doing so, lower the primarily raised mean arterial pressure, and thus the SBP and DBP. These drugs, especially CCBs, are widely and effectively used in systolic hypertension but have a separate, limited, and even controversial effect on aortic stiffness independent of mean arterial pressure (Mackenzie et al., 2009; Ait-Oufella et al., 2010; Ong et al., 2011; Shahin et al., 2012; Townsend et al., 2015). Their limited ability to reduce the aortic stiffness of aging accounts for the therapeutic difficulty encountered clinically in lowering the SBP and PP in older subjects. Nonetheless, there is unequivocal evidence that treatment of isolated systolic hypertension with standard antihypertensive therapy is beneficial (Group, 1991; Staessen et al., 1997; Williamson et al., 2016). However, three observations are important to discuss within this clinical approach. First, the treatment combining ACE inhibition and CCB (Chi et al., 2016) has been shown to be superior to other combinations in term of anti-hypertensive effect. Second, in long-term trials, ACEI, CCBs, beta-blockers, and diuretics all reduce significantly and equally aortic stiffness compared to placebo (Ong et al., 2011). Third, at least in ESRD subjects, drug treatment significantly reduces not only aortic stiffness but also wave reflections (London et al., 2016) through changes in the augmentation index.

There remains an unmet need in the management of hypertension for the large and growing number of affected elderly patients for other agents that more directly focus on therapeutic objectives to improve central artery stiffness (Smulyan et al., 2016b). Aldosterone inhibition is known to have a particular effect on CV fibrosis and stiffness (Benetos et al., 1997; Edwards et al., 2009), particularly regarding some genotypes (Safar et al., 2005), but has not yet been clinically well studied for this indication. Breakers of collagen cross-links, such as alagebrium, more directly attack aortic stiffness (Kass et al., 2001) but have failed due to severe adverse effects. Efforts to delay or reduce aortic elastin fragmentation using matrix metalloproteinase inhibitors (Wang et al., 2012) offer some hope in this direction, but have not been clinically tested. Because of a suspected role for inflammation in aortic stiffness (Roman et al., 2005), anti-inflammatory agents have been tried but only in limited circumstances (Maki-Petaja et al., 2006; Maki-Petaja et al., 2007). A promising recent therapeutic candidate, vasopeptidase inhibitor (sacubitril), inhibits both ACE and neprilysin (a neutral endopeptidase), which inactivates natriuretic peptides such as atrial and brain peptides. The inhibition of neprilysin permits greater activity of atrial and brain natriuretic peptides, both of which have natriuretic and antihypertensive actions. Recent clinical studies using this neprilysin inhibitor in combination with an angiotensin receptor antagonist demonstrated good antihypertensive effect and safety (Reference Values for Arterial Stiffness, 2010; Kario et al., 2014; Williams et al., 2017). However, larger studies are needed in order to confirm safety and evaluate the potentially beneficial effect on arterial stiffness.

## Conclusions and Perspectives

In the vast majority of young and middle-age populations, the lower the BP levels the better the arterial health. In this group and for this reason, BP levels are closely correlated with CV risk. In these subjects, evaluation of arterial stiffness, especially in hypertensive and other high-risk subjects, could add important information on target organ damage and CVD risk. But by comparison, the simplicity of BP measurements has made this measurement a gold standard. However, for DBP after the age of 65 years and for SBP in the very old and frail, low BP levels are often due to an aged arterial system in an aged individual with a high degree of frailty and loss of function and autonomy. This and comorbidities may therefore reflect poor arterial health and a frail general status. Therefore, BP measurements alone can provide erroneous information. In very old populations it is therefore crucial to measure arterial stiffness, a good indicator of arterial health, especially when measured using methods that are less influenced by BP levels. Other biomarkers of vascular aging and systemic frailty could be of major help to better characterize global risk.

## References

Aatola, H., T. Koivistoinen, N. Hutri-Kahonen et al. Lifetime fruit and vegetable consumption and arterial pulse wave velocity in adulthood: The Cardiovascular Risk in Young Finns Study. *Circulation* 2010;122: 2521–8.

Ait-Oufella, H., C. Collin, E. Bozec et al. Long-term reduction in aortic stiffness: A 5.3-year follow-up in routine clinical practice. *J Hypertens*, 2010;28(11): 2336–41.

Akbulut, G., E. Koksal, S. Bilici et al. Metabolic syndrome (MS) in elderly: A cross sectional survey. *Arch Gerontol Geriatr.* 2011;53: e263–6.

Alecu, C., C. Labat, A. Kearney-Schwartz et al. Reference values of aortic pulse wave velocity in the elderly. *J Hypertens*, 2008;26(11): 2207–12.

Al Hazzouri, A. Z., A. B. Newman, E. Simonsick et al. Pulse wave velocity and cognitive decline in elders: The Health, Aging, and Body Composition study. *Stroke*, 2013;44: 388–93.

Ambrosy, A. P., G. C. Fonarow, J. Butler et al. The global health and economic burden of hospitalizations for heart failure: Lessons learned from hospitalized heart failure registries. *J Am Coll Cardiol.* 2014;63: 1123–33.

Aparicio, L. S., L. Thijs, J. Boggia Defining thresholds for home blood pressure monitoring octogenarians. *Hypertension.* 2015;66: 865–73.

Ashor, A. W., M. Siervo, J. Lara, C. Oggioni, J. C. Mathers Antioxidant vitamin supplementation reduces arterial stiffness in adults: A systematic review and meta-analysis of randomized controlled trials. *J Nutr.* 2014;144(10): 1594–602.

Asmar, R., A. Benetos, J. Topouchian et al. Assessment of arterial distensibility by automatic pulse wave velocity measurement. Validation and clinical application studies. *Hypertension*, 1995;26(3): 485–90.

Asmar, R. G., G. M. London, M. E. O'Rourke, and M. E. Safar Improvement in blood pressure, arterial stiffness and wave reflections with a very-low-dose perindopril/ indapamide combination in hypertensive patient: A comparison with atenolol. *Hypertension*, 2001;38: 922–6.

Authors/Task Force M., Mancia G., Fagard R., Narkiewicz K. et al. 2013 ESH/ESC Guidelines for the management of arterial hypertension: The Task Force for the management of arterial hypertension of the European Society of Hypertension (ESH) and of the European Society of Cardiology (ESC). *Eur Heart J.* 2013;34:2159–219.

Avolio, A. P., L. M. Van Bortel, P. Boutouyrie et al. Role of pulse pressure amplification in arterial hypertension: Experts' opinion and review of the data. *Hypertension*, 2009;54(2): 375–83.

Bäck, M., W. S. Powell, S. E. Dahlén et al. Update on leukotriene, lipoxin and oxoeicosanoid receptors: IUPHAR Review 7. *Br J Pharmacol.* 2014;171: 3551

Balkestein, E. J., D. P. van Aggel-Leijssen, M. A. van Baak, H. A. Struijker-Boudier, L. M. Van Bortel The effect of weight loss with or without exercise training on large artery compliance in healthy obese men. *J Hypertens*, 1999;17(12 Pt 2): 1831–5.

Barinas-Mitchell, E., L. H. Kuller, K. Sutton-Tyrrell et al. Effect of weight loss and nutritional intervention on arterial stiffness in type 2 diabetes. *Diabetes Care*, 2006;29(10): 2218–22.

Beckett, N. S., R. Peters, A. E. Fletcher et al. Treatment of hypertension in patients 80 years of age or older. *N Engl J Med*, 2008;358(18): 1887–98.

Benetos, A., S. Gautier, C. Labat et al. Mortality and cardiovascular events are best predicted by low central/peripheral pulse pressure amplification but not by high blood pressure levels in elderly nursing home subjects: The PARTAGE study. *J Am Coll Cardiol.* 2012;60: 1503–11.

Benetos, A., C. Adamopoulos, J. M. Bureau et al. Determinants of accelerated progression of arterial stiffness in normotensive subjects and in treated hypertensive subjects over a 6-year period. *Circulation*, 2002;105(10): 1202–7.

Benetos, A., S. Buatois, P. Salvi et al. Blood pressure and pulse wave velocity values in the institutionalized elderly aged 80 and over: Baseline of the PARTAGE study. *J Hypertens*, 2010;28(1): 41–50.

Benetos, A., C. J. Bulpitt, M. Petrovic et al. An Expert Opinion From the European Society of Hypertension-European Union Geriatric Medicine Society Working Group on the Management of Hypertension in Very Old, Frail Subjects. *Hypertension*, 2016;67(5): 820–5.

Benetos, A., C. Labat, P. Rossignol et al. Treatment with multiple blood pressure medicines, achieved blood pressure, and mortality in older nursing home residents. *JAMA Intern Med.* 2015;175: 989–95

Benetos, A., P. Lacolley, M. E. Safar Prevention of aortic fibrosis by spironolactone in spontaneously hypertensive rats. *Arterioscler Thromb Vasc Biol*, 1997;17(6): 1152–6.

Benetos, A., P. Rossignol, A. Cherubini et al. Polypharmacy in the aging patient: Management of hypertension in octogenarians. *JAMA*, 2015;314(2): 170–80.

Benetos, A., P. Salvi, and P. Lacolley, Blood pressure regulation during the aging process: the end of the "hypertension era"? *J Hypertens*, 2011;29(4): 646–52.

Benetos, A., A. Thomas, L. Joly et al. Pulse pressure amplification, a mechanical biomarker of cardiovascular risk. *J Am Coll Cardiol*, 2010;55: 1032–37.

Benetos, A., M. Zureik, J. Morcet et al. A decrease in diastolic blood pressure combined with an increase in systolic blood pressure is associated with a higher cardiovascular mortality in men. *J Am Coll Cardiol.* 2000;35: 673–80.

Blacher, J., R. Asmar, S. Djane, G. M. London, M. E. Safar Aortic pulse wave velocity as a marker of cardiovascular risk in hypertensive patients. *Hypertension*, 1999a;33(5): 1111–17.

Blacher, J., A. P. Guerin, B. Pannier, S. J. Marchais, M. E. Safar, G. M. London Impact of aortic stiffness on survival in end-stage renal disease. *Circulation*, 1999b;99(18): 2434–9.

Boutouyrie, P., A. I. Tropeano, R. Asmar et al. Aortic stiffness is an independent predictor of primary coronary events in hypertensive patients: A longitudinal study. *Hypertension*, 2002;39(1): 10–15.

Braunwald, E. Heart failure. *JACC Heart Fail.* 2013;1: 1–20.

Cameron, J. D., Dart A. M. Exercise training increases total systemic arterial compliance in humans. *Am J Physiol.* 1994;266(2 Pt 2): H693–H701.

Chi, C., C. Tai, B. Bai et al. Angiotensin system blockade combined with calcium channel blockers is superior to other combinations in cardiovascular protection with similar blood pressure reduction: A meta-analysis in 20,451 hypertensive patients. *J Clin Hypertens (Greenwich)*, 2016;18:801–8.

Cole, C. R., E. H. Blackstone, F. J. Pashkow, C. E. Snader, M. S. Lauer Heart-rate recovery immediately after exercise as a predictor of mortality. *N Engl J Med*, 1999;341(18): 1351–7.

Crichton G. E., M. F. Elias, G. A. Dore, W. P. Abhayaratna, M. A. Robbins Relations between dairy food intake and arterial stiffness. Pulse wave velocity and pulse pressure. *Hypertension* 2012;59: 1044–51.

Dengo, A. L., E. A. Dennis, J. S. Orr et al. Arterial destiffening with weight loss in overweight and obese middle-aged and older adults. *Hypertension*, 2010;55(4): 855–61.

Edwards, N. C., R. P. Steeds, P. M. Stewart, C. J. Ferro, J. N. Townend Effect of spironolactone on left ventricular mass and aortic stiffness in early-stage chronic kidney disease: A randomized controlled trial. *J Am Coll Cardiol*, 2009;54(6): 505–12.

Franklin, S. S., S. A. Khan, N. D. Wong, M. G. Larson, D. Levy Is pulse pressure useful in predicting risk for coronary heart disease? *Circulation.* 1999;100: 354–60.

Genton L., V. L. Karsegard, T. Chevalley, M. P. Kossovsky, P. Darmon, C. Pichard Body composition changes over 9 years in healthy elderly subjects and impact of physical activity. *Clin Nutr.* 2011;30: 436–42.

Group, S. C. R., Prevention of stroke by antihypertensive drug treatment in older persons with isolated systolic hypertension. Final results of the Systolic Hypertension in the Elderly Program (SHEP). SHEP Cooperative Research Group. *JAMA*, 1991;265(24): 3255–64.

Haskell, W. L., I. M. Lee, R. R. Pate et al. Physical activity and public health: Updated recommendation for adults from the American College of Sports Medicine and the American Heart Association. *Med Sci Sports Exerc*, 2007;39(8): 1423–34.

Hayashi, K., Handa H., Nagasawa S., Okumura A., Moritake K. Stiffness and elastic behavior of human intracranial and extracranial arteries. *J Biomechanics* 1980;13: 175–84.

Henry, O. F., J. Blacher, J. Verdavaine, M. Duviquet, M. E. Safar Alpha 1-acid glycoprotein is an independent predictor of in-hospital death in the elderly. *Age Ageing*, 2003a;32(1): 37–42.

Henry, R. M., P. J. Kostense, A. M. Spijkerman et al. Arterial stiffness increases with deteriorating glucose tolerance status: The Hoorn Study. *Circulation.* 2003b;107: 2089–95.

Hughes, T. M., S. Craft, O. L. Lopez. Review of "the potential role of arterial stiffness in the pathogenesis of Alzheimer's disease." *Neurodegener Dis Manag.* 2015;5(2): 121–35.

Joly, L., C. Perret-Guillaume, A. Kearney-Schwartz et al. Pulse wave velocity assessment by external noninvasive devices and phase-contrast magnetic resonance imaging in the obese. *Hypertension*, 2009;54(2): 421–6.

Juonala, M., C. G. Magnussen, G. S. Berenson et al. Childhood adiposity, adult adiposity, and cardiovascular risk factors. *N Eng J Med* 2011;365(20): 1876–85.

Kane, G. C., B. L. Karon, D. W. Mahoney et al. Progression of left ventricular diastolic dysfunction and risk of heart failure. *JAMA*. 2011;306: 856–63.

Kario, K., N. Sun, F. T. Chiang et al. Efficacy and safety of LCZ696, a first-in-class angiotensin receptor neprilysin inhibitor, in Asian patients with hypertension: a randomized, double-blind, placebo-controlled study. *Hypertension*, 2014;63(4): 698–705.

Kass, D. A., E. P. Shapiro, M. Kawaguchi et al. Improved arterial compliance by a novel advanced glycation end-product crosslink breaker. *Circulation*, 2001;104(13): 1464–70.

Kearney-Schwartz, A., P. Rossignol, S. Bracard et al. Vascular structure and function is correlated to cognitive performance and white matter hyperintensities in older hypertensive patients with subjective memory complaints. *Stroke*, 2009;40: 1229–36.

Korotkoff, N., On method of studying blood pressure. *Bull Imperial Acad Med (St Petersburg)*, 1906;365–7.

Korteweg, D. J. Über die Fortpflanzungsgeschwindigkeit des Schalles in Elastischen Röhren. *Annalen der Physik*. 1878;241(12): 525–42.

Lakatta, E. G., Arterial and cardiac aging: Major shareholders in cardiovascular disease enterprises: Part III: cellular and molecular clues to heart and arterial aging. *Circulation*, 2003;107(3): 490–7.

Laurent, S., P. Boutouyrie, R. Asmar et al. Aortic stiffness is an independent predictor of all-cause and cardiovascular mortality in hypertensive patients. *Hypertension*, 2001;37(5): 1236–41.

Laurent, S., J. Cockcroft, L. Van Bortel et al. Expert consensus document on arterial stiffness: Methodological issues and clinical applications. *Eur Heart J*, 2006;27(21): 2588–605.

Laurent, S., S. Katsahian, C. Fassot et al. Aortic stiffness is an independent predictor of fatal stroke in essential hypertension. *Stroke*, 2003;34(5): 1203–6.

Leeper, N. J., F. E. Dewey, E. A. Ashley et al. Prognostic value of heart rate increase at onset of exercise testing. *Circulation*, 2007;115(4): 468–74.

London, G. M., M. E. Safar, B. Pannier. Aortic aging in ESRD: Structural, hemodynamic, and mortality implications. *J Am Soc Nephrol*, 2016;27(6): 1837–46.

London, G. M., R. G. Asmar, M. F. O'Rourke, M. E. Safar, REASON Project Investigators Mechanism(s) of selective systolic blood pressure reduction after a low-dose combination of perindopril/indapamide in hypertensive subjects: Comparison with atenolol. *J Am Coll Cardiol*, 2004;43: 92–9.

Mackenzie, I. S., C. M. McEniery, Z. Dhakam, M. J. Brown, J. R. Cockcroft, I. B. Wilkinson Comparison of the effects of antihypertensive agents on central blood pressure and arterial stiffness in isolated systolic hypertension. *Hypertension*, 2009;54(2): 409–13.

Mahomed, F. The physiology and clinical use of the sphygmograph. *Med Times Gazette*, 1872; 62.

Maki-Petaja, K. M., A. D. Booth, F. C. Hall et al. Ezetimibe and simvastatin reduce inflammation, disease activity, and aortic stiffness and improve endothelial function in rheumatoid arthritis. *J Am Coll Cardiol*, 2007;50(9): 852–8.

Maki-Petaja, K. M., F. C. Hall, A. D. Booth et al. Rheumatoid arthritis is associated with increased aortic pulse-wave velocity, which is reduced by anti-tumor necrosis factor-alpha therapy. *Circulation*, 2006;114(11): 1185–92.

Mattace-Raso, F. U., T. J. van der Cammen, A. Hofman et al. Arterial stiffness and risk of coronary heart disease and stroke: The Rotterdam Study. *Circulation*, 2006;113(5): 657–63.

McEniery, C. M., I. R. Hall, A. Qasem, I. B. Wilkinson, and J. R. Cockcroft Normal vascular aging: Aifferential effects on wave reflection and aortic pulse wave velocity: The Anglo-Cardiff Collaborative Trial (ACCT). *J Am Coll Cardiol*, 2005;46(9): 1753–60.

Meaume, S., A. Benetos, O. F. Henry, A. Rudnichi, and M. E. Safar Aortic pulse wave velocity predicts cardiovascular mortality in subjects >70 years of age. *Arterioscler Thromb Vasc Biol*, 2001;21(12): 2046–50.

Miller S. L., R. R. Wolfe The danger of weight loss in the elderly. *J Nutrition, Health and Aging* 2008;12(7): 2008.

Mitchell, G. F., M. E. Dunlap, W. Warnica et al. Long-term trandolapril treatment is associated with reduced aortic stiffness: The prevention of events with angiotensin-converting enzyme inhibition hemodynamic substudy. *Hypertension*, 2007;49(6): 1271–7.

Miyaki, A., S. Maeda, M. Yoshizawa et al. Effect of weight reduction with dietary intervention on arterial distensibility and endothelial function in obese men. *Angiology*, 2009;60(3): 351–7.

Mobius-Winkler, S., M. Uhlemann, V. Adams et al. Coronary collateral growth induced by physical exercise: Results of the impact of intensive exercise training on coronary collateral circulation in patients with stable coronary artery disease (EXCITE) Trial. *Circulation*, 2016;133(15): 1438–48.

Molander L., H. Lovheim, T. Norman et al. Lower systolic blood pressure is associated with greater mortality in people aged 85 and older. *J Am Geriatr Soc.* 2008;56: 1853–9.

Monahan K. D., R. P. Feehan, C. Blaha, D. J. McLaughlin Effect of omega-3 polyunsaturated fatty acid supplementation on central arterial stiffness and arterial wave reflections in young and older healthy adults. *Physiol Rep.* 2015;3(6) pii: e12438.

Mossello E., M. Pieraccioli, N. Nesti et al. Effects of low blood pressure in cognitively impaired elderly patients treated with antihypertensive drugs. *JAMA Intern Med.* 2015;175: 578–85.

Namasivayam, M., B. J. McDonnell, C. M. McEniery, M. F. O'Rourke, I. Anglo-Cardiff Collaborative Trial Study, Does wave reflection dominate age-related change in aortic blood pressure across the human life span? *Hypertension*, 2009;53(6): 979–85.

Nichols, W. W., M. F. O'Rourke *McDonald's Blood Flow in Arteries. Theoretical, Experimental and Clinical Principles*, fourth ed. 2006, Edward Arnold: London. p. 49–94, 193–233, 339–402, 435–502.

O'Rourke, M. F., E. D. Frolich Pulse pressure: Is this a clinically useful risk factor? *Hypertension.* 1999;34: 372–4.

Oliver, J. J., D. J. Webb Noninvasive assessment of arterial stiffness and risk of atherosclerotic events. *Arterioscler Thromb Vasc Biol*, 2003;23(4): 554–66.

Ong, K. T., S. Delerme, B. Pannier et al. Aortic stiffness is reduced beyond blood pressure lowering by short-term and long-term antihypertensive treatment: A meta-analysis of individual data in 294 patients. *J Hypertens*, 2011;29(6): 1034–42.

O'Rourke, M. F., D. E. Gallagher, Pulse wave analysis. *J Hypertens Suppl*, 1996;14(5): S147–57.

O'Rourke, M. F., Mahomed. Frederick Akbar *Hypertension*, 1992;19(2): 212–17.

O'Rourke, M. F., J. B. Seward, Central arterial pressure regulation during the aging process: new views entering the second century after Korotkoff. *Mayo Clin Proc*, 2006;81: 1057–68.

O'Rourke M. F., Safar M. E., Dzau V. The Cardiovascular Continuum extended: Aging effects on the aorta and microvasculature. *Vasc Med.* 2010;15(6): 461–8.

Pannier, B., A. P. Guerin, S. J. Marchais, M. E. Safar, and G. M. London, Stiffness of capacitive and conduit arteries: Prognostic significance for end-stage renal disease patients. *Hypertension*, 2005;45(4): 592–6.

Pannier B., Thomas F., Eschwege E. et al. Cardiovascular risk markers associated with the metabolic syndrome in a large French population: The "SYMFONIE" study. *Diabetes Metab.* 2006;32: 467–74.

Pase M. P., N. A. Grima, J. Sarris The effects of dietary and nutrient interventions on arterial stiffness: A systematic review. *Am J Clin Nutr* 2011;93: 446–54.

Pauca, A. L., M. F. O'Rourke, and N. D. Kon, Prospective evaluation of a method for estimating ascending aortic pressure from the radial artery pressure waveform. *Hypertension*, 2001;38(4): 932–7.

Piepoli M. F., A. W. Hoes, S. Agewall European Guidelines on cardiovascular disease prevention in clinical practice: The Sixth Joint Task Force of the European Society of Cardiology and Other Societies on Cardiovascular Disease Prevention in Clinical Practice. *European Heart Journal* 2016;37: 2315–81.

Pries, A. R., T. W. Secomb, P. Gaehtgens, Biophysical aspects of blood flow in the microvasculature. *Cardiovasc Res*, 1996;32: 654–67.

Rabkin, S. W. Arterial stiffness: Detection and consequences in cognitive impairment and dementia of the elderly. *Journal of Alzheimer's Disease* 2012;32: 541–9.

Reference Values for Arterial Stiffness, C. Determinants of pulse wave velocity in healthy people and in the presence of cardiovascular risk factors: "Establishing normal and reference values." *Eur Heart J*, 2010;31(19): 2338–50.

Reusz, G. S., O. Cseprekal, M. Temmar et al. Reference values of pulse wave velocity in healthy children and teenagers. *Hypertension*, 2010;56(2): 217–24.

Riva-rocci S. Un nuovo sfigmomanometro. *Gazzetta Medica di Torino*, 1896;50: 981–96.

Roman, M. J., R. B. Devereux, J. E. Schwartz et al. Arterial stiffness in chronic inflammatory diseases. *Hypertension*, 2005;46(1): 194–9.

Rueda-Clausen, C. F., A. A. Ogunleye, A. M. Sharma Health benefits of long-term weight-loss maintenance. *Annu Rev Nutr* 2015;35: 475–516.

Sacre, J. W., G. L. Jennings, B. A. Kingwell Exercise and dietary influences on arterial stiffness in cardiometabolc disease. *Hypertension* 2014;63: 888–93.

Safar, M. E., H. Smulyan Coronary ischemic disease, arterial stiffness, and pulse pressure. *Am J Hypertens.* 2004;17: 724–6.

Safar, M. E., J. Blacher, B. Pannier et al. Central pulse pressure and mortality in end-stage renal disease. *Hypertension*, 2002;39(3): 735–8.

Safar, M. E., V. Cattan, P. Lacolley et al. Aldosterone synthase gene polymorphism, stroke volume and age-related changes in aortic pulse wave velocity in subjects with hypertension. *J Hypertens*, 2005;23: 1159–66.

Safar, M. E., F. Thomas, J. Blacher et al. Metabolic syndrome and age-related progression of aortic stiffness. *J Am Coll Cardiol*, 2006;47(1): 72–5.

Saji, N., K. Kimura, H. Shimizu, Y. Kita. Association between silent brain infarct and arterial stiffness indicated by brachial-ankle pulse wave velocity. *Int Med* 2012;51: 1003–8.

Salvi, P., M. E. Safar, C. Labat et al. Heart disease and changes in pulse wave velocity and pulse pressure amplification in the elderly over 80 years: The PARTAGE Study. *J Hypertens.* 2010;28: 2127–33.

Salvi, P., G. Lio, C. Labat, E. Ricci, B. Pannier, and A. Benetos Validation of a new non-invasive portable tonometer for determining arterial pressure wave and pulse wave velocity: The PulsePen device. *J Hypertens*, 2004;22(12): 2285–93.

Satizabal C. L., A. S. Beiser, V. Chouraki, G. Chene, C. Dufouil, S. Seshadri Incidence of dementia over three decades in the Framingham Heart Study, *N Engl J Med* 2016;374: 523–32.

Scuteri A., M. Tesauro, L. Guglini, D. Lauro, M. Fini, N. Di Daniele Aortic stiffness and hypotension episodes are associated with impaired cognitive function in older subjects with subjective complaints of memory loss. *Intern J Cardiol* 2013;169: 371–7.

Segers, P., E. R. Rietzschel, M. L. De Buyzere et al. Noninvasive (input) impedance, pulse wave velocity, and wave reflection in healthy middle-aged men and women. *Hypertension*, 2007;49(6): 1248–55.

Sehgel, N. L., Y. Zhu, Z. Sun et al. Increased vascular smooth muscle cell stiffness: a novel mechanism for aortic stiffness in hypertension. *Am J Physiol Heart Circ Physiol*, 2013;305(9): H1281–7.

Serhan, C. N. Pro-resolving lipid mediators are leads for resolution physiology. *Nature.* 2014;510: 92.

Services, U.D.o.h.a.H., *Dietary Guidelines for American 2005*, ed. t. ed. 2005, Washington DC: US department of Agriculture.

Shahin, Y., J. A. Khan, I. Chetter, Angiotensin converting enzyme inhibitors effect on arterial stiffness and wave reflections: a meta-analysis and meta-regression of randomised controlled trials. *Atherosclerosis*, 2012;221(1): 18–33.

Shea, M. K., B. J. Nicklas, D. K. Houston et al. The effect of intentional weight loss on all-cause mortality on older adults: Results of a randomized controlled weight-loss trial. *Am J Clin Nutr* 2011;94: 839–46.

Shibata, S., B. D. Levine Effect of exercise training on biologic vascular age in healthy seniors. *Am J Physiol Heart.* 2012;302: H1340–6.

Shirai, K., J. Utino, K. Otsuka, M. Takata A novel blood pressure-independent arterial wall stiffness parameter; Cardio-ankle vascular index (CAVI). *J Atheroscler Thromb* 2006;13: 101–7.

Shoji, T., M. Emoto, K. Shinohara et al., Diabetes mellitus, aortic stiffness, and cardiovascular mortality in end-stage renal disease. *J Am Soc Nephrol*, 2001. 12(10): 2117–24.

Singer, J., J. N. Trollor, B. T. Baune, P. S. Sachdev, E. Smith Arterial stiffness, the brain and cognition: A systematic review. *Ageing Res Rev* 2014;15: 16–27.

Sjöström, L. Review of the key results from the Swedish Obese Subjects (SOS) trial – A prospective controlled intervention study of bariatric surgery. *J Intern Med* 2013;273: 219–234.

Smulyan, H., A. Lieber, M. E. Safar Hypertension, diabetes type II, and their association: Role of arterial stiffness. *Am J Hypertens*, 2016a;29(1): 5–13.

Smulyan, H., S. Mookherjee, M. E. Safar The two faces of hypertension: Role of aortic stiffness. *J Am Soc Hypertens*, 2016b;10(2): 175–83.

Staessen, J. A., R. Fagard, L. Thijs et al. Randomised double-blind comparison of placebo and active treatment for older patients with isolated systolic hypertension. The Systolic Hypertension in Europe (Syst-Eur) Trial Investigators. *Lancet*, 1997;350(9080): 757–64.

Temmar, M., Labat C., Benkhedda S. et al. Prevalence and determinants of hypertension in the Algerian Sahara. *J Hypertens*. 2007;25: 2218–26.

Temmar, T., G. Watfa, L. Joly et al. Algerian elderly women loose the gender-advantage in terms of arterial stiffness and cardiovascular profile. *J Hypertens*. 2013;31:2244–50.

Thul S., C. Labat, M. Temmar, A. Benetos, M. Bäck Low salivary resolvin D1 to leukotriene B4 ratio predicts carotid intima media thickness: a novel biomarker of non-resolving vascular inflammation. *Eur J Prev Cardiol*, 2017;24:903–6.

Toto-Moukouo, J. J., A. Achimastos, R. G. Asmar, C. J. Hugues, M. E. Safar Pulse wave velocity in patients with obesity and hypertension. *Am Heart J*, 1986;112(1):136–40.

Townsend, R. R., I. B. Wilkinson, E. L. Schiffrin et al. Recommendations for improving and standardizing vascular research on arterial stiffness: A scientific statement from the American Heart Association. *Hypertension*, 2015;66(3): 698–722.

Turnbull, F., B. Neal, T. Ninomiya et al. Effects of different regimens to lower blood pressure on major cardiovascular events in older and younger adults: Meta-analysis of randomised trials. *BMJ*. 2008;336: 1121–3.

Upala, S., A. Sanguankeo, S. Congrete, V. Jaruvongvanich Effect of cholecalciferol supplementation on arterial stiffness: A systematic review and meta-analysis. *Scand Cardiovasc J.* 2016;50(4): 230–5.

Valenti, L., H. S. Pantoni Markus Treatment of vascular risk factors in patients with a diagnosis of Alzheimer's disease: A systematic review. *BMC Medicine* 2014;12: 160.

van de Laar, R. J., C. D. Stehouwer, B. C. van Bussel, M. H. Prins, J. W. Twisk, I. Ferreira Adherence to a Mediterranean dietary pattern in early life is associated with lower arterial stiffness in adulthood: The Amsterdam Growth and Health Longitudinal Study *J Intern Med.* 2013;273(1): 79–93.

van Sloten, T. T., A. D. Protogerou, R. M. Henry, M. T. Schram, L. J. Launer Stehouwer CDAssociation between arterial stiffness, cerebral small vessel disease and cognitive impairment: A systematic review and meta-analysis. *Neurosci Biobehav Rev.* 2015;53: 121–30.

Waldstein, S. R., S. C. Rice, J. F. Thayer, S. S. Najjar, A. Scuteri, A. B. Zonderman Pulse pressure and pulse wave velocity are related to cognitive decline in the Baltimore Longitudinal Study of Aging. *Hypertension* 2008;51: 99–104.

Wang, M., J. Zhang, R. Telljohann et al. Chronic matrix metalloproteinase inhibition retards age-associated arterial proinflammation and increase in blood pressure. *Hypertension*, 2012;60(2): 459–66.

Watfa G., A. Benetos, A. Kearney-Schwartz et al. Do arterial hemodynamic parameters predict cognitive decline over a period of 2 years in individuals older than 80 years living in nursing homes? The PARTAGE Study. *J Am Med Dir Assoc.* 2015;16: 598–602.

Wildman, R. P., G. N. Farhat, A. S. Patel et al. Weight change is associated with change in arterial stiffness among healthy young adults. *Hypertension*, 2005;45(2): 187–92.

Williams, B., J. R. Cockcroft, K. Kario et al. Effects of Sacubitril/Valsartan versus Olmesartan on central hemodynamics in the elderly with systolic hypertension. The PARAMETER Study. *Hypertension* 2017;69: 411–20.

Williams, B., P. S. Lacy, S. M. Thom et al. Differential impact of blood pressure-lowering drugs on central aortic pressure and clinical outcomes: principal results of the Conduit Artery Function Evaluation (CAFE) study. *Circulation*, 2006;113(9): 1213–25.

Williamson, J. D., M. A. Supiano, W. B. Applegate et al. Intensive vs. standard blood pressure control and cardiovascular disease outcomes in adults aged >75 years. A randomized clinical trial. *JAMA*. 2016;315: 2673–82.

Willum-Hansen, T., J. A. Staessen, C. Torp-Pedersen et al. Prognostic value of aortic pulse wave velocity as index of arterial stiffness in the general population. *Circulation*, 2006. 113(5): 664–70.

Wu, C., E. Smit, C. A. Peralta, et al. Functional status modifies the association of blood pressure with death in elders: Health and Retirement Study. *J Am Geriatr Soc.* 2017. doi:10.1111/jgs.14816

Young, T., On the function of Heart and arteries (The Cronian lecture). *Philosophical Transaction*, 1809; 99.

Zhong W., K. J. Cruickshanks, C. R. Schubert et al. Pulse wave velocity and cognitive function in older adults. *Alzheimer Dis Assoc Dis* 2014;28: 44–9.

# 10 Prevention of Frailty

Bertrand Fougère and Matteo Cesari

## Introduction

### Global Aging

The remarkable gain of about 30 years in life expectancy in Western Europe, the United States of America, Canada, Australia, and New Zealand, and even larger gains in Japan, Spain, and Italy, stands out as one of the most important accomplishments of the twentieth century. Between 2015 and 2030, the number of people aged 60 years and older in the world is projected to grow by 56 percent (from 901 million to 1.4 billion). By 2050, the global population of older persons is expected to more than double (compared to 2015), reaching nearly 2.1 billion (United Nations, Department of Economic and Social Affairs, 2015). In particular, the subgroup of people aged 80 years and older (i.e., the "oldest-old" population) is growing more rapidly, in absolute and relative terms. Projections indicate that in 2050 the oldest-old population will reach 434 million individuals, threefold higher than in 2015 (when it was constituted by "only" 125 million) (United Nations, Department of Economic and Social Affairs, 2015).

However, a question arises: although we do live longer, are we also living better? Most evidence from people younger than 85 years suggests a certain delay in the incidence of limitations and disabilities occurred over these last years, despite an increase in the prevalence of chronic diseases and clinical conditions. This apparent contradiction can be, at least in part, explained by the capacity of anticipating diagnoses, improvement of interventions, and the amelioration of care for rendering diseases less disabling (Crimmins, 2004; Perenboom et al., 2004; Parker and Thorslund, 2007). For example, it has been estimated that 14–22 percent of the reduction in incident disability has been obtained thanks to the efficacy of preventive campaigns against cardiovascular diseases (Cutler et al., 2016). The wider use of assistive technology and improvements in housing standards, public transport, accessibility to buildings, changes in social policies, and the social perception of disability might have also contributed to loosening the links between diseases and disability (Wolf et al., 2005; Parker and Thorslund, 2007). Similarly, increasing levels of educational attainment and income in older people, improved living and workplace conditions, changes in marital status – toward a rising proportion of couples in older people, and improvements in early childhood conditions can be presented as additional factors explaining the relative decrease of disability (Reynolds et al., 2005; Schoeni et al., 2008).

Thus, aging reflects the ongoing interaction between individuals and the environments they inhabit. This interaction results in trajectories of both intrinsic capacity and functional ability. Even if an individual's intrinsic capacity has fallen below its peak, the person may still be able to do the things that matter to them if they live in a supportive environment. The environment may become increasingly important as decrements in a person's capacity increase. In this context, numerous entry points can be identified for actions to prevent frailty and promote healthy aging, but all will have one goal: to foster functional ability. This can be achieved in two ways: by supporting the building and maintenance of intrinsic capacity, and by enabling those with a decrement in their functional capacity to do the things that are important to them.

### Inadequacy of Traditional Healthcare Models

The aging world is facing huge social and public health challenges, requiring decisive and coordinated action. It is critical to maximize health and vitality in the extra years gained in life expectancy. This relies in the ability of political, economic, and health service delivery systems to make the right compromises between needs, resources, and expectations. However, while all modern societies are committed to providing health and social services to their citizens, these systems are quite dynamic and fluctuant, driven by diverse and evolving national and regional policies.

## Frailty

### Definition of Frailty

Frailty is an age-related condition characterized by decreased reserve and resistance to stressors. It results from cumulative declines across multiple physiological systems, and increases vulnerability to adverse outcomes (Walston et al., 2006; Fried et al., 2009; Clegg et al., 2013), including falls (Kojima, 2015), disability (Fried et al., 2001; Al Snih et al., 2009; Song et al., 2010), long-term care, and mortality (Woods et al., 2005; Cawthon et al., 2007; Graham et al., 2009). Frailty is distinct from comorbidity and disability (Fried et al., 2004). Although there is not an agreed and unique operationalization of frailty, this condition has frequently been depicted as a transition phase between robustness and disability, thus regarded as a sort of pre-disability stage. In particular, Fried and colleagues have proposed that the signs and symptoms of frailty result from dysregulated energetics, involving multiple molecular and physiological pathways, which lead to sarcopenia, inflammation, decreased heart rate variability, altered clotting processes, altered insulin resistance, anemia, altered hormone levels, and micronutrient deficiencies (Walston et al., 2006). These physiological impairments result in the five clinical characteristics of frailty: weakness, low energy, slow walking speed, low physical activity, and weight loss (Fried et al., 2001). The presence of any three of these phenotypes indicates that a person is "frail," one or two phenotypes indicates "pre-frail," and none of these characteristics indicates that a person is "robust." Fried and colleagues went on to validate this concept in two large datasets from the Cardiovascular Health Study (CHS) (Fried et al., 2001) and the Women's Health and Aging Studies (WHAS) (Bandeen-Roche et al., 2006). It is noteworthy that the instrument per se does not exclude the possibility of a coexistence of frailty with disability, as also described by the authors in a report disentangling the relationships between frailty, disability, and comorbidity (Fried et al., 2004; Tavassoli et al., 2014). However, the frailty phenotype is often used in combination with a physical function scale for capturing a condition suitable for applying preventive strategies against disability.

A number of other definitions have also been described in the literature, including FRAIL (Fatigue, Resistance, Ambulation, Illnesses, Loss of weight) by the International Academy of Nutrition and Aging (Abellan van Kan et al., 2008), the Frailty Instrument developed by Primary Care of the Survey of Health, Ageing, and Retirement in Europe (SHARE-FI) (Romero-Ortuno et al., 2010), and the Groningen Frailty Indicator (Peters et al., 2012). All these tools are very interesting in the prevention of frailty but they must be used in association with tools that suppress disability. Other major definition commonly used in the literature for frailty is the so-called frailty index (FI) (Jones et al., 2004), proposed by Rockwood and colleagues. The FI is based on a significant amount of information retrieved from the results of a comprehensive geriatric assessment (CGA) (Jones et al., 2004). It characterizes frailty across multiple dimensions, providing a quantitative and objective estimate of the accumulation of deficits the person has experienced with age (Andrew et al., 2008). However, the FI is difficult to operate in the prevention of frailty because of the need for a CGA – it must be used in second intention.

A systematic review examined operational definitions of frailty and identified fifteen components in the different conceptualizations and screening tools for frailty (e.g., physical function, mobility, cognition) (Sternberg et al., 2011). Major international efforts have been made over the years for reaching a consensus over the frailty definition (Morley et al., 2013). However, although an agreed theoretical definition is available, there is still a lack of consensus for a unique operational definition of frailty. This explains why estimates of frailty prevalence are highly variable, ranging from 4 to 59 percent, depending on the population being studied and the study location (Walston et al., 2002; Puts et al., 2005; Woods et al., 2005; Lally and Crome, 2007; Syddall et al., 2010; Clegg et al., 2013).

## Pathogenesis of Frailty

A large body of literature, mainly accumulated rapidly in the past few years, suggests several important multisystem pathophysiologic processes in the pathogenesis of the frailty syndrome, including chronic inflammation and immune activation, and those in musculoskeletal and endocrine systems. Chronic inflammation is likely a key underlying mechanism that contributes to frailty directly and indirectly through other intermediate pathophysiologic processes. Potential etiologic factors include genetic/epigenetic and metabolic factors, environmental and lifestyle stressors, and acute and chronic diseases.

## Need for Interventions to Prevent Frailty

With the high prevalence of frailty, as well as the costs and the clinical burdens related to it, identifying effective strategies for preventing age-related reduction of homeostatic reserves is needed. Aiming such efforts represents an opportunity for preventing or delaying the onset of frailty for those most at risk, improving the effectiveness of prevention and the delivery of care, and improving the health and quality of life for individuals with complex health needs.

Some reviews have focused on interventions targeting the prevention of frailty, but they address specific interventions, such as screening tools (Pialoux et al., 2012), home-based support (Elkan et al., 2001), home telecare (Barlow et al., 2007), hospital discharge planning (Bauer et al., 2009), physical activity programs (Chou et al., 2012), or health promotion (Gustafsson et al., 2009). Although these specific interventions are important individually, addressing prevention of frailty likely requires a comprehensive approach involving coordination across a broad range of interventions at clinical, public health, and system levels.

## Interventions to Prevent Frailty

First, in developing a response to prevent frailty, it is thus important not just to consider approaches that ameliorate the losses associated with older age but also those that may reinforce recovery and adaptation to stress. These strengths may be particularly important in helping people marshal the resources that will enable them to deal with the health issues that often arise in older age (Huber et al., 2011). In order to prevent frailty, it is necessary to change the organization of care. The rapid demographic transition forces a public health effort. In the last decade, there have been numerous calls for taking preventive actions against frailty (Morley et al., 2013) (Figure 10.1).

## Healthy Aging

A World Health Organization report defines healthy aging as "the process of developing and maintaining the functional ability that enables well-being in older age." In this context, the main goals and priorities to support healthy aging are the promotion of access to appropriate health services and the raising of awareness/knowledge about health and positive lifestyles. A key message by the World Health Organization is that preventive strategies should not be applied at older age, but since young age and adulthood. Evidence suggests

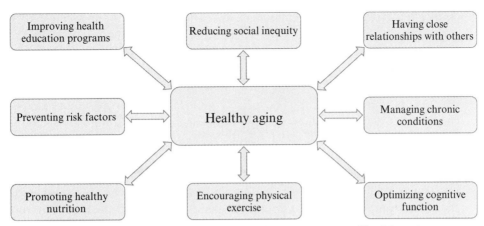

**Figure 10.1.** *Interventions to prevent frailty: components of healthy aging*

that person-centered and integrated care is the best approach for implementing these strategies across older people's lives (Johri et al., 2003; Ouwens et al., 2005; McDonald et al., 2013).

### To Ensure Access to Appropriate Health Services to Older Persons

Access to healthcare services is important for preventing the disabling cascade and promoting successful aging. However, many barriers (in particular, socioeconomic) may limit the access of people (especially at advanced age) to care services. Furthermore, when an older person may have access to care, he/she is frequently faced with models of care organization that are not designed to meet his/her needs. There is indeed a great potential for intervening on the systems for improving the health status of aging populations. Important clinical-level elements of designing care for older people include providing a single point of entry (Esterman and Ben-Tovim, 2002; Chernichovsky and Leibowitz, 2010; Hébert et al., 2010; Goodwin et al., 2016).

### To Pursue Raising Awareness and Improve Health Education Programs

The goal is to have people preserving physical function as long as possible. Thus, strategies aimed at enhancing the capacity of the individual at taking care of him/herself are extremely important. Such empowerment of the individual at taking care of his/her health will facilitate the prompt detection of clinical issues and implementation of interventions at earlier stages. The early detection and treatment of noncommunicable diseases is another area in which action can be taken during this period. The effective management of care for people with, or at high risk for, cardiovascular disease, cancer, chronic respiratory disease, diabetes, and other noncommunicable diseases can prevent the accumulation of functional deficits, reduce the need for hospitalization and costly high-technology interventions, and reduce premature deaths (Fulop et al., 2010; Beck et al., 2013; World Health Organization, 2016). There is a range of effective interventions for preventing and controlling noncommunicable diseases, and many countries – mostly high-income countries – have already achieved major reductions in deaths from chronic disease by implementing these interventions (Epping-Jordan et al., 2005). However, more focused action and political commitments are needed in many parts of the world, especially in low-income and middle-income countries, to close the gap for older people in the treatment of chronic diseases (Lloyd-Sherlock et al., 2014). Guidance is available for implementing interventions in low-resource primary care settings (World Health Organization, 2016). Particular attention needs to be paid to hypertension, which is responsible for a relevant proportion of cardiovascular disease, associated declines in intrinsic capacity, and premature death. Yet, it is possible to minimize these risks if hypertension is detected and treated at an early stage. People with hypertension should have an assessment of their total cardiovascular risk, including tests for diabetes mellitus and other risk factors. Hypertension and diabetes are closely associated, and one cannot be properly managed without giving attention to the other (Weening-Dijksterhuis et al., 2011). Evidence indicates that this total risk approach to treatment decision-making, as opposed to decision-making based on the presence of any single risk factor, helps prevent the use of unnecessary medications and, thus, their side effects (Brown et al., 2000).

Following unhealthy behaviors (e.g., inadequate diet, sedentariness, smoking) is not justified, but effective strategies to target them and their consequences are available (Peto et al., 2000; Michel et al., 2008; Musini et al., 2009; Fulop et al., 2010; Beck et al., 2013; Dorner et al., 2013; Elwood et al., 2013; Estruch et al., 2013; World Health Organization, 2016). Interestingly, the implementation of strategies for improving behaviors has shown to be effective even at older age.

### Physical Exercise

Engaging in physical activity across the life course has many benefits, including increased longevity. For example, a recent pooled analysis of large longitudinal studies found that people who engaged in 150 minutes per week of physical activity at moderate intensity had a 31 percent reduction in mortality compared with those who were less active. The benefit was greatest in those older than 60 years (Arem et al., 2015), indicating that the positive effects of physical exercise are not limited to young individuals or in adulthood, but can be obtained even in the elderly.

To date, exercise is the intervention that has most consistently shown benefits in preventing frailty and its key components (Fiatarone et al., 1994; Gill et al., 2002; Forster et al., 2009; Theou et al., 2011). Exercise exerts multiple physiologic effects in the organism, particularly in favor of the musculoskeletal, endocrine, and immune systems. A large number of trials have demonstrated the positive impact of exercise intervention on key components of the frailty syndrome, including muscle strength and functional mobility, and in both robust as well as already frail elders (Forster et al., 2009; Clegg et al., 2014).

There is evidence to suggest that past leisure time physical activity is related to frailty at advanced age. Savela et al. showed that people with high leisure time physical activity had up to 80 percent lower risk of frailty compared to sedentary subjects (Savela et al., 2013). This conclusion has been confirmed by others who observed that older individuals who regularly engaged in exercise activities were less likely to develop frailty through a 5-year period, compared to those who were sedentary (Brach et al., 2004; Peterson et al., 2009).

The benefits of exercise at improving functional capacities, falls, and quality of life of older adults has been largely reported in reviews and meta-analyses (Weening-Dijksterhuis et al., 2011; Chou et al., 2012; Cadore et al., 2014; Giné-Garriga et al., 2014). Resistance (Chandler et al., 1998; Brown et al., 2000; Izquierdo and Cadore, 2014) and aerobic programs alone, or better, combined (Gill et al., 2002; Pahor et al., 2014), are recommended to older individuals to prevent physical frailty, probably because of the exercises capacity to improve maximal oxygen uptake ($Vo_2max$) (Ehsani et al., 1985) and muscle mass (Sugawara et al., 2002; Harber et al., 2009).

### Nutritional Interventions

Aging is accompanied by physiological changes that can negatively impact nutritional status. Epidemiological studies examining the association between dietary intake or nutritional status and frailty have indeed supported a putative role for nutrition in the development of frailty (Kaiser et al., 2010; Bonnefoy et al., 2015), sarcopenia, and functional decline (Volkert, 1946; Inzitari et al., 2011; Robinson et al., 2012). Sensory impairments, such as a decreased sense of taste and/or smell, may result in reduced appetite. Poor oral health and dental problems can lead to difficulties in chewing, inflammation of the gums, and a monotonous diet, finally resulting in malnutrition (Kshetrimayum et al., 2013).

Given their important role in muscle metabolism, the nutrients most extensively studied for the treatment or prevention of frailty, and especially of sarcopenia, are proteins and essential amino acids. Current evidence indicates that older persons may have reduced ability to use ingested protein for muscle protein synthesis. It is suggested to increase the recommendations for daily protein intake in this age group to at least 1.0–1.2 g/kg body weight/day in order to maintain, or help regain, muscle mass (Millward, 2012; Robinson et al., 2012; Beasley et al., 2013; Deutz et al., 2014; Paddon-Jones and Leidy, 2014; Bonnefoy et al., 2015). To date, reliable evidence from RCTs, including frail older individuals is scarce (Bendayan et al., 2014), and most studies in this area focus on sarcopenia and/or include healthy older persons.

Nutritional supplements that have been tested in older adults, although again, mostly in healthy and not frail persons, and mainly in relation to sarcopenia, are vitamin D, creatine, beta-hydroxy-beta-methylbutyrate (β-HMB), arginine, beta-alanine and citrulline, omega-3 fatty acids, and antioxidants, including carotenoids, selenium, vitamin E and C, and isoflavones (Millward, 2012; Robinson et al., 2012; Deutz et al., 2014; Bonnefoy et al., 2015; Rondanelli et al., 2015). However, to date the number of studies is too small and their designs and results are too heterogeneous to draw reliable conclusions regarding the relevant effects of specific supplementations in the maintenance or restoring of robustness in the older population.

In some studies the combination with exercise and/or physical activity was most effective to reinforce lean/muscle mass and physical performance (Malafarina et al., 2013; Bendayan et al., 2014; Bibas et al., 2014; Nowson and O'Connell, 2015) and to prevent frailty (Epping-Jordan et al., 2005). It is currently recommended to combine both approaches (Volkert, 1946; Morley et al., 2010).

## Comprehensive Geriatric Assessment

The CGA has been demonstrated to improve health outcomes in frail older adults, and represents the gold standard approach against manifest frailty.

The overall objectives of this intervention are to improve physical and psychological function, reduce hospitalization and iatrogenic adverse events, develop adaptive strategies addressing disability and dependence, improve quality of life, and decrease early mortality in older adults (Stuck and Iliffe, 2011). The assessment is interpreted by a care team (usually consisting of a nurse, a social worker, and a physical therapist under the coordination of a geriatrician) followed by the formulation of treatment goals and management plans, developed with the direct participation of the patient and caregivers. The resulting process of assessment, individual care, support planning, and regular review is vital to provide a personal plan of care for treatment of frailty.

It is noteworthy that the accumulation of drugs (and related adverse reactions) with age can be responsible for and/or associated with frailty. Indeed, older adults often have multiple chronic and acute diseases, which progressively and steadily increase in prevalence with age (Marengoni et al., 2011; Onder et al., 2015). The treatment of these diseases usually leads to polypharmacy. It has been estimated that more than 50 percent of persons aged 65 years and older receive five or more drugs concomitantly (Kaufman et al., 2002; Onder et al., 2014). Drug use in the older population might raise several concerns related to an increased risk of drug–drug and drug–disease interactions, poor adherence to treatment, and increased risk of adverse drug reactions (Nobili et al., 2009; Marengoni et al., 2014; Dumbreck et al., 2015). The optimization of drug prescriptions in frail older adults is a key part of the interdisciplinary plan of action against frailty. At the same time, health professionals should closely and carefully monitor drug prescriptions, even in robust individuals for avoiding the onset of iatrogenic consequences responsible for the fragilization of the individual.

## Development of New Models of Care

Raising awareness about frailty among public health authorities, practitioners, and the general population is the first step in a new model of care for the elderly (Rodríguez-Artalejo and Rodríguez-Mañas, 2014). Older people and their caregivers need to be alert to the warning signs of frailty and its consequences. They must have the knowledge and skills to take responsibility for their health status, and to modify their unhealthy behaviors. Health professionals need to be trained to validate signs of frailty. Finally, public health authorities must become familiar with the increasing burdens that frailty will impose on their healthcare systems, and become proactive in planning and implementing counteractive strategies.

Primary care is the first contact point for health services in many countries. It is the place where promoting prevention among robust individuals and supporting care for the frail ones should take place. An important resolution would be to optimize access to care and ensure a universal coverage of health needs. To provide this objective, formalities need to be simplified as much as possible, with a priority on efficiency. This goal might be more easily conducted with a single entry point into the system for frail patients, and the wider implementation of case manager models of care. The screening of frailty must also use any formal and informal contact that the older person may have with healthcare (e.g., emergency departments, outpatient clinics) and social services (e.g., senior centers).

At the same time, prevention of frailty implies the need of targeting information to the general population (among robust and also young individuals) in order to promote healthy lifestyles and behaviors. Preventive campaigns should be directed in a cost-effective fashion and capable of conveying clear and practical messages. The image of "aging" should be modified and improved in our societies (Rowe et al., 2016). Older persons should be transformed from an apparent societal burden into a resource, by maintaining them active and supportive of younger age classes. Tackling ageism will require building and embedding in the thinking of all generations a new understanding of aging. This cannot be based on outdated conceptualizations of older people as burdens or on unrealistic assumptions that older people today have somehow avoided the health challenges of their parents and grandparents. Rather, it demands an acceptance of the wide diversity of the experience of older age, acknowledgment of the inequities that often underlie it, and openness to asking how things might be done better. Actions that may help tackle ageism include: (1) undertaking communication campaigns to increase knowledge about and understanding of aging among the media, general public, policymakers, employers, and service providers; (2) legislating against age-based discrimination; (3) ensuring that a balanced view of aging is presented in the media, for example, by minimizing sensationalist reporting of crimes against older people.

## Conclusion

In summary, the improvement of lifestyle and adhesion to recommendations for successful aging are the key strategies for preventing frailty. Once frailty is onset, its complex nature requires the conduction of a geriatric comprehensive assessment for identifying the underlying causes and mechanism. Interventions failing to comprehensively evaluate the individual may determine a too sectorial and partial view of the entire picture with the risk of implementing suboptimal results. Strategies differentiating biological, socio-behavioral, and environmental causes should be carefully considered in the design of personalized intervention. With increasing understanding of the biologic foundations of frailty, more effective and tailored interventions and innovative geriatric care models will develop.

## References

Abellan van Kan G., Rolland Y., Bergman H., et al. The I.A.N.A Task Force on frailty assessment of older people in clinical practice. *J Nutr Health Aging.* 2008 Jan;12(1):29–37.

Al Snih S., Graham J. E., Ray L. A., et al. Frailty and incidence of activities of daily living disability among older Mexican Americans. *J Rehabil Med.* 2009 Nov;41(11):892–7.

Andrew M. K., Mitnitski A. B., Rockwood K. Social vulnerability, frailty and mortality in elderly people. *PloS One.* 2008;3(5):e2232.

Arem H., Moore S. C., Patel A., et al. Leisure time physical activity and mortality: a detailed pooled analysis of the dose-response relationship. *JAMA Intern Med.* 2015 Jun;175(6):959–67.

Bandeen-Roche K., Xue Q.-L., Ferrucci L., et al. Phenotype of frailty: characterization in the Women's Health and Aging Studies. *J Gerontol A Biol Sci Med Sci.* 2006 Mar;61(3):262–6.

Barlow J., Singh D., Bayer S., Curry R. A systematic review of the benefits of home telecare for frail elderly people and those with long-term conditions. *J Telemed Telecare.* 2007;13(4):172–9.

Bauer M., Fitzgerald L., Haesler E., Manfrin M. Hospital discharge planning for frail older people and their family. Are we delivering best practice? A review of the evidence. *J Clin Nurs.* 2009 Sep;18(18):2539–46.

Beasley J. M., Shikany J. M., Thomson C. A. The role of dietary protein intake in the prevention of sarcopenia of aging. *Nutr Clin Pract Off Publ Am Soc Parenter Enter Nutr.* 2013 Dec;28(6):684–90.

Beck A. M., Kjær S., Hansen B. S., et al. Follow-up home visits with registered dietitians have a positive effect on the functional and nutritional status of geriatric medical patients after discharge: a randomized controlled trial. *Clin Rehabil.* 2013 Jun;27(6):483–93.

Bendayan M., Bibas L., Levi M., et al. Therapeutic interventions for frail elderly patients: part II. Ongoing and unpublished randomized trials. *Prog Cardiovasc Dis.* 2014 Oct;57(2):144–51.

Bibas L., Levi M., Bendayan M., et al. Therapeutic interventions for frail elderly patients: part I. Published randomized trials. *Prog Cardiovasc Dis.* 2014 Oct;57(2):134–43.

Bonnefoy M., Berrut G., Lesourd B., et al. Frailty and nutrition: searching for evidence. *J Nutr Health Aging.* 2015 Mar;19(3):250–7.

Brach J. S., Simonsick E. M., Kritchevsky S., Yaffe K., Newman A. B., Health, Aging and Body Composition Study Research Group. The association between physical function and lifestyle activity and exercise in the health, aging and body composition study. *J Am Geriatr Soc.* 2004 Apr;52(4):502–9.

Brown M., Sinacore D. R., Ehsani A. A., et al. Low-intensity exercise as a modifier of physical frailty in older adults. *Arch Phys Med Rehabil.* 2000 Jul;81(7):960–5.

Cadore E. L., Moneo A. B. B., Mensat M. M., et al. Positive effects of resistance training in frail elderly patients with dementia after long-term physical restraint. *Age Dordr Neth.* 2014 Apr;36(2):801–11.

Cawthon P. M., Marshall L. M., Michael Y., et al. Frailty in older men: prevalence, progression, and relationship with mortality. *J Am Geriatr Soc.* 2007 Aug;55(8):1216–23.

Chandler J. M., Duncan P. W., Kochersberger G., Studenski S. Is lower extremity strength gain associated with improvement in physical performance and disability in frail, community-dwelling elders? *Arch Phys Med Rehabil.* 1998 Jan;79(1):24–30.

Chernichovsky D., Leibowitz A. A. Integrating public health and personal care in a reformed US health care system. *Am J Public Health.* 2010 Feb;100(2):205–11.

Chou C.-H., Hwang C.-L., Wu Y.-T. Effect of exercise on physical function, daily living activities, and quality of life in the frail older adults: a meta-analysis. *Arch Phys Med Rehabil.* 2012 Feb;93(2):237–44.

Clegg A., Barber S., Young J., Iliffe S., Forster A. The Home-based Older People's Exercise (HOPE) trial: a pilot randomised controlled trial of a home-based exercise intervention for older people with frailty. *Age Ageing.* 2014 Sep;43(5):687–95.

Clegg A., Young J., Iliffe S., Rikkert M. O., Rockwood K. Frailty in elderly people. *Lancet.* 2013 Mar 2;381(9868):752–62.

Crimmins E. M. Trends in the health of the elderly. *Annu Rev Public Health.* 2004;25:79–98.

Cutler D. M., Landrum M. B., Stewart K. A. Intensive medical care and cardiovascular disease disability reductions [Internet]. *National Bureau of Economic Research*; 2006 May [cited 2016 Jul 11]. Report No.: 12184. Available from: http://nber.org/papers/w12184

Deutz N. E. P., Bauer J. M., Barazzoni R., et al. Protein intake and exercise for optimal muscle function with aging: recommendations from the ESPEN Expert Group. *Clin Nutr Edinb Scotl.* 2014 Dec;33(6):929–36.

Dorner T. E., Lackinger C., Haider S., et al. Nutritional intervention and physical training in malnourished frail community-dwelling elderly persons carried out by trained lay "buddies": study protocol of a randomized controlled trial. *BMC Public Health.* 2013;13:1232.

Dumbreck S., Flynn A., Nairn M., et al. Drug-disease and drug-drug interactions: systematic examination of recommendations in 12 UK national clinical guidelines. *BMJ.* 2015;350:h949.

Ehsani A. A., Spina R. J., Peterson L. R., et al. Attenuation of cardiovascular adaptations to exercise in frail octogenarians. *J Appl Physiol Bethesda MD* 1985. 2003 Nov;95(5):1781–8.

Elkan R., Kendrick D., Dewey M., et al. Effectiveness of home based support for older people: systematic review and meta-analysis. *BMJ.* 2001 Sep 29;323(7315):719–25.

Elwood P., Galante J., Pickering J., et al. Healthy lifestyles reduce the incidence of chronic diseases and dementia: evidence from the Caerphilly cohort study. *PLoS One.* 2013;8(12):e81877.

Epping-Jordan J. E., Galea G., Tukuitonga C., Beaglehole R. Preventing chronic diseases: taking stepwise action. *Lancet Lond Engl.* 2005 Nov 5;366(9497):1667–71.

Esterman A. J., Ben-Tovim D. I. The Australian coordinated care trials: success or failure? The second round of trials may provide more answers. *Med J Aust.* 2002 Nov 4;177(9):469–70.

Estruch R., Ros E., Salas-Salvadó J., et al. Primary prevention of cardiovascular disease with a Mediterranean diet. *N Engl J Med.* 2013 Apr 4;368(14):1279–90.

Fiatarone M. A., O'Neill E. F., Ryan N. D., et al. Exercise training and nutritional supplementation for physical frailty in very elderly people. *N Engl J Med.* 1994 Jun 23;330(25):1769–75.

Forster A., Lambley R., Hardy J., et al. Rehabilitation for older people in long-term care. *Cochrane Database Syst Rev.* 2009;(1):CD004294.

Fried L. P., Ferrucci L., Darer J., Williamson J. D., Anderson G. Untangling the concepts of disability, frailty, and comorbidity: implications for improved targeting and care. *J Gerontol A Biol Sci Med Sci.* 2004 Mar;59(3):255–63.

Fried L. P., Tangen C. M., Walston J., et al. Frailty in older adults: evidence for a phenotype. *J Gerontol A Biol Sci Med Sci.* 2001 Mar;56(3):M146–56.

Fried L. P., Xue Q.-L., Cappola A. R., et al. Nonlinear multisystem physiological dysregulation associated with frailty in older women: implications for etiology and treatment. *J Gerontol A Biol Sci Med Sci.* 2009 Oct;64(10):1049–57.

Fulop T., Larbi A., Witkowski J. M., et al. Aging, frailty and age-related diseases. *Biogerontology.* 2010 Oct;11(5):547–63.

Gill T. M., Baker D. I., Gottschalk M., et al. A program to prevent functional decline in physically frail, elderly persons who live at home. *N Engl J Med.* 2002 Oct 3;347(14):1068–74.

Giné-Garriga M., Roqué-Fíguls M., Coll-Planas L., Sitjà-Rabert M., Salvà A. Physical exercise interventions for improving performance-based measures of physical function in community-dwelling, frail older adults: a systematic review and meta-analysis. *Arch Phys Med Rehabil.* 2014 Apr;95(4):753–69.e3.

Goodwin N., Sonola L., Thiel V., Kodner D. *Co-ordinated Care for People with Complex Chronic Conditions [Internet].* 2013 [cited 2016 Sep 27]. (London: The King's Fund). Available from: http://kingsfund.org.uk/sites/files/kf/field/field_publication_file/co-ordinated-care-for-peoplewith-complex-chronic-conditions-kingsfund-oct13.pdf

Graham J. E., Snih S. A., Berges I. M., et al. Frailty and 10-year mortality in community-living Mexican American older adults. *Gerontology.* 2009;55(6):644–51.

Gustafsson S., Edberg A.-K., Johansson B., Dahlin-Ivanoff S. Multi-component health promotion and disease prevention for community-dwelling frail elderly persons: a systematic review. *Eur J Ageing.* 2009 Oct 17;6(4):315–29.

Harber M. P., Konopka A. R., Douglass M. D., et al. Aerobic exercise training improves whole muscle and single myofiber size and function in older women. *Am J Physiol Regul Integr Comp Physiol.* 2009 Nov;297(5):R1452–9.

Hébert R., Raîche M., Dubois M.-F., et al. Impact of PRISMA, a coordination-type integrated service delivery system for frail older people in Quebec (Canada): a quasi-experimental study. *J Gerontol B Psychol Sci Soc Sci.* 2010 Jan;65B(1):107–18.

Huber M., Knottnerus J. A., Green L., et al. How should we define health? *BMJ.* 2011;343:d4163.

Inzitari M., Doets E., Bartali B., et al. Nutrition in the age-related disablement process. *J Nutr Health Aging.* 2011 Aug;15(8):599–604.

Izquierdo M., Cadore E. L. Muscle power training in the institutionalized frail: a new approach to counteracting functional declines and very late-life disability. *Curr Med Res Opin.* 2014 Jul;30(7):1385–90.

Johri M., Beland F., Bergman H. International experiments in integrated care for the elderly: a synthesis of the evidence. *Int J Geriatr Psychiatry.* 2003 Mar;18(3):222–35.

Jones D. M., Song X., Rockwood K. Operationalizing a frailty index from a standardized comprehensive geriatric assessment. *J Am Geriatr Soc.* 2004 Nov;52(11):1929–33.

Kaiser M., Bandinelli S., Lunenfeld B. Frailty and the role of nutrition in older people. A review of the current literature. *Acta Bio-Medica Atenei Parm.* 2010;81(Suppl 1):37–45.

Kaufman D. W., Kelly J. P., Rosenberg L., Anderson T. E., Mitchell A. A. Recent patterns of medication use in the ambulatory adult population of the United States: the Slone survey. *JAMA.* 2002 Jan 16;287(3):337–44.

Kojima G. Frailty as a predictor of future falls among community-dwelling older people: a systematic review and meta-analysis. *J Am Med Dir Assoc.* 2015 Dec;16(12):1027–33.

Kshetrimayum N., Reddy C. V. K., Siddhana S., et al. Oral health-related quality of life and nutritional status of institutionalized elderly population aged 60 years and above in Mysore City, India. *Gerodontology.* 2013 Jun;30(2):119–25.

Lally F., Crome P. Understanding frailty. *Postgrad Med J.* 2007 Jan;83(975):16–20.

Lloyd-Sherlock P., Beard J., Minicuci N., Ebrahim S., Chatterji S. Hypertension among older adults in low- and middle-income countries: prevalence, awareness and control. *Int J Epidemiol.* 2014 Feb;43(1):116–28.

Malafarina V., Uriz-Otano F., Iniesta R., Gil-Guerrero L. Effectiveness of nutritional supplementation on muscle mass in treatment of sarcopenia in old age: a systematic review. *J Am Med Dir Assoc.* 2013 Jan;14(1):10–7.

Marengoni A., Angleman S., Melis R., et al. Aging with multimorbidity: a systematic review of the literature. *Ageing Res Rev.* 2011 Sep;10(4):430–9.

Marengoni A., Pasina L., Concoreggi C., et al. Understanding adverse drug reactions in older adults through drug-drug interactions. *Eur J Intern Med.* 2014 Nov;25(9):843–6.

McDonald K. M., Schultz E. M., Chang C. Evaluating the state of quality-improvement science through evidence synthesis: insights from the closing the quality gap series. *Perm J.* 2013;17(4):52–61.

Morley J. E., Argiles J. M., Evans W. J., et al. Nutritional recommendations for the management of sarcopenia. *J Am Med Dir Assoc.* 2010 Jul;11(6):391–6.

Michel J.-P., Newton J. L., Kirkwood T. B. L. Medical challenges of improving the quality of a longer life. *JAMA.* 2008 Feb 13;299(6):688–90.

Morley J. E., Vellas B., van Kan G. A., et al. Frailty consensus: a call to action. *J Am Med Dir Assoc.* 2013 Jun;14(6):392–7.

Millward D. J. Nutrition and sarcopenia: evidence for an interaction. *Proc Nutr Soc.* 2012 Nov;71(4):566–75.

Musini V. M., Tejani A. M., Bassett K., Wright J. M. Pharmacotherapy for hypertension in the elderly. *Cochrane Database Syst Rev.* 2009;(4):CD000028.

Nobili A., Pasina L., Tettamanti M., et al. Potentially severe drug interactions in elderly outpatients: results of an observational study of an administrative prescription database. *J Clin Pharm Ther.* 2009 Aug;34(4):377–86.

Nowson C., O'Connell S. Protein requirements and recommendations for older people: a review. *Nutrients.* 2015 Aug;7(8):6874–99.

Onder G., Bonassi S., Abbatecola A. M., et al. High prevalence of poor quality drug prescribing in older individuals: a nationwide report from the Italian Medicines Agency (AIFA). *J Gerontol A Biol Sci Med Sci.* 2014 Apr;69(4):430–7.

Onder G., Palmer K., Navickas R., et al. Time to face the challenge of multimorbidity. A European perspective from the joint action on chronic diseases and promoting healthy ageing across the life cycle (JA-CHRODIS). *Eur J Intern Med.* 2015 Apr;26(3):157–9.

Ouwens M., Wollersheim H., Hermens R., Hulscher M., Grol R. Integrated care programmes for chronically ill patients: a review of systematic reviews. *Int J Qual Health Care J Int Soc Qual Health Care ISQua.* 2005 Apr;17(2):141–6.

Paddon-Jones D., Leidy H. Dietary protein and muscle in older persons. *Curr Opin Clin Nutr Metab Care.* 2014 Jan;17(1):5–11.

Pahor M., Guralnik J. M., Ambrosius W. T., et al. Effect of structured physical activity on prevention of major mobility disability in older adults: the LIFE study randomized clinical trial. *JAMA.* 2014 Jun 18;311(23):2387–96.

Parker M. G., Thorslund M. Health trends in the elderly population: getting better and getting worse. *The Gerontologist.* 2007 Apr;47(2):150–8.

Perenboom R. J. M., Van Herten L. M., Boshuizen H. C., Van Den Bos G. A. M. Trends in disability-free life expectancy. *Disabil Rehabil.* 2004 Apr 8;26(7):377–86.

Peters L. L., Boter H., Buskens E., Slaets J. P. J. Measurement properties of the Groningen Frailty Indicator in home-dwelling and institutionalized elderly people. *J Am Med Dir Assoc.* 2012 Jul;13(6):546–51.

Peterson M. J., Giuliani C., Morey M. C., et al. Physical activity as a preventative factor for frailty: the health, aging, and body composition study. *J Gerontol A Biol Sci Med Sci.* 2009 Jan;64(1):61–8.

Peto R., Darby S., Deo H., et al. Smoking, smoking cessation, and lung cancer in the UK since 1950: combination of national statistics with two case-control studies. *BMJ.* 2000 Aug 5;321(7257):323–9.

Pialoux T., Goyard J., Lesourd B. Screening tools for frailty in primary health care: a systematic review. *Geriatr Gerontol Int.* 2012 Apr;12(2):189–97.

Puts M. T. E., Lips P., Deeg D. J. H. Static and dynamic measures of frailty predicted decline in performance-based and self-reported physical functioning. *J Clin Epidemiol.* 2005 Nov;58(11):1188–98.

Reynolds S. L., Saito Y., Crimmins E. M. The impact of obesity on active life expectancy in older American men and women. *The Gerontologist.* 2005 Aug;45(4):438–44.

Robinson S., Cooper C., Aihie Sayer A. Nutrition and sarcopenia: a review of the evidence and implications for preventive strategies. *J Aging Res.* 2012;2012:510801.

Rodríguez-Artalejo F., Rodríguez-Mañas L. The frailty syndrome in the public health agenda. *J Epidemiol Community Health.* 2014 Aug;68(8):703–4.

Romero-Ortuno R., Walsh C. D., Lawlor B. A., Kenny R. A. A frailty instrument for primary care: findings from the Survey of Health, Ageing and Retirement in Europe (SHARE). *BMC Geriatr.* 2010;10:57.

Rondanelli M., Faliva M., Monteferrario F., et al. Novel insights on nutrient management of sarcopenia in elderly. *BioMed Res Int.* 2015;2015:524948.

Rowe J. W., Fulmer T., Fried L. Preparing for better health and health care for an aging population. *JAMA.* 2016 Oct 25;316(16):1643–4.

Savela S. L., Koistinen P., Stenholm S., et al. Leisure-time physical activity in midlife is related to old age frailty. *J Gerontol A Biol Sci Med Sci.* 2013 Nov;68(11):1433–8.

Schoeni R. F., Freedman V. A., Martin L. G. Why is late-life disability declining? *Milbank Q.* 2008 Mar;86(1):47–89.

Song X., Mitnitski A., Rockwood K. Prevalence and 10-year outcomes of frailty in older adults in relation to deficit accumulation. *J Am Geriatr Soc.* 2010 Apr;58(4):681–7.

Sternberg S. A., Wershof Schwartz A., Karunananthan S., Bergman H., Mark Clarfield A. The identification of frailty: a systematic literature review. *J Am Geriatr Soc.* 2011 Nov;59(11):2129–38.

Stuck A. E., Iliffe S. Comprehensive geriatric assessment for older adults. *BMJ.* 2011;343:d6799.

Sugawara J., Miyachi M., Moreau K. L., et al. Age-related reductions in appendicular skeletal muscle mass: association with habitual aerobic exercise status. *Clin Physiol Funct Imaging.* 2002 May;22(3):169–72.

Syddall H., Roberts H. C., Evandrou M., et al. Prevalence and correlates of frailty among community-dwelling older men and women: findings from the Hertfordshire Cohort Study. *Age Ageing.* 2010 Mar;39(2):197–203.

Tavassoli N., Guyonnet S., Abellan Van Kan G., et al. Description of 1,108 older patients referred by their physician to the "Geriatric Frailty Clinic (G.F.C) for Assessment of Frailty and Prevention of Disability" at the gerontopole. *J Nutr Health Aging.* 2014 May;18(5):457–64.

Theou O., Stathokostas L., Roland K. P., et al. The effectiveness of exercise interventions for the management of frailty: a systematic review. *J Aging Res.* 2011;2011:569194.

United Nations, Department of Economic and Social Affairs, Population Division. World Population Ageing 2015 [Internet]. 2015. Available from: http://un.org/en/development/desa/population/publications/pdf/ageing/WPA2015_Report.pdf

Volkert D. The role of nutrition in the prevention of sarcopenia. *Wien Med Wochenschr 1946.* 2011 Sep;161(17–18):409–15.

Walston J., Hadley E. C., Ferrucci L., et al. Research agenda for frailty in older adults: toward a better understanding of physiology and etiology: summary from the American Geriatrics Society/National Institute on Aging Research Conference on Frailty in Older Adults. *J Am Geriatr Soc.* 2006 Jun;54(6):991–1001.

Walston J., McBurnie M. A., Newman A., et al. Frailty and activation of the inflammation and coagulation systems with and without clinical comorbidities: results from the Cardiovascular Health Study. *Arch Intern Med.* 2002 Nov 11;162(20):2333–41.

Weening-Dijksterhuis E., de Greef M. H. G., Scherder E. J. A., Slaets J. P. J., van der Schans C. P. Frail institutionalized older persons: a comprehensive review on physical exercise, physical fitness, activities of daily living, and quality-of-life. *Am J Phys Med Rehabil Assoc Acad Physiatr.* 2011 Feb;90(2):156–68.

Wolf D. A., Hunt K., Knickman J. Perspectives on the recent decline in disability at older ages. *Milbank Q.* 2005;83(3):365–95.

Woods N. F., LaCroix A. Z., Gray S. L., et al. Frailty: emergence and consequences in women aged 65 and older in the Women's Health Initiative Observational Study. *J Am Geriatr Soc.* 2005 Aug;53(8):1321–30.

World Health Organization. Prevention and Control of Noncommunicable Diseases: Guidelines for Primary Health Care in Low Resource Settings [Internet]. Geneva: World Health Organization; 2012 [cited 2016 Sep 14]. (WHO Guidelines Approved by the Guidelines Review Committee). Available from: http://ncbi.nlm.nih.gov/books/NBK148622/

Global Action Plan for the Prevention and Control of NCDs 2013–2020 [Internet]. WHO. [cited 2016 Sep 14]. Available from: http://who.int/nmh/events/ncd_action_plan/en/

World Health Organization. Preventing Chronic Diseases: A Vital Investment [Internet]. WHO. [cited 2016 Sep 14]. Available from: http://who.int/chp/chronic_disease_report/contents/en/

# 11 Preventive Effects of Physical Activity in Older People

Timo E. Strandberg

A healthy lifestyle, including physical activity (PA), during the life course is a major modifiable factor for healthy aging (WHO World Report on Aging and Health, 2015), but starting PA in old age is beneficial as well (Stessman et al., 2009) – even for individuals with frailty or cognitive disorders (Weening-Dijksterhuis et al., 2011; Pitkälä et al., 2013a,b). Physical activity is important to maintain functional capacity and prevent chronic diseases and disability, but also as a part of treatment and rehabilitation (Singh, 2002; Salpakoski et al., 2014). However, it is important to adjust PA to a frail patient and his/her medications; in a previously physically inactive person, it is often wise to start PA low and go slow. It is also essential to ask about personal preferences, and thus ensure optimal adherence. This review will focus on relationships between PA and outcomes relevant for old and oldest-old people: functional capacity, frailty, osteoporosis, cognitive disorders, and mental and social aspects. Prevention of specific diseases, such as cardiovascular diseases, is not reviewed.

## Functional Capacity and Mobility

Physical inactivity is an independent risk factor for disability, not being able to do activities of daily living (ADL), but PA, affects the development of chronic non-communicable diseases (NCD) as well (Boyle et al., 2007; Paterson and Warburton, 2010). According to a systematic review, it would be possible for retired persons (65 years and older) to reduce the risk of disability up to 50 percent through regular PA (Paterson and Warburton, 2010). One simple guideline is to have aerobic exercise at least 150 minutes per week and muscle strength, flexibility, and balance training 2 to 3 times per week. In the randomized American Lifestyle Interventions and Independence for Elders (LIFE) trial, this type of exercise for an average of 2.6 years was shown to prevent mobility-disability in home-living, vulnerable individuals aged 70–89 years (Pahor et al., 2014). The effects of physical exercise, similar to that used in LIFE, combined with dietary advice, is currently being tested in an older European population with sarcopenia, who are at risk of disability (Sarcopenia and Physical Frailty in Older People SPRINTT: multi-component treatment strategies, Landi et al., 2017).

Physical activity has positive effects for ADL (e.g., dressing/bathing, eating, walking, toileting, hygiene) and instrumental activities of daily living (IADL) (e.g., housework, using a telephone, handling medications, shopping, preparing meals, transportation within the community) (Boyle et al., 2007). To be most effective in maintaining functional capacity and mobility, PA must be versatile, include not only, for example, walking, but also muscle exercise for strength, flexibility, and balance. The greatest benefits are obtained by those with already reduced capacity (Salpakoski et al., 2014). It has even been possible to improve ADL among frail institutionalized older persons using appropriate exercise for muscle strength and function (Weening-Dijksterhuis et al., 2011).

Maintaining ADL and IADL involves several dimensions: muscle strength of lower extremities (start up and go), joint mobility (dressing, bathing, eating), general endurance, and balance. When functional capacity is already reduced, one size does not fit all and individualized PA programs are needed.

## Frailty and Sarcopenia

Muscle mass and muscle strength decrease gradually, and to a certain degree, are part of the normal aging process. This decrease is, however, accelerated with chronic diseases and physical inactivity. Sarcopenia refers to a pathological loss of muscle tissue with aging, and it is always associated with reduced strength and function (Cruz-Jentoft et al., 2014). The ability of muscle to produce sufficient force in a short time (force-velocity relationship) is decreased faster with aging than maximal force. One reason is the special vulnerability of muscle fast twitch fibers to aging.

Gymnasium-type exercise is the most effective form of PA to increase and maintain muscle mass and strength. Muscle strength and the cross-sectional area of muscle increase in a few months with intensive exercise, and this applies both to robust and frail older persons (Fiatarone et al., 1994). Increasing muscle mass and strength requires sufficient frequency (1–2 times per week) and relatively great resistance, i.e., 60 percent to 80 percent of the maximal resistance at which a person is able to make one repetition (one repetition maximum, 1RM) (Liu and Latham, 2009). There is, however, evidence in healthy older persons that even a lesser resistance, 20 percent to 40 percent of 1RM is sufficient for a positive effect. This requires that repetitions are increased (several dozens) and muscle is exhausted (Van Roie et al., 2013).

If the goal is to increase the muscle force-velocity relationship, exercise should involve great movement velocity and moderate resistance (ca. 40 percent of 1RM) (Reid et al., 2015). Scientific evidence is strong on the effects of physical exercise on muscle power and moderate on the effects on function and muscle mass, in the aged (Liu and Latham, 2009; Cruz-Jentoft et al., 2014). Exercises that increase muscle power have positive effects on functional capacity and mobility, especially among older people with reduced capacity (Fiatarone et al., 1994). Because leaving home and going to a gym can be an obstacle for frail persons, it is important that they can also perform muscle strength promoting exercises at home.

Sarcopenia is a frequent component of the frailty syndrome. Frailty is characterized by a weakening of several physiological functions leading to loss of reserves, vulnerability to stressors, and an increased risk of institutionalization and death (Strandberg et al., 2011). Physical inactivity in midlife is a risk factor for frailty (Savela et al., 2013), and currently the best evidence for frailty prevention is from exercise and optimal nutrition (Strandberg et al., 2011). It has been suggested that treatment of frailty would consist of 45 minutes of physical exercise 3 times per week (Messinger-Rapport et al., 2013), the regimen consisting of aerobic exercise, progressive strength, balance, and functional training (Weening-Dijksterhuis et al., 2011; Messinger-Rapport et al., 2013).

## Bone Density and Osteoporosis

Physical activity has an important role in bone physiology both in young and old age (Kohrt et al., 2004; Marques et al., 2012; Cosman et al., 2014). It contributes to reaching maximal bone mass during childhood and adolescence, preserving bone mass for up to 50 years of age, and slowing the development of osteopenia and osteoporosis in later life. It is even possible to improve bone density in older people with intensive physical exercise (Marques et al., 2012). Physical activity increases bone strength by modifying bone structure and increasing mineral content. Bone cells form new bone tissue where the stress is high and remove tissue from inactive areas. With repeated stress, the outer shell of the compact bone is thickened and the ultrastructure of the inner spongy bone reorganized; consequently, bone as a whole gets stronger without change in total bone mass.

The best stimulus for bones is strike/blow-type stress, like quick turns and jumps, while single maximal stress is more effective than repetitive but milder ones. Aerobics, tennis, and other ball games, as well as gymnastics and muscle training (where stress emerges from muscle power), are efficient types of activity. In order to make stronger bones, exercise should be relatively intensive and long-term, because the positive effect on bones obtained in adult life fades quite rapidly after discontinuation of exercise. While in muscle strength exercise, the goal is at least 50 percent of 1RML, while optimal intensity for bones is 70–80 percent of 1RM (Kohrt et al., 2004).

When the grade of bone density is at the level of osteopenia, it is possible to go in for aerobic, jogging, or muscle strength exercise (50 percent of 1RM) (Kohrt et al., 2004). For an older person with osteoporosis, the primary goal of PA is to improve muscle strength and posture, and with long-term use, resisting further bone loss. Physical activity may reduce back pain and ensuing restrictions typical of osteoporosis. Pathognomonic change of posture in osteoporosis is the accentuation of thoracic kyphosis (hyperkyphosis), and therefore important components of training are strengthening of spinal extensor muscles and improving vertebral stability, for example using a rubber band. The severity of osteoporosis and presence of possible fractures play an essential role for selecting suitable exercise (Cosman et al., 2014; Giangregorio et al., 2015), and a physiotherapist is often needed for exercise planning. General outlines are as follows: a person with mild to moderate osteoporosis should exercise daily, if possible walking briskly or at least avoid sitting and lying down. In grave osteoporosis, suitable ways to maintain muscle strength include exercise in water and movements utilizing own body weight. Strong forward bending and twists, as well as sudden strikes and shock-type movements increase fracture risk in osteoporosis and are therefore contraindicated (Giangregorio et al., 2015).

## Preventing Falls and Fractures

For maximal effect, prevention of fragility fractures requires multifactorial measures: careful assessment of risk of falls, prevention of falls, and in case of falls, protection for fractures using protective devices (like hip pads) and treating osteoporosis adequately (Blain et al., 2016). Physical activity has the potential to reduce the risk of falls and the risk of osteoporosis. There is moderate evidence that PA can reduce hip fractures, and it has been assessed that persons with much PA have 20–70 percent lower risk of hip fractures, compared to physically inactive people. Training leg muscle strength and balance 2 to 3 times per week is the main type of exercise for prevention of falls.

It is essential that exercise be planned according to individual needs and resources. Multi-professional cooperation is often needed, and in practice, exercise can be performed as group sessions or individually at home (or eventually in a nursing home). A gradual, progressive increase of physical challenge in planned exercise is important. In addition, everyday life should be physically active, and staying vertical during the day as much as possible is essential.

## Impaired Cognition and Memory Disorders

Physical activity has potentially several beneficial effects on cognition and brain health in old age (Gorelick et al., 2011; Brown et al., 2013). It may reduce the risk for chronic – especially cardiovascular – diseases and improve cerebrovascular functioning and brain perfusion. Physical activity may also increase brain neurotrophins (e.g., brain-derived neurotropic factor, BDNF), decrease response to stressors, and improve brain plasticity and resilience through synaptogenesis and neurogenesis. All of these may contribute to better preservation of volumes of grey and white matter, hippocampus, and total brain tissue.

Accordingly, in many observational studies midlife PA, especially of the aerobic type, has been associated with less cognitive decline and lower risk of dementia in later life (Gorelick et al., 2011; Lafortune et al., 2016). Also good cardiorespiratory fitness seems to protect generally from cognitive decline and memory disorders. Similarly, encouraging results on cognition has been obtained in randomized, controlled trials, but conclusive evidence about the effect of PA preventing clinical memory diseases, such as Alzheimer's disease, is still scarce (Andrieu et al., 2015; Lafortune et al., 2016).

The main evidence for PA is from the effects of aerobic exercise on executive functioning (i.e., planning, reasoning, decision-making), but there are also reports of positive effects on memory and language functions. Also, resistance training has been reported to beneficially affect cognitive functions (Colcombe and Kramer, 2003; Komulainen et al., 2010; Smith et al., 2010). However, the cognitive part of the large LIFE study could not demonstrate benefit on cognition after 2.6 years of aerobic and resistance training in 70–89 year old individuals (Sink et al., 2015). Multi-domain intervention – not only PA – may be needed for optimal effect. This was tested in a randomized trial of older (70+) individuals at risk of dementia (Finnish Geriatric Intervention Study to Prevent Cognitive Impairment and Disability, FINGER, Ngandu et al., 2015). A 2-year intervention, consisting of aerobic and resistance exercise, cognitive training, dietary advice, and monitoring vascular risk factors, resulted in improvement or maintenance of cognitive functioning in the intervention group as compared to the control group. Whether the proof-of-concept result of less cognitive decline is further reflected in less clinical cognitive disorders will be tested during follow-up.

## Secondary Prevention and Rehabilitation of Clinical Cognitive Disorders

Physical activity is an important part of rehabilitation in cognitive disorders such as Alzheimer's disease. These dementing diseases are sooner or later associated with stiffening of muscles, balance problems, and gait instability, which impair ADL, predispose falls, and interfere with care procedures. Sarcopenia and progressing frailty are also prevalent among patients with dementia. Various interventions utilizing aerobic and resistance exercises, balance training, and interventions aiming to improve functional capacity have been able to improve mobility of dementia patients, and with long-term, regular, and intensive training, functional capacity has been improved (Pitkälä et al., 2013a). This was demonstrated in the Finnish Alzheimer Disease Exercise (FINALEX) study, where home-living Alzheimer patients were randomized to three trial arms: (1) intervention with group-based exercise (4-hour sessions with approximately 1-hour training); (2) intervention with individualized home-based exercise (1-hour training, both twice a week for 1 year); and (3) a control group receiving the usual community care (Pitkälä et al., 2013b). Intervention consisted of both aerobic and resistance training. Mobility and functional capacity were assessed with Functional Independence Measure (FIM) and the Short Physical Performance Battery.

Intervention had significant beneficial effect on physical functioning as compared to the control group and intervention groups. The intervention groups

Table 11.1 *Features of physical activity probably beneficial for brain health*

- Has beneficial effects on chronic – especially cardiovascular – disease risk factors
- Provides mental and social stimuli
- Leads to new surroundings
- Challenges to learn new ways of thinking and functioning
- Activates senses
- Is safe and not too stressful

also had significantly fewer falls than controls during the follow-up year (Öhman et al., 2016a). There was also beneficial effect on executive function, but not in other domains of cognition (Öhman et al., 2016b). It is of note that even the home-based PA intervention in FINALEX was safe and did not increase costs (Pitkälä et al., 2013b).

Because of scarcity of reliable clinical trials, it is not yet possible to give exact recommendations of PA for prevention of cognitive disorders. General conclusions can, however, be drawn from neurophysiology and available clinical studies. Physical activity is probably beneficial for brain health, which includes the features depicted in Table 11.1.

## Mental and Social Dimensions of Physical Activity

Physical activity produces well-being and its beneficial physiological effects are reflected in the psychological state of individuals. Being physically active protects from depression and this applies also to older and functionally impaired people (Strawbridge et al., 2002). Resistance training reduces depressive symptoms and improves sleep quality (Singh et al., 2005). Various exercises improving cardiorespiratory fitness, muscle strength, joint flexibility, and balance have been shown to improve psychological well-being in older people (Windle et al., 2010).

Exercise in group sessions offers a possibility to meet other people and relieve loneliness; ensuing social contacts are a beneficial side effect of such PA. Improving and preserving mobility also permits various social activities: visiting relatives and friends, going shopping, and attending concerts and exhibitions.

## How to Activate Older People to Exercise

There are international guidelines of PA and exercise, which include older people (https://health.gov/paguidelines/pdf/paguide.pdf, WHO, 2010). In Table 11.2, there is a summary of recommendations in various conditions (modified from Savela et al., 2015). In old age it is especially important to train muscle

Table 11.2  *Physical activity in various conditions common in older people*

| Condition or aim | Recommendation |
| --- | --- |
| Maintaining functional capacity, cognition, mood; Prevention of depression | Physical activity according to general guidelines:<br>– Moderate aerobic exercise ≥ 150 min/week or heavy aerobic exercise ≥ 75 min/week<br>– At least moderate muscle strength training ≥ 2×/week, large muscle groups, 8–12 repetitions/ muscle group<br>– Joint flexibility and balance training, especially if risk of falling or chronic disease or disability is affecting mobility and balance |
| Sarcopenia | – Primary: muscle strength training 2–3 ×/week, 60–80 percent of 1RM for large muscle groups, 8–12 repetitions/muscle group |
| Frailty | – Primary: versatile exercise including progressive muscle strength training 40–80 percent of 1RM, progressive balance training, functional training (walking, gait, plays, etc.), and aerobic exercise 3×/week, 45–60 min/session |
| Promotion of bone health | – Primary: progressive muscle strength training 70–80 percent of 1RM, 2–3 series, 8–12 repetitions/series, 2–3×/week<br>– Balance and flexibility training<br>– Moderate aerobic exercise, ≥ 30 min daily |
| Osteopenia | – For the promotion of bone health, but progressive muscle strength training 50 percent of 1RM |
| Osteoporosis | – Primary: strengthening of spinal muscles and correction of posture with mild or moderate efficiency<br>– Balance promoting training 2–3 ×/week<br>– Moderate aerobic exercise ≥ 30 min daily |
| Prevention of falls and fractures | – Primary: progressive muscle strength training 60–80 percent of 1RM, 10–15 repetitions, 2–3 ×/week<br>– Balance and mobility training at least 2 ×/week<br>– Moderate aerobic exercise ≥ 2.5 hours/week |

1RM = one repetition maximum (maximal resistance at which a person is able to make one repetition).

strength in the lower extremities, otherwise many different PA types can be recommended and are important for patient adherence. Most chronic diseases are not contraindications for PA, rather the other way around. However, tailoring PA for specific clinical states and resources is naturally needed.

For those older people who have been physically inactive, have disabilities, and comorbidities, expert consultation (geriatrician, physiotherapist) is recommended for planning an exercise program. It is also worthwhile to check the medication list for possible drugs interfering with PA. It is of utmost importance to guide and motivate the patient to exercise regularly and long-term. For caregivers, their guidance and motivation is naturally instrumental in patients with cognitive disorders and other conditions affecting functional independence.

## Conclusions

Healthy aging, well-being, and functional independence in later life are major issues in aging societies and major goals of good geriatric care. Promoting PA over the life-course and in old age, especially among the frailest, is important to maintain and even improve mobility and functional capacity. It must be possible for all older people – including those in nursing homes and hospitals – to be physically active, but it is necessary to individualize the mode of PA.

## References

Andrieu S., Coley N., Lovestone, Aisen P. S., Vellas B. Prevention of sporadic Alzheimer's disease: lessons learned from clinical trials and future directions. *Lancet Neurol.* 2015;14:926–44.

Blain H., Masud T., Dargent-Molina P., et al. EUGMS Falls and Fracture Interest Group; European Society for Clinical and Economic Aspects of Osteoporosis and Osteoarthritis (ESCEO), Osteoporosis Research and Information Group (GRIO), and International osteoporosis Foundation (IOF). A Comprehensive Fracture Prevention Strategy in Older Adults: The European Union Geriatric Medicine Society (EUGMS) Statement. *J Nutr Health Aging.* 2016;20(6):647–52.

Boyle P. A., Buchman A. S., Wilson R. S., et al. Physical activity is associated with incident disability in community-based older persons. *J Am Geriatr Soc.* 2007;55(2):195–201.

Brown B. M., Peiffer J. J., Martins R. N. Multiple effects of physical activity on molecular and cognitive signs of brain aging: can exercise slow neurodegeneration and delay Alzheimer's disease? *Mol Psychiatry.* 2013;18(8):864–74.

Colcombe S., Kramer A. F. Fitness effects on the cognitive function of older adults: a meta-analytic study. *Psychol Sci.* 2003;14(2):125–30.

Cosman F., de Beur S. J., LeBoff M. S., et al. Clinician's Guide to Prevention and Treatment of Osteoporosis. *Osteoporos Int.* 2014; 25(10):2359–81.

Cruz-Jentoft A. J., Landi F., Schneider S. M., et al. Prevalence of and interventions for sarcopenia in ageing adults: a systematic review. Report of the International Sarcopenia Initiative (EWGSOP and IWGS). *Age Ageing.* 2014;43(6):748–59.

Fiatarone M. A., O'Neill E. F., Ryan N. D., et al. Exercise training and nutritional supplementation for physical frailty in very elderly people. *N Engl J Med.* 1994;330(25):1769–75.

Giangregorio L. M., McGill S., Wark J. D., et al. Too Fit To Fracture: outcomes of a Delphi consensus process on physical activity and exercise recommendations for adults with osteoporosis with or without vertebral fractures. *Osteoporos Int.* 2015;26(3):891–910.

Gorelick P. B., Scuteri A., Black S. E., et al. Vascular contributions to cognitive impairment and dementia. A statement for healthcare professionals from the American Heart /American Stroke Association. *Stroke.* 2011;42:2672–713.

Kohrt W. M., Bloomfield S. A., Little K. D., et al. American College of Sports Medicine Position Stand: physical activity and bone health. *Med Sci Sports Exerc.* 2004;36(11):1985–96.

Komulainen P., Kivipelto M., Lakka T. A., et al. Exercise, fitness and cognition – a randomised controlled trial in older individuals: the DR's EXTRA study. *Eur Geriatr Med.* 2010;1:266–72.

Lafortune L., Martin S., Kelly S., et al. Behavioural risk factors in mid-life associated with successful ageing, disability, dementia and frailty in later life: a rapid systematic review. *PLos One.* 2016;11(2):e0144405. doi:0.1371/journal.pone.0144405

Landi F., Cesari M., Calvani R., et al. The "Sarcopenia and Physical fRailty IN older people: multi-componenT Treatment strategies" (SPRINTT) randomized controlled trial: design and methods. *Aging Clin Exp Res.* 2017;29(1):89–100. doi:10.1007/s40520-016-0715-2

Liu C. J., Latham N. K. Progressive resistance strength training for improving physical function in older adults. *Cochrane Database Syst Rev.* 2009;(3):CD002759.

Marques E. A., Mota J., Carvalho J. Exercise effects on bone mineral density in older adults: a meta-analysis of randomized controlled trials. *Age (Dordr).* 2012; 34:1493–515.

Messinger-Rapport B. J., Gammack J. K., Thomas D. R., et al. Clinical update on nursing home medicine: 2013. *J Am Med Dir Assoc.* 2013;14(12):860–76.

Ngandu T., Lehtisalo J., Solomon A., et al. A 2 year multidomain intervention of diet, exercise, cognitive training, and vascular risk monitoring versus control to prevent cognitive decline in at-risk elderly people (FINGER): a randomised controlled trial. *Lancet* 2015;385(9984):2255–63.

Öhman H., Savikko N., Strandberg T., et al. Effects of exercise on functional performance and fall rate in subjects with mild or advanced Alzheimer's disease: secondary analyses of a randomized controlled study. *Dement Geriatr Cogn Disord.* 2016a;41(3–4):233–41.

Öhman H., Savikko N., Strandberg T. E., et al. Effects of exercise on cognition: the Finnish Alzheimer Disease Exercise Trial (FINALEX): a randomized, controlled trial. *J Am Geriatr Soc.* 2016b; 64:731–8.

Pahor M., Guralnik J. M., Ambrosius W. T., et al. Effect of structured physical activity on prevention of major mobility disability in older adults: the LIFE study randomized clinical trial. *JAMA.* 2014;311(23):2387–96.

Paterson D. H., Warburton D. E. Physical activity and functional limitations in older adults: a systematic review related to Canada's Physical Activity Guidelines. *Int J Behav Nutr Phys Act.* 2010;7:38. doi:10.1186/1479-5868-7-38

Pitkälä K., Savikko N., Pöysti M., Strandberg T., Laakkonen M. L. Efficacy of physical exercise intervention on mobility and physical functioning in older people with dementia: a systematic review. *Exp Gerontol.* 2013a;48:85–93.

Pitkälä K. H., Pöysti M. M., Laakkonen M. L., et al. Effects of the Finnish Alzheimer disease exercise trial (FINALEX): a randomized controlled trial. *JAMA Intern Med.* 2013b;173(10):894–901.

Reid K. F., Martin K. I., Doros G., et al. Comparative effects of light or heavy resistance power training for improving lower extremity power and physical performance in mobility-limited older adults. *J Gerontol A Biol Sci Med Sci.* 2015;70(3):374–80.

Salpakoski A., Törmäkangas T., Edgren J., et al. Effects of a multicomponent home-based physical rehabilitation program on mobility recovery after hip fracture: a randomized controlled trial. *J Am Med Dir Assoc.* 2014;15(5):361–8.

Savela S., Komulainen P., Sipilä S., Strandberg T. Physical activity of the elderly – what kind of and what for? (in Finnish). *Duodecim.* 2015;131(18):1719–25.

Savela S. L., Koistinen P., Stenholm S., et al. Leisure-time physical activity in midlife is related to old age frailty. *J Gerontol A Biol Sci Med Sci.* 2013;68(11):1433–8.

Singh M. A. Exercise comes of age: rationale and recommendations for a geriatric exercise prescription. *J Gerontol A Biol Sci Med Sci.* 2002;57(5):M262–82.

Singh N. A., Stavrinos T. M., Scarbek Y., et al. A randomized controlled trial of high versus low intensity weight training versus general practitioner care for clinical depression in older adults. *J Gerontol A Biol Sci Med Sci.* 2005;60(6):768–76.

Sink K. M., Espeland M. A., Castro C. M., et al. Effect of a 24-month physical activity intervention vs health education on cognitive outcomes in sedentary older adults: the LIFE randomized trial. *JAMA.* 2015;314(8):781–90.

Smith P. J., Blumenthal J. A., Hoffman B. M., et al. Aerobic exercise and neurocognitive performance: a meta-analytic review of randomized controlled trials. *Psychosom Med.* 2010;72(3):239–52.

Stessman J., Hammerman-Rozenberg R., Cohen A., et al. Physical activity, function, and longevity among the very old. *Arch Intern Med.* 2009;169(16):1476–83.

Strandberg T. E., Pitkälä K. H., Tilvis R. S. Frailty in older people. *Eur Geriatr Med.* 2011;2:344–55.

Strawbridge W. J., Deleger S., Roberts R. E., et al. Physical activity reduces the risk of subsequent depression for older adults. *Am J Epidemiol.* 2002;156(4):328–34.

Van Roie E., Delecluse C., Coudyzer W., et al. Strength training at high versus low external resistance in older adults: effects on muscle volume, muscle strength, and force-velocity characteristics. *Exp Gerontol.* 2013;48(11):1351–61.

Weening-Dijksterhuis E., de Greef M. H., Scherder E. J., et al. Frail institutionalized older persons: A comprehensive review on physical exercise, physical fitness, activities of daily living, and quality-of-life. *Am J Phys Med Rehabil.* 2011;90(2):156–68.

WHO. World Report on Ageing and Health. 2015. http://apps.who.int/iris/bitstream/10665/186463/1/9789240694811_eng.pdf

Global recommendations on physical activity for health. *World Health Organization* 2010. ISBN 978 92 4 159 997 9.

Windle G., Hughes D., Linck P., et al. Is exercise effective in promoting mental well-being in older age? A systematic review. *Aging Ment Health.* 2010;14(6):652–69.

# 12 Nutrition and Cognition

Stany Perkisas and Maurits Vandewoude

## Introduction

There is an increasing average life span that is shifting the demographic curve worldwide. The World Health Organization projects that by 2050, the world's population over 60 years old will nearly double, from 12 percent (900 million) to 22 percent (2 billion). This will be accompanied by an increase in chronic conditions, including neurocognitive disorders. An estimated 44 million people worldwide were living with dementia in 2013 with numbers predicted to double every 20 years, reaching 135 million affected by 2050 (World Health Organization, 2012). Although there is still a lack of consensus in measuring quality of life (QoL) in dementia (Bowling et al., 2015), there is abundant evidence that cognitive decline negatively affects the QoL of both the patient and his/her primary caregiver (Thomas et al., 2006; Wetzels et al., 2010; Black et al., 2012; Langlois et al., 2012; Leroi et al., 2012).

In accord with other geriatric syndromes, the processes underlying the development of dementia span a far longer period than previously thought (Shatenstein et al., 2015). Many acquired risk factors for dementia such as hypertension, diabetes, and obesity may be modified by diet (Middleton and Yaffe, 2009). There is an increasing body of evidence that both nutritional status and specific nutrients may have an effect on cognitive function (Gustafson et al., 2015). Currently, there are no dietary recommendations or accepted health claims referring to age-related cognition on the foodstuffs marketed (Vauzour et al., 2016). In this chapter, the current evidence on nutrients and their effect on cognition will be summarized.

## Screening and Assessment of Nutritional Status

One's nutritional state should be regarded as a vital sign, just as blood pressure or heart rate. Evidence supporting the negative health outcomes of malnutrition is ever-growing and includes higher hospitalization/re-hospitalization rates (Lim et al., 2012), longer length of hospital stays (Kyle et al., 2006; Stratton et al., 2006), higher in-hospital complication rates (Putwatana et al., 2005; Sorensen et al., 2008), higher healthcare costs (Lim et al., 2012; Gomes et al., 2016), and increased mortality risk (Henderson et al., 2008; Ozkalkanli et al., 2009; Gomes et al., 2016). However, malnutrition is still widespread, both in hospitalized and community-dwelling persons. Since there is no golden standard by which to assess or diagnose malnutrition, different screening tools and criteria are used.

## Nutritional Status in Cognitive Decline

There is a marked evolution of the nutritional state in persons with cognitive decline. Weight loss is a strong clinical feature herein, being present often in the pre-symptomatic phases and becoming more pronounced with time (Gillette Guyonnet et al., 2007; Albanese et al., 2013; Volkert et al., 2015). There are some hypotheses, although the exact mechanisms are still incompletely understood (Gillette Guyonnet et al., 2007; Smith and Greenwood, 2008). Neurodegeneration in specific brain regions (mesial temporal cortex) involved in appetite regulation and eating behavior could imply a link between limbic system damage and low body weight in Alzheimer's disease (AD) (Grundman et al., 1996; Volkert et al., 2015). Olfactory system decline in AD could lead to decreased appetite and thus weight loss (Braak et al., 1999; Stanciu et al., 2014; Volkert et al., 2015). Apolipoprotein E-e4 allele (APOE) has been related to weight loss in AD and early olfactory loss of function, even before the onset of cognitive impairment (Vanhanen et al., 2001; Olofsson et al., 2010; Volkert et al., 2015). The clinical outing of these mechanisms is a reduced dietary intake and eventually malnutrition. This is exacerbated by certain typical problems in cognitive decline: difficulties with shopping, storing and preparing food, remembering meals, and losing the ability to initiate or continue effective eating strategies (Volkert et al., 2015). Also behavioral problems such as agitation, hyperactivity, or meal refusal make mealtimes difficult and increase energy requirements (Fjellstrom et al., 2010; Silva et al., 2013). In later stages clear pathological symptoms can be seen, such as the inability to recognize food, oral-tactile agnosia, and swallowing and feeding apraxia, leading to dysphasia and increased risk of aspiration and death (Chouinard et al., 1998; Langmore et al., 2002; Volkert et al., 2015). This is sometimes supplemented by already present problems inherent to older age such as anorexia of aging (Malafarina et al., 2013), chewing problems (Laudisio et al., 2014), dental difficulties (Ramsay et al., 2015), and depression (Regan et al., 2013).

## Nutrients

### Antioxidants

Oxidative stress is an important mechanism that plays a central role in brain aging. The brain relies heavily on oxidative phosphorylation as a way for maintaining energy (Vauzour et al., 2016), forming active oxyradicals and various other free radicals that can possibly damage the phospholipid, protein and DNA molecules as also modulate cell signaling pathways and gene expression pattern (Chakrabarti et al., 2011). This poses a great threat to neuronal homeostasis and leads to the development of neurodegenerative diseases (Wang et al., 2014; Vauzour et al., 2016). Overfeeding, high caloric/low dietary fiber diet, consumption of low antioxidant nutrients, sedentary lifestyle, and emotional stress have been reported as key environmental factors for oxidative stress and brain disorders (Martin et al., 2006; Mattson, 2012; Vauzour et al., 2016).

However, some free radical forming is still thought to have a protective effect, since a moderate oxy-radical production can upregulate the mitochondrial biogenesis program and brain antioxidant capacity, thus protecting the brain (Vauzour et al., 2016). This remains a delicate balance (Chakrabarti et al., 2011). Antioxidant supplementation could have a positive effect on cognitive decline, although the literature herein in still limited (Chakrabarti et al., 2011; Rafnsson et al., 2013).

Some trace elements seem to have beneficial effects on the prevention of cognitive decline, probably through their antioxidant properties (Vauzour et al., 2016). Zinc, selenium, and chromium protect against cerebral oxidative stress; a deficiency of these trace elements is linked to cognitive decline (Akbaraly et al., 2007; Roussel et al., 2007; Krikorian et al., 2010; Nuttall and Oteiza, 2014). However, only chromium supplementation has been linked with improved cognitive function (Krikorian et al., 2010).

Regarding the antioxidant effects of certain vitamins, we refer to their specific segment further in this chapter.

## Vitamins

### *Vitamin B*

At present, eight vitamin B subtypes are seen as important cofactors/coenzymes. The strongest evidence regarding cognitive function, however, is found in vitamin B6 (pyridoxine), B9 (folic acid), and B12 (cobalamine), through their inverse relation with homocysteine. Rising homocysteine levels contribute to amyloid/Tau protein accumulation and neuronal death, and are regarded as important risk factors for AD (Clarke et al., 1998; Seshadri et al., 2002; Obeid and Herrmann, 2006; Vauzour et al., 2016). Homocysteine stimulates neurotoxicity, apoptosis, and platelet activation (contributing to white matter lesions, vascular injury, and ischemic strokes) (Vauzour et al., 2016). Supplementation of vitamin B has given inconsistent results. It seemed to have a positive impact on executive and planning function (de Jager et al., 2012), global cognition scores, attention and executive function scores (Moorthy et al., 2012), cognitive decline (de Jager et al., 2012; Alzheimer's Disease International, 2014), slowed shrinkage of the whole brain volume, and reduced cerebral atrophy associated with AD and cognitive decline (Smith et al., 2010; Douaud et al., 2013). Recent reviews (Malouf and Areosa Sastre, 2003), randomized controlled trials (Walker et al., 2012; Douaud et al., 2013; Hankey et al., 2013), and observational studies (Sachdev et al., 2002; Vogiatzoglou et al., 2008; de Lau et al., 2009; Smith et al., 2010; Tangney et al., 2011b) also seem to be leaning more toward a positive effect (Vauzour et al., 2016). Other systematic reviews (Malouf and Areosa Sastre, 2003; O'Leary et al., 2012) and meta-analyses (Ford and Almeida, 2012; Clarke et al., 2014), however, did not procure the same results, with the overall tone being that there was no significant effect of vitamin B supplementation on individual cognitive domains, global cognitive function, or cognitive aging (Vauzour et al., 2016).

## Vitamin C

The role of vitamin C in supporting cognitive function remains controversial (Harrison, 2012). Prospective studies of dietary intake and supplements were predominantly negative, while studies measuring plasma concentration were mostly positive, but limited by their cross-sectional designs. According to the "sink hypothesis," the brain preserves the antioxidant capacity of the central nervous system by obtaining at any cost the essential amount of vitamin C needed from peripheral pools (Bowman, 2012). Additional research needs to clarify the role of vitamin C.

## Vitamin D

Vitamin D is associated with multiple conditions, including osteoporosis, falls, cancer, heart disease, type 2 diabetes mellitus, and stroke (Vauzour et al., 2016). Since vitamin D receptors were found in the brain (Brouwer-Brolsma and de Groot, 2015), investigation points toward an association of vitamin D between all-cause dementia and AD (Anastasiou et al., 2014; Schlogl and Holick, 2014; Annweiler et al., 2015). Current literature has not been able to prove a causal link between vitamin D and cognition, dementia, or neuroimaging abnormalities. There are also no interventional studies proving a causal relationship between vitamin D deficiency and cognitive problems (Balion et al., 2012).

## Vitamin E

Vitamin E is a collective term for eight naturally occurring compounds, four tocopherols (alpha-, beta-, gamma-, and delta-), and four tocotrienols (alpha-, beta-, gamma-, and delta-). A high dietary intake of tocopherols is associated with a reduced incidence of dementia (Mangialasche et al., 2011). However, interventional studies using vitamin E supplementation failed to report positive effects on the risk of AD (Barnard et al., 2014). Initially thought to only have antioxidant properties, more recent investigation shows an effect on the regulation of signal transduction, gene expression, and redox sensing (Joshi and Pratico, 2012). The inconsistent findings from the clinical studies may be partially explained by the use of pure alpha-tocopherol, which is less effective than, for example, gamma-tocopherol in terms of antioxidant and anti-inflammatory properties (Usoro and Mousa, 2010). However, a recent trial suggested possible benefits for alpha-tocopherol in mild to moderate AD by slowing functional decline and decreasing caregiver burden (Dysken et al., 2014). In fact, clinical and epidemiological observations support the idea that the protective role may be related more to the balance between different forms, rather than to the action of the single molecule (Mangialasche et al., 2013).

## Omega-3 Polyunsaturated Fatty Acids (Omega-3 PUFA)

The brain consists of almost 60 percent adipose tissue, and fatty acids are of utmost importance in maintaining cerebral integrity and function (Chang et al., 2009). They are incorporated into cerebral cell membranes and influence different functions such as cellular signaling, transmembrane transport, cerebral inflammation, synthesizing neurotransmitters, and lipid messengers, which participate in signaling cascades that can either promote neuronal injury or neuroprotection (Chang et al., 2009; Janssen and Kiliaan, 2014; Vauzour et al., 2016).

## Polyphenols

Polyphenols are found in vegetables, legumes, fruits, nuts, coffee, tea, wine, and chocolate (Llorach et al., 2012).

There is some evidence regarding polyphenols and positive health effects on certain chronic conditions such as cardiovascular diseases, cancer, osteoporosis, diabetes, and neurodegenerative diseases (Arts and Hollman, 2005; Scalbert et al., 2005; Hooper et al., 2008; McCullough et al., 2012; Cassidy et al., 2013; van Dam et al., 2013; Zamora-Ros et al., 2014; Vauzour et al., 2016). These effects involve modulation of the AMPK-autophagy systems, present in neuronal and glial cells, which could in theory prevent neurodegeneration (Vauzour et al., 2016). However, results are limited and inconsistent (Zamora-Ros et al., 2014), probably due to the polyphenol metabolome, which is characterized by diverse biological properties in about 500 polyphenols, posing a large bias in measurement and dietary assessment (Zamora-Ros et al., 2014). Current literature suggests that perhaps single polyphenols should be targeted instead of the entire group (Zamora-Ros et al., 2012, 2014). One specific polyphenol, found in cinnamon, reversed Tau protein aggregation and broke up Tau filaments *in vitro*, counteracting the increase of amyloid precursor protein (APP) and Tau protein in rat studies (Peterson et al., 2009; Anderson et al., 2013; Vauzour et al., 2016).

## Flavonoids

Flavonoids are part of the polyphenol family, but are discussed separately because of the multitude of studies on this subgroup. This group of phytonutrients, which consists of more than 6,000 different types, is found in almost all fruits and vegetables.

Although it is believed that the primary action of flavonoids is through its antioxidant properties, many other pathways have been proposed: influencing different aspects of synaptic plasticity (Spencer, 2008; Williams and Spencer, 2012; Del Rio et al., 2013), combatting neuronal dysfunction and toxicity, recruiting anti-apoptotic pro-survival signaling pathways, increasing antioxidant gene expression, reducing Aβ pathology (Williams et al., 2004, 2012; Williams and Spencer, 2012), modulating the activation status of neuronal receptors, signaling proteins and gene expression (Williams et al., 2008; Rendeiro et al., 2012, 2013), inhibiting/reducing both βγ-secretase activity and Aβ production, and inhibiting the β-site amyloid precursor protein cleaving enzyme 1 (Cox et al., 2015). There are some animal studies describing changes in synaptic plasticity markers (Spencer, 2009).

Due to the poor bioavailability, the extensively *in vivo* metabolization, and the use in studies of 100 times higher concentrations than found in a normal diet, there is a lack of consensus in interpreting the various studies (Vauzour et al., 2016). There seems to be some evidence of flavonoid-rich foods being associated with cognitive benefits (Macready et al., 2010; Williams and Spencer, 2012), although the exact mechanisms are unclear. A lot of evidence suggests that these effects are due to changes in peripheral vascular function and cerebral blood flow in a nitric oxide mediated way (Attwell et al., 2010). Particular flavanols (Schroeter et al., 2006, 2010) and anthocyanins (Rodriguez-Mateos et al., 2013) can activate endothelial nitric oxide synthesis (Schroeter et al., 2006) and/or inhibit NADPH oxidase activity (Rodriguez-Mateos et al., 2013; Vauzour et al., 2016). This positively affects cerebral arterial dilatation (Atochin and Huang, 2011; Rodriguez-Mateos et al., 2013). Some studies state that neurons can also release nitric oxide, increasing the cerebral blood flow in adjacent arterioles and capillaries (Schroeter et al., 2006; Vauzour et al., 2016). Magnetic resonance imaging studies found an increase of blood flow in particular regions of the brain (Brickman et al., 2014; Lamport et al., 2015), more specifically, the dentate gyrus of the hippocampus, a region responsible for local neurogenesis (Bakker et al., 2008; Yassa et al., 2011; Brickman et al., 2014). However, no cause-effect relationship has been investigated between flavonoid intake, vascular function, and cognitive performance (Williams et al., 2008; Rendeiro et al., 2012, 2013; Corona et al., 2013; Vauzour et al., 2016).

Data on *Ginkgo biloba* (flavonoid) is very inconsistent. It appears to improve memory, attention, and overall cognitive performance (Kanowski et al., 1997; Le Bars et al., 1997), but other studies did not show a difference of reduction in cognitive decline between study groups (Snitz et al., 2009; Vellas et al., 2012), a reduction of incidence rate of dementia (DeKos et al., 2008), or even a significant evidence for a clinical benefit Birks and Evans, 2009).

## Carotenoids

Carotenoids (lycopene, lutein, zeaxanthin, astaxanthin, β-cryptoxanthin, α-carotene, and β-carotene) are found mostly in vegetables and fruits (Vauzour et al., 2016). Only lycopene is associated with cognitive performance

(Polidori et al., 2009; Vauzour et al., 2016). Astaxanthin, phosphatidylserine, and vitamin E supplements improved memory skills in mild cognitive impairment (Zanotta et al., 2014; Vauzour et al., 2016).

## Caffeine

Caffeine is a central nervous system stimulant, but evidence for its effect on cognitive processes is inconsistent. Cross-sectional and longitudinal population-based studies suggest possible protective effects for coffee, tea, and caffeine use against cognitive impairment or decline, but systematic reviews did not find convincing evidence for an association between caffeine intake and cognitive change or risk of dementia (Beydoun et al., 2014; Panza et al., 2015).

## Alcohol

Moderate consumption of alcoholic beverages (<15.0 g of alcohol/day) during late life is associated with higher cognitive functioning and a decreased risk of dementia (Stampfer et al., 2005; Lang et al., 2007). This is consistent with studies that examined the relationship between alcohol consumption during midlife and cognitive functioning in late life (Virtaa et al., 2010; Kesse-Guyot et al., 2012). However, additional research indicates that the protective effects may be influenced by gender (Lyu and Lee, 2012), the presence of APO-E4 alleles (Downer et al., 2014), or genetic differences in metabolizing alcohol (Ritchie et al., 2014). A recent longitudinal study showed that only red wine consumption was consistently associated with less strong cognitive decline (Nooyens et al., 2014). These data suggest that non-alcoholic substances, such as polyphenols in red wine, are responsible for cognition-preserving effects (Nooyens et al., 2014). The anti-inflammatory properties of alcohol and the protective effects against risk factors for dementia such as stroke, coronary heart disease, and type 2 diabetes may contribute to the observed association (Imhof et al., 2001). However, excessive alcohol consumption is associated with significant health risks and increased mortality (Di Castelnuovo et al., 2006). A daily consumption of more than 36 g alcohol (about 360 ml wine) was associated with a faster cognitive decline (Sabia et al., 2014), suggesting that the positive effects of alcohol on cognition are not seen in heavy drinkers.

## Diets

### Calorie Restriction

The effect of calorie restriction (CR) on the brain is derived largely from animal studies and is situated in the process of hippocampal atrophy and neurogenesis. In humans, hippocampal neurogenesis decreases with age, and has been linked to mood and cognition (Stangl and Thuret, 2009; Zainuddin, 2012; Murphy and Thuret, 2014). Limiting intake when compared to unrestricted appeared to enhance hippocampal neurogenesis in a mouse model (Wu et al., 2008b). It is important to note that essential micronutrients (vitamins, minerals, and others) were given in normal amounts. Calorie restriction also seems to have a protective effect on synapses, with an increase in the expression of genes that are involved in synaptic plasticity (Park and Prolla, 2005) and a diminished effect of metabolic and oxidative damage (Mattson, 2012). This data could be vital, since synaptic plasticity is paramount in understanding neurodegenerative processes occurring during AD (Maruszak et al., 2014). Rodents, rats, and mice under long-term CR have shown increased neurogenesis in the hippocampus (Snyder et al., 2011; Mateus-Pinheiro et al., 2013), increased expression of hippocampal NMDA receptors (Yilmaz et al., 2011), and improved working memory (Steinman et al., 2011; Kuhla et al., 2013). Nutrition seems to have an impact on hippocampal neurogenesis and mental health (Murphy et al., 2014). More research is needed to sort out which nutritional components specifically partake in the process of brain plasticity and synaptic function.

## Ketogenic Diets

Ketogenic diets (KD) have been used for almost a hundred years in various settings, such as neurological diseases (Hartman et al., 2007; Baranano and Hartman, 2008), endocrinological diseases (Dashti et al., 2006), cardiovascular problems (Paoli et al., 2011), and weight loss (Paoli et al., 2013). Ketone bodies have a negative effect on the production of reactive oxygen species in neurological tissues, stimulate mitochondrial biogenesis, act as neuroprotective agents by raising ATP levels, and help regulate neuronal membrane excitability by stimulating polyunsaturated fatty acid synthesis (Huffman and Kossoff, 2006; Bough and Rho, 2007).

Rodent studies in a specific dietary variant, the medium chain triglyceride ketogenic diet, have helped unravel the effects in seizure control (Chang et al., 2015). Decanoic acid, provided in the diet, reduced excitatory postsynaptic currents and inhibited α-amino-3-hydroxy-5-methyl-4-isoxazolepropionic acid receptors, which are targeted by certain antiepileptic drugs. This effect is enhanced during synaptic activation. By these effects, reduced seizures were induced in hippocampal slices of rodent brains without the production of ketone bodies (Chang et al., 2013, 2015). This could be an important feature in dementia pathology, since there is a higher incidence of seizures in AD (Palop and Mucke, 2009). One study could correlate the oral administration of medium chain triglycerides with an improved cognitive function in patients with mild cognitive impairment or probable AD (Reger et al., 2004). It is hypothesized that this is due to the increase of serum β-hydroxybutyrate. A stabilization of cognitive function was seen in mild to moderate AD after ingestion of 40 grams of medium chain triglycerides (Craft et al., 2000). It must be said, however, that this last effect was strongly dependent on APO-E genotype.

## Multi-component Approach

It has been long known that lifestyle and diet have an effect on certain diseases, such as cardiovascular ones (Bang et al., 1971, 1980; Estruch et al., 2013). This effect is largely due to the lipid fraction of the diet, which has direct effects on synaptic function and cognitive processes (Wurtman, 2008; Kamphuis and Scheltens, 2010; Shah, 2011; Shah et al., 2013; de Waal et al., 2014; van Wijk et al., 2014). Saturated fatty acids, for example, increase the risk of neurological dysfunction with increased intake (Gomez-Pinilla, 2008; Wu et al., 2008a; Li et al., 2013). Other possible interactions influenced by diet are synaptic transmission, membrane fluidity, signal transduction, neurotransmitter pathways, decreased inflammation, restored cerebral blood flow and volume, inhibited neurodegeneration, and enhanced neural plasticity by increased neurogenesis (Jansen et al., 2013, 2014; Wiesmann et al., 2013; Zerbi et al., 2014; Vauzour et al., 2016).

The evidence presented in this chapter so far has been rather unfavorable in terms of clear results on cognition, either positive or negative. This could partly be explained by multifactorial etiology, the long duration of the asymptomatic phase, and the uncertain evolution of cognitive problems. Perhaps another piece of the puzzle is that single nutrients might not have the same strong action as a multi-component approach (Engelborghs et al., 2014). With this insight, two different options are highlighted: the Mediterranean diet and medical foods.

## The Mediterranean Diet

The Mediterranean diet (MD) is characterized by a high intake of fruits, vegetables, legumes, cereals, fish and seafood, and olive oil, and a moderate intake of alcohol, mainly wine, consumed with meals, and a low intake of meat and dairy products (Trichopoulou et al., 2003; Vauzour et al., 2016). Several other typical compounds of the MD, such as onions, garlic, purslane, and spices (especially, rosemary, thyme, and oregano), deserve further research because their possible effects on cognition are still poorly understood. Table 12.1 summarizes the main nutritional characteristics of these food groups relevant to brain structure and functioning (Vandewoude et al., 2016). It must be noted that there is a great heterogeneity in the definition of the MD between studies, especially in non-Mediterranean countries (Vauzour et al., 2016).

Evidence is still uncertain regarding the MD and cognition. Although there are positive results, where the MD lowers the risk of cognitive decline (Feart et al., 2009; Tangney et al., 2011a; Martinez-Lapiscina et al., 2013; Tsivgoulis et al., 2013; Wengreen et al., 2013), mild cognitive impairment (Scarmeas et al., 2009; Martinez-Lapiscina et al., 2013), and AD (Scarmeas et al., 2006; Psaltopoulou et al., 2013; Singh et al., 2014), although some studies did not find a protective effect (Cherbuin and Anstey, 2012; Vercambre et al., 2012).

Regarding other known risk factors for dementia and cognitive decline, the MD could lower the risk for cardiovascular diseases (Sofi et al., 2010) and diabetes (Kastorini et al., 2011; Salas-Salvado et al., 2011), reduce plasma

Table 12.1 *Nutritional characteristics of the Mediterranean diet (Zerbi et al., 2014)*

| Food groups | Main nutritional components relevant to cognition |
|---|---|
| **High intake** | |
| Fruits and nuts | Vitamins C and E, carotenoids, polyphenols, ω-3 PUFA (mainly alpha-linolenic acid, ALA) |
| Vegetables | Vitamin C, carotenoids, polyphenols, folate |
| Legumes | Low glycemic index |
| Cereals | Low glycemic index, vitamin B6 |
| Fish and seafood | Long-chain ω-3 PUFAs (EPA and DHA), vitamin D |
| Olive oil | Monounsaturated fat (in substitution to other fat types), polyphenols |
| **Moderate intake** | |
| Alcohol (mainly wine) | Polyphenols |
| **Low intake** | |
| Meat | Saturated fat |
| Dairy products | Saturated fat |

ω-3 PUFA: Omega-3 polyunsaturated fatty acid.

homocysteine levels (high intake of vitamin B6 and B9) (Feart et al., 2012), and also have anti-inflammatory effects through the higher intake of omega-3 polyunsaturated fatty acids and antioxidants (e.g., vitamins C and E) (Frisardi et al., 2010; Valls-Pedret et al., 2015).

The low intake of dairy products leading to low calcium intake (Feart et al., 2012), combined with low meat consumption and a moderate consumption of alcoholic beverages may not be recommended for older people, especially those at risk of malnutrition (Zerbi et al., 2014).

### Medical Foods

With increasing age, it seems to become more and more difficult to ingest all the required single nutrients by diet alone. A simple manner in which to replace all of these is by use of medical foods, ensuring a multi-nutrient approach that can work synergistically and be more interesting than single-nutrient supplementation (Engelborghs et al., 2014). Studies executed in patients with early dementia stages given medical foods compared to placebo seemed to show a positive effect on cognition, with positive effects on the memory domain of neuropsychological test batteries (Scheltens et al., 2012), functional connectivity (Scheltens et al., 2012), functional brain network organization (de Waal et al., 2014), and sustained memory improvement (Olde Rikkert et al., 2015; Vauzour et al., 2016). With these products, the aim is to create new, and maintain existing, neuronal structures (Wurtman et al., 2009; Cansev et al., 2015).

## Conclusion

There is still a lack of interventional studies proving the effect of specific nutrients on cognition – a short overview is again given in Table 12.2. This evidence will undoubtedly be hard to acquire, seeing that both the intervention and the underlying pathology require a long period of time to take effect. This gives way to the advice that already in young and midlife adults, an optimal

Table 12.2 *Overview of compounds and their interventions and results*

| Compound | Intervention/observation | Result |
| --- | --- | --- |
| **Nutrients** | | |
| Antioxidants | Antioxidant supplementation | Positive effect on CD |
| | Zinc, selenium, chromium deficiency | Linked to CD |
| | Chromium supplementation | Linked with ↑ cognitive function |
| Vitamin B | Vitamin B supplementation | – Inconsistent results<br>– Possible positive impact on executive and planning function, global cognition scores, attention and executive function scores, and cognitive decline<br>– No significant effect on individual cognitive domains, global cognitive function, or cognitive aging |
| Vitamin C | Vitamin C supplementation | Predominantly negative results |
| Vitamin D | Vitamin D deficiency | No proof of causal relationship with cognitive problems |
| Vitamin E | High dietary intake of tocopherols | Association with ↓ incidence of dementia |
| | Vitamin E supplementation | No positive effects on risk of AD |
| | Alpha-tocopherol supplementation | Possible benefits in AD |
| ω-3 PUFA | (Fish) long-chain ω-3 PUFA supplementation | – Inconsistent results<br>– No effect on cognitive function<br>– Some positive findings in specific cognitive domains |
| Polyphenols | Dietary intake of polyphenols | Results are limited and inconsistent |
| | Specific polyphenol found in cinnamon | – Reversion of Tau protein aggregation<br>– Counteracting increase of amyloid precursor protein and Tau protein in rat studies |

*(cont.)*

Table 12.2 (*cont.*)

| Compound | Intervention/observation | Result |
|---|---|---|
| Flavonoids | Flavanols and anthocyanins | Positive effect on cerebral arterial dilatation |
| | Dietary flavonoid intake | No cause-effect relationship proven with cognitive performance |
| | *Ginkgo biloba* supplementation | – Data is limited and inconsistent<br>– ↑ memory, attention, and overall cognitive performance<br>– No difference of reduction in cognitive decline, incidence rate of dementia<br>– No significant evidence for a clinical benefit |
| Carotenoids | Dietary intake of lycopene | Association with cognitive performance |
| | Astaxanthin, phosphatidylserine, and vitamin E supplementation | ↑ memory skills in MCI |
| Caffeine | Dietary intake of coffee, tea, and caffeine | – Possibly protective against MCI or decline<br>– No association with cognitive change or risk of dementia |
| Alcohol | Moderate consumption of alcoholic beverages (<15.0 g of alcohol/day) during late life | Possible association with ↑ cognitive function and ↓ dementia risk |
| | Dietary intake of red wine | Associated with less strong CD |
| | Dietary intake of >36 g alcohol daily | Association with a faster CD |
| **Diets** | | |
| Calorie restriction | Caloric restriction diet | ↑ of hippocampal neurogenesis in a mouse model |
| Ketogenic diets | Medium chain triglyceride supplementation | ↑ of cognitive function in MCI or probable AD |
| Mediterranean diet | Use of the MD | – Inconsistent results<br>– Possibly ↓ risk of cognitive decline, MCI, and AD |
| Medical foods | Use of medical foods | Positive effect on cognition and on the memory domain of neuropsychological test batteries and sustained memory improvement |

CD: Cognitive decline, AD: Alzheimer dementia, ω-3 PUFA: ω-3 polyunsaturated fatty acids, MCI: mild cognitive impairment, MD: Mediterranean diet.

nutritional health must be pursued, and that nutritional awareness should be more stressed in the education of adolescents.

When malnutrition is detected, in all age ranges, correction is paramount, both for specific depletions, as also overall nutritional status. Using a multi-nutritional approach often has better results than targeting a single nutrient.

Although epidemiological evidence favors the use of the Mediterranean diet, it is valuable to shift through the different types proposed, and while acknowledging their flaws, also take into account the individual. A high proportionate intake of cereals, fruits, fish, vegetables, and olive oil is recommended, but possible low calcium intake, low meat consumption, and moderate consumption of alcoholic beverages may not be recommended for older people.

In summary, although some advice can be given, there is still little evidence for dietary recommendations in the prevention of cognitive decline. Further work is needed on nutritional awareness in younger age groups to increase the effect of possible intervention.

## References

Akbaraly, T. N., I. Hininger-Favier, I. Carriere, et al., Plasma selenium over time and cognitive decline in the elderly. *Epidemiology*, 2007; 18(1): 52–8.

Albanese, E., C. Taylor, M. Siervo, et al., Dementia severity and weight loss: a comparison across eight cohorts. The 10/66 study. *Alzheimers Dement*, 2013; 9(6): 649–56.

Anastasiou, C. A., M. Yannakoulia, N. Scarmeas, Vitamin D and cognition: an update of the current evidence. *J Alzheimers Dis*, 2014; 42(Suppl 3): S71–80.

Anderson, R. A., B. Qin, F. Canini, et al., Cinnamon counteracts the negative effects of a high fat/high fructose diet on behavior, brain insulin signaling and Alzheimer-associated changes. *PLoS ONE*, 2013; 8(12): e83243.

Annweiler, C., E. Dursun, F. Feron, et al., "Vitamin D and cognition in older adults": updated international recommendations. *J Intern Med*, 2015; 277(1): 45–57.

Arts, I. C., P. C. Hollman, Polyphenols and disease risk in epidemiologic studies. *Am J Clin Nutr*, 2005; 81(1 Suppl): 317S–25S.

Atochin, D. N., P. L. Huang, Role of endothelial nitric oxide in cerebrovascular regulation. *Curr Pharm Biotechnol*, 2011; 12(9): 1334–42.

Attwell, D., A. M. Buchan, S. Charpak, et al., Glial and neuronal control of brain blood flow. *Nature*, 2010; 468(7321): 232–43.

Bakker, A., C. B. Kirwan, M. Miller, et al., Pattern separation in the human hippocampal CA3 and dentate gyrus. *Science*, 2008; 319(5870): 1640–2.

Balion, C., L. E. Griffith, L. Strifler, et al., Vitamin D, cognition, and dementia: a systematic review and meta-analysis. *Neurology*, 2012; 79(13): 1397–405.

Bang, H. O., J. Dyerberg, A. B. Nielsen, Plasma lipid and lipoprotein pattern in Greenlandic West-coast Eskimos. *Lancet*, 1971; 1(7710): 1143–5.

Bang, H. O., J. Dyerberg, H. M. Sinclair, The composition of the Eskimo food in north western Greenland. *Am J Clin Nutr*, 1980; 33(12): 2657–61.

Baranano, K. W., A. L. Hartman, The ketogenic diet: uses in epilepsy and other neurologic illnesses. *Curr Treat Options Neurol*, 2008; 10(6): 410–19.

Barberger-Gateau, P., C. Raffaitin, L. Letenneur, et al., Dietary patterns and risk of dementia: the Three-City cohort study. *Neurology*, 2007; 69(20): 1921–30.

Barberger-Gateau, P., L. Letenneur, V. Deschamps, et al., Fish, meat, and risk of dementia: cohort study. *BMJ*, 2002; 325(7370): 932–3.

Barnard, N. D., A. I. Bush, A. Ceccarelli, et al., Dietary and lifestyle guidelines for the prevention of Alzheimer's disease. *Neurobiol Aging*, 2014; 35(Suppl 2): S74–8.

Beydoun, M. A., H. A. Beydoun, A. A. Gamaldo, et al., Epidemiologic studies of modifiable factors associated with cognition and dementia: systematic review and meta-analysis. *BMC Public Health*, 2014; 14: 643.

Birks, J., J. Grimley Evans, *Ginkgo biloba* for cognitive impairment and dementia. *Cochrane Database Syst Rev*, 2009; (1): CD003120.

Black, B. S., D. Johnston, A. Morrison, et al., Quality of life of community-residing persons with dementia based on self-rated and caregiver-rated measures. *Qual Life Res*, 2012; 21(8): 1379–89.

Bough, K. J., J. M. Rho, Anticonvulsant mechanisms of the ketogenic diet. *Epilepsia*, 2007; 48(1): 43–58.

Bowling, A., G. Rowe, S. Adams, et al., Quality of life in dementia: a systematically conducted narrative review of dementia-specific measurement scales. *Aging Ment Health*, 2015; 19(1): 13–31.

Bowman, G. L., Ascorbic acid, cognitive function, and Alzheimer's disease: a current review and future direction. *Biofactors*, 2012; 38(2): 114–22.

Braak, E., K. Griffing, K. Arai, et al., Neuropathology of Alzheimer's disease: what is new since A. Alzheimer? *Eur Arch Psychiatry Clin Neurosci*, 1999; 249(Suppl 3): 14–22.

Brickman, A. M., U. A. Khan, F. A. Provenzano, et al., Enhancing dentate gyrus function with dietary flavanols improves cognition in older adults. *Nat Neurosci*, 2014; 17(12): 1798–803.

Brouwer-Brolsma, E. M., L. C. de Groot, Vitamin D and cognition in older adults: an update of recent findings. *Curr Opin Clin Nutr Metab Care*, 2015; 18(1): 11–16.

Cansev, M., N. van Wijk, M. Turkyilmaz, et al., A specific multi-nutrient enriched diet enhances hippocampal cholinergic transmission in aged rats. *Neurobiol Aging*, 2015; 36(1): 344–51.

Cassidy, A., K. J. Mukamal, L. Liu, et al., High anthocyanin intake is associated with a reduced risk of myocardial infarction in young and middle-aged women. *Circulation*, 2013; 127(2): 188–96.

Cederholm, T., J. Palmblad, Are omega-3 fatty acids options for prevention and treatment of cognitive decline and dementia? *Curr Opin Clin Nutr Metab Care*, 2010; 13(2): 150–5.

Chakrabarti, S., S. Munshi, K. Banerjee, et al., Mitochondrial dysfunction during brain aging: role of oxidative stress and modulation by antioxidant supplementation. *Aging Dis*, 2011; 2(3): 242–56.

Chang, C. Y., D. S. Ke, J. Y. Chen, Essential fatty acids and human brain. *Acta Neurol Taiwan*, 2009; 18(4): 231–41.

Chang, P., N. Terbach, N. Plant, et al., Seizure control by ketogenic diet-associated medium chain fatty acids. *Neuropharmacology*, 2013; 69: 105–14.

Chang, P., K. Augustin, K. Boddum, et al., Seizure control by decanoic acid through direct AMPA receptor inhibition. *Brain*, 2015: 1–13.

Cherbuin, N., K. J. Anstey, The Mediterranean diet is not related to cognitive change in a large prospective investigation: the PATH Through Life study. *Am J Geriatr Psychiatry*, 2012; 20(7): 635–9.

Chouinard, J., E. Lavigne, C. Villeneuve, Weight loss, dysphagia, and outcome in advanced dementia. *Dysphagia*, 1998; 13(3): 151–5.

Clarke, R., A. D. Smith, K. A. Jobst, et al., Folate, vitamin B12, and serum total homocysteine levels in confirmed Alzheimer disease. *Arch Neurol*, 1998; 55(11): 1449–55.

Clarke, R., D. Bennett, S. Parish, et al., Effects of homocysteine lowering with B vitamins on cognitive aging: meta-analysis of 11 trials with cognitive data on 22,000 individuals. *Am J Clin Nutr*, 2014; 100(2): 657–66.

Conklin, S. M., P. J. Gianaros, S. M. Brown, et al., Long-chain omega-3 fatty acid intake is associated positively with corticolimbic gray matter volume in healthy adults. *Neurosci Lett*, 2007; 421(3): 209–12.

Corona, G., D. Vauzour, J. Hercelin, et al., Phenolic acid intake, delivered via moderate champagne wine consumption, improves spatial working memory via the modulation of hippocampal and cortical protein expression/activation. *Antioxid Redox Signal*, 2013; 19(14): 1676–89.

Cox, C. J., F. Choudhry, E. Peacey, et al., Dietary (−)-epicatechin as a potent inhibitor of betagamma-secretase amyloid precursor protein processing. *Neurobiol Aging*, 2015; 36(1): 178–87.

Craft, S., S. Asthana, G. Schellenberg, et al., Insulin effects on glucose metabolism, memory, and plasma amyloid precursor protein in Alzheimer's disease differ according to apolipoprotein-E genotype. *Ann N Y Acad Sci*, 2000; 903: 222–8.

Dangour, A. D., E. Allen, R. Clarke, et al., A randomised controlled trial investigating the effect of vitamin B12 supplementation on neurological function in healthy older people: the Older People and Enhanced Neurological function (OPEN) study protocol [ISRCTN54195799]. *Nutr J*, 2011; 10: 22.

Dashti, H. M., N. S. Al-Zaid, T. C. Mathew, et al., Long term effects of ketogenic diet in obese subjects with high cholesterol level. *Mol Cell Biochem*, 2006; 286(1–2): 1–9.

de Jager, C. A., A. Oulhaj, R. Jacoby, et al., Cognitive and clinical outcomes of homocysteine-lowering B-vitamin treatment in mild cognitive impairment: a randomized controlled trial. *Int J Geriatr Psychiatry*, 2012; 27(6): 592–600.

de Lau, L. M., A. D. Smith, H. Refsum, et al., Plasma vitamin B12 status and cerebral white-matter lesions. *J Neurol Neurosurg Psychiatry*, 2009; 80(2): 149–57.

de Waal, H., C. J. Stam, M. M. Lansbergen, et al., The effect of souvenaid on functional brain network organisation in patients with mild Alzheimer's disease: a randomised controlled study. *PLoS ONE*, 2014; 9(1): e86558.

DeKosky, S. T., J. D. Williamson, A. L. Fitzpatrick, et al., *Ginkgo biloba* for prevention of dementia: a randomized controlled trial. *JAMA*, 2008; 300(19): 2253–62.

Del Rio, D., A. Rodriguez-Mateos, J. P. Spencer, et al., Dietary (poly)phenolics in human health: structures, bioavailability, and evidence of protective effects against chronic diseases. *Antioxid Redox Signal*, 2013; 18(14): 1818–92.

Di Castelnuovo, A., S. Costanzo, V. Bagnardi, et al., Alcohol dosing and total mortality in men and women: an updated meta-analysis of 34 prospective studies. *Arch Intern Med*, 2006; 166(22): 2437–45.

Douaud, G., H. Refsum, C. A. de Jager, et al., Preventing Alzheimer's disease-related gray matter atrophy by B-vitamin treatment. *Proc Natl Acad Sci U S A*, 2013; 110(23): 9523–8.

Downer, B., F. Zanjani, D. W. Fardo, The relationship between midlife and late life alcohol consumption, APOE e4 and the decline in learning and memory among older adults. *Alcohol Alcohol*, 2014; 49(1): 17–22.

Dysken, M. W., M. Sano, S. Asthana, et al., Effect of vitamin E and memantine on functional decline in Alzheimer disease: the TEAM-AD VA cooperative randomized trial. *JAMA*, 2014; 311(1): 33–44.

Engelborghs, S., C. Gilles, A. Ivanoiu, et al., Rationale and clinical data supporting nutritional intervention in Alzheimer's disease. *Acta Clin Belg*, 2014; 69(1): 17–24.

Estruch, R., E. Ros, J. Salas-Salvado, et al., Primary prevention of cardiovascular disease with a Mediterranean diet. *N Engl J Med*, 2013; 368(14): 1279–90.

Feart, C., B. Alles, B. Merle, et al., Adherence to a Mediterranean diet and energy, macro-, and micronutrient intakes in older persons. *J Physiol Biochem*, 2012; 68(4): 691–700.

Feart, C., C. Samieri, V. Rondeau, et al., Adherence to a Mediterranean diet, cognitive decline, and risk of dementia. *JAMA*, 2009; 302(6): 638–48.

Fjellstrom, C., A. Starkenberg, A. Wesslen, et al., To be a good food provider: an exploratory study among spouses of persons with Alzheimer's disease. *Am J Alzheimers Dis Other Demen*, 2010; 25(6): 521–6.

Ford, A. H., O. P. Almeida, Effect of homocysteine lowering treatment on cognitive function: a systematic review and meta-analysis of randomized controlled trials. *J Alzheimers Dis*, 2012; 29(1): 133–49.

Freund-Levi, Y., M. Eriksdotter-Jonhagen, T. Cederholm, et al., Omega-3 fatty acid treatment in 174 patients with mild to moderate Alzheimer disease: OmegAD study: a randomized double-blind trial. *Arch Neurol*, 2006; 63(10): 1402–8.

Frisardi, V., F. Panza, D. Seripa, et al., Nutraceutical properties of Mediterranean diet and cognitive decline: possible underlying mechanisms. *J Alzheimers Dis*, 2010; 22(3): 715–40.

Gillette Guyonnet, S., G. Abellan Van Kan, E. Alix, et al., IANA (International Academy on Nutrition and Aging) Expert Group: weight loss and Alzheimer's disease. *J Nutr Health Aging*, 2007; 11(1): 38–48.

Gomes, F., P. W. Emery, C. E. Weekes, Risk of Malnutrition Is an Independent Predictor of Mortality, Length of Hospital Stay, and Hospitalization Costs in Stroke Patients. *J Stroke Cerebrovasc Dis*, 2016; 25(4): 799–806.

Gomez-Pinilla, F., Brain foods: the effects of nutrients on brain function. *Nat Rev Neurosci*, 2008; 9(7): 568–78.

Grundman, M., J. Corey-Bloom, T. Jernigan, et al., Low body weight in Alzheimer's disease is associated with mesial temporal cortex atrophy. *Neurology*, 1996; 46(6): 1585–91.

Guerchet, M., Prina, M., Prince, M., et al. *Nutrition and Dementia. A Review of Available Research.* London: Alzheimer's Disease International (ADI).

Gustafson, D. R., M. Clare Morris, N. Scarmeas, et al., New perspectives on Alzheimer's disease and nutrition. *J Alzheimers Dis*, 2015; 46(4): 1111–27.

Hankey, G. J., A. H. Ford, Q. Yi, J. W. Eikelboom, et al., Effect of B vitamins and lowering homocysteine on cognitive impairment in patients with previous stroke or transient ischemic attack: a prespecified secondary analysis of a randomized, placebo-controlled trial and meta-analysis. *Stroke*, 2013; 44(8): 2232–9.

Harrison, F. E., A critical review of vitamin C for the prevention of age-related cognitive decline and Alzheimer's disease. *J Alzheimers Dis*, 2012; 29(4): 711–26.

Hartman, A. L., M. Gasior, E. P. Vining, et al., The neuropharmacology of the ketogenic diet. *Pediatr Neurol*, 2007; 36(5): 281–92.

Henderson, S., N. Moore, E. Lee, et al., Do the malnutrition universal screening tool (MUST) and Birmingham nutrition risk (BNR) score predict mortality in older hospitalised patients? *BMC Geriatr*, 2008; 8: 26.

Hooper, L., P. A. Kroon, E. B. Rimm, et al., Flavonoids, flavonoid-rich foods, and cardiovascular risk: a meta-analysis of randomized controlled trials. *Am J Clin Nutr*, 2008; 88(1): 38–50.

Huffman, J., E. H. Kossoff, State of the ketogenic diet(s) in epilepsy. *Curr Neurol Neurosci Rep*, 2006; 6(4): 332–40.

Imhof, A., M. Froehlich, H. Brenner, et al., Effect of alcohol consumption on systemic markers of inflammation. *Lancet*, 2001; 357(9258): 763–7.

Jansen, D., V. Zerbi, I. A. Arnoldussen, et al., Effects of specific multi-nutrient enriched diets on cerebral metabolism, cognition and neuropathology in AbetaPPswe-PS1dE9 mice. *PLoS One*, 2013; 8(9): e75393.

Jansen, D., V. Zerbi, C. I. Janssen, et al., Impact of a multi-nutrient diet on cognition, brain metabolism, hemodynamics, and plasticity in apoE4 carrier and apoE knockout mice. *Brain Struct Funct*, 2014; 219(5): 1841–68.

Janssen, C. I., A. J. Kiliaan, Long-chain polyunsaturated fatty acids (LCPUFA) from genesis to senescence: the influence of LCPUFA on neural development, aging, and neurodegeneration. *Prog Lipid Res*, 2014; 53: 1–17.

Joshi, Y. B., D. Pratico, Vitamin E in aging, dementia, and Alzheimer's disease. *Biofactors*, 2012; 38(2): 90–7.

Kamphuis, P. J., P. Scheltens, Can nutrients prevent or delay onset of Alzheimer's disease? *J Alzheimers Dis*, 2010; 20(3): 765–75.

Kanowski, S., W. M. Herrmann, K. Stephan, et al., Proof of efficacy of the *Ginkgo biloba* special extract EGb 761 in outpatients suffering from mild to moderate primary degenerative dementia of the Alzheimer type or multi-infarct dementia. *Phytomedicine*, 1997; 4(1): 3–13.

Kastorini, C. M., H. J. Milionis, K. Esposito, et al., The effect of Mediterranean diet on metabolic syndrome and its components: a meta-analysis of 50 studies and 534,906 individuals. *J Am Coll Cardiol*, 2011; 57(11): 1299–313.

Kesse-Guyot, E., V. A. Andreeva, C. Jeandel, et al., Alcohol consumption in midlife and cognitive performance assessed 13 years later in the SU.VI.MAX 2 cohort. *PLoS One*, 2012; 7(12): e52311.

Krikorian, R., J. C. Eliassen, E. L. Boespflug, et al., Improved cognitive-cerebral function in older adults with chromium supplementation. *Nutr Neurosci*, 2010; 13(3): 116–22.

Kuhla, A., S. Lange, C. Holzmann, et al., Lifelong caloric restriction increases working memory in mice. *PLoS One*, 2013; 8(7): e68778.

Kyle, U. G., M. P. Kossovsky, V. L. Karsegard, et al., Comparison of tools for nutritional assessment and screening at hospital admission: a population study. *Clin Nutr*, 2006; 25(3): 409–17.

Lamport, D. J., D. Pal, C. Moutsiana, et al., The effect of flavanol-rich cocoa on cerebral perfusion in healthy older adults during conscious resting state: a placebo controlled, crossover, acute trial. *Psychopharmacology (Berl)*, 2015; 232(17): 3227–34.

Lang, I., R. B. Wallace, F. A. Huppert, et al., Moderate alcohol consumption in older adults is associated with better cognition and well-being than abstinence. *Age Ageing*, 2007; 36(3): 256–61.

Langlois, F., T. T. Vu, M. J. Kergoat, et al., The multiple dimensions of frailty: physical capacity, cognition, and quality of life. *Int Psychogeriatr*, 2012; 24(9): 1429–36.

Langmore, S. E., K. A. Skarupski, P. S. Park, et al., Predictors of aspiration pneumonia in nursing home residents. *Dysphagia*, 2002; 17(4): 298–307.

Laudisio, A., Y. Milaneschi, S. Bandinelli, et al., Chewing problems are associated with depression in the elderly: results from the InCHIANTI study. *Int J Geriatr Psychiatry*, 2014; 29(3): 236–44.

Le Bars, P. L., M. M. Katz, N. Berman, et al., A placebo-controlled, double-blind, randomized trial of an extract of *Ginkgo biloba* for dementia. North American EGb Study Group. *JAMA*, 1997; 278(16): 1327–32.

Leroi, I., K. McDonald, H. Pantula, et al., Cognitive impairment in Parkinson disease: impact on quality of life, disability, and caregiver burden. *J Geriatr Psychiatry Neurol*, 2012; 25(4): 208–14.

Li, W., R. Prakash, D. Chawla, et al., Early effects of high-fat diet on neurovascular function and focal ischemic brain injury. *Am J Physiol Regul Integr Comp Physiol*, 2013; 304(11): R1001–8.

Lim, S. L., K. C. Ong, Y. H. Chan, et al., Malnutrition and its impact on cost of hospitalization, length of stay, readmission and 3-year mortality. *Clin Nutr*, 2012; 31(3): 345–50.

Llorach, R., M. Garcia-Aloy, S. Tulipani, et al., Nutrimetabolomic strategies to develop new biomarkers of intake and health effects. *J Agric Food Chem*, 2012; 60(36): 8797–808.

Lyu, J., S. H. Lee, Gender differences in the link between excessive drinking and domain-specific cognitive functioning among older adults. *J Aging Health*, 2012; 24(8): 1380–98.

Macready, A. L., L. T. Butler, O. B. Kennedy, et al., Cognitive tests used in chronic adult human randomised controlled trial micronutrient and phytochemical intervention studies. *Nutr Res Rev*, 2010; 23(2): 200–29.

Malafarina, V., F. Uriz-Otano, L. Gil-Guerrero, et al., The anorexia of ageing: physiopathology, prevalence, associated comorbidity and mortality. A systematic review. *Maturitas*, 2013; 74(4): 293–302.

Malouf, R., A. Areosa Sastre, Vitamin B12 for cognition. *Cochrane Database Syst Rev*, 2003; (3): CD004326.

Mangialasche, F., A. Solomon, I. Kareholt, et al., Serum levels of vitamin E forms and risk of cognitive impairment in a Finnish cohort of older adults. *Exp Gerontol*, 2013; 48(12): 1428–35.

Mangialasche, F., W. Xu, M. Kivipelto, et al., Tocopherols and tocotrienols plasma levels are associated with cognitive impairment. *Neurobiol Aging*, 2011; 33(10): 2282–90.

Martin, B., M. P. Mattson, S. Maudsley, Caloric restriction and intermittent fasting: two potential diets for successful brain aging. *Ageing Res Rev*, 2006; 5(3): 332–53.

Martinez-Lapiscina, E. H., P. Clavero, E. Toledo, et al., Mediterranean diet improves cognition: the PREDIMED-NAVARRA randomised trial. *J Neurol Neurosurg Psychiatry*, 2013; 84(12): 1318–25.

Martinez-Lapiscina, E. H., P. Clavero, E. Toledo,et al., Virgin olive oil supplementation and long-term cognition: the PREDIMED-NAVARRA randomized, trial. *J Nutr Health Aging*, 2013; 17(6): 544–52.

Maruszak, A., A. Pilarski, T. Murphy, et al., Hippocampal neurogenesis in Alzheimer's disease: is there a role for dietary modulation? *J Alzheimers Dis*, 2014; 38(1): 11–38.

Mateus-Pinheiro, A., L. Pinto, J. M. Bessa, et al., Sustained remission from depressive-like behavior depends on hippocampal neurogenesis. *Transl Psychiatry*, 2013; 1: e210.

Mattson, M. P., Energy intake and exercise as determinants of brain health and vulnerability to injury and disease. *Cell Metab*, 2012; 16(6): 706–22.

Mazereeuw, G., K. L. Lanctot, S. A. Chau, et al., Effects of omega-3 fatty acids on cognitive performance: a meta-analysis. *Neurobiol Aging*, 2012; 33(7): 1482. e17–1482.e29.

McCullough, M. L., J. J. Peterson, R. Patel, et al., Flavonoid intake and cardiovascular disease mortality in a prospective cohort of US adults. *Am J Clin Nutr*, 2012; 95(2): 454–64.

Middleton, L. E., K. Yaffe, Promising strategies for the prevention of dementia. *Arch Neurol*, 2009; 66(10): 1210–15.

Moorthy, D., I. Peter, T. M. Scott, et al., Status of vitamins B-12 and B-6 but not of folate, homocysteine, and the methylenetetrahydrofolate reductase C677T polymorphism are associated with impaired cognition and depression in adults. *J Nutr*, 2012; 142(8): 1554–60.

Morris, M. C., D. A. Evans, C. C. Tangney, et al., Fish consumption and cognitive decline with age in a large community study. *Arch Neurol*, 2005; 62(12): 1849–53.

Murphy, T., S. Thuret, The systemic milieu as a mediator of dietary influence on stem cell function during ageing. *Ageing Res Rev*, 2014; 19: 53–64.

Murphy, T., G. P. Dias, S. Thuret, Effects of diet on brain plasticity in animal and human studies: mind the gap. *Neural Plast*, 2014; 2014: 1–32.

Nooyens, A. C., H. B. Bueno-de-Mesquita, B. M. van Gelder, et al., Consumption of alcoholic beverages and cognitive decline at middle age: the Doetinchem Cohort Study. *Br J Nutr*, 2014; 111(4): 715–23.

Nuttall, J. R., P. I. Oteiza, Zinc and the aging brain. *Genes Nutr*, 2014; 9(1): 379.

Obeid, R., W. Herrmann, Mechanisms of homocysteine neurotoxicity in neurodegenerative diseases with special reference to dementia. *FEBS Lett*, 2006; 580(13): 2994–3005.

Olde Rikkert, M. G., F. R. Verhey, R. Blesa, et al., Tolerability and safety of Souvenaid in patients with mild Alzheimer's disease: results of multi-center, 24-week, open-label extension study. *J Alzheimers Dis*, 2015; 44(2): 471–80.

O'Leary, F., M. Allman-Farinelli, S. Samman, Vitamin B12 status, cognitive decline and dementia: a systematic review of prospective cohort studies. *Br J Nutr*, 2012; 108(11): 1948–61.

Olofsson, J. K., S. Nordin, S. Wiens, et al., Odor identification impairment in carriers of ApoE-varepsilon4 is independent of clinical dementia. *Neurobiol Aging*, 2010; 31(4): 567–77.

Ozkalkanli, M. Y., D. T. Ozkalkanli, K. Katircioglu, et al., Comparison of tools for nutrition assessment and screening for predicting the development of complications in orthopedic surgery. *Nutr Clin Pract*, 2009; 24(2): 274–80.

Palop, J. J., L. Mucke, Epilepsy and cognitive impairments in Alzheimer disease. *Arch Neurol*, 2009; 66(4): 435–40.

Panza, F., V. Solfrizzi, M. R. Barulli, et al., Coffee, tea, and caffeine consumption and prevention of late-life cognitive decline and dementia: a systematic review. *J Nutr Health Aging*, 2015; 19(3): 313–28.

Paoli, A., L. Cenci and K. A. Grimaldi, et al., Beyond weight loss: a review of the therapeutic uses of very-low-carbohydrate (ketogenic) diets. *Eur J Clin Nutr*, 2013; 67(8): 789–96.

Paoli, A., L. Cenci, K. A. Grimaldi, Effect of ketogenic Mediterranean diet with phytoextracts and low carbohydrates/high-protein meals on weight, cardiovascular risk factors, body composition and diet compliance in Italian council employees. *Nutr J*, 2011; 10(112): 1–8.

Park, S. K., T. A. Prolla, Lessons learned from gene expression profile studies of aging and caloric restriction. *Ageing Res Rev*, 2005; 4(1): 55–65.

Peterson D. W., R. C. George, F. Scaramozzino, et al., Cinnamon extracts inhibit Tau protein aggregation associated with Alzheimer's disease in vitro. *J Alzheimers Disease*, 2009; 17(3): 585–96.

Polidori, M. C., D. Pratico, F. Mangialasche, et al., High fruit and vegetable intake is positively correlated with antioxidant status and cognitive performance in healthy subjects. *J Alzheimers Dis*, 2009; 17(4): 921–7.

Pottala, J. V., K. Yaffe, J. G. Robinson, et al., Higher RBC EPA + DHA corresponds with larger total brain and hippocampal volumes: WHIMS-MRI Study. *Neurology*, 2014; 82(5): 435–42.

Psaltopoulou, T., T. N. Sergentanis, D. B. Panagiotakos, et al., Mediterranean diet, stroke, cognitive impairment, and depression: a meta-analysis. *Ann Neurol*, 2013; 74(4): 580–91.

Putwatana, P., P. Reodecha, Y. Sirapo-ngam, et al., Nutrition screening tools and the prediction of postoperative infectious and wound complications: comparison of methods in presence of risk adjustment. *Nutrition*, 2005; 21(6): 691–7.

Rafnsson, S. B., V. Dilis, A. Trichopoulou, Antioxidant nutrients and age-related cognitive decline: a systematic review of population-based cohort studies. *Eur J Nutr*, 2013; 52(6): 1553–67.

Ramsay, S. E., P. H. Whincup, R. G. Watt, et al., Burden of poor oral health in older age: findings from a population-based study of older British men. *BMJ Open*, 2015; 5(12): e009476.

Regan, C. O., P. M. Kearney, G. M. Savva, et al., Age and sex differences in prevalence and clinical correlates of depression: first results from the Irish Longitudinal Study on Ageing. *Int J Geriatr Psychiatry*, 2013; 28(12): 1280–7.

Reger, M. A., S. T. Henderson, C. Hale, et al., Effects of beta-hydroxybutyrate on cognition in memory-impaired adults. *Neurobiol Aging*, 2004; 25(3): 311–14.

Rendeiro, C., D. Vauzour, R. J. Kean, et al., Blueberry supplementation induces spatial memory improvements and region-specific regulation of hippocampal BDNF mRNA expression in young rats. *Psychopharmacology*, 2012; 223(3): 319–330.

Rendeiro, C., D. Vauzour, M. Rattray, et al., Dietary levels of pure flavonoids improve spatial memory performance and increase hippocampal brain-derived neurotrophic factor. *PLoS One*, 2013; 8(5): e63535.

Ritchie, S. J., T. C. Bates, J. Corley, et al., Alcohol consumption and lifetime change in cognitive ability: a gene x environment interaction study. *Age (Dordr)*, 2014; 36(3): 9638.

Rodriguez-Mateos, A., C. Rendeiro, T. Bergillos-Meca, et al., Intake and time dependence of blueberry flavonoid-induced improvements in vascular function: a randomized, controlled, double-blind, crossover intervention study with mechanistic insights into biological activity. *Am J Clin Nutr*, 2013; 98(5): 1179–91.

Roussel, A. M., M. Andriollo-Sanchez, M. Ferry, et al., Food chromium content, dietary chromium intake and related biological variables in French free-living elderly. *Br J Nutr*, 2007; 98(2): 326–31.

Sabia, S., A. Elbaz, A. Britton, et al., Alcohol consumption and cognitive decline in early old age. *Neurology*, 2014; 82(4): 332–9.

Sachdev, P. S., M. Valenzuela, X. L. Wang, et al., Relationship between plasma homocysteine levels and brain atrophy in healthy elderly individuals. *Neurology*, 2002; 58(10): 1539–41.

Salas-Salvado, J., M. Bullo, N. Babio, et al., Reduction in the incidence of type 2 diabetes with the Mediterranean diet: results of the PREDIMED-Reus nutrition intervention randomized trial. *Diabetes Care*, 2011; 34(1): 14–19.

Samieri, C., P. Maillard, F. Crivello, et al., Plasma long-chain omega-3 fatty acids and atrophy of the medial temporal lobe. *Neurology*, 2012; 79(7): 642–50.

Samieri, C., S. Lorrain, B. Buaud, et al., Relationship between diet and plasma long-chain n-3 PUFAs in older people: impact of apolipoprotein E genotype. *J Lipid Res*, 2013; 54(9): 2559–67.

Scalbert, A., C. Manach, C. Morand, et al., Dietary polyphenols and the prevention of diseases. *Crit Rev Food Sci Nutr*, 2005; 45(4): 287–306.

Scarmeas, N., Y. Stern, R. Mayeux, et al., Mediterranean diet and mild cognitive impairment. *Arch Neurol*, 2009; 66(2): 216–25.

Scarmeas, N., Y. Stern, M. X. Tang, et al., Mediterranean diet and risk for Alzheimer's disease. *Ann Neurol*, 2006; 59(6): 912–21.

Scheltens, P., J. W. Twisk, R. Blesa, et al., Efficacy of Souvenaid in mild Alzheimer's disease: results from a randomized, controlled trial. *J Alzheimers Dis*, 2012; 31(1): 225–36.

Schlogl, M., M. F. Holick, Vitamin D and neurocognitive function. *Clin Interv Aging*, 2014; 9: 559–68.

Schroeter, H., C. Heiss, J. Balzer, et al., (−)-Epicatechin mediates beneficial effects of flavanol-rich cocoa on vascular function in humans. *Proc Natl Acad Sci U S A*, 2006; 103(4): 1024–9.

Schroeter, H., C. Heiss, J. P. Spencer, et al., Recommending flavanols and procyanidins for cardiovascular health: current knowledge and future needs. *Mol Aspects Med*, 2010; 31(6): 546–57.

Seshadri, S., A. Beiser, J. Selhub, et al., Plasma homocysteine as a risk factor for dementia and Alzheimer's disease. *N Engl J Med*, 2002; 346(7): 476–83.

Shah, R. C., P. J. Kamphuis, S. Leurgans, et al., The S-Connect study: results from a randomized, controlled trial of Souvenaid in mild-to-moderate Alzheimer's disease. *Alzheimers Res Ther*, 2013; 5(6): 1–9.

Shah, R. C. et al., Medical foods for Alzheimer's disease. *Drugs Aging*, 2011; 28(6): 421–8.

Shatenstein, B., P. Barberger-Gateau, P. Mecocci, Prevention of age-related cognitive decline: which strategies, when, and for whom? *J Alzheimers Dis*, 2015; 48(1): 35–53.

Silva, P., M. J. Kergoat, B. Shatenstein, Challenges in managing the diet of older adults with early-stage Alzheimer dementia: a caregiver perspective. *J Nutr Health Aging*, 2013; 17(2): 142–7.

Singh, B., A. K. Parsaik, M. M. Mielke, et al., Association of Mediterranean diet with mild cognitive impairment and Alzheimer's disease: a systematic review and meta-analysis. *J Alzheimers Dis*, 2014; 39(2): 271–82.

Sinn, N., C. M. Milte, S. J. Street, et al., Effects of n-3 fatty acids, EPA v. DHA, on depressive symptoms, quality of life, memory and executive function in older adults with mild cognitive impairment: a 6-month randomised controlled trial. *Br J Nutr*, 2012; 107(11): 1682–93.

Smith, A. D., S. M. Smith, C. A. de Jager, et al., Homocysteine-lowering by B vitamins slows the rate of accelerated brain atrophy in mild cognitive impairment: a randomized controlled trial. *PLoS One*, 2010; 5(9): e12244.

Smith, K. L., C. E. Greenwood, Weight loss and nutritional considerations in Alzheimer disease. *J Nutr Elder*, 2008; 27(3–4): 381–403.

Snitz, B. E., E. S. O'Meara, M. C. Carlson, et al., *Ginkgo biloba* for preventing cognitive decline in older adults: a randomized trial. *JAMA*, 2009; 302(24): 2663–70.

Snyder, J. S., A. Soumier, M. Brewer, et al., Adult hippocampal neurogenesis buffers stress responses and depressive behaviour. *Nature*, 2011; 476(7361): 458–61.

Sofi, F., R. Abbate, G. F. Gensini, et al., Accruing evidence on benefits of adherence to the Mediterranean diet on health: an updated systematic review and meta-analysis. *Am J Clin Nutr*, 2010; 92(5): 1189–96.

Sorensen, J., J. Kondrup, J. Prokopowicz, et al., EuroOOPS: an international, multicentre study to implement nutritional risk screening and evaluate clinical outcome. *Clin Nutr*, 2008; 27(3): 340–9.

Spencer, J. P., Food for thought: the role of dietary flavonoids in enhancing human memory, learning and neuro-cognitive performance. *Proc Nutr Soc*, 2008; 67(2): 238–52.

The impact of flavonoids on memory: physiological and molecular considerations. *Chem Soc Rev*, 2009; 38(4): 1152–61.

Stampfer, M. J., J. H. Kang, J. Chen, et al., Effects of moderate alcohol consumption on cognitive function in women. *N Engl J Med*, 2005; 352(3): 245–53.

Stanciu, I., M. Larsson, S. Nordin, et al., Olfactory impairment and subjective olfactory complaints independently predict conversion to dementia: a longitudinal, population-based study. *J Int Neuropsychol Soc*, 2014; 20(2): 209–17.

Stangl, D., S. Thuret, Impact of diet on adult hippocampal neurogenesis. *Genes Nutr*, 2009; 4(4): 271–82.

Steinman, M. Q., K. K. Crean, B. C. Trainor, Photoperiod interacts with food restriction in performance in the Barnes maze in female California mice. *Eur J Neurosci*, 2011; 33(2): 361–70.

Stratton, R. J., C. L. King, M. A. Stroud, et al., "Malnutrition Universal Screening Tool" predicts mortality and length of hospital stay in acutely ill elderly. *Br J Nutr*, 2006; 95(2): 325–30.

Sydenham, E., A. D. Dangour, W. S. Lim, Omega 3 fatty acid for the prevention of cognitive decline and dementia. *Cochrane Database Syst Rev*, 2012; 6: CD005379.

Tan, Z. S., W. S. Harris, A. S. Beiser, et al., Red blood cell omega-3 fatty acid levels and markers of accelerated brain aging. *Neurology*, 2012; 78(9): 658–64.

Tangney, C. C., M. J. Kwasny, H. Li, et al., Adherence to a Mediterranean-type dietary pattern and cognitive decline in a community population. *Am J Clin Nutr*, 2011a; 93(3): 601–7.

Tangney, C. C., N. T. Aggarwal, H. Li, et al., Vitamin B12, cognition, and brain MRI measures: a cross-sectional examination. *Neurology*, 2011b; 77(13): 1276–82.

Thomas, P., F. Lalloue, P. M. Preux, et al., Dementia patients caregivers quality of life: the PIXEL study. *Int J Geriatr Psychiatry*, 2006; 21(1): 50–6.

Titova, O. E., P. Sjogren, S. J. Brooks, et al., Dietary intake of eicosapentaenoic and docosahexaenoic acids is linked to gray matter volume and cognitive function in elderly. *Age (Dordr)*, 2013; 35(4): 1495–505.

Trichopoulou, A., T. Costacou, C. Bamia, et al., Adherence to a Mediterranean diet and survival in a Greek population. *N Engl J Med*, 2003; 348(26): 2599–608.

Tsivgoulis, G., S. Judd, A. J. Letter, et al., Adherence to a Mediterranean diet and risk of incident cognitive impairment. *Neurology*, 2013; 80(18): 1684–92.

Usoro, O. B., S. A. Mousa, Vitamin E forms in Alzheimer's disease: a review of controversial and clinical experiences. *Crit Rev Food Sci Nutr*, 2010; 50(5): 414–19.

Vakhapova, V., T. Cohen, Y. Richter, et al., Phosphatidylserine containing omega-3 Fatty acids may improve memory abilities in nondemented elderly individuals with memory complaints: results from an open-label extension study. *Dement Geriatr Cogn Disord*, 2014; 38(1–2): 39–45.

Valls-Pedret, C., A. Sala-Vila, M. Serra-Mir, et al., Mediterranean diet and age-related cognitive decline: a randomized clinical trial. *JAMA Intern Med*, 2015; 175(7): 1094–103.

van Dam, R. M., N. Naidoo, R. Landberg, Dietary flavonoids and the development of type 2 diabetes and cardiovascular diseases: review of recent findings. *Curr Opin Lipidol*, 2013; 24(1): 25–33.

van de Rest, O., J. M. Geleijnse, F. J. Kok, et al., Effect of fish-oil supplementation on mental well-being in older subjects: a randomized, double-blind, placebo-controlled trial. *Am J Clin Nutr*, 2008; 88(3): 706–13.

van de Rest, O., A. Spiro, 3rd, E. Krall-Kaye, et al., Intakes of (n-3) fatty acids and fatty fish are not associated with cognitive performance and 6-year cognitive change in men participating in the Veterans Affairs Normative Aging Study. *J Nutr*, 2009; 139(12): 2329–36.

van de Rest, O., L. W. van Hooijdonk, E. Doets, et al., B vitamins and n-3 fatty acids for brain development and function: review of human studies. *Ann Nutr Metab*, 2012; 60(4): 272–92.

van Wijk, N., L. M. Broersen, M. C. de Wilde, et al., Targeting synaptic dysfunction in Alzheimer's disease by administering a specific nutrient combination. *J Alzheimers Dis*, 2014; 38(3): 459–79.

Vandewoude M., et al., Healthy brain ageing and cognition: nutritional factors. *European Geriatric Medicine*, 2016; 7: 77–85.

Vanhanen, M., M. Kivipelto, K. Koivisto, et al., APOE-epsilon4 is associated with weight loss in women with AD: a population-based study. *Neurology*, 2001; 56(5): 655–9.

Vauzour, D., M. Camprubi-Robles, S. Miquel-Kergoat, et al., Nutrition for the ageing brain: towards evidence for an optimal diet. *Ageing Res Rev*, 2016; 35: 222–40.

Vellas, B., N. Coley, P. J. Ousset, et al., Long-term use of standardised *Ginkgo biloba* extract for the prevention of Alzheimer's disease (GuidAge): a randomised placebo-controlled trial. *Lancet Neurol*, 2012; 11(10): 851–9.

Vercambre, M. N., F. Grodstein, C. Berr, et al., Mediterranean diet and cognitive decline in women with cardiovascular disease or risk factors. *J Acad Nutr Diet*, 2012; 112(6): 816–23.

Virtaa, J. J., T. Jarvenpaa, K. Heikkila, et al., Midlife alcohol consumption and later risk of cognitive impairment: a twin follow-up study. *J Alzheimers Dis*, 2010; 22(3): 939–48.

Virtanen, J. K., D. S. Siscovick, W. T. Longstreth, et al., Fish consumption and risk of subclinical brain abnormalities on MRI in older adults. *Neurology*, 2008; 71(6): 439–46.

Vogiatzoglou, A., H. Refsum, C. Johnston, et al., Vitamin B12 status and rate of brain volume loss in community-dwelling elderly. *Neurology*, 2008; 71(11): 826–32.

Volkert, D., M. Chourdakis, G. Faxen-Irving, et al., ESPEN guidelines on nutrition in dementia. *Clin Nutr*, 2015; 34(6): 1052–73.

Walker, J. G., P. J. Batterham, A. J. Mackinnon, et al., Oral folic acid and vitamin B-12 supplementation to prevent cognitive decline in community-dwelling older adults with depressive symptoms – the Beyond Ageing Project: a randomized controlled trial. *Am J Clin Nutr*, 2012; 95(1): 194–203.

Wang, X., W. Wang, L. Li, et al., Oxidative stress and mitochondrial dysfunction in Alzheimer's disease. *Biochim Biophys Acta*, 2014; 1842(8): 1240–7.

Wengreen, H., R. G. Munger, A. Cutler, et al., Prospective study of Dietary Approaches to Stop Hypertension- and Mediterranean-style dietary patterns and age-related cognitive change: the Cache County Study on Memory, Health and Aging. *Am J Clin Nutr*, 2013; 98(5): 1263–71.

Wetzels, R. B., S. U. Zuidema, J. F. de Jonghe, et al., Determinants of quality of life in nursing home residents with dementia. *Dement Geriatr Cogn Disord*, 2010; 29(3): 189–97.

Wiesmann, M., D. Jansen, V. Zerbi, et al., Improved spatial learning strategy and memory in aged Alzheimer AbetaPPswe/PS1dE9 mice on a multi-nutrient diet. *J Alzheimers Dis*, 2013; 37(1): 233–45.

Williams, R. J., J. P. Spencer, C. Rice-Evans, Flavonoids: antioxidants or signalling molecules? *Free Radic Biol Med.*, 2004; 36(7): 838–49.

Williams, C. M., M. A. El Mohsen, D. Vauzour, et al., Blueberry-induced changes in spatial working memory correlate with changes in hippocampal CREB phosphorylation and brain-derived neurotrophic factor (BDNF) levels. *Free Radic Biol Med*, 2008; 45(3): 295–305.

Williams, R. J., J. P. Spencer, Flavonoids, cognition, and dementia: actions, mechanisms, and potential therapeutic utility for Alzheimer disease. *Free Radic Biol Med*, 2012; 52(1): 35–45.

Williamson, R., A. McNeilly, C. Sutherland, Insulin resistance in the brain: an old-age or new-age problem? *Biochem Pharmacol*, 2012; 84(6): 737–45.

Witte, A. V., L. Kerti, H. M. Hermannstadter, et al., Long-chain omega-3 fatty acids improve brain function and structure in older adults. *Cereb Cortex*, 2013; 24(11): 3059–68.

World Health Organization. *Dementia: A Public Health Priority*, 2012. Geneva, Switzerland: WHO Press.

Wu, A., Z. Ying, F. Gomez-Pinilla, Docosahexaenoic acid dietary supplementation enhances the effects of exercise on synaptic plasticity and cognition. *Neuroscience*, 2008a; 155(3): 751–9.

Wu, P., Q. Shen, S. Dong, et al., Calorie restriction ameliorates neurodegenerative phenotypes in forebrain-specific presenilin-1 and presenilin-2 double knockout mice. *Neurobiol Aging*, 2008b; 29(10): 1502–11.

Wurtman, R. J., M. Cansev, T. Sakamoto, et al., Use of phosphatide precursors to promote synaptogenesis. *Annu Rev Nutr*, 2009; 29: 59–87.

Wurtman, R. J., Synapse formation and cognitive brain development: effect of docosahexaenoic acid and other dietary constituents. *Metabolism*, 2008; 57(Suppl 2): S6–10.

Yassa, M. A., J. W. Lacy, S. M. Stark, et al., Pattern separation deficits associated with increased hippocampal CA3 and dentate gyrus activity in nondemented older adults. *Hippocampus*, 2011; 21(9): 968–79.

Yilmaz, N., H. Vural, M. Yilmaz, et al., Calorie restriction modulates hippocampal NMDA receptors in diet-induced obese rats. *J Recept Signal Transduct Res*, 2011; 31(3): 214–19.

Yurko-Mauro, K., D. McCarthy, D. Rom, et al., Beneficial effects of docosahexaenoic acid on cognition in age-related cognitive decline. *Alzheimers Dement*, 2010; 6(6): 456–64.

Zainuddin M. S., S. Thuret, Nutrition, adult hippocampal neurogenesis and mental health. *British Medical Bulletin*, 2012; 103(1): 25.

Zamora-Ros, R., M. Rabassa, R. Llorach, et al., Application of dietary phenolic biomarkers in epidemiology: past, present, and future. *J Agric Food Chem*, 2012; 60(27): 6648–57.

Zamora-Ros, R., M. Touillaud, J. A. Rothwell, et al., Measuring exposure to the polyphenol metabolome in observational epidemiologic studies: current tools and applications and their limits. *Am J Clin Nutr*, 2014; 100(1): 11–26.

Zanotta, D., S. Puricelli, G. Bonoldi, Cognitive effects of a dietary supplement made from extract of *Bacopa monnieri*, astaxanthin, phosphatidylserine, and vitamin E in subjects with mild cognitive impairment: a noncomparative, exploratory clinical study. *Neuropsychiatr Dis Treat*, 2014; 10: 225–30.

Zerbi, V., D. Jansen, M. Wiesmann, et al., Multinutrient diets improve cerebral perfusion and neuroprotection in a murine model of Alzheimer's disease. *Neurobiol Aging*, 2014; 35(3): 600–13.

# 13 Nutrition, Muscle Function, and Mobility in Older People

Rebecca Diekmann and Juergen M. Bauer

Nutrition requires special consideration in the older population, as it is more closely associated with functionality, morbidity, and mortality than in younger adults (FAO, 2001; Rothenberg, 2002). With increasing age, the preservation of independence and autonomy becomes a key issue for quality of life among seniors. For these reasons, all healthcare providers involved in the care of older persons should have a thorough knowledge of the nutritional requirements for healthy older adults and older patients as well. This chapter reviews the current evidence regarding energy requirements and micro- and macronutrient requirements. A special focus will be placed on the relevance of protein, including amino acids and vitamin D for muscle strength, muscle performance, and mobility.

## Basic Requirements of Macro-/Micronutrients in Older Adults

### Energy

In general, energy requirements decline with increasing age. This is a consequence of changes in body composition, including increasing fat mass and decreasing muscle mass. But the decline of physical activity in older age is much more important in this regard. The latter becomes most evident when older persons around age 70 are compared to those around age 90 (Rothenberg, 2002).

According to the Food and Agriculture Organization of the United Nations (FAO), the World Health Organization (WHO), and the United Nations University (UNU) expert consultation in the year 1985, the energy requirements of adults in general should be calculated based on the estimates of habitual total energy expenditure (TEE), which are determined based on the doubly labeled water (DLW) technique and heart rate monitoring (HRM). Total energy expenditure is defined as the energy spent in a 24-hour period by an individual or a group of individuals, reflecting the average amount of energy spent in a typical day. As growth is no longer an energy-demanding factor in the older population, the large diversity of TEE is explained by differences in habitual physical activity and body weight (FAO, 2001). Basal metabolic rate (BMR), which is the minimum rate of energy expenditure compatible with life, is considered as constant in most population groups and is measured under standard conditions that include being awake in the supine position after 10 to 12 hours of fasting and 8 hours of physical rest, as well as being in a state of mental relaxation in an ambient environmental temperature that does not elicit heat-generating or heat-dissipating processes. In most individuals 45–70 percent of daily total energy expenditure, depending on age and lifestyle, equals BMR, which is mainly determined by age, gender, body size, and body composition. Physical activity and body weight (BW) are the main determinants for the individual energy requirement. As shown in Table 13.1a and b, men and women above the age of 60 require between 1,550 and 3,600 kcal, depending on weight, height, and physical activity level. The physical activity level (PAL) is expressed as a multiple of BMR and calculated as TEE/BMR for 24 hours (FAO, 2001).

Total energy expenditure decreases with increasing age. Roberts and Dallal analyzed this fact in 2005. They measured the TEE of 800 adults with an age above 20, and described a decrease with age. Based on their results, an overview of TEE, according to age, was published. Men with normal weight, 60 years and older, exhibited TEE between 1,935 and 2,397 kcal and women with normal weight used between 1,356 and 2,042 kcal/day, depending on age and individual physical activity. The respective values for overweight persons vary more profoundly from those persons with normal weight (see Table 13.2) (Roberts and Dallal, 2005).

In summary, the energy requirements of older individuals depend on gender, age, and physical activity, the latter being closely associated with individual health status, which in turn affects physical activity. Table 13.3 presents a simplified overview on the calculation of energy requirements according to Gaillard and co-workers (Gaillard et al., 2007), which may be suitable for application in clinical routine. However, the adequacy of these calculations has to be checked against individual weight development, as the range of actual requirements may differ significantly.

## Protein

Protein is a key macronutrient and an essential component of all physiological systems. It is highly relevant for the preservation of muscle and its function. The World Health Organization, the US Institute of Medicine, the European Food Safety Authorities (EFSA), and many national societies recommend a dietary protein intake of 0.8 g/kg BW a day across all age groups (WHO, 2015; Food and Nutrition Board, 2014). In general, it should be noted that with declining energy requirements (see above), protein intake might become inadequate in older age, if food is served with the same distribution of macronutrients as in young age. Therefore, in older individuals that are regarded as being at risk of deteriorating functionality, protein intake should be calculated in absolute numbers. The World Health Organization's recommendation of 0.8 g/kg BW/ day is been based solely on nitrogen balance studies that included only a small number of older individuals, who were healthy (Rizzoli et al., 2014; Tang et al., 2014). In recent years, several expert groups reviewed the accumulating scientific

Table 13.1a  *Daily average energy requirement for women aged 18 to 29.9 years* (FAO, 2001)

| Mean weight (kg) | BMR/kg[a] kJ | BMR/kg[a] kcal | 1.45 × BMR MJ | kJ/kg | kcal | kcal/kg | 1.60 × BMR MJ | kJ/kg | kcal | kcal/kg | 1.75 × BMR MJ | kJ/kg | kcal | kcal/kg | 1.90 × BMR MJ | kJ/kg | kcal | kcal/kg | 2.05 × BMR MJ | kJ/kg | kcal | kcal/kg | 2.20 × BMR MJ | kJ/kg | kcal | kcal/kg | Height (m) for BMI values[b] 24.9 | 21.0 | 18 5 |
|---|---|---|---|---|---|---|---|---|---|---|---|---|---|---|---|---|---|---|---|---|---|---|---|---|---|---|---|---|---|
| 45 | 107 | 26 | 7.0 | 155 | 1,650 | 37 | 7.7 | 170 | 1,850 | 41 | 8.4 | 190 | 2,000 | 44 | 9.2 | 205 | 2,200 | 49 | 9.9 | 220 | 2,350 | 52 | 10.6 | 235 | 2,550 | 57 | 1.34 | 1.46 | 1.56 |
| 50 | 103 | 25 | 7.4 | 150 | 1,800 | 36 | 8.2 | 165 | 1,950 | 39 | 9.0 | 180 | 2,150 | 43 | 9.8 | 195 | 2,350 | 47 | 10.5 | 210 | 2,500 | 50 | 11.3 | 225 | 2,700 | 54 | 1.42 | 1.54 | 1.64 |
| 55 | 99 | 24 | 7.9 | 145 | 1,900 | 35 | 8.7 | 160 | 2,100 | 38 | 9.5 | 175 | 2,300 | 42 | 10.3 | 190 | 2,450 | 45 | 11.2 | 205 | 2,650 | 48 | 12.0 | 220 | 2,850 | 52 | 1.49 | 1.62 | 1.72 |
| 60 | 96 | 23 | 8.3 | 140 | 2,000 | 33 | 9.2 | 155 | 2,200 | 37 | 10.1 | 170 | 2,400 | 40 | 10.9 | 180 | 2,600 | 43 | 11.8 | 195 | 2,800 | 47 | 12.7 | 210 | 3,050 | 51 | 1.55 | 1.69 | 1.80 |
| 65 | 93 | 22 | 8.8 | 135 | 2,100 | 32 | 9.7 | 150 | 2,300 | 35 | 10.6 | 165 | 2,550 | 39 | 11.5 | 175 | 2,750 | 42 | 12.4 | 190 | 2,950 | 45 | 13.3 | 205 | 3,200 | 49 | 1.62 | 1.76 | 1.87 |
| 70 | 91 | 22 | 9.2 | 130 | 2,200 | 31 | 10.2 | 145 | 2,450 | 35 | 11.2 | 160 | 2,650 | 38 | 12.1 | 175 | 2,900 | 41 | 13.1 | 185 | 3,100 | 44 | 14.0 | 200 | 3,350 | 48 | 1.68 | 1.83 | 1.95 |
| 75 | 89 | 21 | 9.7 | 130 | 2,300 | 31 | 10.7 | 145 | 2,550 | 34 | 11.7 | 155 | 2,800 | 37 | 12.7 | 170 | 3,050 | 41 | 13.7 | 185 | 3,300 | 44 | 14.7 | 195 | 3,500 | 47 | 1.74 | 1.89 | 2.01 |
| 80 | 87 | 21 | 10.1 | 125 | 2,400 | 30 | 11.2 | 140 | 2,700 | 34 | 12.2 | 155 | 2,950 | 37 | 13.3 | 165 | 3,200 | 40 | 14.3 | 180 | 3,450 | 43 | 15.4 | 190 | 3,700 | 46 | 1.79 | 1.95 | 2.08 |
| 85 | 86 | 21 | 10.6 | 125 | 2,550 | 30 | 11.7 | 140 | 2,800 | 33 | 12.8 | 150 | 3,050 | 36 | 13.9 | 165 | 3,300 | 39 | 15.0 | 175 | 3,600 | 42 | 16.1 | 190 | 3,850 | 45 | 1.85 | 2.01 | 2.14 |

* Values rounded to closest 0.1 MJ/day, 50 kcal/day, 5 kJ/kg/day, 1 kcal/kg/day.

a BMR calculated for each weight from the equations in Table 5.2. Values of BMR/kg are presented for ease of calculations for those who wish to use different PAL values or different weights.

b Height ranges are presented for each mean weight for ease of making dietary energy recommendations to maintain an adequate BMI based on a population's mean height and PAL. For example, the recommended mean energy intake for a female population of this age group with a mean height of 1.70 m and a lifestyle with a mean PAL of 1.75 is about 10.1 MJ (2,400 kcal)/day or 170 kJ (40 kcal)/kg/day to maintain an optimum population median BMI of 21.0 (WHO/FAO, 2002), with an individual range of about 9.5 to 11.2 MJ (2,300 to 2,650 kcal)/day or 160 to 175 kJ (38 to 42 kcal)/kg/day to maintain the individual BMI limits of 18.5 to 24.9 (WHO, 2000).

Table 13.1b  *Daily average energy requirement for women aged ≥ 60 years**

| Mean weight | BMR/kg[a] | | 1.45 × BMR | | | | 1.60 × BMR | | | | 1.75 × BMR | | | | 1.90 × BMR | | | | 2.05 × BMR | | | | 2.20 × BMR | | | | Height (m) for BMI values[b] | | |
|---|---|---|---|---|---|---|---|---|---|---|---|---|---|---|---|---|---|---|---|---|---|---|---|---|---|---|---|---|---|
| | | | | | | | Daily energy requirement according to BMR factor (or PAL) and body weight indicated | | | | | | | | | | | | | | | | | | | | | | |
| kg | kJ | kcal | MJ | kJ/kg | kcal | kcal/kg | MJ | kJ/kg | kcal | kcal/kg | MJ | kJ/kg | kcal | kcal/kg | MJ | kJ/kg | kcal | kcal/kg | MJ | kJ/kg | kcal | kcal/kg | MJ | kJ/kg | kcal | kcal/kg | 24.9 | 21.0 | 18 5 |
| 45 | 99 | 24 | 6.5 | 145 | 1,550 | 34 | 7.1 | 160 | 7,100 | 38 | 7.8 | 175 | 1,850 | 41 | 8 5 | 190 | 2,050 | 45 | 9.2 | 205 | 2,200 | 49 | 9.8 | 220 | 2,350 | 52 | 1.34 | 1.46 | 1.56 |
| 50 | 93 | 22 | 6.7 | 135 | 1,600 | 32 | 7.4 | 150 | 1,800 | 36 | 8.1 | 165 | 1,950 | 39 | 8.8 | 175 | 2,100 | 42 | 9.5 | 190 | 2,300 | 46 | 10.2 | 205 | 2,450 | 49 | 1.42 | 1.54 | 1.64 |
| 55 | 88 | 21 | 7.0 | 130 | 1,700 | 31 | 7.8 | 140 | 1,850 | 34 | 8.5 | 155 | 2,050 | 37 | 9.2 | 165 | 2,200 | 40 | 9.9 | 180 | 2,350 | 43 | 10.7 | 195 | 2,550 | 46 | 1.49 | 1.62 | 1.72 |
| 60 | 84 | 20 | 7.3 | 120 | 1,750 | 29 | 8.1 | 135 | 1,950 | 32 | 8.8 | 145 | 2,100 | 35 | 9.6 | 160 | 2,300 | 38 | 10.3 | 170 | 2,450 | 41 | 11.1 | 185 | 2,650 | 44 | 1.55 | 1.69 | 1.80 |
| 65 | 80 | 19 | 7.6 | 115 | 1,800 | 28 | 8.4 | 130 | 2,000 | 31 | 9.1 | 140 | 2,200 | 34 | 9.9 | 155 | 2,350 | 37 | 10.7 | 165 | 2,550 | 39 | 11.5 | 175 | 2,750 | 42 | 1.62 | 1.76 | 1.87 |
| 70 | 77 | 18 | 7.9 | 110 | 1,900 | 27 | 8.7 | 125 | 2,050 | 30 | 9 5 | 135 | 2,250 | 32 | 10.3 | 145 | 2,450 | 35 | 11.1 | 160 | 2,650 | 38 | 11.9 | 170 | 2,850 | 41 | 1.68 | 1.83 | 1.95 |
| 75 | 75 | 18 | 8.1 | 110 | 1,950 | 26 | 9.0 | 120 | 2,150 | 29 | 9.8 | 130 | 2,350 | 31 | 10.6 | 140 | 2,550 | 34 | 11.5 | 155 | 2,750 | 37 | 12 3 | 165 | 2,950 | 39 | 1.74 | 1.89 | 2.01 |
| 80 | 72 | 17 | 6.4 | 105 | 2,000 | 25 | 9.3 | 115 | 2,200 | 28 | 10.1 | 125 | 2,400 | 30 | 11.0 | 140 | 2,650 | 33 | 11.9 | 150 | 2,850 | 35 | 12.7 | 160 | 3,050 | 38 | 1.79 | 1.95 | 2.08 |
| 85 | 70 | 17 | 6.7 | 100 | 2,050 | 24 | 9.6 | 115 | 2,300 | 27 | 10.5 | 125 | 2,500 | 29 | 11.4 | 135 | 2,700 | 32 | 12.3 | 145 | 2,950 | 34 | 11 2 | 155 | 3,150 | 37 | 1.85 | 2.01 | 2.14 |

* Values rounded to closest 0.1 MJ/day, 50 kcal/day, 5 kJ/kg/day, 1 kcal/kg/day.

[a] BMR calculated for each weight from the equations in Table 5.2. Values of BMR/kg are presented for ease of calculations for those who wish to use different PAL values or different weights.

[b] Height ranges are presented for each mean weight for ease of making dietary energy recommendations to maintain an adequate BMI based on a population's mean height and PAL. For example, the recommended mean energy intake for a female population of this age group with a mean height of 1.70 m and a lifestyle with a mean PAL of 1.75 is about 8.8 MJ (2,100 kcal)/day or 145 kJ (35 kcal/kg/day to maintain an optimum population median BMI of 21.0 (WHO/FAO, 2002), with an individual range of about 8.5 to 9.5 MJ (2,050 to 2,250 kcal)/day or 135 to 155 kJ (32 to 37 kcal)/kg/day to maintain the individual BMI limits of 18.5 to 24.9 (WHO, 2000).

Table 13.2   *Total energy expenditure and physical activity level of adult age in normal weight and overweight men and women. A summary of data collected, according to Bauer et al. (2013)*

| | *n* | weight | TEE | PAL[a] | BMR |
|---|---|---|---|---|---|
| **Normal weight** | | | | | |
| *Males* | | | | | |
| 60–69.9 | 14 | 67.8 ± 6.1 | 2,397 ± 437 | 1.61 ± 0.18 | 1,487 ± 227 |
| 70–79.9 | 30 | 70.0 ± 6.7 | 2,407 ± 374 | 1.62 ± 0.25 | 1,497 ± 183 |
| 80–89.9 | 4 | 67.1 ± 4.0 | 1,700 ± 239 | 1.17 ± 0.15 | 1,457 ± 21 |
| 90–96.5 | 6 | 65.6 ± 7.3 | 1,935 ± 156 | 1.38 ± 0.17 | 1,415 ± 184 |
| *Females* | | | | | |
| 60–69.9 | 48 | 59.0 ± 5.5 | 2,042 ± 343 | 1.69 ± 0.31 | 1,219 ± 161 |
| 70–79.9 | 14 | 59.0 ± 7.7 | 1,888 ± 295 | 1.55 ± 0.26 | 1,229 ± 147 |
| 80–89.9 | 6 | 51.9 ± 3.1 | 1,382 ± 152 | 1.21 ± 0.09 | 1,143 ± 54 |
| 90–96.5 | 9 | 52.2 ± 5.7 | 1,356 ± 166 | 1.17 ± 0.13 | 1,166 ± 153 |
| **Overweight** | | | | | |
| *Males* | | | | | |
| 60–69.9 | 30 | 87.8 ± 12.8 | 2,851 ± 420 | 1.71 ± 0.29 | 1,687 ± 190 |
| 70–79.9 | 34 | 84.8 ± 9.8 | 2,624 ± 461 | 1.55 ± 0.27 | 1,713 ± 254 |
| 80–89.9 | 7 | 78.1 ± 6.6 | 2,294 ± 357 | 1.47 ± 0.16 | 1,558 ± 133 |
| 90–96.5 | 2 | 77.5 ± 10.6 | 1,863 ± 46 | 1.29 ± 0.13 | 1,550 ± 177 |
| *Females* | | | | | |
| 60–69.9 | 46 | 78.2 ± 13.4 | 2,061 ± 294 | 1.52 ± 0.23 | 1,374 ± 190 |
| 70–79.9 | 19 | 69.3 ± 7.9 | 1,868 ± 402 | 1.51 ± 0.28 | 1,234 ± 89 |
| 80–89.9 | 6 | 62.8 ± 5.6 | 1,748 ± 464 | 1.42 ± 0.37 | 1,233 ± 205 |
| 90–96.5 | 7 | 74.8 ± 7.3 | 1,766 ± 292 | 1.33 ± 0.22 | 1,332 ± 125 |

TEE, Total energy expenditure; PAL, physical activity level; BMR, basal metabolic rate.
[a] Using measured BMR values.

Table 13.3   *Simplified calculation of energy requirement*

| | Requirement in kcal/kg body weight/day |
|---|---|
| Basal metabolic rate of older persons | approx. 20 |
| Total metabolic rate | |
| [a] active and healthy older seniors | 30–35[a] |
| [a] seniors with relevant illness and reduced physical activity | 25–30 |
| [a] if underweight (BMI <21 kg/m²) to compensate for recent weight loss | 34–38 |
| [a] hyperactivity (e.g., wandering in dementia) | Up to 40 |

[a] variance dependent on age and gender

Table 13.4    *Overview on protein recommendations by different authorities and expert groups*

|  | Institute of Medicine for adults[a] (Institute of Medicine, 2014) | Recommendations by the PROT-AGE study group[b] (Bauer et al., 2013) | Recommendations by the ESPEN group (Deutz et al., 2014) | ESCEO guidelines for postmenopausal women (Rizzoli et al., 2014) |
|---|---|---|---|---|
| Healthy older adults | 0.8 g/kg BW/day | 1.0–1.2 g/kg BW/day 25–30 g protein/meal, incl. 2.5–2.8 g leucine | 1.0–1.2 g/kg BW/day | 50–71 years: 1.0 g/kg BW/day 71+ years: 1.0–1.2 g/kg BW/day 20–25 g protein/meal |
| Older adults with an acute or chronic illness |  | 1.2–1.5 g/kg BW/day, adults with severe illness or injury or marked malnutrition need as much as 2.0 g/kg BW/day | 1.2–1.5 g/kg BW/day, even higher when severely ill or malnourished |  |

[a] Recommendations are regardless of gender and age for all adults.
[b] All adults >65 years are included, regardless of gender.

evidence on older individuals, and as a consequence, they recommended 1.0–1.2 g protein/kg BW/day for healthy older individuals and up to 1.5 g protein/kg BW/day for older patients with acute or chronic diseases, especially for those who are affected by sarcopenia and frailty (Bauer et al., 2013; Rizzoli et al., 2014). This recommendation refers to an optimal protein intake in an at-risk population for (further) functional decline. The need for higher protein requirements in older persons has been explained by age-associated changes of protein metabolism in this population, which lead to the so-called anabolic resistance of aging. Immobilization is regarded as a major contributing factor for this condition. In addition, older patients may have a greater need of protein as a consequence of inflammatory diseases (Bauer et al., 2013). Tang et al. (2014) determined the dietary protein requirement of older women aged 80 to 87 years (by the minimally invasive indicator amino acid oxidation (IAAO) methodology) and identified a mean protein requirement of 0.85 g/kg BW/day, which was 29 percent higher than the current estimated average requirement (EAR) of 0.66 g/kg/day. While the methodology of this approach is still heavily debated among experts, this study may nevertheless be regarded as being relevant in the ongoing discussion on protein intake in older individuals. Table 13.4 gives an overview on current recommendations of authorities and expert groups with regard to protein intake (see Table 13.4) (Bauer and Diekmann, 2015).

## Vitamins and Minerals

Since the 1980s, considerable research has been carried out on micronutrients to understand their physiological role. Micronutrient deficiencies and low dietary intakes among older adults have been associated with functional decline, frailty, and loss of independence (ter Borg et al., 2015). In most instances recommendations on micronutrient intake have not been specified for older people. This population exhibits a higher risk for nutritional deficiencies as a consequence of age-associated changes of physiological processes. Certain vitamins such as vitamin $B_{12}$, vitamin A, vitamin C, vitamin D, calcium, iron, zinc, and other trace minerals seem to be of special relevance in older age. In 2005, Chernoff reviewed the literature on micronutrient requirements in older women and concluded that there is little specific information in this regard and that the joined effects of chronic diseases, over-the-counter use of supplements, and the highly variable quality of nutritional intake due to immobility and institutionalization, as well as age-associated metabolic changes make it difficult to identify the nutritional needs in this population (Chernoff, 2005). The World Health Organization published recommendations for the requirements of vitamins and minerals in 2004 (WHO, 2015).

Bolzetta et al. (2015) discussed recently whether the recommendations for vitamins are appropriate for older persons by comparing American, European, and Italian recommended dietary allowances (RDAs). The authors concluded that the current RDAs are adequate for older women's intake of riboflavin, vitamin $B_6$, and folic acid, but should be raised for vitamin $B_{12}$ and for vitamin C. In 2015, the intake of micronutrients was calculated for 20 of them based on an international pooled data set. For six nutrients (vitamin D, thiamin, riboflavin, Ca, Mg, and Se) an inadequacy of current recommendations was identified (ter Borg et al., 2015).

## Vitamin D

Vitamin D is of special relevance in the older population, as it is a relevant cofactor for the anabolism of bone as well as muscle. Vitamin D is required for the absorption of calcium from the intestine. Several research groups have analyzed the relationship between vitamin D and muscle (for further details see Bischoff-Ferrari et al., 2004, 2009).

Vitamin $D_3$ is mainly synthesized by exposing bare skin to sunlight (ultraviolet B rays) from the precursor 7-dehydrocholesterol. The use of sun cream, low sun exposure due to immobilization, and cholesterol-lowering drugs may lead to vitamin D insufficiency. As a consequence especially people who are housebound or who live in institutions are usually at a higher risk of vitamin D deficiency. However, skin synthesis of vitamin D also declines naturally as a consequence of dermal aging processes.

Vitamin D may also be ingested with certain food components. A high content of vitamin D is present in oily fish, margarine, eggs, and fortified breakfast cereals. Even with a near optimal intake of the aforementioned foods, vitamin

D intake in older persons may be inadequate and a vitamin D supplementation would be indicated.

The RDA for vitamin D for older people has been 15 μg/day in the United States (Food and Nutrition Board, Institute of Medicine, National Academies), while in Europe, 5 and 20 μg/day (Spiro and Buttriss, 2014) has been recommended. The German Society for Nutrition (Deutsche Gesellschaft für Ernährung DGE) increased its recommendation to 20 μg/day in 2012 (German Nutrition Society, New Reference Values for Vitamin D, 2012). At present the optimal vitamin D level is still debated. Most experts agree that a serum level of 25-hydroxyvitamin D [25(OH)D] ≥ 75 nmol/l (20 ng/ml) should be recommended. The relevance for muscle function and mobility is described in Chapter 2.

## Macro- and Micronutrients with Special Relevance for Muscle Strength and Muscle Function in Older Persons

### Protein and Specific Amino Acids

High protein intake may benefit muscle function, which was shown in a number of recent studies. Several reviews on optimal protein intake for the preservation of functionality in older age have been published in recent years, summarizing the current scientific knowledge (Bauer et al., 2013; Bauer and Diekmann, 2015; Nowson and O'Connell, 2015).

Benefits of a higher protein intake were also documented in human studies. In 2008, Houston et al. focused on changes in total and appendicular lean mass and their association with energy-adjusted protein intake in women 70–79 years of age, who were participating in the Health, Aging, and Body Composition Study (Houston et al., 2008). During a 3-year follow-up, subjects in the highest quintile of protein intake lost less lean mass (approximately 40 percent less) than subjects in the lowest quintile (Figure 13.1). In another longitudinal study, Beasley et al. showed a positive association between calibrated protein intake and physical performance measures (grip strength, number of chair stands in 15 seconds, and a timed 6-m walk). In this analysis, data provided by a baseline food frequency questionnaire, as well as data derived from doubly labeled water studies and 24-hour urinary nitrogen sampling were used to calculate calibrated protein intake (Beasley et al., 2013).

Least-squares means with different superscript letters are significantly different, $p < 0.05$ ($t$ test). Median total protein intake as a percentage of total energy intake (g/kg/day) by quintile (from quintile 1 to quintile 5) was 11.2 percent (0.7 g/kg/day), 12.7 percent (0.7 g/kg/day), 14.1 percent (0.8 g/kg/day), 15.8 percent (0.9 g/kg/day), and 18.2 percent (1.1 g/kg/day) (Houston et al., 2008).

### Optimal Protein Intake

Besides the optimal amount of protein, the distribution over the day has been a recent research interest. In 2014, the group of Mamerow tested the influence of

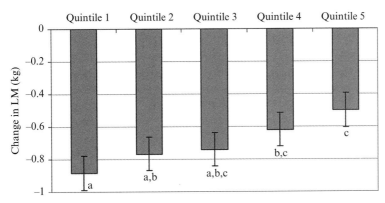

**Figure 13.1.** *Adjusted lean mass (LM) loss by quintile of energy-adjusted total protein intake*

Adjusted for age, sex, race, study site, total energy intake, baseline LM, height, smoking, alcohol use, physical activity, oral steroid use, prevalent disease (diabetes, ischemic heart disease, congestive heart failure, cerebrovascular disease, lung disease, cancer), and interim hospitalizations.

protein distribution over the day on muscle protein fractional synthesis (Beasley et al., 2013). In this study, the effect of an evenly distributed protein intake without carbohydrates at breakfast, lunch, and dinner was compared against a skewed distribution with a high protein meal at dinner. With the evenly distributed protein intake, a 25 percent higher muscle fractional synthesis rate was documented. Focusing on frailty in older individuals, Bollwein et al. (2013) identified a more uneven distribution of protein intake in frail persons in comparison to more robust ones. However, the median of the daily protein intake did not differ between robust, pre-frail, and frail older individuals.

While the above studies favor the recommendation of an even distribution of protein over the day, other studies have challenged this perspective by testing the pulse feeding of protein. In 2013, Bouillanne showed a significant increase in the lean mass index after protein pulse-feeding, in comparison to a more even intake in a group of 66 older patients of a rehabilitation ward, who were malnourished or at risk of malnutrition. In this study 36 subjects received spread protein in four meals and 30 subjects consumed 72 percent of the protein (1.31 g/kg BW/day on average) in one meal at noon (Bouillanne et al., 2013).

Before a final conclusion can be drawn on this topic, both strategies – evenly distributed protein intake and pulse-feeding – must be tested in more extensive studies that include longer intervention periods.

## Branched-Chain Amino Acids

Branched-chain amino acids have been identified as being highly relevant for the anabolic effect of protein. The branched-chain amino acid leucine is regarded as offering the strongest stimulation of muscle protein synthesis. The effects of proteins rich in branched-chain amino acids, and especially in leucine, have been examined in older individuals – in healthy as well as in frail ones. Dillon et al. (2009) documented an increase in lean mass compared to baseline values in a

3-month study with essential amino acids versus placebo in healthy older women. A positive association of branched-chain amino acid metabolites in serum with muscle cross-sectional area and fat-free mass (FFM) index was shown in a cohort of 73 older persons with functional limitations by Lustgarten et al. (2013). In a small study by Wall et al. involving 24 older adults, the effect of casein with or without 2.5 g crystalline leucine on post-prandial incorporation into muscle protein was examined. The authors concluded that post-prandial muscle protein synthesis rates improved significantly with leucine co-ingestion (Tieland et al., 2012). Kramer et al. tested the effect of protein and other macronutrients on muscle protein synthesis rate in 45 non-sarcopenic older men in a single test day study. The muscle protein synthesis rate was measured by: (1) a stable isotope methodology after supplementation of 21 g leucine-enriched whey protein, with carbohydrate and fat, (2) an isonitrogenous amount of 21 g leucine-enriched whey protein, without carbohydrate and fat, or (3) an isocaloric mixture containing carbohydrate und fat only. All subjects consumed the same standardized meal regarding energy and macronutrient amount. The ingestion of the leucine-enriched supplement significantly raised the muscle protein synthesis rates, without a modulation by a co-ingestion of carbohydrate and fat (Collins et al., 2016).

At present experts also discuss the relevance of "fast" and "slow" proteins for muscle anabolism. Fast proteins exhibit a superior rate of digestion, with early and high peaks of their serum concentrations (e.g., whey protein has been considered a fast protein).

In 2014, Gryson et al. showed that the leucine balance in older adults was superior when consuming a high-protein diet of 1.2 g/kg BW/day compared to a diet containing only 1.0 g/kg BW/day (Gryson et al., 2014). This effect was strongest for soluble milk proteins, which are regarded as "fast" proteins. In another study, three different doses of whey protein (10, 20, and 35 g) were tested to measure plasma peak values of marker amino acids, whole body protein net balance, and postprandial muscle protein accretion in 48 older men. The best effect on all three outcome parameters was yielded by the highest protein dose (Pennings et al., 2011).

In the foreseeable future, results of the VIVE2 study will be available. In this multi-center study, the effects on physical function, muscle mass and strength, and body composition after a 6 months supplementation with 20 g whey protein and vitamin D versus a low calorie placebo drink will be identified in a cohort of 150 mobility-limited older adults (Kirn et al., 2015).

## Potential Ceiling Effect of Protein Intake in Older Persons

In recent publications, a ceiling effect for high protein intake with regard to its positive effect on protein synthesis has been discussed. In 2008 the effects on whole body protein synthesis and muscle mitochondrial function in a study involving ten days of a high protein (1.5 g protein * kg FFM/day) versus a very high protein (3.0 g protein * kg FFM/day) diet were compared in healthy younger adults versus healthy older adults. Net daily nitrogen balance increased in both young and older subjects with the very high protein intake but, in parallel, the post-absorptive use of protein as an energy source also increased. The authors concluded that neither whole body protein synthesis nor muscle mitochondrial function were affected positively by a short-term very high protein diet (Reinders et al., 2015). Symons et al. examined muscle protein synthesis by providing either a single moderate protein serving (30 g) or a large protein serving (90 g protein). They showed that an amount exceeding 30 g protein per meal failed to enhance muscle protein synthesis any further. This effect was observed in both younger and older subjects (Jeromson et al., 2015). In this context Deutz and Wolfe focused on the relevance of net protein synthesis by discussing the relative contribution of protein synthesis and protein breakdown. They concluded that there might be no upper limit for the anabolic response to increasing amounts of protein during a meal. While protein synthesis shows a ceiling effect with higher protein intake, this is not the case for the associated decrease in protein breakdown (Smith et al., 2015). The above hypothesis should be tested in adequately powered trials.

## The Relevance of Protein for Frailty and Sarcopenia Treatment

In older age a relevant percentage of the population becomes frail. It is therefore indicated to have a closer look at the relevance of protein intake in this condition, whose prevalence averages 10 percent among older persons beyond age 65 and is associated with negative health outcomes like falls, hospitalization, and institutionalization.

Tieland et al. found a positive effect of supplementation with milk protein on physical function in 62 frail older persons who all underwent a resistance-type exercise-training program during the study period. The intervention group, who received 2 times 15 g milk protein for 24 weeks, achieved a significantly higher Short Physical Performance Battery (SPPB) score than the control group (Tieland et al., 2012). In addition, two recent studies also showed a benefit to a high whey protein intake in similar patient groups. In a multi-center, randomized, controlled, double-blind study among 380 sarcopenic community-living older adults, the effect of a combination of vitamin D and a leucine-enriched whey protein given for 13 months versus an iso-caloric control product was tested. The active product contained, per serving, 20 g whey protein, 3 g total leucine, 9 g carbohydrates, 3 g fat, 800 IU vitamin D, and a mixture of vitamins, minerals, and fibers, whereas the iso-caloric control product did not contain any protein or micronutrients, only carbohydrates, fat, and some trace elements. A positive effect of supplementation was documented for the chair-stand test and for appendicular muscle mass (Bauer et al., 2015). Rondanelli et al. (2016) also showed a positive additive effect of a 12-week supplementation of whey protein on physical function, muscle strength, and muscle mass in 130 sarcopenic older individuals, who attended a physical activity program. The Pro-Elderly study ("Protein Intake and Resistance Training in Aging") included frail subjects and tested the effect of whey protein and creatine co-supplementation versus whey protein supplementation solely. In the 14 weeks of intervention all subjects also undertook a supervised exercise-training program. The authors concluded that creatinine had no additional beneficial effect (Collins et al., 2016).

According to the results that have been described above, a higher intake of protein, especially of proteins with a high percentage of branched-chain amino acids, e.g., leucine, may offer a significant anabolic benefit on muscle mass and muscle function in sarcopenic or frail older individuals. Due to its high content of leucine and digestive kinetics as a fast protein, whey protein has been regarded as protein with superior characteristics in this patient group. However, as some evidence is still inconclusive further studies are still required to verify the clinical relevance of protein, especially whey supplementation.

## Lipids

The percentage of lipids in the daily diet should be around 30 percent energy. This amount is identical for younger and older adults. When focusing on the effect of lipids for overall health, as well as cognitive and physical function, polyunsaturated fatty acids (PUFAs) deserve special consideration. Among them $\omega$-3 and $\omega$-6 fatty acids may be considered as the most beneficial ones. $\omega$-3 fatty acids include $\alpha$-linolenic acid (ALA), docosahexaenoic acid (DHA), and eicosapentaenoic acid (EPA), while $\omega$-6 includes linoleic acid and arachidonic acid. ALA and linolenic acid are essential components of human nutrition.

The relationship of PUFAs and physical function was recently reviewed by Casas-Augustench et al. (2017). Several observational studies have documented a preservation of muscle mass and physical function, with higher PUFA intake or plasma levels. Among the positively affected functional parameters were: hand-grip strength, walking speed, and knee extension strength. In addition, a lower risk of mobility disability has been described (Robinson et al., 2008; Abbatecola et al., 2009; Murphy et al., 2010; Welch et al., 2014; Reinders et al., 2015a, 2015b).

Recent evidence shows that PUFAs are active at the muscle level by increasing the synthesis and by decreasing the breakdown of proteins (Jeromson et al., 2015). In a recent study, Smith et al. (2015) showed that high doses n-3 PUFA (4 g/day) given for 6 months improved muscle mass and performance. The supplementation of fish oil in older women resulted in an increase in resting metabolic rate, exercise-related energy expenditure, and lean body mass, and an improvement of functional capacity (Logan and Spriet, 2015). However, there have also been studies published that could prove no beneficial effect of PUFAs on muscle are available (Krzyminska-Siemaszko et al., 2015). Therefore, additional proof of the relevance of high PUFA intake for muscle mass and muscle function is still needed.

## Vitamin D

The past 10–15 years have been characterized by high research efforts regarding vitamin D and its relationship with functionality in older individuals. Numerous cross-sectional studies identified a significant association between vitamin D levels and strength, as well as mobility.

The authors of the Health ABC study, a cohort of community-dwelling, initially well-functioning older adults, concluded that low 25-hydroxyvitamin D (25(OH)D) was associated with an increased risk of mobility limitation and disability after a six-year follow-up (Houston et al., 2013). Data from the InCHIANTI study showed an association of vitamin D insufficiency with frailty for men, but not for women (in a sub-sample of 444 male and 561 female participants) (Shardell et al., 2009). The Cardiovascular Health Study All Stars examined the association between 25-hydroxyvitamin D levels and physical function in 988 community-dwelling adults aged 77 to 100. Here the authors concluded that vitamin D deficiency was common and that it was associated with poorer physical performance, lower muscle strength, and ADL disability (Houston et al., 2011).

Based on the aforementioned positive association between vitamin D levels and functionality, several interventions have been realized to confirm these observational results. An Australian study with 302 community-dwelling elderly women aged 70 to 90 with serum 25-hydroxyvitamin D (25(OH)D) levels of less than 24 ng/ml was randomized to 1,000 IU/day vitamin D(2) or to placebo. The vitamin D supplementation with vitamin D improved muscle strength and function in those who were the weakest and slowest at baseline (Zhu et al., 2010). In contrast, the placebo-controlled, double-blind supplementation of 150,000 IU every 3 months for 9 months in community-dwelling older women over 70 years did not show any positive effect on muscle strength or mobility (Glendenning et al., 2012). An alternative way to enhance 25(OH)D levels was published in 2011 by Bischoff-Ferrari. In a study of 20 healthy postmenopausal women 25(OH)D$_3$ was tested against vitamin D$_3$ for 4 months. It is known that 25(OH)D$_3$ has hydrophilic properties and a shorter half-life time. It induces a rapid increase in serum 25(OH)D levels. Women on 25(OH)D$_3$ compared with those on vitamin D$_3$ had a 2.8-fold increased odds ratio of maintaining or improving lower extremity function (Bischoff-Ferrari et al., 2012).

A systematic review of the association between vitamin D and muscle strength was published in 2009. Based on the results of 16 studies published since 2004 – eight observational and eight interventional – the authors concluded the evidence was still inconsistent (Annweiler et al., 2009). A meta-analysis, published in 2011, included 13 studies demonstrating that a vitamin D supplementation of 800 to 1,000 IU/day induced a benefit on muscle strength (Muir and Montero-Odasso, 2011). However, one of the most recent papers on this topic summarized that vitamin D has only a small positive effect on muscle strength and that this effect was more evident in older persons who presented a 25-hydroxyvitamin D level <30 nmol/l (Beaudart et al., 2014).

## The Relevance of Body Composition for Muscle Function and Mobility in Older Persons

In older individuals, changes of body composition are to a large extent associated with aging processes. In general the amount of body fat increases and lean mass decreases, even in weight stable persons (Zamboni et al., 2003;

Ding et al., 2007). Furthermore, age-associated changes of fat distribution and the increase of fat infiltration in organ tissues are both significant (Delmonico et al., 2009). The aforementioned processes precipitate a deterioration of physical function in older persons, which may finally affect their activities of daily living (ADL) and their independency. In 2013, a systematic review and an accompanying meta-analysis were published that summarized the relevance of obesity for muscle strength and functional decline based on 50 longitudinal studies (Schaap et al., 2013). Body composition in those studies was described by BMI, abdominal circumference, waist-to-hip ratio, fat mass, muscle mass, and muscle fat infiltration. The authors concluded that obesity as indicated by BMI values $\geq$30 kg/m², a large waist circumference, or a high percentage of body fat were all associated with functional decline. The association of waist circumference with mobility and ADL disability was stronger than the respective associations with BMI. This result may be interpreted as a consequence of the shortcomings of BMI for an estimation of fat mass in older persons and/or as significant evidence for the high relevance of abdominal fat for functionality in this population. As in other analyses, low muscle strength age was associated with functional decline, while no significant association could be shown between low muscle mass and functional decline. In addition, sarcopenia without simultaneous obesity was not a risk factor for instrumental IADL disability in a study with an 8-year follow-up (Baumgartner et al., 2004).

The above data suggest that muscle mass cannot be regarded as a valuable prognostic parameter for functional decline in older persons. Fat mass may be more relevant in this regard, especially in women. To draw firm conclusions, with regard to future preventive programs, more data on muscle quality and its relationship with overall fat mass are required.

## References

Abbatecola A. M., Cherubini A., Guralnik J. M., et al. Plasma polyunsaturated fatty acids and age-related physical performance decline. *Rejuvenation Res* 2009;12:25–32.

Annweiler C., Schott A. M., Berrut G., et al. Vitamin D-related changes in physical performance: a systematic review. *J Nutr Health Aging* 2009;13:893–98.

Bauer J. M., Diekmann R. Protein and older persons. *Clin Geriatr Med* 2015;31:327–38.

Bauer J., Biolo G., Cederholm T., et al. Evidence-based recommendations for optimal dietary protein intake in older people: a position paper from the PROT-AGE Study Group. *J Am Med Dir Assoc* 2013;14:542–59.

Bauer J. M., Verlaan S., Bautmans I., et al. Effects of a vitamin D and leucine-enriched whey protein nutritional supplement on measures of sarcopenia in older adults, the PROVIDE study: a randomized, double-blind, placebo-controlled trial. *J Am Med Directors Assoc* 2015;16:740–7.

Baumgartner R. N., Wayne S. J., Waters D. L., et al. Sarcopenic obesity predicts instrumental activities of daily living disability in the elderly. *Obesity Research* 2004;12:1995–2004.

Beasley J. M., Wertheim B. C., LaCroix A. Z., et al. Biomarker-calibrated protein intake and physical function in the Women's Health Initiative. *J Am Geriatr Soc* 2013;61:1863–71.

Beaudart C., Buckinx F., Rabenda V., et al. The effects of vitamin D on skeletal muscle strength, muscle mass, and muscle power: a systematic review and meta-analysis of randomized controlled trials. *J Clin Endocrinol Metab* 2014;99: 4336–45.

Bischoff-Ferrari H. A., Borchers M., Gudat F., et al. Vitamin D receptor expression in human muscle tissue decreases with age. *J Bone Mineral Res* 2004;19:265–9.

Bischoff-Ferrari H. A., Dawson-Hughes B., Staehelin H. B., et al. Fall prevention with supplemental and active forms of vitamin D: a meta-analysis of randomised controlled trials. *BMJ (Clin Res ed.)* 2009;339:b3692.

Bischoff-Ferrari H. A., Dawson-Hughes B., Stocklin E., et al. Oral supplementation with 25(OH)D3 versus vitamin D3: effects on 25(OH)D levels, lower extremity function, blood pressure, and markers of innate immunity. *J Bone Mineral Res* 2012;27:160–9.

Bollwein J., Diekmann R., Kaiser M. J., et al. Distribution but not amount of protein intake is associated with frailty: a cross-sectional investigation in the region of Nurnberg. *Nutr J* 2013;12:109.

Bolzetta F., Veronese N., de Rui M., et al. Are the recommended dietary allowances for vitamins appropriate for elderly people? *J Acad Nutr Diet* 2015;115:1789–97.

Casas-Agustench P., Cherubini A., Andres-Lacueva C. Lipids and physical function in older adults. *Curr Opin Clin Nutr Metab Care* 2017;20:16–25.

Chernoff R. Micronutrient requirements in older women. *Am J Clin Nutr* 2005;81:1240S–5S.

Collins J., Longhurst G., Roschel H., et al. Resistance training and co-supplementation with creatine and protein in older subjects with frailty. *The Journal of Frailty & Aging* 2016;5:126–34.

Delmonico M. J., Harris T. B., Visser M., et al. Longitudinal study of muscle strength, quality, and adipose tissue infiltration. *The American Journal of Clinical Nutrition* 2009;90:1579–85.

Deutz, Nicolaas E. P., Bauer J. M., Barazzoni R., et al. Protein intake and exercise for optimal muscle function with aging: recommendations from the ESPEN Expert Group. *Clin Nutr* 2014;33:929–36.

Institute of Medicine. Dietary Reference Intakes for Energy, Carbohydrate, Fiber, Fat, Fatty Acids, Cholesterol, Protein, and Amino Acids. www.iom.edu/Reports/2002/Dietary-Reference-Intakes-for-Energy-Carbohydrate-Fiber-Fat-Fatty-Acids-Cholesterol-Protein-and-Amino-Acids.aspx (accessed December 16, 2014).

Dillon E. L., Sheffield-Moore M., Paddon-Jones D., et al. Amino acid supplementation increases lean body mass, basal muscle protein synthesis, and insulin-like growth factor-I expression in older women. *J Clin Endocrinol Metab* 2009;94:1630–7.

Ding J., Kritchevsky S. B., Newman A. B., et al. Effects of birth cohort and age on body composition in a sample of community-based elderly. *The American Journal of Clinical Nutrition* 2007;85:405–10.

FAO. Human energy requirements. Report of a Joint FAO/WHO/UNU Expert Consultation 2001. ftp://ftp.fao.org/docrep/fao/007/y5686e/y5686e00.pdf.

Food and Nutrition Board, Institute of Medicine, National Academies. www
    .nationalacademies.org/hmd/Global/News%20Announcements/~/media/Files/
    Activity%20Files/Nutrition/DRIs/DRI_Summary_Listing.pdf.

Gaillard C., Alix E., Salle A., et al. Energy requirements in frail elderly people: a review
    of the literature. *Clin Nutr* 2007;26:16–24.

German Nutrition Society. New reference values for vitamin D. *Ann Nutr Metab*
    2012:241–6. www.dge.de/wissenschaft/referenzwerte/vitamin-d/https://www
    .dge.de/wissenschaft/referenzwerte/vitamin-d/.

Glendenning P., Zhu K., Inderjeeth C., et al. Effects of three-monthly oral 150,000 IU
    cholecalciferol supplementation on falls, mobility, and muscle strength in older
    postmenopausal women: a randomized controlled trial. *Journal of Bone and
    Mineral Research: The Official Journal of the American Society for Bone and
    Mineral Research* 2012;27:170–6.

Gryson C., Walrand S., Giraudet C., et al. "Fast proteins" with a unique essential amino
    acid content as an optimal nutrition in the elderly: Growing evidence. *Clin Nutr*
    2014;33:642–8.

Houston D. K., Nicklas B. J., Ding J., et al. Dietary protein intake is associated with lean
    mass change in older, community-dwelling adults: the Health, Aging, and Body
    Composition (Health ABC) Study. *Am J Clin Nutr* 2008;87:150–5.

Houston D. K., Tooze J. A., Davis C. C., et al. Serum 25-hydroxyvitamin D and physical
    function in older adults: the Cardiovascular Health Study All Stars. *Journal of
    the American Geriatrics Society* 2011;59:1793–801.

Houston D. K., Neiberg R. H., Tooze J. A., et al. Low 25-hydroxyvitamin D predicts
    the onset of mobility limitation and disability in community-dwelling older
    adults: the Health ABC Study. *The Journals of Gerontology. Series A, Biological
    sciences and medical sciences* 2013;68:181–7.

Jeromson S., Gallagher I. J., Galloway, Stuart D. R., et al. Omega-3 fatty acids and
    skeletal muscle health. *Marine Drugs* 2015;13:6977–7004.

Kirn D. R., Koochek A., Reid K. F., et al. The vitality, independence, and vigor in the
    elderly 2 study (VIVE2): design and methods. *Contemporary Clinical Trials*
    2015;43:164–71.

Krzyminska-Siemaszko R., Czepulis N., Lewandowicz M., et al. The effect of a 12-
    week omega-3 supplementation on body composition, muscle strength and
    physical performance in elderly individuals with decreased muscle mass.
    *International Journal of Environmental Research and Public Health* 2015;12:
    10558–74.

Logan S. L., Spriet L. L. Omega-3 fatty acid supplementation for 12 weeks increases
    resting and exercise metabolic rate in healthy community-dwelling older
    females. *PloS one* 2015;10:e0144828.

Lustgarten M. S., Price L. L., Chale A., et al. Branched chain amino acids are associated
    with muscle mass in functionally limited older adults. *J Gerontol A Biol Sci
    Med Sci* 2013.

Muir S. W., Montero-Odasso M. Effect of vitamin D supplementation on muscle
    strength, gait and balance in older adults: a systematic review and meta-
    analysis. *Journal of the American Geriatrics Society* 2011;59:2291–300.

Murphy R. A., Mourtzakis M., Chu Q. S., et al. Skeletal muscle depletion is associated
    with reduced plasma (n-3) fatty acids in non-small cell lung cancer patients. *The
    Journal of Nutrition* 2010;140:1602–06.

Nowson C., O'Connell S. Protein requirements and recommendations for older people: a review. *Nutrients* 2015;7:6874–99.

Pennings B., Boirie Y., Senden J. M., et al. Whey protein stimulates postprandial muscle protein accretion more effectively than do casein and casein hydrolysate in older men. *Am J Clin Nutr.* 2011;93:997–1005. www.ncbi.nlm.nih.gov/pubmed/?term=pennings+B+AND+boirie+Y.

Reinders I., Murphy R. A., Song X., et al. Polyunsaturated fatty acids in relation to incident mobility disability and decline in gait speed; the Age, Gene/Environment Susceptibility-Reykjavik Study. *European Journal of Clinical Nutrition* 2015a;69:489–93.

Reinders I., Song X., Visser M., et al. Plasma phospholipid PUFAs are associated with greater muscle and knee extension strength but not with changes in muscle parameters in older adults. *The Journal of Nutrition* 2015b;145:105–12.

Rizzoli R., Stevenson J. C., Bauer J. M., et al. The role of dietary protein and vitamin D in maintaining musculoskeletal health in postmenopausal women: a consensus statement from the European Society for Clinical and Economic Aspects of Osteoporosis and Osteoarthritis (ESCEO). *Maturitas* 2014;79:122–32.

Roberts S. B., Dallal G. E. Energy requirements and aging. *Public Health Nutr* 2005;8:1028–36.

Robinson S. M., Jameson K. A., Batelaan S. F., et al. Diet and its relationship with grip strength in community-dwelling older men and women: the Hertfordshire cohort study. *Journal of the American Geriatrics Society* 2008;56:84–90.

Rondanelli M., Klersy C., Terracol G., et al. Whey protein, amino acids, and vitamin D supplementation with physical activity increases fat-free mass and strength, functionality, and quality of life and decreases inflammation in sarcopenic elderly. *The American Journal of Clinical Nutrition* 2016;103:830–40.

Rothenberg E. M. Resting, activity and total energy expenditure at age 91-96 compared to age 73. *The Journal of Nutrition, Health & Aging* 2002;6:177–8.

Schaap L. A., Koster A., Visser M. Adiposity, muscle mass, and muscle strength in relation to functional decline in older persons. *Epidemiologic Reviews* 2013;35:51–65.

Shardell M., Hicks G. E., Miller R. R., et al. Association of low vitamin D levels with the frailty syndrome in men and women. *The Journals of Gerontology. Series A, Biological Sciences and Medical Sciences* 2009;64:69–75.

Smith G. I., Julliand S., Reeds D. N., et al. Fish oil-derived n-3 PUFA therapy increases muscle mass and function in healthy older adults. *The American journal of clinical nutrition* 2015;102:115–22.

Spiro A., Buttriss J. L. Vitamin D: an overview of vitamin D status and intake in Europe. *Nutrition bulletin / BNF* 2014;39:322–50.

Tang M., McCabe G. P., Elango R., et al. Assessment of protein requirement in octogenarian women with use of the indicator amino acid oxidation technique. *Am J Clin Nutr* 2014;99:891–8.

ter Borg S., Verlaan S., Hemsworth J., et al. Micronutrient intakes and potential inadequacies of community-dwelling older adults: a systematic review. *The British Journal of Nutrition* 2015;113:1195–206.

Tieland M., Dirks M. L., van der Zwaluw, N., et al. Protein supplementation increases muscle mass gain during prolonged resistance-type exercise training in frail elderly people: a randomized, double-blind, placebo-controlled trial. *J Am Med Dir Assoc* 2012;13:713–19.

Welch A. A., MacGregor A. J., Minihane A., et al. Dietary fat and fatty acid profile are associated with indices of skeletal muscle mass in women aged 18-79 years. *The Journal of Nutrition* 2014;144:327–34.

World Health Organization. *WHO | Nutrition for older persons.* www.who.int/nutrition/topics/ageing/en/index1.html (accessed January 13, 2015).

Zamboni M., Zoico E., Scartezzini T., et al. Body composition changes in stable-weight elderly subjects: the effect of sex. *Aging Clinical and Experimental Research* 2003;15:321–7.

Zhu K., Austin N., Devine A., et al. A randomized controlled trial of the effects of vitamin D on muscle strength and mobility in older women with vitamin D insufficiency. *Journal of the American Geriatrics Society* 2010;58:2063–8.

# 14 Gerontechnologies and Successful Aging

Daniel Gillain, Sébastien Piccard, Christelle Boulanger, and Jean Petermans

## Introduction

According to the 2012 Ageing Report from the Economic Policy Committee (EPC), the proportion of the population in the EU aged 65 and over will become a much larger share (rising from 18 percent to 30 percent of the population), and those aged 80 and over (rising from 5 percent to 12 percent) will almost become as numerous as the young population in 2060. The number of older people (aged 80 years and above) is projected to increase by even more, almost tripling – from 23.7 million in 2010 to 62.4 million in 2060. The increase in the total age-dependency ratio (people aged 14 and below and people aged 65 and above over the population aged 15–64) is projected to be even larger, rising from 49.3 million in 2010 to 77.9 million in 2060.

Aging is a natural process, which can be classified into three periods at the end of life: (1) entrance into retirement: the aged but active, without disabled disease, often grandparents, with potential social difficulties because of the loss of professional relations; (2) frailty with health diseases, acute and chronic: causing loss of activity and the need for help to continue autonomous living; and (3) disability with cognitive and physical impairment: needing specific healthcare interventions. Aging could be associated with a series of daily problems like loss of autonomy, frailty, illness, and social isolation. Current solutions, particularly in disability, such as placement in specialized hosting institution, show their limit because of the lack of availability and individual and social cost

The increase in life expectancy, number of chronic patients, and healthcare costs, and the shortage of medical and paramedical staff are among the most important challenges in the next few years. In reply to these mutations, the healthcare system evolves gradually, passing from a traditional, paternalistic approach, controlled by the professionals of health, to a patient-centered approach.

Most economists have a very pessimistic vision of the aging of the population. It is indeed the first time in the history of humanity that we are entering a post-transition demographic phase with a significant increase amongst old people. It is a reality and also a challenge.

In this context of change, we can see a rapid and significant development of technologies for old people, and some of these technological innovations could help overcome the potential barriers in aging well.

Indeed, a wide variety of technological devices have emerged in order to help old people to better manage their own health and to compensate for possible difficulties. These technologies, called gerontechnologies, are therefore aimed at promoting successful aging.

In the domain of aging, the concepts of successful aging versus frailty become known in response to the need to build prevention and treatment strategies in the elderly. In summary, it can be considered that frailty represents the intermediate states between aging with complete functional autonomy and irreversible dependency (disability) being the result of pathological aging.

## Successful Aging

The first appearance of the concept of successful aging comes from Robert Havighurst in 1961 (Havighurst, 1961). In 1987, Rowe and Kahn (Rowe and Kahn, 1987, 1998) developed, within the MacArthur Research Network on an Aging Society, a model to characterize those very robust and independent older persons according to three domains: (1) disease risk, (2) physical or cognitive capacity, and (3) engagement with life. Successful aging is in the first part of aging and should be protected as long as possible. A lot of definition has been developed involving a multidimensional approach. The most validated and usual model is the MacArthur model (Figure 14.1).

In 30 years, the model remains applicable but obviously has been widely discussed. In their 2015 paper (Rowe and Kahn, 2015), these same authors criticize the model and have a look at its evolution. The authors note that "a thousand of articles have been written on the concept and its components, and more than 100 variations of the original model have been proposed." By its multidisciplinary character, the model of successful aging presents five main domains of approach already mentioned by Seeman et al. in 1995 (Seeman et al., 1995):

- Physical performance;
- Behavioral factors;
- Social network characteristics;

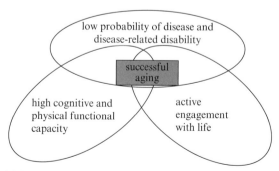

**Figure 14.1.** *The model of successful aging*
*Source:* From Rowe and Kahn (1998)

- Psychological characteristics;
- Sociodemographic characteristics.

The underlying characteristic of this kind of multi-factorial model is that the resultant, i.e., successful aging, is more important than the sum of its components, there is thus, an effect of potentiation.

In a very interesting literature review, Kusumastuti et al. (2016) performed a quantitative analysis of citation networks, exploring the literature on successful aging found in the Web of Science Core Collection Database using the CitNetExplorer software. At that time, the citation network consisted of 3,871 publications, with 10,804 citation links, within the time window from 1902 through 2015. By applying a cluster analysis to this database, the authors isolated two main clusters: the Havighurst-cluster and the Katz-cluster. In the Havighurst-cluster we meet publications concerning successful aging, but from the point-of-view of old persons. Thus, it is a more subjective vision. On the other hand, the Katz-cluster publications are more objective and more quantitative publications, in a perspective of clinical research.

One of the most recent literature reviews in the first cluster is the paper of Deep and Jeste (2006). The authors insist there is a lack of consensus on the definition of the concept. Thus, out of 28 published papers, they count 29 different definitions. Despite the variability between the definitions, about one-third of seniors were classified as successful aging. The majority of these definitions were based on the absence of disability, with less inclusion of psychosocial variables.

The founding publication of the Katz-cluster is the famous paper of Sidney Katz et al., written in 1963 (Katz et al., 1963), with the introduction of the activities of daily living (ADL) and the concept of autonomy.

But the wellness of the person is probably one aspect of healthy aging. In a brief communication in 2011, Thompson et al. (2011) cited Halbert Dunn, who originally defined wellness as "an integrated method for functioning, which is oriented toward maximizing the potential of which the individual is capable. It requires that the individual maintain a continuum of balance and purposeful direction within the environment where he/she is functioning: (1) physical well-being/ fitness, (2) mental and cognitive health, (3) social well-being, and (4) spiritual well-being."

## Gerontechnologies

### The Numeric Revolution

The principle steps of the numerical revolution can be considered:

- 1980–90: first dematerialization with the first personal computers (PC) and the appearance of Internet
- 2000: amplifications and appearance of the first smartphones
- 2010 onward: explosion of application, Internet, connected devices and robotics
- Future: the "quantified self" is the first sign of the next major transformation

Concerning healthcare and the medico social system, it is needed to correlate the route of life into this revolution, putting the person at the center of the transformation process. The individual is the owner of his/her health data, with the ability to choose the best healthcare and concerning technology, giving order according to what is needed and useful in a given situation, and also for the prevention of future incidents (La Révolution du Bien Vieillir, 2015).

## The Birth of Gerontechnologies

Gerontechnology is a discipline dedicated to the use of new technologies in the field of aging. It is based on a cross-disciplinary and multidisciplinary approach between gerontology, which studies aging in its various aspects, and the different techniques (physical, chemical, civil, mechanical, electrical, industrial, information, and communication technologies (ICT) applied to the production of products and services that meet the needs of daily life).

Gerontechnologies brings together new technologies (domotics, robotics, telemedicine, e-health, m-health) that may have an interest in gerontology. The term "gerontechnology" made one of its first appearances in the Proceedings of the First International Conference on Technology and Aging, held in Eindhoven in August 1991. It was finally adopted in October 1996 at the Second International Conference on Gerontechnology in Helsinki, Finland.

This field originated in 1980 at the Eindhoven University of Technology in the Netherlands. Gerontechnology is applied in five major areas of design: prevention, compensation, enhancement, research, and aid to caregivers. Prevention is the most powerful and novel of these applications, since it proposes that aging may be altered by redesign of the environment, products, and services. The Herman Bouma Fund for Gerontechnology Foundation was established in honor of the professor emeritus status of Dr. Herman Bouma, on March 26, 1999. Gerontechnology is defined as an interdisciplinary field of scientific research in which technology is directed toward the aspirations and opportunities of older persons. Gerontechnology aims at good health, full social participation, and independent living up to a high age. Research and Development (R&D), the design of devices and proposed services, must aim to increase the quality of life.

Next, we note the publication of founding articles (Bouma, 1998; Graafmans and Taipale, 1998; Pinto et al., 2000a, b). In their 2003 book, Wahl and Mollenkopf (Wahl and Mollenkopf, 2003) argue that, at the general level, all these approaches conceptualize technology and human development (aging) as an interactional relationship: "placing the person and his environment (including, technological devices) in a dynamic and reciprocal exchange system."

In 1997, the International Society for Gerontechnology was founded and *Gerontechnology* (ISSN/EISSN 1569-1101 1569-111X its quarterly official journal) first appeared in January 2001. Bouma et al. (2007) recalled the evolution of gerontechnologies since 1990.

## Domains of Application

As pointed out by Wu et al. (2015), very simply, there are two categories of technology among older adults technology: technology that targets the overall population and assisting technology with special needs.

For Fozard (2001), applications of gerontechnology are based on five ways of using technology:

- To prevent or delay age-related declines in functioning;
- To compensate for existing age related limitations in functioning;
- To enhance enjoyment and participation in activities that for many older persons may result from changes in work and family responsibilities;
- To support the caregiver of disabled elderly persons with technology;
- To improve applied and basic research on aging using technology that addresses the major scientific problems of gerontology.

Early in the development of the concept of gerontechnologies, five main application domains of daily life are distinguished:

(1) Health and self-esteem;
(2) Housing and daily living;
(3) Mobility and transport;
(4) Communication and governance;
(5) Work and leisure.

These domains are then crossed with the expected technological impacts:

- Enhancement and Satisfaction;
- Prevention and Engagement;
- Compensation and Assistance;
- Care Support and Organization.

A lot of applications can be considered, and technological development is so rapid that it makes it very challenging. The problem is also to make a distinction between useful and needed tools and "gadget" devices. That is one reason why typology and classifications are so important.

## Typology

As early as 2002, attempts to develop taxonomy of gerontechnologies appeared (JEMH et al., 2002). Given the complexity of representing such a large subject, a conceptual schema is used, based on a cross table between the fields of application, in columns, and the technological impacts, in rows.

This representation is taken up by Bouma et al., in a 2009 study where the authors filled cells with the products and services available in the gerontechnology market (Bouma et al., 2009). However, the typology of gerontechnology is not yet well defined. In a systematic review, not previously published, our group demonstrates how gerontechnology can be classified according to their

Typologies

**Finality of the technology**

- Technology for health
- Technology for well-being

- Communication
- Comfort
- Health
- Security

- Technologies for autonomy and communication
- Technologies for autonomy, culture, and spare-time activities
- Technologies for autonomy and comfort
- Technologies for autonomy and security

- Communication support
- Compensation and assistance
- Help for ADL
- Disease follow-up
- Remote treatment
- Rehabilitation
- Distraction / entertainment
- Social and emotional support
- Social and emotional stimulation

**Figure 14.2.** *Typologies of gerontechnologies*
*Source:* Boulanger et al. (unpublished)

finality (Figure 14.2) and how it is actually difficult to find consensual and clear typologies.

However, we propose a classification in two system types: assisting persons and supervising them with possibilities to have alert. In both groups, subclassifications can be proposed according their objectives in health security, social link, and comfort (Figure 14.3). We realize that this type of model is important, but not at all ultimate. Yet, it is a way to try to be able to make sense when the devices are introduced to older persons.

As can be seen in Table 14.1, our group is in the process of developing an updated gerontechnologies application matrix.

## Adoption and Acceptance

In a more health and assistance finality, we have tried to classify the technologies with information and supervision of potential health problems. This can be included in e-health and is one part of the topic. So in healthy aging, these devices could be helpful in the prevention of incident, and diseases, but have yet to prove their effectiveness.

In a study of Thompson et al. (2011) on 27 subjects, with a mean age of 88 years, all residing in an independent retirement community, and who generally rated their baseline overall health as excellent or very good, were followed for 8 weeks. The participants were involved in a wellness platform, integrating a tele-health kiosk that assessed physiological parameters, WebQ (allowing for the administration of questionnaires on functional, social, and spiritual well-being), and Cognifit software, which assessed cognitive parameters. The subjects reported a high level of social support and expressed positive attitudes toward the e-health tools and the holistic assessment of wellness. Several participants commented on the value of receiving feedback and having the ability to monitor their own progress. They explain the desire to understand their own wellness information. Parameters were highly correlated across multiple domains

TECHNOLOGIES

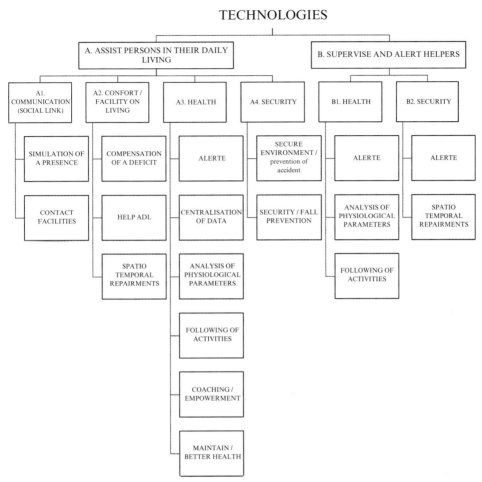

**Figure 14.3.** *Categorization of gerontechnologies*
*Source:* Boulanger et al. (unpublished)

of wellness. Important clusters were formed across cognitive and physiological domains, giving further evidence of the need for an integrated approach to the assessment of wellness.

In Hanson (2010), a web-based research protocol was proposed to a user group of young people (age 30 or younger) and an older user group (age 60 or older). Behavioral analysis of participants was based on eye tracking technique. The observed differences are more about performance and speed, than on understanding. For the author, "older adults represent one such group in danger of exclusion. In some cases, older adults have been disinterested in new technologies. In other cases, however, the technologies fail to take into consideration the strengths and weaknesses of older users that would promote this usability."

A recent report by Aaron Smith (2014) shows that older people are often isolated from digital life, although the use of technology is increasing. Many

Table 14.1 *Applications matrix of gerontechnologies (Boulanger et al., in progress)*

|  | Prevention | Compensation | Alarm/intervention |
|---|---|---|---|
| Classification of technologies | Prevention's technologies: Detect precursor's signs of trouble | Compensation's technologies: The senior is able to keep autonomy | Alarm's technologies: Quick intervention by the formal occurs. Automatic alarms or activated by the senior himself |
| Cognitive functions: Dementia, cognitive disorders (memory, disorientation in space and/or in time) | Ex: Follow activity or stimulate memory | Ex: Compensation such as memory prostheses (recall tasks, medications, etc.) geolocations | Ex: Alarm when a medication has not been, when person is out of a predetermined perimeters or is lot. When a change has been noted in the activity |
| Moving functions: Motor disorders | Ex: Stimulation of physical activity | Ex: Compensation of a motor trouble to help seniors to keep their autonomy in the moving (by light path, specific devices, etc.) | Ex: Falls alarms |
| Vital functions: Cardiac, pulmonary problems, etc. | Ex: Follow health parameters, nutritional coaching, recall to take medications, etc. | Ex: Personalization of recommendation about health, using personal parameters | Ex: Alarm if cardiac, pulmonary, or other problems |
| Sensorial functions: Hearing, sight troubles, etc. |  | Ex: Adapted interfaces, adapted devices |  |
| Social link: Social isolation/ depression | Ex: Facilitation to social link, Internet, and use messaging, etc. Follow activities | Ex: Compensation of social isolation contacts with family, friends, etc. | Ex: Alarm when a change is noted concerning social contacts |

older persons face physical challenges to using new digital devices and need assistance; while others lack interest in technology. These non-interest users of the Internet think they are not missing out on much.

Still, the biggest challenge is to accommodate the need for a holistic integrated service, which means providing personalized services and adapting technology and content to the individual needs of the different stakeholders. Further, cross-disciplinary research that relates informatics and technology to different stages of the aging process and that evaluates the effects of proposed technical solutions is needed (Koch, 2010).

For Ziefle and Schaar (2014), the dilemma between older patient empowerment and their stigmatization requires rethinking traditional concepts according to their potential users. It assumes:

- Rethinking of Information and Communication Technology in the medical context;
- Rethinking of age and aging in greying societies;
- Rethinking technology design: user-centered, hedonic, and affective design.

The authors conclude that, "positive aspects of age and aging – life experience, domain knowledge, skills and expertise, wisdom, lifelong learning, and keeper of values and culture – should be deeply anchored in the public's mind. This seems to be not only a timely duty in nowadays societies; it also secures social and societal traditions, and medical technology development is part of it. If future medical technology adheres to an open-minded age perception, empowerment of the seniors is enabled."

While literature on technology adoption does not include ageism (a discrimination by one age group toward another), this literature is consonant with the hypothesis that ageism may contribute to digital divide. In a recent article (McDonough, 2016), Carol McDonough considers that an additional reason for the digital divide among older people is that some of them have internalized the negative and often wrong messages of ageism, which may lead to a reduction in self-efficacy, and specifically, older adult's inability to use internet technology. Wandke et al. (2012) confirms this idea by discuss six common myths in the field of "human-computer interaction and older people" (i.e., older people are not interested in using computers, older people consider computers as useless and unnecessary, older people simply cannot understand interactive computing technology, etc.). They therefore consider that such myths are problematic because they can lead older people to avoid the use of technologies. Consequently, old people could be fearful and anxious about technology and their ability to use the Internet. If older people do not possess the optimism and innovativeness that are the positive attitude in the technology readiness model, then they are likely to only have the negative message of the model, discomfort and insecurity. A consequence is that these older adults devalue the benefit and usefulness of the Internet, and consequently do not adopt it. The attitude toward technology is a significant determinant of adoption. It can be expected that over time this effect will decrease, because future old generations, having grown up using the Internet and technology will not possess a negative view.

In a systematic review, providing an overview of adults' perception of fall technologies, Hawley-Hague et al. (2014) demonstrated that the technology needs to be clearly described in research and older peoples' attitude toward different sorts of techniques must be clarified, to make specific recommendations. Indeed the positive message about the benefit of falls technology is critical, if it is not simple, and especially when tailored to individual need. In this exploratory study, where a lot of devices (e.g., portable computers, robotics, games consoles) were used, the results demonstrated that one of the barriers of successful use is the lack of adoption and adherence. These two factors are very much linked to the understanding, potential benefits such as independence, increased safety, convenience, and increased social opportunities and confidence. Therefore the adoption and acceptance of a device should be considered at the beginning of the concept. It is important that it is influenced not only by its usefulness, but also by the position of the patient and by the perception by the patient of its "plus value" for their wellness in the successful aging, and not largely influenced by the stereotype of aging.

In a recent review, Dasgupta et al. (2016) have demonstrated a positive impact of tablets on different components of successful aging such as management of chronic conditions, medications, maintenance of physical and cognitive health, and social impact. However, the definition of successful aging of the author includes the management of chronic conditions along with the maintenance of physical, mental, and socio-emotional health. The studies were performed in different settings and with different sample sizes. The impact of the fast evolution of tablets is difficult to measure. With regard to the maintaining of physical health, the studies had small sample sizes, did not take into account gender, age, mood, weather, and chronic conditions, and were not randomized. In cognitive health, the impact of the tablets applications on complex behavior and their transfer effects to other domains of successful aging has not been studied. User interface design seems to change from one cognitive domain to the next. No information has been obtained on the effectiveness of casual games and autonomous training. When defining social support, the studies are limited because of a lack of specificity; the authors consider that comparative evaluations of different ICT tools are needed to demonstrate their effectiveness in improving socio-emotional health of the persons and their privacy implications. Caution must be taken in maintaining privacy and confidentially, but the limited number of long-term studies is also mentioned. Furthermore, the integration with the care provider must also be better developed, which is particularly important in the survey of chronic diseases.

In that matter, the concept of literacy in e-health must be developed further. E-Health literacy names a set of skills and knowledge that are essential for productive interactions with technology-based health tools. Van der Vaart (van der Vaart and Drossaert, 2017) has developed a digital health literacy instrument (DHLI) to make self-report measures using multiple subscales. The DHLI is acceptable, and is now considered as a new measurement tool to assess digital health literacy, measuring six diverse skills. Its self-report scale shows proper reliability and validity. The included performance-based items should be studied and adapted further, to determine their value and their discriminant validity. Future research should examine the acceptability of this instrument in other languages and among different (risk) populations and should explore ways to measure mobile health literacy skills as well. The Digital Health Literacy Instrument, in both Dutch and English, is available and may be used on request via the corresponding author. The researchers show that "acceptance in this stage is influenced by 27 factors, divided into six themes: concerns regarding technology (e.g., high cost, privacy implications and usability factors); expected benefits of technology (e.g., increased safety and perceived usefulness); need for technology (e.g., perceived need and subjective health status); alternatives to technology (e.g., help by family or spouse), social influence (e.g., influence of family, friends and professional caregivers); and characteristics of older adults (e.g., desire to age in place)."

In a very complete systematic review in 2014 (Peek et al., 2014), Peek et al. have reviewed 2,841 articles and selected 16 relevant articles that investigated the acceptance of technology that enhances safety or provides social interaction. They also concluded that we have to differentiate between factors in the pre-implementation stage and factors in the post-implementation stage and that more research is needed to capture the complexity and timeline of the acceptance process of different types of electronic technology for aging in place by community-dwelling older adults. This complexity must be analyzed by models of technology acceptance research, which are dominated by the Technology Acceptance Model (TAM) and the Unified Theory of Acceptance and Use of Technology (UTAUT). To understand the use of these models, reference is made to the article by Kiwanuka in 2015 (Kiwanuka, 2015). The unified model of Venkatesh et al. (2007), known under the abbreviation of UTAUT, represents a simplified version compared to TAM, in the sense of not taking into account the construct "attitude towards new technology," as indeed most models were inspired by TAM. It uses three determinants of intent to use, which are: expected performance, expected effort, and social influences.

It is obvious that the assessment of the acceptability or, in other words, the compliance of gerontechnologies proposed to people is an essential step to avoid the development of inapplicable devices. By way of example, numerous studies on evaluation models used in various gerontechnologies can be found (Barnard et al., 2013; Chen and Chan, 2013, 2014; Cimperman et al., 2013, 2016; Arenas-Gaitán et al., 2015; Magsamen-Conrad, 2015; Axelsson and Wikman, 2016; Ma et al., 2016).

This way of information should help the conceptors of devices, but probably more, the acceptance by older persons, in their knowledge and understanding of the device.

## Ethical Issues

Ethical values are another important field. In gerontechnology, we start from the assumption that the effects of our professional actions should be beneficial to aging persons directly or indirectly. But what are ethics is saying to us? Technology must improve the quality of life of the person with a substantial benefit they can see and better feel. The device must give the assurance of liberty to the user and not give the feeling of being followed by "big brother."

If technology is connected to the way older people live, then they will participate; but if technology negatively alters people's way of life, then that will not be the case (Bowen, 2009). On another hand, in order to give consent, it is generally understood that a person should have the information required to make a decision and to understand the implications of that decision (van Berlo, 2005). As mentioned by Bouma (2010), ethics deals with intended and foreseeable effects of human actions onto others. Direct effects upon one or more persons can be traced one-to-one to earlier actions of one or more actors. More often, indirect effects may be traced back to a number of earlier actions and situations. Then we may speak of foreseeable changes in the likelihood of certain effects. The basic issue is to consider what effects and side effects (risks, misuse) might result from our actions and in what circumstances.

Obviously, "good" and "bad" are not constants, as an all-encompassing term for present law, religion, and custom, but depending on cultural acceptance, behavior and comprehension of the purpose are constants. The wishes of the persons and acceptance are also necessary, but the advice of experts about the real improvement that a machine can bring should be highly valued (van Bronswijk et al., 2002).

But the question is not so easy in chronic diseases and frail persons, especially with cognitive disorders. And quite often, it seems to the caregivers that it is this population who could better benefit from the progress of technologies to let them live at home in a secure environment. In these situations, the principle of beneficence (doing good for others) needs to be considered together with the principle of justice, in terms of progress, security, and dignity (Cornet, 2012).

## Perspectives and Danger

Geriatricians must face the challenges of their education, culture, skills, and clinical practice. However, they need to sustain daily functioning and enhance the quality of care and quality of life of their aged patients. Gerontechnology can help them to face future challenges (Vanbronswijk Bouma 2002). Smart objects will be very often used to maintain health and functional capacity. Information from the environment interacts rapidly with the user. Relevant health information such as diet, physical activity, brain functioning, but also physiological parameters, can have access in real time. But the rare studies on efficiency published, have not been convincing and the participants found the concept unfamiliar and not very interesting (Michel and Franco, 2014). In the prevention and management of disease health, connected platforms can include vital signs and other parameters. Different adherence systems have been created, particularly to optimize medication, and their validity has been proven. However, no gold standard has emerged (Stegemann et al., 2012).

The incorporation of new technologies into the fields of health and social care is already a worldwide phenomenon. But there is a lack of evidence to support this practice. Older people who are not aware of the technologies could be disproportionately affected by the numeric revolution, and geriatricians and caregivers must keep in mind the wide-ranging implications for their patients and also their own practice (Stowe and Harding, 2010).

Therefore, we can consider that it is very important to verify the efficiency in terms of survey help, but also in terms of quality of life. It is regrettable that not enough studies have been conducted to confirm effectiveness, and most often the devices used precede the need or try to impose some new use.

## Conclusions

Successful aging is a multidisciplinary and complex concept. How to distinguish it from similar terms as healthy aging, active aging, well aging, and aging in place? Foster and Walker (2015) and Tesch-Römer and Wahl (2017) suggest lines of thought. While a robust individual obviously benefits with successful aging, the frail show signs of failed aging. For Susan Friedman et al. (2015), "it seems appropriate not only to target prevention efforts toward older adults with chronic medical conditions and the near frail, but also to take a more-active role in promoting and educating successful aging to middle-aged and older individuals with preserved function and few or no comorbidities." The development of a preventive, organized, multidisciplinary, early, and evaluated policy to prevent functional decline instead of loss of autonomy is essential. It could enable the whole population to successfully age, to contain the incidence of loss of autonomy, and limit the extent of disability, thus offering a significant financial impact. Unfortunately, the statistics available on the OECD website show that the share devoted to prevention in overall health expenditure is desperately low (see Figure 14.4).

The goal of gerontechnology used in everyday life is to maintain the physical fitness, cognitive health, social links, and emotional balance of the users. Furthermore, assistive technologies, by replacing or compensating for diminished functionality, can restore some autonomy while relieving caregivers. If old people could retain their capabilities, the need for assistive technologies would be postponed. Therefore, the alternative perspective is more preventive and proactive.

However, radical changes in society will deeply influence the practice of medicine. Tomorrow wireless, from home to hospitals and institutions, will be used to circulate information. All recorded health information will be transferred to personal cellphones from capture on the skin (i.e., miniature epidermal captures

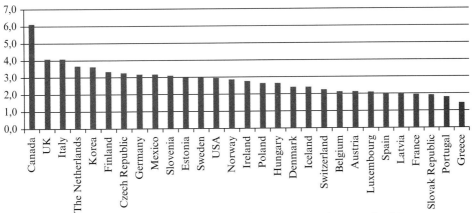

**Figure 14.4.** *Preventive care in share of current expenditure on health*
OECD, 2014, http://stats.oecd.org/Index.aspx?DatasetCode=HEALTH_STAT

or "electronic skin") and users will be constantly updated of their medical situation from the cloud computer. This "informal network of care" will be increasingly important. Even if the applications come quickly to daily life, it seems impossible to imagine the individual aging process without considering the affective surroundings of the person. Nevertheless, in the care system, "companion" robots will not replace humans soon (Michel, 2012).

## References

Arenas-Gaitán J., Peral-Peral B., Ramón-Jerónimo M. Elderly and internet banking: an application of UTAUT2. *Journal of Internet Banking and Commerce*, 2015; 20(1):1–23.

Axelsson S. W., Wikman A. M. Ready for e-health: Swedish older persons' perceptions of mobile health related applications. *Gerontechnology*, 2016; 15(suppl):67s.

Barnard Y., Bradley M. D., Hodgson F., Lloyd A. D. Learning to use new technologies by older adults: perceived difficulties, experimentation behaviour and usability. *Computers in Human Behavior*, 2013; 29:1715–24.

Bouma H. Gerontechnology: emerging technologies and their impact on aging in society. *Stud Health Technol Inform*, 1998; 48:93–104.

Professional ethics in gerontechnology: a pragmatic approach. *Gerontechnology*, 2010; 9:429–32.

Bouma H., Fozard J. L., Bouwhuis D. G., et al. Gerontechnology in perspective. *Gerontechnology*, 2007; 6(4):190–216.

Bouma H., Fozard J. L., van Bronswijk J. E. M. H. Gerontechnology as a field of endeavour. *Gerontechnology*, 2009; 8(2):68–75.

Bowen W. R. *Engineering Ethics: Outline of an Aspirational Approach*, Springer, London, 2009, pp. 78–80.

Chen K., Chan A. H. Use or non-use of gerontechnology – a qualitative study. *Int J Environ Res Public Health*, 2013; 10(10):4645–66.

Gerontechnology acceptance by elderly Hong Kong Chinese: a senior technology acceptance model (STAM). *Ergonomics*, 2014; 57(5):635–52.

Cimperman M., Brenčič M. M., Trkman P., et al. Older adults' perceptions of home telehealth services. *Telemed J E Health*, 2013; 19(10):786–90.

Cimperman M., Makovec Brenčič M., Trkman P. Analyzing older users' home telehealth services acceptance behavior-applying an Extended UTAUT model. *Int J Med Inform*. 2016; 90:22–31.

Cornet G. Alzheimer's disease wandering behaviour: Gerontechnology and ethics in three French Speaking countries. *Gerontechnology*, 2012; 11(2):266–8.

Dasgupta D., Chaudhry B., Koh E., et al. A survey of tablet applications for promoting successful aging in older adults. *IEEE Access*, 2016; 4:9005–17.

Depp C. A., Jeste D. V. Definitions and predictors of successful aging: a comprehensive review of larger quantitative studies. *Am J Geriatr Psychiatry*, 2006; 14(1):6–20.

Economic Policy Committee (EPC). August 2018. *The 2012 Ageing Report: Underlying Assumptions and Projection Methodologies*. EUROPEAN ECONOMY 4/2011. Available at: http://ec.europa.eu/economy_finance/publications/european_economy/2011/ee4_en.htm

Foster L., Walker A. Active and successful aging: a European policy perspective. *Gerontologist*, 2015; 55(1):83–90.

Fozard J. L. Gerontechnology and perceptual motor-function: New opportunities for prevention, compensation, and enhancement. *Gerontechnology*, 2001; 1(1):5–24.

Friedman S. M., Shah K., Hall W. J. Failing to focus on healthy aging: a frailty of our discipline? *J Am Geriatr Soc*, 2015; 63(7):1459–62.

Graafmans J., Taipale V. Gerontechnology. A sustainable investment in the future. *Stud Health Technol Inform*, 1998; 48:3–6.

Hanson V. L. Influencing technology adoption by older adults. *Interact Comput*, 2010; 22(6):502–9.

Havighurst R. J. *Successful aging. Gerontologist*, 1961; 1:8–13.

Hawley-Hague H., Boulton E., Hall A., et al. Older adults' perceptions of technologies aimed at falls prevention, detection or monitoring: a systematic review. *Int J Med Inform*, 2014; 83(6):416–26.

Katz S., Ford A. B., Moskowitz R. W., et al. Studies of illness in the aged the index of ADL: a standardized measure of biological and psychosocial function. *JAMA*, 1963; 185(12):914–19.

Kiwanuka M. Acceptance process: the missing link between UTAUT and diffusion of innovation theory. *American Journal of Information Systems*, 2015; 3(2):40–4.

Koch S. Healthy ageing supported by technology – a cross-disciplinary research challenge. *Inform Health Soc Care*, 2010; 35(3–4):81–91.

Kusumastuti S., Derks M. G., Tellier S., et al. Successful ageing: a study of the literature using citation network analysis. *Maturitas*, 2016; 93:4–12.

"La Révolution du Bien Vieillir: comment le numérique transforme l'action sociale et accélère le développement de la Silver Economie" (Livre Blanc de Syntec Numérique, 2015).

Ma Q., Chan A. H., Chen K. Personal and other factors affecting acceptance of smartphone technology by older Chinese adults. *Appl Ergon*, 2016; 54:62–71.

Magsamen-Conrad K. *Bridging the Divide: Using UTAUT to predict multigenerational tablet adoption practices* (2015). Media and Communications Faculty Publications. Paper 37. http://scholarworks.bgsu.edu/smc_pub/37.

McDonough C. C. The effect of ageism on the digital divide among older adults. *J Gerontol Geriatr Med*, 2016; 2:008.

Michel J. P. The future of geriatric medicine. *European Geriatric Medicine*, 2012; 3(4):233–7.

Michel J. P., Franco A. Geriatricians and technology. *Journal of the American Medical Directors Association*, 2014; 15(12):860–2.

Peek S. T., Wouters E. J., van Hoof J., et al. Factors influencing acceptance of technology for aging in place: a systematic review. *Int J Med Inform*, 2014; 83(4):235–48.

Pinto M. R., De Medici S., Napoli C. Ergonomics, gerontechnology and well-being in older patients with cardiovascular disease. *Int J Cardiol*, 2000; 72(2):187–8.

Pinto M. R., De Medici S., Van Sant C., et al. Ergonomics, gerontechnology, and design for the home-environment. *Appl Ergon*, 2000a; 31(3):317–22.

Rowe J. W., Kahn R. L. Human aging: usual versus successful. *Science*, 1987; 237,143–9. *Successful aging*. New York, NY: Pantheon Books. 1998.

Successful Aging 2.0: Conceptual Expansions for the 21st Century. *J Gerontol B Psychol Sci Soc Sci*, 2015; 70(4):593–6.

Seeman T. E., Berkman L. F., Charpentier P. A., et al. Behavioral and psychosocial predictors of physical performance: MacArthur studies of successful aging. *J Gerontol A Biol Sci Med Sci*, 1995; 50(4):M177–83.

Smith A. Pew Research Center, April 2014, "Older Adults and Technology Use." Available at: www.pewinternet.org/2014/04/03/older-adults-and-technology-use/

Stegemann S., Baeyens J., Cerreta F., et al. Adherence measurement systems and technology for medications in older patient populations. *European Geriatric Medicine*. 2012; 3(4):254–60.

Stowe S., Harding S. Telecare, telehealth and telemedicine. *European Geriatric Medicine* 2010; 1(3):193–7.

Tesch-Römer C., Wahl H. W. Toward a more comprehensive concept of successful aging: disability and care needs. *J Gerontol B Psychol Sci Soc Sci*, 2017; 72(2):310–18.

Thompson H. J., Demiris G., Rue T., et al. A holistic approach to assess older adults' wellness using e-health technologies. *Telemed J E Health*. 2011; 17(10):794–800.

van Berlo A. *Ethics in domotics. Gerontechnology*, 2005; 3(3):170–2.

van Bronswijk J. E. M. H., Bouma H., Fozard J. L. Technology for quality of life: an enriched taxonomy. *Gerontechnology*. 2002; 2(2):169–72.

van der Vaart R., Drossaert C. Development of the digital health literacy instrument: measuring a broad spectrum of health 1.0 and health 2.0 skills. *J Med Internet Res*. 2017; 19(1):e27.

Venkatesh, V., Morris, M. G., Davis, G. B., et al. User acceptance of information technology: toward a unified view. *MIS Quarterly*, 2007; 27(3):425–78.

Wahl H. W., Mollenkopf H. Impact of everyday technology in the home environment on older adults' quality of life. In Charness N., Schaie K. W., editors. *Impact of technology on successful aging*. New York: Springer; 2003. pp. 215–41.

Wandke H., Sengpiel M., Sönksen M. Myths about older people's use of information and communication technology. *Gerontology*, 2012; 58(6):564–70.

Wu Y. H., Damnée S., Kerhervé H., et al. Bridging the digital divide in older adults: a study from an initiative to inform older adults about new technologies. *Clin Interv Aging*, 2015; 10:193–200.

Ziefle M., Schaar A. K. *Handbook of Smart Homes, Health Care and Well-Being*. New York: Springer; 2014. *Technology acceptance by patients: empowerment and stigma*; pp. 30–100.

# 15 Optimization of Drug Use in Older People

A Key Factor for Successful Aging

Mirko Petrovic, Annemie Somers,
Sophie Marien, and Anne Spinewine

## Introduction

### Drug-Related Problems

One of the major challenges in social and economic terms is the growing older population. By 2025, more than 20 percent of the people in Europe will be 65 years or older, with a quick increase in people aged > 80 years (http://ec.europa.eu/health/ageing/policy_en). These older people often suffer from multiple morbidities and therefore often use multiple drugs (polypharmacy, in the case of $\geq$ 5 drugs).

The quality of pharmacotherapy in these patients is an important issue for healthcare practitioners and governments, since literature shows that adverse drug events are more prominent in older patients in comparison to younger patients (Mannesse et al., 2000; Beijer & Blaey, 2002; Onder et al., 2002; Pirmohamed et al., 2004; Leendertse et al., 2008).

Overall, the negative consequences of drug therapy possibly leading to adverse drug events or drug therapy failure are so-called "drug-related problems" (official definition: "an event or circumstance involving drug therapy that actually or potentially interferes with desired health outcomes") (Hepler & Strand, 1990). Drug-related problems include overuse, misuse, and underuse of drugs.

Various factors can explain the high incidence of drug-related problems in older persons (Bemt et al., 2000; Hajjar et al., 2003; Steinman et al., 2006; Lund et al., 2010). Firstly, older people often suffer from different diseases, and consequently are treated with many drugs, with a higher risk of adverse reactions and drug-drug interactions. Secondly, changes in pharmacokinetic and pharmacodynamic properties make older persons more prone to the occurrence of drug-related problems. Thirdly, older patients are often treated by multiple healthcare professionals, in particular, different prescribing physicians. Therefore, it can be difficult to keep an overview of the different medications prescribed in terms of indications, duration of therapy, monitoring of adverse reactions and follow-up of the effectiveness of the drugs for the different medical problems. Fourthly, decreased capability to handle drugs (e.g., taking tablets out of blisters or inhalation techniques) can lead to decreased compliance and inappropriate drug therapy (Swift, 2003; Le Couteur et al., 2004).

The clinical impact of drug-related problems in older persons is illustrated by the high incidence of drug-related hospital admissions. The reported percentages vary, however, considerably from 4 to 30 percent (Mannesse et al., 2000; Beijer & Blaey, 2002; Onder et al., 2002; Pirmohamed et al., 2004; Leendertse et al., 2008). The majority of these problems concern adverse drug reactions, and several studies have estimated that 50–97 percent of drug-related problems in older people were avoidable. When using a broad definition of DRPs and a thorough analysis in a prospective design, a high incidence of drug-related hospital admissions (DRHAs) on the geriatric ward was found, especially in patients using a high number of drugs before admission (Somers et al., 2010).

Although older patients are often hospitalized at acute geriatric wards with professional care, including evidence-based drug therapy, the risk of drug-related problems during hospitalization is still present (Bemt et al., 2000). The prolongation of the pharmacotherapy initiated before hospital admission, in combination with the acute treatment during admission, makes the drug scheme often complex, not only due to numerous drugs but also with regard to the need for careful evaluation of which medicines should be continued, changed, temporarily or definitely stopped, and which drugs should be started with follow-up of effects and side effects.

## Inappropriate Prescribing

Since older patients are more vulnerable to adverse drug-related events, there is a need to ensure appropriate prescribing in order to prevent misuse, overuse, and underuse of drugs. Efforts should be made to detect and prevent inappropriate prescribing for older patients, preferably in a multidisciplinary team consisting of physicians and pharmacists. Different tools have been developed to detect so-called "potentially inappropriate prescribing" or PIP. Application of these tools helps to detect PIP with possible hazardous consequences for older patients. After detection, the team has to decide whether or not to alter the drug therapy by outweighing the benefits and the risks.

## Medication Non-Adherence

Another cause for the occurrence of DRPs in older patients is non-adherence, meaning that there is a significant difference between the intake of drugs by the patient and the prescribed treatment. In a WHO report about long-term therapy, it was concluded that approximately 50 percent of patients do not take medications as prescribed, and that increasing adherence may have a greater effect on health than improvements in specific medical therapy (Sabaté, 2003). Different types of non-adherence exist as well as according actions for improvement, meaning that medication adherence is not exclusively the responsibility of the patient (Brown & Bussell, 2011). When looking at older patients, it is clear that non-adherence represents an important problem for effectiveness of therapy (Hughes, 2004).

## Unintended Medication Discrepancies

Older persons often suffer from multiple chronic conditions and are more hospitalized than younger people, and are often institutionalized, in case living at home is not possible anymore. This can lead to discontinuity of drug therapy, with unintended medication discrepancies as a consequence. Often drugs taken before a hospital admission have been changed when the patient is discharged, and without fluent electronic communication, there is a high possibility of erroneous drug use during hospitalization or after discharge. This can again lead to drug-related problems when patients are taking the wrong drugs or the wrong doses. It has been shown that unintended medication discrepancies in older patients during transition moments are common and therefore efforts should be made toward seamless pharmaceutical care (Kostas et al., 2013).

## Goal of This Chapter

In this chapter the authors wish to explain the difficulties that can arise with drug therapy in older persons, and elaborate the causes of drug-related problems i.e., inappropriate prescribing, medication non-adherence, and unintended medication discrepancies in the three first sections. Furthermore, we will highlight possible solutions to overcome these difficulties in the subsequent three sections, i.e., medication reconciliation, medication review, and tools to improve adherence (Box 15.1).

---

**Box 15.1   Key elements of optimization of drug use in older people**

**Medication reconciliation (Marien et al., 2017)**
   Tools to avoid discrepancies (Smith et al., 2004; Drenth-van Maanen et al., 2011; Claeys et al., 2012)

**Prescribing assessment and optimization**
   Medication review (NHS Cumbria Medicines Management Team, 2013)
   Tools for detection of potentially inappropriate prescribing (Hanlon et al., 1992; Somers et al., 2012; Kaufmann et al., 2014; The American Geriatrics Society, 2015; O'Mahony et al., 2015; Tommelein et al., 2016; Renom-Guiteras et al., 2017),
   Deprescribing (Scott et al., 2015)
   e-Tools to support prescribing optimization (Lesselroth et al., 2011; de Wit et al., 2016)

**Adherence assessment and optimization (Haynes et al., 2008; Conn et al., 2009, 2015)**

**Collaborative and integrated approaches**
   Role of clinical pharmacy and other healthcare providers (Schmader et al., 2004; Scullin et al., 2007; Ellis et al., 2011; Petrovic et al., 2012; Dilles et al., 2013; Onder et al., 2013)
   Patient-centered care (Barry and Edgman-Levitan, 2012; Phillips et al., 2016)

## What Needs to Be Optimized

### Inappropriate Prescribing

Medication appropriateness in older people is understood when medication is safe in terms of its pharmaceutical properties and is cost effective to prescribe. However, a more integrated definition of inappropriate prescribing, beyond this one-dimensional approach, should include the assessment of older persons' prescription medications in the context of their multimorbidity, polypharmacy, complex medication regimes, functional and cognitive status, treatment goals, and life expectancy.

Moreover, a holistic evaluation of prescribing appropriateness should include the domains of overprescribing, misprescribing, and underprescribing.

Overprescribing refers to the prescription of medications for which no obvious clinical indication exists.

Misprescribing concerns the prescription of a medication that increases the risk of a drug-related problem. It includes prescribing that refers to an incorrect dose, frequency, modality of administration, or duration of treatment. Additionally, misprescribing encompasses the use of medications that are likely to cause clinically significant drug-drug or drug-disease interactions. Safer, equally effective alternatives should always be taken into consideration.

Underprescribing refers to the omission of potentially appropriate and useful medications that are clinically indicated for treatment or prevention of an existing disease (O'Connor et al., 2012).

It has been shown that older patients suffer more often from inappropriate prescribing and drug-related problems than middle-aged patients. The relationships between multimorbidity, polypharmacy, inappropriate prescribing, and drug-related problems are important to understand. The tendency to complex medication regimes and greater levels of polypharmacy is additionally influenced by evidence-based guidelines, which often support multiple drug regimens for single diseases. However, the older patient with multimorbidity is often prescribed multiple combinations of evidence-based drug therapies for different diseases at the same time, which may not be well tolerated because of adverse drug-drug and drug-disease interactions. Paradoxically, this evidence-based polypharmacy is often based on large-scale trials that specifically exclude older patients with multimorbidity, polypharmacy, and frailty (Dodd et al., 2011; O'Mahony et al., 2012).

The clinical impact of inappropriate prescribing and drug-related problems in older people is illustrated by the high incidence of drug-related hospital admissions and the related increase of expenditures (Wu et al., 2012). Although older patients are often hospitalized at acute geriatric wards with professional care, including evidence-based pharmacotherapy, the risk of drug-related problems during hospitalization is still present. The prolongation of the pharmacotherapy initiated before hospital admission, in combination with acute treatment during admission, makes the drug scheme often complex, not only due to numerous drugs but also with regard to the need for careful evaluation of which medicines should be continued, changed, temporarily or definitely stopped, and which drugs should be started with follow-up of effects and side effects.

Since older patients are more vulnerable to adverse drug-related events, there is a need to ensure appropriate prescribing in order to prevent overprescribing, misprescribing, and underprescribing.

### *Potentially Inappropriate Medication (PIM)*

Medication appropriateness can be assessed by evaluating the quality of a prescribing decision (i.e., a process measure) and/or the outcome of a prescribing decision (i.e., an outcome measure). On the one hand, an example of a process measure of prescribing appropriateness would be the application of a validated criterion to a patient's prescription and clinical diagnosis. On the other hand, an example of an outcome measure would be to evaluate the medications of older patients presenting with a certain clinical outcome (e.g., confusion or falls); a medication that is known to increase the risk of that same outcome (i.e., confusion or falls) would be inappropriate in that instance. Process measures of appropriateness should however clearly predict outcome measures. Process and outcome measures of prescribing appropriateness can be assessed by means of explicit (criterion-based) or implicit (judgment-based) criteria (O'Connor et al., 2012).

### Non-Adherence

In the past two decades, the influence of adherence to drug therapy has been explored extensively. It has become clear that adherence is an essential step between treatment and outcome (Brown & Bussell, 2011). World Health Organization defined adherence as "the extent to which a person's behavior – taking medication, following a diet, and/or executing lifestyle changes, corresponds with agreed recommendations from a healthcare provider (HCP)" (Sabaté, 2003). This definition concerns an agreed therapy, whereas the previously used term "compliance" describes the degree to which a patient correctly follows medical advice (possibly not agreed upon). In a report about long-term therapy, it was concluded that approximately 50 percent of patients do not take medications as prescribed, and that increasing adherence may have a greater effect on health than improvements in specific medical therapy (Sabaté, 2003).

Two types of non-adherence have been identified, related to different patients' behaviors.

Intentional non-adherence is an active decision of the patient to forego prescribed therapy.

Underlying causes are fear for adverse reactions, not feeling ill, or not realizing the benefit of the medication. Unintentional non-adherence, on the other hand, is a passive process whereby patients fail to adhere to prescribing instructions through forgetfulness, carelessness, or circumstances out of their control (e.g., health literacy). Patients can exhibit both types of non-adherent behaviors (Lehane & McCarthy, 2007).

Adherence can be calculated by dividing the number of pills the patient actually takes by the number of pills prescribed by the physician in that same time period. Patients are generally considered adherent to their medication if their medication adherence percentage is greater than 80 percent (Osterberg & Blaschke, 2005).

### Determinants of Adherence to Pharmacotherapy

Non-adherence risk factors could be medication-related. These include number of medications, medication treatment complexity, duration, packaging, and medication-related adverse events. Patient-related risk factors comprise age-related physiological changes, index disease, comorbidities, cognitive abilities, and patient's affect, psychosocial profile, health literacy, personal values, beliefs, trust, and economic factors. Prescriber's determinants consider education, specialty, psychosocial profile, teamwork, communication, time constraints, and cost restraint pressure.

Other factors, i.e., regarding health system and environment, involve patient-prescriber relationship, access to medication-based health insurance, restrictive formularies, generics, and social support (Gellad et al., 2011).

### Adherence and Older People, Why Are They Vulnerable?

When looking at older patients, it is clear that non-adherence represents an important problem for effectiveness of therapy (Hughes, 2004). Older people are vulnerable to multimorbidity, with a higher risk of polypharmacy, and therefore might be at higher risk of non-adherence to pharmacotherapy compared to their younger counterparts. Non-adherence includes failing to get a first prescription or subsequent repeats dispensed, discontinuing a medicine before the course of therapy is complete, taking more or less medicines than prescribed, and/or taking a dose at the wrong time. Non-adherence is a frequent cause of treatment failure; 40 to 75 percent of older patients do not follow their prescription appropriately. Consequences of non-adherence are noticeable at patients' level in the suboptimal treatment of their condition, the potential harm resulting from suboptimal management, and the deterioration of functional capacities. At public health level, it results in increased expenditures to counter suboptimal treatment and increased clinical risk due to the additional cost of medicines dispensed but not used, and at the societal level, poorly managed long-term conditions can negatively affect the economic contribution individuals make to society.

### Medication Discrepancies at Transition Moments

A complete and accurate medication list is essential for seamless care transition between the community and the hospital. Discrepancies can arise between actual pre-admission medications and those recorded at admission, as home medications are a recognized safety concern among older inpatients (Drenth-van Maanen et al., 2011). Uncorrected discrepancies may continue throughout hospitalization and after discharge, impeding appropriate pharmacotherapy (Villanyi et al., 2011; Cornu et al., 2012). Studies have shown that great variation exists in the reported prevalence of discrepancies in the home medication lists of patients admitted to geriatric wards, ranging from 40 to 92 percent of the sample population (Drenth-van Maanen et al., 2011; Villanyi et al., 2011; Cornu et al., 2012; Perehudoff et al., 2015). Similar problems can arise at discharge, when therapy is not continued as intended (Wong et al., 2008; Cornu et al., 2012).

In section III, the strategy to reduce discrepancies will be discussed in depth. This strategy is called "medicines reconciliation" and is defined as "the process of identifying the most accurate list of a patient's current medicines – including the name, dosage, frequency and route – and comparing them to the current list in use, recognizing discrepancies, and documenting any changes, thus resulting in a complete list of medications, accurately communicated" (Agency for Healthcare Research and Quality US Department of Health and Human Services, 2012).

## Types of Discrepancies

Unintentional discrepancies can be categorized into one of five main types: medicine (i.e., incorrect or duplicate medicine, absent medicine, or brand), dose (i.e., incorrect or absent dose), frequency (i.e., incorrect or absent frequency), time of administration (i.e., incorrect or absent time), and route of administration (i.e., incorrect or absent route) (Kostas et al., 2013). More than one discrepancy type can arise for the same medication. Any discrepancies identified should be immediately updated in the patient's electronic file used by the medical team.

## Potential Clinical Impact

The potential clinical impact of each discrepancy can be adjudicated using a validated three-point scale: discrepancies unlikely to cause, with a potential to cause moderate, and with a potential to cause serious patient discomfort or clinical deterioration (Cornish et al., 2005). At the level of discrepancy, a geriatrician and a hospital pharmacist, who was not involved in the medication reconciliation, should execute assessment independently. The two scores for each discrepancy should then be compared and, in case of disagreement, the highest clinical impact score used in data analysis.

In a systematic review, discrepancy inconsistencies were found across studies, their classification and data sources were used. Standardization and common discrepancy nomenclature is necessary for medication reconciliation outcomes to be compared, and to identify best practices to enhance safety (Agency for Healthcare Research and Quality US Department of Health and Human Services, 2012).

## Optimization of Drug Use

### Medication Reconciliation Definition, Process, Added Value

Medication reconciliation (MedRec) is a formal and collaborative process of obtaining and verifying a complete and accurate list of all patient's current medications – including the name, dosage, frequency, and route – to ensure that precise and comprehensive medication information is transmitted consistently across transitions of care (Agency for Healthcare Research and Quality US Department of Health and Human Services, 2012). Medication reconciliation could also be the first step of a clinical medication review. With or without reviewing the medication list, MedRec aims to enable prescribers making the most appropriate prescribing decisions for the patient (Bell et al., 2011). Several leading international healthcare organizations involved in patient safety, such as the OMS, have listed MedRec as a priority objective to improve healthcare.

The formal and collaborative process of MedRec consists of four steps:

(1) Verification: The first step consists in gathering the Best Possible Medication History (BPMH). This is a particularly difficult step requiring medication information from multiple sources (general practitioner, community pharmacist, specialist, electronic medical record, patient, etc.). Several tools exist to support the clinician taking it.
(2) Identification: In the second step, the clinician compares different lists in order to identify discrepancies – unexplained differences between lists – related to drug name, drug dosages, drug frequency, and route of administration.
(3) Reconciliation: Identified discrepancies are resolved in the third step. While reconciling a list, medications can also be checked for appropriateness.
(4) Communication: The fourth step aims to elaborate the reconciled list. It is essential to document each taken decision and each modification. Finally, with the document reconciled, the list is shared with the patient and every patient's healthcare provider. Patient medication education should also be added to this particular step.

While each MedRec process will be made of the four described steps, the care transition point will modify the lists compared in the second step (Kostas et al., 2013). For example:

(1) At admission: the Best Possible Medication History (BPMH) is compared with admission orders.
(2) During inpatient transfer: the BPMH is compared to pre-transfer medications and transfer medications.
(3) At discharge: the BPMH and current inpatient medications are compared to write the discharge medication list.
(4) At-home or in long-term care: the BPMH is compared to the most current information found in the patient's recorded medication information sources.

## Impact of MedRec

Two systematic reviews have concluded that MedRec interventions prevent medication errors associated with harm (Kwan et al., 2013; Mueller et al., 2013). MedRec interventions are complex interventions to evaluate because they are influenced by many variables (e.g., workflow, leadership, staff skills, training, use of IT, existence of patient safety culture) (Pevnick et al., 2016). Several studies measured adverse drug events but only a few assessed hard clinical outcomes (e.g., hospital readmissions, emergency visits, morbidity, and mortality) (Gillespie et al., 2009), while direct cost savings need to deepen to draw consistent conclusions.

## Tools to Avoid Discrepancies

Because older people are more susceptible to adverse drug reactions and their potentially clinical consequences, and because they frequently transition across settings or care providers, improving continuity of care is particularly important for this group of patients.

MedRec is a complex and resources-intensive process. During the last decade, leading organizations have developed toolkits to support the development, implementation, and improvement of MedRec processes. The "Match Toolkit for MedRec" (Gleason et al., 2012), "A Toolkit to Disseminate Best Practices in Inpatient Medication Reconciliation," from the Marquis Study, and the "Paper to Electronic MedRec Implementation Toolkit" (Schnipper et al., 2009) are three valuable publications.

Because the MedRec process requires method and rigor, some tools are specifically dedicated to each step of the process. Structured questionnaires, such as the Structured History Taking of Medication Use (Drenth-van Maanen et al., 2011) or the Best Possible Medication History Interview Guides (grey literature), can be helpful for the first step. Concerning identification of discrepancies and reconciliation, Claeys's and Smith's tool are precious instruments (Smith et al., 2004; Claeys et al., 2012). Nevertheless, these are more suitable for research because application of these instruments in daily practice is time-consuming.

The use of information technology (IT) appears to be a promising approach, as it can support each step of the MedRec process by reducing the clinician's cognitive overload/burden (by reducing the needed time and concentration). To be a valuable support, IT tools should follow several recommendations (Marien et al., 2017). Furthermore, the electronic exchange of drug lists between the community and the hospital will be an essential step in the near future to avoid discrepancies. However, IT will not solve every problem. Of course, improving information sharing, integration, and IT interoperability will help at gathering the BPMH, but the patient will still be the only one knowing what medication he/she is exactly taking. Patient participation in MedRec needs to be enhanced, even though this is not always easy in the case of older people. If needed, we should learn to empower older patients with their principal caregiver (i.e., family, friend, healthcare professional).

Besides IT and patient participation, multidisciplinary teamwork is essential. The specific role of each team member should be clarified as well as the associated responsibilities related to his/her profession and interpersonal skills. The patient also has a role to play. Indeed, using a shared decision-making (SDM) process could greatly improve MedRec outcomes. Taking patient medication adherence into account could yield better follow-up since it is more suitable to patient preferences.

In addition, healthcare organizations should redesign the drug process and provide enough resources and time for medication reconciliation activities in daily practice and should offer staff training to promote continuous improvement of MedRec skills for healthcare professionals.

## Prescribing Optimization

Medication review (MedRev) is defined as "a structured, critical examination of a patient's medicines with the objective of reaching an agreement with the patient about treatment, optimizing the impact of medicines, minimizing the number of medication related problems and reducing waste" (NHS Cumbria Medicines Management Team, 2017). It is recognized as a cornerstone of medication management to improve patient safety, especially for older people with polypharmacy, where medicines are an important cause of unplanned hospital admissions (Blenkinsopp et al., 2012).

Medication review should ideally be done in the presence of the patient and his current medication.

The process of medication review can be structured in four different steps:

(1) A first step consists of the identification of all the medications that the patient is taking. At each care transition point, this identification of current medication should be joined to a medication reconciliation process.
(2) Secondly, the drug scheme is screened for drug-related problems (DRPs), i.e., any misuse, underuse, or overuse of drugs. Several tools exist to support this drug screening.
(3) Thirdly, possible solutions to the drug-related problems are discussed between the pharmacist and the physician. When possible, these solutions are presented and discussed with the patient.
(4) Finally a medication management plan is created to address any issue. How medications of this plan are best taken, is explained by the pharmacist (or another healthcare provider) to the patient.

### When to Review Medications?

A medication review should be planned on a regular basis. The exact frequency can vary depending on the setting, the needs, and the resources. An annual medication review is often proposed or recommended. There are no international validated criteria or risk scores to identify patients that benefit most from a medication review. However, it is generally agreed that the patients most likely to benefit are patients with a large number of medications, taking high-risk medication(s), having experienced previous adverse drug events, and patients transitioning to a new level of care (e.g., palliative care).

A medication review is usually performed by a physician, if possible in collaboration with a pharmacist, and sometimes a nurse. These healthcare professionals should be appropriately trained.

## Impact of a Reliable Medication Review

The impact of a pharmacist-led MedRev has been widely studied and is known to be positive on drug-related-problem (DRP) detection (Gheewala et al., 2014; Kempen et al., 2014). DRP detection is even more efficient when pharmacists are working in collaboration with physicians. Ideally, improvements in DRP detection should be linked to improvements in hard outcomes such as hospital readmissions and mortality. However, a recent Cochrane review did not find evidence concerning these improvements (Christensen & Lundh, 2016).

Large efforts are currently being done to develop, validate, and test software engines that can reliably and promptly support healthcare professionals who perform complex medication reviews in older people with multimorbidity. The European Union-funded SENATOR and OPERAM clinical trials, initiated in 2012 and 2016, respectively, examine the impact of customized software engines in reducing medication-related morbidity, avoidable excess cost, and rehospitalization in older people with multimorbidity (Lavan et al., 2016).

## Tools for Detection of Potentially Inappropriate Prescribing (PIP)

A systematic review by Kaufmann et al., identified 46 tools to assess appropriateness of prescribing, which were published between 1991 and 2013 (Kaufmann et al., 2014). Since the publication of the 2014 review, the updates of some of these tools have been published in addition to several new tools (The American Geriatrics Society, 2015; O'Mahony et al., 2015; Renom-Guiteras et al., 2015; Tommelein et al., 2016). These tools are categorized as explicit (criterion-based) or implicit (judgment-based) tools.

## Explicit Tools

Explicit tools or criteria used with prescribing data only or with clinical data are often used to detect inappropriate prescribing. Criteria to detect overprescribing comprise of a list of incorrect indications to prescribe a specific medication or medication class. Criteria to detect underprescribing generally states that a medication should be prescribed to prevent or to treat a certain condition, unless in the case of contraindication. Criteria to detect misprescribing usually focus on choice of medication, dose, indications, duration of treatment, duplication of therapy, and follow-up. The medication-to-avoid criteria have been the most often used. They are based on lists of potentially inappropriate medications (PIMs), i.e., medications that should be avoided in older people because the risks outweigh the benefits (i.e., medications that should always be avoided in older people, doses that should not be exceeded, and medications that should be avoided in patients with specific conditions) (Spinewine et al., 2007).

Various explicit tools are available, although only the Beers criteria and the STOPP/START (Screening Tool of Older Persons' Prescriptions and Screening Tool to Alert doctors to Right – appropriate, indicated – Treatment) criteria have been evaluated for predictive validity. Beers criteria, lastly updated in 2015, identify a list of 53 PIMs, or medication classes divided into three categories: PIMs to avoid independent of comorbidities, PIMs to avoid in older people with certain diseases and syndromes, and medications to be used with caution (The American Geriatrics Society, 2015).

The STOPP criteria for screening PIMs, as well as the START criteria for the detection of potential prescribing omissions of indicated, potentially beneficial drugs medications, updated in 2015, are organized according to physiological systems and include both PIP (80 criteria) and omission of potentially beneficial pharmacotherapy (34 criteria) (O'Mahony et al., 2015).

The Beers and the STOPP/START criteria have been compared in terms of impact on the incidence of potentially inappropriate prescribing medication (including prescribing omission), polypharmacy, and clinical relevance of medication changes. The application of both tools improved the prescribing appropriateness, and reduced polypharmacy; they also induced treatment modifications of potential major clinical relevance. The best results were observed with the recent version of the STOPP/START (Boland et al., 2016).

Explicit criteria can be applied with little or no clinical judgment but do not address individual differences between patients.

## Implicit Tools

Implicit tools take into account clinical information of the individual patient to judge appropriateness of prescribing. The Medication Appropriateness Index (MAI) represents a comprehensive and validated implicit tool (Hanlon et al., 1992). It is a judgment-based process measure of prescribing appropriateness that assesses ten elements of prescribing: indication, effectiveness, dose, correct directions, practical directions, DDIs, drug–disease interactions, duplication, duration, and cost. These elements are assessed based on clinical judgment rather than objective measures, and the ratings generate a weighted score that serves as a summary measure of prescribing appropriateness. Recently, an adapted version has been published in which the original MAI was changed to cover more aspects of drug therapy and to reduce the number of questions by grouping certain aspects. Moreover, three questions were omitted (practical directions, duplication of therapy, and cost), one question was rephrased (i.e., "effectiveness" was changed to "right choice"), and one question about adverse drug reactions was added (Somers et al., 2012).

Implicit criteria are time-consuming and more dependent on the user. No single ideal tool exists so far. The choice of a tool may depend on the purpose of use and availability of data. Implementation of such a tool requires that the tool should not only be well-designed and comprehensive, but also still practical in everyday practice. Integration of assessment tools in electronic decision support systems could be a promising approach. These tools are useful for identifying potentially inappropriate prescribing, although they cannot substitute for good clinical decision-making when treating older patients.

## Judicious Drug Cessation or Deprescribing

Deprescribing is defined as the process of withdrawal of inappropriate medication, supervised by a healthcare professional with the goal of managing polypharmacy and improving outcomes (Reeve et al., 2015). This approach is particularly important among older people in whom multimorbidity and polypharmacy are common, but protocols for stopping medication in these circumstances are scarce (Cammen et al., 2014). Deprescribing should be especially considered in any older patient (a) presenting with a new symptom or syndrome suggestive of adverse drug effects; (b) manifesting advanced disease, terminal illness, dementia, extreme frailty, or full dependence; (c) receiving high-risk drugs or combinations; and (d) receiving preventive drugs for scenarios associated with no increased disease risk despite drug cessation (Scott et al., 2015).

A practical approach to deprescribing consists of five steps: first, identification of all medications the patient is currently taking and the indications for each medication; second, consideration of the overall risk of medication-induced harm in an individual patient; third, estimation of the potential for each medication to be deprescribed; fourth, prioritization of drugs to be deprescribed, considering benefits and harms (including risk of withdrawal, reactions, or disease rebound syndromes); and fifth, implementation of a discontinuation regimen and monitoring the patient closely (Scott et al., 2015). The approach must combine patient preference and context, clinical judgment, and scientific data (where it exists). A comprehensive geriatric assessment (CGA) may help with deprescribing (Cammen et al., 2014). SDM is absolutely essential: the patient, family, and other healthcare providers must be engaged in the process. Data suggest that older people and carers are open to the idea of medication withdrawal if they understand why it is being recommended.

Deprescribing can be considered for many different classes of medications. For example, in frail older people with a history of falls, functional or cognitive impairment, deprescribing should be considered for fall-risk-increasing drugs, psychotropic drugs (especially benzodiazepines), certain cardiovascular drugs, and drugs with anticholinergic properties. Other drugs to be considered for deprescribing in older people include proton-pump inhibitors, antihypertensive agents, bisphosphonates, statins, and antidiabetic agents. In addition, at the end of life, careful assessment of medication is necessary, in order to avoid unnecessary treatments and potentially serious adverse drug reactions and events (Cammen et al., 2014).

The evidence so far shows that multidisciplinary interventions can help reduce the drug burden. Their effects on clinical outcomes are less clear, although emerging evidence has shown that deprescribing strategies targeting patients with multimorbidity and older people may improve patient outcomes. For example, a non-randomized trial of polypharmacy reduction in older people showed that over half of drugs could be discontinued and that this reduction in the drug burden was associated with improvements in cognition and global health (Garfinkel & Mangin, 2010). Studies of deprescribing are in progress worldwide and will contribute to better-informed clinical decisions and policies on deprescribing.

## Other Tools to Support Prescribing Optimization

In the past decade, the use of health information technology (IT) has been widespread, and the use of smart phones and tablets has strongly increased. The healthcare system has not been outdone however, as it is currently not possible to record all tools, clinical decision support systems, and applications that have been developed to support clinicians in their daily practice.

Specific electronic tools have been developed to support medication reconciliation (eMedRec tools). Indeed MedRec is a very complex time-consuming task causing cognitive overload for the clinician. E-tools are thus particularly interesting if these are helping the clinician at least for: (1) gathering the BPMH and comparing lists, (2) identifying discrepancies, and (3) resolving these by providing the following options: continue, change, or discontinue a medication. A recent systematic review (Marien et al., 2017) retrieved 11 tools in the literature that fully electronically enabled MedRec. Additional commercial tools were identified but little information about their functioning was collected.

Classic Clinical Decision Support Systems (CDSSs) include alerts, reminders, order sets, drug-dose calculations that automatically remind the clinician of a specific action, or care summary dashboards that provide performance feedback on quality indicators. Because reviewing medication is a resource-intensive task with space for a lot of avoidable human errors, commercially or locally CDSS have been developed. Two recent (Meulendijk et al., 2015; Alagiakrishnan et al., 2016) studies evaluated the appropriateness of MedRev decisions made by clinicians with the support of a CDSS. Both tools positively influenced appropriate decisions made in medication review, but both tools have weaknesses and will need to improve in the upcoming years. One of the biggest challenges MedRev CDSS are facing is the good calibration of alerts, "enough but not too much," with the uprising risk of "alert fatigue." MedRev CDSS algorithms should approach the expertise of the gerontopharmacology meeting (de Wit et al., 2016).

Even if users recognize that e-tools can improve MedRev and MedRec processes (especially patient safety and clinicians' ability) (Lesselroth et al., 2011), and even if they think it is useful and valuable (Meulendijk et al., 2013), long-term acceptance is not acquired. Firstly, because clinicians possess considerable leverage to resist organizational change (Holahan et al., 2015). Secondly, Health IT (HIT) needs to be compatible (i.e., showing consistency and similarities) with existing work processes. Thirdly, the climate around HIT should be positive, encouraging end-users to adapt HIT to the context, support users in mastering HIT, and remove obstacle to the use of HIT (Holahan et al., 2015).

In conclusion, the use of electronic tools is not the solution but it can be a valuable help to improve medication optimization by supporting MedRev and MedRec. How best e-tools are integrated into the workflow and existing software will likely have a baring on how acceptable e-tools will be for clinicians in daily practice and how better pharmacotherapy will be optimized. Finally, behavior changes will not be obtained if users are not convinced about the tool usability, so they should be included at the start of the development of new tools to create a positive organizational climate.

## Adherence Optimization

Presently, no single method is sufficiently accurate and reliable to pick out non-adherence. A combination of methods appears to be most suitable. Moreover, it becomes increasingly evident that adherence, as a process, has to be assessed over time and not just at one evaluation point. In particular, when functional impairments or cognitive deficits may affect reliability of adherence, a comprehensive geriatric assessment should be performed and the caregiver involved (Giardini et al., 2016).

### Optimizing Adherence

A meta-analysis evaluated the adherence outcomes of various interventions (Conn et al., 2009). Medication-related interventions improving adherence include attempts to decrease polypharmacy and prevent adverse drug events, education on medication, rationalization of medication regimen, reduction of complexity, age-friendly dosage and medication labeling, written instructions on medication, and medication review.

Patient-related interventions include assessment of medication taking/managing and identifying problems, education regarding disease, treatment goals, disease symptom self-monitoring, adherence monitoring by healthcare professionals and feedback, medication self-monitoring (e.g., diaries), medication reminders (e.g., calendars, charts, phone, e-mail, computer provided), refill reminders – in addition to dose administration aids (e.g., pillboxes, blister packages, containers), training, developing contextual cues, communication, follow-up on education, or monitoring, psychosocial interventions, specific approaches for older people with cognitive impairment, or professional assistance in medication management.

Prescriber-related interventions comprise education for professionals, medication review, multidisciplinary involvement and role setting, improvement of multidisciplinary communication, and coordination of care.

Health system- and environment-related interventions include concept of concordance, age-friendly access to medication, improved logistics, and policy recognition of healthcare costs of non-adherence.

Behavioral interventions with regard to pillboxes, blisters with multiple medications, special medical containers, reminders for medication taking and self-monitoring of symptoms were mentioned among more effective measures. Moreover, another meta-analysis has shown that reminders and reminder-packaging have a positive impact on medication adherence. Interventions were most effective when they used blister packs and were delivered in pharmacies, while interventions were less effective when studies included older subjects and those with cognitive impairment (Conn et al., 2015).

However in a systematic review, Haynes et al. pointed out that no firm conclusion about the effectiveness of strategies to counteract non-adherence can be drawn, because of methodological limitations (Haynes et al., 2008).

## Optimization of Adherence in Older People with Impairment

Nine studies assessed interventions regarding adherence in older people with multimorbidity and polypharmacy (Hawe & Higgins, 1990; Hanlon et al., 1996; Bernsten et al., 2001; Grymonpre et al., 2001; Nazareth et al., 2001; Volume et al., 2001; Sturgess et al., 2003; Lee et al., 2006; Wu et al., 2006). Five of them found improvement of adherence (Hawe & Higgins, 1990; Bernsten et al., 2001; Sturgess et al., 2003; Lee et al., 2006; Wu et al., 2006). Moreover, better adherence was associated with a reduction in mortality over 2 years, better control of chronic diseases, and decreased healthcare costs. Promising interventions appeared in medication review, focusing on therapy rationalization (in two studies) (Bernsten et al., 2001; Sturgess et al., 2003), patient-tailored education in combination with medication reminders (medication chart) (Hawe & Higgins, 1990), dose administration aid (Lee et al., 2006), or patient follow-up (Sturgess et al., 2003; Lee et al., 2006; Wu et al., 2006). Healthcare professionals can instruct patients by explaining how to take medication(s), addressing any lack of motivation to take medication, and by discussing with patients their knowledge and beliefs about their pharmacotherapy. However, it is difficult to compare interventions because of their heterogeneity and the methodological inconsistencies of some of these studies. Besides, overall functioning, quality of life and utilization of healthcare services were seldom reported. Additionally, the studies did not focus on attitudes and values, motivation, coping strategies, and social support.

Evidence on how to approach adherence in older people with cognitive impairment is limited. In a systematic review, Campbell et al. showed the significance of relational aspects in improving adherence, stressing the need to sustain older people with relationships more than the instrumental aid of information and communication technologies alone (Campbell et al., 2012). For this group of patients, an individualized medication management assessment should include a medication history, proxy information, and repeated medication monitoring. Reducing the number of medications, tailoring the dose regimen to the patient's routine and preferences, coordinating medication dosage, and offering medication organizers and reminders are the most frequently recommended interventions (Topinkova et al., 2012).

In a systematic meta-review, Mistiaen et al. proposed integrated interventions for compensating patients' limitations due to dementia; regular medication reviews and systematic cooperation between physicians and pharmacists provided promising results for a multidisciplinary, multifaceted approach in which adherence is a part of a wider model of collaborative care (Mistiaen et al., 2007).

## Collaborative and Integrated Approaches

### Role of Clinical Pharmacy and Other Healthcare Providers

Multidisciplinary teams in medicine always confer advantages over non-integrated healthcare providers within any system, and geriatrics is a good example. When the complexity of an older patient is considered by the team prior to any pharmacotherapy, the risk of an ADR can be diminished. Preferably, integrated drug management is provided starting with hospital admission and followed up after discharge in a manner that is transparent to the patient, with continuous information flow between hospital physicians and nurses, clinical pharmacists inside or outside the hospital, and primary care physicians. An ultimate patient benefit is that this process leads to optimized drug therapy with reduced length of hospital stay, longer time to readmission, and decreases the number of readmissions (Scullin et al., 2007).

The traditional medical approach to treatment of older patients is not always enough to fully assess all problematic areas. Therefore, a comprehensive geriatric assessment within a multidisciplinary framework may be required to improve the pharmacotherapy and reduce the ADR rate. When this is performed by means of an individual care plan tailored to an older person that includes a more thorough evaluation, it results in enhanced care planning and better quality of care (Ellis et al., 2011). In this process, the issue of pharmacotherapy is seen as a part of the overall treatment plan, embracing a more holistic program in which drug prescribing is one way of treatment that is integrated into others.

As a part of a multidisciplinary team, nurses are responsible for the daily care of older patients. More contact time with patients puts nurses in a position to screen for the presence of ADRs. In practice, however, nurses are not always confident about their participation in drug monitoring. Moreover, a lack of specific pharmacotherapy knowledge and lack of attention to report observations to physicians have been reported. Dilles et al. developed an instrument, Pharmanurse, to facilitate nurse-driven adverse drug reaction (ADR) screening as an input for interdisciplinary medication review in older nursing home residents. The intervention consisted of an interdisciplinary medication review, prepared by nurse observations of potential ADRs using personalized screening lists generated by the Pharmanurse software. Pharmanurse is specifically adapted to use by nurses and to use in nursing homes. In 81 percent of the 418 residents, nurses observed 1,527 potential ADRs (mean per resident 3.7). Physicians confirmed 821 ADRs in 60 percent of the residents (mean per resident 2.0). As a result, 214 medication changes were planned in 21 percent of the residents (mean per resident 0.5) because of ADRs (Dilles et al., 2013).

One further benefit is that the drug prescription plan may be simplified based on pharmacological and healthcare needs of the individual patient with concurrent reductions in drug-related adverse events and increases in the quality of drug prescribing (Petrovic et al., 2012; Onder et al., 2013). In a large study in 11 Veterans Affairs (VA) hospitals, inpatient geriatric unit and outpatient geriatric clinic teams evaluated and managed patients according to published guidelines and VA standards in the intervention arms. A 35 percent reduction in the risk of serious ADRs compared with usual care was observed in outpatient geriatric clinic care and inpatient geriatric unit care, with a significant reduction of unnecessary and inappropriate drug use and underuse. Moreover, outpatient geriatric clinic care significantly reduced the number of clinical conditions that were caused by the omission of drugs (Schmader et al., 2004).

## Patient's Perspectives, Preferences, Participation – Patient-Centered Care

Person-centered care (PCC), defined as "care that is respectful and responsive to individual patient preferences, needs and values and that ensures patient values guide all clinical decisions," has been recognized as a cornerstone of high-quality healthcare (Barry and Edgman-Levitan, 2012; de Silva, 2014; Phillips et al., 2016; American Geriatrics Society Expert Panel on Person-Centered Care, 2016). SDM, "an approach where clinicians and patients share the best available evidence when faced with the task of making decisions, and where patients are supported to consider options, to achieve informed preferences" is the most important attribute of patient-centered care. Actively informing, eliciting, and incorporating patient preferences in decisions are at the heart of SDM (Elwyn et al., 2014).

As part of the medication review process, alignment of drug therapy with the patient's preference is increasingly advocated as a promising strategy to tackle inappropriate polypharmacy in older people (Tannenbaum et al., 2014; Kogan et al., 2016). SDM is considered to be more complicated in the context of older age and multimorbidity. It is however highly relevant. Older patients with multimorbidity often face preference sensitive decisions (i.e., when more than one medically reasonable option is available and when there is no best strategy since the option depends on the patient's personal values and preferences) with regard to starting, continuing, and stopping medications. This occurs because evidence on the benefit- harm ratio of many medications is uncertain in older patients with multiple conditions and there is an increased risk of adverse events due the problem of polypharmacy (Belcher et al., 2006).

Preferences-sensitive decisions may occur for health-related outcome, treatment choice, and process. With regard to outcomes, a patient can, for example, consider maintaining current quality of life as being more important than prolonging life or preventing future morbid events. This will influence treatment choices to be made. Research data suggest that there is large inter-individual variability in the selection of preferred outcomes. This supports individualizing decision-making.

Patient participation in clinical decision-making is not only ethically appropriate but has also been shown to improve outcomes, including reduced length of stay and readmission rates, improved functional capacity and reduced mortality (Phillips et al., 2016), and better patient satisfaction and adherence (Umar et al., 2012; Elwyn et al., 2014).

Despite the scarcity data on PCC in the area of medication review for older people, guidance exists as to how to implement PCC in clinical practice (American Geriatrics Society Expert Panel on the Care of Older Adults with Multimorbidity, 2012a; Jansen et al., 2016). First, the clinician should recognize when the older adult with multimorbidity and polypharmacy is facing a "preference-sensitive decision." If so, the SDM process can start.

The SDM process can be divided into four major steps: choice talk, option talk, preference talk, and decision talk (American Geriatrics Society Expert Panel on the Care of Older Adults with Multimorbidity, 2012b; Elwyn et al., 2012; Stiggelbout et al., 2015; Jansen et al., 2016). These principles seem relevant to apply in the context of medication review, even though there are no or limited data on their feasibility and impact.

In the choice talk, the HCP informs the patient that several options exist, a decision is to be made, and that this will depend on what is important to the patient. In the option talk, the HCP explains the options (including the option of not changing treatment), the advantages and disadvantages of each option, and how likely they are to occur. The HCP and patient then move to the preference talk, whose aim is to discuss the patient's preferences for the different options. The HCP supports the patient in identifying preferences, goals, and priorities. Finally, the decision talk is about making the decision by integrating the patient's preferences and priorities with evidence on benefits and harms. The HCP and patient discuss patient's decisional role preference (decision by patient/HCP or collaboratively), make or defer the decision, and discuss possible follow-up.

Major barriers to the implementation of PCC practices include physician workload, traditional approaches to clinical practice – where most HCPs still function in a traditional role of principal decision-maker, lack of training, provider concerns for risk and safety, and lack of payment structures (AGS). Moreover, SDM in multimorbidity is often limited by the challenge of communicating risks and benefits in the area of multimorbidity. However, especially in an area in which evidence about benefit is uncertain, and given the different values healthcare professionals and patients assign, SDM for medication prescribing is an appropriate approach (Belcher et al., 2006).

## Summary

Older people use more drugs than any other age group. The prescription strategy constitutes a major challenge. Polypharmacy, inappropriate prescribing and drug-related problems in older people are important problem of public health as a link exists with significant morbidity and mortality and with a large waste of health resources. The main target is the balance between an unsustainable number of different prescription drugs to treat various chronic diseases and the failure to take preventive measures in these older patients. In this review, the difficulties in prescribing in the older population and the identification, prevention and optimization of inappropriate prescribing and drug related problems in older people are respectively discussed. Medication reconciliation, medication review, tools for detection of potentially inappropriate prescribing, use of health information technology, adherence optimization, patient-tailored pharmacotherapy, and judicious drug cessation are highlighted as a part of collaborative and integrative approaches.

## References

Agency for Healthcare Research and Quality US Department of Health and Human Services. *Medications at Transitions and Clinical Handoffs (MATCH) Toolkit for Medication Reconciliation.* Publication No. 11(12)-0059, August 2012. Available at: www.ahrq.gov/sites/default/files/publications/files/match.pdf. Last visit: 25 April 2018.

Alagiakrishnan K., Wilson P., Sadowski C. A., et al. Physicians' use of computerized clinical decision supports to improve medication management in the elderly-the Seniors Medication Alert and Review Technology intervention. *Clinical Interventions in Aging.* 2016; 11:73–81.

American Geriatrics Society Expert Panel on Person-Centered Care. Person-Centered Care: A Definition and Essential Elements. *Journal of the American Geriatrics Society.* 2016; 64:15–18.

American Geriatrics Society Expert Panel on the Care of Older Adults with Multimorbidity. Patient-centered care for older adults with multiple chronic conditions: a stepwise approach from the American Geriatrics Society: American Geriatrics Society Expert Panel on the Care of Older Adults with Multimorbidity. *J Am Geriatr Soc.* 2012a; 60:1957–68.

American Geriatrics Society Expert Panel on the Care of Older Adults with Multimorbidity. Guiding principles for the care of older adults with multimorbidity: an approach for clinicians. *Journal of the American Geriatrics Society.* 2012b; 60:E1–E25.

Barry M. J., Edgman-Levitan S. Shared decision making – pinnacle of patient-centered care. *The New England journal of medicine.* 2012; 366:780–1.

Beijer H. J., de Blaey C. J. Hospitalisations caused by adverse drug reactions (ADR): a meta-analysis of observational studies. *Pharm World Sci.* 2002; 24:46–54.

Belcher V. N., Fried T. R., Agostini J. V., et al. Views of older adults on patient participation in medication-related decision making. *Journal of General Internal Medicine.* 2006; 21:298–303.

Bell C., Colquhoun M., Creighton P., et al. *Medication reconciliation in acute care: getting started kit.* 2011. Available at: www.ismp-canada.org/download/MedRec/Medrec_AC_English_GSK_V3.pdf. Last visit: 25 April 2018.

Bernsten C., Bjorkman I., Caramona M., et al. Pharmaceutical care of the elderly in Europe Research (PEER) Group. Improving the well-being of elderly patients via community pharmacy based provision of pharmaceutical care: a multicentre study in seven European countries. *Drugs Aging.* 2001; 18:63–77.

Blenkinsopp A., Bond C., Raynor D. K. Medication reviews. *British Journal of Clinical Pharmacology.* 2012; 74:573–80.

Boland B., Guignard B., Dalleur O., et al. Application of STOPP/START and Beers criteria: compared analysis on identification and relevance of potentially inappropriate prescriptions. *Eur Geriatr Med.* 2016; 7:416–23.

Brown M. T., Bussell J. K. Medication adherence: WHO cares? *Review Mayo Clin Proc.* 2011; 86:304–14.

Campbell N., Boustani M., Skopelja E., et al. Medication adherence in older adults with cognitive impairment: a systematic evidence-based review. *The American Journal of Geriatric Pharmacotherapy.* 2012; 10:165–77.

Christensen M., Lundh A. Medication review in hospitalised patients to reduce morbidity and mortality. *The Cochrane Database of Systematic Reviews.* 2016; 2:CD008986.

Claeys C., Neve J., Tulkens P. M., et al. Content validity and inter-rater reliability of an instrument to characterize unintentional medication discrepancies. *Drugs & Aging.* 2012; 29:577–91.

Conn V., Hafdahl A., Cooper P., et al. Interventions to improve medication adherence among older adults: meta-analysis of adherence outcomes among randomized controlled trials. *Gerontologist.* 2009; 49:447–62.

Conn V., Ruppar T., Chan K., et al. Packaging interventions to increase medication adherence: systematic review and meta-analysis. *Current Medical Research and Opinion.* 2015; 31:145–60.

Cornish P. L., Knowles S. R., Marchesano R., et al. Unintended medication discrepancies at the time of hospital admission. *Arch Intern Med.* 2005; 165:424–9.

Cornu P., Steurbaut S., Leysen T., et al. Effect of medication reconciliation at hospital admission on medication discrepancies during hospitalization and at discharge for geriatric patients. *Ann Pharmacother.* 2012; 46:484–94.

de Silva D. *Helping Measure Person-Centered Care.* London: The Health Foundation 2014.

de Wit H. A., Hurkens K. P., Mestres Gonzalvo C., et al. The support of medication reviews in hospitalised patients using a clinical decision support system. *Springer Plus.* 2016; 5:871.

Dilles T., Vander Stichele R., Van Bortel L., et al. The development and test of an intervention to improve ADR screening in nursing homes. *J Am Med Dir Assoc.* 2013; 14:379.e1–6.

Dodd K. S., Saczynski J. S., Zhao Y., et al. Exclusion of older adults and women from recent trials of acute coronary syndromes. *J Am Geriatr Soc.* 2011; 59: 506–11.

Drenth-van Maanen A. C., Spee J., van Hensbergen L., et al. Structured history taking of medication use reveals iatrogenic harm due to discrepancies in medication histories in hospital and pharmacy records. *J Am Geriatr Soc.* 2011; 59:1976–7.

Ellis G., Whitehead M., Robinson D., et al. Comprehensive geriatric assessment for older adults admitted to hospital: meta-analysis of randomised controlled trials. *BMJ.* 2011; 343:d6553.

Elwyn G., Frosch D., Thomson R., et al. Shared decision making: a model for clinical practice. *Journal of General Internal Medicine.* 2012; 27:1361–7.

Elwyn G., Lloyd A., May C., et al. Collaborative deliberation: a model for patient care. *Patient Education and Counseling.* 2014; 97:158–64.

Garfinkel D., Mangin D. Feasibility study of a systematic approach for discontinuation of multiple medications in older adults: addressing polypharmacy. *Arch Intern Med.* 2010; 170:1648–54.

Gellad W., Grenard J., Marcum Z. A systematic review of barriers to medication adherence in the elderly: looking beyond cost and regimen complexity. *Am J Geriatr Pharmacother.* 2011; 9:11–23.

Gheewala P. A., Peterson G. M., Curtain C. M., et al. Impact of the pharmacist medication review services on drug-related problems and potentially inappropriate prescribing of renally cleared medications in residents of aged care facilities. *Drugs & Aging.* 2014; 31:825–35.

Giardini A., Martin M., Cahir C., et al. Toward appropriate criteria in medication adherence assessment in older persons: Position Paper. *Aging Clin Exp Res.* 2016; 28:371–81.

Gillespie U., Alassaad A., Henrohn D., et al. A comprehensive pharmacist intervention to reduce morbidity in patients 80 years or older: a randomized controlled trial. *Archives of Internal Medicine.* 2009; 169:894–900.

Gleason K. M., Brake H., Agramonte V., et al. Medications at Transitions and Clinical Handoffs (MATCH) Toolkit for Medication Reconciliation. (Prepared by the Island Peer Review Organization, Inc., under Contract No. HHSA2902009000 13C.) AHRQ Publication No. 11(12)-0059. Rockville, MD: Agency for Healthcare Research and Quality. *Revised August* 2012.

Grymonpre R., Williamson D., Montgomery P. Impact of a pharmaceutical care model for non-institutionalized elderly: results of a randomized controlled trial. *Into J Pham Pac.* 2001; 9:235–41.

Hajjar E. R., Hanlon J. T., Artz M. B. et al. Adverse drug reaction risk factors in older outpatients. *Am J Geriatr Pharmacother* 2003; 1:82–89.

Hanlon J., Schmader K.., Samsa G., et al. A method for assessing drug therapy appropriateness. *J Clin Epidemiol.* 1992; 45:1045–51.

Hanlon J., Weinberger M., Samsa G., et al. A randomised, controlled trial of a clinical pharmacist intervention to improve inappropriate prescribing in elderly outpatients with polypharmacy. *Am J Med.* 1996; 100:428–37.

Hawe P., Higgins G. Can medication education improve the drug compliance of the elderly? Evaluation of an inhospital program. *Patient Educ Couns.* 1990; 16:151–60.

Haynes R., Ackloo E., Sahota N., et al. Interventions for enhancing medication adherence. *The Cochrane Database of Systematic Reviews.* 2008(2):CD000011.

Hepler C. D., Strand L. M. Opportunities and responsibilities in pharmaceutical care. *Am J Hosp Pharm.* 1990; 47:533–43.

Holahan P. J., Lesselroth B. J., Adams K., et al. Beyond technology acceptance to effective technology use: a parsimonious and actionable model. *Journal of the American Medical Informatics Association: JAMIA.* 2015; 22:718–29.

http://ec.europa.eu/health/ageing/policy_en. Last visit: 10 April 2017.

Hughes C. M. Medication non-adherence in the elderly: how big is the problem? *Drugs & Aging.* 2004; 21:793–811.

Jansen J., Naganathan V., Carter S. M., et al. Too much medicine in older people? Deprescribing through shared decision making. *BMJ (Clinical Research ed.).* 2016; 353:i2893.

Kaufmann C., Tremp R., Hersberger K., et al. Inappropriate prescribing: a systematic overview of published assessment tools. *Eur J Clin Pharmacol.* 2014; 70:1–11.

Kempen T. G., van de Steeg-van Gompel C. H., Hoogland P., et al. Large scale implementation of clinical medication reviews in Dutch community pharmacies: drug-related problems and interventions. *International Journal of Clinical Pharmacy.* 2014; 36:630–5.

Kogan A. C., Wilber K., Mosqueda L. Person-centered care for older adults with chronic conditions and functional impairment: a systematic literature review. *Journal of the American Geriatrics Society.* 2016; 64:e1–7.

Kostas T., Pacquin A. M., Zimmerman K. M., et al. Characterizing medication discrepancies among older adults during transitions of care; a systematic review focusing on discrepancy synonyms, data sources and classification terms. *Aging Health.* 2013; 9:497–508.

Kwan J. L., Lo L., Sampson M., et al. Medication reconciliation during transitions of care as a patient safety strategy: a systematic review. *Ann Intern Med.* 2013; 158:397–403.

Lavan A. H., Gallagher P. F., O'Mahony D. Methods to reduce prescribing errors in elderly patients with multimorbidity. *Clinical Interventions in Aging.* 2016; 11:857–66.

Le Couteur D. G., Hilmer S. N., Glasgow N., et al. Prescribing in older people. *Aust Fam Physician.* 2004; 33:777–781.

Lee J., Grace K., Taylor A. Effect of a pharmacy care programme on medication adherence and persistence, blood pressure, and low-density lipoprotein cholesterol: a randomized controlled trial. *J Am Med Assoc.* 2006; 296:2563–71.

Leendertse A. J., Egberts A. C., Stoker L. J., et al. Frequency of and risk factors for preventable medication-related hospital admissions in the Netherlands. *Arch Intern Med.* 2008; 168:1890–6.

Lehane E., McCarthy G. Intentional and unintentional medication non-adherence: a comprehensive framework for clinical research and practice? A discussion paper. *Int J Nurs Stud.* 2007, 44:1468–77.

Lesselroth B. J., Holahan P. J., Adams K., et al. Primary care provider perceptions and use of a novel medication reconciliation technology. *Informatics in Primary Care.* 2011; 19:105–18.

Lund B. C., Carnahan R. M., Egge J. A., et al. Inappropriate prescribing predicts adverse drug events in older adults. *Ann Pharmacother.* 2010; 44:957–63.

Mannesse C. K., Derkx F. H., de Ridder M. A., et al. Contribution of adverse drug reactions to hospital admission of older patients. *Age Ageing.* 2000; 29:35–9.

Marien S., Krug B., Spinewine A. Electronic tools to support medication reconciliation-a systematic review. *Journal of the American Medical Informatics Association: JAMIA.* 2017; 24:227–40.

Meulendijk M., Spruit M., Drenth-van Maanen C., et al. General practitioners' attitudes towards decision-supported prescribing: an analysis of the Dutch primary care sector. *Health Informatics Journal.* 2013; 19:247–63.

Meulendijk M. C., Spruit M. R., Drenth-van Maanen A. C., et al. Computerized decision support improves medication review effectiveness: an experiment evaluating the STRIP assistant's usability. *Drugs & Aging.* 2015; 32:495–503.

Mistiaen P., Francke A., Poot E. Interventions aimed at reducing problems in adult patients discharged from hospital to home: a systematic meta-review. *BMC Health Services Research.* 2007; 7:47.

Mueller S. K., Kripalani S., Stein J., et al. A toolkit to disseminate best practices in inpatient medication reconciliation: multi-center medication reconciliation quality improvement study (MARQUIS). *Joint Commission Journal on Quality and Patient Safety / Joint Commission Resources.* 2013; 39:371–82.

Nazareth I., Burton A., Schulman S., et al. A pharmacy discharge plan for hospitalized elderly patients – a randomized controlled trial. *Age Ageing.* 2001; 30:33–40.

NHS Cumbria Medicines Management Team. *Clinical Medication Review A Practice Guide,* February 2013. Available at: www.cumbria.nhs.uk/ProfessionalZone/ MedicinesManagement/Guidelines/MedicationReview-PracticeGuide2011 .pdf. Last visit: 10 April 2017.

O'Connor M., Gallagher P., O'Mahony D. Inappropriate prescribing criteria, detection and prevention. *Drugs Aging.* 2012; 29:437–52.

O'Mahony D., Cherubini A., Petrovic M. Optimizing pharmacotherapy in older patients: a European perspective. *Drugs Aging.* 2012; 29:423–5.

O'Mahony D., O'Sullivan D., Byrne S., et al. STOPP/START criteria for potentially inappropriate prescribing in older people: version 2. *Age Ageing.* 2015; 44:213–18.

Onder G., Pedone C., Landi F., et al. Adverse drug reactions as cause of hospital admissions: results from the Italian Group of Pharmacoepidemiology in the Elderly (GIFA). *J Am Geriatr Soc.* 2002; 50:1962–8.

Onder G., van der Cammen T., Petrovic M., et al. Strategies to reduce the risk of iatrogenic illness in complex older adults. *Age Ageing.* 2013; 42:284–91.

Osterberg L., Blaschke T. Adherence to medication. *N Engl J Med.* 2005; 353:487–97.

Perehudoff K., Azermai M., Somers A., et al. Medication discrepancies in older patients admitted to non-geriatric wards: an exploratory study. *European Geriatric Medicine.* 2015; 6(1):41–5.

Petrovic M., van der Cammen T., Onder G. Adverse drug reactions in older people: detection and prevention. *Drugs Aging.* 2012; 29:453–62.

Pevnick J. M., Shane R., Schnipper J. L. The problem with medication reconciliation. *BMJ Quality and Safety.* 2016; 25:726–30.

Phillips N. M., Street M., Haesler E. A systematic review of reliable and valid tools for the measurement of patient participation in healthcare. *BMJ Quality and Safety.* 2016; 25:110–17.

Pirmohamed M., James S., Meakin S., et al. Adverse drug reactions as cause of admission to hospital: prospective analysis of 18 820 patients. *BMJ.* 2004; 329:15–19.

Reeve E., Gnjidic D., Long J., et al. A systematic review of the emerging definition of 'deprescribing' with network analysis: implications for future research and clinical practice. *Br J Clin Pharmacol.* 2015; 80:1254–68.

Renom-Guiteras A., Meyer G., Thürmann P. A. The EU (7)-PIM list: a list of potentially inappropriate medications for older people consented by experts from seven European countries. *Eur J Clin Pharmacol.* 2015; 71: 861–75.

Sabaté E. (Ed.) *Adherence to Long-Term Therapies: Evidence for Action.* World Health Organization, 2003, Geneva, Switzerland.

Schmader K., Hanlon J., Pieper C., et al. Effects of geriatric evaluation and management on adverse drug reactions and suboptimal prescribing in the frail elderly. *Am J Med.* 2004; 116:394–401.

Schnipper J. L., Hamann C., Ndumele C. D., et al. Effect of an electronic medication reconciliation application and process redesign on potential adverse drug events: a cluster-randomized trial. *Archives of Internal Medicine.* 2009; 169:771–80.

Scott I., Hilmer S., Reeve E., et al. Reducing inappropriate polypharmacy. *JAMA Intern Med.* 2015; 175: 827–34.

Scullin C., Scott M., Hogg A., et al. An innovative approach to integrated medicine management. *J Eval Clin Pract.* 2007; 13:781–88.

Smith J. D., Coleman E. A., Min S. J. A new tool for identifying discrepancies in post acute medications for community-dwelling older adults. *The American Journal of Geriatric Pharmacotherapy.* 2004; 2:141–7.

Somers A., Robays H., Vander Stichele R., et al. Contribution of drug related problems to hospital admission in the elderly. *J Nutr Health Aging.* 2010; 14:475–82.

Somers A., Mallet L., van der Cammen T., et al. Applicability of an adapted medication appropriateness index for detection of drug-related problems in geriatric inpatients. *Am J Geriatr Pharmacother.* 2012; 10:101–9.

Spinewine A., Schmader K., Barber N., et al. Appropriate prescribing in elderly people: how well can it be measured and optimised? *Lancet.* 2007; 370:173–84.

Steinman M. A., Landefeld C. S., Rosenthal G. E., et al. Polypharmacy and prescribing quality in older people. *J Am Geriatr Soc.* 2006; 54:1516–23.

Stiggelbout A. M., Pieterse A. H., De Haes J. C. Shared decision making: concepts, evidence, and practice. *Patient Education and Counseling.* 2015; 98:1172–9.

Sturgess I., McElnay J., Hughes C., et al. Community pharmacy based provision of pharmaceutical care to older patients. *Pharm World Sci.* 2003; 25: 218–26.

Swift C. G. The clinical pharmacology of ageing. *Br J Clin Pharmacol.* 2003; 56: 249–53.

Tannenbaum C., Martin P., Tamblyn R., et al. Reduction of inappropriate benzodiazepine prescriptions among older adults through direct patient education: the EMPOWER cluster randomized trial. *JAMA Internal Medicine.* 2014; 174:890–8.

The American Geriatrics Society 2015 Beers Criteria Update Expert Panel. American Geriatrics Society 2015 updated beers criteria for potentially inappropriate medication use in older adults. *J Am Geriatr Soc.* 2015; 63: 2227–46.

Tommelein E., Petrovic M., Somers A., et al. Older patients' prescriptions screening in the community pharmacy: development of the Ghent Older People's Prescriptions community Pharmacy Screening (GheOP³S) tool. *J Public Health (Oxf).* 2016; 38:e158–70.

Topinkova E., Baeyens J., Michel J., et al. Evidence-based strategies for the optimization of pharmacotherapy in older people. *Drugs Aging.* 2012; 29: 477–94.

Umar N., Litaker D., Schaarschmidt M. L., et al. Outcomes associated with matching patients' treatment preferences to physicians' recommendations: study methodology. *BMC Health Services Research.* 2012; 12:1.

van den Bemt P. M., Egberts A. C., Lenderink A. W., et al. Risk factors for the development of adverse drug events in hospitalized patients. *Pharm World Sci.* 2000; 22:62–6.

van der Cammen T., Rajkumar C., Onder G., et al. Drug cessation in complex older adults: time for action. *Age Ageing.* 2014; 43: 20–5.

Villanyi D., Fok M., Wong R. Y. Medication reconciliation: identifying medication discrepancies in acutely ill hospitalized older adults. *Am J Geriatr Pharmacother.* 2011; 9:339–44.

Volume C., Farris K., Kassam R., et al. Pharmaceutical care research and education project: patient outcomes. *J Am Pharm Assoc.* 2001; 41:411–20.

Wong J. D., Bajcar J. M., Wong G. G., et al. Medication reconciliation at hospital discharge: evaluating discrepancies. *Annals of Pharmacotherapy.* 2008; 42:1373–9.

Wu J., Leung W., Chang S., et al. Effectiveness of telephone counselling by a pharmacist in reducing mortality in patients receiving polypharmacy: randomised controlled trial. *Br Med J.* 2006; 333:522–7.

Wu C., Bell C. M., Wodchis W. P. Incidence and economic burden of adverse drug reactions among elderly patients in Ontario emergency departments, a retrospective study. *Drug Safety* 2012; 35:769–81.

# PART II

# Psychosocial Factors

# 16 Bio-Psycho-Social Bridge

The Psychoneuroimmune System in Successful Aging

Mónica De la Fuente

## Introduction

To achieve successful aging it is necessary to have and maintain good health, and for this, the organism has to show an appropriate balance in its responses when facing all the changes that constantly occur. Although the term most often used to describe this balance is "homeostasis," as nothing is static in life, the term "homeodynamic" should be employed. Nevertheless, since the word "homeostasis" is better known, it will appear in the present chapter referring to the dynamic balance. This balance is necessary for the maintenance of health in all biological responses to molecular, physiological, and social stimuli. With the aging process, which starts at the end of the complete development of the organism, when reproductive activity is reached, that is to say at the adult age, all the physiological systems begin to be impaired, but especially those charged with the maintenance of homeostasis such as the nervous, endocrine, and immune systems. In this context, the aging process may be defined as a progressive and general deterioration of the functions of the organism that leads to a lower ability to adaptively react to changes and to preserve homeostasis. With the passing of time this balance changes or fails, and although aging should not be considered a disease, the risk of suffering and dying increases (De la Fuente & Miquel, 2009).

In addition, the aging process is very heterogeneous; there are different rates of molecular and physiological changes in the various systems of the organism and in the diverse members of a population of the same chronological age. This justifies the introduction of the concept of "biological age," which determines the level of aging experienced by each individual, his/her rate of aging, and therefore his/her life expectancy (Martinez de Toda et al., 2016). Biological age is related to mean longevity, which can be defined as the mean length of time that members of a population, who were born on the same date, live. Subjects of a population with a higher rate of aging show an older biological age and a shorter life span. The aging process, in the subjects of each species, finishes at the end of their maximum life span or maximum longevity, which is the maximum time that an individual belonging to this species can live. For instance, in

This work was supported by grants RETICEF (RD12/0043/0018) and FIS (PI15/01787) from the ISCIII-FEDER of the European Union.

human beings, the maximum longevity is about 122 years, whereas in mouse and rat strains it is only 3 and 4 years, respectively. Since humans currently present about 75–85 years of mean longevity and the aging process starts in adults in their twenties, we therefore spend most of our lives aging. If the maximum longevity is fixed in each species, the mean life span of individual organisms shows marked variability, and it can be increased by environmental factors that allow for the maintenance of good health, and consequently approaching the maximum life span in good condition. A healthy longevity depends on approximately 25 percent genes and 75 percent environmental and lifestyle factors (De la Fuente & Miquel, 2009). As can be seen in Figure 16.1, these genes and factors can affect each individual throughout their life, from fetal state until his/her death. In fetal life and in the neonatal periods, environmental factors are involved in the development and status of the homeostatic systems and consequently in health. Nevertheless, later on, lifestyle factors are the most implicated, especially in the long period of aging. Moreover, since the rate of aging is the result of individual epigenetic mechanisms acting on genes from fetal life throughout the life of the subject, the relationships between genes and environmental factors during the entire life of each subject need to be considered. It is necessary to recognize that the more appropriate physiological characteristics we have in adult age, the more likely it is that healthy aging will occur.

## The Psychoneuroimmune System

Currently, there is abundant work that confirms the existence of bidirectional communication among the homeostatic systems, namely the nervous, endocrine, and immune systems, which is mediated by cytokines, hormones, and neurotransmitters through the presence of the corresponding receptors on the cells of the three systems. Moreover, immune, nervous, and endocrine products coexist in lymphoid, neural, and endocrine tissues, and the cells of these three systems are capable of synthesizing all these mediators. Thus, cytokines, which are mainly produced by leukocytes in their immune response against infections and tumor cells, are also synthetized by nerve cells. These molecules are able to reach neurons and to regulate important brain activities including neurotransmitter metabolism, neuroendocrine function, and synaptic plasticity, as well as the neural circuitry of mood, among other functions. In addition, neurotransmitters and hormones, produced by nerve and endocrine cells but also by leukocytes, modify immune cell functions. This shows the complexity of the regulation of the organism, since this communication among the homeostatic systems is established in long and local circuits and consequently affects the body in general. Presently, a "psychoneuroimmunoendocrine system," also called simply a "psychoneuroimmune system," is generally accepted as existing. This allows the preservation of homeostasis and therefore of health. Moreover, the interaction between regulatory systems involves evolutionarily conserved mechanisms. The scientific confirmation of the communication between these systems has permitted the understanding of why situations of depression, emotional stress, and anxiety are accompanied by a greater vulnerability to infections, cancers, and autoimmune diseases. This agrees with the concept that the immune system is affected. By contrast, pleasant emotions help to maintain good immune function. In addition, any influence exerted on the immune system will have an effect on the nervous and endocrine systems and vice versa (De la Fuente, 2014a; Verburg-van Kemenade et al., 2017).

## The Stress Response in the Context of the Psychoneuroimmune System

Stress is essential for life, since it is "the nonspecific response of the body to any demand," and all organisms are submitted continuously to physical and emotional "stressors" (all stimuli able to induce stress response). If individuals respond adequately to these life stressors they maintain their health, but the failure of adaptation to them can cause disease. The concept of stress is only understandable in the framework of "psychoneuroimmunology." Thus, stressor stimuli induce modifications in the central nervous system (CNS) and in the sympathetic nervous system (SNS), as well as in the neuroendocrine system, more specifically in the hypothalamic-pituitary-adrenal (HPA) axis. Their activation leads to the secretion of neurotransmitters and hormones such as noradrenaline, catecholamine, and glucocorticoids, which play an important role in organizing the stress response by binding to their receptors in brain and peripheral tissues. These neurotransmitters and hormones can act as modifiers of immune functions (Cruces et al., 2014; Ray et al., 2017).

In addition, all living systems have the intrinsic ability to respond, to counteract, and to adapt to external and internal stress. This stress resistance capacity has evolved from a complex set of molecular self-defense mechanisms, which are the basis of the "hormesis process" that will be explained later (De la Fuente et al., 2011).

It should be kept in mind that stress-related physiological changes, and concretely, those in the immune system, are very different. These not only depend on the type, frequency, duration, and intensity of stressors, but also on the characteristics of each individual (e.g., personality, life experiences, social situation, controllability, and perception of the situation, among others), all of which cause a very high inter-individual variability in responses. Thus, the resilience capacity of each subject (i.e., his/her ability to cope with changes) is very relevant to the physiological consequences of stress situations. Hence, any stressor seems to affect individuals differentially, since the resilience or vulnerability to stress of each one, which depends on several factors affecting the subject throughout its life, will be different (Albrecht et al., 2017; Ménard et al., 2017).

When there is an adaptive response to physical or psychological challenges the regulatory systems maintain the homeostatic balance and therefore the health and survival of the individual. However, the inability to cope with stressful situations disrupts the neuroimmunoendocrine network, and the consequent loss of homeostasis favors the appearance of pathologies. Thus, the survival of the individual may be compromised (Cruces et al., 2014).

## Age-Related Changes in the Psychoneuroimmune System

The capacity of homeostasis frequently deteriorates with aging, since many functions of the three homeostatic systems are affected, as well as there being an impairment of the communication among these systems. In fact, only aged individuals who maintain their functions at levels similar to healthy adults achieve very high longevity. Nevertheless, the age-related changes in homeostasis are established at different rates in each subject, which is manifested by differing biological age. Moreover, the age-related failure in the response to stress is related with the loss of homeostasis and the consequent increase in morbidity and mortality that appears with aging. As mentioned by Holliday, senescence and death are the final manifestations of unsuccessful homeostasis (Holliday, 2006).

The age-related changes in the three homeostatic systems and in their communication will be commented upon briefly below.

## Changes in the Nervous System with Aging

With respect to the nervous system, a progressive loss of its general functions with aging is evident. This can be shown, for example, in areas such as sensation, cognition, memory, and motor activity. The neurobiology of aging has been one of the most rapidly expanding areas of scientific endeavor over the past two decades. There is evidence indicating that normal aging of humans and other animals is accompanied by some alterations in the neurotransmitters, with impairment of their levels and synthesis. Moreover, a decrease in synaptic density and an increase in synaptic aberrations appear with increasing age. An age-related characteristic of the brain is the reduction of its capacity for neurogenesis. Thus, the hippocampus, a structure in the CNS equipped with a high degree of flexibility and adaptation due to its capacity for neurogenesis, is clearly affected by aging. This fact explains the learning and cognitive impairment in aged subjects. Moreover, hippocampus neurogenesis may be involved in the regulation of stress-related disorders, and this could be one of the causes of the inappropriate response to stress situations that occur with aging (Thakur & Rattan, 2012; Ojo et al., 2015).

## Changes in the Endocrine System with Aging

In the endocrine system, several changes accompany healthy aging (Jones & Boelaert, 2015). These include the decrease of the growth hormone/insulin-like factor-1 axis (somatopause) and of sexual hormones, namely estradiol (menopause), testosterone (andropause), and dehydroepiandrosterone (adrenopause), which are related to the alterations in the age-determined sexual functions. Another relevant hormone that decreases with aging is melatonin, which explains many of the age-related complaints involving circadian rhythms and sleep disturbances. In addition, the alterations of the HPA axis with age are responsible for decreasing stress adaptability in older subjects. Nevertheless, although levels of cortisol, the principal glucocorticoid of the HPA axis in humans, seem to increase with age, this depends on the emotional regulation and social support of each individual (De la Fuente, 2014b). Thus, resilience resources can modulate the effects of this stress hormone of stress on health in aging.

## Changes in the Immune System with Aging

With the passage of time there is a decrease in resistance to infections and an increase in autoimmune processes and cancers, which indicate the presence of a less competent immune system. Since this system is a good indicator of health, these age-related changes exert a great influence on the increase in morbidity and mortality. In fact, the increased death rate found in aged populations is due in great proportion to cancer and infectious processes. Although there are contradictory data on the impact of aging on immune response, it is presently accepted that almost every component of the immune system undergoes striking age-associated restructuring, leading to changes that may include enhanced, as well as diminished functions, known as immunosenescence (De la Fuente, 2014b; Bauer & De la Fuente, 2016).

## Changes in Nervous-Endocrine-Immune Communication with Aging

In aging, it is difficult to determine whether the deterioration of the nervous, endocrine, and immune systems occurs simultaneously or starts in one and then affects the others. However, many age-related changes happen in the communication between the homeostatic systems, which suffer impairment. This idea was the basis of another theory of aging, which proposed that these changes in neuroimmunoendocrine communication are a probable cause of physiological senescence. Although this theory of aging, like most, is focused on something that happens with aging, not on its cause, it nevertheless shows the relevance of the altered neuroendocrine-immune communication in the aging process.

With age, innervations of immune organs such as sympathetic innervation, as well as the concentration of their neurotransmitters such as noradrenaline (NA), decrease. Although the expression of beta-receptors on immune cells increases during old age, as a compensatory mechanism, higher concentrations of NA are needed for stimulation of these cells. Moreover, several studies have shown that the responses of immune cells to many neurotransmitters worsen depending on the increase in the age of the subject. This defective response to neurotransmitters could contribute to the processes of immunosenescence. Moreover, in the case of catecholamine this could explain the inadequate response to stress that occurs with aging. In addition, the age-related impairment of the immune system could affect the functions of the other regulatory systems, through the increased oxidative and inflammatory stress that immune cells can produce (De la Fuente, 2014b).

## Factors That Could Be Involved in the Contradictory Results Obtained in the Studies on Age-Related Changes of the Homeostatic Systems

Although everybody agrees that the homeostatic systems change with aging and that an age-related impairment of their functions appears, there are many contradictory observations. This may be due to several reasons, such as the age of subjects studied (chronological and biological age), the species and strains analyzed, the location of the cells, the gender differences, the time of day or season in which the functions were studied (the circadian and seasonal rhythms), and the different designs and methods used in the determination of a function, among others. In addition, many researchers are currently considering the peculiar characteristics of each subject (psychological, social, nutritional state, etc.), something previously not taken into account (Alonso-Fernández & De la Fuente, 2011). In addition, new factors are appearing in this scientific field, such as the microbiota of each individual. Microbiota, especially the trillions of microorganisms that colonize the intestine, have coevolved over hundreds of millions of years with metazoan hosts in a symbiotic relationship. These microorganisms, the majority of which are bacteria, permit the maintenance of host health allowing adequate gut functions as well as protecting against colonization by exogenous pathogens. Moreover, they are also able to regulate immune, endocrine, and nervous system functions. Although this is a field that has been poorly studied in the context of aging, it is known that age-related changes in microbiota could be the basis of the impairment functions in nervous and immune cells (Bischoff, 2016; Rea et al., 2016).

## The Immune System as a Marker of Health and the Rate of Aging

It is very difficult to find parameters that measure biological age, which is more appropriate than chronological age to show the rate of aging of a subject. Although there are some proposed biomarkers, they have not been validated. Since it has been demonstrated that the competence of the immune system is an excellent marker of health, and several age-related changes in immune functions have been linked to life span, we decided to find out whether some immune functions could be markers of biological age and therefore predictors of longevity. Recently, we have reported how several immune parameters are useful in this context. Thus, with aging there is a decrease of functions such as the phagocytosis capacity, lymphoproliferative response, the mobility to the infectious focus, or chemotaxis, as well as "natural killer" (NK) activity against tumor cells, all very relevant functions for an appropriate immune response to infection and cancers. This was observed in immune cells from human subjects, in a transversal study, at different ages, and in mice in a longitudinal study, obtaining the leukocytes at the same ages corresponding to humans. Surprisingly, our results showed that the members of the two species present similar age-related changes of the immune parameters studied. Moreover, the validation of the above parameters as markers of biological age was carried out in two ways. First, by showing that the adult individuals with values for those parameters similar to those in older subjects die before their counterparts. This fact, which logically can only be confirmed in experimental animals with a lower life span than humans, was observed in a model of prematurely aging mice in which adult animals showing premature immunosenescence die prematurely. Second, by finding that the subjects reaching a very advanced age present these immune functions at levels similar to those of adults. This was observed in both humans (centenarians) and long-lived mice. Moreover, since the evolution of these immune functions is similar in mice and humans, it may be assumed that those adult humans showing immune parameters at the levels of older subjects have a greater biological age and a shorter longevity (De la Fuente, 2014b; Martinez de Toda et al., 2016).

## Oxidation and Inflammation in the Homeostatic Systems: Friends or Foes?

One of the most widely accepted theories of aging is the free radical or oxidation theory proposed in 1956 (Harman, 1956). Later, the idea of inflamm-aging appeared (Franceschi et al., 2000). The theory of oxidation-inflammation of aging, which we recently proposed (De la Fuente & Miquel, 2009), integrates the previously mentioned theories. According to this theory, the aging process is accompanied by chronic oxidation and inflammatory stress (excess of oxidant and inflammatory compounds facing the antioxidant and anti-inflammatory defenses), which leads to the damage of cell components, including proteins, lipids, and DNA, contributing to the age-related decline of all physiological functions. This is especially true in the cells of the regulatory systems, which are very vulnerable to the effects of oxi-inflamm-aging. Moreover, the immune system, due to its capacity for producing oxidant and inflammatory compounds (oxidation and inflammation are two very related processes) in order to carry out its defensive functions, seems to be involved, if not well-controlled, in the general increase in oxidative and inflammatory stress of the organism and thus in the rate of aging (Figure 16.1).

Although both oxidation and inflammation are relevant processes for life, since they carry out many functions in the nervous and immune systems, this fact depends on the context, intensity, course, and duration, among other characteristics of these processes. Thus, oxidative and inflammatory stresses could be beneficial or detrimental for the homeostatic systems. In general, the excess of oxidation and inflammation is deleterious. For this reason, cells need to maintain a balance between the production of oxidants and pro-inflammatory compounds, and the antioxidant and anti-inflammatory defenses in order to prevent an excess of the former and the resulting oxidative and inflammatory damage. This balance is essential to preserve the functioning of homeostatic system cells, especially those of the immune system due to their above-mentioned characteristics. In fact, immunosenescence seems to be a consequence of an oxidative and inflammatory stress situation in the immune cells. Moreover, this age-related imbalance of oxidation and inflammation in the immune system might be involved in the general oxi-inflamm-aging of the organism (De la Fuente, 2014b; Vida et al., 2014; Bauer & De la Fuente, 2016). In addition, the immune cells move through the body, and if their redox balance is altered they can affect the other cells of the organism and, therefore impair health and increase the rate of aging.

In this context, a relationship has been found between the life span of a subject, the redox, and inflammatory state of his/her immune cells, and the function capacity of these cells. Thus, when an animal shows high oxidative stress in its immune cells, these cells have impaired function and the animal shows decreased longevity in relation to other members of the group of the same chronological age. This happens in chronologically and biologically older experimental animals, such as those with anxiety, depression, or poor response to stress. In contrast, subjects that achieve greater longevity, such as human centenarians and extremely long-lived mice, show a preserved redox state and functions in their immune cells (De la Fuente & Miquel, 2009).

## Environmental and Lifestyle Factors That Modify the Psychoneuroimmune System

There are many factors that can affect the homeostatic systems and their communication, and consequently the health and rate of aging of subjects. Several of these are related to premature alteration of the homeostatic systems and thus with premature aging, which could explain the lower longevity of individuals. Nevertheless, other factors have been proved to produce positive effects on the homeostatic systems, decreasing the biological age of subjects and permitting a healthy longevity.

### Alterations of the Psychoneuroimmune System and Premature Aging

Many studies in humans and experimental animals have shown how several situations that negatively affect the homeostatic systems are related to premature aging. Thus, for example, subjects (humans and experimental animals) with inadequate response to stress, anxiety, depression, and loneliness, among others, show premature aging in their nervous and immune systems, and in the case of experimental animals, shorter longevity than the corresponding controls (De la Fuente & Gimenez-Llort, 2010; Cruces et al., 2015; Martinez de Toda et al., 2016).

It is accepted that an inadequate response to stress is one of the conditions leading to an acceleration of aging, accompanied by an impairment of homeostatic and other physiological systems. In fact, in rodents, life span appears to be inversely related to the intensity of behavioral and neuroendocrine response to stressful stimuli. Moreover, many cellular changes observed in aging are similarly found following stress and chronic glucocorticoid exposure. Thus, it has been shown that mice with chronic hyper-reactivity to stress show premature aging of the homeostatic systems, greater oxidative stress, and a shorter life span (De la Fuente, 2010; Martinez de Toda et al., 2016).

In both humans and experimental animals, those with anxiety and depression also show premature aging, with alterations in the nervous and immune systems, and oxidative stress in adult age, similar to that observed in older subjects. Moreover, in the case of rodents these present a shorter longevity (Vida & De la Fuente, 2013).

Social animals such as rodents and humans are characterized by living in groups, and the maintenance of these organizations ensures the survival and reproductive success of these species, representing an adaptive advantage. Thus, the establishment and maintenance of interactions among the individuals of a group may contribute to the correct functioning of the homeostatic systems and therefore help to maintain the health of each subject. Conversely, the disruption of social interactions has significant negative effects leading to a loss of homeostasis and the development of a wide range of pathologies. For this reason, social isolation or "loneliness" is considered a potent emotional stressor for social species, provoking deterioration of the psychoneuroimmune system, which is postulated as a risk factor of morbidity and mortality. In fact, experimental animals exposed to isolation show altered behavioral responses, which reveal a certain degree of depression, inmunosenescence, and oxidative stress. In these animals and in non-human primates, social isolation reduces the life span of the subjects. Nevertheless, these changes depend on individual resilience and vulnerability to stress. Thus, only animals responding with anxiety to isolation show homeostatic deteriorations and shorter longevity (Cruces et al., 2014, 2015).

## Strategies to Improve the Psychoneuroimmune System

Many strategies have been proposed to enable the maintenance of excellent nervous and immune functions with aging, resulting in a better quality of life, and consequently, greater longevity.

According to the oxidation-inflammation theory of aging, the basis of the age-related deterioration of the homeostatic systems and their communication is chronic oxidative-inflammatory stress, as explained above. Therefore, it is useful to test the effects of lifestyle and environmental strategies on the improvement of redox and inflammatory status, and consequently on regulatory system functions, especially on those of the immune system. Several of these strategies will be discussed below.

### Benefits of Hormesis

The use of the phenomenon called "hormesis" has been proposed to achieve healthy aging, using the stimulation of cellular protection mechanisms to provide beneficial effects in the body in response to single or multiple mild-stress situations. In fact, "hormesis" may be defined as "a process in which exposure to a low amount of chemical agents or environmental factors that are damaging in higher doses, induces an adaptive beneficial effect on the cell or organism." Since the effect of stress on cells and organisms seems to be a dose-dependent process, mild stress induces, after initial disruption in homeostasis, a response of tolerance through an adaptive compensatory process. In this, the maintenance and repair mechanisms of the biological systems are challenged and activated. Thus, whereas excessive stress accelerates the aging process, exposure to low doses of stress agents, such as food and physical and mental activities, among others, produces a variety of beneficial effects including health, and extends the life span of cells and organisms.

In spite of the recent increase in studies on hormesis, the basic nature of this phenomenon remains largely unknown. Nevertheless, it is necessary to take into account that many of the effects of the strategies that will be mentioned seem to be due to their hormetic properties, which allow an improvement in immune and nervous function with aging (De la Fuente et al., 2011, 2014b).

### Nutrition

The ingestion of food of appropriate quality and in appropriate quantity is essential to maintaining good health. Thus, the impaired state of homeostatic systems found even in healthy elderly subjects can be attributed to deficiencies of macronutrients, such as proteins, and micronutrients (vitamins, zinc, etc.), indicating that appropriate nutrition could play a preventive role in the aging process. Older individuals often have multiple nutrient deficiencies because of physiological, social, and economic factors. Thus, the use of "functional foods" seems to positively influence many cellular parameters, which can help to decrease the deleterious effect of the aging process. In this context, nutrients such as dietary fiber, several fatty acids, and specially antioxidant compounds are of particular interest (Figure 16.1).

**Antioxidants**: As previously mentioned, endogenous antioxidants decrease in oxidative stress situations such as aging, because they are spent neutralizing the excess of oxidants, this being very important in cells of the nervous and immune systems. Moreover, biological age and mean longevity seem to be associated with optimal antioxidant protection. Thus, the ingestion of a diet enriched with antioxidants is important to maintain an optimum redox balance and therefore protect the aging organism against oxidative stress. This could be a reasonable way to decrease the rate of aging and the impairment associated with physiological and pathological aging. Some research questions the positive role of the ingestion of antioxidant vitamins in the organism, especially in high doses. This excess could result in a possible decrease in the endogen antioxidant defenses or could even produce "reductive stress." However, many studies have shown the positive effect of diet supplementation with moderate levels of antioxidants on nervous and immune functions in chronologically old and prematurely aging subjects, with a consequent slowing down of their aging process. Moreover, this antioxidant ingestion can produce hormetic effects by activating transcription factors, which result in the induction of several genes encoding, among other molecules, antioxidant defenses. This could explain the positive results obtained during aging in the homeostatic systems with diets enriched with appropriate, in general low, amounts of antioxidants (De la Fuente et al., 2011, 2014b; Pae et al., 2012).

In addition, since microbiota can regulate the oxidation-inflammation state, not only through the regulation that they exercise on immune and nervous system functions, but also due to the fact that many microorganisms show antioxidant and anti-inflammatory properties, the use of probiotics, as another functional food, is being studied in the context of improving homeostatic systems in aging (Kaushal & Kansal, 2012; Pae et al., 2012; Divyashri et al., 2015).

**Caloric restriction:** A large body of research has shown that caloric restriction (CR) can slow down multiple aspects of the aging process. Thus, CR (without malnutrition) seems to be one of the most powerful interventions to increase life span in a variety of animal species, ranging from invertebrates to humans. Most gerontologists agree that CR extends life by decreasing oxidative damage and/or by increasing protective and repair processes. Thus, CR improves homeostatic system functions by decreasing the oxidative stress and making cells more resistant to oxidation (Bouchard & Villeda, 2015; López-Lluch & Navas, 2016). These beneficial effects seem to be the consequence of hormetic mechanisms that permit the slowing down of the aging process (De la Fuente, 2014b).

### *Physical Activity*

Physically active people show a lower risk of illness; habitual moderate exercise is an effective means of preventing or delaying a large number of diseases. Together with the muscular, cardiovascular, and respiratory systems, physical activity strongly modulates the homeostatic systems. Thus, physical activity is deemed to be another lifestyle factor to modulate nervous and immune systems improving health and quality of life, especially in older subjects. However, since physical exercise, even that of moderate intensity, is a stress situation in which changes in the SNS and/or the HPA axis occur, it can cause both beneficial and harmful effects on health, depending on the response (adaptation) to the changes that it produces. The effects of exercise on the homeostatic systems can be summarized by saying that acute heavy training induces an oxidative and inflammatory response and thus can impair many nervous and immune functions. Nevertheless, moderate training exercise leads to clear benefits for these functions and consequently good health and an improved life span. Although it is very difficult to know what the optimal level of exercise is for the appropriate functioning of homeostatic systems in each individual, a physically active life is related to healthy longevity.

The beneficial effects of exercise are mainly mediated by its antioxidant and anti-inflammatory properties. For this reason, exercise has been proposed as a "therapeutic intervention," especially in people with oxidative and inflammatory states, such as chronologically and biologically old subjects. Thus, if exercise is performed as a hormetic intervention, it could well be a good preventive strategy, decreasing oxidative and inflammatory stress, for adequate function of the homeostatic systems (Figure 16.1). Nevertheless, since inappropriate exercise may be harmful in some circumstances, when it clearly deregulates the oxidative and inflammatory responses accelerating the aging process, it would be more helpful (from a physiological point of view) to think in terms of carrying out an active life, and avoiding the modern tendency to lead a sedentary existence (De la Fuente et al., 2011, 2014b; Park et al., 2015).

### Environmental Enrichment

The term "environmental enrichment" (EE) was established to define an experimental approach in animal models that mimics the maintenance of an active social, mental, and physical life in humans. In the previous section the positive effects of physical activity on health were already been commented upon. In this section the effects of mental activity and especially social relationships on the homeostatic systems will be treated. It is known that persons with an active mental life show better nervous and immune function and consequently better health. In experimental animals, the most frequently used EE protocol is the presence in the cages of several types of objects, which are changed every two days. This improves behavioral responses, and nervous, endocrine, and immune functions. Thus, EE increases brain plasticity and neurogenesis, improves some learning and memory abilities, prevents age-related cognitive impairments, and reverses some of the negative consequences of neurodegenerative diseases (De la Fuente & Arranz, 2012). Moreover, EE may confer stress resistance, protecting the animal from the consequences of uncontrollable stress exposure, such as depressive and anxiety-like behaviors. In fact, continuous exposure to new objects and social interactions of the EE could be considered a mild stress condition with hormetic effects. EE has also shown an improvement in functions, redox, and the inflammatory state of the immune system, thereby extending healthy longevity (Arranz et al., 2010, 2011; De la Fuente, 2014b).

In addition, maintaining an active social network and good social relationships seem to be necessary to enhance neural, endocrine, and immune functions, ensuring the maintenance of psychological and physiological health and therefore increasing the life span of individuals (Seeman & Crimmins, 2001; Garrido et al., 2017,

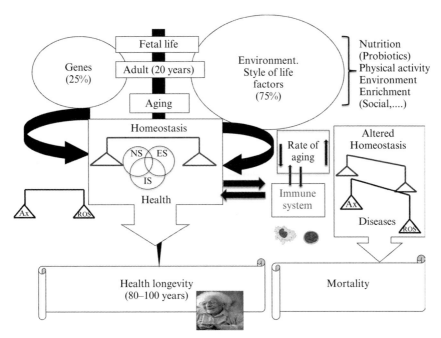

**Figure 16.1.** *Reaching a healthy longevity*
The achievement of a healthy longevity depends on each individual's genes but especially on environmental and lifestyle factors (nutrition, physical activity, ...), which affect the homeostatic systems, namely the nervous, endocrine and immune systems, and the communication between them. The good state of these systems allows the maintenance of health from the beginning of life until its end. This is more evident during the long period of aging. The immune system, due to its characteristics, is an excellent marker of the rate of aging of each subject, and its function capacity is involved in this rate of aging and in reaching a healthy longevity.

2018) (Figure 16.1). In fact, in experimental animals, the cohabitation of chronologically old or of prematurely aging mice with healthy adult animals improves the formers nervous, endocrine, and immune system functions and consequently increases longevity.

## Conclusion and Future

The response to the question "Can we control the rate of aging and achieve healthy longevity?" is clearly "yes." In this chapter the accepted role of the homeostatic systems, namely the nervous, endocrine, and immune systems and their intercommunication in the maintenance of health and thus on the rate of aging and longevity, has been highlighted. In this context, although the genes of each individual are involved in his/her maintenance of health, the epigenetic influence is more relevant, and consequently, lifestyle and environmental factors exert a major influence on health. Thus, we have many tools for modulating our aging. Moreover, if we accept that the basis of age-related physiological deterioration is the increase in oxidative and inflammatory stress, lifestyle factors that decrease oxi-inflamm-aging of the organism will be capable of slowing down the aging process. In addition, the immune system is both a good marker of the biological age of each individual and is involved in the rate of aging. If this system is functioning appropriately and is well regulated, it can contribute to healthy longevity (Figure 16.1).

To reach a good biological age and healthy longevity we have to avoid harmful habits (such as an excess of smoking, alcohol, and stress, and lack of sleep, among others) and maintain adequate nutrition, physical and mental activity, psychological state, and social relationships. All these strategies can exert their effects through hormetic adaptation mechanisms. Thus, if specific medication is needed to control the high number of age-related illnesses, the prevention of these diseases and maintenance of health during the aging process is important to well-being and a prolonged life span. Strategies such as those commented upon in the present chapter are recommended as general non-pharmacological therapeutic interventions. Moreover, they decrease "poly-medication" and the associated side effects, which are very common in aging.

More research is needed in order to uncover the optimal amount, frequency, moment in time, and physiological and psychological situation of each individual in which these strategies would yield increased beneficial effects. Better understanding and application of those lifestyles that improve homeostatic systems, and thus health and life span, are very relevant in slowing down the unavoidable aging process. In this we bear a great responsibility.

## References

Albrecht, A., Müller, I., Ardi, Z., et al. (2017). Neurobiological consequences of juvenile stress: A GABAergic perspective on risk and resilience. *Neurosci Biobehav Rev.*, 74, 21–43.

Alonso-Fernandez, P., De la Fuente, M. (2011). Role of the immune system in aging and longevity. *Curr Aging Sci.*, 4(2), 78–100.

Arranz, L. De Castro, N. M., Baeza, I., et al. (2010). Environmental enrichment improves age-related immune system impairment. Long-term exposure since adulthood increases life span in mice. *Rejuvenation Research.*, 13, 415–28.

Arranz, L. De Castro, N. M., Baeza, I., et al. (2011). Effect of environmental enrichment on the immunoendocrine aging of male and female triple-transgenic 3xTg-AD mice for Alzheimer's disease. *J Alzeimers Dis.*, 25, 727–37.

Bauer, M., De la Fuente, M. (2016). The role of oxidative and inflammatory stress and persistent viral infections in immunosenescence. *Mech Ageing Dev.*, 158, 27–37.

Bischoff, S. C. (2016). Microbiota and aging. *Curr Opin Clin Nutr Metab Care.*, 19, 26–30.

Bouchard, J., Villeda, S. A. (2015). Aging and brain rejuvenation as systemic events. *J Neurochem.*, 132, 5–19.

Cruces, J., Venero, C., Pereda-Pérez, I., et al. (2014). The effect of psychological stress and social isolation on neuroimmunoendocrine communication. *Curr Pharm Des.*, 20, 4608–28.

Cruces, J., Portal-Nuñez, S., Fernandez-Tresguerres, J. A. et al. (2015). Loneliness and social isolation worsen immunity in the elderly. *Aproach Aging Control.*, 19, 7–16.

De la Fuente, M. (2010). Murine models of premature ageing for the study of diet-induced immune changes: improvement of leucocyte functions in two strains of old prematurely ageing mice by dietary supplementation with sulphur-containing antioxidants. *Proc Nutr Soc.*, 69, 651–9.

(2014a). Crosstalk between the nervous and the immune systems in health and sickness. *Curr Pharm Des.*, 20, 4605–7.

(2014b). The immune system, a marker and modulator of the rate of aging. In A. Massoud & N. Rezaei (Eds.), *Immunology of Aging*, pp. 3–23. Springer-Verlag, Berlin Heidelberg.

De la Fuente, M., Arranz, L. (2012). The importance of the environment in brain aging: Be happy, live longer!. In M. K. Thakur & S. I. Rattan (Eds.). *Brain Aging and Therapeutic Interventions*, pp. 79–94. Springer, Science+Business Media, Dordrecht.

De la Fuente, M., Gimenez-Llort, L. (2010). Models of aging of neuroimmunomodulation: strategies for its improvement. *Neuroimmunomodulation*, 17, 213–16.

De la Fuente, M., Miquel, J. (2009). An update of the oxidation-inflammation theory of aging. The involvement of the immune system in oxi-inflamm-aging. *Curr Pharm Des.*, 15, 3003–26.

De la Fuente, M., Cruces, J., Hernandez, O., et al. (2011). Strategies to improve the functions and redox state of the immune system in aged subjects. *Curr Pharm Des.*, 17, 3966–93.

Divyashri, G., Krishna, G., Muralidhara & Prapulla, S. G. (2015). Probiotic attributes, antioxidant, anti-inflammatory and neuromodulatory effects of Enterococcus faecium CFR 3003: in vitro and in vivo evidence. *J Med Microbiol.*, 64, 1527–40.

Franceschi, C., Bonafé, M., Valensin, S., et al. (2000). Inflamm-aging. An evolutionary perspective on immunosenescence. *Ann N Y Acad Sci.*, 908, 244–54.

Garrido, A., Cruces, J., Iriarte, I., et al. (2017). Premature immunosenescence in catecholamines synthesis deficit mice. Effect of social environment. *Rev Esp Geriatr Gerontol.*, 52, 20–26.

Garrido, A., Cruces, J., Ceprian, N., et al. (2018). Improvement in behavior and immune function and increased life span of old mice cohabiting with adult animals. *J Gerontol A Biol Sci Med Sci.*, 73, 873–81.

Harman, D. (1956). Ageing: a theory based on free radical and radiation chemistry. *J Gerontol.*, 2, 298–30.

Holliday, R. (2006). Aging is no longer an unsolved problem in biology. *Ann N Y Acad Sci.*, 1067, 1–9.

Jones, C. M., Boelaert, K. (2015). The endocrinology of ageing: a mini-review. *Gerontology*, 61, 291–300.

Kaushal, D., Kansal, V. K. (2012). Probiotic Dahi containing Lactobacillus acidophilus and Bifidobacterium bifidum alleviates age-inflicted oxidative stress and improves expression of biomarkers of ageing in mice. *Mol Biol Rep.*, 39, 1791–9.

López-Lluch, G., Navas, P. (2016). Calorie restriction as an intervention in ageing. *J Physiol.*, 594, 2043–60.

Martinez de Toda, I., Mate, I., Vida, C., et al. (2016). Immune function parameters as markers of biological age and predictors of longevity. *Aging*, 8, 3110–19.

Ménard, C., Pfau, M. L., Hodes, G. E., et al. (2017). Immune and neuroendocrine mechanisms of stress vulnerability and resilience. *Neuropsychopharmacology*, 42, 62–80.

Ojo, J. O., Rezaie, P., Gabbott, P. L., et al. (2015). Impact of age-related neuroglial cell responses on hippocampal deterioration. *Front Aging Neurosci.*, 7, 57.

Pae, M., Meydani, S. N., Wu, D. (2012). The role of nutrition in enhancing immunity in aging. *Aging and Disease*, 3, 91–129.

Park, K., Lee, S., Hong, Y., et al. (2015). Therapeutic physical exercise in neural injury: friend or foe?. *J Phys Ther Sci.*, 27, 3933–5.

Ray, A., Gulati, K., Rai, N. (2017). Stress, anxiety, and immunomodulation: a pharmacological analysis. *Vitam Horm.*, 103, 1–25.

Rea, K., Dinan, T. G., Cryan, J. F. (2016). The microbiome: a key regulator of stress and neuroinflammation. *Neurobiol Stress*, 4, 23–33.

Seeman, T. E., Crimmins, E. (2001). Social environment effects on health and aging: integrating epidemiologic and demographic approaches and perspectives. *Ann N Y Acad Sci.*, 954, 88–117.

Thakur, M. K., Rattan, S. I. (2012). *Brain Aging and Therapeutic Interventions*. Springer, Science+Business Media, Dordrecht.

Verburg-van Kemenade, B. M., Cohen, N., Chadzinska, M. (2017). Neuroendocrine-immune interaction: Evolutionarily conserved mechanisms that maintain allostasis in an ever-changing environment. *Dev Comp Immunol.*, 66, 2–23.

Vida, C., De la Fuente, M. (2013). Stress-related behavioural responses, immunity and ageing in animal models. Immunosenescence. In J. A. Bosch, C. Phillips, & J. M. Lord (Eds.). *Immunosenescence: Psychosocial and Behavioral Determinants*, pp. 125–44. Springer Media, New York.

Vida, C., Gonzalez, E. M., De la Fuente, M. (2014). Increase of oxidation and inflammation in nervous and immune system with aging and anxiety. *Curr Pharm Des.*, 20, 4656–78.

# 17 The Adaptation Process of Aging

Jana Nikitin and Alexandra M. Freund

## The Adaptation Process of Aging

Most people associate old age with such attributes as "forgetful," "unattractive," "ill," or "lonely" (Kite et al., 2005). At first glance, then, aging primarily implies losses. In fact, the ratio of expected developmental gains (i.e., perceived desirable changes) and losses (i.e., perceived undesirable changes) in a wide range of personality, social, and intellectual characteristics becomes increasingly negative with age, with developmental gains decreasing and developmental losses increasing with age (Heckhausen et al., 1989).

Losses in functional capacity and the availability of resources in old age are only one side of the coin. In his seminal work, Paul Baltes (1987, p. 611) pointed out that any process of development entails an "inherent dynamic between gains and losses" and that no stage in the life course consists only of growth or only of losses. In fact, people still expect gains in old age. Even at age 80 people expect more gains than losses (Heckhausen et al., 1989). Using a very basic definition of successful development as the simultaneous maximization of gains and minimization of losses (Baltes, 1987), the central question of successful development and aging is: "How do people bring about gains and prevent losses and how do they adapt to the changes in the availability of resources throughout their lives?" This is the central question of this chapter.

## Age-Related Adaptations

There is an impressive body of empirical evidence suggesting that most people successfully adapt to changing circumstances as they age. For example, middle-aged and older adults (compared to young adults) expect more desirable changes in old age, have more differentiated expectations regarding aging (Heckhausen et al., 1989), and view aging as increasingly multifaceted (Hummert et al., 1994). It seems that with accumulated experience and knowledge, people also detect more possibilities for successful aging. Moreover, the strength of the

This work was supported by Grant 100019_159399 (Project "Why is social avoidance motivation detrimental to young but not older adults?") from the Swiss National Science Foundation (PI: Jana Nikitin).

correlation between positive expectations regarding aging and life satisfaction increases as people age (Kornadt & Rothermund, 2011), supporting that positive expectations on aging are adaptive for older adults. Regarding the adaptation to critical life events associated with aging, there is broad empirical evidence for older adults' resilience such as the adaptation to severe illnesses (e.g., Deimling et al., 2002). Even at the very end of life, many people still actively shape their development and exert control (Kotter-Grühn et al., 2009).

These findings demonstrate that older people can exert control and achieve positive outcomes even when they encounter increasing losses associated with aging. Development at any age is not just a passive process of maturation and unfolding of abilities and skills, but an ongoing and dynamic interaction of a person with his or her environment (e.g., Baltes et al., 2006). In this chapter, we focus on *motivational* changes as a key factor for understanding the adaptation process in older adulthood. The motivational approach focuses on the role of goals for successful aging. From this perspective, adaptation does not only encompass the adjustment of a person to changes in the availability of internal and external resources and demands of the environment, but also entails that persons proactively place themselves and shape their environment according to their goals. As such, similar to the usage of the term in biology, adaption refers to a process of optimizing the fit between a person and the environment when faced with internal or external changes.

## Motivational Models of Adaptation

In the next part of this chapter, we discuss three prominent motivational theories of successful development that focus on different aspects of successful development. Whereas the model of selection, optimization, and compensation (SOC; Baltes and Baltes, 1990) provides a general framework for the conceptualization of successful aging, the theory of primary and secondary control (OPS; Heckhausen & Schulz, 1995) and the dual-process model of coping (Brandtstädter & Greve, 1994) are centered around the notion of control and coping, respectively. In the following, we will introduce each model, the use of the proposed adaptation strategies across adulthood, and their function for successful aging.

### Selection, Optimization, and Compensation (SOC)

Paul and Margaret Baltes defined successful aging as "an adaptive process involving the components of selection, optimization, and compensation" (Baltes and Baltes, 1990, p. 1). *Selection* channels a person's internal or external resources to a subset of potential options by developing, elaborating, and committing to goals. Selection can either be elective or a response to losses. *Elective selection* is the process of goal development and commitment in order to set priorities that help by focusing on limited resources. *Loss-based selection* is a response to losses in goal-relevant resources that threaten the attainment or maintenance of one's current goals. Loss-based selection involves a revision of goals (e.g., adjusting the goal standards) or a restructuring of the goal hierarchy (e.g., disengaging from blocked goals). Selection is central for adaptive development as it orients a person toward those goals that are most important and thereby provides direction and meaning to behavior. Even a brilliant pianist with great talent has to select the pieces she or he practices to achieve high performance.

In order to pursue selected goals, people acquire and invest in goal-relevant means such as goal-relevant behaviors that augment their resources, maximize gains, and minimize losses (*optimization*). Although means differ with respect to a particular goal, there are several optimization strategies that are generally adaptive for pursuing goals such as monitoring the goal progress, sacrificing momentary temptations for the benefit of long-term goal achievement, and being involved in activities that promote goal achievement. For example, if a runner wants to run a marathon, she will need to intensify her training, change her diet, and monitor her running progress.

*Compensation* is a response to losses resulting in the restriction in the range of plasticity or adaptive potential. When losses threaten the attainment of desirable goals or lead to a standstill in goal progress, loss-based selection is not always an option. Sometimes goals are too important to the person to give them up. In such cases, compensation comes into play. Compensation aims at the avoidance of losses by substituting goal-relevant means through the acquisition of new, or the activation of previously unused, internal or external resources. For example, a woman who can no longer maintain her beloved garden on her own might hire a gardener to do the muscle-heavy jobs.

## The Use of the SOC Strategies Across Adulthood

The use of the SOC strategies decreases from middle to old adulthood, which is probably the case because the use of the SOC strategies itself requires resources (Freund & Baltes, 2002). However, older people seem to be more skillful in the use of the SOC strategies (e.g., Freund & Riediger, 2006), which might compensate for the quantitative reduction of SOC use. Regarding the use of the particular strategies, older adults use more loss-related strategies. This is likely due to the motivational shift from a primary orientation toward gains in young adults to a stronger orientation toward the prevention of losses in old age (Ebner et al., 2006). We discuss the age-related gain and avoidance of loss orientations in more detail later in this chapter.

## The Adaptiveness of the SOC Strategies in Old Age

The SOC strategies are beneficial for successful development across the entire length of adulthood (Freund & Baltes, 2002), but particularly in old age, when resources are scarce. A study with young-old (70–80 years) and old-old adults (80–90 years) (Jopp & Smith, 2006, Study 1) illustrates the benefits of the use of SOC strategies in older adulthood. In the study, the use of SOC strategies was particularly adaptive for satisfaction with aging when personal, social, and cognitive resources, as well as health were low (which is presumably the case in old-old adults). Whereas SOC strategies and resources predicted aging satisfaction independently in young-old adults, they interacted in the prediction of aging satisfaction in old-old adults. In the old-old group, the impact of low resources on aging satisfaction was buffered by SOC. These cross-sectional findings were replicated in a longitudinal study (Jopp & Smith, 2006, Study 2), which found that over the course of one year, resource-poor persons profited more from using SOC strategies than resource-rich persons.

## The Model of Optimization in Primary and Secondary Control (OPS)

The basic tenet of the OPS model is that people generally strive for control over the environment (Heckhausen & Schulz, 1995). This kind of control is called *primary control*. Primary control targets the external world and attempts to achieve effects in the environment in order to shape the environment to fit one's own needs and potentials. Whenever possible, people aspire to maximize the primary control they can exert over the environment. Only when primary control is not possible, *secondary control* comes into play. Secondary control – targeted at the self and attempting to achieve changes within the person – has a compensatory function because the loss of primary control is self-threatening. Secondary control protects emotional well-being and self-esteem after the loss of primary control. In addition, it preserves motivational resources for exerting primary control in the future. Secondary-control strategies are emotion regulation (rather than action), downward adjustments of the ideal self, or downward social comparisons. An additional reason to use secondary control is the finiteness of goal-related resources, which forces people to be selective and to focus only on some goals and inhibit alternatives. Secondary control promotes this process by enhancing the attractiveness of selected goals and reducing the attractiveness of alternatives (Heckhausen & Schulz, 1995).

## Primary and Secondary Control Across Adulthood

Primary and secondary control have different hypothetical developmental trajectories (Heckhausen & Schulz, 1995). Although people strive to maximize overall primary control across the entire life span, the actual capacity to exert primary control decreases as people age. As primary control capacity decreases, people have to invest more and more into secondary-control strategies in order to maintain a subjective sense of primary control, even when the original goal standards had to be lowered or given up entirely. Thus, secondary control striving increases across the life span so that losses in primary control do not undermine a personal sense of primary control.

## Selective and Compensatory Control

The OPS model distinguishes between selective and compensatory control as an additional dimension to primary and secondary control. This results in four different control strategies: (1) *selective primary control* refers to the investment of behavioral resources (e.g., time, effort, and skills) into a pursuit of goals; (2) *selective secondary control* refers to the enhancement and maintenance of motivational commitment to a given goal in the face of obstacles (e.g., positive illusions of attainability, devaluation of attractive alternatives, and valuation of the selected goal); (3) *compensatory primary control* promotes the goal pursuit by the mobilization of external resources (e.g., social support, technical aids); (4) *compensatory secondary control* refers to goal disengagement if the goal is no longer attainable (e.g., distancing from goal, self-protection).

This differentiation is relevant when it comes to the timing of the accomplishment of developmental tasks. Different developmental tasks have different opportunity windows that are defined by sociocultural, age-normative, or biological opportunity structures. For example, graduation and entering the first job should be accomplished before age 30, bearing the first child should not be postponed long after age 40, etc. Off-time accomplishment of developmental goals is more resource intensive because there are fewer internal (e.g., energy) and external (e.g., institutional support such as access to free education) resources available for goal pursuit. For this reason, developmental control strategies have to fit the respective opportunity structures in order to be successful. When approaching a developmental deadline, selective primary and secondary control and compensatory primary control are the most adaptive strategies. After passing the developmental deadline without attaining the developmental goal, the strategies might be best switched to compensatory secondary control.

Empirical evidence supports these assumptions of the OPS model. People engage in goal pursuit when the opportunities for goal attainment are favorable, not only in young but also in old age. For example, Wrosch et al. (2002) examined how the self-reported engagement in health control strategies (i.e., cognitive and behavioral investments toward attaining a health goal such as, "I invest as much time and energy as possible to improve my health") affected the development of depressive symptoms in older adults with ongoing reversible health problems. As expected, engagement in health control strategies predicted reduction of depressive symptoms over time. However, when they cross a developmental deadline, people profit from goal disengagement. This is particularly adaptive in old age. For example, Dunne et al. (2011) investigated if goal disengagement (e.g., withdrawing effort and commitment from unattainable goals) can protect older adults who face functional disabilities from long-term increases in depressive symptoms. Across six years, older adults with poor disengagement capacities experienced an increase in depressive symptoms, whereas older adults who disengaged from unattainable goals did not.

## The Dual-Process Model of Coping

Goal engagement (i.e., *assimilation*) and goal disengagement (i.e., *accommodation*) is also the theoretical centerpiece of the dual-process model of coping

(Brandtstädter & Greve, 1994). The main idea of the dual-process model of coping is that successful adaptation entails a balance of goal engagement and disengagement. Both a rigid pursuit of goals without adaptation to changing circumstances as well as frequent switching from one goal to another are maladaptive for successful development. Successful development needs both continuity as well as adaptive flexibility. The dual-process model of coping focuses on the dynamic interplay of active goal pursuit and goal adjustment to changing circumstances or decreasing resources. The main tenet of the model is that the discrepancy between the actual and the desired developmental outcomes can be reduced either through assimilation or through accommodation.

Assimilation reduces the discrepancy between the actual and desired state by actively changing the situation so that it fits a person's needs and desires (akin to primary control strategies). Accommodation refers to the adjustment of aspiration levels to situational constraints (akin to secondary control strategies). The timing of the switch from assimilative to accommodative coping depends on three main factors: (1) the importance of the goal, (2) the attainability of the goal, and (3) controllability of the goal attainment and goal pursuit. The more important, the more attainable, and the more controllable a goal is, the longer and harder people will try to achieve it.

## Assimilative and Accommodative Coping Across Adulthood

The model proposes that when goals become difficult to achieve, i.e., with increasing age, assimilative strategies are first intensified. However, when many goals are no longer attainable, assimilative strategies decrease and make way for accommodative strategies. Thus, the trajectory of assimilative strategies across adulthood should be an inverted U-shape function. This hypothesis was investigated in a large sample of older adults combining cross-sectional and longitudinal assessment of assimilative activities (such as activities aiming at maintaining or increasing performance) in four different domains of functioning: physical fitness, mental efficiency, physical appearance, and everyday competence (Rothermund & Brandstädter, 2003). The authors found the expected inverted U-shape of assimilative efforts. This development was adaptive, particularly for the oldest groups.

To summarize, motivational theories of aging emphasize the active role of the individual in shaping her or his own development and in adapting to changing circumstances. It is beyond the scope of this chapter to systematically compare and contrast the three models. Suffice it here to note that all three models (SOC, OPS, and the dual-process model) are based on the assumption that people actively set and pursue goals that give people's lives direction and enable the acquisition and maintenance of resources. Strategies of goal engagement and disengagement allow people to keep control over their lives and to shape their development despite declining resources.

## Age-Related Changes in the Cognitive Representation of Goals

Research on motivated cognition demonstrates that the cognitive representation of goals impacts goal pursuit and achievement. In the following section, we elaborate on two central age-related changes in the cognitive representation of goals: (i) goal orientation (toward gains, maintenance, and loss prevention) and (ii) goal focus (on the outcome or the process of goal pursuit).

### Goal Orientation

Although some researchers argue that striving for more and higher levels of functioning and accumulating resources is a basic human need, this does not seem to be the case throughout the entire life span. It appears to be less adaptive to strive for gains in very old age when gains become less attainable. Instead of achieving more, people might better invest their decreasing resources on maintaining the levels of functioning they have already achieved and to avoid potential losses. In line with this assumption, people – as they age – orient their goals less toward gains and more toward maintaining what they have already achieved or toward avoiding losses (Ebner et al., 2006). This shift in goal orientation seems to be closely connected to the expected resource investment. When people experience declining resources, they often choose to invest their resources into less resource-intensive goals directed at maintenance and prevention of losses rather than into more resource-intensive growth goals (Ebner et al., 2006).

The orientation toward growth and loss prevention is accompanied by a preferential processing of the related information. Whereas younger adults attend more to indicators of gains, older adults attend more to indicators of losses. A heightened attention to gains or losses, respectively, enable young and older adults to gather the kind of information that best helps them to achieve gains or prevent losses. For example, Depping and Freund (2013) demonstrated that older adults remember more loss-relevant information than younger adults when they have to make a decision between two relevant options. The authors concluded that older – compared to younger – adults process negative information preferentially when making a decision because negative information is more diagnostic than positive information when attempting to minimize losses.

Does the adaptiveness of an orientation toward growth versus the prevention of loss change across adulthood? This seems to be the case. In a series of experiments, Freund (2006) demonstrated that younger adults are more persistent in a task when they can optimize their level of achievement, whereas older adults are more persistent when they can compensate for losses in their performance. Moreover, the different goal orientations seem to also have different consequences for the subjective well-being of younger and older adults. Whereas younger adults report higher levels of subjective well-being when they orient their goals toward growth, older adults report higher levels of subjective well-being when their goals are oriented toward prevention of losses (Ebner et al., 2006).

## Goal Focus

The orientation toward growth and maintenance has consequences not only for people's choices, information processing, and well-being, but also for their focus on means or outcomes of their goals (Freund et al., 2012). Goals can be defined as cognitive representations linking certain means (or actions) with desired outcomes. People differ in how much they focus on the outcomes or on the means of goals. For example, when training for a marathon, people can focus more strongly on the means (e.g., jogging regularly) or on the outcomes (e.g., winning a marathon race). Generally, focus on the means (i.e., *process focus*) is more beneficial for both goal achievement and goal-related well-being than focus on the outcomes (i.e., *outcome focus*) (Freund et al., 2012).

How are growth and loss-prevention goals related to outcome and process focus? Freund et al. (2012) argued that goals oriented toward growth typically have a clear outcome to be achieved, which might draw attention to this outcome. In contrast, goals directed at the maintenance of functioning and prevention of loss have no clear end point and, therefore, might lead to focus on the means of the goal pursuit. Supporting this rationale, Freund et al. (2010) found that process and outcome focus differ by age. Younger adults focused more on the outcomes of goal pursuit than older adults, whereas older adults were increasingly oriented toward the process of goal pursuit. Moreover, Mustafić and Freund (2012) demonstrated that outcome focus is predicted by growth orientation, whereas process focus is predicted by loss-prevention orientation.

Taken together, goal orientation toward gains, maintenance, and the prevention of losses has different trajectories across adulthood. Whereas young adults adopt a stronger gain orientation in their personal goals with according information processing and well-being outcomes, older adults are increasingly oriented toward and profit from maintenance and the prevention of losses. These differences seem to be driven by expectations of resource investment to the pursuit of gains and prevention of loss goals. Stronger orientation toward the prevention of losses also drives older adults' stronger focus on the means of the goals rather than on the outcomes. Focus on the means, in turn, is more adaptive for the goal pursuit and subjective well-being, thereby contributing to successful aging.

## Age-Related Motivational Changes in Different Life Domains

In the previous parts of this chapter, we discussed age-related motivational changes in general. In the following section, we outline specific motivational changes in the three most important life domains: (i) work and particularly the transition to retirement, (ii) leisure, and (iii) social relationships (see also Table 17.1).

Table 17.1 *Specific regulatory strategies in different life domains*

| | Goal engagement (elective selection, optimization, compensation, primary control, selective secondary control, assimilation) | Goal disengagement (loss-based selection, compensatory secondary control, accommodation) |
|---|---|---|
| Transition to retirement | Continuity of meaningful goals and purpose<br>Retirement planning<br>Control maintenance | Work-goals disengagement<br>Control maintenance |
| Leisure activities | Intensifying participation | Reducing diversity |
| Social relationships | Reducing number of social relationships to the most important ones<br>Increased social participation | Avoidance of negative social encounters<br>Seeking alternative social relationships<br>Dependent behavior |

## Work and Transition to Retirement

Work has many important functions in people's lives. Important for the scope of this chapter, work has structural function, meaning that it structures time into patterns of work and leisure and it structures life paths through career-related goals. When people retire, they lose their work-related roles, meanings, and external structures. As argued by Freund et al. (2009), this might lead to higher importance of regulatory strategies. Retirees need to disengage from their work roles and restructure their lives. Thus, successful retirement requires flexibility and adaptability to available resources as means of maximizing gains and minimizing losses, which accompany the retirement process (Baltes and Rudolph, 2013).

In fact, not all people retire from work successfully. After a short "honeymoon phase" characterized by the experience of freedom from the time demands and daily structure of work life (Atchley, 1975), retirement is often associated with constrains both in the physical (e.g., poorer health and lower activity level) and the psychological domain (e.g., lower levels of happiness) (Richardson & Kilty, 1991). Thus, retirement is a challenging phase that requires the use of regulatory strategies. There is broad research on the adaptation to retirement that demonstrates the benefits of the regulatory strategies as defined within the three motivational models described earlier in this chapter (see Baltes and Rudolph, 2013).

One important adaptation strategy to retirement is *goal continuity*, i.e., maintaining meaningful and stable life goals and purpose. Robbins et al. (1994) interviewed workers who retired earlier within a voluntary retirement program. They found that social support, health, and socioeconomic status influenced post-retirement leisure quality and life satisfaction only through goal continuity.

In other words, goal continuity was an important mediator of early-retirement adaptation, linking personal and social resources to positive outcomes.

A second important adaptation strategy in the retirement process is the *maintenance* of perceived high control (Gall et al., 1997). In a longitudinal study, Gall and colleagues investigated short-term and long-term predictors of retirement adaptation. In the short term, retirees who had more resources (better physical health and higher income), reported higher satisfaction with different areas of retirement (such as leisure activities, financial situation, or social relationships) than retirees with fewer resources. For long-term adjustment, however, locus of control was important for adaptation. Those retirees who kept a strong sense of control over their lives adapted better to retirement than those who felt controlled by external forces. This result supports the notion of the OPS model – that people strive for control over their lives and that maintaining high control is important for the adjustment to developmental changes.

A highly beneficial regulatory strategy in the retirement process is *retirement planning*. Planning strategies for retirement such as building up savings, learning about pension and Social Security benefits, developing hobbies and other leisure time activities, deciding whether to move or not, making sure that medical care will be available, or moving in with children or other relatives (Ferraro, 1990) can be best understood as elective selection and optimization (Baltes and Rudolph, 2013).

Finally, *disengagement* from work-related goals seems to be a beneficial strategy in the retirement process. Atchley (1975) proposed the adaptive function of reorganizing individual's hierarchy of personal goals by replacing work-related goals with alternatives, particularly when work was personally important. As an illustration, Warriner and Lavalle (2008) investigated adaptation to retirement in elite athletes who can be assumed to value sports goals highly. Those athletes who did not disengage from sports goals after retirement suffered more from identity loss and other adjustment problems than those who disengaged. It seems beneficial for the person to replace highly valued work-related goals with new roles and alternative goals that are high in subjective meaning, such as volunteering (Nimrod & Shrira, 2016). These strategies are best described as loss-based selection in terms of the SOC model, compensatory secondary control in terms of the OPS model, and accommodation in terms of the dual-process model of coping.

To summarize, retirement is a challenging process that benefits from regulatory strategies. On the one hand, active planning of retirement, goal continuity, and high control enables the retiree to maintain high levels of physical and psychological well-being. On the other hand, disengagement from highly valued work-related goals and engagement in new, subjectively meaningful goals helps retirees to maintain a purpose in life and to develop new identity after leaving work.

## Leisure

In contrast to work, leisure is a life domain best characterized by a lack of clear normative constraints. As such, leisure is closely connected to older age in the view of many people. But is leisure also beneficial for older adults?

This seems to be the case. There is good empirical evidence that participation in leisure activities ("active aging") promotes life satisfaction and well-being as well as physical and cognitive functioning into old age (Nimrod & Shrira, 2016).

Although participation in leisure activities decreases as people age, leisure activities provide even more benefits for very old people. Nimrod and Shrira (2016) investigated the strength of the association between leisure involvement and change in quality of life in 19 European countries. Respondents with high levels of leisure involvement reported an increase in quality of life over time, whereas non-active respondents reported a decline. These results, held after controlling for socio-demographics, health, and cognitive functioning, suggest the important role of leisure participation, particularly in very old age. As the authors argued, leisure is a source for physical and psychological resilience that helps very old adults to cope with the cumulative risk factors associated with the aging process.

This view was also supported in a representative sample of older adults (Silverstein & Parker, 2002). Older adults, who increased their leisure-activity participation across different domains (e.g., cultural, physical) during a period of 10 years, also experienced improvements in their life conditions. This effect was particularly strong among older adults who became widowed, developed functional impairments, and had relatively low contact with their family. In other words, leisure participation was an adaptive strategy to compensate for social and physical losses in later life.

To summarize, the association between leisure activities and aging is somewhat paradoxical because those older adults who may benefit the most from leisure activities, i.e., very old adults who face cumulative losses, are the ones who face the greatest number of constraints preventing them from engaging in leisure activities (Nimrod & Shrira, 2016). This paradox originates from the different use of the regulatory strategies in resource-rich (i.e., young-old) and resource-poor (i.e., oldest-old) individuals. As Lang et al. (2002) demonstrated, resource-rich older adults (i.e., those high in sensorimotor-cognitive, personality, and social functioning) used more SOC strategies in everyday function including leisure, than resource-poor older adults. A particular strategy of resource-rich older adults in the leisure domain was selection, i.e., reducing the diversity of activities by focusing on most preferred ones. In addition, resource-rich older adults used more optimization strategies by investing more time and effort in the specific activities. Thus, selection and optimization seem to be adaptive strategies for maintaining high functioning in the leisure domain.

## Social Relationships

Satisfying social relationships are fundamental for physical and psychological well-being across the entire life span and they are one of the most critical variables for successful aging (Lang & Carstensen, 1998). However, individuals also actively shape their social environments by selection (e.g., discontinuation of social relationships), optimization (e.g., investment in high-quality relationships), and compensation (e.g., transformation of social relationships) (Lang, 2001).

There is robust evidence that social-network size decreases in the second half of life (see Antonucci et al., 2006). Although a substantial part of the network-size reduction is due to functional losses and mortality of social partners, there is also evidence suggesting that older people deliberately discontinue their relationships with partners who are less close or subjectively less important (Lang & Carstensen, 1998). Older adults become *selective*, i.e., they prefer to invest their decreasing resources to few but emotionally meaningful social relationships. Greater focus on emotionally meaningful social relationships, in turn, is associated with higher well-being in older adulthood (Lang et al., 1998).

Another selection process in the social domain is the avoidance of negative social encounters. Older people not only prefer avoidance-related strategies when facing interpersonal tensions, but they also suffer more than younger adults from negative social encounters when they cannot avoid them (Birditt et al., 2005). The motivation to avoid negative social encounters seems to be driven by older people's vulnerabilities such as prolonged recovery phase from high physiological arousal, greater suffering from sustaining negative events compared to younger adults, and stronger negative emotions when confronted with interpersonal losses (for a summary, see Charles, 2010).

*Optimization* in the social context refers to high investment of individual resources into social participation that enable older adults to profit from the beneficial effects of social relationships on cognitive, mental, and physical functioning (Lang, 2001). Supporting the benefits of optimization in the social context, Lövdén et al. (2005) demonstrated that social participation alleviates cognitive decline into very old age. Social participation is not only beneficial for the prevention of cognitive decline but can also improve people's health and subjective well-being. In an intervention study with nursing home residents, those who took their meals in a family-like style during a period of 6 months reported a subsequently higher overall quality of life, higher motor functioning, and higher body weight than the control group, who received the usual individual pre-plated service (Nijs et al., 2006). The mere presence of other people during the meals led to a significant improvement in health and subjective well-being.

Finally, when social relationships are less available, due to the loss of social partners or functional constraints (e.g., limited mobility), older people might use *compensatory* strategies such as intensifying alternative social contacts or increasing dependent behavior in order to secure social contacts (Lang, 2001). For example, Guiaux et al. (2007) investigated how older adults' social networks change due to widowhood. The authors demonstrated that social contact and social support increased immediately after widowhood and, around 2.5 years later, decreased again. These results support the view that the widowers used compensation strategies after their spouses deceased. Moreover, although contact and support increased for all social relationships, the highest increase was measured for child and sibling relationships, which are presumably the most emotionally meaningful relationships for older adults.

In addition to seeking alternative contacts to social losses, older adults might also show more dependent behavior, as one side effect of dependency is more social contact. Baltes (1996) demonstrated in her research on "learned dependency" that this mechanism is particularly pronounced when dependent behavior is reinforced and independent behavior is largely ignored, as is sometimes the case in nursing homes. When nursing staff responds attentively to independent behavior, the residents change to more independent behavior, supporting the notion that dependent behavior is a compensatory strategy to receive attention and social contact (Baltes, 1996).

To summarize, social relationships are both predictors and outcomes of successful aging. Older people actively use regulatory strategies to build, maintain, and improve social relationships. They concentrate their resources on few but emotionally meaningful relationships, avoid negative social encounters, and seek or intensify alternative relationships after losses. The investment in social relationships, in turn, is beneficial for older people's health and well-being.

## Conclusions and Future Directions

In this chapter, we took a motivational perspective to discuss the adaptation process of aging. We argued that older adults do not only passively react to possible losses associated with aging. Instead, they continue to actively shape their development by the use of regulatory strategies that might be best characterized as goal engagement and goal disengagement. These regulatory strategies enable older adults to maintain high control over their lives despite developmental losses. We discussed how goal-related regulatory strategies can improve functioning and well-being in the domain of work, leisure, and social relationships. As depicted in Table 17.1, both goal-engagement and goal-disengagement strategies are beneficial for adaptation in these three life domains. Some strategies (such as maintaining high control after retirement) are supported by both goal engagement and goal disengagement, highlighting that it is the *orchestration* of the regulatory strategies that is particularly beneficial as people age.

In the last part of this chapter, we briefly address some newer socio-demographic developments and their influence on the adaptation process of aging. It is well known that industrial societies are aging rapidly as the fertility rates steadily decrease and life expectancy increases. This development shifts the age distribution of the populations in all industrialized countries toward older age groups. In addition, people today have a higher life expectancy than people at any time in the history of mankind. Thus, the population of older adults is not only increasing but the phase of older adulthood has extended for more people than ever before. How do the increased longevity and the increasing proportion of older adults affect self-regulation in old age?

We assume that longevity leads to a prolongation of the phase of the life that is associated with relatively few and weak social norms and expectations (i.e., old age), which, in turn, might lead to greater importance of self-regulatory strategies as described in this chapter. As is often stated, people do not just want to add more years to life, but want to add life to these years. Self-regulation might be the key factor for adding life to the additional years in old age. Interestingly, there is evidence demonstrating that older adults become more skilled in self-regulation (Freund & Riediger, 2006). Thus, older adults develop skills that enable them to successfully adapt to the increasing life expectancy. On the other hand, self-regulation of older adults seems to be closely tied to the availability of individual and social resources. Although some older adults do shape their development into very old age (Kotter-Grühn et al., 2009), resource-poor older adults, in general, use less regulatory strategies (Lang et al., 2002). Considering that an increased longevity implies prolonging the phase of very old age for more and more people, more future research is needed to address the question as to whether there are possibilities to increase self-regulation in the group of people who experience multiple losses.

The increasing proportion of older adults challenges societies; due to the negative effects on healthcare spending, retirement policies, the use of long-term care services, and the workforce composition, the increasing proportion of older adults in the society might lead to intergenerational tensions (North & Fiske, 2015). Older adults might be seen as a burden to society, leading to negative stereotypes about aging and age discrimination. Sadly, negative age-related stereotypes and expectations have very detrimental effects on successful aging (Lamont et al., 2015). Thus, how to counteract negative age stereotypes is an important question. North and Fiske (2015) proposed approaches against ageism that involve: (i) changing people's mindsets about older adults and (ii) changing older adults' mindsets about themselves. The former strategies involve recognizing realities about older adults such as, older workers are not less innovative than younger workers, deemphasizing intergenerational competition by creating superordinate goals that improve cooperation between age groups, and changing environments and reframing tasks and activities so that they are less threatening for older people. With respect to older people themselves, strategies such as increasing positive aging self-perceptions, using dual age-identities, strengthening the identification with a generation instead of an age group, and increasing generativity, i.e., responsibility for coming generations, might be promising approaches (Weiss & Lang, 2012).

We propose that self-regulatory abilities of older people might help in implementing these strategies aiming at the reduction of intergenerational tensions. For example, older people might actively adopt strategies that help them to overcame negative stereotypes (such as selecting and pursuing generativity goals) or actively seek environments that fit their needs and abilities. Moreover, such strategies might increase older people's self-efficacy and, thus, improve their positive self-views. In addition, the self-regulation skills of older people need to be recognized by the society, which would improve views of old age and aging itself. For example, as noted earlier, acknowledging older people's independency strivings might not only support older people's independent behavior and positive self-views, but also improve the image of older people in the society. Thus, self-regulation might be an important means to bridging generations.

# References

Antonucci, T. C., Ajrouch, K. J., Birditt, K. S., et al. (2006). Social relations in the third age: Assessing strengths and challenges using the Convoy Model. In J. B. James & P. Wink (Eds.), *Annual Review of Gerontology and Geriatrics* (Vol. 26, pp. 193–209). New York, NY: Springer.

Atchley, R. C. (1975). Adjustment to loss of job at retirement. *The International Journal of Aging and Human Development*, 6, 17–27. doi:10.2190/EHU3-VCRV-VCRJ-04NU.

Baltes, P. B. (1987). Theoretical propositions of life-span developmental psychology: On the dynamics between growth and decline. *Developmental Psychology*, 23, 611–26. doi:10.1037/0012-1649.23.5.611.

Baltes, M. M. (1996). *The many faces of dependency in old age*. New York, NY: Cambridge University Press.

Baltes, P. B., Baltes, M. M. (1990). Psychological perspectives on successful aging: The model of selective optimization with compensation. In P. B. Baltes & M. M. Baltes (Eds.), *Successful Aging: Perspectives from the Behavioral Sciences* (pp. 1–34). New York, NY: Cambridge University Press.

Baltes, B. B., Rudolph, C. W. (2013). The theory of selection, optimization, and compensation. In M. Wang & M. Wang (Eds.), *The Oxford Handbook of Retirement* (pp. 88–101). New York, NY: Oxford University Press.

Baltes, P. B., Lindenberger, U., Staudinger, U. M. (2006). Life span theory in developmental psychology. In R. M. Lerner & W. Damon (Eds.), *Handbook of Child Psychology (6th ed. Vol 1), Theoretical Models of Human Development* (Vol. 1, pp. 569–664). Hoboken, NJ: Wiley.

Birditt, K. S., Fingerman, K. L., Almeida, D. M. (2005). Age differences in exposure and reactions to interpersonal tensions: A daily diary study. *Psychology and Aging*, 20, 330–340. doi:10.1037/0882-7974.20.2.330.

Brandtstädter, J., Greve, W. (1994). The aging self: stabilizing and protective processes. *Developmental Review*, 14, 52–80. doi:10.1006/drev.1994.1003.

Charles, S. T. (2010). Strength and vulnerability integration: a model of emotional well-being across adulthood. *Psychological Bulletin*, 136, 1068–91. doi:10.1037/a0021232.

Deimling, G. T., Kahana, B., Bowman, K. F., et al. (2002). Cancer survivorship and psychological distress in later life. *Psycho-Oncology*, 11, 479–94. doi:10.1002/pon.614.

Depping, M., Freund, A. M. (2013). When choice matters: task-dependent memory effects in older adulthood. *Psychology and Aging*, 28, 923–36. doi:10.1037/a9934520.

Dunne, E., Wrosch, C., Miller, G. E. (2011). Goal disengagement, functional disability, and depressive symptoms in old age. *Health Psychology*, 30, 763–70. doi:10.1037/a0024019.

Ebner, N. C., Freund, A. M., Baltes, P. B. (2006). Developmental changes in personal goal orientation from young to late adulthood: from striving for gains to maintenance and prevention of losses. *Psychology and Aging*, 21, 664–78. doi:10.1037/0882-7974.21.4.664.

Ferraro, K. F. (1990). Cohort analysis of retirement preparation, 1974–1981. *Journal of Gerontology*, 45, S21–S31. doi:10.1093/geronj/45.1.S21.

Freund, A. M. (2006). Age-differential motivational consequences of optimization versus compensation focus in younger and older adults. *Psychology and Aging*, 21, 240–52. doi:10.1037/0882-7974.21.2.240.

Freund, A. M., Baltes, P. B. (2002). Life-management strategies of selection, optimization, and compensation: Measurement by self-report and construct validity. *Journal of Personality and Social Psychology*, 82, 642–62. doi:10.1037/0022-3514.82.4.642.

Freund, A. M., Riediger, M. (2006). Goals as building blocks of personality and development in adulthood. In D. K. Mroczek & T. D. Little (Eds.), *Handbook of Personality Development* (pp. 353–72). Mahwah, NJ: Lawrence Erlbaum.

Freund, A. M., Nikitin, J., Ritter, J. O. (2009). Psychological consequences of longevity: The increasing importance of self-regulation in old age. *Human Development*, 52, 1–37. doi:10.1159/000189213.

Freund, A. M., Hennecke, M., Riediger, M. (2010). Age-related differences in outcome and process goal focus. *European Journal of Developmental Psychology*, 7, 198–222. doi:10.1080/17405620801969585.

Freund, A. M., Hennecke, M., Mustafic, M. (2012). On gains and losses, means and ends: Goal orientation and goal focus across adulthood. In R. M. Ryan (Ed.), *The Oxford Handbook of Human Motivation* (pp. 280–300). New York, NY: Oxford University Press.

Gall, T. L., Evans, D. R., Howard, J. (1997). The retirement adjustment process: changes in the well-being of male retirees across time. *The Journals of Gerontology Series B: Psychological Sciences and Social Sciences*, 52, P110–P117. doi:10.1093/geronb/52B.3.P110.

Guiaux, M., Van Tilburg, T., Broese van Groenou, M. (2007). Changes in contact and support exchange in personal networks after widowhood. *Personal Relationships*, 14, 457–73. doi:10.1111/j.1475-6811.2007.00165.x.

Heckhausen, J., Schulz, R. (1995). A life-span theory of control. *Psychological Review*, 102, 284–304. doi:10.1037/0033-295X.102.2.284.

Heckhausen, J., Dixon, R. A., Baltes, P. B. (1989). Gains and losses in development throughout adulthood as perceived by different adult age groups. *Developmental Psychology*, 25, 109–21. doi:10.1037//0012-1649.25.1.109.

Hummert, M. L., Garstka, T. A., Shaner, J. L., et al. (1994). Stereotypes of the elderly held by young, middle-aged, and elderly adults. *Journal of Gerontology*, 49, P240–P249. doi:10.1093/geronj/49.5.P240.

Jopp, D. S., Smith, J. (2006). Resources and life-management strategies as determinants of successful aging: On the protective effect of selection, optimization, and compensation. *Psychology and Aging*, 21, 253–65. doi:10.1037/0882-7974.21.2.253.

Kite, M. E., Stockdale, G. D., Whitley, B. E., et al. (2005). Attitudes toward younger and older adults: an updated meta-analytic review. *Journal of Social Issues*, 61, 241–66. doi:10.1111/j.1540-4560.2005.00404.x.

Kornadt, A. E., Rothermund, K. (2011). Contexts of aging: assessing evaluative age stereotypes in different life domains. *The Journals of Gerontology Series B: Psychological Sciences and Social Sciences*, 66B, 547–56. doi:10.1093/geronb/gbr036.

Kotter-Grühn, D., Kleinspehn-Ammerlahn, A., Gerstorf, D., et al. (2009). Self-perceptions of aging predict mortality and change with approaching death: 16-year longitudinal results from the Berlin Aging Study. *Psychology and Aging*, 24, 654–67. doi.org/10.1037/a0016510.

Lamont, R. A., Swift, H. J., Abrams, D. (2015). A review and meta-analysis of age-based stereotype threat: negative stereotypes, not facts, do the damage. *Psychology and Aging*, 30, 180–93. doi:10.1037/a0038586.

Lang, F. R. (2001). Regulation of social relationships in later adulthood. *Journals of Gerontology Series B: Psychological Sciences and Social Sciences*, 56, 321–6. doi:10.1093/geronb/56.6.P321.

Lang, F. R., Carstensen, L. L. (1998). Social relationships and adaptation in late life. In A. S. Bellack & M. Hersen (Eds.), *Comprehensive Clinical Psychology* (Vol. 7, pp. 55–72). Oxford, UK: Pergamon.

Lang, F. R., Staudinger, U. M., Carstensen, L. L. (1998). Perspectives on socioemotional selectivity in late life: How personality and social context do (and do not) make a difference. *Journals of Gerontology: Series B: Psychological Sciences and Social Sciences*, 53B, 21–30. doi:10.1037/0882-7974.9.2.315.

Lang, F. R., Rieckmann, N., Baltes, M. M. (2002). Adapting to aging losses: do resources facilitate strategies of selection, compensation, and optimization in everyday functioning? *Journals of Gerontology: Series B: Psychological Sciences and Social Sciences*, 57B, 501–9. doi:10.1093/geronb/57.6.P501.

Lövdén, M., Ghisletta, P., Lindenberger, U. (2005). Social participation attenuates decline in perceptual speed in old and very old age. *Psychology and Aging*, 20, 423–34. doi.org/10.1037/0882-7974.20.3.423.

Mustafić, M., Freund, A. M. (2012). Means or outcomes? Goal orientation predicts process and outcome focus. *European Journal of Developmental Psychology*, 9, 493–9. doi:10.1080/17405629.2012.661411.

Nijs, K. A. N. D., de Graaf, C., Kok, F. J., et al. (2006). Effect of family style mealtimes on quality of life, physical performance, and body weight of nursing home residents: Cluster randomised controlled trial. *BMJ: British Medical Journal*, 332, 1180–3. doi:10.1136/bmj.38825.401181.7C.

Nimrod, G., Shrira, A. (2016). The paradox of leisure in later life. *The Journals of Gerontology: Series B: Psychological Sciences and Social Sciences*, 71B, 106–11. doi:10.1093/geronb/gbu143.

North, M. S., Fiske, S. T. (2015). Modern attitudes toward older adults in the aging world: A cross-cultural meta-analysis. *Psychological Bulletin*, 141, 993–1021. doi:10.1037/a0039469.

Richardson, V., Kilty, K. M. (1991). Adjustment to retirement: Continuity vs. discontinuity. *The International Journal of Aging and Human Development*, 33, 151–69. doi:0.2190/6RPT-U8GN-VUCV-P0TU.

Robbins, S. B., Lee, R. M., Wan, T. T. H. (1994). Goal continuity as a mediator of early retirement adjustment: testing a multidimensional model. *Journal of Counseling Psychology*, 41, 18–26. doi:10.1037/0022-0167.41.1.18.

Rothermund, K., Brandstädter, J. (2003). Coping with deficits and losses in later life: from compensatory action to accommodation. *Psychology and Aging*, 18, 896–905. doi:10.1037/0882-7974.18.4.896.

Silverstein, M., Parker, M. G. (2002). Leisure activities and quality of life among the oldest old in Sweden. *Research on Aging*, 24, 528–47. doi:10.1177/0164027502245003.

Warriner, K., Lavalle, D. (2008). The retirement experiences of elite female gymnasts: Self identity and the physical self. *Journal of Applied Sport Psychology*, 20, 301–17. doi:10.1080/10413200801998564.

Weiss, D., Lang, F. (2012). "They" are old but "I" feel younger: Age-group dissociation as a self-protective strategy in old age. *Psychology and Aging*, 27, 153–63. doi:10.1037/a0024887.

Wrosch, C., Schulz, R., Heckhausen, J. (2002). Health stresses and depressive symptomatology in the elderly: the importance of health engagement control strategies. *Health Psychology*, 21, 340–8. doi:10.1037/0278-6133.21.4.340.

# 18 Behavioral Health

Marta Santacreu, Marcos Alonso Rodríguez, and
María Ángeles Molina

Based on the repercussion of behavior in the process of health and illness and the modifiability of behavioral risk and protective factors, behavioral health is defined as "the application of behavioral and biomedical sciences knowledge and techniques to the maintenance of health and biomedical prevention of illness and dysfunction by a variety of self-initiated individual and shared activities" (Matarazzo, 1984, p. 29).

As it is well-known, human and social developments, scientific advances, and technological progresses produced, from the end of nineteenth century, a strong increment in life expectancy, opening new challenges for the so-called "aging societies." From a biological point of view, the aging process entails a decline of the effectiveness and efficiency of organic and functional systems, associated with an increase of the probability of sickness, disability, and falls, causing greater dependency. Nevertheless, Fries (1989) pointed out two provocative hypotheses: "most of the crucial aspects of aging, including the presence or absence of disease, are under individual control" (*modifiability hypothesis*). Table 18.1 shows negative conditions associated with aging (low functionality, medical problems, and illnesses) and modifiable behaviorally protective or preventive factors. From this perspective emerge Fries's second hypothesis, the *compression of morbidity*, changing the current pessimistic view about the *failure of success* in aging, predicting that scientific advances would be able to prolong not only life expectancy but also disability-free life expectancy, compressing morbimortality at the end of life. Although Fries's hypotheses were not well accepted by the scientific community at that time, there is a vast accumulation of data supporting both hypotheses now (see Fries et al., 2011; Fries, 2012).

Finally, authors outlined basics strategies for changing behaviors: (1) *primordial prevention* prescribes never smoking, never sedentary, and no obesity; (2) *primary prevention* requires increasing exercise, reducing smoking, reducing obesity, and finally, moderating health problems; and (3) *secondary prevention* (when illness already appears and is partially under behavioral control) includes reduction in cholesterol, hypertension control, diabetes control, etc. Although behavioral health implies tertiary prevention, this chapter focuses on primordial, primary, and secondary prevention, clearly stating that in order to ensure successful aging, the promotion of healthy behaviors must be the responsibility of the individual and supported by the community and public policies. In summary,

Table 18.1 *Modifiable aging manifestation suggested by Fries (1989 modified)*

| Problematic features associated to age | Modifying factors |
| --- | --- |
| Physical fitness | Exercise, weight control, nonsmoking |
| Heart reserve | Aerobic exercise |
| Mobility | Stretching exercise |
| Blood pleasure | Exercise, salt intake |
| Intelligence and memory | Practice, training |
| Reaction time | Exercise |
| Isolation | Practice socialization |
| Heart disease | Diet exercise, other health habits |
| Cancer | Diet, nonsmoking, physical exercise |
| Arthritis | Exercise, weight control |
| Agility | Stretching control |

there are several examples of behavioral lifestyles that directly influence the promotion of successful aging, preventing age-related illnesses and declines.

But not all risk factors respond to behavioral changes, there are other environmental risk factor predictors of illness and disability, because the individual has full agency. For example, education and socioeconomic status have been linked to illness and disabilities; data from the United Kingdom revealed a negative correlation between socioeconomic status and overweight/obesity and diabetes. Overall, socioeconomic data is positively correlated with life expectancy and self-reported mental and physical health, and negatively correlated with chronic disease and psychiatric morbidity (see Fernández-Ballesteros, 2008). Likewise, environmental factors play an important role in successful aging. As emphasized by Antonucci et al. (2012) in a proactive model, the trend toward declining levels of physical activity and increasing obesity is recorded in society at the largest levels.

In conclusion, the process of aging successfully is not only the outcome of the application of public policies that support healthy aging, but also requires the result of individuals' behaviors, i.e., avoiding behavioral risk factors and reinforcing protector ones across their life span. The aims of the following sections are: (1) what are the most important lifestyles factors for better aging – now a global goal of the aging countries (Fernández-Ballesteros et al., 2013) and (2) promoting behavioral change and the psychological and educational factors that encourage change and adherence.

## Successful Aging Behaviors and Lifestyles

Aging happens throughout the life span, thus from birth to death we are aging – it is a lifelong process. How we are reaching old age is not random but it depends upon the lifestyle adopted throughout our life. Thus, healthy lifestyles are highlighted as the most important factor to promote health and avoid illnesses (WHO, 2002; Fernández-Ballesteros et al., 2013). Lifestyles are understood as a set of learnt behaviors across a process, incorporated into daily life. In other words, lifestyle is one of the most important behavioral determinants of the different pathways of getting older (Rowe & Khan, 1997; Fernández-Ballesteros et al., 2010). Behaviors and lifestyle factors may promote successful aging (*protective factors*) or be associated with the development of illness and disability (*risk factors*).

There are thousands of studies looking for risk and protective factors across life; one of the first was the *Alameda County Study*, conducted in the United States of American, which was designed to investigate normal daily routines and social-support factors to determine which might be *risk factors* for poor health and mortality in a real community. It started in 1965, but had follow-up studies over the subsequent 30 years (Breslow & Breslow, 1993). In the first wave, risk factors included drinking excessive amounts of alcohol, smoking cigarettes, being obese, sleeping fewer or more than seven to eight hours per night, being physically inactive, eating between meals, and not eating breakfast (Idler & Benyamni, 1997).

Taking into consideration research on healthy lifestyles since, and those proposed by Fries et al. (2011; see also Table 18.1), determining factors now include: regular physical activity, no smoking, low alcohol intake, and a healthy diet (Bogers et al., 2006). Moreover, there are other psychological factors, which have an influence too, such as keeping oneself mentally active, being socially engaged, and having positive emotions and stress control (Anderson & Anderson, 2003; Maes & Karoly, 2005). We will now describe these behavioral lifestyles.

## Physical Exercise

Physical activity has shown not only a positive impact on physical functioning and physical health but also on mental health, and cognitive and social functioning (Chodzko-Zajko et al., 2009). Some of the well-known positive effects include chronic disease prevention (Harmell et al., 2014), better recovery treatment for many diseases, including arthritis and type 2 diabetes (Vincent et al., 2012), improvements in cellular and immune systems functioning (Simpson et al., 2012), and reduction in the likelihood of developing mental health problems (Lavie & Milani, 2011).

Moreover, physically active older adults are likely to live more than those who are sedentary. For example, in a longitudinal study Yates et al. (2008) reported that 72-year-old men, who exercised regularly, had a 30 percent higher probability to being alive at 90 years of age than their sedentary equals. In fact, sedentary people are twice as prone to have a functional limitation and to be socially disconnected (Meisner et al., 2010).

Exercise recommendations for older adults should include aerobic, muscle strengthening, and flexibility exercises (Chodzko-Zajko et al., 2009). For substantial health benefits, the guidelines recommend individuals participate in at least 150 minutes of moderate-intensity aerobic activity, 75 minutes of vigor-ous-intensity aerobic activity, or an equivalent combination of each per week, plus strengthening activities involving all major muscle groups at least 2 days per week (Elsawy & Higgins, 2010).

As mentioned above, physical activity has been related to several positive out-comes beyond that of physical functioning. For example, higher level of physical activity has been related to higher social commitment and higher participation in productive activities (Mendes de Leon et al., 2003). Because physical activity promotes community integration, which in turn helps to improve social partic-ipation that reduces sedentary lifestyle, it also increases the sense of belonging and facilitates participation in voluntary activities (Meisner et al., 2010).

Physical activity has also shown positive effects on cognitive functioning of older people as measured by cognitive ability tasks and neuroimaging tests. Overall the practice of physical activity is positively related to the maintenance of cognitive functioning during the aging process (Geda et al., 2010).

Therefore, keeping oneself physically active contributes to maintaining a good condition in older age, as reflected in terms of good health, increased social participation, and positive cognitive functioning, which are all especially relevant contributors for successful aging.

## Healthy Diet

Several biological and psychological changes affect older adults' nutrition; the process of aging is accompanied by metabolic, physiologic, and biochemical changes that affect older adults' nutritional state. For example, the loss of sen-sitivity in the sense of taste and oral-dental problems can affect swallowing and the enjoyment of food. Other nutritional processes, such as digestion, nutri-ent absorption, and metabolic waste elimination also decline as people age. Unfortunately, these biological changers are often accompanied by social iso-lation, limited economic availability, deficits in nutritional information, and/or limited physical mobility. All these factors represent a threat to follow an accu-rate diet (Minuti et al., 2014), which otherwise is necessary to achieve a success-ful aging, alongside keeping an optimal weight. Overall, the two main threats to achieving successful aging are obesity and malnutrition.

In regard to obesity, daily energy intake should allow keeping weight within the normal limits of the body mass index (BMI), which is a measure of body fat based on height and weight (weight in kilograms divided by the square of height in meters). Normal BMI range is between 20 and 25, and scores over 27 are overweight and over 30 indicates obesity. Being obese or overweight is asso-ciated with several negative consequences on aging: it predicts cognitive demen-tia in old age (Gardener et al., 2012), and other illness such as cardiovascular diseases and diabetes, as well as reducing life expectancy in both qualitatively and quantitatively terms (Peytremann-Bridevaux & Santos-Eggimann, 2008).

At the other end, a score under 20 indicates malnutrition. Several factors such as advanced age, comorbidity, multiple drug consumption, social isolation, economical problems, and mobility impairment are risk factors of this condition. With the aim to maintain a healthy weight and good nutritional parameters, the most recommended diet is Mediterranean, which has been linked to lower instances of coronary diseases and cancer, and increased life expectancy (Renaud et al., 1995; Gardener et al., 2012). Mediterranean diet is characterized by an energy balance that consists of a combination of vegetables, legumes, fruits, nuts, cereals, and olive oil, with a high consumption of fish, a moderate consumption of dairy products, and a low consumption of meat.

The positive effects of a correct diet, such as the Mediterranean one, not only positively impact the maintenance of optimal physical functioning, but also affect the good functioning of cognitive abilities in aging (Joseph et al., 1998; Gardener et al., 2012).

In summary, dietary intake among elderly people has been highlighted as an important modifiable factor contributing to health and well-being (Doets & Kremer, 2016).

## Alcohol and Tobacco Control

Smoking is a habit highly related to several diseases responsible for early death, such as cardiovascular diseases, diseases of the respiratory system, and different types of cancer (Haveman-Nies et al., 2003). Similarly, high alcohol intake is related to the development of more than 200 diseases (WHO, 2015a). While total tobacco cessation is advisable, light alcohol consumption has been recommended in order to prevent coronary diseases and cerebral vascular strokes (Rimm et al., 1999).

Prevalence studies show that the number of smoking declines with age. Traditionally, samples of older adults were composed by former male smokers and never female smokers. However, currently the number of women who smoke is increasing (WHO, 2015b). In the last years, the implementation of public policies aiming at reducing tobacco consumption has proven effective: these include the strict restriction of smoking in public places, high tax increases, banned advertising campaigns, prevention programs, and tobacco cessation programs funded with public money (WHO, 2015b).

In summary, no smoking and moderate alcohol intake are especially recommended habits to reach a successful aging, but it is never too late to adhere to these habits (WHO, 2015a).

## Cognitive Activity

Cognitive functioning preservation has become one of the main contributors to quality of life in aging and a determinant of successful aging (Palmore et al., 1985; Baltes and Baltes, 1990). Moreover, it is a predictor of longevity (Poon et al., 2000) and good health (Palmore et al., 1985; Maier & Smith, 1999).

While all daily life activities require a certain degree of cognition, only highly mentally demanding activities are related to good cognitive functioning as people age. One of the aspects that make activities highly demanding is the time that we have to perform them. Studies have found that processing speed, one of the abilities that firstly declines with age, is at the base of all other mental processes and its training has a positive impact on overall cognitive functioning (Ball et al., 2007).

Empirical evidence supports that the regular practice of cognitive activities is related to cognitive functioning preservation (Fernández-Ballesteros et al., 2012). In fact, the more activities people practice, the better performance they achieve when doing cognitive ability tests. Moreover, in longitudinal studies, those who practice more cognitive activities show a slower pattern of cognitive decline and a delay on the appearance of cognitive impairment symptoms. Therefore, a higher level of cognitive activity practice is related to a lower risk of developing dementia.

Despite the fact that the relationship between cognitive activities and cognitive functioning is still under study, and that the nature of the relationship between activity and functioning remains unspecified, being cognitively active is a must for successful aging (WHO, 2015a).

## Affect, Control, and Coping with Stress

Emotions, which are adaptive responses, not only interact with but also influence the rest of the individual quotidian spheres such as the health, behavior, cognition, and social areas. Emotions are essential for motivation and action readiness. The process of aging inherently involves several physical and social changes that can be appraised as stressful by some individuals; for example, as we age, we must cope with different situations that are potentially problematic; some of them refer to social role changes, chronic diseases, onset and the process of disabilities, death of loved ones, and the awareness of our own mortality. However, across the life span, experience seems to improve emotional functioning, and older people generally experience more complex and heterogeneous emotions, have positive emotional balance, and better emotional self-regulation, and better adaptive capacity. People often feel stress when they appraise a situation as a threat, feel they do not have enough resources to cope with it, and/or cannot control it.

Stress has a direct negative relationship with health; a person suffering from stress is more likely to develop certain diseases or to accelerate the negative consequences of chronic ones. Stress also has a negative indirect relationship with health since people suffering from stress may initiate or accentuate negative health behaviors as a way of coping with stress.

Coping strategies can be regarded as individual resources that act on the individual's biological system in order to initiate self-regulation processes to adapt to or "cope" with conflictive situations. Coping taxonomies tend to distinguish active versus coping dimensions. Active coping strategies are usually described as adaptive strategies that "face the stressor directly," while passive coping strategies consist of avoidance behaviors and are usually considered "maladaptive" strategies (e.g., Lazarus & Folkman, 1984). However, coping is dependent, to a great extent, on the appraisal of the event that is particular to each person. Thus, those situations in which a person lacks internal control may prefer passive strategies to active ones.

Regarding aging, this natural process is not assessed as a particular situation or something to be solved, instead, it is regarded as a natural happening that should be accepted and integrated into the lifespan development, favoring, therefore, the adoption of passive strategies.

Adaptive coping ways are learned throughout one's life. If we understand aging as an adaptation process, learning and adopting adaptive coping methods are likely to help in successful aging.

## Social Engagement

Particular attention has been paid to the evolution of social relationships over the life span and their effect on the process of aging. Different authors have proposed that social relationships affect the way in which one ages and vice versa (Charles & Carstensen, 2010).

Usually, the social functioning of any individual remains stable as a person grows older, however, as time passes, a reduction in his or her social network is expected, due to the decease of family members and friends.

Previous research indicates that both the quantity and the quality of social relationships of the elderly affect the prevention of cognitive impairment (Charles & Carstensen, 2010). Moreover, Blanchard-Fields et al. (2008) have indicated that the satisfaction obtained from social relationships is a key factor in the prevention (and maintenance) of cognitive functioning. Finally, the quality and quantity of social relationships has also been related to better physical and mental health, as well as less mortality (Ryff & Singer, 2001).

## Promoting Healthy Behavior and Lifestyles

Although successful aging is the end result of a live lived in a healthy manner, it is never too late to incorporate healthy life habits that may benefit one's health and functioning (Fernández-Ballesteros, 2008; WHO, 2015a).

Research supports the great plasticity we still conserve at the final stages of our life, and how we can still benefit from adhering to healthy lifestyles, even at the end of life, in terms of improving our health and functioning (WHO, 2015a). There are several variables to take into account in order to promote these behaviors and its maintenance across time. On the one hand, there are comprehensive theoretical models that provide a full explanation of behavioral change and adherence to healthy lifestyles. On the other hand, the effect of individual variables, such as personality and intelligence (or cognitive functioning), on health and healthy lifestyle selection has been broadly studied. Both aspects are reviewed in the following sections.

## Models of Behavioral Change

Several models of health behavior have proposed that *purpose* is the most proximal cause of behavior, i.e., the cognitive antecedent of an act that marks the effort and persistence one will put in order to achieve a desired outcome (Triandis, 1980; Webb & Sheeran, 2006). *Purpose* can be the result of deliberate cognitive processes (e.g., Ajzen, 1991) or just the product of superficial processes (Wood et al., 2002).

These models, which are summarized in the next section, are important since they provide guidelines to develop efficient programs to modify health-related behaviors, which are of special interest given the strong relationship between behavioral risk factors and chronic diseases such as cardiovascular disease, diabetes, and certain types of cancer (World Health Organization, 2008).

### *Theory of Planned Behavior*

The Theory of Planned Behavior (TPB), which is an extension of the Theory of Reasoned Action (TRA), is concerned with motivational factors as determinants of the likelihood of performing a specific behavior (Figure 18.1). The Theory of Planned Behavior assumes that the best predictor of a behavior is the intent to engage in such behavior, which in turn is preceded by the attitude held toward the behavior and social normative behaviors. Moreover, TPB extends TRA by including the concept of perceived behavioral control, i.e., TRA was proposed to explain volitional behaviors or behaviors in which the individual enjoys a great degree of control; however, this is not always the case, and although intent is the main predictor of behaviors, perceived behavioral control is an additional direct determinant that can also moderate the relationship between intent and behavior (Webb & Sheeran, 2006).

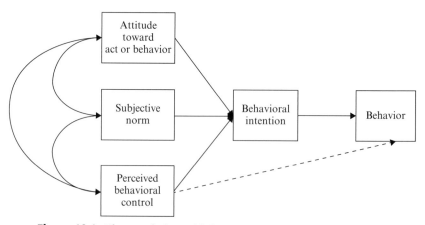

**Figure 18.1.** *Theory of planned behavior*
*Source:* Ajzen (1991)

## Model of Interpersonal Behavior

Similar to the previous model, purpose or intent is regarded as a key predictor of behavior. However, as an important moderator, the Model of Interpersonal Behavior (MIP) also considers the extent to which the behavior is habitual, i.e., intent loses its strength at predicting behavior when such behavior is frequently performed. Behaviors that have been frequently repeated in stable contexts are named habits and they only need sporadic thought to be elicited (Wood et al., 2002).

Therefore, the MIP proposes that the likelihood of performing a behavior is a function of the habit of performing the behavior, the intent, and the facilitating or harmful conditions.

## Protection Motivation Theory

Rogers (1985) explicitly acknowledged the role of emotions in his model of health behavior. The protection motivation theory proposes that individuals obtain information regarding health behaviors from environmental (e.g., verbal persuasion) and intrapersonal (e.g., previous experiences) sources. Then they engage in two different types of appraisal to determine the protection motivation (i.e., intent to perform the health behavior); threat appraisal refers to the assessment of the perceived threat (i.e., severity, susceptibility, and fear), while coping appraisal refers to the response effectiveness and self-efficacy to engage in the recommended behavior.

## Theories of Goal Striving and Self-Regulation

According to Control Theory (Carver & Scheier, 2001), self-regulation is an ongoing process of comparing current performance against the desired standard

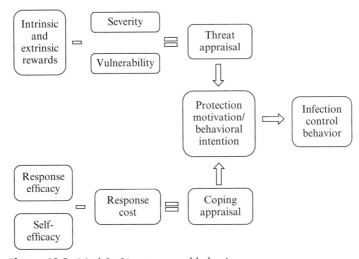

**Figure 18.2.** *Model of interpersonal behavior*

and adjusting behavior accordingly. Standards of comparison stem from the hierarchical structure of the individual's goals, at the top of the hierarchy are the self-related goals, in the middle are the abstract action goals, and at the bottom are the courses of action. Common to any behavior is the previous establishment of an intent or reference value (Carver Charles & Scheier, 1998).

Lastly, the Model of Action Phases (MAP) (Heckhausen & Gollwitzer, 1987) provides a temporal analysis of the phases of goal pursuit; previous to the development of a goal intent, which would lead to the starting point for subsequent goal striving, MAP proposes an action phase called predecisional. In this phase, the person deliberates about the feasibility and desirability of the many wishes and desires he or she may pursue.

### Empirical Support

Several meta-analyses (Sheppard et al., 1988; Randall & Wolff, 1994; Sheeran, 2002) have integrated results from studies that focused on the impact of changing participant's intent on subsequent behavior change.

These studies conclude that goals or intents have strong associations with behavior, even when reporting an effect size of 1.47 for meta-analysis based on correlational studies (see Sheeran, 2002) and a relatively lower effect size for meta-analysis, based on experimental studies ("a medium-to-large change in intent or purpose [d = 0.66] engenders a small-to-medium change in behavior [d = 0.36]") (Webb & Sheeran, 2006, p. 260). Importantly (Webb & Sheeran, 2006), report evidence shows that when the behavior is assessed objectively (i.e., third person), the subsequent change in behavior is sustained in time and the effect size in even increments to medium-to-large. However, generalization of these results to older population needs to be taken with caution; the ability to form and implement intent is likely to be hampered by the natural decrease in the executive functioning of the older population (French et al., 2014). Consequently, it is important to pay specific attention to research that has focused on both older population and specific health behavior. Since a specific review is beyond the scope of this chapter, we will focus on a specific health behavior that is regarded as essential for successful aging: physical activity.

### Promoting Physical Activity: An Example of Behavioral Change in Older People

As noted before, physical inactivity ranks among the fourth highest risk factor for mortality (WHO, 2011), and despite efforts made, as people get older the tendency is to reduce physical activity (Hallal et al., 2012).

Different approaches have been tested in order to understand what increases the engagement in physical activity among the older population. Adopting a qualitative approach, Devereux-Fitzgerald and colleagues (Devereux-Fitzgerald et al., 2016) reported in a meta-synthesis conducted in non-clinical samples that *awareness of benefits* (psychosocial or physical) and *feeling of enjoyment* are the key factors for the acceptability of physical activity. In particular, it appears that programs running within a community tailored to this population, and providing a sense of meaningful benefits, including the formation of new social contacts, facilitate engagement in exercise in later life.

Studies using quantitative methodology tend to test health behavior models (see above). In their meta-analysis of the theories of reasoning actions and its relationship to exercise, Hagger et al. (2002) found that age is a moderator factor in such a way that older people samples were more likely to perceive their intents than younger samples. This is probably due to the instability of purposes among younger samples and their relative inexperience with the target behavior. These intents have been, in turn, found to precede participants' attitudes toward behavior and to a less extent, their perceived behavioral control and self-efficacy (Hagger et al., 2002). This is according to Conn and collaborators (Conn et al., 2003). In a study with a sample ($N = 225$) of women aged 65 and older, Conn et al. reported that significant predictors of exercise behavior were from perceived control beliefs and behavioral beliefs. In the same line, Brenes et al. (1998), in a study with an older adult sample (53 to 84 years) participating in an exercise program, reported that among the different determinants to be engaged in, behavioral control in physical activity was perceived as the most significant and unique predictor of intent to exercise and the proper engagement in exercise behavior during a 1 month period. A practical issue, however, is to evaluate the effect in time of interventions in this segment of the population.

Regarding the setting interventions provided, Conn et al. (2011) performed a meta-analysis: behavioral interventions (versus cognitive interventions), administered directly to individuals (versus community interventions), and face-to-face interventions (versus mediated interventions) were the most effective ones. Conn et al. (2011) reported an effect size of 0.19 in the short- to mid-term.

Addressing long-term effectiveness of interventions aimed at promoting physical activity in adults aged 55 to 70 years, Hobbs et al. (2013) suggested that tailoring interventions are more effective in increasing physical activity level (versus generic interventions), although the mode of delivery is not necessary important for the effectiveness. Likewise, Hobbs et al. (2013) reported that low frequency of interventions (<11) had more lasting effects than those based on high frequency (≥11) contact.

Interestingly, Hobbs et al. (2013) also found that multi-modal intervention in conjunction with behavioral-cognitive technique was the most adequate for increasing short-term engagement in physical activity among those at risk of chronic behavioral control, and that it was the most significant and unique predictor of intent to exercise and the proper engagement in exercise behavior conditions. It appears that for this subtype of the old population, it is important to design interventions short in duration, with exercises that can be completed at home (Clegg et al., 2011).

In sum: (1) awareness of benefits (psychosocial or physical) and feeling of enjoyment seem to be the most important motivational factors for physical exercise adherence, while behavioral control is the most significant and unique predictor of intent to exercise and the proper engagement in exercise behavior; (2) older people samples were more likely to perceive their intents than younger samples; and (3) tailoring and face-to-face interventions seem to increase physically active participation.

## Personality and Health Behavioral Change

The probability of being involved in any new action requires individual decisions; along the history of behavioral change, a question has emerged: could personality be involved in the adherence to treatment? Taken into consideration, the Big Five Model by Costa and McCrae (1988) proposes that *conscientiousness* is the most relevant factor for behavioral change. Conscientiousness describes individuals with a propensity for impulse control, who facilitate task- and goal-directed behavior, and who tend to stay healthier and live longer as a result. In fact, the effect of conscientiousness is equal to or greater than that of many known biomedical risk factors (Friedman & Kern, 2014). Overall, recent meta-analysis indicates that conscientiousness is a strong predictor of longevity (Friedman et al., 1993), lower mortality risk (Kern & Friedman, 2008), reduced disease development (Chapman et al., 2007), and better coping (Connor-Smith & Flachsbart, 2007), while low conscientiousness has been linked to Alzheimer's disease and related cognitive problems (Wilson et al., 2007).

To understand the powerful effects of conscientiousness on health-related outcomes we may rely on different perspectives; first, as Clark and Watson (1999) have put forward, healthy behaviors tend to be associated with constraint, which in turn is the opposite to disinhibition. That is, while disinhibited individuals tend to be impulsive, somewhat reckless and with a tendency for searching immediate rewards, constrained individuals (e.g., high conscientiousness) plan carefully, avoid risk-taking behavior, and are more aware of the longer-term consequences of their behavior (Clark & Watson, 1999). In other words, individuals low in conscientiousness (i.e., low in constraint/high in disinhibition) are more likely to engage in unhealthy behaviors characterized by both immediate gratifying effects and disregard for future consequences. Second, the problem-behavior theory (Donovan et al., 1991) considers health-related behaviors to explain the interaction of three systems, namely the personality system, the perceived environment system, and the behavior system. Related to all systems is the dimension of conventionality-unconventionality, i.e., "an orientation toward, commitment to, and involvement in ... established institutions" (Donovan et al., 1991, p. 52). As the reader may notice, this definition taps into several aspects of conscientiousness (e.g., upholding social norms and traditions, avoiding trouble). Research indicates that "highly conventionality" is positively related to healthy behaviors such as exercising regularly or eating healthier food (Donovan et al., 1991). These two theoretical perspectives help to understand why conscientiousness often interacts with unhealthy stressors (e.g., emotional challenges) and other unhealthy personality traits (e.g., neuroticism) in such a way that it reduces their detrimental effects. Likewise, highly conscientious individuals are likely to reduce health-related risk with their daily decisions (Friedman & Kern, 2014). Finally, conscientiousness is related to occupational success in such a way that highly conscientious individuals are more likely to have better education, more successful and meaningful careers, and enjoy higher incomes, which are all factors related to better health, well-being, and a longer life prospect (Hampson et al., 2007).

Finally, it is important to mention that the role of conscientiousness in the engagement of healthy behaviors also impacts adherence, not only by following medical orders, keeping recommended weight, and engaging in exercise (i.e., wellness maintenance) (see Booth-Kewley & Vickers, 1994; Edmonds et al., 2009), but also by taking a high degree of self-care in specific diseases such as renal disease, cholesterol, and diabetes (see Hill & Roberts, 2011). Interestingly, Bogg and Roberts (2004) meta-analysis suggested that the relationship between conscientiousness and health might differ across life span; as such, mid-late adulthood is characterized by the presence of new health issues triggered by the aging process (e.g., slower metabolism). Therefore mid-late adulthood individuals who are high on conscientiousness may benefit from this personality trait since they are likely to strive for maintaining a good health status. Keeping a good health status also involves listening and following doctors' advice (e.g., changes in lifestyle, medication adherence). In particular, Hill and Roberts (2011) found that medication adherence only holds for adults over 51 years of age, which indicates otherwise – that the age in which following one's medication regime becomes greatly consequential (Shanahan et al., 2014).

## Health Literacy and Successful Aging

As it is very well known, education is a relevant determinant for health and aging. The field of *health literacy* has gained considerable importance across the world in recent years, given the growing demand derived from the life expectancy increase, the complexity of healthcare, and its relationship with health promotion (WHO, 2013). Health literacy is a broad and complex concept. The definition of health literacy emphasizes two elements of the term: (1) the skills required to access and use the healthcare system, and (2) the ability to change lifestyles or living conditions in response to this information (WHO, 2013). Therefore, "health literacy" is dependent upon not only basic literacy skills but also the ability of self-efficacy to enhance and maintain behavior changes (WHO, 2013).

The term of health literacy has emerged from two different angles: as a clinical risk factor and as health protective factor. From the medical perspective, attention is focused on reducing the impact of illness, what has been called *medical literacy*. From a broader approach, the study of health literacy concept emphasizes the importance of educational research into literacy, models of adult learning, and health promotion (Nutbeam, 2009; Peerson & Saunders, 2009).

The European Health Literacy Survey collected data from 1000 people in eight European countries: Austria, Bulgaria, Germany, Greece, Ireland, the

Netherlands, Poland, and Spain (World Health Organization, 2013). From the whole sample, more than 60 percent of 75-year-old and older had limited (inadequate or problematic) health literacy. Austria, Bulgaria, Greece, and Spain had more prevalence (over 70 percent), while the Netherlands had the least (29 percent). Prevalence of low health literacy in older adults from United States is similar to these results: 70 percent of adults aged over 65 years showed low health literacy (Kutner et al., 2006).

Low health literacy has appeared as the strongest predictor of an individual's health status, even after adjusting for age, income and educational level, baseline health, cognitive functioning, and health behaviors (Kellerman, 1999; Marcus, 2006; Bostok and Steptoe, 2012). Low health literacy in old age appears as a risk factor for several health outcomes, such as health problems and health status, disease prevalence and incidence (Berkman et al., 2011), adherence (Chew et al., 2004), hospitalization (Baker et al., 2002), diseases control and medication management (Schillinger et al., 2002), participating in screening and prevention programs (Kobayashi et al., 2013), and mortality (Bostok & Steptoe, 2012).

Better health literacy can help improve individual health and successful aging (Peerson & Saunders, 2009). Thus, researchers and policy makers must put their attention on developing strategies to improve health literacy as a policy to close the gap in regards to health management inequalities stemming from the lack of literacy skills and consequently promoting successful aging.

In particular, the European Commission's policy area on Lifelong Learning in Making a European Area of Lifelong Learning a Reality pointed out health literacy as one of the most economically relevant basic literacies (European Commission, 2001). Here, older people are considered a target population for the need of strengthening health literacy in Europe; since this must be done within a broader approach strategy, it must take into account lifelong learning and understand the complex process of aging. Moreover, the WHO's Active Ageing Initiative proposed improved health literacy as a tool to promote active aging throughout Europe.

To enhance health literacy and reduce older adults' health literacy inequalities, several aspects have been highlighted. First, the need to improve people's health literacy requires enhanced consciousness of the need to be as literate as possible to age well (Kickbusch, 2001, 2008). Moreover, health literacy has been related to general cognition skills (Berkman et al., 2011), which have several implications. On the one hand, keeping a high cognitive functioning is associated with a delay of the health literacy decline among old people (Kobayashi et al., 2013, 2015). On the other hand, general cognitive ability, which tends to be a long-term stable characteristic, has direct implications in health literacy interventions (Mõttus et al., 2014). Interventions to increase skills of managing one's general health may be suboptimal when a wider range of cognitive skills is implicated. That is why efforts to tackle the low literacy *per se* seem to not be ideal, while intensive interventions with the aim to manage a specific health-related problem produce more efficient results (Berkman et al., 2011).

In regards to healthy behaviors, Taggart et al. (2012) made a systematic review of treatments to improve health literacy and promote positive change in lifestyle behaviors for smoking, nutrition, alcohol, physical activity, and/or weight. The interventions consisted of individual motivational interviewing and counseling, group education, written materials, telephone coaching or counseling, or a combination of the interventions. All of them appeared to be effective in improving health literacy and reducing risk behaviors at some point. Moreover, the likelihood of interventions being effective did not appear to be related to the intensity (i.e., extension, cost, and clinicians commitment) of the intervention. Therefore, low cost intervention to improve health literacy can produce a high benefit.

Finally, the increasing development of e-health and the rapidity with which the Internet has become the main source in providing health information, contribute to the inequality of older adults' health literacy. Hence, the importance of how controlling Internet use affects health literacy has become relevant.

More research is needed into the role of individuals' motivation for health literacy, as well as involvement in the educational system and health promotion initiatives. Furthermore, the complex way in which health literacy is related to diagnoses of health conditions, physical and cognitive functioning, and experiences with the healthcare system remain short of studies, including research on its overall potential influences on successful lifestyle behaviors.

## Conclusions

This chapter highlights the importance of individual behaviors in order to achieve successful aging. Two key points are considered: (1) the healthy lifestyles that contribute to achieved successful aging and (2) the models of behavioral change and other relevant variables that contribute to the adherence to these healthy behaviors and avoidance of behavioral risk.

Several studies have reported the key behaviors that preserve and promote good health and functioning in all life areas (physical, cognitive, social, and emotional). However, more research is needed in order to maximize the benefits of these behaviors, i.e., what are the characteristics that make the best of these behaviors?

Regarding the promotion of successful lifestyles, there are still several questions to be answered. Despite the fact that there are several models of behavioral change that allow us to explain how people adhere to healthy behavioral plans, there is still a lot of withdrawal, and it is difficult to make people follow these programs across time. More research is needed in order to achieve better adherence to healthy lifestyles.

The rapid dissemination of technological innovation might be a new opportunity to study the impact of healthy behaviors and promote people to age well. Smartphone technology allows us to face both problems related with successful aging: defining better the specific beneficial behaviors for living better and increased adherence to them. On the one hand, these devices let us collect a great amount of data and a wide range of measures, with a high level of detail and sensitive metric, which highly improve research opportunities about how to reach successful ageing. On the other hand, smartphone technology might play an important role in helping older adults handle challenges in their daily lives and improve task completion. It seems that improved positive attitude toward aging motivates the elderly to utilize smartphones to compensate for aging-related deficits in daily life (Sun et al., 2016).

Research on the impact of smartphone technology on different aspects of successful aging is in its early stage. However, growing empirical research supports its positive effects on different components of successful aging such as the management of chronic conditions, the maintenance of physical and cognitive health, and social engagement (Sun et al., 2016). Thus, an iterative, user-centered design approach would make this technology acceptable among older adults. Nevertheless, exceptional caution is required in order to design and implement these programs, especially with maintaining privacy and confidentiality.

As we emphasized, the process for successful aging is a long journey that we should adopt at the earliest possible time in our life. To walk along this journey requires sacrifices, as the road might be paved with plenty of barriers and impediments. Likewise, gratification is postponed and long-term companions might not be attracted to the final reward, which is the enjoyment of a full and successful life in all possible aspects. Importantly, it is necessary to remind the reader that it is never too late to take this walk and to enjoy the journey.

## References

Ajzen, I. (1991). The theory of planned behavior. *Organizational Behavior and Human Decision Processes*, 50(2), 179–211.

Anderson, N. B., Anderson, P. E. (2003). *Emotional Longevity: What Really Determines How Long You Live*. New York: Viking Press.

Antonucci, T.C., et al. (2012). The Right to Move: A Multidisciplinary Lifespan Conceptual Framework. In Fernández-Ballesteros, R. Robine, J.M., Walker, A. & Kalache, A. (Eds.), *Active Aging. A Global Goal*. Current Gerontology and Geriatric Research, Special Issue.

Baker, D. W., Gazmararian, J. A., Williams, M. V., et al. (2002). Functional health literacy and the risk of hospital admission among Medicare managed care enrollees. *American Journal of Public Health*, 92(8), 1278–83.

Ball, K., Edwards, J. D., Ross, L. A. (2007). The impact of speed of processing training on cognitive and everyday functions. *The Journals of Gerontology Series B: Psychological Sciences and Social Sciences*, 62(1), 19–31.

Baltes, P. B., Baltes, M. M. (1990). Psychological perspectives on successful aging: The model of selective optimization with compensation. In P. B. Baltes &

M. M. Baltes (Eds.), *Successful Aging: Perspectives from the Behavioral Sciences* (pp. 1–34). New York: Cambridge University Press.

Berkman, N. D., Sheridan, S. L., Donahue, K. E., et al. (2011). *Health literacy interventions and outcomes: An update of the literacy and health outcomes systematic review of the literature (Evidence Report/Technology Assessment, Number 199*. Prepared by RTI International-University of North Carolina Evidence-based Practice Center under Contract No. 290–2007-10056-I. AHRQ Publication Number 11-E006). Rockville, MD: Agency for Healthcare Research and Quality.

Blanchard-Fields, F., Horhota, M., Mienaltowski, A. (2008). Social context and cognition. In S. M. Hofer & D. F. Alwin (Eds.), *Handbook of Cognitive Aging: Interdisciplinary Perspectives* (pp. 614–28). Thousand Oaks, CA: SAGE.

Bogers, R. P., Tijhuis, M. A. R., Van Gelder, B. M., et al. (2006). *Final report of the HALE (Healthy Ageing: a Longitudinal study in Europe) project*. Bilthoven, NL: Centre for Prevention and Health Services Research.

Bogg, T., Roberts, B. W. (2004). Conscientiousness and health-related behaviors: a meta-analysis of the leading behavioral contributors to mortality. *Psychological Bulletin*, 130(6), 887.

Booth-Kewley, S., Vickers, R. R. (1994). Associations between major domains of personality and health behavior. *Journal of Personality*, 62(3), 281–98.

Bostock, S., Steptoe, A. (2012). Association between low functional health literacy and mortality in older adults: Longitudinal cohort study. *British Medical Journal*, 344, e1602.

Brenes, G. A., Strube, M. J., Storandt, M. (1998). An application of the theory of planned behavior to exercise among older adults. *Journal of Applied Social Psychology*, 28(24), 2274–90.

Breslow, L., Breslow, N. (1993). Health practices and disability: Some evidence from Alameda County. *Preventive Medicine*. 22, 86–95.

Carver, C. S., Scheier, M. F. (1998). *On the Self-regulation of Behavior*. Cambridge: Cambridge University Press.

(2001). *On the Self-regulation of Behavior*. Cambridge University Press.

Charles, S. T., Carstensen, L. L. (2010). Social and emotional aging. *Annual Review of Psychology*, 61, 383–409.

Chapman, B. P., Duberstein, P. R., Lyness, J. M. (2007). The distressed personality type: replicability and general health associations. *European Journal of Personality*, 21(7), 911–29.

Chew, L. D., Bradley, K. A., Flum, D. R., et al. (2004). The impact of low health literacy on surgical practice. *The American Journal of Surgery*, 188(3), 250–3.

Chodzko-Zajko, W., Schwingel, A., Park, C. H. (2009). Successful aging: the role of physical activity. *American Journal of Lifestyle Medicine*, 3(1), 20–8.

Clark, L. A., Watson, D. (1999). Temperament: a new paradigm for trait psychology. In L. Pervin & O. John (Eds.), *Handbook of Personality: Theory and Research* (2nd ed., pp. 399–423). New York: Guilford Press.

Clegg, A. P., Barber, S. E., Young, J.B., et al. (2011). Do home-based exercise interventions improve outcomes for frail older people? Findings from a systematic review. *Reviews in Clinical Gerontology*, 22(01), 68–78.

Conn, V. S., Tripp Reimer, T., Maas, M. L. (2003). Older women and exercise: Theory of planned behavior beliefs. *Public Health Nursing*, 20(2), 153–63.

Conn, V. S., Hafdahl, A. R., Mehr, D. R. (2011). Interventions to increase physical activity among healthy adults: meta-analysis of outcomes. *American Journal of Public Health*, 101(4), 751–8.

Connor-Smith, J. K., Flachsbart, C. (2007). Relations between personality and coping: a meta-analysis. *Journal of Personality and Social Psychology*, 93(6), 1080.

Costa, P. T., McCrae, R. R. (1988). From catalog to classification: Murray's needs and the five-factor model. *Journal of Personality and Social Psychology*, 55, 258–65.

Devereux-Fitzgerald, A., Powell, R., Dewhurst, A., et al. (2016). The acceptability of physical activity interventions to older adults: A systematic review and meta-synthesis, *Social Science & Medicine*, 158, 14–23.

Doets, E. L., Kremer, S. (2016). The silver sensory experience–A review of senior consumers' food perception, liking and intake. *Food Quality and Preference*, 48, 316–32.

Donovan, J. E., Jessor, R., Costa, F. M. (1991). Adolescent health behavior and conventionality–unconventionality: An extension of problem-behavior therapy. *Health Psychology*, 10(1), 52.

Edmonds, G. W., Bogg, T., Roberts, B. W. (2009). Are personality and behavioral measures of impulse control convergent or distinct predictors of health behaviors?. *Journal of Research in Personality*, 43(5), 806–14.

Elsawy, B., Higgins, K. E. (2010). Physical activity guidelines for older adults. *American Family Physician*, 81(1), 55–9.

European Commission (EC). (2001). *Making a European Area of Lifelong Learning a Reality*. http://viaa.gov.lv/files/free/48/748/pol_10_com_en.pdf

Fernández-Ballesteros, R. (2008). *Active Aging. The Contribution of Psychology*. Göttingen: Hogrefe.

Fernández-Ballesteros, R., Zamarrón, M. D., López-Bravo, M. D., et al. (2010). Envejecimiento con éxito: criterios y predictores. *Psicothema*, 22(4), 641–7.

Fernández-Ballesteros, R., Zamarrón, M. D., Molina, M.A., et al. (2012). Cognitive plasticity in normal and pathological aging. *Clinical Intervention on Aging*, 7, 15–25.

Fernández-Ballesteros, R. Robine, J. M., Walker, A. et al. (2013). Current gerontology and geriatric research, Active Aging. *A Global Goal (Special Issue)*.

French, D. P., Olander, E. K., Chisholm, A., et al. (2014). Which behaviour change techniques are most effective at increasing older adults' self-efficacy and physical activity behaviour? A systematic review. *Annals of Behavioral Medicine*, 48(2), 225–34.

Friedman, H. S., Kern, M. L. (2014). Personality, well-being, and health. *Annual Review of Psychology*, 65, 719–42.

Friedman, H. S., Tucker, J. S., Tomlinson-Keasey, C., et al. (1993). Does childhood personality predict longevity? *Journal of Personality and Social Psychology*, 65(1), 176.

Fries, J. F. (1989). *Aging Well*. Grands Rapid: Michigan Addison-Wesley Co.

(2012). The theory and practice of active aging. In Fernández-Ballesteros, R. Robine, J. M., Walker, A., et al. (Eds.), *Current Gerontology and Geriatric Research*, Active Aging. A Global Goal (Special Issue).

Fries, J. F., Bruce, B., Chakravarty, E. (2011). Compression of morbidity 1980–2011: a focused review of paradigms and progress. *Journal of Aging Research*, 2011(3), 1–10.

Gardener, S., Gu, Y., Rainey-Smith, S. R., et al. (2012). Adherence to a mediterranean diet and Alzheimer's disease risk in an Australian population. *Translational Psychiatry*, 2(10), e164.

Geda, Y. E., Roberts, R. O., Knopman, D. S., et al. (2010). Physical exercise, aging, and mild cognitive impairment: a population-based study. *Archives of Neurology*, 67(1), 80–6.

Hagger, M. S., Chatzisarantis, N. L., Biddle, S. J. (2002). A meta-analytic review of the theories of reasoned action and planned behavior in physical activity: Predictive validity and the contribution of additional variables. *Journal of Sport and Exercise Psychology*, 24(1), 3–32.

Hallal, P. C., Andersen, L. B., Bull, F. C., et al. Lancet Physical Activity Series Working Group. (2012). Global physical activity levels: surveillance progress, pitfalls, and prospects. *The Lancet*, 380(9838), 247–57.

Hampson, S. E., Goldberg, L. R., Vogt, T. M., et al. (2007). Mechanisms by which childhood personality traits influence adult health status: Educational attainment and healthy behaviors. *Health Psychology*, *26*, 121–5.

Harmell, A. L., Jeste, D., Depp, C. (2014). Strategies for successful aging: a research update. *Current Psychiatry Reports*, 16(10), 476–11.

Haveman-Nies, A., De Groot, L. C., Van Staveren, W. A. (2003). Dietary quality, lifestyle factors and healthy ageing in Europe: the SENECA study. *Age and Ageing*, 32(4), 427–34.

Heckhausen, H., Gollwitzer, P. M. (1987). Thought contents and cognitive functioning in motivational versus volitional states of mind. *Motivation and Emotion*, 11(2), 101–20.

Hill, P. L., Roberts, B. W. (2011). The role of adherence in the relationship between conscientiousness and perceived health. *Health Psychology*, 30(6), 797.

Hobbs, N., Godfrey, A., Lara, J., et al. (2013). Are behavioral interventions effective in increasing physical activity at 12 to 36 months in adults aged 55 to 70 years? a systematic review and meta-analysis. *BMC Medicine*, 11(1), 75.

Idler, E. L., Benyamni, Y. (1997). Self-rated health and mortality: a review of twenty-seven community studies. *Journal of Health and Social Behavior*, 38(1): 21–37.

Joseph, J. A., Shukitt-Hale, B., Denisova, N. A., et al. (1998). Long-term dietary strawberry, spinach, or vitamin E supplementation retards the onset of age-related neuronal signal-transduction and cognitive behavioral deficits. *The Journal of Neuroscience*, 18(19), 8047–55.

Kellerman, R. (1999). Health literacy: report of the council on scientific affairs. *Journal of the American Medical Association*, 281(6), 552–7.

Kern, M. L., Friedman, H. S. (2008). Do conscientious individuals live longer? A quantitative review. Problem-behavior therapy. *Health Psychology*, 10, 52–61.

Kickbusch, I. S. (2001). Health literacy: addressing the health and education divide. *Health Promotion International*, 16(3), 289–97.
   (2008). Health literacy: an essential skill for the twenty-first century. *Health Education*, 108(2), 101–4.

Kobayashi, L. C., Wardle, J., von Wagner, C. (2013). Limited health literacy is a barrier to colorectal cancer screening in England: evidence from the English Longitudinal Study of Ageing. *Preventive Medicine*, 61, 100–5.

Kobayashi, L. C., Wardle, J., Wolf, M. S., et al. (2015). Cognitive function and health literacy decline in a cohort of aging English adults. *Journal of General Internal Medicine*, 30(7), 958–64.

Kutner, M., Greenberg, E., Jin, Y., et al. (2006). *The Health Literacy of America's Adults: Results from the 2003 National Assessment of Adult Literacy (NCES 2006–483)*. Washington, DC: U.S. Department of Education, National Center For Education Statistics.

Lazarus, R. S., Folkman, S. (1984). *Stress, Appraisal, and Coping*. New York: Springer.

Lavie, C. J., Milani, R. V. (2011). Cardiac rehabilitation and exercise training in secondary coronary heart disease prevention. *Progress in Cardiovascular Diseases*, 53(6), 397–403.

Maes, S., Karoly, P. (2005). Self-regulation assessment and intervention in physical health and illness: A review. *Applied Psychology*, 54(2), 267–99.

Maier, H. Smith, J. (1999). Psychological predictors of mortality in old age. *Journal of Gerontology*, 54, 44–54.

Marcus, E. N. (2006). The silent epidemic – the health effects of illiteracy. *New England Journal of Medicine*, 355(4), 339–41.

Matarazzo, J. D. (1984) Behavioral health. In J.D. Matarazzo et al. (Eds.), *Behavioral Health. A Handbook for Health Enhancement and Disease Prevention*. New York: John Wiley and Sons.

Meisner, B. A., Dogra, S., Logan, A. J., et al. (2010). Do or decline? Comparing the effects of physical inactivity on biopsychosocial components of successful aging. *Journal of Health Psychology*, 15(5), 688–96.

Mendes de Leon, C. F., Glass, T. A., Berkman, L. F. (2003). Social engagement and disability in a community population of older adults the new haven EPESE. *American Journal of Epidemiology*, 157(7), 633–42.

Minuti, A., Patrone, V., Giuberti, G., et al. (2014). Nutrition and ageing. In G. Riva, P. Ajmone-Marsan, & C. Grassi (Eds.), *Active Ageing and Healthy Living: A Human Centered Approach in Research and Innovation as Source of Quality of Life*. IOS Press.

Mõttus, R., Johnson, W., Murray, C., et al. (2014). Towards understanding the links between health literacy and physical health. *Health Psychology*, 33(2), 164.

Nutbeam, D. (2009). The evolving concept of health literacy. *Social Science and Medicine*, 67(12), 2072–8.

Palmore, E., Busse, E. W., Maddox, G. L., et al. (Eds.) (1985). *Normal Aging III*. Durham: Duke University Press.

Peerson, A., Saunders, M. (2009). Health literacy revisited: what do we mean and why does it matter?. *Health Promotion International*, 24(3), 285–96.

Peytremann-Bridevaux, I., Santos-Eggimann, B. (2008). Health correlates of overweight and obesity in adults aged 50 years and over: results from the Survey of Health, Ageing and Retirement in Europe (SHARE). *Swiss Medical Weekly*, 138(17–18), 261–6.

Poon, L. W., Johnson, M. A., Davey, A., et al. (2000). Psycho-social predictors of survival among centenarians. In Martin, P., Rott, C., Hagberg, B., et al. (Eds.), *Autonomy versus Dependence in the Oldest Old*. Serdi, Paris, France, pp. 77–89.

Randall, D. M., Wolff, J. A. (1994). The time interval in the intention-behaviour relationship: Meta-analysis. *British Journal of Social Psychology*, 33(4), 405–18.

Renaud, S., de Lorgeril, M., Delaye, J., et al. (1995). Cretan Mediterranean diet for prevention of coronary heart disease. *The American Journal of Clinical Nutrition*, 61(6), 1360S–67S.

Rimm, E. B., Williams, P., Fosher, K., et al. (1999). Moderate alcohol intake and lower risk of coronary heart disease: meta-analysis of effects on lipids and haemostatic factors. *BMJ*, 319(7224), 1523–8.

Rogers, R. W. (1985). Attitude change and information integration in fear appeals. *Psychological Reports*, 56, 179–82.

Rowe, J. W., Kahn, R. L. (1997). Successful aging. *The Gerontologist*, 37(4), 433–40.

Ryff, C. D., Singer, B. H. (Eds.). (2001). *Emotion, Social Relationships, and Health*. Oxford University Press.

Schillinger, D., Grumbach, K., Piette, J., et al. (2002). Association of health literacy with diabetes outcomes. *JAMA*, 288(4), 475–82.

Shanahan, M. J., Hill, P. L., Roberts, B. W., et al. (2014). Conscientiousness, health, and aging: the life course of personality model. *Developmental Psychology*, 50(5), 1407.

Sheeran, P. (2002). Intention—behavior relations: A conceptual and empirical review. *European Review of Social Psychology*, 12(1), 1–36.

Sheppard, B. H., Hartwick, J., Warshaw, P. R. (1988). The theory of reasoned action: A meta-analysis of past research with recommendations for modifications and future research. *Journal of Consumer Research*, 15(3), 325–43.

Simpson, R. J., Lowder, T. W., Spielmann, G., et al. (2012). Exercise and the aging immune system. *Ageing Research Reviews*, 11(3), 404–20.

Sun, Y., McLaughlin, M. L., Cody, M. J. (2016). *Using the Smartphone to Support Successful Aging: Technology Acceptance with Selective Optimization and Compensation Among Older Adults. In International Conference on Human Aspects of IT for the Aged Population* (pp. 490–500). Springer International Publishing.

Taggart, J., Williams, A., Dennis, S., et al. (2012). A systematic review of interventions in primary care to improve health literacy for chronic disease behavioral risk factors. *BMC Family Practice*, 13(1), 49.

Triandis, H. C. (1980). Theoretical reflections on applied behavioral science. *Journal of Applied Behavioral Science*, 16, 229–30.

Vincent, H. K., Raiser, S. N., Vincent, K. R. (2012). The aging musculoskeletal system and obesity-related considerations with exercise. *Ageing Research Reviews*, 11(3), 361–73.

Webb, T. L., Sheeran, P. (2006). Does changing behavioral intentions engender behavior change? A meta-analysis of the experimental evidence. *Psychological Bulletin*, 132(2), 249–68.

Wilson, R. S., Schneider, J. A., Arnold, S. E., et al. (2007). Conscientiousness and the incidence of Alzheimer disease and mild cognitive impairment. *Archives of General Psychiatry*, 64(10), 1204–12.

Wood, W., Quinn, J. M., Kashy, D. A. (2002). Habits in everyday life: Thought, emotion, and action. *Journal of Personality and Social Psychology*, 83(6), 1281–97.

World Health Organization. (2002). *Active ageing. A policy framework*. Geneva: World Health Organization.

(2008). *WHO Global Report on Falls Prevention in Older Age*. World Health Organization.

(2011). *Global status report on noncommunicable diseases 2010*. Geneva: World Health Organization.

(2013). *Health Literacy. The Solid Facts*. Denmark: World Health Organization.

(2015a). *World Report on Ageing and Health*. Geneva: World Health Organization.

(2015b). *WHO Global Report on Trends in Prevalence of Tobacco Smoking 2015*. World Health Organization.

# 19 Effects of Environmental Enrichment and Training across Life Span in Cognition

María Dolores Calero

## Introduction

As people age, a slow but progressive natural decline in certain cognitive skills can be observed. The literature has accepted this phenomenon, referring to it as cognitive aging (Deary et al., 2009), and research has sought to determine its limits – the degree of decline and the variables that can positively or negatively affect this loss (Wischenka et al., 2016).

The traditional view of old age as a stage of general decline, with no possibility of improvement, led to a pessimistic attitude toward the elderly and a passive acceptance of this cognitive aging. This attitude has long been upheld. However, starting in the 1970s, a number of research studies led by Baltes began to break away from a negative aging perspective. To begin, Baltes and Willis launched ADEPT: The *Adult Developmental and Enrichment Project* at Pennsylvania State University. Later, beginning in 1987, the Baltes team intervened in *The Berlin Aging Study* at the *Berlin-Brandenburg Academy of Sciences*. Based on these early publications, aging is perceived as a stage of individualized development, determined by multiple variables (biological, physical, social, and personal), with different phases of losses and gains. Furthermore, these researchers demonstrated the possibility of cognitive improvement in healthy old people; they developed the concept of cognitive plasticity, and established cognitive differences between healthy old people and pathological aging.

In later decades, different groups have continued to investigate these topics, confirming the effectiveness of certain types of training for maintaining the cognitive status of older people, the variables that are involved in optimal aging, and the limits and physiological correlates of cognitive plasticity. In recent years, topics such as transfer of training and factors that determine active aging have been incorporated into the agenda.

The past 40 years have brought an important change in the view of aging: it is now understood and accepted that old people are the managers of their own physical and mental health, although some require the aid of social and healthcare agents in order to maintain their autonomy. The environment, fundamentally the social environment, is considered an important variable in promoting active aging, because it influences cognitive maintenance in older people in very diverse ways. The post-retirement years are conceived as productive, with collaborations that can be enriching for the elderly themselves and for the society they live in. This view is promoted in Europe as a method to cope with demographic aging in developed countries. There is both a social interest, to prolong independent functioning and defer the costs of elder care; and an individual interest, to improve quality of life in old age. Along with this comes increased priority given to research that evaluates the effects of any procedures that may promote autonomous, active, and effective maintenance in older people.

The time has come for a detailed analysis that helps us better understand the meaning of environmental enrichment, the effects it produces, and how it can be encouraged. This analysis is needed both for normal aging and for pathological aging, since the clinical/pathological data suggest that differences between the two states are mainly quantitative. Consequently, this review will not differentiate between normal aging and/or situations of cognitive impairment; put differently, age-related cognitive evolution will be considered a continuum that extends from normal aging to cognitive impairment to dementia. As in the case of other authors (Hertzog et al., 2009), this approach allows us to address, in a single chapter, studies carried out with old people who suffer impairment and/or dementia, and old people who have normal and/or optimal aging. The following pages will examine the findings from the past four decades of research.

## Theoretical Bases

Before going further into research studies that describe the effects of environmental enrichment in older people, we must first try to define and delimit the different theoretical and methodological concepts that are foundational to this topic. The first concept needing definition is *environmental enrichment.*

## Environmental Enrichment

According to Baroncelli et al. (2010), even though most human beings experience a high degree of environmental complexity and novelty, levels of cognitive, social, and physical stimulation vary greatly among individuals and at different periods of life. Out of all these environmental experiences, *environmental enrichment* can be defined as those physical, sensory, affective, and/or cognitive experiences that take place throughout one's lifetime and contribute to optimizing a person's physical, cognitive, and/or emotional repertories. For a human being, the environment under consideration is eminently social, affective, and cognitive, and this environment becomes an enriching experience when it exceeds the limits of what is strictly needed for a person to carry on with his/her activity. As such, it encourages, or gives rise to, new and enriching skills, behaviors, sensations, or feelings. In short, environmental enrichment describes a situation where the environment stimulates learning. Enrichment takes place in a natural way throughout one's life, where a person acquires cognitive, affective, and experiential equipment that protect against damage or losses due to age or illness (in other words, they form part of their cognitive reserve or plasticity). As we shall see later, a large number of epidemiological studies demonstrate how high levels of physical and/or mental activity are associated with less cognitive impairment and less risk for dementia (Baroncelli et al., 2010). But environmental enrichment can also take place at a specific time, in a premeditated or voluntary way, as an intervention to change a person's natural cognitive course at a specific moment in their life. This idea has been accepted as natural for small children, and is called early stimulation, early care, cognitive education, etc.; it has also been used for some time with older people, through the application and assessment of different training programs. Environmental enrichment thus constitutes a procedure that directly affects skill maintenance, as though it were a kind of continuous refresher course.

At any rate, this is a construct in which multiple variables – physiological, physical, and cognitive – have a bidirectional influence, so it must be considered within a broader context rather than the purely cognitive (Hertzog et al., 2009). Some of these variables are part of the individual's attempt to adopt a healthier lifestyle, while others may belong to the behavioral repertoire or to the environment, without any cognition-related intention (e.g., pursuing hobbies or family relationships). All of these are associated with changes in the brain (i.e., functional, anatomical, or chemical), and require simultaneous consideration of plasticity at the different social, behavioral, and neuronal levels of analysis (Baltes et al., 2006; Lindenberger et al., 2006; Fernández-Ballesteros et al., 2007).

To accept the possibility of environmental enrichment means accepting that individuals' neurobiological state is influenced by their social context and by their personal behavior, and vice versa (Cacioppo, 2002; Li & Lindenberger, 2002; Baltes et al., 2006; Hertzog et al., 2009). Different findings encourage us to look at brain-behavior relations as dynamic and reciprocal (Lindenberger et al., 2006), and along these lines, one can analyze the effects of an enriched environment on older people (Brown et al., 2003; Jessberger & Gage, 2008).

## Life Span Theory

Other concepts to keep in mind relate to cognitive aging. In this direction, the theory developed by Baltes and his team is essential, and serves as the foundation for later research on the effects of environmental enrichment on older people.

The Adult Developmental and Enrichment Project (ADEPT) is one of the most important research programs on cognitive training in the elderly. Its main objective was to examine the intellectual modifiability of older people through a series of interrelated longitudinal studies, involving a total of 500 participants, who had good health and a high level of education, with a mean age of 70 (Baltes & Willis, 1982). The project tested inter-individual variability in the level and direction of intellectual functioning, its multidimensionality, and its plasticity. The difference between performance and potential was established, and they adopted Cattell and Horn's two-factor model of intelligence (Cattell, 1963; Horn & Cattell, 1966) to explain its development. They also verified that healthy old people significantly benefit from exposure to conditions that enhance performance, whereby they assert that individual plasticity in old age is at least as ample as the decreases that are observed on standard psychometric tests of intellectual functioning in this life stage. The main results from their work have already been reviewed (Calero & Navarro, 2006; Hertzog et al., 2009) and can be summarized as follows: older adults significantly improve their skills after a brief training. This improvement can compensate for age-related impairment, it is maintained for a one- or two-year period, and is also seen in the very old. The effects of training do not alter the factor structure of the skill and they can be cumulative in the elderly person, such that the skill may be maintained with a few sessions from time to time (Schaie & Willis, 1986; Willis & Schaie, 1986; Schaie et al., 1987; Willis & Nesselroade, 1990).

Later on, as part of the Berlin Aging Study (BAS), the Baltes team proposes that aging includes a process of Selective Optimization with Compensation, or SOC (Baltes, 1987). According to this process, people select life domains that are important to them, they optimize any resources and aids that facilitate their success in these domains, compensate for any losses in these domains, and create an environment for being successful in the course of their life. The process of optimization is a process whereby new resources are acquired, new skills are developed, ideas are copied or drawn from the success resources of others, and one's own energy is used to reach personal goals. Through this process, old people develop skills in order to effectively adapt to the requirements of their surroundings; this ensures that, even when they have losses, these are compensated, thus maintaining similar performance to when they were young in those aspects that they habitually practice. Moreover, there is a possibility of intra-individual cognitive modifiability (cognitive plasticity).

## Theory of Disuse

A parallel theory, also foundational to the studies of Baltes and to later researchers, is Denney's Theory of Disuse (Denney, 1982), according to which, performance in certain skills diminishes with age because these skills are not used. This hypothesis offers an alternative explanation to the differential course of certain skills, traditionally explained by Cattell and Horn's two-factor theory (Cattell, 1963; Horn & Cattell, 1966). According to the two-factory theory, there are two types of skills: the genetically determined *fluid skills*, which begin to decline at age 50, and the environmentally related *crystallized skills*, which are maintained throughout one's life span. According to Denney, different skills are not necessarily under the control of different variables, but all of them reflect the influence of biological and environmental factors. For this reason, fluid skills (reasoning, spatial orientation, etc.) would correspond to an individual's unexercised potential. In other words, they are a function of the biological potential and of the standard environmental experience, and if these diminish with age, it is because the individual stops using them regularly, as he or she becomes further removed from formal education. However, optimally exercised (language, knowledge, etc.) crystallized skills will be maintained throughout one's life cycle because they correspond to the individual's optimally (habitually) exercised potential. This implies, according to the author, that whether by training or by compensation, age-related differences in performance in different skills could be reduced (Calero, 2000).

## Cognitive Plasticity

Another important theoretical question that frames the research studies to be discussed has to do with relations between *brain plasticity*, or *brain reserve* (Satz, 1993; Stern, 2002), and *cognitive plasticity*. As Fernández-Ballesteros et al. (2007) explain, the two terms involve different levels of one construct, a neurobiological level (brain reserve) and a behavioral level (cognitive plasticity); the latter can be observed through a methodology involving cognitive training, such as *testing-in-the-limits*, while the former has certain limitations to being measured (Richards & Deary, 2005). According to Jones et al. (2006), cognitive plasticity is a multi-factor concept that reflects an individual's potential to improve their performance after training.

Greenwood and Parasuraman (2010) sustain that successful cognitive aging requires interactions between neuronal plasticity and cognitive plasticity, stimulated by environmental demands, and supported by lifestyle factors (such as exercise and diet) that improve the integrity of the brain. Accordingly, if an adult brain preserves the normal mechanisms of neuronal plasticity and is stimulated by new experiences, including new learning, then it will be able to successfully adapt to age-related cognitive changes. These changes (following Baltes) would be compensatory in many cases and strategic in others; that is to say, these authors consider that changes in processing modes may occur due to experience and new learning – a fact that has been verified in animals and in humans (Rosenzweig & Bennett, 1996; Calero & Navarro, 2006; Brehmer et al., 2014). This confirms therefore, that plasticity is a prerequisite for environmental enrichment to protect against cognitive impairment in old age.

In an attempt to complete this view of cognitive plasticity, Lövden et al. (2010) incorporate a second term, that of *flexibility*. They suggest that plasticity reflects a secondary change in response to a principal change in the system. For example, in brain injury, the brain's capacity to change is not revealed by the damage sustained, but by the brain's reaction of restoration and compensation. Flexibility, then, indicates the ability to optimize performance within the current structural limitations imposed by the brain. Thus, plasticity is related to changes in structure, while flexibility indicates reconfiguration of the existing behavior repertory – without any structural change – by making use of prior neuronal resources (Lövden et al., 2010; Kühn & Lindenberger, 2016). It is therefore synonymous with functional capacity. In one of their most recent publications, Kühn and Lindenberger (2016) indicate that plasticity diminishes from childhood to old age, while flexibility increases from childhood until midlife and then diminishes thereafter. According to these authors, plasticity in old age would allow for maintenance, but not growth.

This differentiation can be very interesting when analyzing the effects obtained by cognitive training in the elderly, if we consider plasticity to be associated with structural changes that would affect cognitive processes and their efficiency, while flexibility would be related to strategy acquisition, i.e., purely functional changes.

## Methodological Bases

### Measuring Plasticity

In order to assess cognitive plasticity, the Baltes group proposed a *testing-in-the-limits* procedure where three parameters are distinguished: performance baseline (i.e., a person's performance without assistance), baseline reserve capacity (i.e., a person's performance in a situation optimized by means of certain systematic training, thereby indicating their plasticity), and development of the reserve capacity (i.e., training to optimize the individual's performance and potential) (Lindenberger & Baltes, 1995). By applying learning potential (LP) assessment to the elderly this procedure has been extended (Fernández-Ballesteros et al., 2007), and its validity and reliability have been verified. With the learning potential methodology, cognitive plasticity is operationalized in terms of the amount of improvement that a person shows after a specific, short-term training, administered between two applications of a standard skills test. This improvement score (pretest-posttest) has demonstrated reliability, with gains maintained for different periods of time (3 months to 2 years) (Willis & Nesselroade, 1990; Stingdotter & Bäckman, 1993; Fernández-Ballesteros & Calero, 1995): (1) construct validity, where gains are generalized to different tests, i.e., there is agreement between gains obtained (Calero, 2004), (2) discriminant validity between healthy old people and old people with Mild Cognitive Impairment (MCI) and with dementia (Fernández-Ballesteros et al., 2003; Calero & Navarro, 2004; Fernández-Ballesteros et al., 2005), (3) predictive validity for gains obtained after long-term training (Calero & Navarro, 2007a,b; Boosman et al., 2014), and (4) for cognitive maintenance or impairment due to the passing of time, over 2-year intervals (Calero & Navarro, 2004).

### Designs Used

Different approaches have been taken with regard to research designs, namely: retrospective ex post facto or simple prospective designs (epidemiological), developmental designs (cross-sectional and longitudinal), and quasi-experimental designs that include training groups.

Cross-sectional studies form the bulk of the initial studies that attempted to compare older people's cognitive skills with those of young people. These studies supplied the foundation for the classic idea of cognitive aging, and were highly criticized for their seriously compromised validity (Schaie, 1978). Beginning in the 1970s, longitudinal studies started to use direct observation of the specific rates of age-related change in cognitive skills in an attempt to overcome the limitations of the prior studies. Even though many studies point out countless sources of error (see Hertzog et al., 2012; Salthouse, 2010a,b), these longitudinal studies have supplied the main source of data for present-day theories of cognitive aging, moreover, Hertzog et al. (2009) focus their review on these studies. Likewise, epidemiological studies on MCI and dementia, many of them either longitudinal or mixed-type, have contributed valuable information in this field.

Another important group of data comes from the studies that include training. These generally quasi-experimental studies may also have certain methodological limitations, due to ethical questions during sample selection, but they provide better help for confirming hypotheses about cognitive change. We must distinguish between two types of intervention studies: (1) studies that focus on measuring cognitive plasticity through an LP procedure, i.e., by including training to verify the existence of cognitive plasticity in the elderly, beginning with ADEPT and continuing to this day, and (2) studies that seek to develop the reserve capacity, as Baltes said, i.e., to apply long-term training aimed at improving a certain skill. In the first group, usually short-term training is included (1 to 6 sessions), specific to the skill being studied: the purpose is to establish whether old people with different characteristics are able to learn, to what degree they can do so, and the stability or transfer of such learning.

This group of studies has served to establish the characteristics and limits of cognitive plasticity, and in this sense, they have fulfilled an important role. Nonetheless, they have received (sometimes unjustified) criticism, because they have not responded to questions that were not related to their initial objectives. For example, the procedure for achieving transfers to untrained tasks and skills or to daily life (Hertzog et al., 2009).

The second group contains studies that evaluate intervention programs applied to old people for maintaining or increasing cognitive skills. This set of longer-term programs incorporates very diverse tasks and designs. These programs were developed based on effects reported in the prior group of studies, and so this line of work appears in the 1990s and continues until 2010. These studies have also been highly criticized, due to the heterogeneity of designs, procedures, criteria, and techniques used to evaluate effects; the results produced are sometimes contradictory, other times negative or inconsistent. From this point forward, almost all the studies carried out are systematic studies or meta-analyses of research performed in the past years.

The meta-analyses are one of the great methodological contributions to this field, because they have synthesized and brought to light the value of the findings obtained with such highly questioned designs as we have just reviewed. This line of work has also had its difficulties and limitations due to the heterogeneity of the studies that they seek to compare, as discussed above. Nonetheless, the conclusions obtained therein have guided research in recent years, leading to a more accurate understanding of the effects of environmental enrichment in the elderly, and especially, the best means for providing enrichment strategies that target cognitive maintenance.

In short, though being aware of the methodological limitations of the different research studies carried out in this field, we shall attempt to review their most important contributions. We focus primarily on longitudinal studies with training, and on meta-analyses, in order to identify the conclusions that consistently appear in the more recent studies that address this topic.

## Lifelong Environmental Enrichment

One of the first longitudinal studies was from Katzman et al. (1989) in Shanghai, with a sample of 5,055 people over the age of 55. In this study, he reveals that low educational level was a main factor in risk for dementia, and an important determinant in prevalence of dementia. He likewise found that, after the age of 75, there was a very marked increase in the prevalence of dementia among illiterate people and people with low educational levels. Very similar results were found in other countries such as Italy (Rocca et al., 1990), France, where no case of dementia was found among persons with university studies (Dartigues et al., 1991), Sweden (Fratiglioni et al., 1991), and Israel (Korczyn et al., 1991).

Later, the *Seattle Longitudinal Study*, initiated in 1956 and led by Schaie, assessed more than 5,000 adults between the ages of 22 and 70 every 7 years, and identified a number of variables that reduce risk for dementia (Schaie, 1994; Schaie et al., 2004):

(1) Absence of chronic diseases. According to the authors, having chronic disease reflects a lifestyle that is unsuitable for maintaining a high level of daily activity.
(2) Living in favorable environments, such as in the case of people with high socioeconomic status. These circumstances include above-average education, a work history involving a high level of complexity and low routine, above-average financial income, and maintenance of family ties.
(3) Carrying on complex activities that involve intellectual stimulation, such as reading, attending cultural events, pursuing educational activities and participating in associations.
(4) Having a flexible personality style.
(5) Being married to a person with a high level of cognitive functioning.
(6) Being satisfied with one's life in old age.

In the *Berlin Aging Study*, which collected data from 516 persons between the ages of 70 and 103, stratified by age and gender and assessed every 6 years (Baltes &

Ulrich-Meyer, 1999), similar results were obtained in these aspects. The authors affirm that persons with medium to high levels of education, and with prestigious and cognitively demanding professions show high cognitive levels at advanced ages, even though their rate of decline at these ages is similar to the others'.

Conclusions similar to those reflected in these early longitudinal studies have been found repeatedly; in general terms, education and a high social level consistently appear as variables that protect against dementia (Katzman et al., 1989; Andel et al., 2006; López & Calero, 2009; Wu et al., 2015). In addition to the importance of educational level, other notable protectors are recreational activities (Fabrigoule et al., 1995) that involve mental stimulation (Hultsch et al., 1999; Menec, 2003) and mentally demanding employment (Bosma et al., 2002).

With regard to social activities, Fratiglioni et al. (2000) indicated three risk factors for developing dementia: (1) living alone and not having friends or family members, (2) the absence of close social ties, and (3) having a very small social network. By contrast, in people with a broad network of social relations characterized by living with another person and having visits and satisfactory daily contact with family members and friends, the incidence of dementia was very low (1.9 percent per year, compared to 15.6 percent per year of persons who met the three risk criteria mentioned above). Other studies confirm these results and incorporate other positive social factors such as participating in different social groups or in productive social activities (e.g., volunteering) (Seeman et al., 2001). However, analyses of social network size have had mixed results (Seeman et al., 2001; Barnes et al., 2004).

Scarmeas et al. (2001) did a seven-year longitudinal study where they monitored an initial sample of 1,772 people over the age of 65 without dementia. The sample was divided into two groups: persons with a high level of activity and persons with a low level of activity. Results showed that persons in the high activity group had 38 percent less risk of developing dementia than did the other group. Specifically, they found that the activities most closely associated with low risk for dementia were social, physical, and intellectual activities, the latter being most important. Another interesting data point from this study was that, for each new activity carried out, the risk of developing dementia was reduced by about 12 percent. In fact, this significant, inverse relationship between risk for dementia and active lifestyle continued to be present even after controlling for variables that might be contaminating the results, such as performance on the initial assessment, the presence of cerebrovascular disease, health limitations, depression, educational level and type of job. These results have been confirmed by later research (Zahodne et al., 2014).

Molina et al. (2011), who studied persons over age 90 that were independent and maintained their cognitive capacity, also sought to analyze the relationship between global level of activity (productive, social, and intellectual) and cognitive functioning. Their results led to the following conclusions: (1) a higher level of productive and recreational activity in very old people, cross-sectionally, is associated with better cognitive functioning; and (2) also cross-sectionally, significant differences are found between groups with high and low cognitive functioning, in their level of productive and intellectual activities; however, no significant differences were found with regard to social or leisure activities. Furthermore, carrying out intellectual activities alone predicts cognitive functioning in the follow-up assessment.

Physical activity has also been related to cognitive maintenance in older people (Gajewski & Falkenstein, 2016). According to different authors, its effects relate to a higher level of neural network activation (Verghese et al., 2003) and/ or to the delay of neurodegenerative processes and therefore a postponement of decline and risk for cardiovascular disease (Laurin et al., 2001; Salthouse, 2009). Geda et al. (2010) found that moderate to intense exercise in middle to advanced age reduced the probability of suffering mild cognitive impairment and, in the same direction, Snyder et al. (2014) indicated that low physical activity stands out as a comorbid condition in elderly people with dementia. Later studies reached similar conclusions (Wischenka et al., 2016).

Several hypotheses have been suggested as possible explanations for the relationship between physical exercise and cognitive health. A systematic review carried out by Fratiglioni et al. (2004) cites three main ideas: (a) the cognitive reserve hypothesis, where physical activity and exercise are assumed to improve brain components, leading to greater cognitive reserve; (b) the vascular hypothesis, postulating that exercise reduces the risk of cardiovascular disease, a factor that is strongly associated with dementia in general (Langa & Levine, 2014); and (c) the stress hypothesis, which emphasizes the advantages of exercise for reducing stress, a factor that increases susceptibility to dementia (Van Uffelen et al., 2008).

In summary, epidemiological and longitudinal studies seem to demonstrate that maintaining an active lifestyle in old age – physically, mentally, and socially – can protect against cognitive impairment. Educational level has an important role in protecting against age-related cognitive impairment, not only as a direct effect, but also because it can foster greater cognitive activity in different areas of life (Andel et al., 2006; Gabryelewicz et al., 2007). The effects of education are reinforced by all kinds of activities, including cultural activities and physical activities, which seem to have an important part in the cognitive maintenance of older people. In short, as Hertzog et al. (2009) propose, the results from different research strategies concur in pointing to the positive effect of environmental enrichment, understood in a broad sense, on cognitive maintenance during aging, indicating its protective effect against impairment and dementia and thus confirming the disuse hypothesis posed by Denney in 1982 (Gow et al., 2013).

## Lifelong Learning

The above review shows that widely varying types of research, from epidemiological studies of dementia to studies of elders with optimal aging, have highlighted the role of both formal and self-managed education in cognitive maintenance. Repeatedly, low educational and socioeconomic levels are related to a greater risk for dementia (Andel et al., 2006; Alley et al., 2007; Britton et al., 2008 Wu et al., 2015), although the influence of education on cognitive status has been confirmed primarily in regard to verbal domains (Zahodne et al., 2011).

These results, in conjunction with the increasing priority given to promotion of active aging, and social interest in equal educational opportunities (Kim & Merriam, 2004; Field, 2006), together have given rise to the development of educational programs for older people. Very diverse types of programs, promoted by European and American institutions, seek to enhance elders' quality of life, increase their activity, and encourage adaptation to social changes (Olajide & Mojirade, 2016). In general, these initiatives start from the assumption that an educational program for adults is a form of environmental stimulation that can lead to positive changes in cognition. However, there are practically no studies that assess these supposed effects. The studies by Fernandez-Ballesteros and her team (Fernández-Ballesteros et al., 2012, 2013), on the effects of attending a 3-year University Program for Older Adults at the Autonomous University of Madrid, or a 1-year program at four Spanish and Latin-American universities, reveal significant increases in self-perception and positive affect, and in scores on the Digit-Symbol subtest of the Wechsler Scale, in the participating older adults, as compared to a control group.

By comparison, the effects of bilingualism have been much more thoroughly investigated. Different studies report its beneficial effects on cognitive reserve (Perani & Abutalebi, 2015; Abutalebib et al., 2015) and protective role against the appearance of dementia (Gold, 2015; Back, 2016; Bialystoka et al., 2016). These benefits seem to be maintained even when controlling for bilingualism produced because of immigration, involving the so-called *healthy migrant effect*, – "a self-selection, such that healthier people are more likely to decide to migrate," according to Fuller-Thomson and Kuh (2014) – in other words, the concurrence of different education and survival-related variables in the sample selection (Back, 2016).

## Environmental Enrichment in Old Age

### In Relation to Cognitive Plasticity

In 2007, Calero, Navarro, and Muñoz analyzed the relationship between life-long level of activity, cognitive functioning, and cognitive plasticity in old age. Participating in this study were 176 people with a mean age of 76; they were evaluated using different tests and a structured interview in order to make a prospective, concurrent analysis of the activities they carried out, whether educational, work-related, social, leisure, cultural, and/or physical. Structural equations analysis of relationships between activity levels, cognitive status, and cognitive plasticity demonstrated the important influence on cognitive plasticity from one's global level of activity after retirement (including the physical, cultural, educational, and social). In other words, while pre-retirement activity was related fundamentally to the old person's cognitive status (as shown above from prior studies), the level of activity that the elders maintained after retirement (at the time they were being evaluated) was fundamentally related to their cognitive plasticity.

Later, Reed et al. (2011) carried out a study of 652 cases (without dementia at the start of the analyses) from two longitudinal studies that used 17 neuropsychological tests to measure activity at three moments in the life of the participants, and an autopsy to evaluate brain damage. They performed a set of multiple regressions in order to define the independent and combined effects of four types of demographic and life experience variables on cognitive plasticity. Cognitive plasticity is operationalized as the discrepancy between the expected effect in the brain (from diagnosed levels of dementia) and the performance level observed on the tests. In the analyses that were carried out, the strongest correlation with cognitive plasticity was cognitive stimulation in one's free time after the age of 40. Cognitive activities at the start of the investigation or at the end (closer to when plasticity was measured) also had a significant but lesser effect. The study suggests, then, that cognitive activity during middle age is especially important for cognitive plasticity. Moreover, regardless of when it was carried out, cognitive activity had greater effects on plasticity than did education. In this study, no relationship was found between education and cognitive plasticity, not even when education was the single predictor in the model.

In short, these studies indicate that after completing one's formal education, work and leisure activities and cognitive activities that provide mental exercise and stimulation are the most important for development and maintenance of plasticity. One might therefore interpret that cognitive activity in adulthood can compensate for a person's low educational level. Consequently, cognitive activities can raise the level of plasticity that might be expected from an elder's level of education, just as a decrease in cognitive activities – from what might be expected with one's level of education – could be reflected in lower cognitive plasticity (Lachman et al., 2009).

## Studies on Cognitive Training in Old Age

As we have indicated, studies that include training can be divided into two basic groups: those that focus on analyzing cognitive plasticity and those that assess cognitive interventions and/or physical activity over the long term.

## On Cognitive Plasticity

After the studies from Baltes and his group, research has focused on different topics, as identified by Navarro and Calero (2009):

## Determination of Neurological Correlates of Cognitive Plasticity

A number of studies have attempted to determine the connections between cognitive plasticity evaluated through dynamic techniques and neurological changes indicating the existence of brain reserve. In this approach, the dynamic assessment procedure has been used in tasks with a close approximation to physiological correlates, such as attention control tasks (Bherer et al., 2006), perception speed tasks (Jones et al., 2006), or dual-task training (Erickson et al., 2007). Additionally, measures of cerebral activity during LP assessment have shown that improvements in performance after memory training are associated with changes in functional brain activity (Nyberg et al., 2003; Dahlin et al., 2008b) and correlate with changes in activation of cerebral regions (Rossi & Rossini, 2004; Jones et al., 2006; Erickson et al., 2007). All of these studies show the relationship between cognitive plasticity and brain reserve, and the influence of short-term cognitive training on brain structure or function.

## Determination of the Capacity of LP Assessment to Diagnose Cognitive Impairment

Prior studies from Margret Baltes and collaborators reached the conclusion that people with a risk of dementia do not benefit from cognitive training programs, due to a lack of plasticity (Baltes et al., 1992, 1995; Baltes & Raykov, 1996), and therefore, the methodology for assessing plasticity can be used for early diagnosis of dementia (Baltes et al., 1995; Raykov et al., 2002). However, other researchers have found improvements in people with dementia after cognitive training that was part of the LP assessment, although to a reduced extent. Consequently, the discriminant validity of this methodology has been verified (Heun et al., 1997; Fernández-Ballesteros et al., 2003; Calero & Navarro, 2004; Blaskewicz et al., 2007; Schreiber & Schneider, 2007).

## Determination of Age-Related Limits in the Quantity and/or Domains of Plasticity (Plasticity in the Oldest-Old)

Findings in this line of research seem to confirm that age is associated with decline in cognitive plasticity, even though old and very old people can benefit from training. For instance, Singer et al. (2003) and Yang et al. (2006) found that the elderly show plasticity beyond the age of 80, but with smaller gains in comparison to the younger elders. Singer et al. found significant but smaller improvements than in the younger elders, while the post hoc tests reflected that 85 percent of very old elders (ages 75–101) could not improve memory performance after training. Yang et al. (2006) report that very old elders (>80 years) showed improvement after training, although there were significant differences from younger elders (<79 years) at both pretest and posttest. These studies would seem to reflect the distinction made in the specialized literature between the *young old* (under 80) and the *oldest old* (from 80 to 85) (Baltes & Smith, 2003). Specifically, in the under-80 age group, healthy elders present significantly superior performance and higher plasticity than elders with cognitive impairment, but this is not the case in the older group. This finding is particularly interesting since it suggests that plasticity measures are able to discriminate between different levels of cognitive functioning for the young old, but not for the oldest old (Navarro & Calero, 2009).

## Long-Term Training

Cognitive training programs for the elderly have gone through several stages of development: the first stage sought to evaluate strategy-focused training programs, i.e., training on specific rules (Karbach & Verhaeghen, 2014). The vast majority of these programs worked on improving memory through the use of several strategies. Initially, the participants were healthy old people and the results were very encouraging; there were positive effects on the skills trained and they were maintained for several months, without great differences between programs (see the meta-analysis by Verhaeghen, Marcoen, & Goossens, 1992, which addresses studies carried out until 1990). Differences were detected between objective and subjective measures of memory, in favor of the former. This may be because subjective memory is more resistant to change, as it involves the subject's expectations about his/her performance in daily life (Floyd & Scogin, 1997).

Later, elders with MCI were included as participants and the meta-analyses were more demanding of the studies reviewed; they focused on controlled studies, evidence-based programs, and objective measures of skill. The results continued to show significant improvements in the groups receiving training, although somewhat lower for old people with MCI than for healthy elders (ver Zhender et al., 2009; Gross et al., 2012; Reijnder et al., 2013). These studies reflect the heterogeneity of programs in use, whether in their design, the skill measurements that were included, or the strategies trained. Despite this, positive results were consistently obtained and gains were maintained as long as 1 year after the training. Regarding transfer, it appears that programs that train a larger number of strategies show some transfer to proximal tasks (Gross et al., 2012); however, most of the studies did not include measures of transfer to untrained tasks or to daily life, and when they are included, very few obtained significant results (only one study, by Smith et al., 2009, out of 35 studies from the period 2007–2012, reviewed in the meta-analysis, Reijnder et al., 2013).

A second stage focused on process-based training, in this case, the group is much more heterogeneous. The programs that were applied offered training in very diverse processes (reasoning, memory, language, attention, processing speed, executive memory, etc.) and used very diverse training methods, including repeated practice, use of feedback, process questions, guided practice, mediational strategies, and so on. As a whole, however, the results seem to be better than in the prior group. One US macro-program, ACTIVE, included 2,832 volunteer participants, who lived in different centers for independent elders. Three types of cognitive interventions were applied over 2 years (Ball et al., 2002). Participants showed improvement in skills trained (reasoning, memory, and processing speed), with effects maintained as long as 5 years after the training, but without generalization to daily life. Later meta-analyses confirmed the gains obtained, indicating some small or moderate transfer to measures of cognitive status (MMSE: *Mini Mental State Examination*) and subjects' self-perception (Li et al., 2011). In evaluating these programs, patients with dementia were also included among the participants, and in all cases, positive results are seen, with effect sizes larger than in strategy-focused training (Sitzer et al., 2006). However, as reported in the systematic reviews, practically no study included measures to estimate transfer of effects to daily life (Belleville, 2008), and when they were included, effectiveness was limited and depended on multiple factors (Zajac-Lampaska & Trempala, 2016).

In recent years, studies have sought to solve the problem of transfer by investigating different possibilities, namely: self-generated strategies (Derwinger et al., 2005; Hertzog et al., 2012), training in metacognition (Bailey et al., 2010), and especially, training in executive functions, based on the assumption that transfer will be made possible by focusing on more basic processes that are involved in a larger number of tasks, or what some authors have called *functional overlap of processes* (von Bastian et al., 2013). In 2014, two meta-analyses were carried out that focused on treating executive function and working memory, emphasizing transfer of training. Both of these indicate significant gains in comparison to control groups, higher when the control group is passive (Karbach & Vergahegen, 2014) than when it is active; evidence of near transfer in healthy old people; and to some extent, evidence of far transfer pertaining to functioning in daily life (Von Bastian & Oberauer, 2014).

## Incorporation of Physical Activity and Computer Programs

Starting in 2000, parallel to the development of cognitive programs, new programs began to appear that incorporated physical exercise or computer programs as a frame or an alternative to the cognitive programs.

In studies that evaluate programs using increased physical activity as a means to maintain cognitive functions in the elderly, a considerable number of cross-sectional studies have shown that regular exercise (understood as a minimum of 20–30 minutes of aerobic exercise that increases heartbeat and oxygen demand) has benefits for cognitive functioning (see Wischenka et al., 2016). It increases executive control processes, such as selective attention, planning, inhibition, executive function, and working memory (Baker et al., 2010; Desjardins-Crépeau et al., 2014) and seems to reduce risk for cognitive impairment and dementia (Laurin et al., 2001). Moreover, several studies show effects of physical exercise at the brain level (Colcombe et al., 2006), associating it with a higher volume of gray matter in the hippocampus (Erickson et al., 2014), greater functional activation in the cortical regions (Hayes et al., 2013), and increased cerebral blood flow (Voelcker-Rehage & Niemann, 2013).

Meta-analyses have similar results and find that for healthy old people, programs that combine aerobic activities and strength training have greater positive benefits on cognition, with moderate, stable effects – higher for executive control processes (Colcombe & Kramer, 2003; Smith et al., 2010; Hindin & Zelinski, 2012; Kelly et al., 2014) (for more information see Gajewski & Falkenstein,

2016). Positive effects in old people with dementia have also been confirmed and maintained for a period of 1 year or more (Van Uffelen et al., 2008; Lautenschlager et al., 2008).

In recent years there has been an attempt to register the effects of combined physical and cognitive programs as dual or sequential interventions. Based on meta-analyses from Lauenroth et al. (2016) and Zhu et al. (2016), significant effects are obtained in physical aptitude and moderate effects in certain cognitive functions (fundamentally visuospatial skills), both in healthy old people and those with dementia, but there were no significant differences in programs that trained in physical activity only. Participants' age was also noted as a moderating variable in the effects. The fundamental conclusion, nonetheless, was the impossibility of determining any superiority of the combined effects or to define the differential influence of each training type.

Also since the year 2000, there have been a great number of computerized training programs supported by the supposed advantages of this methodology. Computerized cognitive interventions have been seen as an alternative channel for traditional training programs, much easier to make available, reaching special or geographically dispersed populations. Due to their lower economic cost and the idea of being a more flexible approach (adjustable to each person and providing real-time performance feedback), a large number of such programs have been published, claiming to improve memory, attention, and different cognitive processes, and thereby staving off cognitive decline in healthy old people. However, few of these programs have been rigorously evaluated (Kueider et al., 2012).

Due to the great variability among these programs, Kueider et al. (2012) grouped them into three fundamental types: (1) computerized cognitive training programs, (2) neuropsychological software programs, and (3) videogames. Each group has well differentiated objectives. The first group aimed to substitute standard cognitive training in basic functions like attention, memory, language, executive function, etc. The second group was designed to improve multiple cognitive processes by using a variety of tasks to increase mastery through repeated exercise; these programs for the most part are self-guided, allowing participants to progress at their own pace, and are designed for people of different ages. The third group reproduces more complex tasks and contexts, where several cognitive functions intervene (multi-tasks).

Different meta-analyses have described their variability. Focusing on studies that deal with old people, we found that videogames seem to significantly improve reaction time and processing speed (Kueider et al., 2012; Shao et al., 2015); neurocognitive programs show medium effect sizes in spatial skills and memory, large effect sizes in processing speed, and small effect sizes in attention and working memory (Kueider et al., 2012; Shao et al., 2015). Some authors explain in detail the physiological changes associated with these effects, such as increased blood flow in the frontal region after training (Reichman et al., 2010). The effect sizes obtained with computerized cognitive training programs are comparable to those produced through non-computerized cognitive training programs, with respect to memory, visuospatial skills, and processing speed, and contradictory, with respect to working memory (Li et al., 2011; Kueider et al., 2012; Lampit et al., 2014). Maintenance of effects seems to be similar to that of face-to-face programs (Lampit et al., 2014; Shao et al., 2015). Interestingly, in the Lampit et al. (2014) meta-analysis, significant differences are noted between applications of the computerized program in a group versus individualized setting, with greater effects in the former situation.

In recent years, computerized programs have also focused on training working memory. In the meta-analysis by Cândea et al. (2016), covering 32 articles published between 2008 and 2015, they found that despite program diversity, in general the effects are positive for healthy old people, though smaller than for young people, and effects are mixed in the case of elders with MCI. They also found that certain programs reported transfer to other tasks in healthy old people, and these programs seem to be the ones that work on multiple functions simultaneously (Cândea et al., 2016).

Concerning the effectiveness of computerized cognitive training, we can point to the controversy aroused by a paper called *Consensus on the Brain Training Industry from the Scientific Community*, published on October 20, 2014, and signed by the United States "Institute of Longevity" and by the German "Max Planck Institute of Human Development," as a reflection of the present state of the question. This document suggested that, even though research has generated positive effects that show cognitive plasticity in old age and the usefulness of computerized training for increasing certain skills, as well as the health benefits of physical exercise, the results do not warrant the assertion that computer programs offer consumers a scientifically founded means of reducing or reversing cognitive impairment. There have been many responses to this letter from other scientists, such as the creation of the COGNITIVE TRAINING DATA website, maintained by Michael Merzenich, or the open letter signed by more than 100 researchers, in an attempt to qualify these affirmations, presenting scientific evidence of training effects and well-executed research studies that show positive results. In general, these researchers consider that a single affirmation cannot be generalized, nor should advertising be confused with scientific evidence. This situation leads to the conclusion that, as subscribed in the present study, there is a requirement for further, careful research and continuous validation in this field. Above all, we must distinguish well-designed studies that assess interventions from simple program applications, without any scientific guarantee.

## Caregivers as Trainers

As a final development in cognitive training programs, we must consider studies that have been developed by adjacent professions devoted to elder care, such as nursing and occupational therapy. In these fields, approaches to cognitive training seek to foster more activity and autonomy in elders with dementia. In this line, which its authors position as a development of Baltes's life span theory (Karen & Shannon, 2008), new forms of care are promoted in order to stimulate and enrich these persons' environment, seeking to foster independence and to maintain cognitive and instrumental skills as much as possible. The approach of "function-focused care" falls within this category, proposing caregiver training programs that would facilitate elders' physical activity as a method of reducing functional decline, with significant results (Thinnes & Padilla, 2011; Resnick & Galik, 2013). Also to be considered are caregiver training programs developed within the approach of "person focused care." Caregivers learn to incorporate into their daily tasks training activities in language and cognitive functions for the elders under their care, with promising results (Goyder et al., 2012; Stein-Parbury et al., 2012). Finally, from a multisensorial approach (Monsalve Robajo & Rozo Reyes, 2007), sensory integration techniques are being developed in order to maintain and/or activate cognitive functions in decline. To date, the few assessments of these initiatives seem to present them as a promising means for integrating cognitive training into the daily life of persons with impairment and/or dementia.

In summary, despite the great variability of all the factors that intervene in evaluating training programs – everything from their design and their sample to measurement criteria – there is consistent evidence of the positive effect of stimulating cognitive maintenance in the elderly. We might say, in the line of Lövden et al. (2010), that maintenance is achieved, rather than an increase above the baseline; but according to the data gathered, there are detectable effects at the brain level (plasticity), maintained for considerable lengths of time, which are not simply functional or behavioral changes in the individual. Another question altogether is the utility of these effects in the elders' daily life.

Therefore, with the stage of enthusiasm behind us, it is time to establish evidence-based interventions, to determine what variable produces what effect, and be able to design programs that ensure transfer of gains to the daily life context of the person being trained. The present situation brings us to a time of reflection. A sampling of the current state of affairs is found in the *Psychological Research* monograph published in October 2014, coordinated by Schubert, Strobach, and Karbach, and dedicated to methodological questions, physiological measures, and variables that can determine the transfer of cognitive training in the elderly. Some of its contributions will be reviewed below.

## Conclusions and Future Directions

Research on the influence of environmental enrichment on cognitive status and cognitive plasticity in older people has consistently shown how this enrichment throughout an individual's life span is associated with maintenance of skills until very advanced ages, holding back cognitive decline. Positive influence on cognitive maintenance has also been shown from one's educational level, a cognitively demanding profession, and the realization of social, cultural, and even physical activities, and that these distinguish successfully aging elders from other groups. However, there are old people who, with a low educational level, participate in cultural activities beyond what might be expected, and they achieve this positive effect on their cognitive status. Regarding cognitive plasticity, the few studies on the effects of environmental enrichment seem to establish that activities carried out as an adult or an older person have the most influence, more than the educational or professional level that the individual has obtained throughout his/her life. Although plasticity can be considered more limited in old age, as suggested by Lövden et al. (2010), thereby reducing the possibility for new learning, there is a proven possibility of action that helps maintain skills previously attained. In this line, future research should continue to investigate the limits of plasticity.

The problem is that, for a variety of reasons, environmental enrichment diminishes with age. The old person's lack of motivation, the end of productive activities, illnesses that isolate him/her, and motor and/or sensory deficits cause a decline in stimulation, and access to cognitively stimulating activities is reduced, impeding the preventive effects of environmental enrichment. In this situation, training should be incorporated to hold back possible cognitive losses. Therefore, there is a fundamental need for cognitive training in elders who are healthy or have impairment and for action from caregivers when dementia is already under way. More work is needed in the design and evaluation of such efforts.

The evidence regarding the effects of cognitive training tells us that it can improve the performance of elders in the areas trained, with moderate effects, and that these effects are detected by psychological tests or objective skill measures. Furthermore, functional change in the brain has also been shown – activation of brain areas related to positive change, not occurring in elders who do not improve (Brehmer et al., 2014) – as have structural changes (volumetric increases), which have been interpreted as evidence of plasticity in older adults (Brehmer et al., 2011; Lövden et al., 2012a).

However, not all the conclusions are as positive as one might hope (Noack et al., 2014). The principal, unresolved problem of cognitive training programs is, as we repeatedly mentioned, the transfer of effects to untrained tasks or to daily life (e.g., Ball et al., 2002; Willis et al., 2006). Admittedly, there seems to be a difference between some programs and others, and in fact, in the review by Hertzog et al. (2009), two potentially important exceptions are highlighted: programs designed to act on executive function and working memory (e.g., Dahlin et al., 2008a; Li et al., 2008; von Bastian et al., 2013; von Bastian & Oberauer, 2014) and metacognitively oriented interventions (Bailey et al., 2010), which seem to increase generalization to other contexts and tasks. Nonetheless, transfer to daily life has rarely been examined, and is even excluded from certain meta-analyses (Guye et al., 2016). Such transfer is the key issue in evaluating cognitive training programs, not only in the elderly, but also in children (Partanen et al., 2015; Traverso et al., 2015).

In recent years, several different initiatives have attempted to address this issue.

First, to review all the methodological problems of measuring change: the type of design, sample selection, inclusion of active control groups, controlling effects of the retest, factorial invariance of the measures used, and the meaning of age-related change, which Salthouse (2010a, 2012) put forward. But incorporating these questions into the studies is still not a customary practice.

Second, a theoretical model to explain transfer must be elaborated. This would include both the definition of the training objective and the hypotheses about its relations (Noack et al., 2014). The model must be precise enough to allow affirmative or null predictions about it. Existing proposals seem to be insufficient to resolve this problem. One example, the neuronal overlap hypothesis, postulates that transfer can only be expected if there is a certain overlap in the neuron activation between the trained task and the tasks used to measure transfer (e.g., Dahlin et al., 2008a; Lustig et al., 2009; Thorell et al., 2009). There is also the classic classification of transfer levels as near, medium, and far, as Campione et al. (1985) used in many of the studies reviewed (e.g., Singley & Anderson, 1989; Perkins & Salomon, 1992; Karbach & Kray, 2009; Henry et al., 2014).

In an attempt to structure the field of knowledge, different criteria have been proposed for classifying the training programs. The first classification, which we have followed in our presentation of the training programs, is to divide them into treatments that focus on specific strategies versus focusing on processes (Lustig, et al., 2009; Lövden et al., 2012b). The former group has shown its compensatory power, i.e., its utility for increasing or recovering a lost skill (Reichman et al., 2010; Hering et al., 2014); hence the reason for their lack of transfer might be in the specificity of strategies trained, and their limited applicability to other situations. The second group, training in processes, seems to show greater transfer to untrained tasks as well as longer-term maintenance of effects (Schmidt & Bjork, 1992; Taatgen, 2013; Kelly et al., 2014; Schubert et al., 2014). The trained processes are supposed to be relevant in different tasks, such that transfer would be more likely. The programs on working memory, mentioned above, would fall into this group. Results have shown significant effects in near transfer (Hering et al., 2014) and in certain skills relevant to daily life (Brown et al., 2013). Combined interventions have also appeared, such as the one from Cavallini et al. (2010), where a metacognitive intervention is associated with mnemonics training in order to increase its transfer.

This classification would fit with the proposal from Lövden et al. (2010); we would understand accordingly that in the first (strategy focused) group, functional changes would take place (flexibility), while in the second group, there would be structural changes (plasticity). A definitive confirmation of structural change and transfer to daily life in this latest generation of training programs continues to be an open question for research.

Recently, in search of a model, von Bastian and Oberauer (2014) attempted to provide a schema that considers all variables that can intervene in the transfer of training in working memory. This schema could be generalized to other possible types of training. We will try to follow it, and then put forward the variables that should be taken into account:

### Type of Training

Von Bastian and Oberauer (2014) classify the type of training in working memory according to three approaches: (1) training that uses individual paradigms (e.g., memory of digits), (2) training that uses multiple paradigms based on a broad cognitive construct (e.g., short-term memory), and (3) multi-factorial, training that addresses multiple cognitive skills (e.g., working memory and executive function). They are based on *functional overlap of processes* between tasks (Von Bastian et al., 2013), as mentioned above, and assume that interventions that simultaneously address multiple cognitive skills could lead to broader transfer effects and have greater ecological validity than those addressing a single skill (Guye et al., 2016). This schema may adequately account for the types of training that are implemented; a clear differentiation of effects of the three groups remains to be established.

### Length of Sessions and Length of Training

Training programs vary greatly in duration and intensity. For example, the number of training sessions ranges from 3 sessions (Borella et al., 2010) to more than 100 (Schmiedek et al., 2010; Bürki et al., 2014), and the duration of training sessions varies from just 10 minutes (Owen et al., 2010) to 30 or 45 minutes (for example, Calero & Navarro, 2007b; Von Bastian & Oberauer, 2014). However, few studies have analyzed the intensity and duration needed in order to produce an optimal effect (Von Bastian et al., 2013). In this regard, we would mention once more that many of the meta-analyses mix training that is designed to measure plasticity in the elderly, usually lasting from 1 to 6 sessions, with training that seeks to produce a significant change in the subjects' cognitive performance, having as few as 6 sessions up to a large number of sessions involving several years of continued training. Moreover, while some studies seem to indicate that number and duration of sessions may not have an important role in the effectiveness of the training (e.g., Holmes et al., 2009; Brehmer et al., 2012; Karbach & Verhaeghen, 2014; Kelly et al., 2014), others indicate the effects of long-duration training on fatigue and motivation (Verhaeghen et al., 1992; Lampit et al., 2014). This question, then, remains in the agenda for future research.

### Age

Age is the differentiating factor that has been most thoroughly investigated with regard to training and transfer of gains. Recent meta-analyses on training in working memory and on LP assessment have reported that the younger elders benefit more from training than those more advanced in age (Swanson & Lussier, 2001; Melby-Lervag & Hulme, 2013). A certain number of studies, however, indicate no differences between younger and older elders, either in the size of gains, or in the length of time they are maintained, even when the elderly are very old (80+ years) (Ball et al., 2002; Dahlin et al., 2008b; Bürki et al., 2014). Differences do appear in transfer to other tasks, which is found in the younger elders and not in the very old (Dahlin et al., 2008b), or where transfer in the elderly appears only in proximal tasks, but not in more distant tasks (Schmiedek et al., 2010; Bürki et al., 2014). To explain this heterogeneity of age-related effects (Brehmer et al., 2012; Guye et al., 2016), some appeal to different activation patterns between young and old is needed (Shuch et al., 2008) or to implicit, age-related limits to learning (Guye et al., 2016), or to the different level of operation of plasticity, being more general in youth, and more local (limiting transfer) in the elderly (Kühn & Lindenberger, 2016). But in any case, this topic also remains open, and as Kühn and Lindenberger (2016) indicate, it would be necessary to investigate age-graded changes in plasticity.

## Previous Skill Level

Analyses reveal that fluid intelligence is a significant predictor of the pretest training score, regardless of age group, but does not predict gains made. Not only so, but from a methodological viewpoint, as Salthouse (2012) indicates, a large number of studies reveal that a lower initial level is related to greater effects in gains and transfer (see Katz et al., 2014; Von Bastian & Oberauer, 2014). It is reasonable to think that an individual's possibilities for improvement depend on his/her initial skill level and on the reason for this level; a low skill level from disuse is not the same thing as a low skill level due to dementia. Studies of plasticity have demonstrated that old people with low educational and cultural levels improve as much as or more than those with a high educational level in skills they do not usually use (e.g., fluid reasoning, spatial orientation) (Fernández-Ballesteros & Calero, 1995; Calero & García-Berben, 1997). However, persons with low scores due to impairment or dementia require more assistance, more precise instructions, and a larger number of environmental props in order to achieve a significant result (Bäckman, 1992, 1996). In this direction, Kühn and Lindenberger (2016) propose that interventions address skills that show greater decline; the results of these initiatives should also be verified.

## Task Design

Other authors have suggested that task design – whether graded according to difficulty (Green & Bavelier, 2008) or having a multidimensional model that presents problems to be trained according to different inputs (Bäckman, 1996) – can determine transfer. Other studies also report that verbal content shows more reduced gains than visuospatial content (Salthouse, 2010b). This fact has also been confirmed in meta-analyses of LP assessment (Swanson & Lussier, 2001), and is in line with Denney's theory, whereby the range of improvement is much less in tasks that draw from crystallized intelligence, because these tasks in general are optimally performed.

Although task design must be taken into account in training, the results reviewed to date seem to favor a multimodal design in order to ensure transfer. Further investigations are needed in order to confirm this.

## Design of Training

We have already discussed how process-focused and metacognitive training seem to produce better results in gains and in transfer. It has been confirmed that mere practice has no significant effects (Swanson & Lussier, 2001; Parente & Stapleton, 1997). Group training, in one study, has also registered better effects than individual training (Guye et al., 2016) and differences have been found between training at home and training in institutions (Kelly et al., 2014; Lampit et al., 2014), but no conclusions have been reached. In some cases, the type of feedback offered during training has been shown to influence its effects. Backman speaks of procedural training (Backman, 1996) and Bottiroli et al. (2013) propose a learner-oriented approach as a more active, self-regulated orientation to learning, in order to promote transfer. Also, LP studies have verified that the best results are produced by training in general strategies, fundamental scaffolding, or mediational (Swanson & Lussier, 2001). In summary, it seems that training based on an interaction around a process, carried out in a group, with a well-designed task that has increasing levels of difficulty and different modes of presentation, can encourage generalization of effects. In addition to taking into account all the individual characteristics that influence results, as mentioned above, the design of training for transfer must also be considered (an issue that has long been posed in psychological therapy). Some authors indicate homework assignments; others speak of taking learning home (Bailey et al., 2010).

In summary, all these parameters must be considered in order to evaluate the effects of an intervention. It is necessary to check the individual effect of each one in order to meet the proposed objective, and by following a schema of evidence-based interventions, to design training that fosters environmental enrichment, and is adjusted to the objective being pursued and to the characteristics of the elder. Returning to the controversy about the effects of computerized cognitive training, there is evidence of significant positive effects from training and from environmental enrichment on the cognitive status of older people, but there is also data to show that not everything works for everyone, or in the same way. Now it is a matter of designing the assessment of each component, the effect of each variable, and how each personal characteristic or technique modulates the maintenance or improvement of each skill in a certain person; all this requires continued work on the design of a structured model of analysis for intervention programs.

## References

Abutalebi, J., Guidi, L., Borsa, V., et al. (2015). A bilingualism provides a neural reserve for aging populations. *Neuropsychologia*, 69, 201–10.

Alley, D., Suthers, K., Crimmins, E. (2007). Education and cognitive decline in older Americans: Results from de AHEAD simple. *Research Aging*, 29, 73–94.

Andel, R., Vigen, C., Mack, W. J., et al. (2006). The effect of educational and occupational complexity on rate of cognitive decline in Alzheimer patients. *Journal International Neuropsychological Society*, 12, 147–52.

Bäckman, L. (1992). Memory training and memory improvement in Alzheimer disease: rules and exceptions. *Acta Neurologica Scandinavia*, 139, 84–9.

   (1996). Utilizing compensatory task conditions for episodic memory in Alzheimer's disease. *Acta Neurologica Scandinavia*, 165, 109–13.

Bailey, H., Dunlosky, J., Hertzog, Ch. (2010). Metacognitive training at home: does it improve older adults' learning?. *Gerontology*, 56, 414–20. DOI: 10.1159/000266030.

Back, T. H. (2016). The impact of bilingualism on cognitive ageing and dementia. Finding a path through a forest of confounding variables. *Linguistic Approaches to Bilingualism*, 6(1/2), 205–26. DOI: 10.1075/lab.15002.bak.

Baker, L. D., Frank, L. L., Foster-Schubert, K., et al. (2010). Effects of aerobic exercise on mild cognitive impairment: A controlled trial. *Archives of Neurology*, 67(1), 71–9.

Ball, K., Berch, D. B., Helmer, K. F., et al. (2002). Effects of cognitive training interventions with older adults: A randomized controlled trial. *Journal of the American Medical Association*, 288, 2271–81.

Baltes, P. B. (1987). Theoretical propositions of life-span developmental psychology: On the dynamics between growth and decline. *Developmental Psychology*, 23, 611–26.

Baltes, P. B., Willis, S. L. (1982). Plasticity and enhancement of intellectual functioning in old age: Penn State's Adult Development and Enrichment Project (ADEPT). In F. I. M. Craik & S. E. Trehub (Eds.), *Aging and cognitive processes* (pp. 353–89). New York: Plenum Press.

Baltes, M. M., Raykov, T. (1996). Prospective validity of cognitive plasticity in the diagnosis of mental status: a structural equation model. *Neuropsychology*, 10, 549–56.

Baltes, P., Ulrich-Meyer, K. (1999). *The Berlin Aging Study: Aging from 70 to 100*. Cambridge: Cambridge University Press.

Baltes, P. B., Smith, J. (2003). New frontiers in the future of aging: from successful aging of the young-old to the dilemmas of the fourth age. *Gerontology*, 49, 123–35.

Baltes, M. M., Kuhl, K. P., Sowarka, D. (1992). Testing for limits of cognitive reserve capacity: A promising strategy for early diagnosis of dementia?. *Journals of Gerontology: Psychological Sciences*, 47, P165–P167.

Baltes, M. M., Kuhl, K. P., Sowarka, D., et al. (1995). Potential of cognitive plasticity as a diagnostic instrument: Across validation and extension. *Psychology and Aging*, 10, 167–72.

Baltes, P. B., Reuter-Lorenz, P., Rösler, F. (Eds.). (2006). *Lifespan development and the brain: The perspective of biocultural co-constructivism*. Cambridge, England: Cambridge University Press.

Barnes, L. L., Mendes de Leon, C. F., Wilson, R. S., et al. (2004). Social resources and cognitive decline in a population of older African Americans and Whites. *Neurology*, 63, 2322–6.

Baroncelli, L., Braschi, C., Spolidoro, M., et al. (2010). Nurturing brain plasticity: impact of environmental enrichment. *Cell Death and Differentiation*, 17, 1092–103.

Bastian, C. C. von, Langer, N., Jäncke, L., et al. (2013). Effects of working memory training in young and old adults. *Memory & Cognition*, 41(4), 611–24. Doi: 10.3758/s13421-012-0280-7.

Bastian, C. C. von, Oberauer, K. (2014). Effects and mechanisms of working memory training: A review. *Psychological Research*, 78(6), 803–20. Doi: 10.1007/s00426-013-0524-6.

Belleville, S. (2008). Cognitive training for persons with mild cognitive impairment. *International Psychogeriatrics*, 20(1), 57–66. Doi: 10.1017/S104161020700631X.

Bherer, L., Kramer, A. F., Peterson, M. S., et al. (2006). Testing the limits of cognitive plasticity in older adults: Application to attentional control. *Acta Psychologica*, 123, 261–278.

Bialystoka, E., Abutalebi, J., Bak, T. H., et al. (2016). Aging in two languages: Implications for public health. *Ageing Research Reviews*, 27, 56–60.

Blaskewicz, J., Willis, S. L., Schaie, K. W. (2007). Cognitive training gains as a predictor of mental status. *Journal of Gerontology: Psychological Sciences*, 62B, 45–52.

Boosman, H. Thamar, J. H., Eerdt, B., et al. (2014). Dynamic testing of learning potential in adults with Cognitive impairments: A systematic review of methodology and predictive value. *Journal of Neuropsychology*, 11, 1–25. DOI: 10.1111/jnp.12063.

Borella, E., Carretti, B., Riboldi, F., et al. (2010). Working memory training in older adults, evidence of transfer and maintenance effects. *Psychology and Aging*, 25(4), 767–78. doi: 10.1037/a0020683.

Bosma, H., van Boxtel, M. P., Ponds, R. W., et al. (2002). Engaged lifestyle and cognitive function in middle and old-aged, non-demented persons: A reciprocal association? *Zeitschrift für Gerontologie und Geriatrie*, 35, 575–81.

Bottiroli, S., Cavallini, E., Dunlosky, J., et al. (2013). The importance of training strategy adaptation: a learner-oriented approach for improving older adults' memory and transfer. *Journal of Experimental Psychology*, 19(3), 205–18.

Brehmer, Y., Rieckmann, A., Bellander, M., et al. (2011). Neural correlates of training-related working-memory gains in old age. *NeuroImage*, 58(4), 1110–20. Doi: 10.1016/j.neuroimage.2011.06.079.

Brehmer, Y., Westerberg, H., Bäckman, L. (2012). Working-memory training in younger and older adults: training gains, transfer, and maintenance. *Frontiers in Human Neuroscience*, 6, Article 63. Doi: 10.3389/fnhum.2012.00063.

Brehmer, Y., Kalpouzos, G., Wenger, E., et al. (2014). Plasticity of brain and cognition in older adults. *Psychological Research*, 78, 790–802. Doi 10.1007/s00426-014-0587-z.

Britton, A., Shipley, M., Singh-Manoux, A., et al. (2008). Successful aging: the contribution of early-life and midlife risk factors. *Journal of the American Geriatrics Society*, 56, 1098–105.

Brown, J., Cooper-Kuhn, C. M., Kemperman, G., et al. (2003). Enriched environment and physical activity stimulate hippocampal but not olfactory bulb neurogenesis. *European Journal of Neuroscience*, 17, 2042–6.

Brown, B. M., Peiffer, J. J., Martins, R. N. (2013). Multiple effects of physical activity on molecular and cognitive signs of brain aging: can exercise slow neurodegeneration and delay Alzheimer's disease?. *Mol Psychiatry*, 18, 864–74.

Bürki, C. N., Ludwig, C., Chicherio, C., et al. (2014). Individual differences in cognitive plasticity: An investigation of training curves in younger and older adults. *Psychological Research*, 78(6), 821–35. Doi: 10.1007/s00426-014-0559-3.

Cacioppo, J. T. (2002). Social neuroscience: Understanding the pieces fosters understanding the whole and vice versa. *American Psychologist*, 57, 819–31.

Calero, M. D. (2000). Psicología de la vejez: funcionamiento cognitivo. In R. Fernández-Ballesteros (Ed.), *Gerontología social* (pp. 201–27). Madrid: Pirámide.

(2004). La validez de las técnicas de evaluación del potencial de aprendizaje. *Psicothema*, 216(2), 217–21.

Calero, M. D., Garcia-Berben, T. M. (1997). A self-training program in inductive reasoning for low-education elderly: tutor-guided training vs. self-training. *Archives of Gerontology and Geriatrics*, (24), 249–59.

Calero, M. D., Navarro, E. (2006). *La plasticidad cognitiva en la vejez*. Barcelona: Editorial Octaedro.

(2004). Relationship between plasticity, mild cognitive impairment and cognitive decline. *Archives of Clinical Neuropsychology*, 19, 653–60.

(2007a). Cognitive plasticity as a modulating variable on the effects of memory training in elderly persons. *Archives of Clinical Neuropsychology*, 22, 63–72.

(2007b). Effectiveness of a memory training programme in the maintenance of status in elderly people with and without cognitive decline. *Psychology in Spain*, 11, 106–12.

Calero, M. D., Navarro, E., Muñoz, L. (2007). Influence of activity on cognitive performance and cognitive plasticity in elderly persons. *Archives of Gerontology and Geriatrics*, 45(3), 307–18.

Campione, J. C., Brown, A. L., Ferrara, R. A., et al. (1985). Breakdowns in flexible use of information: Intelligence-related differences in transfer following equivalent learning performance. *Intelligence*, 9(4), 297–315.

Cândea, D. M., Cotet, C. D., Stefan, S., et al. (2016). Computerized cognitive training for working memory in older adults: A review. *Erdelyi Pszichologiai Szemle = Transylvanian Journal of Psychology*, 16(2), 141–61.

Cattell, R. B. (1963). Theory of fluid and crystallized intelligence: a critical experiment. *Journal of Educational Psychology*, 54, 1–22.

Cavallini, E., Dunlosky, J., Bottiroli, S., et al. (2010). Promoting transfer in memory training for older adults. *Aging Clinical Experimental Research*, 22(4), 314–23.

Colcombe, S., Kramer, A. F. (2003). Fitness effects on the cognitive function of older adults: A meta-analytic study. *Psychological Science*, 14, 125–30.

Colcombe, S. J., Erickson, K. I., Scalf, P., et al. (2006). Aerobic exercise training increases brain volume in aging humans: Evidence from a randomized clinical trial. *Journal of Gerontology: Medical Sciences*, 61B, 1166–70.

Dahlin, E., Nyberg, L., Bäckman, L., et al. (2008a). Plasticity of executive functioning in young and older adults: immediate training gains, transfer, and long-term maintenance. *Psychology and Aging*, 23(4), 720–30. Doi: 10.1037/a0014296.

Dahlin, E., Stigsdotter Neely, A. S., Larsson, A., et al. (2008b). Transfer of learning after updating training mediated by the striatum. *Science*, 320(5882), 1510–12. Doi: 10.1126/science.1155466.

Dartigues, J., Gagnon, M., Michel, P. (1991). Le programme de recherche pâquis sur l'épidémiologie de la demence méthodes et résultats initiaux. *Revista de Neurología*, 147, 225–30.

Deary, I. J., Corley, J., Gow, A. J., et al. (2009). Age-associated cognitive decline. *British Medical Bulletin*, 92(1), 135–52. Doi: 10.1093/bmb/ldp033.

Denney, N. W. (1982). Aging and cognitive changes. In B. B. Wolman (Ed.), *Handbook of Developmental Psychology* (pp. 807–28). New Jersey: Prentice Hall.

Derwinger, A., Stigsdotter, A., Bäckman, L. (2005). Design your own memory strategies! Self-generated strategy training versus mnemonic training in old age: An 8-month follow-up. *Neuropsychological Rehabilitation*, 15(1), 37–54.

Desjardins-Crépeau, L., Berryman, N., Vu, T. T., et al. (2014). Physical functioning is associated with processing speed and executive functions in community-dwelling older adults. *Journal Gerontology: Psychological Sciences*, 69, 837–44.

Erickson, K. I., Colcombe, S. J., Wadhwa, R., et al. (2007). Training-induced plasticity in older adults: Effects of training on hemispheric asymmetry. *Neurobiology of Aging*, 28, 272–83.

Erickson, K. I., Leckie, R. L., Weinstein, A. M. (2014). Physical activity, fitness, and gray matter volume. *Neurobiological Aging*, 35, 20–8.

Fabrigoule, C., Letenneur, L., Dartigues, J. F., et al. (1995). Social and leisure activities and risk of dementia: A prospective longitudinal study. *Journal of the American Geriatrics Society*, 43, 485–90.

Fernández-Ballesteros, R., Calero, M. D. (1995). Training effects on the intelligence of older persons. *Archives of Gerontology and Geriatrics*, 20, 135–48.

Fernández-Ballesteros, R., Zamarrón, M., Tárraga, L., et al. (2003). Cognitive plasticity in healthy, mild cognitive impairment subjects and Alzheimer´s disease patients: a research project in Spain. *European Psychologist*, 8, 148–59.

   (2005). Learning potential: a new method for assessing cognitive impairment. *International Psychogeriatrics*, 17, 119–28.

Fernández-Ballesteros, R., Zamarrón, M. D., Calero, M. D. et al. (2007). Cognitive plasticity and cognitive impairment. In R. Fernández-Ballesteros (Ed.), *GeroPsychology. European Perspectives for an Ageing World* (pp. 145–64). Göttingen: Hogrefe and Huber.

Fernández-Ballesteros, R., Molina, M. A., Schettini, R., et al. (2012). Promoting active aging through university programs for older adults: an evaluation study. *GeroPsych*, 25(3), 321–43.

Fernández-Ballesteros, R. Caprara, M., Schettini, R. et al., (2013). Effects of university programs for older adults: changes in cultural and group stereotype, self-perception of aging, and emotional balance. *Educational Gerontology*, 39, 119–31. Doi: 10.1080/03601277.2012.699817.

Field, J. (2006). *Lifelong learning and the new educational order*. London: Trentham Books.

Floyd, M., Scogin, F. (1997). Effects of memory training on the subjective memory functioning and mental health of older adults: A meta-analysis. *Psychology and Aging*, 12, 150–61.

Fratiglioni, L., Grut, M., Forsell, Y. (1991). Prevalence of Alzheimer disease and other dementias in an elderly urban population: relationship with age, sex, and education. *Neurology*, 41, 1886–92.

Fratiglioni, L., Wang, H., Ericsson, K., et al. (2000). Influence of social network on occurrence of dementia: a community-based longitudinal study. *The Lancet*, 335, 1315–19.

Fratiglioni, L., Paillard-Borg, S., Winblad, B. (2004). An active and socially integrated lifestyle in late life might protect against dementia. *The Lancet Neurology*, 3(6), 343–53.

Fuller-Thomson, E., Kuh, D. (2014). The healthy migrant effect may confound the link between bilingualism and delayed onset of Alzheimer's disease. *Cortex; a journal devoted to the study of the nervous system and behavior*, 52, 128. Doi: 10.1016/j.cortex.2013.08.009.

Gabryelewicz, T., Styczynska, M., Luczywek, E., et al. (2007). The rate of conversion of mild cognitive impairment to dementia: Predictive role of depression. International *Journal of Geriatric Psychosomatic*, 22, 563–7.

Gajewski, P. D., Falkenstein, M. (2016). Physical activity and neurocognitive functioning in aging – a condensed updated review. *European Review of Aging and Physical Activity*, 13(1). Doi: 10.1186/s11556-016-0161-3.

Geda, Y. E., Roberts, R. O., Knopman, D. S., et al. (2010). Physical exercise, aging, and mild cognitive impairment: A population-based study. *Archives of Neurology*, 67(1), 80–6.

Gold, B. T. (2015). Lifelong bilingualism and neural reserve against Alzheimer's disease: A review of findings and potential mechanisms. *Behavioural Brain Research*, 281, 9–15.

Gow, A. J., Corley, J., Starr, J. M., et al. (2013). Which social network or support factors are associated with cognitive abilities in old age?. *Gerontology*, 59, 454–63. Doi: 10.1159/000351265.

Goyder, J., Orrell, M., Wenborn, J., et al. (2012). Staff training using STAR: a pilot study in UK care homes. *International Psychogeriatrics*, 24(06) 911–20.

Green, C. S., Bavelier, D. (2008). Exercising your brain: A review of human brain plasticity and training-induced learning. *Psychology and Aging*, 23(4), 692–701.

Greenwood, P. M., Parasuraman, R. (2010). Neuronal and cognitive plasticity: a neurocognitive framework for ameliorating cognitive aging. *Frontiers in Aging Neuroscience*, 10(2), 1–14.

Gross, A. L., Parisi, J. M., Spira, A. P., et al. (2012). Memory training interventions for older adults: A meta-analysis. *Aging & Mental Health*, 16(6), 722–34.

Guye, S., Röcke, C., Mérillat, S., et al. (2016) Adult Lifespan. In T. Strobach & J. Karbach (Eds.), *Cognitive Training: An Overview of Features and Applications* (pp. 134–56). Berlin/New York: Springer.

Hayes, S. M., Hayes, J. P., Cadden, M., et al. (2013). Review of cardiorespiratory fitness-related neuroplasticity in the aging brain. *Frontier in Aging Neuroscience*, 5, 31–41.

Henry, L. A., Messer, D. J., Nash, G. (2014). Testing for near and far transfer effects with a short, face-to-face adaptive working memory training intervention in typical children. *Infant and Child Development*, 23, 84–103. Doi: 10.1002/icd.1816.

Hering, A., Rendell, P., Rose, N., et al. (2014). Prospective memory training in older adults and its relevance for successful aging. *Psychological Research*, 7(2), 25–46.

Hertzog, C., Kramer, A. F., Wilson, R. S., et al. (2009). Enrichment effects on adult cognitive development. can the functional capacity of older adults be preserved and enhanced?. *Psychological Science*, 9(1), 1–64.

Hertzog, C., Prince, J., Dunlosky, J. (2012). Age differences in the effects of experimenter-instructed versus self-generated strategy use. *Experimental Aging Research*, 38, 42–62.

Heun, R., Burkart, M., Benkert, O. (1997). Improvement of picture recall by repetition in patients with dementia of Alzheimer type. *International Journal of Geriatric Psychiatry*, 12, 85–92.

Hindin, S. B., Zelinski, E. M. (2012). Extended practice and aerobic exercise interventions benefit untrained cognitive outcomes in older adults: a meta-analysis. *Journal American Geriatric Society*, 60, 136–41. Doi: http://dx.doi.org/10.1111/j.1532-5415.2011.03761.x.

Holmes, J., Gathercole, S. E., Dunning, D. L. (2009). Adaptive training leads to sustained enhancement of poor working memory in children. *Developmental Science*, 12(4), F9–F15. Doi: 10.1111/j.1467-7687.2009.00848.x.

Horn, J. L., Cattell, R. B. (1966). Refinement and test of the theory of fluid and crystallized intelligence. *Journal of Educational Psychology*, 57, 253–70.

Hultsch, D. F., Small, B. J., Hertzog, C., et al. (1999). Use it or lose it: Engaged lifestyle as a buffer of cognitive decline in aging. *Psychology and Aging*, 14, 245–63.

Jessberger, S., Gage, F. H. (2008). Structural and functional plasticity of the aging hippocampus. *Psychology & Aging*, 23, 684–91.

Jones, S., Nyber, L., Sandblom, J., et al. (2006). Cognitive and neural plasticity in aging: General and task-specific limitation. *Neuroscience and Biobehavioral Research*, 30, 864–72.

Karbach, J., Kray, J. (2009). How useful is executive control training? Age differences in near and far transfer of tasks witching training. *Developmental Science*, 12(6), 978–90.

Karbach, J., Verhaeghen, P. (2014). Making working memory work: a meta-analysis of executive-control and working memory training in older adults. *Psychological Science*, 25(11), 2027–37. Doi: 10.1177/0956797614548725.

Karen, E., Shannon, J. (2008). Family caregivers of older adults: a life span perspective. *Family Relations*; 57(1), 100–11.

Katz, B., Jaeggi, S., Buschkuehl, M., et al. (2014). Differential effect of motivational features on training improvements in school-based cognitive training. *Frontier Human Neuroscience*, 24. http://dx.doi.org/10.3389/fnhum.2014.00242.

Katzman, R., Aronson, M., Fuld, P., et al. (1989). Development of dementing illnesses in an 80-year-old volunteer cohort. *Annals of Neurology*, 25, 317–24.

Kelly, M. E., Loughrey, D., Lawlor, B. A., et al. (2014). The impact of exercise on the cognitive functioning of healthy older adults: A systematic review and meta-analysis. *Ageing Research Review*, 16, 12–31.

Kim, A., Merriam, S. (2004). Motivations for learning among older adults in a learning-in-retirement institute. *Educational Gerontology*, 30, 441–55.

Korczyn, A. D., Kahana, E., Galper, Y. (1991). Epidemiology of dementia in Ashkelon, Israel. *Neuroepidemiology*, 10(1), 00.

Kueider, A. M., Parisi, J. M., Gross, A. L., et al. (2012). Computerized cognitive training with older adults: a systematic review. *PLoS ONE*, 7(7), e40588.

Kühn, S., Linderberger, U. (2016). Research on human plasticity in adulthood: a lifespan agenda. In K. W. Schaie & S. L. Willis (Eds.), *Handbook of the Psychology of Aging* (Eighth edition, pp. 105–23). London: Elsevier.

Lachman, M. E., Agrigoroaei, S., Murphy, C., et al. (2009). Frequent cognitive activity compensates for education differences in episodic memory. *American Journal of Geriatric Psychiatry*, 18(1), 4–10.

Lampit, A. Hallock, H., Valenzuela, M. (2014). Computerized cognitive training in cognitively healthy older adults: a systematic review and meta-analysis of effect modifiers. *PLOS Medicine*, 11(11), e1001756.

Langa, K. M., Levine, D. A. (2014). The diagnosis and management of mild cognitive impairment: A clinical review. *The Journal of the American Medical Association*, 312(23), 2551–61.

Lauenroth, A., Ioannidis, A. E., Teichmann, B. (2016). Influence of combined physical and cognitive training on cognition: a systematic review. *BMC Geriatrics*, 16, 141. Doi: 10.1186/s12877-016-0315-1.

Laurin, D., Verreault, R., Lindsay, J., et al. (2001). Physical activity and risk of cognitive impairment and dementia in elderly persons. *Archives of Neurology*, 58(3), 498–504.

Lautenschlager, N. T., Cox, K. L., Flicker, L., et al. (2008). Effect of physical activity on cognitive function in older adults at risk for Alzheimer disease: A randomized trial. *The Journal of the American Medical Association*, 300(9), 1027–37.

Li, S. C., Lindenberger, U. (2002). Constructed functionality instead of functional normality. *Behavioral and Brain Sciences*, 25, 761–2.

Li, S. C., Schmiedek, F., Huxhold, O., et al. (2008). Working memory plasticity in old age: practice gain, transfer, and maintenance. *Psychology and Aging*, 23(4), 731–42. Doi: 10.1037/a0014343.

Li, H., Li, J., Li, N., et al. (2011). Cognitive intervention for persons with mild cognitive impairment: A meta-analysis. *Ageing Research Reviews*, 10, 285–96.

Lindenberger, U., Baltes, P. B. (1995). Testing the limits and experimental simulation methods to explicate the role of learning in development. *Human Development*, 38, 349–60.

Lindenberger, U., Li, S. C., Bäckman, L. (2006). Delineating brain behavior mappings across the lifespan: Substantive and methodological advances in developmental neuroscience. *Neuroscience and Biobehavioral Reviews*, 30, 713–17.

López, A., Calero, M. D. (2009). Predictors of Cognitive Impairment in Aging. *Spanish Journal of Geriatrics and Gerontology*, 44(4), 26–58.

Lövden, M., Bäckman, L., Lindenberger, U., et al. (2010). A theoretical framework for the study of adult cognitive plasticity. *Psychological Bulletin*, 136(4), 659–76.

Lövdén, M., Schaefer, S., Noack, H., et al. (2012a). Spatial navigation training protects the hippocampus against age-related changes during early and late adulthood. *Neurobiology of Aging*, 33(3), 620. e9. Doi: 10.1016/j.neurobiolaging.2011.02.013.

Lövdén, M., Brehmer, Y., Li, S., et al. (2012b). Training-induced compensation versus magnification of individual differences in memory performance *Frontiers in Human Neuroscience*, 6, 141. Doi: 10.3389/fnhum.2012.00141.

Lustig, C., Shah, P., Seidler, R., et al. (2009). Aging, training, and the brain: a review and future directions. *Neuropsychology Review*, 19(4), 504–22. Doi: 10.1007/s11065-009-9119-9.

Melby-Lervag, M., Hulme, C. (2013). Is working memory training effective? A meta-analytic review. *Developmental Psychology*, 49(2), 270–91. Doi: 10.1037/a0028228.

Menec, V. H. (2003). The Relation Between Everyday Activities and Successful Aging: A 6-Year Longitudinal Study. *Journal of Gerontology: Social Sciences*, 58B(2), S74–S82.

Molina, M. A., Schettini, R., López-Bravo, M. D., et al. (2011). Actividades cognitivas y funcionamiento cognitivo en personas muy mayores. *Revista Española de Geriatría y Gerontología*, 46(6), 297–302.

Monsalve Robajo, A. M., Rozo Reyes, C. M. (2007). Aproximación conceptual al uso de la integración sensorial en personas con demencia tipo Alzheimer. *Revista Colombiana de Psiquiatría*, XXXVI(2), 321–31.

Navarro, E., Calero, M. D. (2009). Estimation of cognitive plasticity in old adults using dynamic assessment techniques. *Journal of Cognitive Education and Psychology*, 8(1), 38–51.

Noack, H., Lövden, M., Schmiedek, F. (2014). On the validity and generality of transfer effects in cognitive training research. *Psychological Research*, 78, 773–89. Doi: 10.1007/s00426-014-0564-6.

Nyberg, L., Sandblom, J., Stingdotter Neely, A., et al. (2003). Neural correlates of training-related memory improvement in adulthood and aging. *Proceeding of the N. Academic Sciences of the USA*, 100(23), 1328–33.

Olajide, O. E. Ayantunji Mojirade, M. M. (2016). Gerontology and its implications for adult education. *European Scientific Journal*, 12(13), 321–8.

Owen, A. M., Hampshire, A., Grahn, J. A., et al. (2010). Putting brain training to the test. *Nature*, 465(7299), U775–U776. Doi: 10.1038/nature09042.

Parente, R., Stapleton, M. (1997). History and system of cognitive rehabilitation. *Neurorehabilitation*, 8, 3–11.

Partanen, P., Jansson, B., Lisspers, J., et al. (2015). Metacognitive strategy training adds to the effects of working memory training in children with special educational needs. *International Journal of Psychological Studies*, 7, 130–40. Doi: 10.5539/ijps.v7n3p13.

Perani, D., Abutalebi, J. (2015). Bilingualism, dementia, cognitive and neural reserve. *Current Opinion Neurology*, 28, 618–25. DOI: 10.1097/WCO.0000000000000267.

Perkins, D. N., Salomon, G. (1992). Transfer of learning. In *International Encyclopedia of Education, Second Edition*. Oxford, England: Pergamon Press.

Raykov, T., Baltes, M., Neher, K., et al. (2002). A comparative study of two psychometric approaches to detect risk status for dementia. *Gerontology*, 48, 185–93.

Reed, B. R., Dowling, M., Tomaszewski, S., et al. (2011) Cognitive activities during adulthood are more important than education in building reserve. *Journal of the International Neuropsychological Society*, 17, 615–24.

Reichman, W. E., Fiocco, A. F., Rose, N. S. (2010). Exercising the brain to avoid cognitive decline: examining the evidence. *Aging Health*, 6(5), 565–84.

Reijnder, J., van Heugten, C., van Boxtel, M. (2013) Cognitive interventions in healthy older adults and people with mild cognitive impairment: A systematic review. *Ageing Research Reviews*, 12, 263–75.

Resnick, B., Galik, E. (2013). Using function-focused care to increase physical activity among older adults. In *Annual Review of Nursing Research* (pp. 176–208). http://dx.doi.org/10.1891/0739-6686.31.175.

Richards, M., Deary, I. J. (2005). A life course approach to cognitive reserve: a model for cognitive aging and development?. *Annual Neurology*, 58, 617–22.

Rocca, W., Banaiuto, S., Lippi, A. (1990). Prevalence of Alzheimer's disease and other dementing disorders: a door to door survey in Appignano, Macerata Province, Italy. *Neurology*, 40, 626–31.

Rosenzweig, M. R., Bennett, E. L. (1996). Psychobiology of plasticity: Effects of training and experience on brain and behavior. *Behavioral Brain Research*, 78, 57–65.

Rossi, S., Rossini, P. M. (2004). TMS in cognitive plasticity and the potential for rehabilitation. *TRENDS in Cognitive Sciences*, 8(6), 273–9.

Salthouse, T. A. (2009). When does age-related cognitive decline begin?. *Neurobiology and Aging*, 30(4), 507–14. Doi: 10.1016/j.neurobiolaging. 2008.09.023.

(2010a). The paradox of cognitive change. *Journal Clinical Experimental Neuropsychology*, 32(6), 622–9. Doi: 10.1080/13803390903401310.

(2010b). Does the meaning of neurocognitive change, change with age?. *Neuropsychology*, 24(2), 273–8.

(2012). Does the direction and magnitude of cognitive change depend on initial level of ability?. *Intelligence*, 40, 352–61.

Satz, P. (1993). Brain reserve capacity on symptom onset after brain injury: A formulation and review of evidence for threshold theory. *Neuropsychology*, 7, 273–95.

Scarmeas, N., Levy, G., Tang, M., et al. (2001). Influence of leisure activity on the incidence of Alzheimer´s disease. *Neurology*, 57, 2236–42.

Schaie, K. W. (1978). Externar validity in the assessment of intellectual development in adulthood. *Journal of Gerontology*, 33(5), 695–701.

(1994). The course of adult intellectual development. *American Psychologist*, 49, 304–13.

Schaie, K. W., Willis, S. L. (1986). Can intellectual decline be reversed?. *Developmental Psychology*, 22, 223–32.

Schaie, K. W., Willis, S. L., Caskie, G. I. L. (2004). The Seattle Longitudinal Study: relationship between personality and cognition. *Journal Aging, Neuropsychology and Cognition*, 11(2–3), 304–24.

Schaie, K. W., Willis, S. L., Hertzog, C., et al. (1987). Effects of cognitive training on primary metal ability structure. *Psychology and Aging*, 2, 233–42.

Schmidt, R. A., Bjork, R. A. (1992). New conceptualizations of practice: common principles suggest new concepts for training. *Psychological Science*, 3(4), 207–17.

Schmiedek, F., Lövdén, M., Lindenberger, U. (2010). Hundred days of cognitive training enhance broad cognitive abilities in adulthood: findings from the COGITO study. *Frontiers in Aging Neuroscience*, 2. DOI: 10.3389/fnagi.2010.00027.

Schreiber, M., Schneider, R. (2007). Cognitive plasticity in people at risk for dementia: Optimising the testing-the-limits-approach. *Aging & Mental Health*, 11(1), 75–81.

Schubert, T., Strobach, T., Karbach, J. (2014). New directions in cognitive training: on methods, transfer, and application. *Psychological Research*, 78, 749–55. DOI: 10.1007/s00426-014-0619-8.

Seeman, T. E., Lusignolo, T. M., Albert, M., et al. (2001). Social relationships, social support, and patterns of cognitive aging in healthy, high-functioning older adults: MacArthur Studies of Successful Aging. *Health Psychology*, 20, 243–55.

Shao, Y., Mang, J., Li, P., et al. (2015). Computer-based cognitive programs for improvement of memory, processing speed and executive function during age-related cognitive decline: a meta-analysis. *PLOS ONE*. Doi:10.1371/journal.pone.0130831.

Shuch, P., Buschkuehl, M., Jaeggi, S. M., et al. (2008). Impact of working memory training on memory performance in old–old adults. *Psychology and Aging*, 23(4), 743–53. DOI: 10.1037/a0014342.

Singer, T., Lindenberger, U., Baltes, P. B. (2003). Plasticity of memory for new learning in very old age: A story of major loss?. *Psychology and Aging*, 18, 306–17.

Singley, M. K., Anderson, J. R. (1989). *The Transfer of Cognitive Skill*. New York: Harvard University Press.

Sitzer, D. I., Twamley, E. W., Jeste, D. V. (2006). Cognitive training in Alzheimer's disease: A meta-analysis of the literature. *Acta Psychiatric Scandinavia*, 114, 75–90. DOI: 10.1111/j.1600-0447.2006.00789.x.

Smith, G. E., Housen, P., Yafe, K., et al. (2009). A cognitive training program based on principles of brain plasticity: results from the Improvement in Memory with Plasticity-based Adaptive Cognitive Training (IMPACT) study. *Journal of the American Geriatrics Society*, 57(4), 594–603.

Smith, P. J., Blumenthal, J. A., Hoffman, B. M., et al. (2010). Aerobic exercise and neurocognitive performance: A meta-analytic review of randomized controlled trials. *Psychosomatic Medicine*, 72(3), 239–52. http://dx.doi.org/10.1097/psy.0b013e3181d14633.

Snyder, H. M., Corriveau, R. A., Craft, S., et al. (2014). Vascular contributions to cognitive impairment and dementia including Alzheimer's disease. *Alzheimer's & Dementia*, 11(6), 710–17.

Stein-Parbury, J., Chenoweth, L., Jeon, Y. H., et al. (2012). Implementing person-centered care in residential dementia care. *Clinical Gerontologist*, 35(5), 404–24.

Stern, Y. (2002). What is cognitive reserve? Theory and research application of the reserve concept. *Journal of the International Neuropsychological Society*, 8, 448–60.

Stingdotter, A., Bäckman, L. (1993). Long-term maintenance of gains from memory training in older adults: 2 3–1/2-year follow-up studies. *Journal of Gerontology: Psychological Sciences*, 48, 233–7.

Swanson, H. L., Lussier, C. M. (2001). A selective synthesis of the experimental literature on dynamic assessment. *Review of Educational Research*, 71(2), 321–63.

Taatgen, N. A. (2013). The nature and transfer of cognitive skills. *Psychological Review*, 120(3), 439–71.

Thinnes, A., Padilla, R. (2011). Effect of educational and supportive strategies on the ability of caregivers of people with dementia to maintain participation in that role. *The American Journal of Occupational Therapy*, 65(5), 541–9.

Thorell, L. B., Lindqvist, S., Nutley, S. B., et al. (2009). Training and transfer effects of executive functions in preschool children. *Developmental Science*, 12(1), 106–13. DOI: 10.1111/j.1467-7687.2008.00745.x.

Traverso, L., Viterbori, P., Usai, M. C. (2015). Improving executive function in childhood: evaluation of a training intervention for 5-year-old children. *Frontiers in Psychology*, 6(525), 1–14. DOI:10.3389/fpsyg.2015.00525.

Van Uffelen, J. G., Chin, A., Paw, M. J., et al. (2008). The effects of exercise on cognition in older adults with and without cognitive decline: A systematic review. *Clinical Journal of Sport Medicine: Official Journal of the Canadian Academy of Sport Medicine*, 18(6), 486–500. http://dx.doi.org/10.1097/jsm.0b013e3181845f0b.

Verghese, J., Lipton, R. B., Katz, M. J., et al. (2003). Leisure activities and the risk of dementia in the elderly. *New England Journal of Medicine*, 348(25), 2508–16.

Verhaeghen, P., Marcoen, A., Goossens, L. (1992). Improving memory performance in the aged through mnemonic training: A meta-analytic study. *Psychology and Aging*, 7, 242–51.

Voelcker-Rehage, C., Niemann, C. (2013). Structural and functional brain changes related to different types of physical activity across the life span. *Neuroscience Biobehavioral Review*, 37, 2268–95.

Willis, S. L., Tennstedt, S. L., Marsiske, M., et al. (2006). Long-term effects of cognitive training on everyday functional outcomes in older adults. *Journal of the American Medical Association*, 296(23), 2805–14. Doi: 10.1001/jama.296.23.2805.

Willis, S. L., Schaie, W. (1986). Training the elderly on the ability factor of spatial orientation and inductive reasoning. *Psychology and Aging*, 1(3), 239–47.

Willis, S. L., Nesselroade, C. S. (1990). Long-term effects of fluid ability training in old-old age. *Developmental Psychology*, 26, 905–10.

Wischenka, M., Marquez, C., Friberg Felsted, K. (2016). Benefits of physical activity on cognitive functioning in older adults. *Annual Review of Gerontology and Geriatrics*, 36, 103–22.

Wu, Y., Prina, A. M., Brayne, C. (2015). The association between community environment and cognitive function: a systematic review. *Soc. Psychiatry Psychiatrics Epidemiology*, 50, 351–62. Doi: 10.1007/s00127-014-0945-6.

Yang, L., Krampe, R. T., Baltes, P. B. (2006). Basic forms of cognitive plasticity extended to the oldest-old: Retest learning, age, and cognitive functioning. *Psychology and Aging*, 21, 372–8.

Zahodne, L. B., Glymour, M. M., Sparks, C., et al. (2011). Education does not slow cognitive decline with aging: 12-year evidence from the Victoria longitudinal study. *Journal of the International Neuropsychological Society*, 17, 1039–46. Doi: 10.1017/S1355617711001044.

Zahodne, L. B., Nowinski, C. J., Gershon, R. C., et al. (2014). Which psychosocial factors best predict cognitive performance in older adults?. *Journal of the International Neuropsychological Society*, 20, 487–95. Doi: 10.1017/S1355617714000186.

Zajac-Lampaska, L., Trempala, J. (2016). Effects of working memory and attentional control training and their transfer onto fluid intelligence in early and late adulthood. *Health Psychology Report*, 4(1), 41–53.

Zhender, F., Martin, M., Altgassen, M., et al. (2009). Memory training effects in old age as markers of plasticity: A meta-analysis. *Restorative Neurology and Neuroscience*, 27, 507–20.

Zhu, X., Yinb, S., Langa, M., et al. (2016). The more the better? A meta-analysis on effects of combined cognitive and physical intervention on cognition in healthy older adults. *Ageing Research Reviews*. Doi: 10.1016/j.arr.2016.07.003.

# 20 Wisdom

The Royal Road to Personality Growth

Ute Kunzmann

## Introduction

The three elements of high subjective well-being – high life satisfaction, the frequent experience of positive affect, and the infrequent experience of negative affect – are among the most often studied psychological indicators of successful development over the adult life span (e.g., Baltes & Baltes, 1990; Freund et al., 2012). Psychological approaches to successful aging would be incomplete, however, if they failed to incorporate human strengths such as altruism, morality, or personality growth orientation, even if these characteristics are likely to be incompatible with a constant experience of happiness, as they require the ability to tolerate and make use of mixed and negative experiences (e.g., Aspinwall & Staudinger, 2003; Labouvie-Vief, 2003).

In this chapter, wisdom is considered a human strength, which has been prized since antiquity in philosophical and religious writings (e.g., Assmann, 1994; Kekes, 1996). In many writings, wisdom has been linked to the ancient idea of a good life, which has been thought to involve a perfect synergy between mind and character (e.g., Kekes, 1996; Baltes & Staudinger, 2000). Given their interest in self-realization and the maximization of a common good, wise people are likely to partake in behavior that contributes, rather than consumes, resources (Sternberg, 1998; Kunzmann & Baltes, 2003, 2005). Also, an interest in understanding the significance and deeper meaning of phenomena, including the blending of developmental gains and losses, seems to involve a tolerance for ambivalent and negative feelings (Kunzmann & Baltes, 2005; Labouvie-Vief, 1990, 2003). Based on these characterizations, wisdom is not necessarily associated with self-centered success and happiness, but rather with thoughts and behaviors that transcend self-interest and reflect a deep understanding of the dialectics between the positive and the negative.

The following shall first provide an overview of the different psychological approaches to the definition and assessment of wisdom. In subsequent sections, two related research topics will be discussed. The first pertains to the question of whether wisdom is an attribute of old age and, thus, shows a normative increase during the adult years. The second topic refers to the question of whether and how wisdom contributes to a successful development during the adult life span. Hopefully the reader will see that wisdom is a worthwhile research topic, even if it is a rare attribute that will neither automatically increase with age nor foster an optimally adjusted, easy, and happy life. Rather, what wisdom promises is a deep understanding of phenomena and an orientation toward growth, creating resources for the self and others to develop their potential. In this sense, wisdom is closely linked to and can be considered a catalyzer for lifelong learning, often defined as a voluntary, self-motivated pursuit of knowledge about the self and the world that is not confined to childhood or the classroom, but takes place throughout life in formal and informal settings (e.g., Aspin & Chapman, 2007).

## Defining and Assessing Wisdom in Psychological Research

Although the psychology of wisdom is a relatively small field, several promising theoretical and operational definitions of wisdom have been developed during the last decades (reviews: Sternberg, 1990, 1998; Baltes & Staudinger, 2000; Kramer, 2000; Kunzmann & Baltes, 2005; Baltes & Smith, 2008; Staudinger & Glück, 2011). In these models, wisdom is thought to be different from other human strengths in that it facilitates an integrative and holistic approach toward life's challenges and problems – an approach that embraces past, present, and future dimensions of phenomena, values different points of views, considers contextual variations, and acknowledges the uncertainties inherent in any sense-making of the past, present, and future.

There are generally two ways of studying wisdom in psychological research (Kunzmann & Baltes, 2005). A first approach, which is grounded in social and personality psychology, is to focus on the nature of wise persons. This line of research has developed self-report trait questionnaires to assess person-related characteristics thought to be associated with the wise personality (e.g., Wink and Helson, 1997; Webster, 2003; Ardelt, 2004).

Perhaps the most popular and well-established approach in this tradition has been Ardelt's three-dimensional wisdom paradigm (e.g., Ardelt, 2003, 2004, 2010). Ardelt has defined wisdom as an integration of reflective, cognitive, and affective elements, and considers the reflective dimension as a prerequisite for the acquisition of the cognitive and emotional elements. More specifically, reflection refers to a person's willingness and ability to overcome subjectivity and projections by looking at phenomena and events from different perspectives. The cognitive element is defined as a person's ability to understand life, i.e., to comprehend the significance and deeper meaning of phenomena. The affective dimension of wisdom reflects a philanthropic attitude and, thus, the frequent experience of empathic positive feelings such as sympathy and compassion, as well as the infrequent experience of negative feelings such as indifference, hostility, or contempt.

Ardelt developed a psychometrically sound self-report questionnaire to assess these dimensions of wisdom in samples of adults. Fourteen items were selected to represent the cognitive dimension of wisdom (e.g., "I often do not understand people's behavior"; reversed), 13 items were indicative of the affective dimension (e.g., "I am easily irritated by people who argue with me"; reversed), and 12 items assessed the reflective dimensions (e.g., "I always try to look at all sides of a problem"). The three wisdom dimensions show positive intercorrelations of moderate size, corroborating the idea that wisdom is a multidimensional concept.

A second approach to studying wisdom has proceeded from a definition of wisdom as a body of highly developed knowledge about human nature and the life course (e.g., Baltes & Smith, 1990; Sternberg, 1998; Baltes & Staudinger, 2000; Grossman et al., 2010). In this tradition, wisdom has been assessed on the basis of performance-based measures.

The Berlin wisdom model is perhaps best known for this approach, proceeding from and integrating work on the aging mind and personality, life span developmental theory, and cultural-historical work on wisdom. In the Berlin paradigm, wisdom has been defined as highly valued and outstanding in knowledge about existential questions and problems related to the meaning and conduct of life (e.g., Dixon & Baltes, 1986; Baltes & Smith, 1990; Dittmann-Kohli & Baltes, 1990; Baltes & Staudinger, 2000). Five criteria were developed to describe this body of knowledge in greater detail: (a) rich factual knowledge about human nature and the life course, (b) rich procedural knowledge about ways of dealing with life problems, (c) life span contextualism, i.e., an awareness and understanding of the many contexts of life, how they relate to each other, and change over the life span, (d) value relativism, i.e., an acknowledgment of individual, social, and cultural differences in values and life priorities, and (e) knowledge about handling uncertainty, including the limits of one's own knowledge.

The assessment of wisdom-related knowledge in the Berlin paradigm has been based on a modified version of the method of "thinking aloud" (Ericsson & Simon, 1984). Specifically, after a warm-up phase, participants are instructed to say out loud everything that crosses their minds when they think about a given hypothetical life problem. One might be: "Imagine that someone gets a call from a good friend who says that he or she cannot go on anymore and wants to commit suicide." Another problem reads: "A 15-year-old girl wants to get married right away. What could one consider and do?" During the interview, the interviewer does not interfere or pose any additional questions. Thus, the participant basically engages in a monologue and, in this sense, the paradigm does not involve any social exchange about the given problem. Trained "raters" evaluate responses to those problems by using the five criteria that were specified as defining wisdom-related knowledge. Past studies have shown that the assessment of wisdom-related knowledge on the basis of these criteria exhibits satisfactory reliability and validity. For example, middle-aged and older public figures from Berlin nominated as life experienced and wise by a panel of journalists – independently of the Berlin definition of wisdom, were among the top performers in laboratory wisdom tasks and outperformed same-aged adults who were not nominated (Baltes et al., 1995).

Although the Berlin wisdom paradigm has dominated much of the work interested in wisdom as knowledge, several valuable extensions and modifications of this paradigm have been suggested in the literature. To this end, Staudinger and colleagues (Mickler & Staudinger, 2008; Staudinger & Glück, 2011) extended the Berlin paradigm, focusing on general wisdom (i.e., wisdom as knowledge about difficult and uncertain problems in general), including personal wisdom (i.e., wisdom as knowledge about the self) as well. To assess personal wisdom, Mickler and Staudinger (2008) presented to their participants a vignette that referred to how they see themselves as a friend (i.e., "Please think aloud about yourself as a friend. What are your typical behaviors? How do you act in difficult situations? Can you think of examples? Can you think of reasons for your behavior? What are your strengths and weaknesses, what would you like to change?"). The think-aloud responses to this question were rated in terms of five wisdom criteria that are similar to the five Berlin criteria in terms of content and structure, but that focused on knowledge about the self rather than life in general. These criteria are (a) rich self-knowledge, i.e., deep insight into oneself and one's own life, (b) heuristics of growth and self-regulation, (c) awareness of the contextual embeddedness of one's own behavior, thoughts, and feelings, (d) self-relativism, and (e) awareness of ambiguity.

Other wisdom researchers have also been interested in personal wisdom, but gave participants the choice to select an instance in which they believed they had been wise (e.g., Bluck & Glück, 2004; König & Glück, 2012). According to Glück and colleagues, the most frequent types of selected situations refer to important life decisions (e.g., deciding for a particular career path) and reactions to difficult life events (e.g., coming to terms with the death of a loved-one). The most frequent wise behaviors reflect empathy and support to others, high self-determination, and deep knowledge and insight (e.g., Bluck & Glück, 2004; Glück et al., 2005). Helson and colleagues, who also asked their participants to give an example of wisdom they had acquired, rated the resulting think-aloud protocols in the tradition of performance-based approaches to wisdom, i.e., in terms of the degree to which they matched priori-defined wisdom criteria. As described by Helson and Wink (1987), a response was considered wise if it was abstract (transcended the personal) and insightful (not obvious), reflected philosophical or spiritual depth, and showed an integration of thought and affect, as well as an awareness of the complexity and limits of knowledge (see also Helson & Srivastava, 2002).

Finally, Grossman and colleagues introduced an approach to the assessment of wisdom that has focused on wise knowledge about intergroup and interpersonal conflicts. Consistent with the Berlin paradigm, the authors were interested in wisdom as knowledge about difficult and uncertain problems in general. In contrast to the Berlin tasks, however, Grossman's tasks focus on one particular problem type (social conflict) and his tasks are comparably context-rich (i.e., they provide detailed information about the people or parties involved in a given conflict, for example, their concerns, motives, and feelings). Grossman and colleagues have rated their participants' open-ended responses on the basis of six wisdom criteria, that seem to have considerable overlap with the Berlin criteria, but are formulated so as to specifically apply to problem vignettes dealing with social conflict: (a) perspective shifting from one's own point of view to the point of view of people involved in the conflict, (b) recognition of the likelihood of change, (c) prediction flexibility, as indicated by multiple possible predictions of how the conflict might unfold, (d) recognition of uncertainty and the limits of knowledge, (e) search for conflict resolution, and (f) search for compromise.

## Conclusions

Although no universally accepted definition of wisdom exists to date, there is much overlap among the specific definitions in that they all consider wisdom as a multidimensional concept that consists of distinct social and cognitive facets, particularly deep insight and sound judgment enabled through the ability to reflect and analyze, as well as an unbiased and philanthropic attitude. Several promising self-report and performance-based measures have been developed to assess wisdom. Given that these measures have focused on slightly different aspects, they will be specifically referred to in the subsequent review of past work, with particular interest in the dynamics between wisdom and successful aging across the adult life span.

## Wisdom: A Theme of Gain in Old Age?

Societal beliefs suggest that wisdom is an attribute of older and experienced individuals (e.g., Clayton & Birren, 1980; Heckhausen et al., 1989). There are also suggestions in the literature that wisdom and old age are closely intertwined. For example, Erikson postulated in his personality theory that generativity and wisdom constitute advanced stages in personality development during the second half of life (Erikson, 1959).

But what is the empirical evidence? Pasupathi et al. (2001) reported that wisdom-related knowledge, as assessed by the Berlin wisdom paradigm, considerably increased during adolescence and young adulthood (i.e., between age 14 and 20). However, there has been little evidence for further age-related increases during adulthood and old age. Specifically, in four studies with a total sample size of 533 individuals ranging in age from 20 to 89 years, the relationship between wisdom-related knowledge and chronological age was almost zero and nonsignificant. In addition, mean levels of wisdom-related knowledge were generally below the mean of the wisdom scales (Staudinger, 1999). This evidence may not come as a surprise if one considers that the development of wisdom is resource demanding and requires a deliberate, intensive, and extended period of time dealing with difficult and uncertain life problems. In addition, a range of supportive person-related and contextual factors are likely involved in this process. Some wisdom-facilitating resources have been shown to decline with age (e.g., openness to new experience), others remain stable (e.g., psychological mindedness), and yet others increase (e.g., emotional stability), suggesting a zero-sum game and age-related stability in overall wisdom-related knowledge (e.g., Staudinger, 1999).

## Differential Age-Related Change in Wisdom

The absence of significant age differences in wisdom is, of course, not incompatible with the idea that at least some adults will experience an age-related increase in wisdom-related knowledge. More specifically, the association between age and wisdom-related knowledge may be positive for those people who are willing and able to learn from life experience or are less affected from normative declines in wisdom-conducive resources such as high openness to new experience or cognitive functioning. Evidence for this differential aging view (see also Ardelt, 2010) comes from a longitudinal study conducted by Wink and Helson (1997). The results suggested that what the authors labeled as practical wisdom (assessed by self-reported cognitive, reflective, and mature adjectives from the Adjective Check List) increased over a 25-year period, particularly among clinical psychologists who might have had more opportunities and a stronger motivation to learn from their own and others' experience with challenges and problems than adults with other occupations (see also Staudinger et al., 1992). In follow-up research, Helson and Srivastava (2002) created an aggregate measure of wisdom, consisting of practical wisdom (as determined by self-report), transcendent wisdom (as determined by ratings of the participants' examples of their own wisdom), and general wisdom-related knowledge (as determined by ratings of think-aloud responses to a Berlin wisdom task). A main finding from this study was that women who pursued a psychological or spiritual career path earlier in life and, thus, presumably had more opportunities and motivation to acquire wisdom, tended to have a higher wisdom score at age 61 than women with other career paths.

## Multidirectional Age Differences in Specific Forms of Wisdom

Adding to the complexity involved in the link between age and wisdom, a differentiation between distinct facets of wisdom suggests multidirectional age differences. To begin, a conceptualization of wisdom-related knowledge as a mean toward decentration and, thus, a contributor to a differentiated and multifaceted view of a given problem, is relatively cognitively demanding and, therefore unlikely to be a particular strength of older adults. By contrast, wisdom-related knowledge as a mean toward self-other integration and, thus, contributor to a deep understanding of a given problem on the basis of one's own concrete experiences with similar problems and processes of affect sharing, is relatively less cognitively demanding and, therefore, more likely to be associated with old age. These two wisdom conceptualizations can ideally be characterized by two more specific wisdom criteria: value relativism, as defined in the Berlin wisdom paradigm (Staudinger et al., 1997), and perspective taking, as defined by Grossman and colleagues (Grossman et al., 2010).

Value relativism has been defined as comprising the ability to (a) distance oneself from one's own perspective and personal values, (b) recognize and understand that problems can be considered from multiple points of view, and

(c) tailor advice to different values and life priorities. What makes this approach toward complex problems cognitively demanding is that individuals have to inhibit their own point of view, the default mode, for many if not all individuals (Decety & Jackson, 2006), to then consider the many perspectives that other individuals might have, and to use this knowledge when giving advice and suggesting problem solutions. Although value relativism involves knowledge about human motivation and emotion, the process of decentration and value-related relativism arguably involves fluid cognitive abilities (e.g., logical thinking, inhibition, and working memory).

Grossman and colleagues have proposed a wisdom criterion, perspective taking, that, at first sight, is highly similar to value relativism. However, a closer look at the exact definition of perspective taking reveals important differences. More specifically, according to Grossman (2012, p. 6), wise perspective taking entails (a) consideration of nonobvious perspectives, i.e., information that is not a salient feature of a given problem and how it is presented, (b) affective involvement when reflecting upon a given problem, and (c) analysis of the problem from the viewpoint of the people involved. According to this definition, a core aspect of perspective taking has been to immerse oneself into another's problem. In this vein, perspective taking involves the activation rather than inhibition of one's own point of view and past experience (e.g., How would I act if I had the problem? What additional information would I consider? What advice can I give to others, given my own experience with similar problem constellations?).

Past evidence strongly suggests that age differences in value relativism and perspective taking are multidirectional. To this end, Grossman and colleagues (Grossman et al., 2010) conducted a laboratory study in which they asked their young, middle-aged, and older participants to think-aloud about political intergroup and private interpersonal problems. Coding of the think-aloud protocols in terms of perspective taking consistently revealed higher perspective taking ability in older than middle-aged or younger adults. An additional finding was that perspective taking, as one of six wisdom criteria, was unrelated to two measures of fluid intelligence (working memory and perceptual speed) and positively related to two measures of crystallized intelligence (comprehension and vocabulary). By contrast, past studies using the Berlin wisdom paradigm and, thus, an operationalization of value relativism as a means to inhibit one's own perspective and consider others, have suggested that value relativism does not change with age or even decrease across age groups (e.g., Staudinger, 1999; Mickler & Staudinger, 2008; Thomas & Kunzmann, 2014). In addition, value relativism, as one of five Berlin wisdom criteria, is typically related to both types of intelligence, i.e., fluid cognitive abilities and crystallized cognitive abilities (e.g., Staudinger et al., 1997; Mickler & Staudinger, 2008).

Together the evidence is consistent with the idea that the relationship between age and wisdom-related knowledge may be dependent on the exact definition of the wisdom criteria. One factor that may be responsible for multidirectional age differences in wisdom is academic intelligence, particularly, fluid cognitive abilities that typically decline with age (e.g., Baltes et al., 2006) and are involved in cognitively demanding facets of wisdom, but not necessarily in more affect-driven components.

## Age Differences in Wisdom: A Question of Context

There is yet another factor that may moderate the effects of age or time on wisdom, i.e., the problem domain to which this body of knowledge is applied. Thomas and Kunzmann (2014) have argued that, even if most individuals do not possess high levels of wisdom-related knowledge, they may still be able to gain some wisdom about some problems, namely the problems that are particularly salient in their own current life (e.g., Thomas & Kunzmann, 2014). Life span developmental researchers would suggest that the problems an individual has a high need to deal with and solve are at least partly influenced by the individual's age (e.g., Baltes et al., 2006). In a similar vein, Erikson (1959) proposed that in each stage of the life cycle, a person faces specific challenges and tasks. For example, old age has been described as a period of loss during which individuals need to let go of many goals and find meaning in their lives as lived. Eventually, because of their greater exposure to the theme of loss, older adults may be more likely than their younger counterparts to gain wisdom-related knowledge about the problems and challenges that surround this theme. This does not necessarily mean, however, that older adults generally have greater wisdom-related knowledge than younger people. As with any type of knowledge, wisdom-related knowledge may be less likely to be available and may even vanish if it is of little salience to the individual and, thus, not regularly used (e.g., Jarvis, 1987; Förster et al., 2005). Seen in this light, there may be problems that elicit greater wisdom-related knowledge in younger than in older adults, namely, problems that are particularly relevant in young adulthood but not in old age. In a recent study, the authors provided first evidence for the idea that conflict in intimate relationships may be such a domain (Thomas & Kunzmann, 2014). In this study with 200 adults spanning the adult life span, wisdom-related knowledge about marital conflict, a problem that is more common in young adulthood than in old age (e.g., Birditt et al., 2005), was highest in the youngest age group studied (20 to 29 years of age) and linearly decreased across the subsequent age groups. Follow-up analyses revealed that young adults' greater exposure to serious conflicts and greater willingness to engage in conflicts partly accounted for the age differences in wisdom-related knowledge about marital conflict. In contrast, wisdom-related knowledge about suicide, a non-normative life event that is not particularly likely to occur at a specific age during the adult life span, remained stable across age groups.

In sum, this evidence is consistent with the idea that young adults can be wiser in some domains than older adults and that the development of wisdom-related knowledge may not be cumulative, but rather described as a sequential process of gain and loss: most individuals are likely to gain a certain degree of wisdom-related knowledge about the problems that are highly salient in their current life; however, this knowledge may become less available and may even vanish if it is not adaptive anymore.

## Conclusions

Past evidence has generally supported the view that wisdom does not automatically come with age. First, given that individuals have limited resources, they have to be selective and can neither acquire wisdom-related knowledge in all possible life domains nor maintain wisdom-related knowledge that they had previously acquired if this knowledge has lost its relevance. Second, only for very few individuals, and only if a rare constellation of facilitating factors and processes are present, can domain-specific wisdom-related knowledge be a stepping-stone to wisdom-related knowledge in a more generalized sense that transcends a particular problem type and shows normative increases well into old and very old age. Finally, some facets of wisdom-related knowledge may be more likely to show lifelong age-related increases than other facets (e.g., cognitively demanding and transcendent aspects of wisdom). Expressed positively, although normative increases in wisdom with age may be the exception rather than the rule, some individuals with the right constellation of wisdom-conducive resources are likely to experience a lifelong increase in wisdom, particularly in those aspects that are closely tied to their own current experiences and that refer to social-affective processes (compassion, advice-giving), rather than cognitively demanding processes (decentering, abstract analyses).

## Wisdom and Successful Aging

There has been a debate about the relationship between wisdom and indicators of successful aging, particularly happiness, life satisfaction, and the absence of negative affect. Some wisdom researchers have argued that wisdom should correlate positively with such indicators (e.g., Ardelt, 2003; Grossman et al., 2013). However, the relatively few studies that have investigated the links between wisdom and subjective well-being measures have been inconsistent and suggest that such relationships do exist, but that they are typically small (i.e., below $r = 0.30$) and not robust across studies. For example, Grossman and colleagues reported that their measure of wisdom showed a weak positive correlation with life satisfaction and a weak negative correlation with negative affect, however, wisdom was unrelated to positive affect (Grossmann et al., 2013). In contrast, Kunzmann and Baltes (2003) reported that wisdom-related knowledge, as assessed in the Berlin paradigm, was unrelated to negative affect, did correlate with certain positive feelings (e.g., interest, inspiration), but not with other positive feelings (e.g., amusement, happiness, or pride). Together this and similar evidence (e.g., Wink & Helson, 1997) suggests that wisdom may not be among the strongest predictors of successful aging, at least if hedonically oriented indicators such as happiness and satisfaction with one's life are being considered.

This is not to say, however, that wisdom-related knowledge does not make significant differences in people's lives. With regard to the question of how wisdom contributes to a good life, it is helpful to distinguish two distinct ways of developing successfully. This distinction has gone by several different names, for example, researchers have differentiated social and intrapsychic maturity (Helson & Wink, 1987), affect optimization and affect complexity (Labouvie-Vief, 2003), hedonic and eudemonic well-being (e.g., Ryan & Deci, 2001), or adjustment and growth (Staudinger & Kunzmann, 2005). Common to these concept pairs is that one concept refers to how well individuals adjust and make the most of their given circumstances, whereas the other concept refers to how well individuals can shape circumstances and, thus, push boundaries that can result from various sources, including norms and expectations set by society or vulnerabilities and blind spots associated with one's own biography.

Individuals focusing on adjustment are foremost concerned with fulfilling the tasks and expectations within a given context (e.g., family, society); they contribute to things running smoothly, and regard values such as emotional security, social reward, embeddedness, and happiness as particularly important. People focusing on growth strongly adhere to what has been called the reality-principle (Labouvie-Vief, 2003); they are truly interested in understanding the deeper meaning of phenomena and, thus, tend to question the given and, if they come to recognize that this step is necessary and appropriate, transcend it. Values that are particularly important to individuals focusing on growth include self-actualization, purpose in life, and autonomy, as well as generativity and an orientation toward maximizing the common good.

Although questions about the dynamics between these two orientations remain, there is general agreement that, depending on the evaluation criteria and outcomes that are being considered, both are highly desirable (e.g., Loevinger, 1976; Kohlberg, 1976; Helson & Wink, 1987; Labouvie-Vief, 2003; Staudinger & Kunzmann, 2005; Wink & Staudinger, 2015). To this end, many researchers have argued that the functioning of any community is dependent on people who strive for a happy and satisfying personal life in accordance with existing social rules and norms. It is also obvious that individuals who successfully adhere to the rules and norms set by a group and who master the tasks that are generally regarded as normative will be rewarded by the group with social esteem, material wealth, and protection; these rewards surly are an important foundation for further happiness and life satisfaction. At the same time, it has not gone unnoticed that no community can survive without individuals who are willing and able to question the given in the face of ever-changing experiences and increasing knowledge and information. This questioning and, where appropriate, transcending may refer societal rules and norms (and the respective social expectations) or intrapsychic "truths" and self-perceptions. Given that reconsidering beliefs and changing accustomed ways of thinking and behaving often is discomforting and can even be threatening, a growth orientation may not be reliably rewarding in terms of emotional or materialistic outcomes. However, such an orientation may foster a sense of autonomy, meaning, and purpose in life, while creating new contexts and producing resources for others to develop.

Wisdom arguably is a human strength that is ideally suited to facilitate a growth orientation (e.g., Helson & Srivastava, 2002; Kunzmann & Baltes, 2003, 2005; Staudinger & Glück, 2011). As discussed above, wisdom not only has an emphasis on the common good, it also involves that ability to analyze and reflect upon difficult and uncertain issues related to the meaning and conduct of life. Consistently, a small but growing body of evidence corroborates the idea that wisdom-related knowledge is an antecedent, correlate, and consequence of a growth orientation.

To this end, Kunzmann and Baltes (2003) reported that adults with higher levels of wisdom-related knowledge, as assessed by the Berlin wisdom paradigm, reported less preference for self-oriented values revolving around a comfortable, secure, and pleasurable life. Instead, they reported preferring self-oriented values such as personal growth and insight, as well as a preference for other-oriented values related to environmental protection, societal engagement, and the well-being of friends. People with high levels of wisdom-related knowledge also showed less preference for conflict management strategies that reflect either a one-sided concern with one's own interests (i.e., dominance), a one-sided concern with others' interests (i.e., submission), or no concern at all (i.e., avoidance). As predicted, they preferred a cooperative approach reflecting a joint concern for one's own and his/her opponent's interests (i.e., cooperation). Finally, people with high levels of wisdom-related knowledge reported that they experience self-centered pleasant feelings less frequently (e.g., happiness, amusement) but process-oriented and environment-centered positive emotions more frequently (e.g., interest, inspiration).

Other research provided similar evidence, for example, wisdom-related knowledge, as assessed by the Berlin paradigm, has been shown to be associated with openness to new experiences, psychological mindedness (i.e., an interest in understanding psychological issues), and ego level (Mickler & Staudinger, 2008; Staudinger et al., 1997). Using their measures of practical and transcendent wisdom, Helson and Wink (1987) reported positive associations of both measures with observer-based ratings of autonomy, unconventionality of thinking, and high self-aspiration, all of which reflect growth-related indicators of successful aging. Using multiple measures of both orientations, growth and adjustment, Wink and Staudinger (2015) were able to show via structural equation modeling that growth, but not adjustment, is associated with wisdom-related knowledge, as assessed by the Berlin paradigm.

## Conclusion

Together these findings suggest that although wisdom may not make one particularly happy, wealthy, and well-adjusted in terms of accomplishing normative tasks (e.g., creating a family in young adulthood or climbing to the top of the career ladder in middle adulthood), it substantially contributes to a good life by fostering what has been labeled personality growth, intrapsychic or affect complexity, and eudemonic well-being.

## Concluding Remarks and Future Perspectives

### Age and Wisdom

As discussed above, the current evidence speaks against normative age-related gains in wisdom. At the same time, under favorable conditions, it may be possible for some individuals to continue to develop and attain increasingly higher levels of wisdom as they age and accumulate experience and knowledge about human nature and the life course. This idea would be consistent with evidence from wisdom nomination studies, strongly and consistently suggesting that most wise individuals are old, although most older individuals are not wise (review: Staudinger & Glück, 2011).

It also deserves special note that many of the resources and conditions facilitative of higher levels of wisdom are not beyond personal control. These factors include openness to new experiences, emotion regulatory abilities, as well as certain motivational orientations (e.g., Glück & Bluck, 2014). Given the evidence for positive associations between such factors and performance-based measures of wisdom-related knowledge (e.g., Staudinger et al., 1997), one exciting direction for future research is to create and implement appropriate intervention programs that have the potential to move adults of any age forward along the road to greater wisdom (e.g., Ferrari & Potworowski, 2008). Such intervention programs may include teaching modules that refer to more distal resources for higher levels of wisdom (e.g., openness to new experiences) and modules that more directly target wisdom-conducive ways of thinking about wisdom problems (e.g., Sternberg, 2004).

Promising evidence comes from a past laboratory study, demonstrating that both younger and older adults can activate their existing wisdom-related knowledge via relatively simple heuristics and strategies; for example, if they imagine what another person they consider close to wisdom would think about a problem before they themselves respond to the problem (Staudinger & Baltes, 1996). Implementing such "interactive mind" strategies when dealing with a wisdom problem leads to improved wisdom performance (i.e., responses that score higher on wisdom criteria such as value tolerance, life span contextualism, or uncertainty management). Thus, wisdom-related knowledge can be improved and does show plasticity, i.e., within-person variability across the adult life span, including old age (see also Grossman et al., 2016). An open question refers to whether it will also be possible to help individuals acquire new bodies of knowledge rather than "only" facilitate the activation of already existing wisdom-related knowledge. Given the evidence from past intervention work in cognitive domains, realizing what has been called individuals' developmental rather than actual reserve capacity most likely requires more extensive, longer-term interventions (e.g., Baltes et al., 2006).

### Wisdom and Successful Aging

Past work interested in the dynamics between wisdom and successful aging focused on two highly distinct processes of successful aging: adjustment and growth, each contributing to a different set of criteria or outcome measures. To this end, adjustment has been thought to be associated with high life satisfaction, a high social reputation, and satisfying social relationships, whereas growth has been thought to be closely linked to generativity and a concern for the common good, a sense of purpose in life, cognitive differentiation, and insight into the deeper meaning of phenomena. Obviously, individuals with a growth orientation sometimes pursue self-related interests and goals related to personal happiness, whereas individuals focusing on adjustment sometimes pursue other-oriented interests and goals related to meaning-making; however, the relative importance placed on these different value types differs and these different priorities may be most striking when values compete, e.g., in situations in which the pursuit of personal happiness would require sacrificing one's need for autonomy and self-determination or in situations in which the meaning-making of certain experiences would involve highly unpleasant feelings. As to the latter conflict, individuals with a growth orientation are far more likely than individuals with an adjustment orientation to pursue their insight-related and knowledge-related goals, despite the negative emotional burden. This, in turn, may explain the weak or sometimes even nonsignificant overall association between wisdom, closely linked to growth orientation, and hedonically oriented facets of successful aging.

One important direction of future research is to investigate the associations between wisdom and successful aging more comprehensively by considering that successful aging is a truly complex and multidimensional concept. To this end, successful aging has been described as encompassing psychological, social, and biological or health-related criteria (e.g., Baltes & Baltes, 1990; Freund et al., 2012). Some researchers have proposed that it is only if an individual meets all these criteria that he or she can be considered a successfully aging individual (Rowe & Kahn, 1997). Although other approaches are more liberal (it seems to some that meeting all criteria of successful aging, particularly health-related criteria, can only be reached if one does not age), it would be interesting to learn more about the relationships between wisdom and physical health. As reviewed, there is evidence that wiser individuals are likely to be socially productive and oriented toward personality growth, however, it appears that theoretical and empirical work interested in wisdom and physical health does not exist to date. This question may be particularly relevant from an aging perspective, given that most, if not all, older individuals are eventually faced with a diagnosis of risk factors for diseases (e.g., hypertension) as well as actual chronic (e.g., coronary heart disease) and life-threatening (e.g., cancer) diseases. Could wisdom help a person deal with and live with these conditions successfully? Might it even help prevent certain types of health-related losses? These are exciting questions that await future research.

Even if wisdom should be considered an ideal that most individuals cannot even come close to, it is worth the effort to strive for wisdom. The way toward wisdom is demanding and, thus, it does not come as a surprise that only very few individuals, if any, score high on performance-based measures of wisdom-related knowledge. There is also no evidence for the idea that wisdom automatically comes with age, or that wiser individuals are better adjusted, e.g., higher life satisfaction, better jobs and careers, or more fulfilling social lives. And yet, wisdom-related knowledge is an essential element of the good life; it fosters generativity and the common good, and can give guidance in times of crises because it is grounded in deep insight into human nature and the life course. Wisdom suggests constructive ways of making sense of existential issues that may be threatening to many, but that need to be addressed in order to fully exploit what it means to be human.

## References

Ardelt, M. (2003). Empirical assessment of a three-dimensional wisdom scale. *Research on Aging*, 25, 275–324.
  (2004). Wisdom as expert knowledge system: A critical review of a contemporary operationalization of an ancient concept. *Human Development*, 47, 257–85.
  (2010). Are older adults wiser than college students? A comparison of two age cohorts. *Journal of Adult Development*, 17, 193–207.
Aspin, D. N., Chapman, J. D. (2007). Lifelong Learning Concepts and Conceptions. In David N. Aspin (Ed.), *Philosophical Perspectives on Lifelong Learning*, Springer.
Aspinwall, L. G., Staudinger, U. M. (Eds.) (2003). *A psychology of human strengths: Fundamental questions and future directions for a positive psychology.* Washington, DC: American Psychological Association.
Assmann, A. (1994). Wholesome knowledge: Concepts of wisdom in a historical and cross-cultural perspective. In D. L. Featherman, R. M. Lerner, & M. Perlmutter (Eds.), *Life-span development and behavior* (Vol. 12, pp. 187–224). Hillsdale, NJ: Erlbaum.
Baltes, P. B. Baltes, M. M. (1990). Psychological perspectives on successful aging: The model of selective optimization with compensation. In P. B. Baltes & M. M. Baltes (Eds.), *Successful aging: Perspectives from the behavioral sciences* (pp. 27–34). Cambridge: Cambridge University Press.
Baltes, P. B., Smith, J. (1990). The psychology of wisdom and its ontogenesis. In R. J. Sternberg (Ed.), *Wisdom: Its nature, origins, and development* (pp. 87–120). New York: Cambridge University Press.
  (2008). The fascination of wisdom: Its nature, ontogeny, and function. *Perspectives on Psychological Science*, 3, 56–74.
Baltes, P. B., Staudinger, U. M. (2000). Wisdom: A metaheuristic (pragmatic) to orchestrate mind and virtue toward excellence. *American Psychologist*, 55, 122–36.
Baltes, P. B., Staudinger, U. M., Märcker, A., et al. (1995). People nominated as wise: A comparative study of wisdom-related knowledge. *Psychology and Aging*, 10, 155–66.
Baltes, P. B., Lindenberger, U., Staudinger, U. M. (2006). Life span theory in developmental psychology. In W. Damon & R. M. Lerner (Eds.), *Handbook of child psychology: Vol. 1. Theoretical models of human development* (Vol. 6, pp. 569–664). New York: Wiley.

Birditt, K. S., Fingerman, K. L., Almeida, D. M. (2005). Age differences in exposure and reactions to interpersonal tensions: A daily diary study. *Psychology and Aging*, 20, 330–40.

Bluck, S., Glück, J. (2004). Making things better and learning a lesson: experiencing wisdom across the lifespan. *Journal of Personality*, 72, 543–73.

Clayton, V., Birren, J. E. (1980). The development of wisdom across the lifespan: A reexamination of an ancient topic. In P. B. Baltes & O. G. Brim (Eds.), *Life-span development and behavior* (Vol. 3, pp. 103–135). New York: Academic Press.

Decety, J., Jackson, P. L. (2006). A social-neuroscience perspective on empathy. *Current Directions in Psychological Science*, 15, 54–8.

Dittmann-Kohli, F., Baltes, P. B. (1990). Toward a neofunctionalist conception of adult intellectual development: Wisdom as a prototypical case of intellectual growth. In *Higher stages of human development* (pp. 54–78). New York: Oxford University.

Dixon, R. A., Baltes, P. B. (1986). Toward life-span research on the functions and pragmatics of intelligence. In R. J. Sternberg & R. K. Wagner (Eds.), *Practical intelligence: Nature and origins of competence in the everyday world* (pp. 203–35). Cambridge, England: Cambridge University Press.

Ericsson, K. A., Simon, H. A. (1984). *Protocol analysis: Verbal reports as data.* Cambridge, MA: MIT Press.

Erikson, E. H. (1959). *Identity and the life cycle.* New York: International University Press.

Ferrari, M., Potworowski, G. (Eds.) (2008). *Teaching for wisdom: cross-cultural perspectives on fostering wisdom.* Heidelberg: Springer.

Förster, J., Liberman, N., Higgins, E. T. (2005). Accessibility from active and fulfilled goals. *Journal of Experimental Social Psychology*, 41, 220–39.

Freund, A. M., Nikitin, J., Riediger, M. (2012). Successful aging. In R. M. Lerner, M. A. Easterbrooks & J. Mistry (Eds.), *Handbook of psychology, Vol. 6. Developmental psychology* (2nd ed., pp. 615–38). New York, NY: Wiley.

Glück, J., Bluck, S. (2014). The MORE Life Experience Model: A theory of the development of personal wisdom. In M. Ferrari & N. Weststrate (Eds.), *The Scientific Study of Personal Wisdom* (pp. 75–98). New York: Springer.

Glück, J., Bluck, S., Baron, J., et al. (2005). The wisdom of experience: Autobiographical narratives across adulthood. *International Journal of Behavioral Development*, 29, 197–208.

Grossman, I. (2012). *Wise reasoning: Technical manual.* Waterloo, Ontario: University of Waterloo.

Grossmann, I., Na, J., Varnum, M. E.W., et al. (2010). Reasoning about social conflicts improves into old age. *Proceedings of the National Academy of Sciences of the United States of America*, 107, 7246–50.

Grossmann, I., Na, J., Varnum, M. E. W., et al. (2013). A route to well-being: Intelligence vs. wise reasoning. *Journal of Experimental Psychology: General*, 142, 944–53.

Grossmann, I., Gerlach, T.M., Denissen, J.J.A. (2016). Wise reasoning in the face of everyday life challenges. *Social Psychological and Personality Science*, 7(7), 611–22.

Heckhausen, J., Dixon, R. A., Baltes, P. B. (1989). Gains and losses in development throughout adulthood as perceived by different adult age groups. *Developmental Psychology*, 25, 109–121.

Helson, R., Srivastava, S. (2002). Creative and wise people: Similarities, differences and how they develop. *Personality and Social Psychology Bulletin*, 28, 1430–40.

Helson, R., Wink, P. (1987). Two conceptions of maturity examined in the findings of a longitudinal study. *Journal of Personality and Social Psychology*, 53, 531–41.

Jarvis, P. (1987). Meaningful and meaningless experience: Towards an analysis of learning from life. *Adult Education Quarterly*, 37, 164–72.

Kekes, J. (1996). *Moral wisdom and good lives*. Ithaca, NY: Cornell University Press.

Kohlberg, L. (1976). Moral stages and moralization: The cognitive-developmental approach. In T. Lickona (Ed.), *Moral development and behavior: theory, research and societal issues* (pp. 31–53). New York: Holt, Rinehart, & Winston.

König, S., Glück, J. (2012). Situations in which I was wise: Autobiographical wisdom memories of children and adolescents. *Journal of Research on Adolescence*, 22, 512–25.

Kramer, D. A. (2000). Wisdom as a classical source of human strength: Conceptualizing and empirical inquiry. *Journal of Social and Clinical Psychology*, 19, 83–101.

Kunzmann, U., Baltes, P. B. (2003). Wisdom-related knowledge: Affective, motivational, and interpersonal correlates. *Personality and Social Psychology Bulletin*, 29, 1104–19.

(2005). The psychology of wisdom: Theoretical and empirical challenges. In R. J. Sternberg & J. Jordan (Eds.), *Handbook of wisdom* (pp. 110–35). New York, NY: Cambridge University Press.

Labouvie-Vief, G. (1990). Wisdom as integrated thought: historical and developmental perspectives. In R. J. Sternberg (Ed.), *Wisdom: Its nature, origins, and development* (pp. 52–83). Cambridge, NY: Cambridge University Press.

(2003). Dynamic integration: affect, cognition, and the self in adulthood. *Current Directions in Psychological Science*, 12, 201–6.

Loevinger, J. (1976). *Ego development: Conception and theory*. San Francisco: Jossey-Bass.

Mickler, C., Staudinger, U. M. (2008). Personal wisdom: Validation and age-related differences of a performance measure. *Psychology and Aging*, 23, 787–99.

Pasupathi, M., Staudinger, U. M., Baltes, P. B. (2001). Seeds of wisdom: adolescents' knowledge and judgment about difficult life problems. *Developmental Psychology*, 37, 351–61.

Rowe, J. W., Kahn, R. L. (1997). Successful aging. *The Gerontologist*, 37, 433–40.

Ryan, M. R., Deci, E. L. (2011). On happiness and human potential: A review of research on hedonic and eudemonic well-being. *Annual Review of Psychology*, 52, 141–66.

Staudinger, U. M. (1999). Older and wiser? Integrating results on the relationship between age and wisdom-related performance. *International Journal of Behavioral Development*, 23, 641–64.

Staudinger, U. M., Baltes, P. B. (1996). Interactive minds: A facilitating setting for wisdom-related knowledge? *Journal of Personality and Social Psychology*, 71, 746–62.

Staudinger, U. M., Kunzmann, U. (2005). Positive adult personality development: Adjustment and/or growth? *European Psychologist*, 10, 320–9.

Staudinger, U. M., Glück, J. (2011). Psychological wisdom research: Commonalities and differences in a growing field. *Annual Review of Psychology*, 62, 215–41.

Staudinger, U. M., Smith, J., Baltes, P. B. (1992). Wisdom-related knowledge in a life review task: Age differences and the role of professional specialization. *Psychology and Aging*, 7, 271–81.

Staudinger, U. M., Lopez, D. F., Baltes, P. B. (1997). The psychometric location of wisdom-related performance: Intelligence, personality, and more? *Personality and Social Psychology Bulletin*, 23, 1200–14.

Sternberg, R. J. (Ed.). (1990). *Wisdom: Its nature, origins, and development*. New York: Cambridge University Press.

  (1998). A balance theory of wisdom. *Review of General Psychology*, 2, 347–65.

  (2004). What is wisdom and how can we develop it? *Annals of the American Academy of Political and Social Science*, 591, 164–74.

Thomas, S., Kunzmann, U. (2014). Age differences in wisdom-related knowledge: Does the age-relevance of the task matter? *The Journals of Gerontology, Series B: Psychological Sciences and Social Sciences*, 69, 897–905.

Webster, J. D. (2003). An explorative analysis of a self-assessed wisdom scale. *Journal of Adult Development*, 10, 13–22.

Wink, P., Helson, R. (1997). Practical and transcendent wisdom: Their nature and some longitudinal findings. *Journal of Adult Development*, 4, 1–15.

Wink, P., Staudinger, U. M. (2015). Wisdom and psychosocial functioning in late life. *Journal of Personality*, 84, 306–18.

# 21 Emotions and Successful Aging

Constança Paúl

## Introduction

Successful aging appears as a multidimensional construct with interrelated, but to some extent, independent components, organized in a hierarchical order: (1) low risk of disease and disease-related disability, (2) high mental and physical function, and (3) active engagement with life (Rowe & Kahn, 1997). There is an extended debate about the concept of successful aging, because it often ignores the relevance of subjective health evaluation and the fact that the majority of old people have health problems (e.g., Bowling, 2007; Pruchno et al., 2010; Paúl et al., 2015). Most studies about successful aging consider very few psychosocial variables, and emphasize the role of absence of disease or disability in successful aging (Depp & Jeste, 2006), yet other variables, from the affective spectrum, seem to be very relevant.

Affect is assumed in this chapter, following Gross (2014), as a broader category that includes emotions, and is one of the main areas of human behavior, relating individuals to the social and physical environment and promoting choices in life. Emotions suppose a physiological, cognitive, and behavioral response, as well as a subjective experience in face of relevant stimuli. After completing the ontogenetic development of the full range of emotions, individuals keep developing affect in parallel with cognitive capacity, and learn how to regulate emotions. Emotional regulation is the psychological process of managing intensity and duration of response to emotional-eliciting stimuli. It indicates the appraisal of good or bad stimuli, considering personal goals (Urry, 2016). In the perspective of Gross (2014), it is the process that allows individuals to influence the type, intensity, and frequency of their affective state.

Emotional regulation appears related to health by multiple pathways, at the physiological level (through the immune system), at the emotional level (through experiences, the generation of psychological resources, and the eliciting of social support to deal with adversity), and finally, at the motivation level (through health-relevant behaviors) (Salovey et al., 2000). However, we have to differentiate the effect of positive versus negative emotions, as positive emotions protect physical health independently of negative emotions (e.g., Kubzansky & Boehm, 2016).

The association between emotion regulation and health can be extended to successful aging as a broadened concept that includes health. Davis and colleagues (2007, p. 262) state that "the ability to maintain an awareness of our positive emotions in the face of life's inevitable difficulties, including challenges to health, may be a hidden key to resilience as we age."

Affectivity has a particular role during aging, to preserve well-being and to facilitate coping with age associated challenges. The regulation of affect maintains people on track with major developmental life tasks, adapting the individual to the challenges of aging. The emotional system seems quite resistant to aging and it is generally accepted that old people are effective in regulating emotions and coping with emotional stimuli (Blanchard-Fields et al., 2011), which seems to be very important for successful aging.

The main objective with this chapter is to explore emotions during aging and the contribution of emotional balance to successful aging. We explore some major affective routes to successful aging, focusing on the theories of wisdom and socioemotional selectivity theory. Followed by the contribution of positive psychology, happiness, and the broaden-and-built theory. Finally we discuss positivity in old age and stress learning as the key to explaining the evolution toward positive regulation of emotions in old age and its contribution to successful aging.

## Routes toward Successful Aging

In 1990, Birren and Fisher (Birren & Fisher, 1990, p. 326) defined wisdom as "the integration of the affective, conative, and cognitive aspects of human abilities in response to life's tasks and problems. Wisdom is a balance between the opposing valences of intense emotion and detachment, action and inaction, and knowledge and doubts." This multidimensional view of wisdom is clearly present in the perspective of Baltes and Staudinger (2000), to whom wisdom is difficult to achieve but recognizable, and includes questions about: (1) the meaning of life, (2) knowledge about limits and uncertainties of the world, (3) superior level of knowledge and judgment, (4) deep and balanced knowledge, (5) harmony between mind and character, and (6) serving oneself, as well as others. Wisdom, being an adaptive value and an ideal attainment of human development, derives its relevance mainly from not showing age-related declines (Staudinger & Leipold, 2003). Based in an affective and balanced look over life and the world, wisdom combines cognition, emotion, and motivation.

There are two major theories about wisdom: one is the development theory of Erikson (1959) that includes wisdom as the final stage of development when people accept peacefully life and death, balancing integrity and despair without major regrets, and turn toward humanity and universality. The other theory of wisdom is based on expertise derived from the "fundamental pragmatic of life" and selectivity, optimization, and compensation strategies, the SOC model, of Baltes and colleagues (e.g., Baltes & Staudinger, 2000).

In both life span perspectives, the attainment of wisdom is not mandatory and it appears as a final achievement of a long process that includes personal characteristics, learning, and experience in context. The idea of balance is present in both Erikson and Baltes, although, in considering different paths to wisdom, they both take into consideration a sage equilibrium and a relativistic look over life that configures tolerance toward the self and others, relativism, and a sense of transcendence, which is progressively acquired along the life span. Reichstadt and colleagues (2010) found that if there were a balance between self-acceptance/self-contentment and engagement with life/self-growth, this would lead to wisdom, which appears as a major contributor to successful aging.

Mature people seem to have attained the capacity to relativize things, and to put them into perspective. Although not consensual, post formal intelligence includes the concept of relativeness and dialectics, bringing contradiction back to reasoning (e.g., Riegel, 1976). Labouvie-Vief and colleagues (1989) postulate that emotions become more and more integrated with cognition with a peak in midlife and introduce the idea of relativism of logic thinking against the absolutism of logic thinking. These theories are decisive to understanding the subjectivity that assumes progressively more relevance during an adult's life, and probably inform the way people live, giving more space to social relationships and valuing the *relation* over the *performance* and the *being* over the *having*. This theoretical line derives from the cognitive development of Piaget, adding to the developmental stages completed until young adulthood, the post formal stage of adult thinking – as a kind of thinking that becomes more complex and dialectic, accepting multi-causality, as well as multiple solutions, the existence of paradoxes and contradictions, uncertainty, and compromise. This later development that brings affect to logic thinking sheds light over the change in the way people regulate emotions, and also over the association between emotional and cognitive behavior across the life span.

A different line of work is the socioemotional selectivity theory (SST). In the 1990s, Carstensen and others (e.g., Carstensen, 1992; Carstensen et al., 1999, 2003) arrived at the formulation of the socioemotional selectivity theory, postulating that due to a limited time perspective – notion of finitude - older people turn to emotional experiences and emotional regulation, and report less negative experiences than younger individuals. The SST explains how old people deal with the notion of the finitude of lifetime as a core issue for adaptation in old age. The theory predicts that people choose social goals that are consistent with their self-perception of time left in life, and that this congruency leads to adaptation. The SST inspires a huge amount of research and experiments looking at the effect of the notion of finitude and positivity in several spheres of life, namely health behaviors.

Lockenhoff and Carstensen (2004) report that present-oriented goals related to emotional meaning, limit the behavior of seeking health information and decision-making by favoring positive material over negative information. Recently, English and Carstensen (2015) found that older adults in relatively poor health showed less positivity in health-related decisions than in unrelated health decisions. The age-related positivity effect reflects goal-directed cognitive processing, depending on relevance and contextual factors of the person. This finding is crucial, as otherwise older people could avoid negative health information, and thus prevent themselves from changing toward a healthier behavior.

The ability to regulate emotions remains stable or improves across the adult life span, which may be explained by the SST reflecting the prioritization of emotional goals. Older adults show relatively high levels of interference in tasks of categorical judgments about emotional and non-emotional stimuli and reduced cognitive control during non-emotional tasks, although they appear to be able to reduce interference during emotional tasks (Samanez-Larkin & Robertson, 2009; Samanez-Larkin et al., 2014).

The communication patterns of autobiographical narratives also corroborate the SST. Robertson and Hopko (2013) reported that young adults are focused on information gathering, whereas older adults become increasingly motivated to regulate emotions. Older adults use more affective words and second and third person pronouns during autobiographical narratives, although varying with the specific narrative valence.

In sum, the attainment of wisdom encompasses a new attitude toward the self, others, and the challenges of aging. These main theoretical perspectives about aging constitute, in our view, an inexorable contribution to the discussion of affect and successful aging.

## The Contribution of Positive Psychology to Understand Affectivity and Successful Aging

Happiness is defined by Seligman (2002) by three main aspects: pleasure or positive emotions, engagement, and meaning. There are several ways to improve happiness, like cultivating gratitude, forgiveness, mindfulness, and building hope, among others. Positive emotion leads to physical benefits, like better health or faster recovery (e.g., Fredrickson, 2001).

Both engagement and meaning are different pathways to happiness, involving emotions. By expressing preferences and attributing (positive/negative) meaning to life and events, people choose to participate in old age. Keeping engaged with tasks and pursuing gratification from a particular behavior, as well as obtaining meaning out of life through, for example, religiosity, are additional ways to achieve a "full life" (Seligman et al., 2005). Social relationships are proven to contribute to health and well-being across life (e.g., Cohen, 2004) and are closely related with health outcomes and happiness.

Human strength enhances successful aging, and combined with virtues (e.g., altruism, joy, health, responsibility), facilitates healthy development and adaptation, and acts as a buffer to illness. In the same route, healthy processes (e.g., mastery, resilience) may be seen as facilitating adaptation, growth, and attainment of fulfillment. Human fulfillment refers to well-being and the sense of meaning and connectivity in all spheres of life (Lopez et al., 2003). On the opposite side, according to the same authors, weaknesses, unhealthy processes, and voids impede positive outcomes, namely successful aging.

On the scope of positive psychology, the broaden-and-build theory of Fredrickson (2001, 2003) focuses on the adaptive role of positive emotions.

While negative emotions tend to help solve problems of immediate survival, which may explain why negative stimuli are usually more prominent, positive emotions tend to help solve problems concerning personal growth and development (Isaacowitz & Riediger, 2011). The experiences of positive emotions help individuals reorganize thinking, broadening personal perspectives and helping to build resources for life. However, there is still a lack of longitudinal evidence about the effect of positive emotions in future resilience.

Fredrickson and Losada (2005) have suggested that there is a cut-off point of positivity, and although this seems difficult to prove, and has been contested (e.g., Brown et al., 2013), the work of Fredrickson has motivated a large amount of fruitful research and may be very relevant to understanding emotional balance and affectivity in old age. From a geropsychological perspective, we can probably observe the development effect, previewed by Fredrickson on the broaden and build theory, in the way older persons behave, as they emphasize positive emotions and disregard negative ones, and by so doing, adapt to the challenges of aging and preserve well-being and happiness.

In sum, positive psychology, although not devoted specifically to explain older adult behavior, is an excellent model to understand old age and the development and role of positive emotions in the process of adaptation and successful aging.

## Perspectives on Positivity in Old Age

There is an aging paradox where the stability or increase of affective well-being across adulthood coincides with cognition or physical health decline (Riediger & Luong, 2016). In fact, there is a wide consensus that older people are generally more positive and report more positive emotions – positivity – than younger adults (e.g., Carstensen et al., 2011; Martins & Mather, 2016; Riediger & Luong, 2016).

A large amount of research on emotion regulation during old age is being done in labs and focuses on neuropsychological mechanisms. This line of studies may be grouped in a theory of deficit. This perspective explains the observed positive emotional bias of older people by their lack of capacity to deal with emotional stimuli in an effective manner. Authors like Martins and Mather (2016) refer to the paradox of the emotional resilience of older adults, showing that as executive lateral structures decline, emotional regulation improves. Other studies stressed that emotional experiences of old people are in fact less complex and diverse (e.g., Brose et al., 2015), while the increase in reaction time in old people could explain the positivity bias, as young people, with a negative bias, became more positive when encouraged to take time in their evaluation (e.g., Neta & Tong, 2016).

However the "deficit perspective" is far from being consensual, as positivity bias was observed in the absence of cognitive decline (e.g., Kalenzaga et al., 2016) and the adaptive trend of positivity continues to evolve in extreme old adults, narrowing the positivity toward, for example, meaningful religious self-relevant information (e.g., Fairfield et al., 2013; Araújo et al., 2016). These results support the idea of an adaptive developmental process of affectivity in old age.

As we suggested above, it is generally agreed that negative stimulus implies a threat to the individual, and is more potent at eliciting an emotional response, i.e., "negative dominance" (Isaacowitz & Riediger, 2011). However, older adults show a positivity bias, focusing and retaining essentially positive stimuli and events, contrary to what is observed in younger individuals who are more attentive to negative stimuli.

Castelli and Lanza (2011) noticed that the social world is organized based on semantic knowledge and emotional response categorization, and that the tendency to group stimuli on the basis of the emotion they evoke increases with age. Older adults seem to be more sensitive to emotional context, employing diverse behaviors, and at the same time, dealing with internal states, i.e., self-regulating emotions (Burton & Bonanno, 2016).

The strength and vulnerability integration theory (SAVI) of Charles (2010) predicts that older adults manage emotions by preventing them from occurring, or withdrawing from them. Over time people gain experience and knowledge about emotions and what elicits them, leading to anticipation of what will probably happen, and therefore having the chance to avoid the negative emotions or create positive ones.

Mikels and Shuster (2016) studied the way people interpret ambiguous situations to make sense of the world, either by using rose-colored or dark glasses. Older people favor less negative interpretations, which supports age-related positivity and a different approach in creating emotional meaning than young adults.

Longitudinal change in positive affect as a component of subjective well-being was examined over a period of 22 years by Gana and colleagues (2015). They found a pattern of positive affect, indicating linear growth before a decline phase. Self-perceived health is a significant predictor of change, but explains a very small proportion (3 percent) of the variation in positive affect. Globally these findings corroborate the idea of significant changes in positive affect in advanced years, when either considering chronological aging or time-to-death (e.g., Vogel et al., 2013).

Culture also shapes emotional experience (e.g., Wirtz et al., 2009; Grossmann et al., 2014). Based on the idea that older adults' goals are to maintain positive experiences and avoid negative ones, they tested their hypothesis that this would be clearer in Western cultures than in Eastern cultures. By comparing reports of positive and negative emotional experiences from random samples of Americans and Japanese they found that older Americans reported significantly less negative emotions in unpleasant situations compared to younger Americans. No such aging effects were observed in the Japanese respondents, which can be explained by a different cultural approach to well-being. With closest social partners, the emotional responses to social interactions varied according to the context of daily social experiences, as well as accumulated social experiences over time (Mejía & Hooker, 2015).

378 CONSTANÇA PAÚL

Taken into account, it becomes clear that emotional regulation and the shift to "positivity" in old age contribute decisively to adaptation, well-being, and successful aging, at least for younger old adults.

## The Central Role of Learning Emotional Balance in Old Age

Learning is a basic process of human behavior, yet it is so basic that it often goes unnoticed from a personal and a scientific point of view. Nevertheless learning, be it operant learning (Skinner, 1953) or vicarious learning (Bandura, 1962), is arguably the most powerful developmental process. People learn throughout their life by different types and schemes of reinforcement, and by observation of the consequences of others' behavior. This last type of learning is considered the more relevant in what concerns social and emotional behaviors, and at the same time it is the less self-determined. People learn with life experience, and by observing and sharing experiences with others, which are the more effective behaviors to succeed. Lefebvre and colleagues (2017) corroborate the hypothesis that optimistic reinforcement learning is specific to instrumental conditioning. A higher learning rate for positive, compared with negative, prediction errors was observed by the authors in a simple instrumental learning task, showing that the prevalence of good news over bad news is a core psychological process that generates and maintains unrealistic optimism.

People differ in their characteristics, and although personality is considered stable across life span, there are adjustments and observable changes in personality-induced behaviors. Therefore, it is likely that people who are more positive will accentuate this characteristic, while those who are more negative will evolve to a more positive emotional control, as experience will teach them what is a more adaptive behavior. As we have also pointed out above, there are cultural differences (e.g., Grossmann et al., 2014) in the positivity shift that cannot corroborate the neuropsychological deficit perspective, and on the contrary, supports the idea of learning in context.

It seems that old people became wise, be it through an internal conflict between contradictory forces facing context and biographical achievements, as Erikson puts it, or by life pragmatic, as in the sense of Baltes, where learning to solve problems is from experience about efficacy mechanisms.

Carstensen (1992), with the socioemotional selectivity theory, showed older adults actively turn toward rewarding meaningful emotional relationships and stimuli and avoiding/forgetting negative ones. This process of adaptation serves as an energy saver and optimizes well-being, probably in the direction of transcendence. The idea of finitude is, according to Carstensen (1992), the core concept ruling older people's choices and leading to the positivity shift. The SAVI model of Charles (2010) integrates the socioemotional selectivity theory and the finitude concept with the idea of experience and knowledge, which results from past years of recognizing of the role of learning how to better regulate emotions.

With the broaden and build theory (Fredrickson, 1998), we learned that positive emotions contribute to the widening of people's perspectives and opportunities, and constitute an occasion to build future resilience to adversity by a feedback mechanism that seems to be no more than a learning process.

While the notion of finitude might develop as people age, we doubt it guides people's lives. Older people seem not to value too much longevity, as Fernandez-Ballesteros and colleagues (2010) showed by comparing countries in regard to the lay concept of aging well. One of the items that received the lowest mean scores in most of the countries was "living a very long time," concluding that contrary to what may be expected on the scope of a biomedical perspective on successful aging, greater longevity was not considered important.

We argue that people look back to the past and learn that it is not effective to spend time and energy paying attention to negative stimuli, or to let negative feelings overrule life experiences. Learning, namely from Baltes and Fredrikson, seems to be the key process to explain the positivity and close relationship orientation of old people.

We arrive to the virtuous circle, where people getting older cultivate close relationships and avoid negative social interaction, which contributes to their health and well-being, and foster relationships. But, is it because they cannot do it differently? Is it because they think they are approaching the end of their lives, and so they turn toward positive emotion and invest in social relationships? Or is it just because they learn through life that this is clearly more effective?

People learn by experience that when they feel happy, they feel healthy, when they deal with positive things, they do not get upset and nervous and they feel better, successively reinforcing their choice. For some people it can take more time to learn, while others may never learn that it is better to concentrate on positive things, like compassion, forgiveness, and gratitude. Yet, positivity seems to be the elixir of successful aging, and what we all are ultimately looking for; it is so simple and so close, that it is often hard to see.

Life looks short from middle life on, but people report that they don't think too much on this issue, they just do not need to compete so much anymore for power, for job positions, or for social status, and they can concentrate more on themselves, avoiding negative things, and focusing on the good and kindness of life, and in those few individuals they have learned to trust. Depp and Jeste (2009, p. 9) draw as a first conclusion about successful aging that "longevity is not necessarily the ideal phenotype; certainly extending longevity is a less ideal goal than maximizing the number of well years, howsoever defined." Thus, the finitude issue appears not to be a main concern for older adults. Fernandez-Ballesteros (2008) concluded that, in addition to Rowe and Kahn's (1997) three domains of successful aging (i.e., low risk of disease and related disability, high mental and physical functioning, and active engagement with life) a fourth domain, emotion and motivation (e.g., positive balance, sense of control, coping with stress), must be included. No matter the objective health issues, no matter the slowness of reactions, if people can manage their life with autonomy, they will be happy and concentrate on what makes them feel good. This way older people keep/find the meaning of life – gerotranscendence – when everything changes around them, having some close relationships, good memories that last, a precise sense of worthiness of self and others, a relativism perspective over life and people in a universal cosmic perspective of being. According to Tornstam (2005), old age is different from mid-life bringing a new understanding about the world, oneself and the relationships with others. Gerotranscendence corresponds to a change from a rational perspective to a more transcendent one, usually followed by higher life satisfaction (Tornstam, 1989, 2011). Probably this last perspective better suits the very old shift rather than the younger-old shift toward positivity (e.g., Fairfield et al., 2013; Gana et al., 2015; Araújo et al., 2016)

## Concluding Remarks

Emotional balance is a key aspect of successful aging. The trend to positivity and the recuperation of subjectivity in logic thinking appears to be a development of cognitive and emotional aging along the life span. Learning is probably the mechanism underlying this evolution, as life experience teaches people about the relative efficacy of strategies used to deal with life challenges. The objectives and expectancies of older adults also change, and bring the prioritizing of affective issues to the top. Health challenges may activate initial hope and trust accomplishments, as seen in the first stages of the Erikson et al. (1986) model, and motivate a broader view of mankind and universal values. This happens, not because people are incapable of behaving differently or are pressured by approaching the end of life, but because affect progresses, and life learning is a basic human condition.

## References

Araújo, L., Ribeiro, O., Paúl, C. (2016). The role of existential beliefs within the relation of centenarians' health and well-being. *J Relig Health*. DOI: 10.1007/s10943-016-0297-5.

Baltes, P., Staudinger, U. (2000). Wisdom, a metaheuristic (pragmatic) to orchestrate mind and virtue toward excellence, *American Psychologist*, 55(1), 122–36. DOI: 10.1037//0003-066X.55.1.122.

Bandura, A. (1962). Social learning through imitation. In M. R. Jones (Ed.), *Nebraska Symposium on Motivation*. Lincoln: University of Nebraska Press.

Birren, J. E., Fisher, L. M. (1990). The elements of wisdom: overview and integration. In R. J. Sternberg (Ed.), *Wisdom, Its Nature, Origins and Development* (pp. 317–32). Cambridge: Cambridge University Press.

Blanchard-Fields, F., Mienaltowski, A., Seay, R. (2011). Age differences in everyday problem-solving effectiveness: older adults select more effective strategies for interpersonal problems. *Journal of Gerontology: Psychological Sciences*, 62B(1), P61–4.

Bowling, A. (2007). Aspiration for older age in the 21st century: what is successful ageing? *International Journal of Ageing and Human Development*, 64(3), 263–97.

Brose, A., Roover, K., Ceulemans, E., et al. (2015). Older adults' affective experiences across 100 days are less variable and less complex than younger adults. *Psychology and Aging*, 30(1), 194–208.

Brown, N., Sokal, A., Friedman, H. (2013). The complex dynamics of wishful thinking: the critical positivity ratio, *American Psychologist*, 68, 801–13, http://dx.doi .org/10.1037/a0032850.

Burton, C., Bonanno, G. (2016). Regulatory flexibility and its role in adaptation to aversive events throughout the lifespan. In A. Ong & C. Lockenhoff (Eds.), *Emotion, Aging, and Health*. Washington: American Psychological Association, pp. 7–30.

Carstensen, L. (1992). Social and emotional patterns in adulthood: support for socioemotional selectivity theory. *Psychology and Aging*, 7, 331–8.

Carstensen, L., Isaacowitz, D., Charles, S. (1999). Taking time seriously: a theory of socioemotional selectivity, *American Psychologist*, 54(3), 165–81.

Carstensen, L., Fung, H., Charles, S. (2003). Socioemotional selectivity theory and the regulation of emotion in the second half of life. *Motivation and Emotion*, 27(2), 103–23.

Carstensen, L., Turan, B., Scheibe, S., et al. (2011). Emotional experience improves with age: evidence based on over 10 years of experience sampling, *Psychol Aging*. 26(1), 21–33. doi: 10.1037/a0021285.

Castelli, L., Lanza, F. (2011). Long life to emotions: emotional response categorisation across the lifespan. *Cognition and Emotion*, 25(8), 1520–5.

Charles, S. (2010). Strength and vulnerability integration (SAVI): a model of emotional well-being across adulthood. *Psychological Bulletin*, 136, 1068–91. http:// dx.doi.org/10.1037/a0021232.

Cohen, S. (2004). Social relationships and health. *American Psychologist*, 59, 676–84.

Davis, M., Zautra, A., Johnson, L., et al. (2007). Psychosocial stress. Emotion regulation, and resilience among older adults. In C. Aldwin, C. Park, & A. Spiro (Eds.), *Handbook of Health Psychology and Aging*. NY: Guilford, ch. 13, 250–66.

Depp, C. A., Jeste, D. V. (2006). Definitions and predictors of successful aging: A comprehensive review of larger quantitative studies. *American Journal of Geriatric Psychiatry*, *14*(1), 6–20.

(2009). Phenotypes of successful aging. In C. A. Depp & D. V., Jeste, D. V. (Eds.), *Successful Cognitive and Emotional Aging*. Washington, DC: American Psychiatric Press, Inc., 2009 (419 pages). Inc ch 1 pp. 1–14.

English, T., Carstensen, L. (2015). Does positivity operate when the stakes are high? health status and decision making among older adults, *Psychology and Aging*, 30(2), 348–55.

Erikson, E. H. (1959). *Identity and the Life Cycle*. New York: International Universities Press.

Erikson, E., Erikson, J., Kivnick, H. (1986). *Vital Involvement in Old Age*. New York: W.W. Norton & Company.

Fairfield, B., Mammarella, N., Domenico, A. (2013). Centenarians' "Holy" memory: is being positive enough? *The Journal of Genetic Psychology*, 174(1), 42–50.

Fernandez-Ballesteros, R. (2008). *Active Ageing: The Contribution of Psychology*. GottingeÅNn: Hogrefe and Huber.

Fernandez-Ballesteros, R., Garcia, L. F., Abarca, D., et al. (2010). The concept of "ageing well" in ten Latin American and European countries. *Ageing & Society*, 30, 41–56. doi: 10.1017/S0144686X09008587.

Fredrickson, B. L. (1998). What good are positive emotions? *Review of General Psychology*, 2(3), 300–19.

(2001). The role of positive emotions in positive psychology: The broaden-and-build theory of positive emotions. *American Psychologist*, 56, 218–26. doi: 10.1037/0003-066X.56.3.218.

(2003). The value of positive emotions. *American Scientist*, 91(4), 330–5.

Fredrickson, B.L., Losada, M. F. (2005). Positive affect and the complex dynamics of human flourishing. *American Psychologist*, 60(7), 678.

Gana, K., Saada, Y., Amieva, H. (2015). Does positive affect change in old age? Results from a 22-year longitudinal study. *Psychology and Aging*, 30(1), 172–9.

Gross, J. (2014). Emotion regulation: conceptual and empirical foundation. In J. Gross (Ed.), *Handbook of Emotion Regulation* (2nd ed., pp. 3–20). New York: Guilford Press.

Grossmann, I., Karasawa, M., Kan, C., et al. (2014). A cultural perspective on emotional experiences across the life span. *Emotion*, *14*(4), 679–92.

Isaacowitz, D., Riediger, M. (2011). When age matters: Developmental perspectives on "cognition and emotion." *Cognition and Emotion*, 25(6), 957–67.

Kalenzaga, S., Lamidey, V., Ergis, A.-M., et al. (2016). The positivity bias in aging: motivation or degradation? *Emotion*. Advance online publication. http://dx.doi.org/10.1037/emo0000170.

Kubzansky, L. D., Boehm, J. K. (2016). Positive psychological functioning: an enduring asset for healthy aging. In A. D. Ong & C. E. Lockenhoff (Eds.), *Emotion, Aging, and Health*. Washington, DC: American Psychological Association.

Labouvie-Vief, G., DeVoe, M., Bulka, D. (1989). Speaking about feelings: conceptions of emotion across life span. *Psychology and Aging*, 4(4), 425–37.

Lefebvre, G., Lebreton, M., Meyniel, F., et al. (2017). Behavioural and neural characterization of optimistic reinforcement learning, *Nature Human Behaviour*, 1, 0067, doi: 10.1038/s41562-017-0067.

Lockenhoff, C., Carstensen, L. (2004). Socioemotional selectivity theory, aging, and health: the increasingly delicate balance between regulating emotions and making tough choices. *Journal of Personality*, 72(6).

Lopez, S., Snyder, C., Rasmussen, H. (2003). Striking a vital balance: developing a complementary focus on human weakness and strength through positive psychological assessment. In S. Lopez & C. R. Snyder (Eds.), *Positive Psychological Assessment, a Handbook of models and measures*. Washington, DC: APA.

Martins, B., Mather, M. (2016). Default mode network and later-life emotion regulation: linking functional connectivity patterns and emotional outcomes. In A. Ong & C. Lockenhoff (Eds.), *Emotion, Aging, and Health* (pp. 7–30), Washington, DC: APA.

Mejía, S., Hooker, K. (2015). Emotional well-being and interactions with older adults' close social partners: daily variation in social context matters. *Psychology and Aging*, 30(3), 517–28.

Mikels, J., Shuster, M. (2016). The interpretative lenses of older adults are not rose-colored—just less dark: aging and the interpretation of ambiguous scenarios. *Emotion*, 16(1), 94–100.

Neta, M., Tong, T. (2016). Don't like what you see? give it time: longer reaction times associated with increased positive affect. *Emotion*. Advance online publication. http://dx.doi.org/10.1037/emo0000181.

Paúl, C., Teixeira, L., Ribeiro, O. (2015). Positive aging beyond "success": towards a more inclusive perspective of high level functioning in old age. *Educational Gerontology*, doi: 10.1080/03601277.2015.1071590.

Pruchno, R. A., Wilson-Genderson, M., Rose, M., et al. (2010). Successful aging: early influences and contemporary characteristics. *Gerontologist*, *50*(6), 821–33.

Reichstadt, J., Sengupta, G., Depp, C. A., et al. (2010). Older adults' perspectives on successful aging: qualitative interviews. *Am J Geriatr Psychiatry*, *18*(7), 567–75.

Riediger, M., Luong, G. (2016). Happy to be unhappy? Pro and contrahedonic motivation from adolescence to old age. In A. Ong & C. Lockenhoff (Eds.), *Emotion, Aging, and Health* (pp. 97–118). Washington, DC: APA.

Riegel, K. (1976). The dialectics of human development, *American Psychologist*, 31(10), 689–700. http://dx.doi.org/10.1037/0003-066X.31.10.689.

Robertson, S., Hopko, D. (2013). Emotional expression during autobiographical narratives as a function of aging: support for the socioemotional selectivity theory. *J Adult Dev*. 20, 76–86. doi: 10.1007/s10804-013-9158-6.

Rowe, J. W., Kahn, R. L. (1997). Successful aging. *Gerontologist*, *37*(4), 433–40.

Salovey, P., Rothman, A., Detweiler, J., et al. (2000). Emotional states and physical health. *American Psychologist*, 55(1), 110–21.

Samanez-Larkin, G. R., Robertson, E. R. (2009). Selective attention to emotion in the aging brain. *Psychology and Aging*, 24(3), 519–29.

Samanez-Larkin, G., Robertson, E., Mikels, J., et al. (2014). Selective attention to emotion in the aging brain. *Motivation Science*, 1(S), 49–63.

Seligman, M. (2002). *Authentic Happiness: Using the New Positive Psychology to Realize Your Potential for Lasting Fulfillment*. New York: Free Press.

Seligman, M., Parks, A., Steen, T. (2005). A balanced psychology and a full life. In F. Huppert, N. Baylis, & B. Keverne (Eds.), *The Science of Well-being* (ch 10, pp. 275–83). New York: Oxford.

Skinner, B. F. (1953). *Science and Human Behavior*, Pearson Education, Inc.

Staudinger, U. M., Leipold, B. (2003). The assessment of wisdom-related performance. In S. J. Lopez & C. R. Snyder (Eds.), *The Handbook of Positive Psychology Assessment* (pp. 171–84). Washington, DC: APA.

Tornstam, L. (1989). Gero-transcendence: A reformulation of the disengagement theory. *Aging*, 1, 55–63.

  (2005). *Gerotranscendence: A Developmental Theory of Positive Aging*. New York: Springer Publishing Company.

  (2011). Maturing into gerotranscendence. *The Journal of Transpersonal Psychology*, 43(2).

Urry, H. (2016). Resources for emotion regulation in older age: linking cognitive resources with cognitive reappraisal. In A. Ong & C. Lockenhoff (Eds.), *Emotion, Aging, and Health* (pp. 97–118). Washington, DC: APA.

Vogel, N., Schilling, O. K., Wahl, H. W., et al. (2013). Time-to-death-related change in positive and negative affect among older adults approaching the end of life. *Psychology and Aging*, 28, 128–41. http://dx.doi.org/10.1037/a0030471.

Wirtz, D., Chiu, C., Diener, E., et al. (2009). What constitutes a good life? Cultural differences in the role of positive and negative affect in subjective well-being, *Journal of Personality*, 77(4), 1167–96. doi: 10.1111/j.1467-6494.2009.00578.x.

# 22 Personal Control and Successful Aging

Katherine E. Bercovitz, Christelle Ngnoumen, and Ellen J. Langer

## Introduction: Defining Control

Researchers in the field of psychology have long investigated the phenomenon of personal control and have adopted many terms to describe the various theoretical nuances assumed under the concept of "control." These areas of research include the illusion of control (Langer, 1975; Langer & Roth, 1975), learned helplessness (Seligman, 1972), internal and external locus of control (Rotter, 1966), primary and secondary control (Rothbaum et al., 1982), self-efficacy (Bandura, 1977), and self-mastery (Adler, 1927). Personal control reflects individuals' beliefs regarding the extent to which they are able to control or influence outcomes. One important distinction made in this literature concerns the difference between actual (objective) control over one's life and one's perceived (subjective) control over life. There is much evidence to suggest that perceived personal control influences a person's behaviors, emotions, and health more strongly than actual (objective) control (e.g., Langer, 1975; McAndrew et al., 2010).

Psychological theory and research suggest that personal control beliefs strongly predict future behavior, health, and illness (e.g., Peterson and Stunkard, 1992). Positive correlations between personal control and health suggest that belief in one's control is closely tied to physical well-being (e.g., Langer et al., 1975), while belief in one's helplessness is linked to mortality and morbidity. This chapter will focus on the effects of perceived personal control and how it relates to successful aging, along with the factors that limit it. We will also discuss strategies that can help older people maximize perceived personal control, with a special focus on mindfulness without meditation.

## The Illusion of Control

In 1967, sociologist James Henslin observed that people attempted to control the outcome of a die roll (Henslin, 1967). Specifically, Henslin observed that some people threw the die softly in an attempt to produce a low number or threw more rigorously to produce a high number. Experimental investigations have shown that when a chance-governed situation incorporates characteristics relevant to skill-determined situations (e.g., choice, familiarity, involvement, competition), people often respond to the situation as if it is skill-determined and behave as though they can control chance events. This skill orientation in a chance situation is known as the illusion of control (Langer, 1975). Langer's research on the illusion of control provided empirical support for this view and has shown that it is even more extensive than Henslin suggested. Examples of how people apply skill orientations in chance situations include actively engaging with the experience and familiarizing themselves with the materials. In one study, participants were given the chance to select a lottery ticket and then given the opportunity to exchange the ticket for one they were told had a better chance of winning. Despite the increased odds associated with the new ticket, participants were significantly more likely to keep their original ticket. This was the harbinger of the endowment effect (Carmon & Ariely, 2000). In a similar vein, studies have demonstrated how participants mistake luck for skill (Myers & Fort, 1963; Langer & Roth, 1975).

Myers and Fort (1963) presented participants with a series of gambles and the option of accepting or rejecting any particular gamble. Participants were shown the outcome of each trial whether or not the gamble was accepted. They found that if participants had accepted the previous gamble and won, they were more likely to accept the next gamble, compared to it if they had accepted and lost, even though in a chance-based task winning or losing should not influence confidence on subsequent trials because trials are independent. Langer (1975) found that participants were more confident that they would win a game of chance when playing against an awkward confederate, as opposed to a more confident one. Participants were also more likely to rate a chance game (e.g., predicting a series of coin tosses on a fair coin) as one requiring skill after having a series of initial successes (Langer & Roth, 1975).

The associated advantages of feeling in control suggest that the illusion of control is an adaptive process. Some researchers have argued that positive illusions, such as our failures to recognize our incompetence and our tendency to overestimate our ability to control events, are evolutionarily adaptive errors that have served us in creating and maintaining a sense of consistency – and thus reducing negative emotional experiences – as we navigate the world (Taylor & Brown, 1988; Ehrlinger & Dunning, 2003). Illusions of control are adaptive biases, as they enable people to feel hopeful in situations where they perceive uncertainty and risk. Research finds that people who feel they have control of a situation are likely to exhibit behaviors that will better enable them to cope with potentially threatening situations compared to those who believe that chance or other non-controllable factors determine whether their behavior will be successful (Monty et al., 1973). The full discussion of the benefits of perceived control can be found later in this chapter.

## Personal Control and Social Stereotypes about Older Adults

Interestingly, people believe they can control chance events, but at the same time, they perceive the aging process as one of increased disability and uncontrollable decline (Langer, 1989b; Fiske et al., 2002). Associations between old age and ill-health – fostered by societal messages, negative labeling, and stigmatization of older adults – lend to expectations of decline and of incompetence among this age group, which causes them to give up control and lowers self-esteem (Langer, 1979; Rodin & Langer, 1980).

The venerable qualities originally subsumed in the term "elderly" are largely overlooked in its colloquial use. In its original form, the term described a wise and respected individual of advanced age; however, its contemporary use has come to ascribe it with the same assumptions of instability and uncontrollability as labels of chronic illness and decline. Similar to labels of chronic illness, our society's labels for aging individuals have managed to foster implicit negative attitudes about older adults as being inflexible, incompetent, low in personal control, and susceptible to ill-health. Drastic increases in life expectancy over the past century, coinciding with a shift in leading causes of death from acute to chronic illness, may have contributed to a view of aging and chronic illness as inextricably linked. While it is typically assumed that susceptibility to chronic illnesses and disabilities increases with age, contrary to expectations, poor health is not an inevitable consequence of aging (Rowe & Kahn, 1987). Moreover, no direct evidence that age changes are governed by a genetic program have been found (Hayflick, 2007). In fact, there is more direct evidence that shows that aging is governed by psychological, behavioral, and environmental factors within the individual's control.

One of the most significant factors that leads to a relinquishing of personal control and to an illusion of incompetence are premature cognitive commitments (Langer, 1979). Premature cognitive commitments form when we accept initial impressions or pieces of information at face value, without thinking critically about their context-dependent nature, and allow those initial impressions to settle and crystallize in our minds until similar signals from the world call up these impressions or information again. At this point, however, now later in time and in a much different context, we nevertheless respond to those initial impressions and information in the same way as we had the first time; i.e., even though the previously learned information does not dictate behavior in the current context in which it is now triggered, we still act according to the old information. Premature cognitive commitments therefore reflect a mindless process in so far as previously learned information is no longer available for conscious processing and evaluation.

In the case of aging, we learn as children what it means to be "old." This information is learned free of context and is later unpacked, just as it was initially learned for reference once people reach older age. The specific "facts" that Western children learn characterize the aging process as one of inevitable and largely uncontrollable decline. These attitudes are pervasive in Western society to such an extent that even young children espouse these attitudes; even before entering elementary school, children demonstrate negative stereotypes toward older adults (Isaacs & Bearison, 1986). Moreover, there is evidence to suggest that as a person ages these stereotypes become self-views (Rothermund, 2005). Not only do people explicitly stereotype older adults, but they also hold implicit stereotypes about this age group (Levy & Banaji, 2004).

The primary stereotypes held about older adults are that they are high in "warmth" dimensions (e.g., "kind"), but low in competence dimensions (e.g., "frail") (Fiske et al., 2002; Cuddy & Fiske, 2004). While age-based stereotypes are multifaceted and include both positive and negative aspects (Cuddy et al., 2008), the negative aspects are generally more emphasized, with older adults generally stereotyped as forgetful, slow, timid, weak, and rigid (Nelson, 2004).

It is of little surprise that people of all ages hold implicit and explicit stereotypes of older adults, given how deeply they insinuate themselves into Western culture. This is reflected in and perpetuated by linguistic patterns. Specifically, a textual analysis spanning English material across a 200-year period of time demonstrated a linear trajectory of negative age-based stereotypes (Ng et al., 2015). For example, negative societal expectations about the aging process are reflected in common expressions, including "senior moments," which semantically links age and forgetfulness (Bonnesen & Burgess, 2004), and "over the hill," a phrase indicating decline.

Pertinent to the current discussion of perceived control and successful aging, societal stereotypes of old age contribute to personal experiences of decreased perceived control in older adults. Specifically, expectations of aging as a process of increasing dependence on others can negatively affect older adults' experience of self-efficacy and control. The language of aging and age-related cues dictate functioning as individuals' identities crystallize around assumptions that then become self-fulfilling prophecies or situation-inferred losses of control.

Consistent with Langer's mind/body unity theory, the stereotype embodiment theory (Levy, 2009) describes how people age in accordance with their stereotypes about older people. For example, individuals from cultures with predominantly strong negative beliefs about older people were more likely to experience memory problems (Levy & Langer, 1994). These attitudes not only affected their memory, but predicted longevity; survival analyses revealed that people with positive attitudes of aging lived about 7.5 years more than those who held negative beliefs about the aging process (Levy et al., 2002). Studies have shown that the self-perception of memory decline, as well as stereotypic beliefs of aging, are strong predictors of actual memory decline (Cook & Marsiske, 2006). Moreover, perceived memory decline was implicated in subsequent global cerebral metabolic decline (Ercoli et al., 2006). People who held more negative age stereotypes earlier showed significantly steeper loss of hippocampal volume and more accumulation of neurofrillary tangles and amyloid plaques, both of which are associated with Alzheimer's disease (Levy et al., 2016).

## Benefits of Perceived Personal Control

A vast amount of literature provides strong evidence for the powerful influence of perceived control on health and well-being (Langer et al., 1975; Langer & Rodin, 1976; Rodin & Langer, 1977; Presson & Benassi, 1996; McKay & Dennett, 2009). Research shows that perceived control predicts the development of positive health behaviors and stress-management strategies that, overtime, prevent future health problems. Higher perceived control is linked to lower psychological stress, fewer acute and chronic illnesses, lower obesity rates, and reduced mortality risks.

Individuals with greater perceived control demonstrate greater use of problem-focused coping efforts during stressful situations (Compas et al., 2006). Problem-focused coping strategies, which involve problem-solving, time management, and obtaining instrumental social support, more directly reduce sources of stress compared to emotion-focused methods (e.g., distractions, thought suppression, eating, drinking, drug use). In general, people who use problem-focused strategies report less stress and greater psychological well-being (Penley et al., 2012).

Perceived control also predicts cardiovascular health. In a study by Kozela et al. (2015), higher perceived control was strongly associated with lower cardiovascular mortality in a Polish sample of older adults, and this relationship remained after controlling for age, sex, education, marital status, hypertension, hypercholesterolemia, smoking, body mass index, diabetes, and history of cardiovascular disease. Using a mediation model, Lachman and Firth (2004) found support for the prediction that control beliefs predict health via their influence on exercise and healthy diet. In this study, women reporting greater perceived control, greater general and cardiovascular health, and lower waist-hip ratios tended to engage in regular exercise and other health-promoting behaviors such as maintaining balanced eating regimens and complying with medical treatments.

Perceived control has been shown to reduce mortality risk. Langer and Rodin (1976) found that institutionalized older adults who were encouraged to assume a more engaged role in their lives by making more decisions about their living environments (e.g., arranging their own furniture and taking care of a plant) reported greater perceived control and became more alert, more active, happier, and healthier compared to a second group of control participants whose care was entirely determined by nursing home staff. Follow-up data 18 months later revealed that the experimental group also lived longer than the comparison group. At the time of the follow-up, 15 percent of the experimental group had died compared to 30 percent of the comparison group (Rodin & Langer, 1977).

Higher levels of perceived personal control among older individuals with arthritis was also associated with lower use of health services (e.g., visited their physicians less frequently, had fewer laboratory tests, spent less time in hospitals) compared to their low-control counterparts (Chipperfield & Greenslade, 1999). High levels of perceived control has similarly been linked to better adjustment to chronic disease including heart attacks and cancer. Heart attack survivors who attributed the causes of their heart attacks to stress and to other people demonstrated more severe symptoms 1 year following their attacks compared to patients who made fewer attributions (Affleck et al., 1987). Taylor and colleagues (1984) similarly found that attributions of responsibility for cancer to others were significantly associated with poorer adjustment. Breast cancer patients who believed that they could control their cancer in the present (as opposed to the future) demonstrated significantly greater adjustment.

Altogether, these results demonstrate that increasing older adults' sense of perceived control, such as by introducing the elements of choice and personal responsibility, improves health and promotes longevity. These findings have implications for the design of healthcare services; they suggest that increasing older adult patients' active involvement in their own care can increase levels of perceived control over more or less controllable aspects of illness, and in a manner that promotes adjustment.

## Mindfulness and Successful Aging

Given the multitude of benefits associated with feeling a sense of personal control, researchers have focused on outlining methods by which an individual might increase his/her sense of control. In this section we will describe socio-cognitive mindfulness (also called Langerian mindfulness), a multifaceted concept that has been developed over 40 years of research (Langer, 1989b), and is therefore not associated with meditation. Specifically, we will describe its key features and how they may help individuals experience more control over the aging process.

### Two Ways of Being: Mindlessness/Mindfulness

In the 1970s, Langer and colleagues observed empirically how people are quick to recycle a previously learned rule or formula, even when the context is no longer appropriate to use said rule or formula (Langer et al., 1978). These observations led to the theory that people spend the majority of their time in a "mindless" state (Chanowitz & Langer, 1980; Langer, 1989a), which can be understood as operating on "automatic pilot." When a person is mindless, he or she automatically applies either old information or an old mode of thinking to the current context. In this automatic processing model, the person searches for information that is hypothesis supporting. In contrast, when a person is in a "mindful" state, he/she actively notices new things about the current situation and draws novel distinctions; he/she is sensitive to subtle changes in the context. Mindfulness as described by Langer, is about considering alternative perspectives and being open to new possibilities (Langer, 1989b; Langer & Moldoveanu, 2000).[1] According to this theory, a mindful moment starts with the simple act of noticing something on purpose. For example, a person may notice how something is different from how he or she expected it, even if the deviation is quite subtle. In this active process of noticing, the person is open to different possibilities and avenues of choice.

1 Note that we are not referring to "mindfulness" as it is often used in the Eastern tradition, which is achieved through regular practice of meditation.

## Mindfulness and Control in the Individual

Mindfulness can promote a sense of control in at least two ways, namely by attention to variability and by attention to context/nuance. First we will consider how paying attention to the constant changes in the environment, interpersonal relationships, and the self can lead to a sense of personal control.

It may seem like a paradox that someone can gain control from understanding that the world is in constant change. Most people consider the process of change as a negative chaotic force that should be avoided at all costs. Empirical work from over 40 years in our lab, however, has shown that noticing change in symptoms is associated with improved health and psychological well-being (Langer, 1989b). Consider people with "chronic" health conditions who come to believe that they experience their symptoms all the time. When these people are taught to pay attention to how their symptoms change over time, they benefit in at least two ways. First, they experience a general sense of control over their illness by realizing that their symptoms are not present all the time. Second, they begin to notice patterns in their symptoms; namely, that certain contexts make their symptoms more or less severe. In noticing and analyzing these contexts, they can then begin to control their symptoms. Both patients and caregivers, who are more mindful, have been shown to experience more positive well-being, decreased rates of decline and less burnout (Pagnini et al., 2015, 2016).

Consider someone who experiences chronic fatigue. Because their fatigue has been labeled as "chronic," they begin to believe that they are tired all the time. When they are asked to notice times throughout the day that they are more and less tired, they begin to question the control of the illness over their lives. Moreover, they can notice the circumstances under which they are more fatigued and alter their schedules accordingly. An individual may consistently notice more fatigue after meeting with a specific person. If possible, the individual can enact control by avoiding meeting with this person or meeting for a shorter period of time.

The same paradigm of attending to variability can be applied to beliefs around personal abilities. Instead of adhering to the belief that he/she cannot do "X" activity, the individual can ask, "Under what circumstances *can* I do 'X' activity?" and "What parts of 'X' activity can I do?" It may be the case that an individual can complete part of an activity (e.g., they can turn on the water and squeeze the shampoo bottle), but are assumed to be incapable of completing any part of the activity (e.g., unable to shower at all). This belief can manifest as a caregiver performing all parts of the activity, hurting not only individual's sense of ability, but also his or her actual ability over time. If a person is presumed unable to shower at all, soon he or she will lose the hand strength necessary for squeezing the shampoo bottle. In other cases, an individual may be able to complete the full activity, albeit in twice the time he/she (or the caregiver) expects the activity to take. Accepting that certain activities may take some extra time is a small price to pay for continued control over the environment. While it may be easier just to wheel an individual to and from the car in a wheelchair, this may communicate the message that the individual is not able to make the trip independently. Budgeting extra time and exhibiting patience can help an individual feel more confident in trying the activity.

Paying attention to the context of an experience is another way mindfulness can improve well-being and sense of control. Instead of looking for an absolute, mindful individuals constantly search for nuance. When people are trained to pay attention to context, they can learn to see how actions always make sense to the actor from the actor's perspective. For example, a friend described as "rigid" or "uptight," can be seen as dependable with learn mindfulness. Similarly, a colleague seen as "flaky" or "undependable" can also be understood to be spontaneous. Using this sensitivity to context, an individual can also detect the meaningful difference between "can't" and "doesn't want to." Without this perspective, an older person may seem unable to pay attention, but are actually just bored with the topic of discussion.

Setting the same expectations of our past and present selves out of automatic habit is similarly mindless. For example, an individual may become discouraged when he or she needs to buy a shower seat. Instead of focusing on how the seat allows completion of the activity, the focus is on how showering in the standing position is no longer possible. Over time, the shower seat may serve as a physical reminder that the individual cannot shower as he or she once did, leading to feelings of decreased control. An older adult can bolster a sense of control by breaking the activity into smaller parts and determining how to meet those subordinate goals in the current context:

• What parts of this activity can I do completely by myself?
• What parts of this activity can I do partially by myself?
• What parts of this activity do I think I cannot do? How do I know this? How might I be wrong?
• What parts of this activity could I do if I were not in a rush?
• What parts of this activity could I do if I were feeling confident?
• What parts of this activity could I do considering how I am feeling today?

In addition to considering the circumstances under which an individual can and cannot complete an activity, one could also consider the personal motivation for completing the activity. When mindful, people will question whether the fact that they used to complete an activity independently necessarily means they wish to continue in that fashion. For example, no longer being able to drive may be a relief for an individual who never enjoyed the responsibility of driving and enjoys the ride from the passenger seat. Just because others may experience loss of independence when they are no longer permitted to drive does not mean that an individual has to feel that way. An individual may also inappropriately overgeneralize not being able to drive a car as not being able to do anything independently. While not driving may not bother the individual, the larger idea of being a dependent (being "old") may in turn, contribute to decreased control.

When an individual is sensitive to context, he or she can notice how daily routine can be seen as a constant stream of opportunities to make choices. All people can discover more choice in life by examining their set of daily activities. Oftentimes people do not consider that things can be done another way. For example, someone might have a cup of hot coffee every morning. If he/she could consider drinking tea or even a glass of iced coffee as an alternative, then drinking hot coffee becomes a choice. In this way, people can take more control of their everyday life by a simple shift in mindset. Some other examples include realizing that one can take another route home, or brush their teeth with the other hand. In realizing how we can change our daily activities subtly, we can discover a greater freedom of personal choice. Even when we reject the alternatives, noticing that we could have chosen them has been shown to improve perceptions of control (Perlmuter & Langer, 1983).

Reconsidering and reframing the concept of "old age" can also increase perceptions of control. In addition to premature cognitive commitments that limit one's conception of what completing an activity independently may look like, people also hold limiting beliefs about what they, the agent, can achieve, once they reach a certain age. These limiting views can arise from internalization of societal ideas about aging as a process of decline. For example, an older people may wish to stay connected with friends and family over social media, but feel limited by age; they may perceive that as an older person, social media is not designed for them or that they will be "bad at" technology. Indeed, research has suggested that older adults tend to underestimate their technological skills, which may lead to difficulty mastering new technology (Marquié et al., 2002).

How might older adults loosen their premature cognitive commitment about the aging process? Mindfulness theory suggests that noticing new things about the environment (including the self) allows a person to broaden his or her fixed schemas (Langer, 1989b). Specifically, once a person realizes that everything is subject to constant flux, he/she could begin to recognize the wider range of personal attributes that have changed over time. Using this mindful framework, an individual can notice skills that are improving (e.g., wisdom and emotional freedom). Another potential strategy in helping an older person expand a schema is to encourage him/her to identify an even older person achieving the goals that he/she wants to achieve. Identifying a salient role model of aging allows the person to broaden his/her conception of what being "old" can mean. For example, an 80-year-old wanting to feel intellectually stimulated may feel inspired by a story of a 100-year-old earning a college degree. Research has shown that having "young" grandparents growing up was related to a longer life (Hsu et al., 2010), suggesting that one's early schemas of "old" may affect their own longevity (Langer et al., 1988). This loosening of labels is an inherently mindful process.

Another avenue for changing attitudes is subliminal priming methods, which retrain the person to associate the concept of "old" and the concept of "good." Research has shown that this type of training over a few months significantly improves perceptions of control (Levy et al., 2014). If a person has an especially strong and overlearned association of "old" and "bad," another method is to remove cues from the environment that he or she have come to associate with old age. This idea was demonstrated most powerfully by a study conducted in

1979, which warrants a detailed description. In this experiment (Langer 1989b, 2009; Langer et al., 1990), researchers tested the hypothesis that when older people bring their minds back to a more youthful period, their bodies will also become more youthful. To test this hypothesis, 80-year-old men lived together for 5 days in a house retrofitted with furniture and décor from 1959 (20 years before). Participants were instructed to live as though it was actually 1959. The researchers provided magazines, television programs, songs and movies that were popular just 20 years before. Participants were instructed to talk about events that happened in 1959 as though they were current events and not to refer to anything that happened after that date (including personal experiences).

Older men who were randomly assigned to a control group also attended the retreat at the retrofitted house at a separate time, but these men were not asked to live as though it was 1959; instead, they were asked to reminisce about that time in their lives, surrounded by the same cues of 1959. Because the retreat was novel and mindfulness inducing, participants in both the control and experimental groups improved significantly on many measures, which challenged the decline model of aging. Participants in both groups improved on measures of physical health including better hearing, stronger hand strength, and increased appetites. Participants also improved on tasks testing figure memory ability. In regards to engagement, researchers observed that participants took the initiative to prepare their own meals and clean up after themselves, a marked difference from initial reports of dependence on caregivers. These results suggested that removing cues of age and inserting cues of youth affect one's perception of control and health.

Moreover, compared to those who were asked to reminisce about this period, those who "became" their younger selves improved more on measures of vision, joint flexibility, posture, manual dexterity, and digit-symbol substitution. Just by "being" their younger selves, the older adults in the experimental group were able to significantly improve their own health, even on measures that were thought to be irreversible. Moreover, at the end of the study participants looked significantly younger than at the study's start. This suggested that age-related cues affected both physical and cognitive health in dramatic ways.

These findings were corroborated by evidence from Hsu and colleagues (2010), who examined the effects of age cues on health and longevity across five very different settings. One of the primary findings was that women who think they look younger after having their hair colored or cut show a decrease in blood pressure and appear younger in photographs presented to blind raters. In the same study, the researchers discovered that clothing, unlike uniforms, could function as an age-related cue, such that those who wear work uniforms have lower morbidity than those who earn the same amount of money and do not wear work uniforms. They also found that baldness cues old age; male participants who went bald prematurely saw themselves as older, aged faster, and had an increased risk of getting prostate cancer and coronary heart disease compared to male counterparts who did not prematurely bald. Older mothers also demonstrated a longer life expectancy compared to women who bore children earlier in life, possibly due to their exposure to younger age-related cues. Lastly, Hsu et al. found that in domestic relationships involving partners of significantly varying ages, younger spouses lived shorter lives while older spouses lived longer lives, presumably due to their exposures to older and younger age-related cues, respectively.

## Mindful Design to Encourage Perceived Control

Here we consider how our society can incorporate personal control into design and public/institutional policies. Specifically, we look at how to mindfully consider alternatives to current ways of approaching it.

Promoting control in older adults occurs when public and institutional policies encourage individual decision-making and readily provide personal-choice alternatives. As described in the above section, Langer and Rodin (1976) demonstrated that nursing home residents who were provided with choices over their schedules showed more engagement and lived longer than those in the control group. Providing residents with more individualized choice is something that can be easily implemented in an institutional setting.

In the case of assisted living facilities, institutional policy can prevent residents from enacting control. Policies are generally designed to keep all residents safe, sometimes at the expense of personal freedom. Policies are typically designed with the "average person" in mind. In failing to flexibly accommodate individual differences, however, institutions will not be able to support personal control. Consider the example of a person who, before entering an assisted living facility, took a shower every other day. To comply with the institutional protocol, the nurses insist that she shower every day. This blanket policy does not serve the individual and needlessly limits personal control. A more flexible model would consider each resident's needs and not over-apply a principle that does not make sense for an individual.

Rigid stereotypes of aging held by caregivers (family members or professionals) can also affect the extent to which an older person feels in control. Efforts to reduce age stereotypes in caregivers by teaching the principles of mindfulness theory could significantly help older people experience more control. While it may be inconvenient for a caregiver to wait longer for an older person to walk with a walker or finish a meal, these small acts will contribute to the older person's sense of control. In fact, efforts to "help" rather than "encourage" led to disability in nursing home residents (Avorn & Langer, 1982). Similarly, community residents and their social partners (home nurses and family members) have been shown to follow a "dependence support script" (Baltes & Wahl, 1992).

Beyond the context of the institution, policymakers are considering avenues that will allow for greater choice in the society at large. One such effort is the expansion of transportation choices. Driving is closely related to personal freedom, and when older adults are no longer able to drive, they often experience depression, isolation, decreased community involvement, and restriction of lifestyle (e.g., Marottoli et al., 2000; Windsor et al., 2007). Policymakers have communicated the need to accommodate the aging population by improving walkways and making public transportation more convenient and accessible. Self-driving cars may eventually solve this problem. Even subtle changes in city planning can make a difference in improving one's sense of control, especially when driving is no longer an option. For example, timing the traffic light just a bit longer can make it safer for slower walkers to cross the street. Another example is adding more curbs to sidewalks to allow electric scooters to utilize them.

Encouraging continued contribution to society among older adults is also an important mechanism by which they can experience a continued sense of mastery. Sometimes older people can feel invisible or obsolete in a society that values youth over wisdom. Programs in which older adults volunteer their time and skills have been shown to serve a protective role in older adults' psychological well-being (Greenfield & Marks, 2004). Past research has shown that the positive effects of volunteerism are mediated by perceptions of personal control (Mellor et al., 2008).

## Conclusions and Future Directions

### Aging as a Choice

Successful aging is a product of expectation and, ultimately, the exercise of choice. The data on aging stereotypes, and of their self-fulfilling impacts on actual health and well-being, suggest that aging is a choice and an evaluation. From a young age, we are repeatedly told the same story – a story about chronological (actual) aging, which is a natural phenomenon all humans experience. For some of us, however, this story will be interpreted mindlessly and unconditionally, such that we will come to view certain arbitrary experiences (e.g., lower back pain at age 50) as definitive markers of an uncontrollable aging process. That is, some of us will choose to create a reality of aging by reinforcing it through our interpretations of personal experiences (e.g., lower back pain at age 50 must necessarily mean I'm aging and declining, rather than being related to the gardening activities I am currently engaging in).

### Defining Aging

It also remains unclear what exactly we mean when we talk about "aging." The reality of most of our life experiences is that they exist as multiple, separate, and temporary states (e.g., lower back pain and forgetting where keys are at age 50 may be two separate, unrelated, and temporary experiences). Our inclination, however, is to try to connect isolated experiences into a coherent story. The "aging" story seems to have evolved as a way to link together all experiences of loss or decline occurring at a later chronological stage. Moreover, this linking of seemingly related experiences contributes to a view of "aging" as an ongoing, uncontrollable, and permanent process. There is a lot of variance in the aging process, however. In fact, there is as much variation among "older adults" as there is among "younger adults," which suggests that there is not one monolithic aging experience, but rather that there are multiple ones, perhaps as many aging experiences as there are older adults in the world.

## Adaptive Aging

Aging stereotypes and their associated stigmas also divert attention away from the potential benefits of aging. Mindlessly instilled fears of decline prevent us from seeing age as a time of necessary loss and of growing wisdom (e.g., increased efficiency). Research has shown, for example, that older adults are less inclined to engage in certain activities compared to their younger counterparts *not* because they can no longer do them, but because the perceived value of the activities decreases over time (see Chanowitz & Langer, 1980). Older adults' transitions away from 40-hour work weeks is an example of such a shift; as individuals get older and attain financial security, the perceived value of work and of financial compensation gets replaced with other kinds of values and needs, including increased interests in hobbies, volunteer work, spending time with extended family, shopping, and traveling. Older adults' decreased engagement in work-related activities therefore does not need to reflect incompetence, but rather may speak to a more differentiated and evolved valuation system. In a similar vein, lower memory recall among older adults on standard memory tasks tends to be interpreted as evidence of general memory decline in old age. Few researchers, however, have sought to determine whether older adults' recall truly declines or merely shifts toward content that is of greater relevance to them, as Langer and colleagues (1979) suggested. If it turned out that older adults' memory remained intact for relevant items only, then this would reflect increased efficiency in memory rather than general memory loss. That is, the aging story would once again shift from one of decline to one of growth. If the aging experience were, in fact, to reflect a progression toward increased efficiency, then preconceptions of aging will need to shift toward understanding it as an adaptive aging process. Future research therefore needs to more closely understand the qualitative nature of the memory changes that occur later in life, as opposed to merely focusing on the total number of words older adults remember from a list generated by an unrepresentative (e.g., younger) sample.

Observed shifts in older adults' values from work and financial gains to volunteering and hobbies also suggest that older age is necessarily a time for innovation and for trying new things. Older adults are more emotionally resilient and less concerned with what other people will think of them than younger adults. These traits may encourage creative solutions that younger people are afraid to suggest.

The upside of aging also shows that as people get older they feel relatively younger. For example, among adults aged 65 and older, 60 percent expressed feeling younger than their age, compared with 32 percent who said they felt exactly their age and 3 percent who said they felt older than their age. In contrast, among 18- to 29-year-olds, half said they felt their age, while about a quarter said they felt older than their age and another quarter said they felt younger than their age. The gap in years between actual (chronological) age and psychological age therefore widens as people grow older (Pew Research Center, 2009). Data on subjective age suggest that older adults understand intuitively what researchers are just beginning to discover: that age is just a number.

## References

Adler, A. (1927). *Understanding Human Nature*. New York: Greenburg.

Affleck, G., Tennen, H., Croog, S., et al. (1987). Causal attribution, perceived control, and recovery from a heart attack. *Journal of Social and Clinical Psychology*, 5(3), 339–55.

Avorn, J., Langer, E. (1982). Induced disability in nursing home patients: a controlled trial. *Journal of American Geriatric Society*, 30, 397–400.

Baltes, M. M., Wahl, H. W. (1992). The dependency-support script in institutions: generalization to community settings. *Psychology and Aging*, 7(3), 409.

Bandura, A. (1977). Self-efficacy: Toward a unified theory of behavioral change. *Psychological Reviews*, 84, 191–215.

Bonnesen, J. L., Burgess, E. O. (2004). Senior moments: The acceptability of an ageist phrase. *Journal of Aging Studies*, 18(2), 123–42.

Carmon, Z., Ariely, D. (2000). Focusing on the forgone: How value can appear so different to buyers and sellers. *Journal of Consumer Research*, 27(3), 360–70.

Chanowitz, B., Langer, E. (1980). Knowing more (or less) than you can show: Understanding control through the mindlessness-mindfulness distinction. In M. E. P. Seligman & J. Garber (Eds.), *Human Helplessness: Theory and Applications*. New York: Academic Press.

Chipperfield, J. G., Greenslade, L. (1999). Perceived control as a buffer in the use of health care services. *Psychological Sciences*, 54B(3), 146–54.

Compas, B. E., Boyer, M. C., Stanger, C., et al. (2006). Latent variable analysis of coping, anxiety/depression, and somatic symptoms in adolescents with chronic pain. *Journal of Consulting and Clinical Psychology*, 74, 1132–42.

Cook, S., Marsiske, M. (2006). Subjective memory beliefs and cognitive performance in normal and mildly impaired older adults. *Aging and Mental Health*, 10(4), 413–23.

Cuddy, A. J., Fiske, S. T. (2004). Doddering but dear: Process, content, and function in stereotyping of older persons. In T. D. Nelson (Ed.), *Ageism: Stereotyping and Prejudice Against Older Persons* (pp. 3–26). Cambridge, MA: MIT Press.

Cuddy, A. J., Fiske, S. T., Glick, P. (2008). Warmth and competence as universal dimensions of social perception: The stereotype content model and the BIAS map. *Advances in Experimental Social Psychology*, 40, 61–149.

Ehrlinger, J., Dunning, D. (2003). How chronic self-views influence (and potentially mislead) estimates of performance. *Journal of Personality and Social Psychology*, 84, 5–17.

Ercoli, L., Siddarth, P., Huang, S. C., et al. (2006). Perceived loss of memory ability and cerebral metabolic decline in persons with the apolipoprotein E-IV genetic risk for Alzheimer disease. *Archives of General Psychiatry*, 63(4), 442–8.

Fiske, S. T., Cuddy, A. J., Glick, P., et al. (2002). A model of (often mixed) stereotype content: Competence and warmth respectively follow from perceived status and competition. *Journal of Personality and Social Psychology*, 82(6), 878.

Greenfield, E. A., Marks, N. F. (2004). Formal volunteering as a protective factor for older adults' psychological well-being. *The Journals of Gerontology Series B: Psychological Sciences and Social Sciences*, 59(5), S258–S264.

Hayflick, L. (2007). Entropy explains aging, genetic determinism explains longevity, and undefined terminology explains misunderstanding both. *PLoS Genetics*, 3(12), e220. http://doi.org/10.1371/journal.pgen.0030220.

Henslin, J. M. (1967). Craps and magic. *American Journal of Sociology*, 316–30.

Hsu, L. M., Chung, J., Langer, E. J. (2010). The influence of age-related cues on health and longevity. *Perspectives on Psychological Science*, 5, 632–48.

Isaacs, L. W., Bearison, D. J. (1986). The development of children's prejudice against the aged. *The International Journal of Aging and Human Development*, 23(3), 175–94.

Kozela, M., Dorynska, A., Stepaniak, U., et al. (2015). Perceived control as a predictor of cardiovascular disease mortality in Poland: The Hapiee study. *Cardiology Journal*, 22, 404–12.

Lachman, M. E., Firth, K. M. (2004). The adaptive value of feeling in control during midlife. In O. G. Brim, C. D. Ryff & R. Kessler (Eds.), *How healthy are we? A national study of well-being at midlife* (pp. 320–49). Chicago: University of Chicago Press.

Langer, E. J. (1975). The illusion of control. *Journal of Personality and Social Psychology*, 32(2), 311–28.

(1979). The illusion of incompetence. In L. Perlmuter & R. Monty (Eds.), *Choice and Perceived Control*. New Jersey: Lawrence Erlbaum.

(1989a). Minding matters: The consequences of mindlessness mindfulness. *Advances in Experimental Social Psychology*, 22(12), 137–73.

(1989b). *Mindfulness*. Reading: Addison-Wesley/Addison Wesley Longman.

(2009). *Counterclockwise: Mindful health and the power of possibility*. New York, NY: Ballantine Books.

Langer, E., Roth, J. (1975). Heads I win, tails it's chance: The illusion of control as a function of the sequence of outcomes in a purely chance task. *Journal of Personality and Social Psychology*, 32, 951–5.

Langer, E. J., Rodin, J. (1976). The effects of choice and enhanced personal responsibility for the aged: a field experiment in an institutional setting. *Journal of Personality and Social Psychology*, 34(2), 191.

Langer, E. J., Moldoveanu, M. (2000). The construct of mindfulness. *Journal of Social Issues*, 56(1), 1–9.

Langer, E. J., Janis, I. L., Wolfer, J. A. (1975). Reduction of psychological stress in surgical patients. *Journal of Experimental Social Psychology*, 11(2), 155–65.

Langer, E., Blank, A., Chanowitz, B. (1978). The mindlessness of ostensibly thoughtful action: The role of placebic information in interpersonal interaction. *Journal of Personality and Social Psychology*, 36, 635–42.

Langer, E., Rodin, J., Beck, P., et al. (1979). Environmental determinants of memory improvement in late adulthood. *Journal of Personality and Social Psychology*, 37, 2003–13.

Langer, E., Perlmuter, L., Chanowitz, B., et al. (1988). Two new applications of mindlessness theory: Aging and alcoholism. *Journal of Aging Studies*, 2, 289–99.

Langer, E., Chanowitz, B., Jacobs, S., et al. (1990). Nonsequential development and aging. In C. Alexander & E. Langer (Eds.), *Higher Stages of Human Development*. New York: Oxford University Press.

Levy, B. (2009). Stereotype embodiment a psychosocial approach to aging. *Current Directions in Psychological Science*, *18*(6), 332–6.

Levy, B., Langer, E. (1994). Aging free from negative stereotypes: Successful memory in China among the American deaf. *Journal of Personality and Social Psychology*, 66(6), 989.

Levy, B. R., Banaji, M. R. (2004). Implicit ageism. In T.D. Nelson (Ed.), *Ageism: Stereotyping and prejudice against older persons* (pp. 49–75). Cambridge, MA: MIT Press.

Levy, B. R., Slade, M. D., Kunkel, S. R., et al. (2002). Longevity increased by positive self-perceptions of aging. *Journal of Personality and Social Psychology*, 83(2), 261.

Levy, B. R., Pilver, C., Chung, P. H., et al. (2014). Subliminal strengthening improving older individuals' physical function over time with an implicit-age-stereotype intervention. *Psychological Science*, 25(12), 2127–35.

Levy, B. R., Ferrucci, L., Zonderman, A. B., et al. (2016). A culture–brain link: Negative age stereotypes predict Alzheimer's disease biomarkers. *Psychology and Aging*, *31*(1), 82.

Marottoli, R. A., de Leon, C. F. M., Glass, T. A., et al. (2000). Consequences of driving cessation decreased out-of-home activity levels. *The Journals of Gerontology Series B: Psychological Sciences and Social Sciences*, 55(6), S334–S340.

Marquié, J. C., Jourdan-Boddaert, L., Huet, N. (2002). Do older adults underestimate their actual computer knowledge?. *Behaviour and Information Technology*, 21(4), 273–80.

McAndrew, L. M., Horowitz, C. R., Lancaster, K. J., et al. (2010). Factors related to perceived diabetes control are not related to actual glucose control for minority patients with diabetes. *Diabetes Care*, 33(4), 736–8.

McKay, R. T., Dennett, D. C. (2009). The evolution of misbelief. *Behavioral and Brain Sciences*, 32(06), 493–510.

Mellor, D., Hayashi, Y., Firth, L., et al. (2008). Volunteering and well-being: Do self-esteem, optimism, and perceived control mediate the relationship?. *Journal of Social Service Research*, 34(4), 61–70.

Monty, R. A., Rosenberger, M. A., Perlmuter, L. C. (1973). Amount and locus of choice as sources of motivation in paired-associate learning. *Journal of Experimental Psychology*, 97, 16–21.

Myers, J. L., Fort, J. G. (1963). Sequential analysis of gambling behavior. *Journal of General Psychology*, 69, 299–309.

Nelson, T. D. (2004). *Ageism: Stereotyping and prejudice against older persons*. MIT press.

Ng, R., Allore, H. G., Trentalange, M., et al. (2015). Increasing negativity of age stereotypes across 200 years: evidence from a database of 400 million words. *PloS One*, 10(2), e0117086.

Pagnini, F., Phillips, D., Bosma, C. M., et al. (2015). Mindfulness, physical impairment and psychological well-being in people with amyotrophic lateral sclerosis. *Psychology and Health*, 30(5), 503–17.

Pagnini, F., Phillips, D., Bosma, C. M., et al. (2016). Mindfulness as a protective factor for the burden of caregivers of amyotrophic lateral sclerosis patients. *Journal of Clinical Psychology*, 72(1), 101–11.

Penley, J. A., Tomaka, J., Wiebe, J. S. (2002). The association of coping to physical and psychological health outcomes: A meta-analytic review. *Journal of Behavioral Medicine*, *25*(6), 551–603.

Perlmuter, L., Langer, E. (1983). The effects of behavioral monitoring on the perception of control. *The Clinical Gerontologist*, 1, 37–43.

Peterson, C., Stunkard, A. J. (1992). Cognates of personal control: Locus of control, self-efficacy, and explanatory style. *Applied and Preventive Psychology*, 1, 111–17.

Pew Research Center Social and Demographics Trends. (2009). *Growing old in America: Expectations vs. reality*. Washington, DC. http://assets.pewresearch.org/wp-content/uploads/sites/3/2010/10/Getting-Old-in-America.pdf.

Presson, P. K., Benassi, V. A. (1996). Illusion of control: A meta-analytic review. *Journal of Social Behavior and Personality*, 11(3), 493–510.

Rodin, J., Langer, E. J. (1977). Long-term effects of a control-relevant intervention with the institutionalized aged. *Journal of Personality and Social Psychology*, *35*(12), 897.

(1980). Aging labels: The decline of control and the fall of self-esteem. *Journal of Social Issues*, 36(2), 12–29.

Rothbaum, F., Weisz, J. R., Snyder, S. S. (1982). Changing the world and changing the self: A two-process model of perceived control. *Journal of Personality and Social Psychology*, 42(1), 5.

Rothermund, K. (2005). Effects of age stereotypes on self views and adaptation. In W. Greve, K. Rothermund, & D. Wentura (Eds.), *The adaptive self: Personal continuity and intentional self-development* (pp. 223–242). Göttingen, Germany: Hogrefe & Huber.

Rotter, J. B. (1966). Generalized expectancies for internal versus external control of reinforcement. *Journal of Educational Research*, 74(3), 185–90.

Rowe, J. W., Kahn, R. L. (1987). Human aging: Usual and successful. *Science*, *237*(4811), 143–9.

Seligman, M. E. (1972). Learned helplessness. *Annual Review of Medicine*, *23*(1), 407–12.

Taylor, S. E., Brown, J. D. (1988). Illusion and well-being: A social psychological perspective on mental health. *Psychological Bulletin*, *103*(2), 193–210.

Taylor, S. E., Lichtman, R. R., Wood, J. V. (1984). Attributions, beliefs in control, and adjustment to breast cancer. *Journal of Personality and Social Psychology*, *46*, 489–502.

Windsor, T. D., Anstey, K. J., Butterworth, P., et al. (2007). The role of perceived control in explaining depressive symptoms associated with driving cessation in a longitudinal study. *The Gerontologist*, *47*(2), 215–23.

# 23 Coping Mechanisms through Successful Aging

María Márquez-González, Sheung-Tak Cheng, and Andrés Losada

The process of aging brings along many changes in a variety of areas of functioning. Many of these changes involve losses, such as objective biological declines and social losses. As we get older, we have to face important *life transitions* – changes in relevant contexts and in roles that are central elements of our identities. Some of these changes involve a certain loss in control or mastery of the environment, which place many older adults in a state of vulnerability, when compared to younger adults. A good example in this regard is retirement, and the associated loss of the "productive role" and all the resources associated with the job context (e.g., social relationships, social validation).

The challenging nature of aging helps us understand that the ability of the individual to effectively cope with life changes and demands is a cornerstone of psychological health and adaptation in old age. In fact, some of the main gerontological models, namely, the model of Selection, Optimization, and Compensation (SOC) of the life span perspective (Baltes & Baltes, 1990), the theory of Primary and Secondary Control (Heckhausen & Schulz, 1995), and the model of Assimilative and Accommodative coping (Brandtstädter & Greve, 1994), explain adaptation in aging as a process mainly based on coping, motivation, and goal setting. These models have been addressed in other chapters of this handbook. Hence, there is consensus that coping is at the core of personal growth, learning, and adaptation throughout the life span.

But, what is coping? Coping is a transactional process, which involves the interaction between the environment and the person, and can be defined as "the constantly changing cognitive and behavioral efforts to manage specific external and/or internal demands that are appraised as taxing or exceeding the resources of the person" (Lazarus & Folkman, 1984: 141). In other words, coping refers to the behavioral, cognitive and emotional mechanisms used by the person to deal with a stressful situation

The coping process can be described as developing in three steps: (1) appraisal of the environmental demand as benign, threatening, potentially harming (for oneself or for important others), challenging or annoying (primary appraisal); (2) appraisal of one's own personal resources and the available choices to appropriately deal with the demand (secondary appraisal); and (3) development of specific coping strategies. As we can see, the process of coping is inextricably linked to cognitive processes involved in the appraisal of events, which include perception, interpretation, and reasoning. Beliefs and personal dispositions such as optimism, self-efficacy, perceived control, personal goals, or resiliency are essential factors shaping appraisal processes and, by extension, coping strategies.

There are many individual differences in how people cope with stressors and demands. Besides personal tendencies or dispositions commented above, the social (e.g., social network) and environmental resources (e.g., access to education, economy, urban versus rural context) people can access are also central determinants of the appraisal and coping process. Fortunately, coping is a dynamic and changeable process, so there is wide room for learning and optimizing our coping strategies throughout the life course. In fact, negative life events and life crises across the life span (e.g., bereavement) can have a "bright side," in the sense that they can provide a context for learning new coping skills and experiencing personal growth.

This chapter briefly outlines the main findings of research on the stress and coping process in older adults, analyzes the essential importance of coping for older adults' adaptation and health, and includes a review of empirical studies analyzing specific coping strategies in older adults facing diverse stressful situations, as well as the description of some interventions aimed at improving older adults' ability to cope effectively.

## The Stress and Coping Process in Old Age

Since its beginning in the 1960s, general literature on stress and coping has evolved from a rather simplistic and linear conceptualization of coping (the restoration of the homeostasis after its alteration by stressors), in which coping was considered to be a stable characteristic of the person (coping style as a "trait"), to a more complex picture, which includes the assumption that the stress and coping process: (a) involve the interaction between many different levels of human functioning, i.e., biological (cellular, genetic, etc.), cognitive, emotional, behavioral, social, and sociocultural, what makes a multidisciplinary approach completely necessary to understand them (Spiro, 2007); (b) is largely shaped by environmental or contextual factors, which can be normative (e.g., retirement) or cohort-specific (e.g., socioeconomic status, access to education), and by personal variables (preferences, tendencies, and abilities), which shape personal trajectories of aging across the life span; (c) is dynamic and plastic, with learning processes and neural and behavioral plasticity being at the base of that dynamism; it is also recursive, as the individuals learn from their coping actions and modify these actions according to their goals (Aldwin et al., 2011); (d) is an adaptive process, inherent to development and growth across the life course; (e) is not an individual or isolated process, as it is embedded in social relationships (e.g., dyadic coping) in which higher-order social contexts (Aldwin et al., 2011) involve a complex and sophisticated set of processes, which are highly influenced by specific environmental demands and individual characteristics. In this sense, coping presents high inter- but also intra-variability, which makes it more interesting to analyze the coping process people display in the different and specific coping contexts (intraindividual differences) they face than the more traditionally studied "coping styles" (Yancura & Aldwin, 2008).

As we know, variability and heterogeneity are central hallmarks of aging, and coping is no exception in this regard. There are many individual differences in how aging affects the process of stress and coping of each individual (trajectories of change). Furthermore, the term "old age" includes people aged 65 to over 100, and this wide age range has important implications with regard to the demands and stressors people have to face and the resources they can rely on: while relatively good health, activity, and functionality are usually present up to age 80, chronic illnesses, frailty, and disability are likely to appear after this age (Collard et al., 2012). Hence, there is great consensus that age-subgroups should be considered in order to develop appropriate research on stress and coping in older adults. A rather extended proposal is to distinguish between young-old (65–74), middle-old (75–84), and oldest-old (85+).

The heterogeneity in stress and coping responses seems to be especially higher in late life (Ong & Bergeman, 2004). According to some authors, most age-related changes in stress and coping processes are shaped by changes in the social context across the life course, including factors such as changes in social roles (e.g., retirement, empty nest, grandparenthood), social resources, and socioeconomic status (Spiro, 2007). Health factors are also central determinants of coping strategies. As already commented above, the way a person appraises a demand or stressful event is closely associated with the type of coping strategies that are more likely to be displayed by that person. Along this line, Moos et al. (2006) found that older adults appraising events as challenging were more likely to rely on positive reappraisal and problem-solving coping strategies to cope with that event, and they had better event outcomes; they also experienced more growth or benefit from those experiences. Personal factors such as personal mastery, previous experience with similar demands, self-efficacy, or resilience may moderate the appraisal and coping processes (Kobasa et al., 1985).

This being assumed, as we advance into old age, the nature of stressors may change from episodic to chronic (e.g., chronic illnesses or functional limitations, persistent family conflicts) (Aldwin, Sutton, Chiara, and Spiro III, 1996). Also, there is some evidence suggesting that older adults are less prone than younger ones to appraise events as problems and, when they do, their stress ratings are usually lower (Boeninger et al., 2009). Older adults' tendency to appraise problems as less stressful may be related to: (a) their greater experience and higher expertise in coping with different life situations; and (b) their previous experience of extremely stressful events (e.g., death of loved ones), which may make everyday stressors seem less serious and easier to deal with (Aldwin et al., 1996). Another reason why older adults may be able to respond to certain stressful events with more calmness or lower perceptions of stress is because they are accepted as "normal" in old age and somehow expected (e.g., medical illnesses), and therefore they are more likely to be shielded from any negative effects (Cheng et al., 2009). On the other hand, the literature shows that the frequency and intensity of traumatic experiences and life events are not higher in old age, and that daily stressors or hassles are even less frequent in this life stage, with the exception of health-related stressors (Aldwin et al., 1996).

However, vulnerability to stress may increase with age. Aldwin et al. (2007) reviewed studies on this topic, and concluded that the immune (Gruenewald & Kemeny, 2007) and neuroendocrine systems (Epel et al., 2007), as well as the cardiovascular response to demands (cardiovascular reactivity; Cooper et al., 2007), show increasing dysregulation with age, which leads to greater health vulnerability to stress, in general, and especially, to psychosocial stress. Important potentiators of this vulnerability are chronic illness, cognitive impairment, and neuroticism (Aldwin, 2011).

The analysis of age differences in coping strategies is very complex, and the literature is not clear in this regard. Furthermore, age-related differences in coping strategies may be a function of the type of situations and demands they have to cope with, which are more chronic or unchangeable (e.g., retirement, widowhood, chronic illness). However, McCrae (1982) found that controlling for the type of problem eliminates the usual empirical finding that older adults use problem-focused coping strategies less frequently than younger ones. In fact, there is evidence suggesting that older adults may be more differentiated in their use of coping strategies, relying on one type of strategy or another depending on the specific situation. As an example, Coats and Blanchard-Fields (2008) found that older adults relied more than younger ones on problem-focused coping strategies for financial problems, but used more avoidant coping strategies for interpersonal problems.

In general, older adults seem to use a lower number of coping strategies (less coping effort, which may reflect their attempt to optimize resources). However, they seem to be equally effective in coping with stressful events when compared to younger adults. This could be explained by their greater experience and knowledge about what strategies work better (Aldwin, 2011; Aldwin et al., 1996).

An interesting characteristic of older adults' coping, and closely related to compensation processes, is *dyadic coping* (Revenson & DeLongis, 2011), which involves collaborative coping between two persons (usually, a couple) who deal jointly with a specific situation. This is more frequently used by older than younger adults (Berg & Upchurch, 2007). Constructive dyadic coping includes sharing and communicating stress and other feelings, provision of support, direct assistance, advice or help with cognitive reappraisal, joint problem-solving, joint relaxation, and so on (Cutrona & Gardner, 2006; Aldwin et al., 2011). This type of collaborative coping can be considered to be a compensation mechanism for cognitive changes occurring in old age, and has, in fact, been found to be related to lower distress and better individual health (Cutrona & Gardner, 2006). Also, finding enjoyment in dyadic coping is associated with higher marital satisfaction in middle-aged and older couples (Berg et al., 2011).

Finally, it has been suggested (Aldwin, 1997) that older adults may be especially skilled with regard to *proactive coping* (Aspinwall & Taylor, 1997), or organizing their lives to avoid taxing situations as much as possible in light of their declining resources. This preventive coping may help older adults

conserve resources for optimization and compensation, thus facilitating continued engagement in valuable personal goals, which are the main contributors
to subjective well-being (Ouwehand et al., 2007). This is completely consistent
with the model of Strength and Vulnerability Integration (SAVI; Charles, 2010),
which highlights age-related enhancement in the use of strategies that serve to
avoid or minimize exposure to negative stimuli, but also the age-related increased
vulnerability to high levels of sustained emotional arousal (Charles, 2010).

All the above said, there are empirical reasons to be optimistic about coping in old age: most people seem to adapt rather well to the challenges of
aging. As we have learned from the theoretical models in gerontology, many
people, as they age, manage to display processes of selection, compensation,
and optimization of behaviors and functions, which allow them to keep on
pursuing relevant goals and values, which in turn, continue filling their lives
with meaning and purpose (Baltes & Baltes, 1990). This successful adaptation
seems to involve many secondary-control coping (Heckhausen & Schulz, 1995)
and accommodative strategies (Brandtstädter & Greve, 1994) that help people
make a healthy *readjustment* of their goals. Successful execution of this strategy requires acknowledgment and acceptance of personal and environmental
limitations or constraints, adjusting personal preferences and goal orientations
to these constraints (Brandtstädter & Renner, 1990), relinquishing unattainable
personal goals, and turning to new realistic goals. One type of secondary control
strategy, namely, specific emotion regulation skills, seems to increase in effectiveness with advancing age, which has been explained as reflecting the priority
of emotion regulation and well-being optimization goals for older adults (see
Socioemotional Selectivity Theory) (Carstensen et al., 2003). This is the case of
the proactive coping strategy called situation selection (e.g., in the social context) (Carstensen et al., 2003) and attentional deployment of positive emotional
information (Isaacowitz et al., 2008) or cognitive reappraisal (Wadsworth et al.,
2004). A coping strategy based on reappraisal, and frequently used by older
adults is downward social comparison (to compare oneself to people who are in
worse conditions) (Cheng et al., 2009), which has been found to be a mediator
between objective life conditions and perceived quality of life (e.g., Beaumont
& Kenealy, 2004). These accommodative processes should not be interpreted as
passivity, as they are highly adaptive and allow older adults to maintain their
well-being and appropriate levels of functioning, in spite of age-related losses
and declines (Aldwin, 2011).

## Coping with Life Transitions

Many of the major negative life events older adults face are part of normative or expected life transitions, such as retirement, role changes (e.g., empty
nest, grandparenthood), and important changes in other areas (e.g., physical
functioning, health, social network, housing, income loss). These transitions
represent a great and stressful challenge for older adults, as they set the need

for a readjustment of many central aspects of personal functioning: identity (roles and fundamental beliefs about oneself and the world), values, goals, and everyday routines, among others. Life transitions frequently involve changes in other factors, such as social network, the pattern of interpersonal relationships, or the physical context. However, major life events also represent opportunities for learning and growth.

Older adults' vulnerability to the effects of life transitions depends on the nature of the transition (expected, desirable, ego-threatening, etc.), the circumstances under which it occurs (degree of choice/control over the transition, concurrent stressors or transitions, coping resources, social support), and the broader context (historical and present, personal and social) in which it is embedded (Szinovacz, 2003). The main gerontological models of SOC (Baltes & Baltes, 1990), theory of Primary and Secondary Control (Heckhausen & Schulz, 1995), and Assimilative and Accommodative Coping (Brandtstädter & Greve, 1994), together with theoretical models such as the Crisis Theory (Turner & Avison, 1992) or the Continuity Theory (Atchley, 1999), offer interesting insights into understanding the diverse coping processes and strategies that are involved in the successful adaptation to these transitions. According to Schumacher et al. (1999), a very helpful attitude for coping with life transitions is an openness to new experiences, an ability to discover new values and sources of meaning, and a willingness to get involved in new roles and new relationships or to learn new abilities. Another adaptive process is to remain in contact with as many continuity factors as possible, which help maintain the stability of identity and personal relationships and life context. In this regard, to recover the routines and usual activities which continue being possible and important for the person is an adaptive coping strategy, which provides perception of control (Schumacher et al., 1999). The main gerontological models agree that one of the keys to successful adaptation is to remain involved, during and after the transitions, in the pursuit of personal values and their associated life goals, which brings purpose and meaning to one's life. In this regard, a person can have planned goals and aspirations pursued specifically after expected life transition occurs (e.g., "When the time for my retirement comes, I will make this one-month trip to Africa that I have always dreamed of."). In close relation with the pursuit of values and goals, a crucial coping process emerges: the ability to perform a flexible readjustment of goals and values when life transitions impose limitations for their achievement. This process involves disengaging from unrealistic or extremely difficult goals or values, and substituting them with new ones that can continue feeding the person's life with purpose, meaning, or positive experiences; this process has been found to buffer the influence of negative resource conditions (e.g., health constraints) (Rothermund & Brandtstädter, 2003).

As an example, Julia has just retired from her job as a teacher at an elementary school. She really enjoyed her work, as it allowed her to fulfill her value of helping children learn and grow, and to feel helpful to other people. After her retirement, she decided to get involved as a volunteer in a center for children with learning disabilities, which helped her to remain connected to her important values. Some coping strategies involved in the flexible goal adjustment are cognitive processes such as reappraisal or reframing: the enhancement of attainable goals that are valued, both for old and new goals, and the devaluation of both competing goals and goals which are unrealistic or extremely difficult to attain. Heckhausen and Schulz (1993) offer an interesting conceptualization of these strategies in terms of primary versus secondary and selective versus compensatory control strategies, framed in Baltes and Baltes's (1990) life span perspective or SOC model.

## Coping and Health in Old Age

There is a great body of empirical evidence supporting the central role of coping strategies in people' differential vulnerability to negative life events and stressors (see review by Holahan et al., 1997). With regard to physical health, research studies clearly support that psychological stress in the general population is linked to the incidence and, more clearly, the progression of health problems such as depression, cardiovascular disease, upper respiratory tract infections, or autoimmune diseases, among others (see review by Cohen et al., 2007). Many studies raise evidence supporting, specifically, the relevance of stress and coping for older adults' health (biomedical and disease outcomes) (Yancura & Aldwin, 2008). Chronic stress seems to be particularly harmful for older adults, given age-related changes in organic systems, such as the progressive loss of immune function (immunosenescence) (e.g., Aw et al., 2007). In fact, an interaction between age and chronic stress is observed for several immune outcomes, such as the antibody increase to influenza vaccination (Gouin et al., 2008). Coping has been found to moderate the effects of stress on immune outcomes in older adults, and its relevance for immune functioning seems to be higher for older than for younger adults (e.g., Thompsen et al., 2004). Specifically, active coping was associated with a greater proliferative response of peripheral blood leukocytes under conditions of high stress (Stowell et al., 2001).

With regard to cardiovascular health, Vitaliano et al. (1995) examined cardiovascular recovery from laboratory stressors in older adults, finding evidence that avoidance coping was significantly associated with diastolic blood pressure and heart rate. In their experimental study with elderly Alzheimer caregivers, Aschbacher et al. (2005) measured the hypercoagulability marker D-dimer before, immediately after, and during recovery from an acute stressor (3-minute speech). They found that caregivers reporting a low reliance on planful problem-solving showed greater increases in D-dimer from baseline to speech and recovery time points, as compared with controls; the authors interpreted these findings as evidence suggesting the salutogenic effects of approach and problem-solving coping strategies, which seem to buffer the impact of acute stress on procoagulant activity.

Stowell et al. (2001) reviewed studies analyzing the relationship between stress, coping, and health, and found enough evidence suggesting that active coping attenuated the effects of stress on mental and physical health, while avoidance coping was usually found to potentiate the detrimental effects of stress on health. However, these authors found that the benefits of active versus avoidance coping seemed to depend on the level of perceived stress: while higher levels of active coping were associated with a better immune response at high stress levels, at low levels of stress it was avoidant coping that was related to a better functioning of the immune system.

## Coping Strategies: Variability and Measurement

The research literature on the types of coping strategies is rather complex, as different classifications have been proposed. Cronkite and Moos (1995) presented a multidimensional model of coping, classifying strategies as a function of their focus (orientation toward the problem: approach versus avoidance) and the coping method (cognitive versus behavioral mechanisms). These two dimensions combine to produce eight coping strategies under four categories: (a) cognitive approach coping (positive reappraisal and logical analysis), (b) behavioral approach coping (problem solving and seeking guidance), (c) cognitive avoidance coping (cognitive avoidance and acceptance/resignation), and (d) behavioral avoidance coping (emotional discharge and seeking alternative rewards). According to Aldwin (2007), a rather extended classification approach groups coping strategies into five main categories: (a) problem-focused coping (e.g., problem solving, seeking information), (b) emotion-focused coping (e.g., avoidance, emotional expression, withdrawal), (c) social support (e.g., seeking emotional support or advice), (d) religious coping (e.g., praying), and (e) cognitive reframing (e.g., "meaning making" and "reinterpretation" processes). Strategies with overlapping goals may be further combined into higher-order categories. Broadly speaking, the various coping strategies are often contrasted in terms of: (a) whether efforts are directed at tackling the problem (i.e., problem-focused coping) or at reducing emotional distress (i.e., emotion-focused coping) or (b) whether one is actively engaged in dealing with the situation (i.e., active or approach coping) or tries to avoid dealing with it (i.e., avoidant coping). However, these higher-order categories of coping strategies overlap somewhat. Seeking information or planned problem-solving are examples of both active and problem-focused coping, whereas cognitive reappraisal, use of humor, and seeking emotional support are examples of active and emotion-focused coping (Carver et al., 1989). Examples of avoidant coping include behavioral disengagement, distraction, denial, and acceptance/resignation.

Coping strategies in old age can be measured using different methods. Traditionally, self-report questionnaires have been used, which assess how people usually cope, assuming a rather "stable" or trait-like conceptualization of coping. As an encompassing concept, the coping strategies covered by the different coping scales vary a lot from one instrument to another. The most widely used instruments to measure coping strategies in older adults are the Coping Responses Inventory

(CRI) (Moos, 1993), the Ways of Coping Questionnaire (WCQ) (Folkman & Lazarus, 1980), and the Coping Inventory for Stressful Situations (CISS) (Endler & Parker, 1990). These measures, however, have not been developed specifically for older adults, but for the adult population in general. In this regard, some authors have suggested that available coping measures are not entirely appropriate for older adults, as they do not include the more nuanced, complex, and sophisticated strategies that seem to emerge in late life (Labouvie-Vief et al., 1987). Besides the general coping measures, there are domain-specific instruments designed to measure the strategies people develop to cope with specific stressors, such as the Coping with Illness Inventory (CWI) (Felton & Revenson, 1984) or the Chronic Pain Coping Inventory (CPCI) (Jensen et al., 1995).

Over the past decades, research on coping has increasingly assumed an ideographic approach, represented by the use of process measures, which allow for the assessment of how the person responds to a specific stressor or demand that has been recently experienced. Here we find the *daily diary methodology*, in which people are asked to record events occurring during a set of days, their coping responses to those events, and some well-being measure, such as their mood state. This can be done with electronic devices, such as palm diaries. Other assessment procedures such as the experience sampling method (ESM) (Csikszentmihalyi & Larson, 1987) and the ecological momentary assessment (EMA) (Stone & Shiffman, 1994) have been developed, as assessment methods consisting of real-time self-reports at random occasions during the time the person is awake along a normal week, frequently using electronic devices. Some authors raise questions about the appropriateness of these modern methods for assessing coping in older adults (Newth & DeLongis, 2000).

## Psychological Variables Related to Coping

Perceiving control or believing that whatever happens in life can be managed, bringing about the desired outcomes, and feeling efficacious to cope with stressors are important facilitators of adaptive coping (Lachman et al., 1994). These characteristics increase the likelihood that older people appraise stressors as challenges, and invest more coping efforts in generating and implementing appropriate solutions, using coping outcomes as feedback to revise the coping process and learn from it. This type of coping is more likely to lead to effective results and solve problems, thus reinforcing the person's perception of control and self-efficacy (Aldwin et al., 2011). The motivation to exert primary control is present across the entire life span. But age-related changes in health or in the social context (among others) impose limitations to primary control, and perceptions of control have been found to decline with advancing age (Heckhausen & Schulz, 1993). Sense of control has been associated with good physical and mental health among the elderly (Heckhausen & Schultz, 1993).

Despite the fact that some authors have suggested that active coping strategies such as problem-solving may not be appropriate for older adults, given the unchangeable nature of many of the stressors and problems they have to deal with, there is great evidence that relying on active and problem-focused coping strategies (primary control) continues to be adaptive into old age, as the elderly are more likely to solve problematic situations (e.g., Moos et al., 2006). As we will discuss later in this chapter, the adaptiveness of the different types of coping strategies depends on the specific nature of the stressor and the whole context of the stress experience.

Other personality variables, such as sense of coherence (Antonovsky, 1979), hardiness (commitment, control, and challenge) (Kobasa, 1979), and optimism have been analyzed by researchers and are currently considered to be relevant facilitators of adaptive coping through the life span. Optimism or the generalized expectancy that good things will happen is associated with higher levels of general health perceptions, vitality, and mental health in older adults (Achat et al., 2000), and with more adherence to health-promoting habits and healthier coping strategies when faced with chronic illnesses that are controllable to a certain degree, such as type 1 diabetes or rheumatoid arthritis (Fournier et al., 2002). It also seems to mediate in the relationship between older adults' pain and life satisfaction (Ferreira & Sherman, 2007).

Resilience has been defined as "the process of adapting well in the face of adversity, trauma, tragedy, threats, or significant sources of stress" (APA, 2015) or "positive adaptation in the context of significant risk or adversity" (Ong et al., 2009). Although resilience is mainly considered to be a process, some argue that it can also be seen as a trait with implications for coping. Some authors assume that resilience is a hallmark of aging well (Wild et al., 2013). Despite increased biological vulnerability to stress, research suggests that older adults have the capacity for considerable resilience in the face of stressful challenges (Staudinger et al., 1995). In this line, Manning, Carr, & Kail (2016) found that resilience plays a moderating role in the relation between onset of chronic disease and the development of basic (ADL) and instrumental (IADL) activities of daily living disabilities in older adults – when developing a new chronic health problem, older adults with high resilience displayed lower ADL and IADL disabilities. Resilience has been found to be associated not only with better psychological health (e.g., perceived quality of life, self-perceived successful aging, improved resistance to stress or lower rates of depression), but also with better physical health (e.g., physical functioning, ADL independence, faster cardiovascular recovery) and increased longevity/lower mortality risk (see review by MacLeod et al., 2016). An interesting mechanism of action of resilience identified in some studies is its association with coping strategies that facilitate the elicitation of positive emotions, such as positive reappraisal (Affleck & Tennen, 1996), humor, and infusing ordinary events with positive meaning (Ong et al., 2004), among others, to regulate negative emotional experiences. The topic of resilience raises the interesting issue of positive aspect of stress, represented by the constructs "post-traumatic growth" (Tedeschi & Calhoun, 2004) or "stress-related growth" (Park & Fenster, 2004). Hence, negative life events can have positive consequences, in the form of personal development, learning, or growth. There is evidence that specific coping strategies, such as problem-focused coping, taking perspective, and self-regulation help older people benefit from stressful experiences (Aldwin et al., 1996).

## Coping and Adaptation to Stress in Old Age: A Review of Empirical Studies

When reviewing the literature on coping and adaptation to stress, concerns appear regarding data interpretation in studies using cross-sectional designs or change scores between two time points. The way one copes is supposed to mediate the effect of stressors on outcomes such as psychological distress or quality of life. However, in cross-sectional studies, one may paradoxically find presumably adaptive strategies to be positively correlated with negative outcomes (e.g., Catanzaro et al., 1995) because coping behaviors are increased during rough times. In terms of examining predictors of successful aging, it is important to be able to ascertain whether the coping strategies are indeed adaptive. For this reason, we will focus more on longitudinal studies that look at the predictive value of coping at an earlier time point. Moreover, special attention will be paid to older adults dealing with significant threats, including acute or chronic illnesses, disability, and trauma, in order to find out whether certain kinds of coping strategies can promote resilience in the face of decline or severe stress.

Differentiating problem-focused from emotion-focused coping, or active from avoidant coping, has implications for successful aging, as attempts to master or control many age-related declines and losses may not be adaptive (Schulz & Heckhausen, 1996). Together with the already commented upon motivation to prioritize emotional goals in later life (Samanez-Larkin et al., 2009), one may expect emotion-focused or avoidant coping to be more appropriate coping strategies for older adults. Along this line, Martin and colleagues (2008) found that centenarians reported less use of active behavioral coping (similar to problem-focused coping) than octogenarians and sexagenarians. Many months later, active behavioral coping decreased in the centenarians and octogenarians but increased in the sexagenarians. Furthermore, active behavioral coping and cognitive reappraisal at baseline predicted better functional health and social relations at the long-term follow-up, whereas avoidant coping predicted more negative affect, but the researchers did not test whether these effects differed by age groups (by including interaction terms with age) (artin et al., 2008). The relative beneficial effect of active over avoidant coping across three life domains (health, interpersonal, and financial/work) was also demonstrated in the study of 297 late midlife and older adults followed at least three times over 10 years (Moos et al., 2006). In this interesting study, the authors found data suggesting that, in all life domains: (1) older adults experiencing more chronic stressors were more likely to appraise events (in all domains) as threatening and use cognitive avoidance and emotional discharge coping strategies; and (2) the use of cognitive avoidance and emotional discharge coping was associated with higher levels of depression and drinking problems in all three domains, which is consistent with previous findings (e.g., Penley et al., 2002). More longitudinal evidence of the detrimental effects of avoidance coping in middle-aged and older adults can be found in Holahan et al. (2005).

The debate on whether one type of coping strategy is more adaptive than others is currently outdated somehow, because the adaptiveness of coping strategies depends on the nature of the situation and the stressor being confronted. Coping is situation-specific and, hence flexibility in the use of strategies is important, especially in the course of declines and losses in later life (Boerner, 2004). There is not a one-size-fit-all approach when it comes to coping with stress. Although active coping is found to be more adaptive than avoidant coping in general, there are situations for which avoidant coping is appropriate. If the situation is malleable and mastering it is obviously desirable, active coping will be the strategy of choice. But if the situation is not changeable or overly demanding, or if changing it makes little sense, emotion-focused or avoidant coping may be more useful. The crucial aspect for adaptation seems to be a wide repertoire of coping strategies and having the flexibility to rely on one or another strategy depending on the nature of the stressor and other characteristics of the context. Flexibility may be more important than coping skills, *per se*, for maintaining functioning in later life. Through lifelong experience, older adults may be more capable of matching coping options to situational demands. The principle guiding the use of coping strategies is the same regardless of age, although the preference tends to swing toward emotion-focused or avoidant strategies in later life, due to declining resources vis-à-vis situational demands. In other words, the cost of active coping vis-à-vis potential returns is higher in later life, whereas the same is true for avoidant coping in young age. We will explore this theme by looking at coping with major or critical physical and health conditions, everyday interpersonal tension, occupational demands and retirement, interpersonal stressors and bereavement, and other important life events such as the dementia caregiving situation.

## Coping with Health-Related Stressors

With regard to health stressors, Moos et al. (2006) found evidence suggesting that these negative events activate more avoidance coping strategies than problems in the other life domains, which is consistent with previous studies (e.g., Patterson et al., 1990). However, approach strategies were also frequently used by older adults to confront health problems, reflecting older adults' maintenance of reliance on active strategies, with regard to decision-making and management of their health problems when they were deemed appropriate.

In a study of patients with newly diagnosed medium-to-late stage head/neck cancer, who were followed for 6 and 12 months, older and midlife patients did not differ in terms of quality of life or depressive symptoms, while the former used more religious coping and the latter used more active coping and had a higher sense of internal locus of control. The use of avoidant coping was asso-ciated with worse outcomes at follow-up, but the effect was less pronounced in older patients (Derks et al., 2005). In another study of older patients with oste-oarthritis, active coping predicted less negative mood after 3 months, whereas avoidant coping had the opposite effect (Hampson et al., 1996). This pattern of results was echoed in cross-sectional studies of patients suffering from myocar-dial infarction (Chung et al., 2008), heart failure (Klein et al., 2007), or cancer (Aarts et al., 2015), among other health issues. To the extent that avoidance implies giving up, these results were not surprising.

With regard to chronic pain, Regier and Parmelee (2015) reviewed studies finding that disengaged (avoidant) and emotion-centered coping were associated with greater depression, higher levels of pain, and greater functional impairment (e.g., Perrot et al., 2008; Somers et al., 2009). In a longitudinal study, negative thoughts about consequences of pain, catastrophizing, and activity avoidance coping contributed to a deteriorated physical function in older adults with joint pain and comorbidity with other health problems (Hermsen et al., 2011).

Although avoidant coping in the face of serious illness may be dysfunctional, there is nonetheless a need to manage the negative emotional reactions to diag-nosis, treatment, and prognosis. As a form of emotion-focused coping, religious coping behaviors (e.g., praying, seeking support from church members) in a sample of older medical inpatients, of whom over 95 percent were Christian, were found to predict stress-related growth 2 years later (Pargament et al., 2004), an effect probably dependent on faith rather than age (Ai et al., 2006). Another study nicely illustrated the adaptiveness of religious coping at different stages of treatment in 335 patients undergoing surgery for a range of medical conditions. Data collection occurred 2 days prior to surgery and 1 month after surgery. Results showed that, controlling for baseline physical status and mood symp-toms, preoperative religious coping predicted better functional health at the 1-month follow-up, but higher levels of such coping reported at the follow-up interview were correlated with poorer functional health (Ai et al., 2006), proba-bly because after surgery, more active coping is needed for recovery and rehabil-itation. Unfortunately, this study did not measure other coping approaches or the benefits of strategies other than religious coping.

## Coping with Work/Occupational Stressors and Retirement

While the studies reviewed above analyze events that have a significant downside risk to safety and physical functioning, how older people cope in the workplace will be an increasingly important topic for successful aging as more and more, especially the young-olds, remain in the workforce. In a two-wave lon-gitudinal study of 676 workers aged 17–73 years, older workers were found to use more active coping at baseline, which in turn predicted less strain 8 months later. On the contrary, younger workers used more behavioral disengagement when job control was low, which also predicted lower strain at follow-up. There was no age difference in the use of positive reappraisal in this study (Hertel et al., 2015). In an environment where performance is critical, older people may rely less on avoidant coping and focus more on active coping in order to compensate for their decline in resources.

With regard to retirement, it seems to be a stressful event for a significant proportion of older adults, mainly due to the circumstances under which it occurs (expectedness, voluntariness, economic conditions, etc.) (Bossé et al., 1997) and the impact it has on other personal areas, such as marital and family relationships. Empirical evidence supports the relevance that variables, such as sense of personal control or good self-rated health, have for retirement adjustment (e.g., Lowis et al., 2009). Also, emotion-focused strategies seem to foster retirees to experience more emotional stability, happiness, and satisfaction in their lives (Brandtstadter & Renner, 1990); yet, the use of avoidance coping appears to be inversely associated with psychological well-being, and seems to hamper adjustment to retirement (e.g., Sharpley & Yardley, 1999).

## Coping with Interpersonal Stressors and Bereavement

Some authors have suggested that interpersonal problems or negative social interactions seem to be especially difficult for older adults to cope with, partly due to their frequency and saliency (Okun & Keith, 1998; Krause & Rook, 2003). An experience sampling study on interpersonal conflict illustrates the usefulness of avoidant coping in certain contexts. In this study, 1,031 adults aged 25–74 years old were interviewed via telephone for 8 consecutive days about various stressors they had experienced on that day. The researchers focused on events that involved disagreements with other people and the participants' responses to them. The results showed that avoiding argument was associated with less affective reactivity in older, than in midlife and young adults, whereas no age difference in affective reactivity was found when participants engaged in argument (Charles et al., 2009). In later life, minimizing tension and maintaining good relationships with other people may make more sense than trying to change personal attitudes and opinions, especially when they have learned through experience that certain arguments are not worthwhile. At the same time, maintaining positive relationships may be crucial to obtaining social support when it is needed in this life stage. Their relative coping success in this domain may be facilitated by the preferential treatment of others toward older people as well.

One of the strongest interpersonal stressors is the loss of a loved one. Bereavement has been found to be one of the most central risk factors for depression among the elderly (Cole & Dendukuri, 2003). However, it affects older adults in different ways, depending on many factors, such as the type and quality of the relationship with that person (Carr et al., 2000) and degree of unresolved issues and regrets (e.g., self-blame, non-acceptance) (Field & Horowitz, 1998). Despite its relevance, the empirical evidence on older adults' coping with bereavement is rather sparse. Using a multilevel daily process design, Ong et al.

(2004) found that the experience of positive emotions and the ability to find humor in stressful situations (humor coping) had a significant positive role for older adults in the regulation of their depressive symptoms during conjugal bereavement. On the contrary, ruminative coping has been found to be associated with maladjustment to loss in the general population (Nolen-Hoeksema et al., 1994).

## Coping with Other Stressful Situations

With regard to how older adults respond to unexpected acute stressors or disasters "out of the blue," events such as the Severe Acute Respiratory Syndrome (SARS) pandemic in 2003 provided an exceptional circumstance to study coping in the face of a totally unexpected, yet prolonged and severe threat. Yeung and Fung (2007) telephone-interviewed 385 Hong Kong Chinese adults during the peak of the pandemic and 2 months afterwards when the pandemic was over. Although none of the participants were infected with the virus, SARS was highly contagious in the crowded living environment of Hong Kong. The researchers found no age differences in the use of problem-focused coping strategies, as well as in the decreased reliance on these strategies when the pandemic was brought under control. However, whereas young adults used more emotion-focused coping at the crisis peak, older adults reported a larger increase in emotion-focused coping over time so that by the end of the pandemic, they reported slightly more emotion-focused coping than young adults. Both problem-focused and emotion-focused coping at crisis peak predicted reduced sadness at end of crisis, but only emotion-focused coping predicted reduced anger; the latter finding was noteworthy because young adults reported more anger than older adults at crisis peak, but by end of crisis, their anger levels were no different from each other. The overall results suggest that older adults may be less reactive to certain stressors than young adults, but they are equally capable to recruit a variety of coping strategies when necessary. In a similar vein, a study of traffic accident victims found essentially no difference among young, midlife, and older victims in terms of coping strategies and posttraumatic symptoms (Chung et al., 2004).

A stressful and chronic situation, which has even been described as a natural experiment of extreme stress, is caring for a relative with Alzheimer's disease or related disorders. Even though some evidence has been found for the stability of caregivers coping patterns (Powers et al., 2002), longitudinal studies done with spouse caregivers or samples composed mostly of spouses provide support to the positive association between avoidant coping and depression, suggesting that the impact of care-recipients' behavioral problems on depression is mediated by escape-avoidant coping (Mausbach et al., 2006; Powers et al., 2002). Mausbach et al. (2007) also found that personal mastery attenuated the effects of stressors on caregivers' mental and physical health in a 5-year longitudinal study. In samples composed not only or mostly of spouse caregivers, similar findings have been found regarding avoidant coping (e.g., Cooper et al., 2008). However, regarding problem-focused strategies or approach coping, mixed findings have been reported. For example, in a 1-year longitudinal study, Goode et al. (1998) found that those caregivers who reported more approach coping in the first interview reported better physical health 1 year later than those reporting lower approach coping. On the other side, Cooper et al. (2008) found that the use of problem-focused strategies predicted higher anxiety 1 year later. Cooper et al. (2008) suggested that these findings could be because the use of problem-focused strategies for situations that cannot be changed may be ineffective and may generate frustration. Okabayashi et al. (2008) found results that support Cooper et al. (2008) findings. Specifically, in their longitudinal study they found that those caregivers who used the "diversion" coping strategy (considered as an avoidance strategy by the authors) were associated with lower burden. On the contrary, approach coping was associated with burden. The authors consider that in order to provide high quality care for long stressful periods, caregivers need to have time away from caregiving obligations, a strategy that also contributes to health maintenance.

## Interventions to Promote Adaptive Coping

Given the amplitude of the construct of coping, its intraindividual variability, and the importance of the specific stress situation to understand and assess coping efficacy, there is a great variability of interventions aimed at promoting adaptive coping in older adults. The empirical evidence presented in this chapter supports the importance of developing prevention and intervention programs to train older adults in the identification of sources of stress, the use of effective coping skills, and the development of psychological resources (resilience, sense of coherence, etc.). According to Moos et al. (2006), the outcome variables (objectives) of interventions to promote adaptive coping should not only be reductions in emotional distress (anxiety, stress, or depression), but also increases in coping effectiveness, and the experience of growth or obtaining meaning from stressful situations. The focus on prevention would help older adults to be better prepared to manage a problematic situation when it emerges.

Intervention programs aimed at promoting successful aging usually include older adults' training in adaptive strategies (realization of pleasant activities, cognitive reappraisal, etc.) to cope with normal aging challenges and life transitions. An example of these programs is Vital Aging (Fernández-Ballesteros et al., 2004), which has been shown to improve older adults' self-perceptions, self-efficacy, and their vision of aging, while increasing frequency of physical exercise, and cultural, intellectual, affective, and social activities (Fernández-Ballesteros et al., 2004). Another example of a program devoted to the promotion of successful aging has been more recently tested by Bode et al. (2007), who developed an intervention for the promotion of proactive coping competencies in people aged between 50 and 75 years. An increase in participants' levels of proactive competences with regard to future-related behaviors was observed at the end of the intervention, which was sustained 3 months after the end of the program.

With regard to programs aimed at training participants in coping strategies for reducing their levels of distress (e.g., depressive or anxious symptomatology), there is increasing research supporting the efficacy of skills-oriented therapies (e.g., cognitive behavior therapy [CBT], including problem-solving therapy and behavioral interventions) for improving older adults' distress associated with depression (Pinquart et al., 2007), insomnia (Germain et al., 2006), anxiety (Ayers et al., 2007), complicated grief (Shear et al., 2014), chronic pain (Cook, 1998), or health problems such as macular degeneration (Rovner & Casten, 2008). There are also studies that recommend matching the type of intervention to the preferred coping style (Fry & Wong, 1991), although problem-focused intervention strategies were found by these authors to provide the best results. The idea of adapting the intervention to participant characteristics, or the specific nature of the problem that is impacting their lives, seems to be a good way of maximizing the probability of obtaining better outcomes through the interventions. In this sense, for example, research seems to recommend the use of cognitive-behavioral based interventions for problems that may be solved (e.g., depressive symptoms associated with a decreased behavioral activation) and acceptance-based interventions for problems that are associated with irremediable changes or losses that are frequent in the elderly (e.g., chronic pain) (for a review, see Márquez-González & Losada, 2015). Even though there is already enough research available as to recommend CBT therapies for problems such as depression, generalized anxiety disorder, pain, insomnia, health problems, or dementia caregivers levels of distress, recent studies seem to provide support to the use of acceptance-based interventions for these problems in the elderly (Wetherell et al., 2011; Losada et al., 2015; Alonso-Fernández et al., 2015).

## Conclusions and Future Directions

Old age is a period marked by major transitions and life events that may threaten one's functioning and subjective well-being. The way older persons cope with these events plays an important role in aging successfully. The traditional stress and coping framework, which views stress as a result of the interplay between the perceived demands of a situation and one's capacity to deal with the demands, provides a useful starting point to examine this question. Models of successful aging, such as SOC, the Primary and Secondary Control theory, or the model of Assimilative and Accommodative Coping, may be seen as a special case of stress and coping theory in the context of aging.

As coping requires behavioral, cognitive, and emotional efforts, changes in biological processes leading to, for example, physical and cognitive decline, pose challenges for coping in later life. Moreover, older people often suffer loss of resources that facilitate coping, such as financial means and long-term social partners. Thus, coping successfully requires one to optimize resources to focus on manageable situations while giving up goals that are unattainable, by realistically assessing objective threats, and one's ability and resources. Such an assessment is facilitated by lifelong learning and experience in dealing with stressful events and the fact that many life events in old age (e.g., retirement, health problems, and bereavement) are normative, meaning that a person can be more prepared to face them through planned efforts. Being able to anticipate problematic situations in everyday life through experience also helps older people to avoid these situations as much as possible (i.e., proactive coping) and to reduce exposure to events that may tax their coping capacity. Also, personal variables such as perceived control, sense of coherence or resilience are very helpful to cope effectively with life stressors.

In addition, being able to shift flexibly between goal engagement and disengagement is key to successful aging, as continuous engagement in unattainable goals is potentially harmful. While such a flexibility is important for any life stage, it is especially important for later life because of the risk of fixation on long-cherished goals and habitual coping approaches, and also because of the continuous shift in the balance between strengths and vulnerabilities in old age. Such flexibility requires cognitive mechanisms such as attentional control and cognitive reappraisal to enable one to disengage from negative stimuli and to see things from a new perspective that gives larger meaning and purpose to previously less valued goals. Thus, the important issue here is not whether active or avoidance strategies are more adaptive in later life, but rather, the ability of older adults to make a flexible and differentiated use of these strategies as determined by the situation.

While the literature has shown active coping to be superior to avoidance coping in older people, this may simply reflect the fact that active coping is still required to handle many everyday problems, although avoidance or disengagement becomes increasingly salient in this life period. This is reflected in interventions for older people who increasingly focus on helping older adults to develop a variety of coping skills, including passive acceptance, when the situation becomes unmanageable.

Future studies are needed to analyze coping strategies from a more idiographic approach – analyzing how they vary from one situation or life domain to another and exploring its association with older people's personal characteristics, such as perceived control or resiliency, and other resources (e.g., health, social support). Also, further research is needed on the validity and reliability of experience sampling methods or ecological momentary assessment in older adults, especially when they include electronic devices.

## References

Aarts, J. W. F., Deckx, L., van Abbema, D. L., et al. (2015). The relation between depression, coping and health locus of control: Differences between older and younger patients, with and without cancer. *Psycho-Oncology*, 24, 950–7.

Achat, H., Kawachi, I., Spiro III, A., et al. (2000). Optimism and depression as predictors of physical and mental health functioning. *The Normative Aging Study. Annals of Behavioral Medicine*, 22, 127–30.

Affleck, G., Tennen, H. (1996). Construing benefits from adversity: Adaptational significance and dispositional underpinnings. *Journal of Personality*, 64, 899–922.

Ai, A. L., Peterson, C., Bolling, S. F., et al. (2006). Depression, faith-based coping, and short-term postoperative global functioning in adult and older patients undergoing cardiac surgery. *Journal of Psychosomatic Research*, 60, 21–8.

Aldwin, C. M. (2007). *Stress, Coping, and Development* (2nd Ed.). New York: Guilford.

Aldwin, C. M., Sutton, K. J., Chiara, G., & Spiro, A., III. (1996). Age differences in stress, coping, and appraisal: findings from the Normative Aging Study. *Journals of Gerontology. Series B: Psychological Sciences and Social Sciences*, 51, 179–88.

Aldwin, C. M., Park, C. L., Spiro, I. A. (2007). Health psychology and aging: an introduction. In C. M. Aldwin, C. L. Park, & A. Spiro, III (Eds.), *Handbook of Health Psychology and Aging* (pp. 413–24). New York: Guilford Press.

Aldwin, C. M., Skinner, E. A., Zimmer-Gembeck, M., et al. (2011). Coping and self-regulation across the life span. In K. Fingerman, C. Berg, J. Smith, & T. Antonucci (Eds.), *Handbook of Life-Span Development* (pp. 561–87). United States: Springer Pub. Co.

Alonso-Fernández, M., López-López, A., Losada, A., et al. (2015). Acceptance and Commitment Therapy and selective optimization with compensation for institutionalized older people with chronic pain. *Pain Medicine*, 17, 264–77.

American Psychological Association (2015). *The Road to Resilience* ©, www.apa.org/helpcenter/road-resilience.aspx Accessed 15.01.17.

Antonovsky, A. (1979). *Health, Stress and Coping*. San Francisco: Jossey-Bass.

Aschbacher, K., Patterson, T. L., von Känel, R., et al. (2005). Coping processes and hemostatic reactivity to acute stress in dementia caregivers. *Psychosomatic Medicine*, 67, 964–71.

Aspinwall, L. G., Taylor, S. E. (1997). A stitch in time: Self-regulation and proactive coping. *Psychological Bulletin*, 121, 417–36.

Atchley, R. C. (1999). *Continuity and Adaptation in Aging: Creating. Positive Experiences*. Baltimore, MD: Johns Hopkins University Press.

Ayers, C. R., Sorrell, J. T., Thorp, S. R., et al. (2007). Evidence-based psychological treatments for late-life anxiety. *Psychology and Aging*, 22, 8–17.

Aw, D., Silva, A. B., Palmer, D. B. (2007). Immunosenescence: Emerging challenges for an ageing population. *Immunology*, 120, 435–46.

Baltes, P. B., Baltes, M. M. (1990). Psychological perspectives on successful aging: The model of selective optimization with compensation. In P. B. Baltes & M. M. Baltes (Eds.), *Successful Aging: Perspectives from the Behavioral Sciences* (pp. 1–34). New York: Cambridge University Press.

Beaumont, J.G., Kenealy, P. M. (2004). Quality of life perceptions and social comparisons in healthy old age. *Ageing and Society*, 24, 755–69.

Berg, C. A., Upchurch, R. (2007). A developmental-contextual model of couples coping with chronic illness across the adult life span. *Psychological Bulletin*, 133, 920–54.

Berg, C. A., Schindler, I., Smith, T. W., et al. (2011). Perceptions of the cognitive compensation and interpersonal enjoyment functions of collaboration among middle-aged and older married couples. *Psychology and Aging*, 26, 167–73.

Bode, C., de Ridder, D. T. D., Kuijer, R. G., et al. (2007). Effects of an intervention promoting proactive coping competencies in middle and late adulthood. *The Gerontologist*, 47, 42–51.

Boeninger, D. K., Shiraishi, R. W., Aldwin, C. M. et al. (2009). Why do older men report lower stress ratings? Findings from the Normative Aging Study. *International Journal of Aging and Human Development*, 68, 149–70.

Boerner, K. (2004). Adaptation to disability among middle-aged and older adults: The role of assimilative and accommodative Coping. *Journal of Gerontology: Psychological Sciences*, 59, P35–P42.

Bossé, R., Spiro, A., III, Levenson, M. R. (1997). Retirement as a stressful life event. In T. W. Williams (Ed.), *Clinical Disorders and Stressful Life Events* (pp. 325–50). Madison, CT: International Universities Press.

Brandtstädter, J., Greve, W. (1994). The aging self: stabilizing and protective processes. *Developmental Review*, 14, 52–80.

Brandtstädter, J., Renner, G. (1990). Tenacious goal pursuit and flexible goal adjustment: Explication and age-related analysis of assimilative and accommodative strategies of coping. *Psychology and Aging*, 5, 58–67.

Carr, D., House, J. S., Kessler, R. C., et al. (2000). Marital quality and psychological adjustment to widowhood among older adults: a longitudinal analysis. *Journal of Gerontology: Social Sciences*, 55B, S197–S207.

Carstensen, L. L., Fung, H., Charles, S. (2003). Socioemotional selectivity theory and the regulation of emotion in the second half of life. *Motivation and Emotion*, 27, 103–23.

Carver, C., S., Weintraub, J., K., Scheier, M., F. (1989). Assessing coping strategies: A theoretically based approach. *Journal of Personality and Social Psychology*, 56(2), 267–83.

Catanzaro, S. J., Horaney, F., Creasey, G. (1995). Hassles, coping, and depressive symptoms in an elderly community sample: The role of mood regulation expectancies. *Journal of Counseling Psychology*, 42, 259–65.

Charles, S. T. (2010). Strength and vulnerability integration (SAVI): a model of emotional well-being across adulthood. *Psychological Bulletin*, 136, 1068–91.

Charles, S. T., Piazza, J. R., Luong, G., et al. (2009). Now you see it, now you don't: Age differences in affective reactivity to social tensions. *Psychology and Aging*, 24, 645–53.

Cheng, S. -T., Fung, H. H., Chan, A. C. M. (2007). Maintaining self-rated health through social comparison in old age. *Journal of Gerontology: Psychological Sciences*, 62B, P277–P285.

(2009). Self-perception and psychological well-being: The benefits of foreseeing a worse future. *Psychology and Aging*, 24, 623–33.

Chung, M. C., Werrett, J., Easthope, Y., et al. (2004). Coping with post-traumatic stress: Young, middle-aged and elderly comparisons. *International Journal of Geriatric Psychiatry*, 19, 333–43.

Chung, M. C., Berger, Z., Jones, R., et al. (2008). Posttraumatic stress and co-morbidity following myocardial infarction among older patients: The role of coping. *Aging and Mental Health*, 12, 124–33.

Coats, A. H., Blanchard-Fields, F. (2008). Emotion regulation in interpersonal problems: The role of cognitive-emotional complexity, emotion regulation goals, and expressivity. *Psychology and Aging*, 8, 39–5.

Cohen, S., Janicki-Deverts, D., Miller, G. E. (2007). Psychological stress and disease. *Journal of the American Medical Association*, 298, 1685–7.

Collard, R. M., Boter, H., Schoevers, R. A., Oude Voshaar, R. C. (2012). Prevalence of frailty in community-dwelling older persons: a systematic review. *Journal of American Geriatric Society*, 60, 1487–92.

Cook, A. J. (1998). Cognitive-behavioral pain management for elderly nursing home residents. *Journals of Gerontology*, 538, P51–P59.

Cooper, D. C., Katzel, L. I., Waldstein, S. R. (2007). Cardiovascular reactivity in older adults. In C. A. Aldwin, C. L. Park & A. Spiro (Eds.), *Handbook of Health Psychology and Aging* (pp. 142–64). New York: Guilford Press.

Cooper, C., Katona, C., Orrell, M., et al. (2008). Coping strategies, anxiety and depression in caregivers of people with Alzheimer's disease. *International Journal of Geriatric Psychiatry*, 23, 929–36.

Cole, M.G., Dendukuri, N. (2003). Risk factors for depression among elderly community subjects: a systematic review and meta-analysis. *American Journal of Psychiatry*, 160, 1147–56.

Cronkite, R. C., Moos, R. H. (1995). Life context, coping processes and depression. In E. E. Beckham & W. R. Leber (Eds.), *Handbook of Depression* (pp. 569–90). New York: Guilford Press.

Csikszentmihalyi, M., Larson, R. (1987). Validity and reliability of the experience sampling method. *Journal of Nervous and Mental Disease*. 175, 526–36.

Cutrona, C. E., Gardner, K. A. (2006). Stress in couples: The process of dyadic coping. In A. L. Vangelisti & D. Perlman (Eds.), *The Cambridge Handbook of Personal Relationships* (pp. 501–15). New York: Cambridge University Press.

Derks, W., Leeuw, J. R. J., Hordijk, G. J., et al. (2005). Differences in coping style and locus of control between older and younger patients with head and neck cancer. *Clinical Otolaryngology*, 30, 186–92.

Endler, N. S., Parker, J. D. A. (1990). Multidimensional assessment of coping: a critical evaluation. *Journal of Personality and Social Psychology*, 58, 844–54.

Epel, E. S., Burke, H. M., Wolkowitz, O. M. (2007). The psychoneuroendocrinology of aging: Anabolic and catabolic hormones. In C. M. Aldwin, C. L. Park & A. Spiro (Eds.), *Handbook of Health Psychology and Aging* (pp. 119–41). New York: Guilford.

Felton, B.J., Revenson, T. A. (1984). Coping with chronic illness: A study of illness controlability and the influence of coping strategies on psychological adjustment. *Journal of Consulting and Clinical Psychology*, 52, 343–53.

Fernández-Ballesteros, R., Caprara, M. G., García, L. F. (2004): Vivir con Vitalidad-m®. Un Programa Europeo Multimedia. *Intervención social*, 13, 65–85.

Ferreira, V.M., Sherman, A. M. (2007). The relationship of optimism, pain and social support to well-being in older adults with osteoarthritis, *Aging and Mental Health*, 11, 89–98.

Field, N. P., Horowitz, M. J. (1998). Applying an empty-chair monologue paradigm to examine unresolved grief. *Psychiatry*, 61, 279–87.

Folkman, S., Lazarus, R. S. (1980). An analysis of coping in a middle aged community sample. *Journal of Health and Social Behavior*, 21, 219–39.

Fournier, M., de Ridder, D. T. D., Bensing, J. (2002). Optimism and adaptation to chronic disease: The role of optimism in relation to self-care options of type 1 diabetes mellitus, rheumatoid arthritis and multiple sclerosis. *British Journal of Health Psychology*, 7, 409–32.

Fry, P. S., Wong, P. T. (1991). Pain management training in the elderly: Matching interventions with subjects' coping styles. *Stress Medicine*, 7, 93–8.

Germain, A., Moul, D. E., Franzen, P. L., et al. (2006). Effects of a brief behavioral treatment for late-life insomnia: preliminary findings. *Journal of Clinical Sleep Medicine*, 2, 403–6.

Goode, K. T., Haley, E. H., Roth, D. L., et al. (1998). Predicting longitudinal changes in caregiver physical and mental health: A stress process model. *Health Psychology*, 17, 190–8.

Gouin, J. P., Hantsoo, L., Kiecolt-Glaser, J. K. (2008). Immune dysregulation and chronic stress among older adults: a review. *Neuroimmunomodulation*, 15, 251–9.

Gruenewald, T. L., Kemeny, M. E. (2007). Psychoneuroimmunological processes in aging and health. In C. M. Aldwin, C. L. Park & A. I. Spiro (Eds.), *Handbook of Health Psychology and Aging* (pp. 97–118). New York, NY: Guilford Press.

Hampson, S. E., Glasgow, R. E., Zeiss, A. M. (1996). Coping with osteoarthritis by older adults. *Arthritis Care and Research*, 9, 133–41.

Heckhausen, J., Schulz, R. (1993). Optimization by selection and compensation: balancing primary and secondary control in life span development. *International Journal of Behavioral Development*, 16, 287–303.

  (1995). A life-span theory of control. *Psychological Review*, 102, 284–304.

Hermsen, L. A., Leone, S. S., van der Windt, D. A., et al. (2011). Functional outcome in older adults with joint pain and comorbidity: design of a prospective cohort study. *BMC Musculoskeletal Disorders*, 12, 241.

Hertel, G., Rauschenbach, C., Thielgen, M. M., et al. (2015). Are older workers more active copers? Longitudinal effects of age-contingent coping on strain at work. *Journal of Organizational Behavior*, 36, 514–37.

Holahan, C. J., Moos, R. H., Bonin, L. (1997). Social support, coping, and adjustment: A resources model. In G. Pierce, B. Lakey, I. G. Sarason & B. Sarason (Eds.), *Sourcebook of Theory and Research on Social Support and Personality*. New York: Plenum.

Holahan, C. J., Moos, R. H., Holahan, C. K., et al. (2005). Stress generation, avoidant coping, and depressive symptoms: A 10-year model. *Journal of Consulting and Clinical Psychology*, 73, 658–66.

Isaacowitz, D. M., Toner, K., Goren, D., et al. (2008). Looking while unhappy: Mood congruent gaze in young adults, positive gaze in older adults. *Psychological Science*, 19, 848–53.

Jensen, M. P., Turner, A. P., Romano, J. M., et al. (1995). The Chronic Pain Coping Inventory: Development and preliminary validation. *Pain*, 60, 203–16.

Klein, D. M., Turvey, C. L., Pies, C. J. (2007). Relationship of coping styles with quality of life and depressive symptoms in older heart failure patients. *Journal of Aging and Health*, 19, 22–38.

Kobasa, S. C., Maddi, S. R., Puccetti, M. C., & Zola, M. A. (1985). Effectiveness of hardiness, exercise and social support as resources against illness. *Journal of Psychosomatic Research*, 29, 525–33.

Konnert, C., Dobson, K., Stelmach, L. (2009). The prevention of depression in nursing home residents: a randomized clinical trial of cognitive–behavioral therapy. *Aging and Mental Health*, 13, 288–99.

Kobasa, S. C. (1979). Stressful life events, personality, and health. An inquiry into hardiness. *Journal of Personality and Social Psychology*, 37, 1–11.

Krause, N., Rook, K. S. (2003). Negative interaction in late life: Issues in the stability and generalizability of conflict across relationships. *Journal of Gerontology: Psychological Sciences*, 57B, P88–P99.

Lachman, M. E., Ziff, M., Spiro, A. (1994). Maintaining a sense of control in later life. In M. Ory (Ed.), *Aging and Quality of Life* (pp. 116–32). New York: Sage.

Lazarus, R. S., Folkman, S. (1984). *Stress, Appraisal, and Coping*. New York: Springer.

Losada, A., Márquez-González, M., Romero-Moreno, R., et al. (2015). Cognitive–Behavioral Therapy (CBT) versus Acceptance and Commitment Therapy (ACT) for dementia family caregivers with significant depressive symptoms: Results of a randomized clinical trial. *Journal of Consulting and Clinical Psychology*, 83, 760–72.

Lowis, M. J., Edwards, A. C., Burton, M. (2009). Coping with retirement: Well-being, health, and religion. *Journal of Psychology*, 143, 427–48.

MacLeod, S., Musich, S., Hawkins, K., et al. (2016). The impact of resilience among older adults. *Geriatric Nursing*, 37, 266–72.

Manning, L. K., Carr, D. C., Kail, B. L. (2016). Do higher levels of resilience buffer the deleterious impact of chronic illness on disability in later life? *The Gerontologist*, 56, 514–24.

Martin, P., Kliegel, M., Rott, C., et al. (2008). Age differences and changes of coping behavior in three age groups: Findings from the Georgia Centenarian Study. *The International Journal of Aging and Human Development*, 66, 97–114.

Márquez-González, M., Losada, A. (2015). Acceptance and Commitment Therapy. In N. Pachana (Ed.), *Encyclopedia of Geropsychology*. Singapore: Springer.

Mausbach, B. T., Aschbacher, K., Patterson, T. L., et al. (2006). Avoidant coping partially mediates the relationship between patient problem behaviors and depressive symptoms in spousal Alzheimer caregivers. *Journal of Geriatric Psychiatry*, 14, 299–306.

Mausbach, B. T., Patterson, T. L., von Känel, R.,et al. (2007). The attenuating effect of personal mastery on the relations between stress and Alzheimer caregiver health: A five-year longitudinal analysis. *Aging and Mental Health*, 11, 7–644.

McCrae, R. R. (1982). Age differences in the use of coping mechanisms. *Journal of Gerontology*, 37, 454–60.

Moos, R. (1993). *Coping Responses Inventory: Adult Form manual*. Odessa, FL: Psychological Assessment Resources.

Moos, R. H., Brennan, P. L., Schutte, K. K., et al. (2006). Older adults' coping with negative life events: Common processes of managing health, interpersonal, and financial/ work stressors. *The International Journal of Aging and Human Development*, 62, 39–59.

Newth, S., DeLongis, A. (2000). Individual differences, mood, and coping with chronic pain in rheumatoid arthritis: a daily process analysis. *Psychological Health*, 19, 283–305.

Nolen-Hoeksema, S., Parker, L. E., Larson, J. (1994). Ruminative coping with depressed mood following loss. *Journal of Personality and Social Psychology*, 67, 92–104.

Okabayashi, H., Sugisawa, H., Takanashi, K., et al. (2008). A longitudinal study of coping and burnout among Japanese family caregivers of frail elders. *Aging and Mental Health*, 12, 434–43.

Okun, M. A., Keith, V. M. (1998). Effects of positive and negative social exchanges with various sources on depressive symptoms in younger and older adults. *Journal of Gerontology*, 53, P4–20.

Ong, A. D., Bergeman, C. S. (2004). Resilience and adaptation to stress in later life: empirical perspectives and conceptual implications. *Ageing International*, 29, 219–46.

Ong, A. D., Bergeman, C. S., Bisconti, T. L. (2004). The role of daily positive emotions during conjugal bereavement. *Journals of Gerontology, Series B: Psychological Sciences and Social Sciences*, 59, P168–P176.

Ong, A. D., Bergeman, C. S., Boker, S. M. (2009). Resilience comes of age: Defining features in later adulthood. *Journal of Personality*, 77, 1777–804.

Ouwehand, C., de Ridder, D., Bensing, J. (2007). A review of successful aging models: proposing proactive coping as an important additional strategy. *Clinical Psychology Review*, 27, 873–84.

Pargament, K. I., Koenig, H. G., Tarakeshwar, N., et al. (2004). Religious coping methods as predictors of psychological, physical and spiritual outcomes among medically ill elderly patients: a two-year longitudinal study. *Journal of Health Psychology*, 9, 713–30.

Park, C. L., Fenster, J. R. (2004). Stress-related growth: Predictors of occurrence and correlates with psychological adjustment. *Journal of Social and Clinical Psychology*, 23, 195–215.

Patterson, T. L., Smith, L. W., Grant, I. (1990). Internal vs. external determinants of coping responses to stressful life-events in the elderly. *British Journal of Medical Psychology*, 63, 149–60.

Penley, J. A., Tomaka, J., Wiebe, J. S. (2002). The association of coping to physical and psychological health outcomes: A meta-analytic review. *Journal of Behavioral Medicine*, 6, 551–603.

Perrot, S., Poiraudeau, S., Kabir, M., et al. (2008). Active or passive pain coping strategies in hip and knee osteoarthritis? Results of a national survey of 4,719 patients in a primary care setting. *Arthritis Care and Research*, 59, 1555–62.

Pinquart, M., Duberstein, P. R., Lyness, J. M. (2007). Effects of psychotherapy and other behavioral interventions on clinically depressed older adults: A meta-analysis. *Aging and Mental Health*, 11, 645–57.

Powers, D. V., Gallagher-Thompson, D., Kraemer, H. C. (2002). Coping and depression in Alzheimer's caregivers: Longitudinal evidence of stability. *Journals of Gerontology: Psychological Sciences and Social Sciences*, 57, 205–11.

Regier, N. G., Parmelee, P. A. (2015). The stability of coping strategies in older adults with osteoarthritis and the ability of these strategies to predict changes in depression, disability, and pain. *Aging and Mental Health*, 19, 1113–22.

Revenson, T. A., De Longis, A. (2011). Couples coping with chronic illness. In S. Folkman (Ed.), *The Oxford Handbook of Stress, Health, and Coping* (pp. 101–23). New York, NY: Oxford University Press.

Rothermund, K., Brandtstädter, J. (2003). Coping with deficits and losses in later life: From compensatory action to accommodation. *Psychology and Aging*, 18, 896–905.

Rovner, B. W., Casten, R. J. (2008). Preventing late-life depression in age-related macular degeneration. *American Journal of Geriatric Psychiatry*, 16, 454–9.

Samanez-Larkin, G., Robertson, E. R., Mikels, J. A., et al. (2009). Selective attention to emotion in the aging brain. *Psychology and Aging*, 24, 519–29.

Sharpley, C., Yardley, P. (1999). The relationship between Cognitive Hardiness, Explanatory style and Happiness-Depression in post-retirement men and women. *Australian Psychologist*, 34, 82–101.

Shear, M. K., Wang, Y., Skritskaya, N., et al. (2014). Treatment of complicated grief in elderly persons: A randomized clinical trial. *Journal of American Medical Association. Psychiatry*, 71, 1287–95.

Schulz, R., Heckhausen, J. (1996). A life span model of successful aging. *American Psychologist*, 51, 702–14.

Schumacher, K. L., Jones, P. S., Meleis, A. I. (1999). Helping elderly persons in transition: A framework for research and practice. In E. A. Swanson & T. Tripp-Reimer

(Eds.), *Life Transitions in the Older Adult: Issues for Nurses and Other Health Professionals* (pp. 1–26). New York: Springer.

Somers, T. J., Keefe, F. J., Pells, J. J., et al. (2009). Pain catastrophizing and pain-related fear in osteoarthritis patients: Relationship to pain and disability. *Journal of Pain and Symptom Management*, 37, 863–72.

Spiro, A. III. (2007). The relevance of a lifespan developmental approach to health. In C. M. Aldwin, C. L. Park & A. Spiro III (Eds.), *Handbook of Health Psychology and Aging* (pp. 75–93). New York: Guilford.

Staudinger, U. M., Marsiske, M., Baltes, P. B. (1995). Resilience and reserve capacity in later adulthood: Potentials and limits of development across the life span. In D. J. Cohen & D. Cicchetti (Eds.), *Developmental Psychopathology: Risk, Disorder, and Adaptation* (Vol. 2, pp. 801–47). Oxford, England: Wiley.

Stone, A. A., Shiffman, S. (1994). Ecological momentary assessment (EMA) in behavioral medicine. *Annals of Behavioral Medicine*, 16, 199–202.

Stowell, J. R., Kiecolt-Glaser, J. K., Glaser, R. (2001). Perceived stress and cellular immunity: when coping counts. *Journal of Behavioral Medicine*, 24, 323–39.

Szinovacz, M. E. (2003). Contexts and pathways: Retirement as institution, process, and experience. In G. A. Adams & T. A. Beehr (Eds.), *Retirement: Reasons, Processes, and Results* (pp. 6–52). New York: Springer.

Tedeschi, R. G., Calhoun, L. G. (2004). Posttraumatic growth: Conceptual foundations and empirical evidence. *Psychological Inquiry*, 15, 1–18.

Thompsen, D. K., Mehlsen, M. Y., Hokland, M., et al. (2004). Negative thoughts and health: associations among rumination immunity, and health care utilization in a young and elderly sample. *Psychosomatic Medicine*, 66, 363–71.

Turner, R. J., Avison, W. R. (1992). Innovations in the measurement of life stress: crisis theory and the significance of event resolution. *Journal of Health and Social Behavior*, 33, 36–50.

Vitaliano, P. P., Russo, J., Paulsen, V. M., et al. (1995). Cardiovascular recovery from laboratory stress: Biopsychosocial concomitants in older adults. *Journal of Psychosomatic Research*, 39, 361–77.

Wadsworth, M. E., Gudmundsen, G. R., Raviv, T., et al. (2004). Coping with terrorism: Age and gender differences in effortful and involuntary responses to September 11th. *Applied Developmental Science*, 8, 143–57.

Wild, K., Wiles, J. L., Allen, R. E. S. (2013). Resilience: Thoughts on the value of the concept for critical gerontology. *Ageing and Society*, 33, 137–58.

Wetherell, J. L., Afari, N., Ayers, C., et al. (2011). Acceptance and commitment therapy for generalized anxiety disorder in older adults: A preliminary report. *Behavior Therapy*, 42, 127–34.

Yancura, L., Aldwin, C. (2008). Coping and health in older adults. *Current Psychiatric Reports*, 10, 10–15.

Yeung, D. Y., Fung, H. H. (2007). Age differences in coping and emotional responses toward SARS: A longitudinal study of Hong Kong Chinese. *Aging and Mental Health*, 11, 579–87.

# 24 Spirituality and Transcendence

Andreas Kruse and Eric Schmitt

## Introduction

### The Spiritual Self as the Core of Personality

William James (1842–1910) was a professor of psychology (1876–1885) and a professor of philosophy (1885–1907) at Harvard University. In the International Encyclopedia of Philosophy he is acknowledged as the most famous American psychologist and philosopher of his time. James's *The Principles of Psychology* (1890), an unprecedented analysis of the discipline's international state (Ricouer, 1992), is regularly cited as the most important text in the history of modern psychology. His prominence in the history of psychology is due to his commitment to ground psychological perspectives in the facts of nervous physiology, the respective new perspectives he introduced as a trained doctor and psychologist, and his philosophical background, which is particularly reflected when dealing with problems of the mind, the relationship between mind and body, or the continuity of the self. Together with Charles Sanders Peirce and John Dewey, William James belongs to the main exponents of pragmatism. Following the epistemology of pragmatism, beliefs must not be considered as mental entities that somehow correspond to, or deviate from, external facts or realities. Instead, beliefs are conceptualized as ways of acting with reference to specific environments. According to philosophical pragmatism, stating that beliefs are true or false refers to the respective "cash value," i.e., to the efficacy for adaptation to specific environments (James, 1907). The respective insight is also reflected in contemporary perspectives on narrative identity, guided autobiography, and narrative therapy, which accentuate that self-understanding is a creative process of reconfiguration and mediating the past, present, and future person, society, and culture, is and ought, and, not least, selfhood and sameness (ipse and idem) (Ricoeur, 1992).

James (1890) defined the self, in its widest possible sense "the sum total of all that he CAN call his, not only his body and his psychic powers, but his clothes and his house, his wife and children, his ancestors and friends, his reputation and works, his lands and horses, and yacht and bank-account. All these things give him the same emotions. If they wax and prosper, he feels triumphant; if they dwindle and die away, he feels cast down, – not necessarily in the same degree for each thing, but in much the same way for all. Since the line between what an individual calls me, and what is simply called mine, is difficult to draw, dealing with the empirical self means dealing with fluctuating material" (p. 279).

According to James, "personality implies the incessant presence of two elements, an objective person, known by a passing subjective thought and recognized as continuing in time" (p. 239). Consequently, James's theory of the self – which is particularly important for the present contribution – proceeds from the differentiation between the self as known, and the self as knower. The former is also characterized as the "Me," or, "Empirical Self," and the latter as the "I," or, "Pure Ego" (James, 1890). The "Me" can be thought of as a result of a person's experiences. James further differentiates between the Material Self, the Social Self, and the Spiritual Self.

The core of the material self is the body. All things "that belong to us or that we belong to" contribute to our material self. Social self refers to "what we are in a given social situation." James stated that, "properly speaking, a man has as many social selves as there are individuals who recognize him and carry an image of him in their mind … But as the individuals who carry the images fall naturally into classes, we may practically say that he has as many different social selves as there are distinct groups of persons about whose opinion he cares" (p. 294). The spiritual self refers to a man's inner or subjective being, to "who we are at our core." The spiritual self is more enduring and intimate than the aforementioned selves. James describes considering our spiritual self as a "reflective process." Spiritual selves reflect the human ability to abandon external perspectives and to "think of subjectivity as such, to think ourselves as thinkers." The "I" or pure ego is responsible for our experience of continuity in the stream of consciousness; it must not be thought of as a substance and therefore cannot be examined by science.

In William James's *Theory of the Self*, the aforementioned constituents arouse corresponding feelings and emotions, particularly self-complacency and self-dissatisfaction, which are considered to be "two opposite classes of affection [that] seem to be direct and elementary endowments of our nature" (p. 306). Moreover, constituents of the Self prompt respective actions of self-seeking and self-preservation, which are considered to be "fundamental instinctive impulses." Following James, spiritual self-seeking includes "every impulse towards psychic progress, whether intellectual, moral, or spiritual in the narrow sense of the term"; however, he goes on to say, "much that commonly passes for spiritual self-seeking in this narrow sense is only material and social self-seeking beyond the grave." Nowadays the concepts of self-preservation and self-seeking are reflected in propositions of needs for self-consistency, self-verification, and self-enhancement as basic motivational factors for human thought, experience, and action, as well as in the idea of lowering aspirations and increasing successes as two basic, alternative strategies of the management of self-esteem. More basically, these concepts correspond with the idea of self-actualization as a basic tendency of the psyche.

Although development of the self basically refers to perspectives of the other, social positions, and social interaction, self-understanding should not be reduced to perspective-taking. William James considered this point with the juxtaposition of the social self and the spiritual self (with the latter as the core of personality).

The aforementioned work of William James elucidates that spirituality refers to the core of our understanding of the self and the world, inspiring perspectives on what we are, as well as perception, reflections, evaluation, and anticipation of the world outside, the past, and future to come.

## A Narrative Perspective on Self-Understanding and Ethics

Explaining the idea of narrative identity, Paul Ricouer argues that what we call knowledge about the self or self-identity is not discovered in the world outside, but reconfigured, i.e., "self-understanding is an interpretation; interpretation of the self, in turn, finds in the narrative, among other signs and symbols, a privileged form of mediation" (Ricouer, 1992, p. 114). Charles Taylor (1985) points out that self-narration must always be orientated toward events, the significance of which, however, does not exist independently of the person narrating and which, in addition, is changed by the narration itself, i.e., "our attempts to formulate what we hold important must, like descriptions, strive to be faithful to something, but what they strive to be faithful to is not an independent object ... but rather a largely inarticulate sense of what is of decisive importance. An articulation of this 'object' tends to make it something different from what it was before" (p. 38). Following Charles Taylor, self-interpretations increase in significance when considering self-definition, i.e., "narratives are (i) an optional medium for articulating some of our implicit self-interpretations and strong evaluations. Narratives alone enable us to (ii) care about our lives as wholes and to (iii) interpret our movements in a moral space. Further, narrative thinking provides a way of providing concordance to (iv) diachronous and (v) synchronous dissonances in our strong evaluations" (Laitinen, 2002, p. 67).

At the beginning of an essay on spirituality and ethics at the end of life, Sulmasy (2013) quotes the aphorism from Aristotle's *Poetics*, "every ethos implies a mythos." Whereas the original meaning intended by Aristotle was that in dramatic work, character development (ethos) requires a plot (mythos), Sulmasy puts forward the thesis "that every system of ethics depends, either implicitly or explicitly, on some very fundamental story about some very basic questions, such as the nature of the universe, the meaning of the human, the nature of value, the purposes (or lack thereof) of human freedom, and others" (Sulmasy, 2013, p. 447), implying "that our fundamental self-identifying and morally originating commitments regarding the most profound questions that all human beings must face – questions that lurk always beneath the surface of medical practice – inform our attitudes and shape our actions in the work we do in caring for those who are dying" (p. 449).

Respective narratives might be seldom told in everyday life, but, particularly in the contexts of palliative care, they regularly come closer to the surface. Treatment preferences and decisions are implicitly or explicitly based on "strong evaluations" (Taylor, 1989), giving answers to questions like: Where did I come from? Where am I going? How am I to live? Here, many patients, relatives, caregivers, and practitioners explicitly refer to religious belief, while others may refer to what Taylor (2007, p. 726) called "immanent transcendence" – i.e., "a belief in something that transcends the person and his or her needs and preferences, but is circumscribed by the bounds of society or humankind or the world or the universe and is not "supernatural" in the sense of being beyond nature." Nevertheless, "even if these self-identifying and morally originating commitments are not religious, these comprehensive sets of assumptions are really sets of religion-like beliefs. As the saying goes, it takes a lot of faith to be an atheist." Sulmasy concludes that, particularly when caring for patients at the end of life, "practitioners should strive to be more conscious of the narratives that undergird their own spiritual and ethical positions, as well as seek to understand those of the patients they serve" (Sulmasy, 2013, p. 450).

## Self-Actualization

A differentiated review of one's own life, and at the end, the composed and hopeful view of one's own vulnerability and finitude (hopeful in the sense of enduring dying and death internally "unscathed"), is significant for a constructive life in old age. "Constructive" here means that the self can express and communicate itself, and that it can even differentiate further (actual genesis). The respective processes are referred to as self-actualization.

Following Goldstein, who coined the term self-actualization, "there is only one motive by which human activity is set going: the tendency to actualize oneself" (Goldstein, 1939, p. 196). This idea can be traced back to the writings of Spinoza who understood development as "becoming what one was intended to be and nothing other than that, no matter how exalted the alternative might appear to be" (Millon, 2003, p. 23).

In our understanding, the term self-actualization describes the realization of values, capabilities, tendencies, and needs, and the consistency of the situation experienced in this process (which can also be understood as a person's experienced sense of purpose). Here, the statement that the person comprises many different types of quality is important for an appropriate understanding of self-actualization: in an approximate differentiation, we can distinguish between the physical, the cognitive, the emotional, the perception-related, the social-communicative, the aesthetic, and the everyday-practical qualities, and each of these qualities alone can already form the source of a self-actualization.

In the language of the existence psychology of Viktor Frankl (2014), self-actualization is to be understood as the striving of mankind for the development of values. Here, Viktor Frankl differentiates between three fundamental value forms in which our comprehensive understanding of a person and their possibilities for development of values are expressed: (a) *homo faber* as the creating person, (b) *homo amans* as the loving, experiencing, perceiving person, and (c) *homo patiens* as the suffering, enduring person who accepts this suffering.

Worthy of mention in Frankl's theory is the statement according to which self-actualization is possible – and Frankl goes so far as to say that this is possible in particular in limit situations. In the realization of adjustment values, meaning the capability of achieving a new attitude toward life in a limit situation (homo patiens); here Frankl even sees the highest form of value realization. Processes of self-actualization also form the core of psychological-humanist theories, which are based on the assumption that the striving for self-realization drives forward development across our entire life span; here we must mention Charlotte Buehler, the founder of humanist psychology.

## Spirituality and Transcendence in the Psychology of Aging

In an essay on self-recognition in old age, the philosopher, Arthur Schopenhauer (1788–1860), describes the process as follows:

> Towards the end of life, much the same happens as at the end of a masked ball when the masks are removed. We now see who those really were with whom we had come in contact during the course of our life. Characters have revealed themselves, deeds have borne fruit, achievements have been justly appreciated, and all illusions have crumbled away. But, for all this, time was necessary. The curious thing, however, is that only towards the end of our lives do we really recognise and understand even ourselves, our real aim and object, especially in our relations to the world and others. Very often, but not always, we shall have to assign to ourselves a lower place than we had previously thought was our due. Sometimes we shall give ourselves a higher, the reason for this being that we had no adequate notion of the baseness of the world, and accordingly set our aim higher than it. Incidentally, we come to know what we have in ourselves. (Schopenhauer, 2000, p. 491)

Elsewhere, we (Kruse, 2014) suggested that very old age has three possible sources of developmental potential: self-reflection, openness to experience, or the susceptibility to new impressions, experiences, and insights. Generativity is a conviction that each individual has his or her place in the succession of generations and the willingness to assume responsibility within the succession of generations. In very old age, the limitations and finiteness of existence becomes increasingly salient, and thus requires concentrated, in-depth self-analysis (Erikson, 1963, 1998). Ideally, processes of self-reflection and life-review result in the achievement of ego integrity, i.e., the awareness of self-sameness and continuity in life and the ability to accept one's life as a whole, including lost opportunities and unfulfilled aspirations and expectations (Erikson, 1998). Furthermore, self-reflection and life-review in older people are promoted by openness to new impressions, experiences, and insights (Randall, 2013). Such openness is paraphrased in psychological literature with the concept of cathectic flexibility, which has also been referred to as "transcendence of the body" in old age and as "transcendence of the self" in very old age (Peck, 1968; Tornstam, 1989; Brown & Lowis, 2003). A lack of cathectic flexibility (i.e., cathectic impoverishment), means preoccupation with physical processes and a lack of sensitivity to emotional, mental, and social processes. As a result, older people may develop neither a sense of living-on in subsequent generations, nor the corresponding generative concerns, nor an appreciation of the spiritual forces of human existence, nor the related attitudes of serenity and confidence (Ardelt et al., 2013; Wink et al., 2013). In contrast, optimum development in very old age involves seeing oneself as a link in the chain of generations and sharing life experience with younger people.

In the past decades, there has been a notable increase of interest and respective research on spirituality and religion, in particular on the relationship between these concepts, i.e., psychological well-being and mental health (Bonelli & Koenig, 2013). However, there is substantial controversy concerning the appropriate definition of the term spirituality (Koenig, 2008, 2011). Overlap between the concepts of religion and spirituality becomes apparent in the respective definitions suggested by Koenig and colleagues (Koenig et al., 2012). According to these authors, religion involves beliefs, practices, and rituals related to the transcendent that may be held or practiced in private or public settings but which are, in some way, derived from established traditions that developed over time within a community. Here, religion is understood as an organized system designed: (a) to facilitate closeness to the transcendent, and (b) to foster an understanding of one's relationship and responsibility to others in living together in a community. Likewise, spirituality is distinguished from humanism, values, morals, and mental health by its connection to the transcendent. Spirituality is understood as something intimately connected to the supernatural, the mystical, and to organized religion. However, the authors further argue that spirituality also extends beyond organized religion and begins before it: "Spirituality includes both a search for the transcendent and the discovery of the transcendent and so involves travelling along the path that leads from non-consideration to questioning, to either staunch non-belief or belief and, if belief, then ultimately to devotion and finally, surrender" (Koenig et al., 2012, p. 3).

The Fetzer Institute/NIA Working Group provided similar definitions of religion, and spirituality and religion (1999). Here, religion is aimed at "fostering and nourishing spiritual life," involving "a system of worship and doctrine," whereas spirituality is defined as, "the transcendent, addressing the ultimate questions about life's meaning with the assumption that there is more to life than what we can see or fully understand" (Fetzer Institute 1999, p. 2).

Besides the similarity in definition of the two terms, research on spirituality regularly considers questions assessing religion also appropriate for assessing spirituality. As a consequence, religion and spirituality are used interchangeable in research reviews. (Koenig, 2012; Park et al., 2013; Tuck & Anderson, 2014).

Generativity, ego-integrity, and gerotranscendence are seen as psychological constructs, which are of particularly significance in understanding the psychological effects of religiousness and spirituality on "active aging."

## Generativity

According to Erikson (1963), the realization of generativity becomes an important developmental task in middle adulthood in the seventh of a total of eight psychosocial crises. Generativity can be defined as "concern in establishing and guiding the next generation" (p. 267). As such, generativity is related to, but also conceptually distinguished from, the concepts of empathy, altruism and intergenerational solidarity. In our understanding, the term empathy accentuates the "capacity to be affected by, and share in, the emotional state of another," whereas the term altruism refers to "behavior that benefits a recipient at a cost to the actor" (de Waal, 2008); intergenerational solidarity can be defined in terms of "social cohesion between generations" (Bengtson & Oyama, 2007). Generativity can reflect individual needs, social norms, or both. Ideally, generative behavior proceeds from an empathic understanding of the needs, interests, and preferences of the younger generation. However, concerns for the next generation do not necessarily reflect the perspectives of younger people. Although generative behavior often implies older peoples' willingness to bear the costs for the benefit of others, engagement for younger generations can reflect selfish, as well as altruistic, motives. Basically, generativity is both motivated by intergenerational solidarity and contributing to maintaining and strengthening intergenerational ties. However, generative behavior is not always requested and accepted by younger people.

Our understanding of generativity follows the conceptual and methodological framework provided by McAdams and colleagues (McAdams et al., 2006; Kruse & Schmitt, 2012). From this perspective, there are two motivational sources of generativity, i.e., cultural demand and inner desire. Cultural demand, as a facet of generativity, can be further explicated as reflecting the age structure of society (Riley et al., 1992) and normative developmental expectations. In this context, it should also be considered that cultural demand for generativity can substantially change over time, e.g., against the background of demographic change, interest in the possibilities and preconditions of development and effective use of strengths and potentials of old age has grown worldwide. However, generativity is not only prompted by society and not only societies benefit from generative action. Inner desire, as a second motivational source of generativity, refers to two complementary basic human needs, i.e., a "need to be needed," to have meaningful relations to others, and a need for "symbolic immortality," i.e., to invest resources and potentials into things that outlive the self (Kotre, 1996). The aforementioned motivational sources of generativity are reflected in two further facets of generativity, i.e., a conscious concern for the next generation and a commitment to take responsibility for the next generation. The translation of concern and commitment into generative action depends on what has been described as "belief in the species," i.e., "to place hope in the advancement and betterment of human life in succeeding generations, even in the face of strong evidence of human destructiveness and deprivation" (McAdams & de St. Aubin, 1992). Moreover, generativity is conceived within the larger context of the life-story theory of adult identity (McAdams et al., 1997, 2006; McAdams, 2013). From this perspective, adults construct, and try to live out, a "generativity script" that not only reflects past generative action, but is also important for current generative concerns and commitments, as well as an understanding of what is worth to outlive the self and what can and should be transmitted to others to live on through generative efforts. Religiousness and spirituality do positively affect generativity in old age if the human being in relationships, as well as parishioners and shared responsibility had been a personally significant issue in the biography. Here, the high potential of religiousness and spirituality for the understanding of the human being as *a being in relationships*, and consequently for generativity, is highlighted.

## Ego-Integrity

In his philosophy of the present, George Herbert Mead wrote: "We speak of the past as final and irrevocable. There is nothing that is less so ... the past (or some meaningful structure of the past) is as hypothetical as the future" (Mead, 1932, p. 12). Life is organized and structured by people themselves, even back in adolescence, people begin to create a coherent life story that – in normal circumstances – becomes more and more a definite story, a basis for reconstructing and understanding the past, for interpreting and evaluating the present, as well as for anticipating the future, setting aims, making plans, and goal pursuit and goal adjustment. In psychology, there is a long-standing controversy as to whether self-consistency is even more important a need than self-respect and self-enhancement, as coping with stress and challenges or more general self-regulation processes seem impossible without establishing and maintaining at least some kind of continuity. Following the life span developmental theory of Erikson (1967; Erikson et al., 1986), establishing ego-integrity in the context of life-review is an indispensable task at the end of human life – if people do not succeed in confronting this task, they are expected to suffer from despair and feelings of disgust about their own lives.

If the detailed description of Hearn and colleagues (2012) that "integrated persons have realistic and insightful self-awareness, can explain the main influences that formed their characters, and are reasonably optimistic" is followed, then such individuals are able to acknowledge regrets and accept losses and inabilities, are involved in sustainable social relationships, and committed to their own values and aspirations, while also understanding and tolerating perspectives resulting from different ethnic and cultural backgrounds; furthermore, they are still curious and engaged, but nevertheless satisfied with their own experiences and achievements. In contrast, "despairing persons are depressed about disappointments, failures, and missed chances in life ... have not accommodated their ways of interpreting the world, or their circumstances, sufficiently to attain reasonable life satisfaction. They frequently express sadness, regret, or failure, sometimes in the form of self-denigrations or sarcasm, or in remarks implying a sense of futility or triviality" (Hearn et al., 2012, pp. 2–3). These authors propose the distinguishing of two additional intermediary identity statuses: non-exploratory persons who "have engaged in little self-examination about values, purpose, or the meaning in life," who "stay within a circumscribed comfort zone of thoughts, motions, and attitudes," and pseudo-integrated persons who "may offer excessively coherent self-presentations from lack of self-awareness, unwillingness to examine problems, or from the wish to appear successful" (Hearn et al., 2012, p. 3).

Erikson's last psycho-social crisis is initiated by changes in older people's situatedness at the end of life and further reinforced by social demand. Ego-integrity is conceptualized as a positive ending point of lifelong identity development, with identity defined as awareness of self-sameness and continuity, and the style of one's individuality coinciding with the sameness and continuity with one's sameness and continuity as perceived by significant others (1968, p. 50). Achieving ego-integrity implies being able to accept one's life as a whole, including lost opportunities and unfulfilled aspirations and expectations. Similarly, more recent gerontological theories, e.g., the continuity theory proposed by Robert Atchley, and the socioemotional selectivity theory proposed by Laura Carstensen (Carstensen et al., 1999; Carstensen & Löckenhoff, 2004), conceptualize continuity as a precondition for satisfaction with life and subjective well-being. In theoretical works, a relationship is very often established between integrity and religiosity or spirituality (e.g., Dalai Lama & Cutler, 1998). Should the condition of a positively perceived religious socialization exist, then there is an age-related increase in the willingness to incorporate one's own life into full terms of reference, which are often interpreted as "divine"; these full terms, or divine references, motivate the individual to perceive the individual life course as necessary and good – this is also true when a lot of limitations and limits are remembered (Kruse, 2007; Härle, 2010).

In a posthumous, extended edition of *The life Cycle Completed*, Joan Erikson proposed adding a ninth stage to her husband's theory of personality development: "Old age in one's 80s and 90s brings with it new demands, re-evaluations, and daily difficulties. These concerns can only be adequately discussed, and confronted, by designating a new ninth stage to clarify these challenges" (in Erikson, 1998, p. 105). As a consequence of growing vulnerability and decline in old age, former solutions of psychosocial crisis have to be confronted again, and modified, with the dystonic pole giving higher prominence. However, drawing extensively on Lars Tornstam's theory of gerotranscendence, Joan Erikson stresses the potential of the respective tension to be a source of growth and strength (see also Brown & Lowis, 2003).

## Gerotranscendence

The theory of gerotranscendence (Tornstam, 1989, 2011) postulates that there is an age-increasing willingness for incorporating one's own life into comprehensive (or "full") terms of reference. Being beyond one's self – as the key element of gerotranscendence – encompasses the feeling of being absorbed into other people's lives (especially into the life of younger generations), as well as the feeling of being embedded into an extensive context or cosmic order (Kruse, 2005; Rosenmayr, 2010).

Tornstam (1997) argues that living into old age, and facing its challenges, brings about a shift in meta-perspective from a materialistic and rational view of the world to a more cosmic and transcendent one. This shift in meta-perspective involves "ontological changes on three levels: the cosmic-level, the self-level, and the social-and-individual-relations level (Tornstam, 1996, pp. 42–3). Developing gerotranscendence implies experience of a redefinition of self and social relationships, as well as a new understanding of fundamental existential questions. "The individual might become less self-occupied, and experience a decreased interest in material things and a greater need for solitary 'meditation.' There is also often a feeling of cosmic communion with the spirit of the universe, and a redefinition of time, space, life and death. There is an increased feeling of affinity with past generations and a decreased interest in superfluous social interaction" (Ahmadi Lewin, 2001, p. 395).

Tornstam (2011) elucidates that developing gerotranscendence goes beyond Erikson's identity status of ego-integrity: "In Erikson's theory, ego-integration primarily refers to an integration of the elements in the life that has passed. The individual reaches a fundamental acceptance of the life lived. In this way, the ego-integrity described by Erikson is more of a reverse integration process within the same definition of the world as before, while the process of gerotranscendence implies more of a forward or outward direction, including a redefinition of reality" (Tornstam, 2011, p. 172).

For characterizing gerotranscendence, it is helpful to take up the differentiation between life time (*Lebenszeit*) and universal time (*Weltzeit*), which had been introduced by Blumenberg (1986). Differentiating between individual life time and cosmic universal time is highlighting the human being's motive for *transcendence* that can be defined as the motive for feeling embedded into a cosmic order in which he or she can trust.

Development of gerotranscendence is seen as a continuous, endogenous process, normally for individuals, instinctive and transcultural, already determined by genetics: "Ageing, or rather living, implies a process during which the degree of gerotranscendence increases" (Tornstam, 1996, p. 41). However, not all people do develop gerotranscendence when aging, since the process can be accelerated or retarded by external factors, not least cultural settings: "In most Western cultures, neither guidance towards, nor acceptance of, the wise gerotranscendent state of mind exists. In our culture, a person who displays the changes accompanying the gerotranscendence state-of-mind runs the risk of being judged as deviant, asocial or mentally disturbed" (Tornstam, 1996, p. 45).

Gerotranscendence is also discussed in the context of religiosity or spirituality – empirical results point out the increasing willingness of older people to interpret their own lives from a universal perspective where a positively evaluated religious socialization exists (cf. Wittrahm, 2010). In this case, the universal perspective does not only refer to a cosmic transcendence, but also includes the advance toward generativity, meaning identification with younger people's lives, feeling with them, sharing their concerns, motivating, and supporting them. Ahmadi Lewin (2001) analyzed three studies on gerotranscendence in Sweden, Iran, and Turkey. Results further support the hypothesis that "in a cultural setting where mystical-type ideas are not integrated into people's ways of thinking – like the Turkish one – secular people may be expected to have a limited ability to develop toward gerotranscendence," whereas societies in which religion is integrated into social and cultural life "provide fertile soil for individuals to develop toward gerotranscendence" (Ahmadi Lewin, 2001, p. 412).

## Spirituality and Transcendence in Physical Health

In their review on different pathways between religiousness, spirituality, and health, Aldwin and colleagues (2014) distinguish between several models aimed at explaining the well-established positive effects of religiousness and spirituality on psychological distress and depressive symptoms, health-related quality of life, morbidity, and mortality (Chida et al., 2009; Krause, 2011; Masters & Hooker, 2013; Park & Slattery, 2013). For example, in a "classical model" (Koenig, 2008), mental health is seen as the mediator of the relationship. Following the propositions of this model, spirituality and religiousness contribute to perceptions of meaning, connectedness, and psychological well-being (Bamonti et al., 2016; Van Cappelen et al., 2016). Respective increases in mental health are supposed to have a positive impact on psychoneuroimmunological factors, thereby reducing levels of cardiovascular disease, cancer, and mortality (Hulett & Armer, 2016). In a related model, Cotton and colleagues (2006), following a proposition of Pargament (1997), conceptualize religiousness – in terms of religious participation – as a distant, and spirituality as a proximal, variable. Here, spirituality is a mediator of the relationship between religiosity and health, implying perceptions of meaning, religious coping, and support. More differentiated models have been proposed by Park (2012), Levin (1996), and Krause (2011). In Park's model, a distinction is made between the general influences of religiosity and spirituality, specific beliefs and interpretations, and influences under crisis situations. Levin (1996) distinguishes between eight aspects that might have an impact on physical health via different pathways, mediators, and salutogenic effects, i.e., religious commitment, identity, involvement, practice, and obedience to, beliefs, faith, and experiences. Krause (2011) distinguishes five basic needs satisfied by religiosity that might have direct and indirect effects on physical health, i.e., the need for the search for self-transcendence, the need for church attendance, the need for sociality, the need for control, and the need for meaning.

Proceeding from self-regulation theory as an integrative perspective, Aldwin and colleagues (2014) hypothesized that religiousness, spirituality, and religious alienation have an impact on physical health via different pathways. Here, religiousness refers to affiliation and service attendance, whereas spirituality refers to mediation and self-transcendence. The authors hypothesized that religiousness has an impact on the behavioral self-regulation of health habits, whereas spirituality has an impact on emotion regulation, which is, in turn, related to inflammatory processes underlying chronic illnesses, such as cardiovascular disease and cancer. Behavioral self-regulation primarily elucidates the preventive aspect of religion and spirituality; emotional regulation primarily elucidates their impact on the course of illness. Moreover, potential adverse effects of "religious alienation," i.e., "the state in which one feels disaffected from one's church and/or abandoned by one's God – in other words, that one's previous understanding and faith may have been badly misplaced" (Aldwin et al., 2016, p. 15) are conceptualized as mediated by both behavioral and emotional regulation processes. Aldwin and colleagues report comprehensive evidence for the proposed model in their review of the respective research: "There is a fair amount of evidence supporting the idea that religiousness and spirituality have different effects on health, and that these effects are mediated primarily by health behaviors and by inflammation-related biomarkers, respectively" (Aldwin et al., 2014, p. 35).

Database searches indicated that religious people show better health behavior habits, e.g., in terms of smoking, alcohol consumption, and medical screenings, but there was only a weak relationship between religiousness and inflammatory biomarkers. In contrast, spirituality was strongly linked to biomarkers, including blood pressure, cardiac reactivity, immune factors, and disease progression. As predicted, religious alienation had a negative impact on physical health due to both aforementioned pathways.

## Spirituality and Transcendence in Psychological Well-Being and Mental Health

Proceeding from the insight that the considerable research concerned with happiness, satisfaction with life, and positive affect in the 1980s largely omitted to address the deeper question of what constitutes the essential features of well-being, particularly neglecting the deep philosophical roots of happiness (which can be traced back to the ancient Greeks) and conceptions of positive human functioning in humanistic, existential, developmental, and clinical psychology (e.g., What does it mean to be self-actualized, individuated, fully functioning or optimally developed?), Carol D. Ryff developed a comprehensive model of psychological well-being (Ryff, 1989, 2013). Points of convergence between different conceptions became the basis for the differentiation of the following six dimensions: (1) purpose in life, i.e., "the extent to which respondents felt their lives had meaning, purpose, and direction"; (2) autonomy, i.e., "whether they viewed themselves to be living in accord with their own personal convictions"; (3) personal growth, i.e., "the extent to which they were making use of their personal talents and potential"; (4) environmental mastery, i.e., "how well they were managing their life situations"; (5) positive relationship, i.e., "the depth of connection they had in ties with significant others"; and (6) self-acceptance, i.e., "the knowledge and acceptance they had of themselves, including awareness of personal limitations" (Ryff, 2013, p. 11).

Following Aristotle's *Nicomachean Ethics*, particularly Aristotle's understanding of eudaimonia, this model accentuates that "the highest of all human goods is not happiness, feeling good, or satisfying appetites. Instead, it is about activities of the soul that are in accord with virtue, which Aristotle elaborated to mean striving to achieve the best that is within us. Eudaimonia thus captured the essence of the two great Greek imperatives: first, to know yourself, and second, to become what you are" (Ryff, 2013, p. 11). Thus, well-being is conceptually related to personal growth, not least also in terms of a comprehensive understanding of the self and world. This approach is supported by empirical studies, particularly in the context of Erikson's stages of identity formation, which suggest a substantial correlation between higher levels of ego development and higher well-being (Ryff, 2013).

Apparently, spirituality and transcendence can be an intellectual and emotional foundation for personal growth. This point can be illustrated by Viktor Frankl's existential analysis – one of which explicitly refers to the "spiritual dimension" (Frankl, 1959) – and particularly by his understanding of self-actualization and realization of values. Hans Thomae, one of the central proponents of the biographical perspective in personality and developmental psychology, considered the experience of consistency in situations as a result of interaction between the personal event structures of a person (how they express themselves in their guiding principles and their dominating life topics) and the content of a situation. When considering the term self-actualization, the differentiation undertaken by Viktor Frankl – which distinguishes between homo faber, homo amans, and homo patiens – is of fundamental importance, as this shows us that, in experiencing and loving, and also in encounters, lie central sources of value realization and a sense of meaning. This differentiation corresponds with the necessity – emphasized in particular in psychological research – that attention should always be paid to recording the different qualities of a personality.

In a review on mental disorders, religion, and spirituality, Bonelli and Koenig (2013) identified 43 research studies in the top 32 psychiatry and 41 neurology journals for the period 1990–2010 (search criteria was the term "religio" or "spiritu" in the article title). Similar to earlier research reviews for the period 1978–89 (Larson et al., 1986, 1992), these authors reported that about three-quarters of the studies found a significant positive relationship between religious involvement and better mental health. Division of results into ICD-10 diagnostic groups and the evaluation of study methodology (design, execution) showed that there is good evidence for a correlation between religious and three major domains of mental health, i.e., depression, substance abuse, and suicide. Some evidence was found for stress-related disorders and organic mental disorder, insufficient evidence (due to low quality of methodology) for the correlation between religiosity/spirituality and bipolar disorders and schizophrenia, and no evidence for a correlation between religiosity/spirituality and other psychiatric disorders such as eating disorders, sexual disorders, phobic anxiety disorders, obsessive compulsive disorders, dissociative disorders, somatoform disorders, personality disorders, mental retardation, or psychiatric disorders in children (authors indicate that "no evidence" must not be mistaken as "no relationship," but rather it means that respective relationships have not yet been studied). According to these authors, a main result of their review is that the topic has been neglected in many high-quality journals: no respective articles were found in 41 percent of psychiatry and 69 percent of neurology journals published in the 20-year period. Notably, Koenig and colleagues (2012) identified close to 2,500 original articles with about three-quarters focusing on religion/spirituality and mental health. Bonelli and Koenig (2013) therefore concluded, "religious involvement may still be the 'forgotten factor' in the study of many mental disorders" (Bonelli & Koenig, 2013, p. 669). The authors argue that particularly the finding that religious involvement is associated with less depression and suicide is remarkable, since it has been traditionally assumed that religion may imply moral restrictions contributing to feelings of guilt and depression. However, the latter perspective is somehow supported by findings, suggesting that extremely high religiosity, like low religiosity, is associated with depression. Following Bonelli and Koenig (2013), it can be hypothesized that "religious life to be truly healthy (like love) needs a certain amount of inner freedom and flexibility" (p. 669).

## Resilience, Spirituality, and Transcendence

Following Michael Rutter, the concept of resilience can be defined as a "reduced vulnerability to environmental risk experience, the overcoming of stress or adversity, or a relatively good outcome despite risk experience" (Rutter, 2012, p. 336). Resilience is considered to have its origins in the universal finding "that there is huge heterogeneity in response to all manners of environmental hazards: physical and psychosocial." It is an "interactive concept," insofar as its presence has to be inferred inter-individual differences in outcomes after experiencing stress and adversity (Rutter, 1987, 2006, 2012). Likewise, Luthar and colleagues (Luthar et al., 2014, 2015) define resilience as "a phenomenon or process reflecting relatively positive adaptation despite significant adversity or trauma," and "a superordinate construct subsuming two distinct dimensions – adversity and positive adaptation" which cannot be directly measured, but must be inferred based on evidence of the two subsumed constructs. Luthar and colleagues (2014, 2015) further differentiate resilience from the related concepts of competence and ego-resiliency. Considering the construct of competence, authors argue that: (1) only resilience presupposes risk or adversity, (2) resilience refers to both presence of health and absence of disorder, whereas competence reflects only the former, (3) resilience refers to both behavioral and emotional characteristics, whereas competence focuses on observable behaviors, and (4) resilience is a superordinate construct subsuming competence (along with exposure to risk). Considering ego-resiliency, i.e., "a personal trait reflecting general resourcefulness, sturdiness of character, and flexibility in response to environmental circumstances" (Block & Block, 1980). Luthar and colleagues argue that: (1) again, only resilience presupposes risk or adversity, (2) resilience is not a personality trait, but a process or phenomenon, and (3) ego-resiliency belongs to those personal attributes "that can foster resilient adaptation, mitigating the negative effects of stressful life experiences" (Luthar et al., 2015, p. 252).

Elucidating the concept of resilience, Lösel and Bliesener (1990) state that while etiological research in developmental psychology traditionally concentrated on risk factors of problem behavior, more recent research has paid more attention to positive outcomes. "This investigation of 'the other side of the coin' – the healthy child in an unhealthy setting – places more emphasis than before on the flexibility of human development. Not only can it increase the proportion of variance explained in etiology, but it can also contribute to the destigmatization of 'risk groups' and to prevention in the natural context." These authors add that resilience must not be mistaken as an absolute, genetically determined resistance to stress, "what is meant is rather a relatively stable ability to resist stressful living conditions and events, involving protective factors from nature–nurture interactions, that can vary across time and circumstances" (Lösel & Bliesener, 1990, p. 299).

Staudinger and colleagues (1995) propose a differentiation between resilience as the maintenance of development despite the presence of risk, and resilience as recovery from trauma. These authors accentuate the idea of reserve capacity, i.e., an individual's potential for positive change (see also Ryff & Singer, 2003). From a gerontological perspective, it can be argued that management of developmental losses in old age is another important facet of resilience (Staudinger et al., 1999).

Manning (2013) conducted a grounded theory analysis on the interplay of spirituality and resilience over the life-course based on 30 qualitative interviews with 6 women aged 80 years and older. This study shows that, particularly in old age, spirituality can promote healthy aging by strengthening and maintaining resilience.

In another qualitative study, Foster and colleagues (2015) analyzed the process of integrating sexual orientation and spirituality in a sample of 27 lesbian and gay Christians for whom religion had high salience. The authors conclude that the process of recognizing incongruence between Christian attitudes to morality and their own sexual preferences has a resilience-building potential. Notably, engagement for social justice in congregations was a substantial part of the resilience-building process in some participants. More generally, critical evaluation of extant and potential support systems, redefining scripture and tradition (transforming theological meaning), and transforming communities are discussed as important decision points for lesbian and gay Christians.

From a study by Kandasamy and colleagues (2011), it can be concluded that spiritual well-being is an important component of quality-of-life in patients suffering from advanced cancer. Here, spiritual well-being was operationalized as a total score of two subscales; one measured a sense of meaning and peace, the other measured the role of faith in illness; quality of life was assessed via the FACIT-sp (Peterman et al., 2002), differentiating physical well-being (reports of physical symptoms), social/family well-being (social support and communication), emotional well-being (mood and emotional responses to illness), and functional well-being (participating in and enjoying daily activities). In the sample of 50 patients (all in hospices, mean age 49.7 years, age range 17–64 years), spiritual well-being was significantly correlated with all five dimensions of quality-of-life (QOL). Moreover, people scoring higher in spiritual well-being had a lower risk of depression, anxiety, fatigue, distress, memory disturbance, loss of appetite, drowsiness, dry mouth, and sadness. Since spiritual well-being is correlated both with physical and psychological indicators of distress, the authors conclude that "spirituality needs to be formally assessed and integrated into the management of patients with advanced cancers and those undergoing palliative care. The attitude of 'therapeutic nihilism' among doctors needs to be changed, and active help should be provided in improving the QOL of the patients which, in turn, will ease the inevitable process of dying" (p. 59).

Proceeding from the insight that spiritual care is an important part of health-care, Pearce and colleagues (2012) addressed the following two questions in a sample of 150 advanced cancer patients in a medical center: Do oncology inpatients receive spiritual care consistent with their needs? When inconsistent, are there deleterious effects on patient outcomes? Patients with advanced cancer ($N = 150$) were surveyed during their inpatient stay at a south-eastern medical center. In this study, 91 percent of the patients reported having spiritual needs. Most of them desired and received spiritual care from healthcare providers, the religious community, and the hospital chaplain. Out of the 150 patients, 42 of them (35 percent) received less care than desired from at least one of the afore-mentioned sources of support. Subjective deficits in received support were associated with more symptoms of depression and lower perceptions of meaning and peace.

Similar results are reported by Vallurupalli and colleagues (2012). In this study, 84 percent of a sample of advanced cancer patients receiving palliative radiation therapy indicated their reliance on religious or spiritual beliefs when coping with their disease. Those who referred to spirituality or religion as a coping resource showed higher levels of quality-of-life. Moreover, most patients perceived spiritual care as an important part of the care received by doctors and nurses.

Using SEM analysis, Currier and colleagues (2016) examined direct and indirect relationships between multidimensional measures of spirituality (considering general religiousness and spirituality, daily spiritual experiences, spiritual values, private spiritual practices, positive and negative religious coping, and organizational religiousness), forgiveness (considering self, interpersonal, and divine forms), and quality-of-life (considering physical, social, psychological, and environmental domains) in a sample of 678 military veterans with PTSD. After control of the PTSD severity, combat exposure, and demographic factors, greater spirituality and greater forgiveness were positively correlated and both significantly associated with quality-of-life. Further analyses show that the impact of spirituality on the quality-of-life was mediated by forgiveness. In interpreting their findings, the authors argue that the unexpected lack of a direct relationship between their comprehensive measure of spirituality and quality-of-life should not be mistaken as an argument for ruling out other possible mechanisms suggested in the field of coping with trauma. In particular, they refer to five complementary mechanisms suggested by former research:

> Spirituality could be associated with better QOL among veterans via (a) reduction of health risks and maladaptive behaviours with an emphasis on personal/social morality, healthy lifestyles, and other behavioural norms in spiritual communities (e.g., less alcohol misuse, drug use, smoking); (b) expanded relational networks and possible social support through participation in a church or other type of spiritual community; (c) possible sense of attachment security and support through a personal relationship with God or a Higher Power; (d) enhancement of positive coping skills and helpful cognitive appraisals that may affirm or even help a veteran to adaptively revise his or her view(s) of God or a Higher Power, or possible other objects/relationships to which he or she might assign ultimate significance in life; and (e) spiritual practices, such as worship, prayer, or meditation which can promote positive emotion (e.g. joy, peace) and reduce the physiological arousal that typically characterizes PTSD. (Currier et al., 2016, pp. 167–8)

Currier and colleagues (2016) discuss alternative explanations for the empirical relationship between spirituality and forgiveness: (a) veterans with greater spirituality could be more likely to engage in forgiveness, (b) veterans whose spirituality decreases as a consequence of the trauma, or who were less spiritual from the beginning, might lack the cognitive, social, and environmental resources that support forgiveness and quality-of-life, and (c) problems with forgiveness might result in a larger spiritual/existential struggle, contributing to a more complicated PTSD-symptomatology that seriously impairs quality-of-life, where "such stressors may challenge some veterans' beliefs about God's character and capability of ordering and effectively intervening in the universe. In these cases, feelings of anger towards God may contribute to negative religious coping and chronic doubts, questions, and inner conflicts about spiritual beliefs" (Currier et al., 2016, p. 168).

In a study on the implications of spirituality for health and well-being, Park and colleagues (Park et al., 2013) developed empirically based typologies of religiousness/spirituality in a nationally representative household survey of 1,445 English-speaking US adults who were 18 and older. Proceeding from data on religious service attendance, prayer, positive religious coping, and daily spiritual experiences, a latent profile analysis extracted a four cluster-model which differentiates between highly religious, moderately religious, somewhat religious, and minimally religious or non-religious participants. Analyses suggest that the highly religious group was most likely to be happy and satisfied with finances and least likely to be psychologically distressed; as regards socio-demographic variables, this group was more likely to be older, female, Afro-American, married, and to have high socioeconomic status. In contrast, the minimally religious group was least likely to be happy and satisfied with their financial situation; they were less likely to be psychologically distressed than the aforementioned group, with no significant differences to the moderately religious and somewhat religious groups in this variable. As regards socio-demographic variables, participants in the minimally religious group were more likely to be younger, male, non-Black, not married, and to have high socio economic status. Cluster membership was not significantly associated with subject health. Park and colleagues concluded that differences in well-being and socio-demographic characteristics elucidate the usefulness of typology in decisions about interventions. Whereas the highly religious people tended to be least at risk in terms of well-being and financial satisfaction, the moderately religious group and the somewhat religious group were more likely to be in need of interventions.

Hayward and colleagues (2016) stated that, although the proportion of non-religious people substantially increased the implication of this development for health and well-being, this has rarely been a topic of empirical research. In their own study, these authors used data from a US survey on religion and health, comparing members of religious groups ($N = 2,401$) with atheists ($N = 83$), agnostics ($N = 189$), and people without religious preference. Results suggest that religious non-affiliates do not significantly differ from affiliates in physical health. However, they showed worse positive psychological functioning characteristics, social support relationships, and health behaviors. As regards dimensions of psychological well-being, no difference was found between people with religious affiliation and those without religious preference, whereas atheists and agnostics had worse outcomes than the aforementioned two groups in these respects. The authors concluded from their results that changes in religious composition have implications for future healthcare needs. In line with other survey research on religiousness (Kosmin & Keysar, 2009; Pew Forum on Religion and Public Life, 2015), the likelihood of non-affiliation was higher in younger people. Proceeding from the assumption that changes in religious affiliation are primarily due to generational change, and that aging has only a minor impact on religious affiliation, Hayward and colleagues emphasize a risk of negative population-level changes when today's younger generations enter later, more vulnerable stages of life: "Poorer psychological well-being, the relative lack of certain positive psychology factors, lower levels of social support, and worse health behaviour, may have some potentially detrimental impacts on overall levels of health problems in the population. Although secular alternatives exist, and may be capable of fulfilling equivalent social and psychological roles, the present findings suggest that their potential may not be fully realised in the population of individuals with no religious affiliation" (Hayward et al., 2016, p. 1034).

Van Cappelen and colleagues (2016) report results from two cross-sectional studies on the mechanisms of how religion and spirituality might exert their impact on subjective well-being, one with churchgoers in Europe and one with university employees interested in mediation in the United States. Whereas most researchers primarily consider social (contact, common activities) and cognitive (meaning, purpose in life) aspects as potential mediators of the relationship, these authors focus on a "surprisingly neglected mechanism," i.e., positive emotions. In both studies, an aggregate measure of positive emotions was a significant mediator for explaining the relationship between religion or spirituality and subjective well-being. Further analyses show that, more precisely, self-transcendent emotions (awe, gratitude, love, and peace), but not other positive emotions (amusement and pride), account for this relationship.

## Life Issues and Spirituality, and Transcendence

Successful aging is a lifelong process. An analysis of the significance of spirituality and transcendence for successful aging must therefore also consider life issues, i.e., dominant concerns, goals, attitudes and perspectives, which are formed in the context of a continuous involvement in tasks, challenges, and the possibilities of changing life situations. According to Hans Thomae (1968), the total structure of life issues is the preferable reference point of a comprehensive analysis of individual behavior and experience, i.e., behavior and experience in a specific situation cannot be understood adequately without a knowledge of basic beliefs, concerns, and goals. Life issues do not constitute stable personality traits. Instead, they are conceptualized as dynamic qualities referring to an understanding of personality as a process. Life issues condense biographical experience, but nevertheless can – and regularly do – change under the impression of new experience (Kruse & Schmitt, 2011).

The analysis of life issues basically ensues from a biographical perspective, asking for processes that brought about "chronic" (outlasting) thematic structures, as well as for processes that initiated changes in respective structures and the degree of openness of a given personality for new experiences, which might initiate further changes of thematic structure (Kruse, 2005). This understanding of life issues comes close to the construct of life structures introduced by Daniel Levinson (1986).

In one of Levinson's formulations of adult development, presented in 1986, the concept of life structure is introduced, through which he describes the underlying pattern or design of a person's life at a given time. Levinson clarifies the meaning of this concept by contrasting it with the concept of personality structure. Theories of the latter are described as ways of conceptualizing answers to the question: "What kind of person am I?" Whereas theories of the former are described as conceptualizing answers to another specific question, i.e., the question: "What is my life like now?" Constituting a "mediating zone between personality structure and social structure," the concept of life structure takes both a developmental and a socialization perspective on human development

> because the life structure is not solely a property of the individual, its evolution cannot be understood from an intra-organismic, developmental perspective; because the life structure is not simply a matter of externally-imposed events and roles, its evolution cannot be understood simply from a socialisation perspective. It is necessary, instead, to create a new perspective that combines development and socialisation and that draws equally on biology, psychology, and social sciences, as well as on the humanities. (Levinson, 1986, p. 13)

The central components of the life structure make up the subjective meaningful relationships of the individual to "various others" in the external world. "Various others" can take the form of people, a group, an institution, a culture, or a particular place. According to Levinson, significant relationships require the following condition as a starting point: there is a high level of investment of the self in the relationship, and, furthermore, the self does experience enrichment in the relationship, e.g., encouragement and stimulation, and the self can adjust itself further from the effect of this enrichment. Consequently, the following central conclusion can be drawn: "The central components are those that have the greatest significance for the self and the evolving life course" (Levinson, 1986, p. 13).

## Results from the Generali Study of Very Old Age

The Generali Study of very old age (Generali Future Funds, 2014) is a comprehensive mixed-method study on life issues, shared responsibility, and forms of engagement in care for others, and social inclusion in very old people (85 to 99 years, mean age 89.5 years), considering both older people's perspectives, values, and aspirations, and perceptions of fourth age and respective opportunity structures in members of institutional staff. The data collected consists of biographical interviews with 400 older persons recruited through collaboration with charitable organizations, educational institutions, churches, and residential homes for the elderly in urban and rural regions of six federal states of Germany (Baden-Wuerttemberg, Hessen, North Rhine-Westphalia, Rhineland-Palatinate, Saxony, and Thuringia), and a standardized survey of 800 employees of municipalities and voluntary organizations (Kruse & Schmitt, 2015).

Table 24.1 presents 27 categories of life issues reconstructed from the participants' narratives (for methodological issues, see Kruse & Schmitt, 2015). Feelings of shared responsibility and motives for engagement in family and community, especially for younger generations, were highly prevalent among the very old participants. Results showed that self-transcendence in the form of engagement for others and, most of all, preoccupation with their life situation, were an integral part of participants' lives. However, some of the reconstructed life issues, such as worrying about loss of autonomy and deteriorating health (see, e.g., categories 5, 9, 10, 12, 13, 16, 19, and 22 in Table 24.1), elucidating that increased vulnerability was also a salient theme. On the positive side, our findings suggested that the very old participants were much more concerned with realizing shared responsibility in social relationships than with personal vulnerability (see, e.g., categories 1, 2, and 3). Social relationships were a significant source of pleasure and fulfillment to the majority of the participants (see category 2). Even though a significant minority of the participants were intensively preoccupied with the finitude of life (see categories 14, 15, and 20), this preoccupation did not seem to imply disengagement from others. Intense preoccupation with the life situation and development of significant others, particularly members of their own family and succeeding generations (see category 2) clearly outnumbers more self-centered concerns. The significance of social relationships to participants was obviously not restricted to the desire to come together with other people, rather, participants expressed the desire to do something for other people. For the majority of the participants, engagement for others was an important source of pleasure and fulfillment (see category 3 in Table 24.1), whereas about one-fourth of the participants were concerned with an unfulfilled need to engage for other people (see category 17). Moreover, almost half of the participants believed that their knowledge and experience might be useful to younger people (see category 7). Thus, our analysis of life issues in very old age supported the assumption that generativity is a basic human motive, also beyond middle adulthood.

Findings from the Generali Study of the very old significantly contribute to understanding transcendence and spirituality in very old age. Life issues referring to the finitude of their own existence – intense preoccupation with the finitude of their own existence, intense preoccupation with the after-life embedded in religious and spiritual contexts, and intense preoccupation with dying and the place of death – were reconstructed only in a minor part of participants' narratives. However, it must be considered that the three categories accentuate an *intense preoccupation*, i.e., the respective life issues somehow *dominated* experience (thematic structure) in respective participants. For them, distancing themselves from these issues is possible only with difficulty. Preoccupation with the finitude of their own existence was strongly associated with a preoccupation with the after-life; in 97 participants, evidence was found for both life issues. Respective accounts in participants' narratives were closely connected and embedded in an elaborated, individual story about religion and/or spirituality.

Three life issues further accentuated a preoccupation with symbolic immortality, i.e., questions about what will be remembered by others, what will have a lasting impact beyond their own existence, and what will outlive the self. Intense preoccupation was observed with their life situation and development of significant others, particularly members of their own family and succeeding generations; the need to be needed and respected, particularly by succeeding generations; belief in their own knowledge and experience as enriching and helpful for succeeding generations. Finitude of their own existence and self-transcendence were strongly connected, particularly in accentuating responsibility for following generations and the need to share and pass knowledge, insights, and experiences in intergenerational relationships. Participants perceived themselves as part of a chain of generations, in the sense of taking from the former and giving to future generations, as living-on in younger people, including those not yet born. Narratives further suggest that being a part of a chain of generations is a substantial resource in coping with their own finitude.

Notably, among the sample of the Generali Study, the very prominence of old life issues accentuating symbolic immortality and shared responsibility was substantially higher than the prominence of life issues referring to finitude of their own existence, death, and dying, thus suggesting generativity to be a significant motive in the very old. To sum up, the findings of the Generali Study of the very

Table 24.1 *Life issues reconstructed from the narratives of the very old participants*
*(N = 400) (Kruse & Schmitt, 2015)*

| Category | Percent |
|---|---|
| 1. Pleasure and fulfillment in emotionally meaningful encounters with other people | 76 |
| 2. Intense preoccupation with the life situation and development of significant others, | 62 |
| 3. particularly members of one's own family and succeeding generations | |
| 4. Pleasure and fulfillment in engagement for other people | 61 |
| 5. Need to be needed and respected, particularly by succeeding generations | 60 |
| 6. Worry about loss of autonomy (self-responsibility and independence) | 59 |
| 7. Commitment to preserving (relative) health and (relative) independence | 55 |
| 8. Belief in own knowledge and experience as enriching and helpful for succeeding generations | 44 |
| 9. Self-reflection, intense preoccupation with own development and self-consistency | 41 |
| 10. Phases of loneliness | 39 |
| 11. Lacking or greatly reduced control of body and somatic functions, worry about further | 36 |
| 12. bodily symptoms | |
| 13. Intense preoccupation with a change of residence (needs to preserve independence, | 34 |
| 14. participation, and well-being) | |
| 15. Phases of despondency | 31 |
| 16. Chronic or temporary pain and striving for control | 30 |
| 17. Intense preoccupation with the finitude of own existence | 30 |
| 18. Intense preoccupation with after-life embedded in religious and spiritual contexts | 28 |
| 19. Worry about a lack of financial security | 24 |
| 20. Unfulfilled need to engage for other people | 23 |
| 21. A lack of respect, approval, and attention from family members | 23 |
| 22. Self-doubts concerning one's attractiveness to other people | 20 |
| 23. Intense preoccupation with dying and place of death | 19 |
| 24. Taking pleasure in own activities, feelings of fulfillment through activity | 18 |
| 25. Perceived cognitive decline and worry about dementia | 17 |
| 26. Intense preoccupation with life and fate of personally significant groups and places (e.g., their 15 hometown) | |
| 27. A lack of respect and attention from others, also alienation from other people, conflicts and misunderstanding | 13 |
| 28. Unfulfilled need for sympathetic and profound communication with succeeding generations | 12 |
| 29. Intense preoccupation with the human creature | 11 |
| 30. Intense preoccupation with the lives of decedents who have been important for own life | 10 |

old show that self-transcendence is a basic part of not only self-understanding, but also of self and world-design in very old age. The finitude of their own existence is thereby subjectively experienced as a part of the human condition, an insight put forward by increasing vulnerability. Particularly in old age – but also at younger ages, since biographical interviews pointed to substantial continuity – spiritual and religious beliefs and commitments provided an important context for coping with challenges and losses in life, a basis for understanding the self and world, and – not least – personal aspirations and projects.

## Concluding Remarks and Future Perspectives

Theoretical conceptions point to spirituality and transcendence as an essential part of human personality, self-understanding, developmental tasks, and well-being. All that time ago, William James, the founder of scientific psychology, described the spiritual self as referring to "who we are at our core," besides and beyond external perspectives, associated with feelings of self-complacency and self-satisfaction, prompting processes of self-seeking and self-preservation. More recent perspectives on narrative identity and ethics (Ricouer, 1992; Sulmasy, 2013) accentuate self-understanding as a (re)constructive process, reflecting more or less explicit fundamental stories on basic questions of human nature, referring to "religion-like morally-originating commitments" (Sulmasy, 2013), "strong evaluations" (Taylor, 1989) which, although seldom told, always lie beneath the surface of individual preferences, aspirations, and values and become apparent in processes of self-actualization (Goldstein, 1939; Frankl, 1959). Theoretical accounts on lifelong development suggest that spirituality and transcendence gain additional importance in old age, due to living into old age and facing its challenges, in the context of normative psychosocial crisis in adulthood, generativity, and ego-integrity (Erikson, Mc Adams), as well as in the context of a "shift in meta-perspective" (Tornstam), an increasing motive for generativity, implying a need for symbolic immortality (Kotre, 1996; Kruse & Schmitt, 2012; McAdams, 2013). As a source of meaning and purpose, spirituality and transcendence not only contribute to, but are also considered an essential part of, subjective well-being (Ryff, 1989).

However, the impact of spirituality and transcendence on quality-of-life and successful aging is not only apparent from a comprehensive understanding of respective concepts. Empirical research provides considerable evidence that spirituality and transcendence substantially contribute to the perceived quality-of-life, establishing and maintaining resilience, coping with crisis and trauma, as well as to engagement in activities and interpersonal relationships.

In empirical research, spirituality and transcendence are regularly operationalized when referring to religious communities, beliefs, and commitments. In research reviews, particularly the terms spirituality and religion, are often used interchangeably. This seems natural due to the substantial overlap between these concepts (Koenig, 2011). However, although religion and spirituality are both concerned with transcendence and refer to strong evaluations, providing purpose and meaning by giving answers to fundamental questions of human nature, future research (and theory development) should give more attention to the differences between these concepts. The Generali Study of the very old shows that life issues reflect different forms of transcendence. A profound understanding of the mechanisms that link religion and spirituality to successful aging (a precondition for the development of promising intervention measures) might require closer consideration of individual beliefs and commitments.

## References

Ahmadi Lewin, F. (2001). Gerotranscendence and different cultural settings. *Ageing and Society*, 21, 395–415

Aldwin, C. M., Park, C. L., Jeong, Y. J., et al. (2014). Differing pathways between religiousness, spirituality, and health: A self-regulation perspective. *Psychology of Religion and Spirituality*, 6(1), 9–21.

Ardelt, M., Landes, S. D., Gerlach, K. R., et al. (2013). Rediscovering internal strengths of the aged: The beneficial impact of wisdom, mastery, purpose in life, and spirituality on aging well. In J. D. Sinnott (Ed.), *Positive Psychology* (pp. 97–119). New York, NY: Springer.

Atchley, R. C. (1989). Continuity theory of normal aging. *The Gerontologist* 29, 183–90.

Bamonti, P., Lombardi, S., Duberstein, P. R., et al. (2016). Spirituality attenuates the association between depression symptom severity and meaning in life. *Aging & Mental Health*, 20(5), 494–9.

Bengtson, V. L., Oyama, P. S. (2007). *Intergenerational Solidarity: Strengthening Economic and Social Ties*. Background Paper, United Nations Headquarters, New York, NY, USA, 2007, www.un.org/esa/socdev/unyin/documents/egmunhqoct07 bengtson.pdf.

Block, J. H., Block, J. (1980). The role of ego-control and ego-resiliency in the organization of behavior. In W.A. Collins (Ed.), *Development of cognition, affect, and social relations* (pp. 39–101). Hillsdale: Erlbaum.

Blumenberg, H. (1986). *Lebenszeit und Weltzeit*. Frankfurt: Suhrkamp.

Bonelli, R. M., Koenig, H. G. (2013). Mental disorders, religion and spirituality 1990 to 2010: a systematic evidence-based review. *Journal of Religion and Health*, 52(2), 657–73.

Brown, C., Lowis, M. J. (2003). Psychosocial development in the elderly: An investigation into Erikson's ninth stage. *Journal of Aging Studies*, 17, 415–26.

Bühler, C. (1933). *Der menschliche Lebenslauf als psychologisches Problem*. Leipzig: Hirzel.

Carstensen, L. L. Löckenhoff, C. E. (2004). Aging, emotion, and evolution: The bigger picture. In P. Ekman, J. J. Campos, R. J. Davidson, & F. B. M. de Waal (Eds.), *Emotions Inside Out: 130 Years after Darwin's The Expression of the Emotions in Man and Animals* (Vol. 1000, pp. 152–79). New York: Annals of the New York Academy of Sciences.

Carstensen, L. L., Isaacowitz, D. M., Charles, S. T. (1999). Taking time seriously: A theory of socioemotional selectivity. *American Psychologist*, 54, 165–81.

Chida, Y., Steptoe, A., Powell, L. H. (2009). Religiosity/spirituality and mortality. A systematic quantitative review. *Psychotherapy and Psychosomatics*, 78, 81–90.

Cotton, S., Zebracki, K., Rosenthal, S. L., et al. (2006). Religion/spirituality and adolescent health outcomes: A review. *Journal of Adolescent Health*, 38(4), 472–80.

Currier, J. M., Drescher, K. D., Holland, J. M., et al. (2016). Spirituality, forgiveness, and quality of life: Testing a mediational model with military veterans with PTSD. *The International Journal for the Psychology of Religion*, 26(2), 167–79.

Dalai Lama & Cutler, H. C. (1998). *The art of happiness*. New York: Riverhead.

De Waal, F. B. M. (2008). Putting the altruism back into altruism: the evolution of empathy. *Annual Review of Psychology*, 59, 279–300.

Erikson, E. H. (1963). *Childhood and Society* (2nd ed.). New York: Norton.
    (1967). The problem of ego integrity. In M. R. Stein, A. J. Vidich, & M. White (Eds.), *Identity and Anxiety* (pp. 37–87). New York: Free Press.
    (1998). *The life cycle completed. Extended version with new chapters on the ninth stage by Joan M. Erikson*. New York: Norton.

Erikson, E. H., Erikson, J. M., Kivnick, H. Q. (1986). *Vital Involvement in Old Age*. New York: Norton.

Fetzer Institute. (1999). *Multidimensional Measurement of Religiousness/Spirituality for Use in Health Research*. Kalamazoo, MI: Fetzer Institute.

Foster, K. A., Bowland, S. E., Vosler, A. N. (2015). All the pain along with all the joy: Spiritual resilience in lesbian and gay Christians. *American Journal of Community Psychology*, 55(1–2), 191–201.

Frankl, V. E. (1959). The spiritual dimension in existential analysis and logotherapy. *J Individ Psychol*, 15, 157–165.
    (2014). *The Will to Meaning*. New York: Penguin.

Generali Future Funds. (2014). *Der Ältesten Rat. Generali Hochaltrigenstudie: Teilhabe im hohen Alter [Advice of the eldest. Generali Study of the very old: Participation in advanced age]*. http://zukunftsfonds.generalideutschland.de/online/portal/gdinternet/zukunftsfonds/content/314342/1010874.

Goldstein, K. (1939). *The Organism. A Holistic Approach to Biology Derived from Pathological Data in Man*. New York: Zone Books.

Härle, W. (2010). *Würde. Groß vom Menschen denken*. München

Hayward, R. D., Krause, N., Ironson, G., et al. (2016). Health and well-being among the non-religious: atheists, agnostics, and no preference compared with religious group members. *Journal of Religion and Health*, 55(3), 1024–37.

Hearn, S., Saulnier, G., Strayer, J., et al. (2012). Between integrity and despair: Toward construct validation of Erikson's eighth stage. *Journal of Adult Development*, 19(1), 1–20.

Hulett, J. M., Armer, J. M. (2016). A systematic review of spiritually based interventions and psycho-neuro-immunological outcomes in breast cancer survivorship. *Integrative Cancer Therapies*, 15, 405–23.

James, W. (1890). *The Principles of Psychology*. New York: Holt.
    (1907). *Pragmatism. A New Name for Some Old Ways of Thinking*. www.encyclopaedia.com/pdfs/8/869.pdf.

Kandasamy, A., Chaturvedi, S. K., Desai, G. (2011). Spirituality, distress, depression, anxiety, and quality of life in patients with advanced cancer. *Indian Journal of Cancer*, 48(1), 55–9.

Koenig, H. G. (2008). Concerns about measuring spirituality in research, *Journal of Nervous and Mental Disease*, 196(5), 349–55.

(2011). Definitions. In H.G. Koenig (Ed.). *Spirituality and Health Research: Methods, Measurement, Statistics, and Resources* (pp. 193–206). Philadelphia: Templeton Foundation Press.

(2012). Religion, spirituality, and health: The research and clinical implications. *ISRN Psychiatry, 2012*. Article ID 278730, 33 pages. doi:10.5402/2012/278730.

Koenig, H. G., King, D. E., Carson, V. B. (2012). *Handbook of Religion and Health*. New York: Oxford University Press.

Kosmin, B. A., Keysar, A. (2009). *American Nones: The Profile of the No Religion Population*. Hartford, CT: Institute for the Study of Secularism in Society & Culture. http://commons.trincoll.edu/aris/publications/2008-2/american-nones-the-profile-of-the-noreligion-population/.

Kotre, J. N. (1996). *Outliving the Self: How We Live on in Future Generations*. New York: Norton.

Krause, N. (2011). Religion and health: making sense of a disheveled literature. *Journal of Religion and Health*, 50, 20–35. doi:10.1007/s10943-010-9373-4.

Kruse, A. (2005). Selbstständigkeit, Selbstverantwortung, bewusst angenommene Abhängigkeit und Mitverantwortung als Kategorien einer Ethik des Alters. *Zeitschrift für Gerontologie & Geriatrie*, 38, 223–37.

(2007). *Das letzte Lebensjahr. Die körperliche, psychische und soziale Situation des alten Menschen am Ende seines Lebens*. Stuttgart: Kohlhammer.

(2014). Entwicklungspotenziale und Verletzlichkeit im hohen und sehr hohen Alter [Developmental potential and vulnerability in old and very old age]. *Psychotherapie im Alter*, 42, 177–98.

Kruse, A., Schmitt, E. (2011). Daseinsthemen: Die Erfassung individueller, dynamischer Einheiten der Persönlichkeit als Aufgabe der psychologisch-biographischen Diagnostik. In G. Jüttemann (Hrsg.), *Biographische Diagnostik* (S. 74–81). Lengerich: Pabst Science Publishers.

(2012). Generativity as a route to active ageing. *Current Gerontology and Geriatrics Research*, Article ID 647650, 9 pages, doi:10.1155/2012/647650.

(2015). Shared responsibility and civic engagement in very old age. *Research in Human Development*, 12(1–2), 133–48.

Laitinen, A. (2002). Charles Taylor and Paul Ricoeur on self-interpretations and narrative identity. In R. Huttunen, H. L. T. Heikkinen, & L. Syrjälä (Eds.), *Narrative Research. Voices of Teachers and Philosophers* (pp. 57–71). SoPhi, 67. Jyväskylä, Finland: SoPhi.

Larson, D. B., Pattison, E. M., Blazer, D. G., et al. (1986). Systematic analysis of research on religious variables in four major psychiatric journals, 1978–1982. *The American Journal of Psychiatry*, 143(3), 329–34.

Larson, D. B., Sherrill, K. A., Lyons, J. S., et al. (1992). Associations between dimensions of religious commitment and mental health reported in the American Journal of Psychiatry and Archives of General Psychiatry: 1978–1989. *American Journal of Psychiatry*, 149(4), 557–9.

Levin, J. S. (1996). How religion influences morbidity and health: Reflections on natural history, salutogenesis and host resistance. *Social Science & Medicine*, 43, 849–64. doi:10.1016/0277-9536(96)00150-5.

Lösel, F., Bliesener, T. (1990). Resilience in adolescence: A study on the generalizability of protective factors. In K. Hurrelmann & F. Lösel (Eds.), *Health Hazards in Adolescence* (pp. 299–320). Berlin: de Gruyter.

Luthar, S. S., Lyman, E. L., Crossman, E. J. (2014). Resilience and positive psychology. In *Handbook of Developmental Psychopathology* (pp. 125–40). United States: Springer.

Luthar, S. S., Crossman, E. J., Small, P. J. (2015). Resilience and adversity. *Handbook of Child Psychology and Developmental Science* (pp. 247–86). New York: Wiley.

Manning, L. K. (2013). Navigating Hardships in Old Age, Exploring the Relationship between Spirituality and Resilience in Later Life. *Qualitative health research*, 1049732312471730.

Masters, K. S., Hooker, S. A. (2013). Religion, spirituality, and health. In R. F. Paloutzian & C. L. Park (Eds.), *Handbook of the Psychology of Religion and Spirituality* (2nd ed., pp. 519–39). New York: Guilford.

McAdams, D. P. (2013). *The Redemptive Self: Stories Americans Live By-Revised and Expanded Edition*. Oxford University Press.

McAdams, D.P., de St. Aubin, E. (1992). A theory of generativity and its assessment through self-report, behavioral acts, and narrative themes in autobiography. *Journal of Personality and Social Psychology*, 62, 1003–15.

McAdams, D. P., Diamond, A., de St. Aubin, E., et al. (1997). Stories of commitment: The psychosocial construction of generative lives. *Journal of Personality and Social Psychology*, 72, 678–94.

McAdams, D. P., Josselson, R., Lieblich, A. (2006). *Identity and Story: Creating Self in Narrative*. Washington: APA Books.

Mead, G. H. (1932). *Philosophy of the Present*. Chicago: The Open Court Publishing Company.

Millon, T. (2003). Evolution: A generative source for conceptualizing the attributes of personality. In T. Millon & M. J. Lerner (Eds.), *Handbook of Psychology, Volume 5: Personality and Social Psychology* (pp. 3–30). New York: Wiley.

Pargament, K. I. (1997). *The Psychology of Religion and Coping: Theory, Research, Practice*. New York: Guilford.

Park, C. L. (2012). Meaning, spirituality, and growth: Protective and resilience factors in health and illness. In A. S. Baum, T. A., Revenson & J. E. Singer (Eds.), *Handbook of Health Psychology* (2nd ed., pp. 405–30). New York: Taylor & Francis.

Park, C. L., Slattery, J. (2013). Religiousness/spirituality and mental health. In R. F. Paloutzian & C. L. Park (Eds.), *Handbook of the Psychology of Religion and Spirituality* (2nd ed., pp. 540–59). New York: Guilford.

Park, N. S., Lee, B. S., Sun, F., et al. (2013). Typologies of religiousness/spirituality: Implications for health and well-being. *Journal of Religion and Health*, 52(3), 828–39.

Pearce, M. J., Coan, A. D., Herndon II, J. E., et al. (2012). Unmet spiritual care needs impact emotional and spiritual well-being in advanced cancer patients. *Supportive Care in Cancer*, 20(10), 2269–76.

Peck, R. (1968). Psychological developments in the second half of life. In B. Neugarten (Ed.). *Middle Age and Aging*. Chicago: Chicago University Press.

Peterman, A. H., Fitchett, G., Brady, M. J., et al. (2002). Measuring spiritual well-being in people with cancer: the Functional Assessment of Chronic Illness Therapy-Spiritual Well-being Scale (FACIT-Sp). *Ann Behav Med*, 24, 49–58.

Pew Forum on Religion and Public Life. (2015). *America's Changing Religious Landscape*. Washington, DC: Pew Research Center.

Ricouer, P. (1992). *Oneself as Another*. The University of Chicago Press: Chicago.

Riley, M. W., Johnson, M. E., Foner, A. (1992). *Aging and Society* (Vol. 3). New York: Russell Sage.

Rosenmayr, L. (2010). Über Offenlegung und Geheimnis von Kreativität. In A. Kruse (Ed.), *Kreativität im Alter* (S. 125–69). Heidelberg: Universitätsverlag Winter.

Rutter, M. (1987). Psychosocial resilience and protective mechanisms. *American Journal of Orthopsychiatry*, 57, 316–31.

Rutter, M. (2006). Implications of resilience concepts for scientific understanding. *Annals of the New York Academy of Sciences*, 1094, 1–12.

(2012). Resilience as a dynamic concept. *Development and Psychopathology*, 24(02), 335–44.

Ryff, C. D. (1989). Happiness is everything, or is it? Explorations on the meaning of psychological well-being. *J Pers Soc Psychol*, 57, 1069–81.

(2013). Psychological well-being revisited: Advances in the science and practice of eudaimonia. *Psychotherapy and Psychosomatics*, 83(1), 10–28.

Ryff, C. D., Singer, B. (2003). Flourishing under fire: Resilience as a prototype of challenging thriving. In C. L. M. Keyes & J. Haidt (Eds.), *Flourishing Positive Psychology and the Life Well-Lived* (pp. 15–36). Washington, DC: American Psychological Association.

Schopenhauer, A. (2000). *Parerga and Paralipomena: Short Philosophical Essays.* Oxford: Clarendon Press.

Staudinger, U. M., Marsiske, M., Baltes, P. B. (1995). Resilience and reserve capacity in later adulthood: Potentials and limits of development across the life span. *Developmental Psychopathology*, 2, 801–47.

Staudinger, U. M., Freund, A. M., Linden, M., et al. (1999). Self, personality and life regulation: Facets of psychological resilience in old age. In P. B. Baltes & K. U. Mayer (Eds.), *The Berlin Aging Study: Aging from 70 to 100* (pp. 302–28). New York, NY: Cambridge University Press.

Sulmasy, D. P. (2013). Ethos, mythos, and thanatos: spirituality and ethics at the end of life. *Journal of Pain and Symptom Management*, 46(3), 447–51.

Taylor, C. (1985). *Philosophical Papers.* Cambridge: Cambridge University Press.

(1989). *Sources of the Self: The Making of the Modern Identity.* Cambridge: Cambridge University Press.

(2007). *Secular Age.* Cambridge, MA: The Belknap Press of Harvard University Press.

Thomae, H. (1968). *Das Individuum und seine Welt.* Göttingen: Hogrefe.

(1996). *Das Individuum und seine Welt (The person and his world).* Bern: Huber.

Tornstam, L. (1989). Gero-transcendence: A meta-theoretical re-formulation of the Disengagement Theory. *Aging*, 1, 55–63.

(1996). Gerotranscendence – a theory about maturing in old age. *Journal of Aging and Identity*, 1, 37–50.

(1997). Life crises and gerotranscendence. *Journal of Aging and Identity*, 2, 117–31.

(2011). Maturing into gerotranscendence. *Journal of Transpersonal Psychology*, 43(2), 166–80.

Tuck, I., Anderson, L. (2014). Forgiveness, flourishing, and resilience: The influences of expressions of spirituality on mental health recovery. *Issues in Mental Health Nursing*, 35(4), 277–82.

Vallurupalli, M. M., Lauderdale, M. K., Balboni, M. J., et al. (2012). The role of spirituality and religious coping in the quality of life of patients with advanced cancer receiving palliative radiation therapy. *The Journal of Supportive Oncology*, 10(2), 81–87.

Van Cappelen, P., Toth-Gauthier, M., Saroglou, V., et al. (2016). Religion and well-being: The mediating role of positive emotions. *Journal of Happiness Studies*, 17(2), 485–505.

Wink, P., Ader, J. M., Dillon, M. (2013). Developmental and narrative perspectives on religious and spiritual identity for clinicians. In J. D. Aten, K. A. O'Grady, L. Everett & J. R. Worthington (Eds.), *The Psychology of Religion and Spirituality for Clinicians* (pp. 19–68). London: Routledge.

Wittrahm, A. (2010). Unsere Tage zu zählen lehre uns …"Theologische Bausteine zu einem Altern in Freiheit und Würde." In A. Kruse (Ed.), *Potenziale im Altern. Chancen und Aufgaben für Individuum und Gesellschaft* (S. 131–43). Heidelberg: Akademische Verlagsgesellschaft.

# 25 Intergenerational Family Relationships and Successful Aging

Ariela Lowenstein, Ruth Katz, and Aviad Tur-Sinai

## Introduction

Global aging is diversifying individual life courses, as well as family behavioral patterns (Lowenstein, 2005). These changes have important implications for successful aging for all family members.

The family constitutes perhaps the most basic social institution, representing the very first group into which one enters at birth, and these ties remain primary over the life course (Wahl et al., 2007). The modern family is a family of relationships, having to assure for each of its members conditions for the construction of people's personal and social identity (Lowenstein & Katz, 2010). The theory of Intergenerational Solidarity itemized the sentiments, behaviors, attitudes, values, and geographic arrangements that bind the generations (Roberts et al., 1991). The solidarity paradigm provides a systematic conceptual language to organize the multiple ways that family members are interconnected. In studying family relations, we chose to relate to the behavioral aspects and to geographic propinquity.

Current variation in family types might create uncertainty in intergenerational family relations and expectations (Bengtson & Lowenstein, 2003). An implication of the demographic and social-familial changes is that a new architecture for social relations may begin to emerge (Katz et al., 2005). One can ask then: "Does elders' successful aging depend on the quality of their intergenerational family relations?" In light of the constant increase in aging populations and changes in family structures, norms and behaviors in most Western countries, linkages between intergenerational family relations, and successful aging of older parents takes on added significance. Fewer young people mean fewer children and grandchildren. These trends create challenges of seeking new modes of generational communication, social inclusion, and social participation.

Demographic shifts represent an ever-present structural change in modern society. Increased life expectancies mean that an individual will be a member of a three or four generation family for longer time periods (e.g., collapse in fertility, changes in timing of family transitions, especially marriage, parenthood, and grandparenthood). These trends imply that intergenerational bonds among adult family members may be more important today than in earlier decades, and needs of elders and their ability to age successfully are best understood within a family context (Bengtson, 2001; Katz & Lowenstein, 2003; Lowenstein et al.,

2007). As White (2013: 216) indicates "today's social problems are the problems of generations."

One of the most influential conceptualizations was introduced by Rowe and Kahn (1997, p. 439; 1998), who defined successful aging as the "avoidance of disease and disability, maintenance of high physical and cognitive function, and sustained engagement in social and productive activities." However, several scholars, like Hank (2011), tend to accept McLaughlin and colleagues (2010, p. 224) view that Rowe and Kahn's concept of successful aging might be too narrow for specific public health purposes and that additional dimensions are needed.

Thus, we decided to use broad, multifaceted constructs that require both subjective and objective measures, focusing on subjective well-being and active aging – involvement with life. Pinquart and Sörensen (2000), in their meta-analysis on findings from 286 empirical studies on subjective well-being, concluded that in order to interpret the findings "more research is needed that investigates associations between subjective well-being and those aspects of life that show increased risk of loss and decline in old age" (p. 187). Family relations and family structures are changing (Bengtson, 2001; Lavee & Katz, 2003) and family generational research is mixed on whether families continue to be the safe haven in which resources are exchanged. Thus, it is imperative to study associations between successful aging and intergenerational family exchange and support (Katz, 2009a, b). Maintaining high levels of subjective well-being and involvement with life are considered to be important aspects of successful aging (Freund & Baltes, 1998; Fernandez-Ballesteros, 2013).

Data suggest that family relations buffer effects of potentially stressful life events and health crises (Davey et al., 2005). Studies of family solidarity effects on coping with crisis situations have revealed that higher solidarity contributes to better adjustment in situations such as widowhood or immigration (Katz & Lowenstein, 1999; Lowenstein & Katz, 2005). Intergenerational family relationships were generally found to contribute to subjective well-being and involvement with life of individuals throughout their life- course (Rossi & Rossi, 1990; Silverstein et al., 2013). Subjective well-being refers to evaluations that people make about their lives (e.g., Shmotkin, 2005), and is defined as a broad concept comprising a wide range of distinct dimensions (Kunzmann et al., 2000). As such, there are different approaches to the meaning and measurement of this construct. Ryff posits yet another approach to the well-being construct and generated a multidimensional model, including six distinct components of positive psychological functioning like personal growth, purpose in life, and self-acceptance (Ryff, 1989).

Active aging is multidimensional, with related concepts like: productive aging, healthy aging, vital aging, and more. It is defined as a process of optimizing opportunities for health, participation, and security to attain good quality of life as people age. Elders are redefining their careers, learning new skills, developing new leisure pursuits, enrolling in educational courses, volunteering for social causes, including involvement in politics (The Johnson County Consortium on Successful Aging, 2006). Biggs and Lowenstein (2011) introduced three interpretations of "new aging" approaches, relevant to societal solidarity: (1) policy priority to encourage older workers to stay longer at work; (2) elders contributing to society in the workplace, as active family members and volunteers, and other "productive" roles; and (3) elders maintaining a healthy life style, by the offering of more opportunities and reducing the "aging burden" on younger generations and society. The World Health Organization (2002) policy program defines active aging as an extraction of health opportunities, social participation, and personal safety. Active aging – aging with well-being and a high quality of life – is one of the main issues facing science and society today. This chapter will focus on the dimension of involvement with life as one central component of active aging.

The present chapter will thus, contribute to the body of research on the associations among socioeconomic resources, health, and economic status, family intergenerational relations, involvement with life, and subjective well-being. It will be achieved by analyzing data on these two dimensions of successful aging – subjective well-being and involvement with life – in European countries and Israel (based on SHARE data). The countries differ in their cultural and social contexts, particularly, family traditions and welfare development.

To sum, intergenerational family relationships were viewed as a significant contributor to successful coping, social integration, and involvement with life in old age (Silverstein & Bengtson, 1991; Silverstein et al., 2013). As a substantial number of studies on the topic were conducted within one culture, it is imperative to continue and study these associations further in a wider comparative perspective. Thus, the chapter will contribute new insights into associations between family relationships and successful aging.

Given these trends, our goal is threefold: (1) to analyze several dimensions of generational relations between older parents and their adult children; (2) to identify main activities of involvement with life and dimensions of subjective well-being; and (3) to study associations between the above variables, comparing European regions and Israel.

## Research Models – Successful Aging

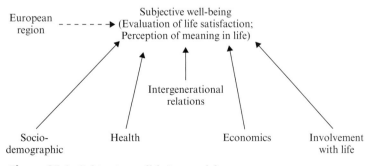

**Figure 25.1.** *Subjective well-being model*

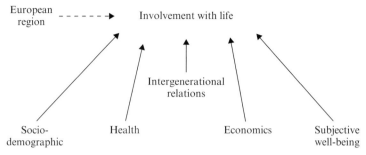

**Figure 25.2.** *Involvement with life model*

## Methods

### Research Population

We used secondary data analyses of SHARE (Survey of Health, Ageing and Retirement in Europe) fifth wave, conducted in 15 European countries (including Israel) during 2013, to achieve the study goals. The SHARE survey was developed 12 years ago as a longitudinal study in order to gain knowledge on changing demographic trends in Europe, interviewing respondents aged 50 or over (Börsch-Supan et al., 2013; Achdut et al., 2015). Among other issues, such as health and family relations, the survey provides a rich database on major economic measures, well-being, and active aging. Our focus was on the population aged 65 and over. The countries were: Austria, Belgium, Czech Republic, Denmark, Estonia, France, Germany, Italy, Netherlands, Slovenia, Spain, Luxemburg, Sweden, Switzerland, and Israel. We relate in our analyses to four clusters of the participating countries according to geographical regions (*Northern Europe*: Denmark, Sweden, Netherlands; *Central Europe*: Austria, Belgium, France, Germany, Luxemburg, Switzerland; *Southern Europe*: Israel, Italy, Spain; *Eastern Europe*: Czech Republic, Estonia, Slovenia [See Antonova et al., 2015; Wallace et al., 2015]). Regional differences were taken into account by adding a categorical variable with four different values, one for each region, with the Northern region serving as the reference category.

The four country groups were defined based on differences in sociocultural context and their level of effective social security systems. The state has a larger social role in Northern and Central European countries compared to Southern and Eastern Europe. These regional variations also correspond quite well with variations in welfare state policies affecting, for example, elders' healthcare and preventive services utilization (e.g., Santos-Eggimann et al., 2005) or participation in socially productive activities, and thus their capacity to age successfully (Hank, 2011).

As a first step, primary respondents aged 50 and above in the household and family modules were selected (60,427). From this sample, respondents who were younger than 65 were excluded, as well as respondents without children and grandchildren (30,431). After this selection process the sample consisted of 29,996 respondents.

## Research Variables and Descriptive Statistics

**Independent variables**: Table 25.1 provides descriptive statistics (means and SD, or percentages for categorical variables, according to the four regions).

**Socio-demographics resources**: (1) gender – percentage of males ranging from 40.5 percent in Eastern Europe to 47.72 in Northern Europe; (2) age average – 74 years in all regions; (3) education, average in years – the lowest was 8.7 in Southern Europe, whereas the highest in Eastern Europe was 11.2; (4) living alone – ranging from 21.2 in Southern Europe to 37.4 in Eastern Europe; (5) number of children, average – the lowest in Eastern Europe was 2.2; and (6) number of grandchildren, average – the highest in Northern Europe was 4.3.

**Health and functioning**: (1) number of chronic diseases – lowest was in Northern Europe with an average of 1.9; (2) ADL – the lowest level of functioning was in Southern Europe, whereas the highest was in Northern Europe; and (3) self-health assessment – the highest was in Northern Europe and the lowest was in the East.

**Economic resources**: (1) rate of employment – the highest was in Northern Europe (5.2) and the lowest was in Central Europe (2.3); (2) household income – the lowest was in Eastern Europe and the highest was in the Northern countries; and (3) makes ends meet – was more so in Northern and Central Europe, with the lowest in the other two regions.

**Intergenerational relations**: (1) social support – the highest provided was in Northern Europe and the highest received was in Eastern Europe; (2) financial support provided – highest in Northern and Central Europe; (3) financial support received – highest in Eastern Europe; and (4) taking care of grandchildren – highest in Northern Europe.

*Dependent variable* of successful aging was measured by two components: subjective well-being, which was based on 7 questions, one asking about evaluation of life satisfaction rated on a scale from 0 to 10 (0 being the lowest). Six other questions asked about perception of meaning in life on a scale from 1 to 4. Factor analysis revealed an eigenvalue of 1.798 (proportion: 1.042). The second component was involvement with life – the respondents' activities during the last year, like volunteering, sports club activities, political involvement, etc. Factor analysis revealed an eigenvalue of 3.561 (proportion: 1.059).

## Statistical Analyses

Two hierarchical regressions, with five models for each of the dependent variables, according to Figures 25.1 and 25.2 were performed. This was performed in order to find the contribution of each to successful aging, but mainly, to examine whether there was a contribution of intergenerational family relations to the explained findings, after controlling for all other variables.

Table 25.1  *Variable distribution (percent/average)*

|  | All | Northern Europe | Central Europe | Southern Europe | Eastern Europe |
|---|---|---|---|---|---|
| Gender (ref=male) (%) | 45.27 | 47.72 | 45.76 | 47.34 | 40.54 |
| Age (avg.) | 73.96 (6.79) | 73.39 (6.79) | 74.12 (6.90) | 74.41 (6.88) | 73.82 (6.48) |
| Education (avg.) | 10.42 (4.24) | 10.79 (4.05) | 10.69 (4.26) | 8.67(4.66) | 11.19 (3.52) |
| Living Arrangement (ref=alone) (%) | 29.11 | 25.17 | 30.51 | 21.24 | 37.39 |
| Children (avg.) | 2.45 (1.29) | 2.53 (1.18) | 2.45 (1.30) | 2.67 (1.55) | 2.16 (1.02) |
| Grandchildren (avg.) | 3.88 (3.11) | 4.30 (3.06) | 3.71 (3.14) | 3.88 (3.54) | 3.78 (2.63) |
| Chronic (avg.) | 2.08 (1.63) | 1.88 (1.54) | 2.03 (1.61) | 2.22 (1.71) | 2.22 (1.64) |
| ADL (avg.) | 0.29 (0.92) | 0.16 (0.65) | 0.29 (0.88) | 0.38 (1.15) | 0.35 (0.95) |
| Self Health Assessment (avg.)[a] | 3.29 (1.05) | 2.81 (1.11) | 3.19 (0.99) | 3.47 (1.01) | 3.70 (0.91) |
| Employment Status (ref: Retired) (%) | 86.06 | 89.39 | 88.06 | 71.67 | 92.82 |
| Income (M, Euro) (avg.) | 19 (3) | 34 (2) | 30 (2) | 15 (3) | 7.5 (2) |
| Makes Ends Meet (avg.)[b] | 2.99 (0.96) | 3.47 (0.77) | 3.24 (0.82) | 2.57 (0.97) | 2.54 (0.91) |
| Involvement with Life (avg.)[c] | 2.11 (1.46) | 2.86 (1.36) | 2.46 (1.44) | 1.09 (1.23) | 1.83 (1.18) |
| Subjective Well-Being (avg.)[d] | 18.47 (3.43) | 19.98 (2.71) | 19.18 (3.16) | 17.13 (3.54) | 17.26 (3.46) |
| Gave Support (%) | 22.44 | 27.50 | 22.73 | 16.93 | 22.38 |
| Received Support (%) | 24.41 | 19.93 | 22.76 | 21.48 | 33.42 |
| Taking Care of Grandchild (%) | 27.33 | 35.81 | 28.55 | 22.66 | 22.20 |
| Gave Financial (%) | 28.80 | 32.94 | 32.76 | 23.23 | 24.08 |
| Received Financial (%) | 6.62 | 4.79 | 5.64 | 4.50 | 11.59 |
| *N* | 29,996 | 6,203 | 10,589 | 6,172 | 7,032 |

Note: Parentheses denote standard deviation value.
[a] 1= Excellent; 5=Poor.
[b] 1= Very hardly; 4=easily.
[c] Number of activities: range 0–8.
[d] Range 6–34.

The first model controlled for all effects of socio-demographic background characteristics, in relation to subjective well-being and to involvement with life outcomes. Model 2 added the effects of health and functioning controls. Model 3 added effects of economics controls. Model 4 examined linkages between the two dependent variables, namely, subjective well-being and involvement with life, as shown in Figures 25.1 and 25.2. Model 5 considered intergenerational family relations above and beyond all other variables. Tables 25.2 and 25.3 present these analyses for the whole population, whereas Tables 25.4 and 25.5 present the final fifth model for the four different regions.

Table 25.2 *Subjective well-being model*

| | Model 1 | Model 2 | Model 3 | Model 4 | Model 5 |
|---|---|---|---|---|---|
| Gender (ref=male) | 0.149*** | 0.007 | −0.049 | 0.002 | −0.035 |
| | (0.04) | (0.03) | (0.03) | (0.03) | (0.04) |
| Age | −0.086*** | −0.029*** | −0.034*** | −0.026*** | −0.020*** |
| | (0.00) | (0.00) | (0.00) | (0.00) | (0.00) |
| Education | 0.072*** | 0.035*** | 0.011** | −0.004 | −0.004 |
| | (0.00) | (0.00) | (0.00) | (0.00) | (0.00) |
| Living arrangement (ref=alone) | −0.729*** | −0.666*** | −0.446*** | −0.464*** | −0.441*** |
| | (0.04) | (0.04) | (0.04) | (0.04) | (0.04) |
| Children (No.) | 0.016 | 0.040* | 0.065*** | 0.068*** | 0.068*** |
| | (0.02) | (0.02) | (0.02) | (0.02) | (0.02) |
| Grandchildren (No.) | 0.033*** | 0.030*** | 0.029*** | 0.026*** | 0.024** |
| | (0.01) | (0.01) | (0.01) | (0.01) | (0.01) |
| Central Europe | −0.667*** | −0.185*** | −0.064 | 0.002 | −0.008 |
| | (0.05) | (0.04) | (0.04) | (0.04) | (0.05) |
| Southern Europe | −2.623*** | −1.823*** | −1.204*** | −0.868*** | −0.881*** |
| | (0.06) | (0.05) | (0.05) | (0.06) | (0.06) |
| Eastern Europe | −2.591*** | −1.435*** | −0.762*** | −0.604*** | −0.589*** |
| | (0.05) | (0.05) | (0.06) | (0.06) | (0.06) |
| Chronic | | −0.136*** | −0.125*** | −0.135*** | −0.125*** |
| | | (0.01) | (0.01) | (0.01) | (0.01) |
| ADL | | −0.598*** | −0.548*** | −0.519*** | −0.465*** |
| | | (0.02) | (0.02) | (0.02) | (0.02) |
| Self Health Assessment | | −1.155*** | −1.032*** | −0.977*** | −0.957*** |
| | | (0.02) | (0.02) | (0.02) | (0.02) |
| Employment Status (ref: Retired)[a] | | | 0.197* | 0.202* | 0.144 |
| | | | (0.08) | (0.08) | (0.09) |

*(cont.)*

Table 25.2  (*cont.*)

|  | Model 1 | Model 2 | Model 3 | Model 4 | Model 5 |
|---|---|---|---|---|---|
| Income (ln) |  |  | 0.141*** | 0.108*** | 0.083*** |
|  |  |  | (0.02) | (0.02) | (0.02) |
| Makes End Meet |  |  | 0.661*** | 0.620*** | 0.626*** |
|  |  |  | (0.02) | (0.02) | (0.02) |
| Involvement with Life |  |  |  | 0.280*** | 0.275*** |
|  |  |  |  | (0.01) | (0.01) |
| Gave Support |  |  |  |  | −0.142*** |
|  |  |  |  |  | (0.04) |
| Received Support |  |  |  |  | −0.440*** |
|  |  |  |  |  | (0.04) |
| Taking Care of Grandchild |  |  |  |  | 0.135*** |
|  |  |  |  |  | (0.04) |
| Gave Financial |  |  |  |  | 0.064 |
|  |  |  |  |  | (0.04) |
| Received Financial |  |  |  |  | 0.128* |
|  |  |  |  |  | (0.05) |
| Constant | 25.414*** | 25.290*** | 21.670*** | 20.822*** | 20.611*** |
|  | (0.22) | (0.20) | (0.29) | (0.29) | (0.32) |
| R-squared | 0.176 | 0.261 | 0.288 | 0.298 | 0.402 |
| N | 29,996 | 29,982 | 29,393 | 29,393 | 26,288 |

* $p<0.05$, ** $p<0.01$, *** $p<0.001$.
[a] Job status included another category (not shown) – other employment status (i.e., unemployed, permanently sick or disabled, homemaker).

## Results

The findings in Table 25.2 reveal that five clusters of variables had an impact on subjective well-being.

**Socio-demographic resources**: gender (men), age (younger), level of education (higher), living arrangements (with family members), and number of children and grandchildren (higher).

**Health and functioning**: chronic diseases (less), ADL functioning (less restricted), and subjective evaluation of health (higher) contributes the most.

**Economic resources**: job status (employed), household income (higher), subjective evaluation of economic welfare (higher), and household income and "makes ends meet" had a significant contribution to subjective well-being (positive).

A positive association was found between involvement with life and subjective well-being.

**Intergenerational relations:** The last module, receiving and providing personal care from children and other family relatives reduced subjective well-being. However, we found that providing care reduces well-being by 14 percent, whereas receiving support reduces it by 3 times (44 percent), taking care of grandchildren (higher), and receiving financial support from children (higher). Thus, we can see that intergenerational family relations contribute above and beyond all other variables to the explained subjective well-being – 34.8 percent.

The findings in Table 25.3 reveal that five clusters of variables had an impact on involvement with life.

**Socio-demographic resources**: gender (women), age (younger), level of education (higher), and number of grandchildren (higher).

**Health and functioning**: chronic diseases (less), ADL functioning (less restricted), and self-health assessment (higher).

**Economic resources**: household income (higher), subjective evaluation of economic welfare (higher).

A positive association was found between subjective well-being and involvement with life.

Table 25.3 *Involvement with life model*

|  | Model 1 | Model 2 | Model 3 | Model 4 | Model 5 |
|---|---|---|---|---|---|
| Gender (ref=male) | −0.124*** | −0.137*** | −0.182*** | −0.179*** | −0.160*** |
|  | (0.02) | (0.02) | (0.02) | (0.02) | (0.02) |
| Age | −0.035*** | −0.026*** | −0.026*** | −0.024*** | −0.019*** |
|  | (0.00) | (0.00) | (0.00) | (0.00) | (0.00) |
| Education | 0.068*** | 0.061*** | 0.053*** | 0.053*** | 0.051*** |
|  | (0.00) | (0.00) | (0.00) | (0.00) | (0.00) |
| Living Arrangement (ref=alone) | −0.028 | −0.022 | 0.066*** | 0.093*** | 0.061*** |
|  | (0.02) | (0.02) | (0.02) | (0.02) | (0.02) |
| Children (No.) | −0.022** | −0.018* | −0.009 | −0.013 | −0.01 |
|  | (0.01) | (0.01) | (0.01) | (0.01) | (0.01) |
| Grandchildren (No.) | 0.009** | 0.008** | 0.008** | 0.007* | 0.003 |
|  | (0.00) | (0.00) | (0.00) | (0.00) | (0.00) |
| Central Europe | −0.362*** | −0.272*** | −0.238*** | −0.234*** | −0.224*** |
|  | (0.02) | (0.02) | (0.02) | (0.02) | (0.02) |
| Southern Europe | −1.580*** | −1.435*** | −1.200*** | −1.129*** | −1.143*** |

*(cont.)*

Table 25.3  (*cont.*)

|  | Model 1 | Model 2 | Model 3 | Model 4 | Model 5 |
|---|---|---|---|---|---|
|  | (0.02) | (0.02) | (0.02) | (0.02) | (0.03) |
| Eastern Europe | $-1.050^{***}$ | $-0.834^{***}$ | $-0.565^{***}$ | $-0.519^{***}$ | $-0.545^{***}$ |
|  | (0.02) | (0.02) | (0.03) | (0.03) | (0.03) |
| Chronic |  | $0.034^{***}$ | $-0.037^{***}$ | $-0.044^{***}$ | $-0.037^{***}$ |
|  |  | (0.01) | (0.00) | (0.00) | (0.01) |
| ADL |  | $-0.115^{***}$ | $-0.106^{***}$ | $-0.074^{***}$ | $-0.074^{***}$ |
|  |  | (0.01) | (0.01) | (0.01) | (0.01) |
| Self Health Assessment |  | $-0.231^{***}$ | $-0.196^{***}$ | $-0.135^{***}$ | $-0.128^{***}$ |
|  |  | (0.01) | (0.01) | (0.01) | (0.01) |
| Employment Status (ref: Retired)[a] |  |  | $-0.016$ | $-0.028$ | $-0.006$ |
|  |  |  | (0.04) | (0.04) | (0.04) |
| Income (ln) |  |  | $0.120^{***}$ | $0.112^{***}$ | $0.090^{***}$ |
|  |  |  | (0.01) | (0.01) | (0.01) |
| Makes End Meet |  |  | $0.146^{***}$ | $0.106^{***}$ | $0.093^{***}$ |
|  |  |  | (0.01) | (0.01) | (0.010 |
| Subjective Well-Being |  |  |  | $0.059^{***}$ | $0.057^{***}$ |
|  |  |  |  | (0.00) | (0.00) |
| Gave Support |  |  |  |  | $0.180^{***}$ |
|  |  |  |  |  | (0.02) |
| Received Support |  |  |  |  | 0.02 |
|  |  |  |  |  | (0.02) |
| Taking Care of Grandchild |  |  |  |  | $0.201^{***}$ |
|  |  |  |  |  | (0.02) |
| Gave Financial |  |  |  |  | $0.210^{***}$ |
|  |  |  |  |  | (0.02) |
| Received Financial |  |  |  |  | $0.165^{***}$ |
|  |  |  |  |  | (0.03) |
| Constant | $4.740^{***}$ | $4.779^{***}$ | $3.032^{***}$ | $1.748^{***}$ | $1.526^{***}$ |
|  | (0.09) | (0.09) | (0.14) | (0.15) | (0.15) |
| R-squared | 0.256 | 0.285 | 0.297 | 0.309 | 0.380 |
| *N* | 29,994 | 29,650 | 29,393 | 29,393 | 26,288 |

* $p<0.05$, ** $p<0.01$, *** $p<0.001$.
[a] Job status included another category (not shown) – other employment status (i.e., unemployed, permanently sick or disabled, homemaker).

**Intergenerational relations**: Included providing social support, providing and receiving financial support from/to household members, and caretaking of grandchildren. Thus, we can see that intergenerational relations contributed above and beyond other variables to the explained variable of involvement with life – 22.9 percent.

Differences between regions (Tables 25.4 and 25.5) were found regarding the two dimensions of successful aging (subjective well-being and involvement with life), which reveal large cross-national variations in successful aging. Structural variability was observed in both dimensions, where the highest was in countries of Central and Northern Europe, followed by Eastern European countries, with the lowest in countries of Southern Europe.

Table 25.4 *Subjective well-being model, by geographical region*

| | Northern Europe | Central Europe | Southern Europe | Eastern Europe |
|---|---|---|---|---|
| Gender (ref = male) | −0.112 | 0.033 | 0.163 | −0.239** |
| | (0.06) | (0.06) | (0.09) | (0.08) |
| Age | −0.049*** | −0.009* | −0.019** | −0.013* |
| | (0.01) | (0.00) | (0.01) | (0.01) |
| Education | −0.004 | −0.027*** | 0.025** | −0.003 |
| | (0.01) | (0.01) | (0.01) | (0.01) |
| Living Arrangement (ref=alone) | −0.271*** | −0.472*** | −0.565*** | −0.520*** |
| | (0.08) | (0.07) | (0.10) | (0.09) |
| Children (No.) | 0.023 | 0.056* | 0.129*** | 0.051 |
| | (0.03) | (0.03) | (0.03) | (0.05) |
| Grandchildren (No.) | 0.050*** | 0.001 | 0.038* | 0.026 |
| | (0.01) | (0.01) | (0.02) | (0.02) |
| Chronic | −0.057* | −0.135*** | −0.171*** | −0.122*** |
| | (0.02) | (0.02) | (0.03) | (0.02) |
| ADL | −0.556*** | −0.405*** | −0.483*** | −0.392*** |
| | (0.06) | (0.04) | (0.04) | (0.04) |
| Self Health Assessment | −0.777*** | −0.984*** | −0.934*** | −1.170*** |
| | (0.03) | (0.03) | (0.05) | (0.05) |
| Employment Status (ref: Retired)[a] | 0.143 | 0.045 | 0.140 | 0.134 |
| | (0.15) | (0.20) | (0.21) | (0.18) |
| Income (ln) | −0.012 | 0.170*** | 0.014 | 0.068 |
| | (0.06) | (0.03) | (0.04) | (0.05) |

*(cont.)*

Table 25.4 *Subjective well-being model, by geographical region*

| | Northern Europe | Central Europe | Southern Europe | Eastern Europe |
|---|---|---|---|---|
| Makes End Meet | 0.459*** | 0.609*** | 0.614*** | 0.705*** |
| | (0.04) | (0.03) | (0.04) | (0.04) |
| Involvement with Life | 0.182*** | 0.282*** | 0.281*** | 0.354*** |
| | (0.02) | (0.02) | (0.04) | (0.03) |
| Gave Support | 0.125 | −0.132* | −0.417*** | −0.212* |
| | (0.07) | (0.07) | (0.11) | (0.09) |
| Received Support | −0.325*** | −0.333*** | −0.743*** | −0.419*** |
| | (0.08) | (0.07) | (0.11) | (0.08) |
| Taking Care of Grandchild | 0.025 | 0.177** | 0.201* | 0.113 |
| | (0.07) | (0.06) | (0.10) | (0.09) |
| Gave Financial | −0.039 | 0.141* | 0.119 | −0.012 |
| | (0.07) | (0.06) | (0.10) | (0.09) |
| Received Financial | −0.048 | 0.155 | −0.135 | 0.220 |
| | (0.14) | (0.12) | (0.19) | (0.12) |
| Constant | 23.866*** | 19.259*** | 19.921*** | 20.162*** |
| | (0.75) | (0.52) | (0.65) | (0.66) |
| R-squared | 0.283 | 0.325 | 0.374 | 0.313 |
| N | 5,576 | 9,022 | 5,242 | 6,448 |

* $p<0.05$, ** $p<0.01$, *** $p<0.001$.
[a] Job status included another category (not shown) – other employment status (i.e., unemployed, permanently sick or disabled, homemaker).

First, considering the two dimensions of successful aging, looking at background characteristics, similarities, and differences between regions were found. Regarding subjective well-being: being younger had an impact in all regions, especially in the North; however, living alone is less important in the North, whereas the number of children is more important in the South and Central regions. Caretaking of grandchildren is more significant in the North, which may point to differences in formal services provision to elders. Health and functioning and subjective assessments of economic situation have an impact in all regions. This is universal, as personal attributes are related to quality of life in all stages of the life course. Economic resources like income are significant only in Central Europe, whereas subjective evaluation of economic situations (makes ends meet) are linked to subjective well-being in all regions. Regarding family relations, receiving social support reduces well-being in all regions; giving

Table 25.5 *Involvement with life model, by geographical region*

| | Northern Europe | Central Europe | Southern Europe | Eastern Europe |
|---|---|---|---|---|
| Gender | −0.325*** | −0.142*** | 0.003 | −0.122*** |
| | (0.04) | (0.03) | (0.04) | (0.03) |
| Age | −0.021*** | −0.027*** | −0.007** | −0.018*** |
| | (0.00) | (0.00) | (0.00) | (0.00) |
| Education | 0.034*** | 0.045*** | 0.060*** | 0.078*** |
| | (0.00) | (0.00) | (0.00) | (0.00) |
| Living Arrangement | −0.035 | 0.028 | 0.155*** | 0.124*** |
| | (0.04) | (0.03) | (0.04) | (0.03) |
| Children (No.) | −0.002 | −0.003 | −0.006 | −0.025 |
| | (0.02) | (0.01) | (0.01) | (0.02) |
| Grandchildren (No.) | 0.009 | 0.004 | −0.004 | 0.006 |
| | (0.01) | (0.01) | (0.01) | (0.01) |
| Chronic | −0.011 | −0.034*** | −0.055*** | −0.041*** |
| | (0.01) | (0.01) | (0.01) | (0.01) |
| ADL | −0.119*** | −0.142*** | −0.025 | −0.049** |
| | (0.03) | (0.02) | (0.01) | (0.02) |
| Self Health Assessment | −0.146*** | −0.125*** | −0.088*** | −0.131*** |
| | (0.02) | (0.02) | (0.02) | (0.02) |
| Employment Status (ref: Retired)[a] | −0.182* | 0.017 | −0.155 | 0.305*** |
| | (0.08) | (0.10) | (0.08) | (0.07) |
| Income (ln) | 0.058 | 0.106*** | 0.093*** | 0.060*** |
| | (0.03) | (0.02) | (0.02) | (0.02) |
| Makes End Meet | 0.067** | 0.071*** | 0.134*** | 0.091*** |
| | (0.02) | (0.02) | (0.02) | (0.02) |
| Subjective Well-Being | 0.057*** | 0.074*** | 0.042*** | 0.046*** |
| | (0.01) | (0.01) | (0.01) | (0.00) |
| Gave Support | 0.138*** | 0.199*** | 0.177*** | 0.176*** |
| | (0.04) | (0.03) | (0.04) | (0.03) |
| Received Support | 0.134** | 0.054 | −0.098* | −0.015 |
| | (0.05) | (0.04) | (0.04) | (0.03) |
| Taking Care of Grandchild | 0.146*** | 0.159*** | 0.305*** | 0.201*** |
| | (0.04) | (0.03) | (0.04) | (0.03) |
| Gave Financial | 0.185*** | 0.173*** | 0.382*** | 0.165*** |
| | (0.04) | (0.03) | (0.04) | (0.03) |

(cont.)

Table 25.5 *(cont.)*

|  | Northern Europe | Central Europe | Southern Europe | Eastern Europe |
|---|---|---|---|---|
| Received Financial | 0.135 | 0.081 | 0.183[*] | 0.212[***] |
|  | (0.08) | (0.06) | (0.07) | (0.04) |
| Constant | 2.434[***] | 1.537[***] | −0.803[**] | 1.003[***] |
|  | (0.46) | (0.28) | (0.27) | (0.26) |
| R-squared | 0.133 | 0.175 | 0.231 | 0.235 |
| *N* | 5,576 | 9,022 | 5,242 | 6,448 |

[*] $p<0.05$, [**] $p<0.01$, [***] $p<0.001$.
[a] Job status included another category (not shown) – other employment status (i.e., unemployed, permanently sick or disabled, homemaker).

support is negatively related to well-being, except in Northern Europe; providing financial support is positively related only in Central Europe.

A somewhat different picture is seen regarding involvement with life (Table 25.5). Younger age, higher education, higher subjective assessment of health and economic situation, ability to provide social support and financial help, and taking care of grandchildren are important in all regions. However, having chronic illness and the level of income were not related to involvement with life, except in the Northern region.

## Discussion

We explored similarities and differences between four European regions regarding associations between: personal and economic resources, health and functioning, with particular attention to the impact of intergenerational family relations on successful aging. Two dimensions of successful aging were investigated in this chapter: subjective well-being and involvement with life. An important focus in well-being research is on subjective well-being (SWB), a cognitive and emotional evaluation of one's well-being (Diener & Lucas, 1999). Involvement with life is a major component of active aging (e.g., doing voluntary work, participating in sport club, reading books, taking part in political/community related organizations, and more), which was found to contribute to successful aging. It is well established in empirical studies that being active promotes well-being (Walker, 2009; Biggs & Lowenstein, 2011).

Using SHARE data, we were able to compare findings from 15 countries. Bengtson et al. (2002) indicated that it is important to look outside national borders in order to construct global conceptualizations of families, age, and well-being. This is particularly meaningful because a large number of studies may have an unacknowledged ethnocentric bias, since they are conducted in a single country. From comparative findings we might map some future directions and key challenges that family intergenerational relationships currently present (Katz et al., 2005). We adopted this perspective that might foster understanding of factors impacting successful aging in the four European regions (Northern, Central, Southern, and Eastern), including Israel. Our study attempts to draw a more broad and multi-dimensional picture of successful aging. However, the limitation here is that we did not look at other dimensions, like bio-medical and environmental.

This chapter contributed to the least studied aspects of exploring linkages between personal, economic, health, and familial resources and successful aging. Some studies have focused on European differences in levels of older people's SWB, but did not examine variation in the impact of factors associated with it (Ferring et al., 2004; Katz, 2009a), or focused mainly on the similarities (Fagerström et al., 2007).

As expected, some personal resources contributed significantly to linkages with successful aging across the 15 countries, like being younger, more educated, living with others, and having grandchildren (Jeste et al., 2013). Additionally, being healthier with less chronic diseases, and having fewer ADL limitations, as well as having positive subjective health assessments contributed to successful aging (Lagiewka & Antunes, 2011). Economic resources like higher household income and higher self-evaluation of income were also strong predictors of both successful aging components (Cho et al., 2015). Interestingly, being male contributed to subjective well-being, whereas being female contributed more to involvement with life, and having children and being employed contributed to subjective well-being only.

A most significant finding was the strong association between intergenerational family relations (including all its components) and successful aging (the two dimensions), even after controlling for background resources, including health and functioning, economic attributes, and other variables. This means that predicting the decline of family relations was not proven in our research. Bengtson suggested it in 2001, because family members are the main support providers at later ages (Van Tilburg, 1995; Bengtson, 2001).

Many studies have shown that throughout Europe, families are highly involved in providing care to older people, even though there are cultural differences in patterns of intergenerational support.

Intergenerational family relations had shown some expected well-established results and some surprising findings that call for more in-depth inquiries. For example, taking care of grandchildren was found to positively contribute to subjective well-being and involvement with life (Bulanda & Jendrek, 2016). It is well recognized in gerontological literature, that close relations with grandchildren has a positive impact on successful aging (Mahne & Huxhold, 2015). However, giving and receiving economic support contributed positively to involvement with life. Subjective well-being was influenced by receiving financial support, but not by providing it, which contradicts a number of findings from other studies (Lee et al., 2014; Zeng et al., 2016). Providing support to others, though, had a positive impact on involvement with life.

Other studies found that daily and regular contact with adult children had a significant positive impact on subjective well-being in Northern and Eastern Europe, while there was no effect found in Central and Southern Europe. According to Daatland and Lowenstein (2005) intergenerational relationships in Southern Europe seem to be duty-driven, while in the North ideals offer more room for negotiation. In Northern Europe, contact with adult children is therefore likely to be in accordance with older adults needs and more frequent contact might then lead to higher subjective well-being. Moreover, the availability of services in Northern Europe might help older adults to have independent relationships (Daatland & Lowenstein, 2005). Frequent contact with children might then exist together with welfare services, while frequent contact in Central and Southern Europe might be based on legal obligations for the family.

Moreover, the role of children is more important in countries where people rely on familial support (Margolis & Myrskylä, 2010), even though state support and family support do not exclude each other (Attias-Donfut et al., 2005). Countries in Northern Europe have the most generous support systems (Esping-Andersen, 2013). The state has a larger social role in Central Europe compared to the South. Eastern countries are characterized by lower levels of welfare provision (Fenger, 2007; Niedzwiedz et al., 2014).

Family is still the main and primary caregiver in times of need and relations with family members across generations, whether social, financial, and/or helping with grandchildren are meaningful and of great importance to older people. A current review notes that "family generational research shows mixed findings on whether families continue to be the safe haven in which resources are exchanged and members supported. The transfer of resources from older to younger family generations is contingent on the nature of family structure and solidarity, as well as broader contexts such as welfare regimes" (Keating et al., 2015, p. 4). Analyzing and comparing generational solidarity between parents and their adult children is based on several international databases: SHARE (first two waves) and OASIS. We found that even in Modern Era, generational solidarity is still strong in most European countries and Israel (Katz et al., 2015), although variations were found in the strengths of the different solidarity dimensions between the countries, which might reflect national and cultural idiosyncrasies in family cultures, behavioral patterns, and social policy traditions (Katz & Lowenstein, 2003).

Regarding generational relations, giving and receiving social support in the South is negatively connected to subjective well-being. Providing financial support is positively related to it in Central Europe. In another cross-national study (Lowenstein et al., 2007), it was found that the capacity to be an active provider in exchange relations enhances elder's life satisfaction, while being mainly a recipient of support from adult children is related to a lower level of well-being. Taking care of grandchildren is beneficial to subjective well-being in Central and Southern Europe.

## Limitations and Future Recommendations

This study has several limitations. First, our choice of a successful aging measure, although composed of two dimensions, obviously affects both prevalence estimates and observed associations and impacts. Despite a focus on subjective well-being and involvement with life, there are other components like biomedical and environmental dimensions of successful aging.

Additionally, an emphasis on active engagement as an indicator of success discriminates against elders who are unable or unwilling to engage in productive activities, e.g., elders who find meaning in old age in other ways (e.g., Holstein & Minkler, 2003). Studies also suggest that specific domains of successful aging might be valued differently by older people across cultures (e.g., Fernández-Ballesteros et al., 2008; Hung et al., 2010).

In order to understand country differences better, future studies could examine the impact of personal economic, health related, and familial variables on successful aging for individual countries. By taking a cross-nationally comparative perspective, one can add another, macro-level dimension of potentially relevant structural (e.g., welfare state) factors affecting individuals' opportunities for successful aging to the analysis.

The study used only one wave of SHARE data. We recommend that future research examine the impact of changes to welfare policies and to family structures and norms, by analyzing several waves of SHARE or other longitudinal databases.

Why should the future of the family interest policymakers? Helping policymakers identify upcoming issues and stimulate debates on long-term policy for society offers a prism through which one can consider how society might change over coming decades, and be better prepared for those changes. Understanding variations in policy environment across various European countries might present a wider picture of the interplay between factors at the societal, familial, and individual level (Wolf & Ballal, 2006), potentially informing family policy development.

## References

Achdut, L., Tur-Sinai, A., Troitsky, R. (2015). Transitions among states of labor force participation in old age. *European Journal of Ageing*, 12(1), 39–49.

Antonova, L., Aranda, L., Havari, E., et al. (2015). Is there a European land of opportunity? Cross-country differences in inter-generational mobility in 14 European countries and Israel. In A. Börsch-Supan, et al. (Eds.), *Ageing in Europe: Supporting Policies for an Inclusive Society*. Berlin: De Gruyter, 209–22.

Attias-Donfut, C., Ogg, J., Wolff, F. C. (2005). European patterns of intergenerational financial and time transfers. *European Journal of Ageing*, 2(3), 161–73.

Bengtson, V. L. (2001). Beyond the nuclear family: The increasing importance of multigenerational bonds. *Journal of Marriage and Family*, 63(1), 1–16.

Bengtson, V. L., Lowenstein, A. (Eds.) (2003). *Global Aging and Challenges to Families*. New York and Berlin: Aldine De Gruyter.

Bengtson, V., Giarrusso, R., Mabry, J. B., et al. (2002). Solidarity, conflict, and ambivalence: Complementary or competing perspectives on intergenerational relationships? *Journal of Marriage and Family*, 64(3), 568–76.

Bengtson, V. L., Acock, A. C., Allen, K. R., et al. (Eds.), *Sourcebook on Family Theory and Research* (pp. 393–407). Sage Publications.

Biggs, S., Lowenstein, A. (2011). *Generational Intelligence: A Critical Approach to Age Relations*. London: Routledge.

Börsch-Supan, A., Brandt, M., Hunkler, C., et al. (2013). Data resource profile: The survey of health, ageing and retirement in Europe (SHARE). *International Journal of Epidemiology*, 1–10.

Bulanda, J. R., Jendrek, M. P. (2016). Grandparenting roles and volunteer activity. *Journal of Gerontology; Social Sciences*, 71(1), 129–40.

Cho, J., Martin, P., Poon, L. W., and Georgia Centenarian Study. (2015). Successful aging and subjective well-being among oldest-old adults. *The Gerontologist*, 55(1), 132–43.

Daatland, S. O., Lowenstein, A. (2005). Intergenerational solidarity and the family–welfare state balance. *European Journal of Ageing*, 2(3), 174–82.

Davey, B., Levin, E., Iliffe, S., et al. (2005). Integrating health and social care: implications for joint working and community care outcomes for older people. *Journal of Interprofessional Care*, 19(1), 22–34.

Diener, E., Lucas, R. E. (1999). 11 Personality and Subjective Well-Being. *Well-being: Foundations of Hedonic Psychology*, 213.

Esping-Andersen, G. (2013). *The Three Worlds of Welfare Capitalism*. John Wiley & Sons.

Fagerström, C., Borg, C., Balducci, C., et al. (2007). Life satisfaction and associated factors among people aged 60 years and above in six European countries. *Applied Research in Quality of life*, 2(1), 33–50.

Fenger, M. (2007). Welfare regimes in Central and Eastern Europe: Incorporating post-communist countries in a welfare regime typology. *Contemporary Issues and Ideas in Social Sciences*, 3(2), 1–30.

Fernández-Ballesteros, R. (2013). Possibilities and limitations of age. *Promoting Conscious and Active Learning and Aging*, 25–74.

Fernández-Ballesteros, R., Garcιá, L. F., Abarca, A., et al. (2008). Lay concept of ageing well: Cross-cultural comparisons. *Journal of the American Geriatrics Society*, 56, 950–2.

Ferring, D., Balducci, C., Burholt, V., et al. (2004). Life satisfaction of older people in six European countries: findings from the European study on adult well-being. *European Journal of Ageing*, 1(1), 15–25.

Freund, A. M., Baltes, P. B. (1998). Selection, optimization, and compensation as strategies of life management: correlations with subjective indicators of successful aging. *Psychology and Aging*, 13(4), 531.

Hank, K. (2011). How "successful" do older europeans age? findings from share. *Journal of Gerontology: Social Sciences*, 66B(2), 230–6.

Holstein, M. B., Minkler, M. (2003). Self, society, and the "new gerontology." *The Gerontologist*, 43(6), 787–96.

Hung, L. W., Kempen, G. I. J. M., De Vries, N. K. (2010). Cross-cultural comparison between academic and lay views of healthy ageing: A literature review. *Ageing and Society*, 30(8), 1373–91.

Jeste, D. V., Savla, G. N., Thompson, W. K. et al. (2013). Association between older age and more successful aging: critical role of resilience and depression. *American Journal of Psychiatry*, 170(2), 188–96.

Successful aging in Johnson County: Transportation report (2006). *The Johnson County Consortium on Successful Aging* (1–35).

Katz, R. (2009a). Intergenerational family relations and subjective well-being in old age: a cross-national study. *European Journal of Ageing*, 6, 79–90.

(2009b). Intergenerational family relations and life satisfaction among three elderly population groups in transition in the Israeli multi-cultural society. *Journal of Cross Cultural Gerontology*, 24, 77–91.

Katz, R., Lowenstein, A. (1999). Adjustment of older Soviet immigrants and their adult children residing in shared households: An intergenerational comparison. *Journal of Family Relations*, 48, 43–50.

(2003). Elders' quality of life and intergenerational relations: A cross-national comparison. *Hallym International Journal on Aging*, 5(2), 131–58.

Katz, R., Lowenstein, A., Phillips, J. et al. (2005). Theorizing intergenerational solidarity, conflict and ambivalence in a comparative cross-national perspective. In Katz, R., Lowenstein, A., Halperin, D., et al. (2015). Generational Solidarity in Europe and Israel. *Canadian Journal on Aging/La Revue canadienne du vieillissement*. Special Section on Aging Families in International Context, 34(3), 342–55.

Keating, N., Kwan, D., Hillcoat-Nalletamby, S., et al. (2015). *Evidence Review of Intergenerational Relationships: Experiences and Attitudes in the New Millennium*. Centre for Innovative Ageing, Swansea University. Foresight, Government Office for Science.

Kunzmann, U., Little, T. D., Smith, J. (2000). Is age-related stability of subjective well-being a paradox? Cross-sectional and longitudinal evidence from the Berlin Aging Study. *Psychology and Aging*, 15(3), 511.

Lagiewka, K., Antunes, J. P. (2011). European innovation partnership on active and healthy ageing–how is the EU connecting the dots between smart innovation and ageing boom. *Review of Applied Socio-Economic Research*, 1(2), 95–103.

Lavee, Y., Katz, R. (2003). The family in Israel: Between tradition and modernity. *Marriage & Family Review*, 34(1–2), 193–217.

Lee, H. J., Lyu, J., Lee, C. M., et al. (2014). Intergenerational financial exchange and the psychological well-being of older adults in the Republic of Korea. *Aging & Mental Health*, 18(1), 30–39.

Lowenstein, A. (2005). Global aging and the challenges to families. In M. Johnson, V. L. Bengtson, P. G. Coleman & T. Kirkwood (Eds.), *Cambridge Handbook on Age and Aging*. Cambridge: Cambridge University Press, pp. 403–13.

Lowenstein, A., Katz, R. (2005). Living arrangements, family solidarity and life satisfaction of two generations of immigrants. *Ageing and Society*, 25, 1–19.

(2010). Family and age in global perspectives. In C. Phillipson & D. Dannefer (Eds.), *Handbook of Social Gerontology*. London: Sage Publications, pp. 190–201.

Lowenstein, A., Katz, R., Gur-Yaish, N. (2007). Reciprocity in parent-child exchange and life satisfaction among the elderly in cross-national perspective. *Journal of Social Issues*, 63(4), 865–83.

McLaughlin, S. J., Connell, C. M., Heeringa, S. G., et al. (2010). Successful aging in the United States: Prevalence estimates from a national sample of older adults. *Journal of Gerontology: Social Sciences*, 65B, 216–26.

Mahne, K., Huxhold, O. (2015). Grandparenthood and subjective well-being: Moderating effects of educational level. *Journal of Gerontology; Social Sciences*, 70(5), 782–92.

Niedzwiedz, C. L., Katikireddi, S. V., Pell, J. P., et al. (2014). The association between life course socioeconomic position and life satisfaction in different welfare states: European comparative study of individuals in early old age. *Age and Ageing*, 43(3), 431–6.

Pinquart, M., Sörensen, S. (2000). Influences of socioeconomic status, social network, and competence on subjective well-being in later life: a meta-analysis. *Psychology and Aging*, 15(2), 187.

Roberts, R. E., Richards, L. N., Bengtson, V. (1991). Intergenerational solidarity in families: Untangling the ties that bind. *Marriage & Family Review*, *16*(1–2), 11–46.

Rossi, A. S., Rossi, P. H. (1990). *Of human Bonding: Parent-Child Relations across the Life Course*. New York: Aldine de Gruyter.

Rowe, J. W., Kahn, R. L. (1997). Successful aging. *The Gerontologist*, 37(4), 433–40.
    (1998). *Successful Aging: The MacArthur Foundation Study*. New York: Pantheon.

Ryff, C. D. (1989). Beyond Ponce de Leon and life satisfaction: New directions in quest of successful ageing. *International Journal of Behavioral Development*, 12(1), 35–55.

Santos-Eggimann, B., Junod, J., Cornaz, S. (2005). Health services utilisation in older Europeans. *Health, ageing and retirement in Europe: First results from the survey of healthy ageing and retirement in Europe*. Mannheim, Mannheim Research Institute for the Economics of Ageing, 131–40.

Shmotkin, D. (2005). Happiness in the face of adversity: Reformulating the dynamic and modular bases of subjective well-being. *Review of General Psychology*, 9(4), 291.

Silverstein, M., Bengtson, V. L. (1991). Do close parent-child relations reduce the mortality risk of older parents? *Journal of Health and Social Behavior*, 382–95.

Silverstein, M., Lowenstein, A., Katz, R., et al. (2013). Intergenerational support and the emotional well-being of older Jews and Arabs in Israel. *Journal of Marriage and Family*, 75, 950–63.

Van Tilburg, T. G. (1995). Delineation of the social network and differences in network size. *Living Arrangements and Social Networks of Older Adults*, 83–96.

Wahl, H. W., Tesch-Römer, C., Hoff, A. (2007). *New Dynamics in Old Age: Individual, Environmental, and Societal Perspectives*. Baywood Pub Co.

Walker, A. (2009). The emergence and application of active ageing in Europe. *Journal of Aging & Social Policy*, 21, 75–93.

Wallace, L. M., Theou, O., Pena, F., et al. (2015). Social vulnerability as a predictor of mortality and disability: cross-country differences in the survey of health, aging, and retirement in Europe (SHARE). *Aging Clinical and Experimental Research*, 27(3), 365–72.

White, J. (2013). Thinking generations. *The British Journal of Sociology*, 64(2), 216–47.

WHO, A. A. (2002). *A Policy Framework. Geneva, Switzerland: World Health Organization*.

Wolf, D. A., Ballal, S. S. (2006). Family support for older people in an era of demographic change and policy constraints. *Ageing and Society*, 26(05), 693–706.

Zeng, Y., Brasher, M. S., Gu, D., et al. (2016). Older parents benefit more in health outcome from daughters' than sons' emotional care in China. *Journal of Aging and Health*, 28(8), 1426–47.

# 26 Involvement with Life and Social Networks

A Pathway for Successful Aging

Toni C. Antonucci and Noah J. Webster

## Introduction

It has been said that the 1987 Rowe and Kahn *Science* article initiated "a sea change" in the field of gerontology and geriatrics, by emphasizing the variability of the aging process and its causes, rather than the previous emphasis on the inevitable central tendency of age-related reduction in functions (Pruchno, 2015). Nevertheless, the model of successful aging has not been without critics. In this chapter we cite briefly several positive effects of the Rowe–Kahn model, as well as summarize the major arguments against and criticisms of the model itself. We then suggest an integration of the convoy model of social relations into the successful aging model as a potentially useful approach for addressing at least some of these criticisms. We next describe two field experiments originally designed to test the successful aging model and demonstrate how social networks provide a unique pathway to successful aging that can be useful for all populations, rather than a privileged minority. The chapter concludes with a call to further integrate social networks and social relationships into the model of successful aging, thus recognizing the pervasive potential of social relations to influence and create unique models of successful aging appropriate to individuals in varying and challenging circumstances.

## Critics and Criticisms

Concepts, if they are influential at all, are likely to have unintended consequences in addition to those intended by their authors, and so it has been for successful aging. The term itself was not new; as Baltes and Baltes (1990) pointed out, it had appeared in publications for decades, usually without definition. In the 1987 article, Rowe and Kahn came close to a definition in their discussion of age-related physiological changes: "In many data sets that

This research was supported in part by a grant from the MacArthur Foundation through the How Housing Matters Program. The authors would like to express deep gratitude to Dr. Robert L. Kahn, who has been a partner in every step of this endeavor. The authors would also like to thank Masterpiece Living, LLC and Beacon Communities for their collaboration on this project, as well as Dr. Jessica Hehman, whose help and generosity in identifying excellent student research assistants to assist with the intervention was greatly appreciated. N.W. and his work on this paper was supported in part by grants from the National Institutes of Health (UL1TR000433, UL1TR002240, AG024824-12).

show substantial average decline with age, one can find older persons with minimal physiologic loss, or none at all … These people might be viewed as having aged successfully with regard to the particular variable under study" (Rowe & Kahn, 1987). A more explicit definition came a decade later, in the *Gerontologist* (Rowe & Kahn, 1997): "We define successful aging as including three main components: low probability of disease and disease-related disability, high cognitive and physical functional capacity, and active engagement with life." Along with these efforts at definition was the authors' recommendation to researchers: Gerontological research should incorporate the distinction between usual and successful aging. That in turn means including the full functional range of the outcome variables under study. It also means undertaking the task of explaining the heterogeneity of older people with respect to these functions.

To the extent that research on aging during the past 10 or 15 years has undertaken that task, Rowe and Kahn's hopes for the field are being realized. At the same time, there have been unintended effects, as represented by some of its major critics. The criticisms range from friendly suggestions to accusations. Examples include Dillaway and Byrnes's (2009) argument that using the concept risks "buying into an exclusionary, ageist, and even discriminatory perspective." Masoro (2001) was no less critical but more specific. He stated that the concept of successful aging downplays the importance of genetics, ignores the species-determined deterioration of late life, and is therefore misleading to individuals and policymakers. Current research on aging shows little or no evidence of the dire predictions. It would be difficult to argue that the concept has stifled genetics research. In fact, research on genetic risk factors has increased and policymakers show no sign of being misled (or, unfortunately, influenced at all) by research, either in support of or contrary to the concept of successful aging. Rowe and Kahn readily agreed with Matilda Riley's (1998) observation that the successful aging model needed enlargement to include the societal factors that define the demands, opportunities, and resources to which older people must respond. In their 1998 book, the final chapter, "Prescriptions for an Aging Society," was a first attempt to address this issue and more sustained efforts are now under way.

Several critics of the Rowe–Kahn model objected to the use of the term successful, arguing that it implied failure for all but a fortunate gifted minority. Rowe and Kahn suggested that the problem with the term "successful" is cultural rather than lexicographical. The dictionary definition of successful is having a favorable or desired outcome, and some synonyms – thriving, flourishing – are consistent with their intentions for the term. They argue that their intention was to establish a multidimensional concept of successful aging, in which most people would find themselves doing well on some dimensions and less well on others. We believe they have accomplished this and their cited examples of Franklin Roosevelt and Stephen Hawking (Rowe & Kahn, 1998, p. 38), whose lives demonstrate remarkable accomplishment (success) in many respects, in spite of severe disabilities, certainly indicate a broader perspective on the meaning of the term "successful." Nevertheless, Rowe and Kahn concede that the cultural tendency to insist on dichotomies – winners and losers – has created a problem for the term.

## Lifetime Influences and Convoys of Support

The field of gerontology and geriatrics owes a great debt to Rowe and Kahn for creating the "sea change," as Pruchno (2015), regarding the aging experience, referred to it. That it did so much with a single concept must be recognized. That some modifications or further specifications would be necessary seems only a testament to how well the concept captured the field and the desire of many who continue to update and make it current. Aging in our society is changing, as is the society itself. It should come as no surprise that a concept introduced in its most modern form in 1987 requires updating or further explications. In truth, given their writings, it would be difficult to assume that Rowe and Kahn would disagree.

In this chapter, we attempt to modestly contribute to this updating by addressing the implied or explicit criticisms that the successful aging model is elitist and lacked recognition that lifetime experiences and circumstances fundamentally influence whether and how one ages, i.e., successful aging. In addition, although the basic successful aging model does include continued engagement with life, we further explicate this engagement by suggesting the incorporation of the convoy model of social relations to highlight how social relations, both contemporaneously and longitudinally, can influence all three aspects of successful aging, i.e., minimizing the risk of disease and disability, maintaining cognitive and physical functioning, and continued engagement in life.

As early as 1975, Kahn applied the term "convoy" to describe the support and socialization usually experienced by an individual embedded in a cohort or network. Kahn and Antonucci (1980; and later Antonucci & Akiyama, 1995; Antonucci et al., 2006, 2009, 2011, 2014) further explicated the model by noting the importance of the individual's personal (i.e., age, gender, race, religion) and situational (i.e., roles, norms, and expectations identified through families, organizations, and society) characteristics as factors influencing an individual's social network and social relations, all of which influence health and well-being, both contemporaneously and longitudinally. We propose that the incorporation of the convoy model of social relations into the successful aging conceptualization will permit individualization in terms of specific personal and situational characteristics and social relations as important determinants of an individualized conceptualization of health and well-being. This provides the potential to age successfully to individuals from all economic strata and with a wide range of life experiences. Further, an important benefit of incorporating the convoy model is that since social relations are a naturally occurring phenomenon, they are accessible and available to all, rather than an elite few. At the same time, the model permits further specification according to the unique personal and situational characteristics of the individual. In the following sections we review two experimental interventions aimed at improving the probability of successful aging. The first conducted among a more advantaged population, and the second in a less advantaged population. By focusing on a less advantaged population and naturally occurring opportunities therein, we begin to address one criticism of the successful aging model and interventions based on its premises, i.e., the model ignores those with fewer lifetime material resources. A cause for considerable optimism, successful aging intervention showed modest but significant effects in *both* populations. Also important, social networks and the resources they provide were individualized for each circumstance but, nevertheless, played an important role in the optimization of both interventions.

## Masterpiece Living: An Experiment in Successful Aging

A research experiment based on Rowe and Kahn's model was initiated in two Florida Masterpiece Living Continuous Care Retirement Communities (CCRCs). The two CCRCs are expensive and are, therefore, generally populated by affluent people who can reasonably be described as benefitting from a lifetime or near lifetime of advantaged circumstances. The research is best described as an ambitious pilot study in an independent living, relatively luxurious, setting. (Toni Antonucci joined the study team after the initial study design and data collection).

Experimental changes were introduced in five areas. Changes in physical facilities were made as needed to provide ample space and equipment for exercise (e.g., treadmills, stationary bicycles, step machines, weights). Swimming pools included ramps for easy access and water was maintained at temperatures comfortable for elderly people. Menus showed the calories and fat content of dishes, and chefs were brought in to plan health-relevant choices. To encourage intellectual activity, book clubs and discussion groups were organized and arrangements were made to tap local resources. For example, in a retirement community located near a university campus, residents were allowed to attend courses tuition-free. Closed-circuit television enabled residents to participate if the commute to the university was inconvenient. Opportunity and invitation to participate in voluntary activities were offered in two ways: resident involvement in the governance of the retirement community itself and visits from leaders of voluntary organizations in the larger community. Finally, a new staff position, Lifestyle Coordinator, was created. This person had overall responsibility for bringing the program to life, as well as for the collection and utilization of research data. These changes were regarded as improving the opportunity structure of the community, but not addressing directly the motivation of residents to respond. The experiment included two elements designed to do so: information to each person that dealt directly with his or her health and social support for residents who chose to share this information.

Health relevant information for each person came from three data sources: an assessment of risk factors developed by the Mayo Clinic, an assessment of mobility (gait, balance, and reach) conducted by the Lifestyle Coordinator, and the Lifestyle Review, a questionnaire that included measures of self-reported health and well-being, activities engaged in, social relations, religious and/or spiritual beliefs, and overall life satisfaction. Feedback information to individual residents came from several sources. Performance on the mobility tests was reported by the Lifestyle Coordinator. Performance on the Mayo Clinic risk factors was available to residents on the Internet. In addition, each resident received his or her own responses to the Lifestyle Review. This information showed base-line data at first, with subsequent updates showing responses after 6 months, and again after 12 months, so that each resident could see gain, loss, or stability in each domain.

When the initial (baseline) information had been distributed, residents were invited to meet in small groups to discuss results and plan appropriate responses. In these informal feedback sessions, each resident had the average responses for all participants, plus his or her own data, and national norms. No resident had information about any other individual. How much personal information was shared in the course of group discussion thus became a matter of individual choice and, as might be expected, people differed greatly in what they chose to reveal. These discussions, with the Lifestyle Coordinator present as facilitator, included plans for individual improvement, suggestions for staff support and assistance, and proposals for improving facilities and equipment. Pairs or small subgroups sometimes formed to work together in various ways. Thus social integration, social support, and personal feedback were all integral parts of the program.

Results indicate that overall perceptions of health from 2002 to 2003, the first year of the program, showed modest gains in the proportion of residents who rated their own health as excellent or very good. The proportion who considered their health only good dropped slightly, while there was a slight increase in the number who rated their health as only fair. Whether this reflected a more realistic assessment is unclear. With respect to medical and lifestyle risk factors, participants in this experiment showed reduction in all five of the measured risk factors: blood pressure, blood sugar, cholesterol/HDL ratio, triglyceride level, and overweight. They also showed improvement, sometimes very small, in the six lifestyle risk factors: lack of exercise, excess dietary fat, inadequate amount of fruits and vegetables, cigarette smoking, excessive use of alcohol (defined as more than two drinks per day for men and one for women), and failure to fasten seatbelts while driving or riding in a car. Participants showed improvement in all these risk factors, although some improvements were not statistically significant. And finally, residents showed improvement in mobility – measured in gait, balance, and stability in the measurement of reach.

**Comparisons with national data**: The overall pattern of these experimental findings shows small but consistent improvement – "stability-plus." The absence of a control group makes interpretation difficult. Some comparison can be made, however, with data from Americans' Changing Lives (ACL), a longitudinal survey of a national sample of 3,617 adults (House et al., 2005). The national data show that the proportion of people without functional limitations decreases with age. The onset of significant decline, however, is strongly affected by level of education, which of course is an indicator of socioeconomic status. Most people with the highest level of education are quite free of functional limitations until age 75; people with the least education show some limitations by age 75. But by age 85, most people, regardless of education level, report some limitations in function. This last point seems especially relevant for interpreting the experimental results. The experimental participants, aged 80 or more, showed stability and small improvements at a time of life when even stability is an accomplishment (for detailed data on the experiment, see Petrossi, 2005). These results left us eager to test the findings among people less advantaged in socioeconomic status, and to do so with a stronger experimental design.

## The MacHouse Affordable Housing Intervention

The MacArthur Foundation (see Figure 26.1) offered an opportunity for the current authors, along with R. L. Kahn, through their How Housing Matters initiative, to adapt and implement the successful aging based intervention in affordable senior housing. Generally speaking, affordable housing is means-tested government subsidized housing. These properties are occupied by people currently living in limited financial circumstances. In fact, they most often have experienced a lifetime of limited financial resources (see Figure 26.1, Box A). Our goal was to explore the extent to which we could develop, create, support, and encourage changes within the communities that would improve the living circumstances of these individuals, but do so in a manner that could be accomplished with limited additional individual or institutional resources and, therefore, be sustained after the completion of the intervention. The changes made were multifaceted and grounded in the successful aging model's three main tenants of minimizing the risk of disease and disability, maintaining mental and physical function, and continuing engagement with life. We saw an opportunity to address multiple aspects of the model with each programmatic aspect and activity implemented. Specifically, we tried to include a social component to all aspects of the intervention (see Figure 26.1, Box B). For example, a physical activity program was implemented in group settings so as to encourage exercise, while simultaneously fostering social connections, engagement, and support between residents. We felt that although these residents did not have significant financial resources, they did have social networks that occurred naturally, could be used to encourage each other, and were, therefore, potential resources to facilitate successful aging.

**Comparison of Affordable Senior Housing and CCRC Residents**

**Demographics** (see Figure 26.1, Box C1): Demographic differences across the two populations are described in Table 26.1. Masterpiece Living provided the CCRC data. The affordable senior housing resident data were collected as baseline data for the MacHouse project in 2012–13. These data are from three affordable senior housing communities.

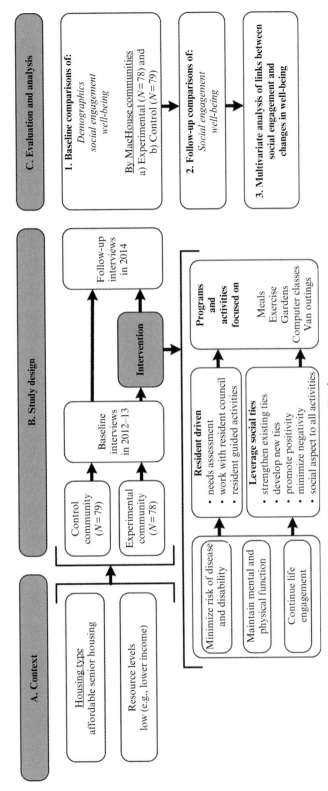

**Figure 26.1.** *The MacHouse Affordable Housing Intervention Study*

Table 26.1 *Demographic comparison of older adults living in affordable housing and CCRCs*

| | CCRC residents (N = 10,114) | Affordable housing residents (N = 157) | | |
| --- | --- | --- | --- | --- |
| | | Experimental (N = 78) | Control (N = 79) | |
| | | Mean (SD) or % | | Sig.[c] |
| Age (60–99) | 83.3 (7.0) | 75.1 (9.8) | 73.7 (8.9) | |
| Gender (% Female) | 67 | 83 | 70 | * |
| Education Level (%) | | | | |
| Less than H.S. | 2 | 16 | 24 | |
| H.S. degree | 15 | 35 | 22 | |
| Some college or more | 83 | 49 | 54 | |
| Marital Status (%)[a] | | | | |
| Married/In Relationship | 49 | 10 | 4 | |
| Widowed | 43 | 37 | 33 | |
| Single[b] | 9 | 53 | 63 | |
| Years Living in Community (%)[a] | | | | |
| <1 year | 11 | 22 | 27 | |
| 1–2 years | 19 | 21 | 20 | |
| 3–5 years | 38 | 24 | 20 | |
| >5 years | 33 | 33 | 33 | |

*$p$-value< 0.05.
[a] Percentages do not sum to 100 percent due to rounding to the nearest whole number.
[b] Includes divorced, separated, and never married.
[c] Test of significant difference between experimental and control communities. Mean differences tested with independent samples t test and proportion differences tested with chi-square test.

The affordable housing residents were younger, more likely to be female, and less educated compared to the CCRC residents. They were also less likely to be married, more likely to be single, but nearly equally likely to be widowed. Lastly, affordable housing and CCRC residents resided in their current housing for similar periods of time, with 33 percent of both groups having lived in their current communities for 5 or more years. The MacHouse experimental and control communities were very similar demographically, except that the experimental communities had significantly more females.

**Social Engagement**: We also compared baseline data for the two groups of residents in terms of social engagement (see Table 26.2). At baseline, the affordable senior housing residents reported similar levels of social engagement as the CCRC residents. This included similarly high levels of ability to get help and support from others, satisfaction with their communities, and frequency of getting out of their individual housing units (e.g., apartments). These similarities suggest social resources are naturally occurring in both housing contexts. One exception we found was that affordable senior housing residents reported participating in social activities less often than their CCRC counterparts. However, this difference we expect may be more a function of the greater resources available in CCRCs leading to more activities than a difference in propensity to participate in social activities. Lastly, in terms of good social ties with other residents, a measure not available among the CCRC residents, we found that affordable senior housing residents at baseline reported that between most and all of their relationships with other residents and staff within the community were good. When comparing the experimental and control affordable senior housing communities to each other there were no statistically significant differences in social engagement. Overall these similarities in social connections and engagement between CCRC and affordable senior housing residents provide evidence of social relations as a naturally occurring resource independent of material resource availability. Furthermore, the findings also indicate the potential for social relationships in affordable senior housing to be an important resource for promoting health and well-being in a context with relatively fewer economic resources.

**Well-Being**: We also compared baseline well-being measures (see Table 26.2) for the two groups. The affordable senior housing residents from both the MacHouse experimental and control communities reported more visits to emergency room physicians in the past year, more falls in the past year, lower self-rated health, greater limitation of social activities because of health (i.e., functional health limitations), less energy, worse sleep quality, and less frequent engagement in muscle strengthening activities compared to CCRC residents. Affordable senior housing residents in the MacHouse experimental communities were similar to CCRC residents in terms of life satisfaction and memory, while residents in the control community were similar to CCRC residents in terms of frequency of aerobic activity. Lastly in terms of feeling depressed, the MacHouse experimental community residents reported feeling so the least often, followed by CCRC residents, and control community residents reporting feeling depressed the most often. The only significant difference when comparing residents in the MacHouse communities was in regard to participation on moderate intensity aerobic activity, with residents in the experimental communities reporting more frequent activity. In contrast to the many similarities observed in terms of social engagement when comparing CCRC to affordable senior housing residents, comparison on well-being indicates many disparities, with affordable senior housing residents generally being worse off. These findings are consistent with the literature and empirical data cited above from the ACL study linking socioeconomic differences with disparities in well-being outcomes in later life. These comparisons also highlighted the great need for and importance of implementing a successful aging program to promote well-being

Table 26.2 *Social engagement comparison of older adults living in affordable housing versus CCRCs*

| | CCRC residents (N=10,114) | Affordable housing residents (N=157) | | | | | | |
| --- | --- | --- | --- | --- | --- | --- | --- | --- |
| | | Experimental (N=78) | | Control (N=79) | | | | |
| | | Mean (SD) | | | | | | |
| | | Baseline | Follow-up | Baseline | Follow-up | 1 | 2 | 3 |
| **Social Engagement** | | | | | | | | |
| Satisfaction with getting help/support from others[a] | 4.2 (0.7) | 4.1 (0.9) | 4.4 (0.7) | 4.2 (0.8) | 4.3 (0.8) | ** | | |
| Satisfaction with community[a] | 4.3 (0.7) | 4.3 (0.9) | 4.3 (0.9) | 4.2 (0.9) | 4.3 (0.8) | | | |
| How often get out of house/apartment[b] | 4.4 (1.0) | 4.4 (0.8) | 4.4 (0.8) | 4.6 (0.7) | 4.4 (0.9) | | | * |
| How often participate in social activities[c] | 4.4 (1.4) | 3.9 (1.5) | 4.1 (1.5) | 4.1 (1.8) | 4.0 (1.8) | | | |
| Good relationships in the community[d] | N/A | 4.1 (0.9) | | 4.1 (0.9) | | - | - | - |
| Good relationships with staff | | | 4.6 (0.6) | | 4.7 (0.5) | - | - | - |
| Good relationships with other residents | | | 3.9 (0.9) | | 4.1 (0.9) | - | - | - |
| **Well-Being** | | | | | | | | |
| Life satisfaction[e] | 4.0 (0.8) | 4.0 (1.0) | 4.0 (0.9) | 3.9 (1.0) | 3.8 (1.1) | | | |
| Depressed (past 4 weeks)[f] | 1.7 (0.8) | 1.6 (1.0) | 1.8 (1.1) | 1.9 (1.1) | 2.0 (1.1) | | | |
| Memory compared to others[g] | 3.5 (0.9) | 3.5 (1.0) | 3.6 (0.9) | 3.6 (1.0) | 3.8 (1.0) | | | |
| Times seen by ER physician in past year[h] | 1.4 (0.7) | 1.9 (1.1) | 1.7 (1.0) | 1.7 (0.9) | 1.8 (1.0) | | | |
| Falls in past year[i] | 1.5 (0.8) | 1.9 (1.1) | 1.6 (1.0) | 1.6 (1.0) | 1.7 (1.0) | * | | |

| | | | | | | |
|---|---|---|---|---|---|---|
| Overall self-rated health (past 4 weeks)[j] | 4.4 (1.0) | 3.6 (1.1) | 3.7 (1.1) | 3.9 (1.0) | 3.7 (1.0) | * |
| Physical health limitations (past 4 weeks)[k] | 1.7 (0.9) | 1.9 (1.2) | 2.3 (1.3) | 1.8 (1.2) | 2.1 (1.4) | * |
| Amount of energy (past 4 weeks)[l] | 3.4 (0.8) | 3.3 (1.0) | 3.3 (1.0) | 3.3 (1.1) | 3.0 (1.0) | * |
| Sleep quality (past 4 weeks)[m] | 3.2 (0.7) | 2.9 (1.0) | 2.9 (1.0) | 2.9 (1.0) | 2.9 (1.0) | |
| Participation in moderate intensity aerobic activity[n] | 3.4 (2.0) | 4.2 (2.0) | 3.8 (2.1) | 3.4 (2.2) | 3.2 (2.2) | * |
| Participation in muscle strengthening activity[n] | 2.6 (1.8) | 2.3 (1.8) | 2.5 (2.0) | 2.4 (2.0) | 1.9 (1.7) | * |

*$p$-value < 0.05; **$p$-value < 0.01.

[a] 1 (very dissatisfied) to 5 (very satisfied).

[b] 1 (less than once per week) to 5 (two or more times a day).

[c] 1 (never/not currently participating) to 6 (5–7 times per week).

[d] 1 (never/not currently participating) to 6 (5–7 times per week); at baseline was asked as "Would you say that all, most, some, a few, or none of your relationships *with other residents and staff are good?*" and at follow-up was asked *"With other residents are good?"*

[e] 1 (very dissatisfied) to 5 (very satisfied).

[f] 1 (not at all) to 5 (extremely).

[g] 1 (much worse) to 5 (much better).

[h] 1 (not at all) to 4 (3+ times).

[i] 1 (0) to 5 (7+).

[j] 1 (very poor) to 6 (excellent).

[k] 1 (not at all) to 5 (could not do usual social activities).

[l] 1 (almost none) to 5 (very much energy).

[m] 1 (very bad) to 4 (very good).

[n] 1 (not currently participating in activity) to 6 (5–7 times a week). 1 = test of difference between experimental baseline and follow-up scores.

2 = test of difference between experimental baseline and follow-up scores.

3 = test of difference between control baseline and follow-up scores.

in affordable senior housing communities. Furthermore, the availability of naturally occurring social connections and resources within the affordable senior housing communities suggested a good avenue and central theme through which to accomplish these goals of helping the residents successfully age.

Overview of Intervention

**To Begin** (see Figure 26.1, Box B): The project was a partnership of three organizations representing a non-profit educational institution (the University of Michigan), a for-profit life-style intervention corporation (Masterpiece Living), and a non-profit housing organization (Beacon Communities, formerly known as ABHOW), with ties to government programs such as Housing and Urban Development (HUD). Our first step was to hire a Life Style Coordinator, interviewers, and research staff. The Life Style Coordinator, a key position, would be the on-site supervisor. For interviewers and research staff we hired local students from a nearby college upon the recommendation of a professor. In addition, a number of local staff volunteered to be trained and also conduct interviews.

**Preliminary Steps**: The first official phase of the project was the baseline interviews, data from which were reported above. After several months of preparation piloting the questionnaire and training interviewers, we organized Kick-Off Day in late 2012. This was widely advertised, included local dignitaries, members of the research team, games, prizes, and a festive lunch. We explained to the residents that the goal of the project was to improve the quality of their life by reinforcing what they liked and addressing things they did not. We emphasized that all information was confidential. The staff was amazed that in the end we obtained an 80 percent baseline response rate.

After the baseline interviews, we began the intervention phase of the project. We emphasized to residents that we were only interested in interventions that the residents wanted and that could continue after we left. Based on resident and staff feedback we decided to focus on meals, exercise, computers, vegetable gardens, and outings. Also, our aim was to incorporate a social element into all aspects of the intervention in order to draw upon and continue to foster a sense of community, and within community, obligation for supporting and helping others. Below we provide an overview regarding each aspect of the intervention.

**Meals**: Given evidence that older people often do not provide themselves with nutritious meals, we invested heavily in this intervention. There were complaints about the quality of the food, that it was often cold, and that the atmosphere was not welcoming. We met with the food preparers about addressing these complaints. The Life Style Coordinator assisted by adding table games, announcements, and other activities during the congregate meals. And finally, the meals were provided free to the residents (subsidized by the project) for a limited time. Participation increased threefold; residents were appreciative. Staff reported that the residents were more engaged, energetic, and happier, they felt, because of the nutritious meals. However, there were also downsides. As soon as we reduced the subsidy, although the meals were still subsidized by 50 percent, the number of participants dropped. Clearly, cost was an issue. Residents also reported that food still sometimes arrived cold and was occasionally of very low quality. We feel it is important to note that in addition to nutrition, these group meals provided a significant opportunity for social engagement, networking, and activity planning.

**Exercise**: Another important area was exercise. Both of the two intervention residences included "gyms," but they were quite limited in terms of size and equipment. The Life Style Coordinator organized programs for residents of varying functional abilities, e.g., individual and group walking activities, tai chi, chair yoga, and chair exercises. We also needed more exercise equipment. Nu-Step provided 8 Recumbent Cross Trainers (6 on loan and 2 donated). The Keiser Corporation lent low impact pneumatic resistance equipment for strength building activities. The larger gym was renovated to be more user-friendly and staff members were trained to lead group exercise classes. Participation rates soared and most classes were at capacity.

**Gardens**: Another project involved vegetable gardens. Several residents were very interested. After much discussion and research, including consultation with local experts, it was decided that we would begin with four raised gardens as a pilot project. The Life Style Coordinator bought supplies including soil, plants, and tools. Residents with garden boxes added their own plants and other accoutrements. There was much excitement; many residents enjoyed watching the gardens grow. Again, some problems did arise. The person who initially agreed to lead this effort had some health problems and disputes with other residents. She resigned from her position and quit the garden project, though she did eventually return. Another woman watered the gardens incessantly, her own and everyone else's. This made several people angry and some felt she ruined their garden. Residents then asked if they could move their gardens onto their private balconies, thus protecting them from the "watering" lady. Permission was granted. However, this development reduced the group and social element of the program.

**Computer Classes**: One resident offered to provide computer classes to the residents. He was willing to teach others how to send emails and how to use Skype. There were publicly available computers and some residents had their own laptops. Despite interest in the program, there were barriers, including the computers needed repairs. Fortunately, these problems were addressed, resolved, and the computer classes began.

**Van Outings**: In the original proposal we highlighted the importance of group outings and emphasized the need to offset the cost of van rides. Trips for local shopping increased, as did leisure trips to nearby and distant points of interest. However, even this did not proceed flawlessly. For example, the van was old and in need of several thousand dollars of repairs. Fortunately, we were able to fix the van, but this was clearly a temporary fix. At the project conclusion a number of residents were planning to fund raising campaign and/or solicit funds from both external and internal sources for a new, larger bus, a wonderful example of naturally occurring social resources being mobilized to address group goals.

**Unforeseen Circumstances and Unintended Consequences**: We did learn that working in less affluent circumstances is associated with a constant array of challenges. In addition to the issues outlined above, other, more general, difficulties arose. There was an almost complete turnover in administrative local community staff during the project period. Major construction projects began, finished, and changed with almost no consultation by corporate staff. As the examples illustrate, several negative serendipitous or purposefully unfortunate events occurred.

In sum, our efforts to implement programs and activities that promoted well-being while simultaneously encouraging engagement with life and others, both within and outside community, were both frustrating and rewarding. While residents were definitely suspicious initially, the residents living in the two experimental communities were incredibly thankful when successful interventions were achieved. We recognized that the true test of the intervention's success is the degree to which changes endure and residents are empowered after the project ends.

**Follow-up interviews** (see Figure 26.1, Box B): In 2014, approximately 14 months after the last of the baseline interviews were conducted we began the process of re-interviewing all the residents at the two experimental communities and the control community.

**Changes in social engagement** (see Figure 26.1, Box C2): From baseline to follow-up the affordable senior housing residents living in the MacHouse experimental communities reported a significant increase in terms of how satisfied they were with their ability to get help and support from others. In all other aspects of social engagement (satisfaction with community, getting out of their apartment, and frequency of participation in social activities) the residents showed stability over time. Residents living in the control community showed similar levels of stability over time in terms of social engagement and quality of relationships, with the exception of reporting a significant decline in how often they got out of their apartments. This suggests intervention efforts focused on social relations and increasing opportunities for social activities within the experimental communities may have made an impact.

**Changes in well-being** (see Figure 26.1, Box C2): As for changes in well-being, residents in the MacHouse experimental communities reported a significant reduction in the number of falls experienced in the past year. On one dimension (health-related functional imitations), residents reported a significant decline from baseline to follow-up over a year later. In all other areas of well-being (life satisfaction, feeling depressed, memory, ER visits, self-rated health, energy, sleep quality, and participation in both aerobic and muscle strengthening activity) the residents showed stability. In contrast, and as preliminary evidence of the success of the intervention, residents in the control community showed no improvement in well-being. In fact they reported significant declines in self-rated health, energy, and frequency of participation in muscle strengthening activity. On all other well-being domains they showed stability. For the most part, reports of both social engagement and well-being were largely stable for residents in both the experimental and control communities. Stability at this stage of the life span and in this generally disadvantaged group, as discussed earlier, can be viewed as a success. Furthermore, within the experimental communities, an improvement such as those observed in the area of fall reduction can be viewed as a higher-level indication of success.

**Links between social engagement and well-being (see** Figure 26.1, Box C3)**:** To examine associations between social engagement and well-being among the affordable senior housing residents we conducted multiple regression models separately for the experimental and control communities. These 11 models predicted each aspect of well-being at follow-up, and included the five social engagement indicators (see Table 26.2) at follow-up as predictors, controlling for the relevant well-being indicator at baseline. Many interesting findings were observed, highlighting the important role of social engagement in promoting positive changes in well-being over time. Among residents living in the MacHouse experimental communities, more frequent participation in social activities at follow-up was associated with an increase in life satisfaction. Contrary to our expectation, greater participation in social activities was also associated with an increase in falls, potentially due to residents being more active. In contrast to this counterintuitive finding, residents who reported getting out of their apartments more often reported both a decline in health-related functional limitations, as well as an increase in energy.

Among residents living in the MacHouse control community, greater satisfaction with one's ability to get needed help and support was associated with an increase in life satisfaction, and declines in feeling depressed and the number of falls experienced in the past year. Similarly, and as expected, getting out of the apartment more often was associated with an increase in aerobic activity, and greater participation in social activities was associated with both an increase in self-rated health and a decrease in functional limitations.

Overall these findings highlight the positive role of social engagement and social relations in facilitating improvements in multiple aspects of well-being. The important role of social relations in the control community highlights the naturally occurring nature of social relations and their ability to help older adults successfully age. In the context of the experimental communities, we found success in providing increased opportunities for residents to get out of their apartments and participate in activities. However, the findings also give guidance that increased opportunities for social activities may need to also be paired with fall prevention programming.

## Conclusion and Future Perspectives

The Rowe and Kahn model of successful aging has fundamentally changed our view of aging from a deficit to a resource model. Nevertheless, attention is needed to assure that successful aging includes people of all types, histories, and resources. Successful aging should include not only those rich in material resources and, thereby uniquely privileged with regard to disease and disability, cognitive and physical functioning and engagement in life. Interventions within privileged communities indicate that success is possible in late life. Results from the intervention among less advantaged populations indicate that improvement and "success" can also be achieved among people who have experienced a lifetime of significantly greater challenges. We hypothesized, and results support, the suggestion that integrating the convoy model of social relations into the successful aging model will help facilitate achieving this goal. As we have shown, social networks provide a naturally occurring resource available to all individuals, including those with limited material resources. We suggest that this resource be integrated into future conceptualizations of and interventions designed to maximize successful aging for people of all ages and backgrounds.

## References

Antonucci, T. C., Akiyama, H. (1995). Convoys of social relations: Family and friendships within a life span context. In R. Blieszner & V. H. Bedford(Eds.), *Handbook of Aging and the Family* (pp. 355–72). Westport, CT: Greenwood Press.

Antonucci, T. C., Ajrouch, K. J., Birditt, K. S. (2006). Social relations in the third age: Assessing strengths and challenges using the Convoy Model. In K. W. Schaie (Series Ed.) and J. B. James, P. Wink (Vol. Eds.), *Annual Review of Gerontology and Geriatrics: Vol. 26. The Crown of Life Dynamics of the Early Postretirement Period* (pp. 193–209). New York: Springer Publishing Co.

Antonucci, T. C., Birditt, K. S., Akiyama, H. (2009). Convoys of social relations: An interdisciplinary approach. In V. Bengston, M. Silverstein, N. Putney & D. Gans (Eds.), *Handbook of Theories of Aging*. New York: Springer Publishing Company.

Antonucci, T. C., Birditt, K. S., Ajrouch, K. (2011). Convoys of social relations: Past, present, and future. In K. L. Fingerman, C.A. Berg, J. Smith & T. C. Antonucci (Eds.), *Handbook of Lifespan Development*. New York: Springer Publishing Company, pp. 161–82.

Antonucci, T. C., Ajrouch, K. J., Birditt, K. S. (2014). The convoy model: Explaining social relations from a multidisciplinary perspective. *The Gerontologist*, 54(1), 82–92.

Baltes, P. B., Baltes, M. M. (1990). Psychological perspectives on successful aging: The model of selective optimization with compensation. In E. B. Baltes & M.M. Baltes (Eds.), *Successful Aging: Perspectives from the Behavioral Sciences* (pp. 1–34). New York: Cambridge University Press. http://dx.doi.org/10.1017/CBO9780511665684

Dillaway, H. E., Byrnes, M. (2009). Reconsidering successful aging a call for renewed and expanded academic critiques and conceptualizations. *Journal of Applied Gerontology*, 28(6), 702–22. http://dx.doi.org/10.1177/0733464809333882

House, J. S., Lantz, P. M., Herd, P. (2005). Continuity and change in the social stratification of aging and health over the life course: evidence from a nationally representative longitudinal study from 1986 to 2001/2002 (Americans' Changing Lives Study). *The Journals of Gerontology Series B: Psychological Sciences and Social Sciences*, 60(Special Issue 2), S15–S26.

Masoro, E. J. (2001). "Successful aging"-Useful or misleading concept?. *The Gerontologist*, 41(3), 415–18.

Petrossi, K. H. (2005). *Expanding the science of successful aging: Older adults living in continuing care retirement communities (ccrcs) (Doctoral dissertation, University of South Florida).*

Pruchno, R. (2015). Successful aging: Contentious past, productive future. The *Gerontologist*, 55(1), 1–4. doi: https://doi.org/10.1093/geront/gnv002

Riley, M. W. (1998). Successful aging. *The Gerontologist*, 38(2), 151.

Rowe, J. W., Kahn, R. L. (1987). Human aging: usual and successful. *Science*, 237(4811), 143–9. http://dx.doi.org/10.1126/science.3299702

(1997). Successful aging. *The Gerontologist*, 37(4), 433–40. http://dx.doi.org/10.1093/geront/37.4.433

(1998). *Successful Aging*. New York: Random House.

# 27 Defining "Success" in Exceptional Longevity

Oscar Ribeiro and Lia Araújo

## Introduction

Demographic aging has been one of the most crucial phenomena of the last and current centuries. A notable trend of the global aging process is the increasing longevity of contemporary populations and the aging of the older population itself. The oldest-old group (85+) is growing faster than any younger segment of the population, and for the first time in human history it is becoming normal to experience old-old age (European Commission, 2014). Within this frame, reaching 100 years old is likely to become more common.

In 2015, there were nearly half a million centenarians worldwide, more than four times as many as in 1990, and projections suggest there will be 3.7 million in 2050, and up to more than 10 million centenarians in 2100 (United Nations, 2015). This growing number of individuals reaching advanced ages posits important questions about the need for understanding and treating pathological aging (e.g., detecting early prodromes of neurocognitive disorders, such as Alzheimer's disease), but also for differentiating "successful" aging from normal aging among the oldest-old.

Aging often is not a matter of chronology, but of restricted activity, and those who have reached the landmark of 100 years old are frequently portrayed as a model for healthy aging both in the media and across studies within the gerontology field. There is some evidence that many centenarians are healthy and independent for most of their lives (Hitt et al., 1999), and proofs of their resilience and psychological robustness are documented (Zeng & Shen, 2010). But as it happens with most complex phenotypes, exceptional longevity is thought to reflect a wide range of influences (e.g., genetic factors, lifestyle choices, environment), and defining what it is to be "successful" at 100 years seems to be far more complex than defining longevity.

Today it is generally accepted that chronological age is vastly inadequate for classifying the level of success among individuals who reach up to the age of 100 or more, and it is also acknowledged that aging successfully is not just a matter of having the right genes or having the best material resources – it also depends on how individuals actively regulate their life and behaviors to optimize health and well-being. But what are the conceptualizations of successful aging in exceptional longevity? And what do we measure when assessing successful aging in the oldest-old? This chapter surveys the breadth of definitions and operationalization of such concepts by providing a scope review on how success has been approached in centenarian studies.

## The Roots of Successful Aging and the Concept's Complexity

The most widely used definition of what it means to be "successful" in later life derives from the pioneering work of Rowe and Kahn (1987), who posited that successful aging is on the upper end of a continuum that extends from pathology to normal aging. Their definition, extensively studied in the MacArthur's Studies (e.g., Berkman et al., 1993), is based on objective measures used by researchers to assess freedom from chronic disease and disability, along with high physical and cognitive functioning, and social engagement. Although other models have conceptualized successful adaptation to aging in developmental terms, including interlocking components (e.g., Baltes' selective optimization and compensation model; Baltes, 1997), or by positing that older adults prioritize the goal of emotional regulation (e.g., the socio-emotional selectivity theory; Carstensen & Turk-Charles, 1994), it is Rowe and Kahn's classic definition that has stimulated the largest body of research.

Either by aiming to further elaborate on what exactly constitutes successful aging and/or quantify the number of individuals who can be labeled as "successful agers" (e.g., Hank, 2011), and/or how to promote successful aging in practical context, research on the successful aging concept has grown increasingly over the last years, stimulating strong debates among researchers worldwide. In 2005, when summarizing the available scientific literature, Bowling and Dieppe (2005) identified two distinct approaches within theoretical definitions: (1) the biomedical models, which consider absence of disease and good physical and mental functioning as successful aging, and (2) the sociopsychological models, which emphasize life satisfaction, social functioning and participation, or psychological resources. A year later, in a comprehensive review of larger quantitative studies, Depp and Jeste (2006) came up with at least 10 different domains in English-language articles published between 1978 and 2005 and available in PubMed. The most frequently appearing components were disability and/or physical functioning (26 out of 29 studies), followed by cognitive function (13), life satisfaction/well-being (9), and social and productive functioning (8). In a more recent publication, Cosco and colleagues (2013) presented a review of successful aging studies, published before March 2013, including non-English articles. Of the 105 operational definitions that the authors were able to identify, the majority included physiological constructs ($n = 97$), followed by engagement constructs ($n = 52$), well-being constructs ($n = 51$), personal resources ($n = 27$), and extrinsic factors ($n = 6$).

Although different investigators agree that successful aging is a multidimensional construct, some studies still present single constructs (34 according to Cosco and colleagues' mentioned review); furthermore, physical health variables have been studied more often than psychological ones, such as cognition and emotion (Jeste et al., 2010). Echoing the need for accounting both medical and non-medical aspects when defining "success" at old age, several scholars have debated the dimensions that should be included in its conceptualization and operationalization. A remarkable work has been developed regarding this issue, and several multidimensional models that include physical, social, and psychological components have been proposed. That was the case of Férnandez-Ballesteros (2011), who presented a structure with five independent factors: health, cognition, activity, affect, and physical fitness. Health was the most important factor, accounting for 21.43 percent of the variance, followed by cognition (account variance 10.98 percent), and activity (account variance 7.60 percent). An important addition to previous models is the emotional and evaluative component of successful aging (account variance 7.02 percent), which was integrated by positive mood, life satisfaction, and perceived self-efficacy for aging. The fifth factor, physical fitness (account variance 6.71 percent), included physical activity and nutrition as indicators of healthy aging (Férnandez-Ballesteros, 2011).

Also Young and colleagues (2009) proposed a multidimensional model of successful aging, postulating that even in the presence of chronic illness successful aging can occur if an individual uses adaptive mechanisms and resources to compensate for physical limitations and environmental challenges; in doing so, it is possible to achieve a strong sense of well-being, quality-of-life, and personal fulfillment. This model of successful aging, as well as several others focusing on additional factors such as leisure activities (e.g., Lee et al., 2011) and spirituality (e.g., Crowther et al., 2002), has called for modifications to the biomedically based MacArthur model of successful aging. It is currently estimated that there are at least 100 variations to the model (Rowe & Kahn, 2015).

When compiling the non-biomedical factors associated with successful aging used in the recent research, Carver and Buchanan (2016) revealed that common constructs included engagement, optimism and/or positive attitude, resilience, spirituality and/or religiosity, self-efficacy and/or self-esteem, and gerotranscendence. According to this authors' scoping review, these contemporary constructs can be used in successful aging model building in the hopes of encouraging future research that is inclusive for those aging with illness. Molton and Yorkston (2016) recently highlighted this concern when claiming for a nuanced application of the successful aging paradigm in those individuals with long-term physical disabilities.

Along with the increased recognition of widening the scope of the successful aging definition, a complementary line of research on subjectively determined successful aging has been gaining force (e.g., Pruchno et al., 2010; Jeste et al., 2013). Several studies that include subjective perceptions on aging have described that some older adults report feeling successful aging despite substantive physical challenges (e.g., Von Faber et al., 2001). Cosco's systematic review and comparison of quantitative operational definitions of successful aging – with qualitative, layperson perspectives – revealed that there are noticeable differences between researchers and laypersons. Whereas qualitative studies demonstrated a greater emphasis on psychosocial aspects of successful aging (e.g., attitude), quantitative studies were generally bio-medically focused, stressing aspects related to functioning/disability (Cosco et al., 2014). Again, the need for recognizing the concept's complexity and enlarging its breadth is highlighted.

Presently, successful aging remains a somewhat elusive construct, as no single dimension or attribute used to measure the construct appears to be satisfactory, and strong divergences exists between objective and subjective definitions (Depp & Jeste, 2010). Considering that longevity may not necessarily be the ideal phenotype of successful aging, one important question relates to how it has been described in extremely old age and if centenarians may constitute a paradigm of successful aging.

## A Scope Review on Successful Aging in Centenarians

The exceptional capacity of some centenarians to deal and overcome constrains in such an advanced age has motivated many researchers to look for associated key factors and traits. Over the last years several papers examined centenarians' phenotype as a model for healthy aging (e.g., Hitt et al., 1999; Engberg et al., 2009) and successful aging (e.g., Motta et al., 2005; Cho et al., 2012). In order to evaluate the joint frequency of "successful aging" and "centenarian" labels in journal articles over the last years, we performed a scan of the literature across PubMed and ISI Web of Knowledge. The search strategy included "successful aging" or "successful ageing," along with the term "centenarians" to be present in the title, keywords, and/or abstract. Searches were conducted initially for a 20 year span (between September 1, 1996, and September 1, 2016), but considering the dearth of publications with the specific word combinations, all literature published before September 1, 2016, was considered eligible for inclusion. For selecting the studies in the first stage, titles, keywords, and abstracts were read using the following exclusion criteria: studies relying on samples with no centenarians, and studies from biological sciences (e.g., genetics). In the second stage, all the full-texts ($n = 27$) were read. Studies without approaching a successful aging definition or its components ($n = 11$) and review papers ($n = 4$) were also excluded. This resulted in 12 studies, which became the focus of this scoping review (Figure 27.1).

Overall, 125 studies were identified as having the main focus on "successful aging" and "centenarians." Interestingly, the majority ($n = 97$) came from biological sciences and presented centenarians as a model of successful aging *per se*. Indeed, most of these studies only referred to successful aging in the beginning of the abstract as the paradigm represented by individuals who reach exceptional longevity (100+ years of age), and/or concluded that the results obtained with centenarians may reveal the factors of successful aging. The other 27 studies were multidisciplinary or from health/psychology/social sciences and aimed to understand how successful aging was effectively approached in oldest-old individuals. Nevertheless, 11 studies did not address successful aging,

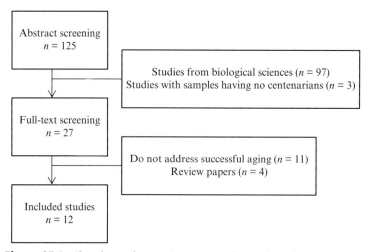

**Figure 27.1.** *Flowchart of screening process for study inclusion*

i.e., they included single references to the concept but were not consolidated studies in the sense of reporting a successful aging definition and/or its components. Information regarding the successful aging conceptualization, the main objectives of the research, sample, type of study, and main conclusions from the remaining 12 studies were extracted and summarized in Table 27.1. Aiming to provide a comprehensive summary of the definitions used of successful aging, a set of review/theoretical articles ($n = 4$) (Antonini et al., 2008; Berr et al., 2012; Martin et al., 2015; Jopp et al., 2016) were also analyzed and their main thoughts incorporated into the present analysis.

The results of this review demonstrate the recent and growing interest of this topic: nine out of the eleven papers were published in the last 6 years (from 2010 to 2016), one dates back to the 1990s (1996), and the others were published in 2005 and 2007. This reflects the recent longevity phenomenon worldwide and the fact that centenarian studies, like most centenarians themselves, have been a phenomenon of recent decades. But this can also reflect the very recent focus on their living circumstances from a psychosocial perspective (e.g., Jopp et al., 2016), and an emergent interest in understanding successful adaptations to extreme longevity within both well-established conceptual frameworks and emergent conceptualizations.

In what regards methodological issues, ten studies are quantitative studies, one is a qualitative research, and one uses both a quantitative and qualitative approach. In seven studies the sample includes only participants aged 100 and over, who are mostly female, due to the sex ratio in oldest-old samples. The other five studies also included near centenarians and younger participants, because the comparison between centenarians and octogenarians was a goal (e.g., Cho et al., 2015).

Five studies expressed a notorious concern in quantifying the number of cases falling into the category of objective "success." Although the rates vary across studies due to the wideness of criteria used to composite indices of successful aging, the number of centenarians fulfilling all domains as presented in Rowe and Kahn's (1997) original model is very low, ranging from 0.0 percent (Cho et al., 2012) to 2.8 percent (Araújo et al., 2016a). Even in studies assuming a wider range of multidimensional criteria (Cheung & Lau, 2016) or based in autonomy (Ozaki et al., 2007) and health (Motta et al., 2005), the proportion of centenarians fulfilling the criteria of "success" was 5.8 percent, 10.4 percent and 20.0 percent respectively (see Table 27.1).

Regardless of this "counting cases approach," the analysis of the 12 empirical studies evidences an effort from different researchers in comprehensively exploring the successful aging concept: some of them call on existing models, particularly Rowe and Kahn's (1997) model, Martin and Martin's (2002) Developmental Adaptation Model, and Young et al. (2009) Multidimensional concept of successful aging, but the majority present new configuration of variables, highlighting the relevance of complementary constructs and the salience of subjectivity.

## Rowe and Kahn's Legacy and the Use of Comprehensive Alternative Models

The successful aging model was assumed as a new paradigm in 1997, and Rowe and Kahn's conceptualization was the framework of important studies (e.g., MacArthur's Studies) and still is largely valued as a reference model (Martin & Gillen, 2014). Examples include research coming from large-scale studies, such as the study conducted by Hank (2011), with a sample from the Survey of Health, Ageing, and Retirement in Europe (SHARE; $n = 21,493$), and McLaughlin and colleagues (2010), with data from the USA Health and Retirement Study (HRS; $n = 37,106$), both based on Rowe and Kahn's model. However, when focusing on this review's findings, we realized that this model was only approached in three centenarian studies, and even these present different alternatives to Rowe and Kahn's objective criteria.

Araújo et al. (2016a) and Cho et al. (2012), from the Oporto Centenarian Study and the Georgia Centenarian Study, respectively, concluded that the prevalence of successful centenarians was dependent on its measurement. When confronting Rowe and Kahn's objective criteria with questions regarding centenarians' appraisals for the same domains (no major disease or disability, high physical and cognitive functioning, active engagement with life), the Portuguese researchers found that many centenarians feel successful despite not being objectively considered as so. In the same way, Cho and colleagues (2012) demonstrated that from a sample of 234 centenarians that did not fulfill all Rowe and Kahn's original criteria, 47.5 percent could be classified as "successful" if subjective health, perceived happiness, and better perceived economic status were used as definitions of successful aging (Cho et al., 2012). Later, in the third paper focusing on Rowe and Kahn's (1997) model, Cho and colleagues (2015) presented a combination of its components with Martin and Martin's (2002)

Table 27.1 *Summary of studies selected for inclusion in the scope review*

| Authors/Year | Conceptualization | Aim(s) | Sample and Method | Operationalization of SA | Conclusions |
|---|---|---|---|---|---|
| Araújo et al. (2016a) | Rowe and Kahn (1997) Successful Aging model | (1) Clarify whether centenarians are able to be successful agers according to objective and subjective criteria.<br>(2) Investigate whether socio-demographic factors, psychological, social, and economic resources are related to successful aging profiles. | 70 centenarians with cognitive capacity to self-report Mean age 109.1 (SD 1.37) Quantitative study | Domains of SA (included both objective and subjective measures):<br>– No major disease or disability<br>– High physical and cognitive functioning<br>– Active engagement with life | Centenarians do not represent the prototype of successful aging, but self-ratings demonstrate that many of them feel successful, despite not being objectively considered as such.<br>Only 1 person met simultaneously both objective and subjective criteria in all three components of successful aging (1.4%); 2 centenarians (2.8%) met exclusively the objective criteria, and 4 centenarians (5.6%) met solely the subjective criteria.<br>Those who were considered successful agers presented higher values of self-efficacy, hope, and purpose in life, as well as few difficulties in covering financial expenses. |

| Reference | Model | Objectives | Sample/Method | Domains of SA | Findings |
|---|---|---|---|---|---|
| Araújo et al. (2016b) | Young, Phelan, and Frick (2009) Multidimensional Model of Successful Aging | (1) Identify subgroups of centenarians sharing communalities in successful aging profiles. (2) Determine the role of socio-demographic factors and psychological, social, and economic resources on successful aging. | 80 centenarians with cognitive capacity to self-report Mean age 101.01 (SD 1.31) Quantitative study | Domains of SA: – Physiological domain – Cognitive domain – Well-being domain – Social domain | Two distinct clusters were grouped, with 40 centenarians in each, one of presenting better results in all domains. Male sex and better income adequacy were the best predictors of successful aging. |
| Cheung & Lau (2016) | New multidimensional model | Investigated associations of SA with biomedical and psychosocial demographic factors. | 120 near-centenarians and centenarians Age between 95–108 years Quantitative study | Domains of SA: – Physical and functional health – Psychological well-being and cognition – Social engagement and family support – Economic resources and financial security | Only a small proportion of participants fulfilled all four dimensions of SA (5.8%); 86.7% participants achieved SA on at least one dimension. Living with family or friends, high levels of optimism, fewer diseases, and fewer barriers to social activities were independent predictors of SA index score. The results also provide support for the presence of psychological resilience and cognitive reserve among very long-lived adults. |

*(cont.)*

Table 27.1 (*cont.*)

| Authors/Year | Conceptualization | Aim(s) | Sample and Method | Operationalization of SA | Conclusions |
|---|---|---|---|---|---|
| Cho et al. (2012) | Rowe and Kahn's Successful Aging model (1997) and an alternative subjective model | (1) Explore whether oldest-old adults are successful agers or not. (2) Explore whether oldest-old adults are satisfied based on the criteria of successful aging, and to expand the psychological concept of successful aging among oldest-old adults. | 375 old participants (72 octogenarians and 234 centenarians) Quantitative study | Original domains of SA: – Low probability of disease – High cognitive/physical capacity – Active engagement with life Alternative domains of SA: – Subjective health – Perceived economic status – Happiness | About 15% of octogenarians and none of centenarians satisfied all three components of successful aging. In the alternative model focused on psychosocial aspects, a total of 62.3% of octogenarians and 47.5% of centenarians were considered successful agers. The results suggest that additional criteria of successful aging should be considered thereby expanding the concept and multidimensional aspects of successful aging among oldest-old adults. |
| Cho et al. (2015) | Combination of Rowe and Kahn (1997) Successful Aging Model and Martin and Martin's (2002) Developmental Adaptation Model | Expand the concept of aging to a spectrum of past and current individual life influences by examining successful developmental adaptation among oldest-old adults. | 375 old participants (72 octogenarians and 234 centenarians) Quantitative study | Successful aging as outcome: – Subjective Well-Being Components: – Physical functioning – Physical health impairment – Cognitive functioning – Social resources – Perceives economic status – Education – Past life experiences | Significant direct effects of social resources and physical health impairment on positive affect; noteworthy indirect effects of cognitive functioning and education on positive affect. Integrating two different models (i.e., successful aging and developmental adaptation) provided a comprehensive view of the aging process and successful adaptation from a developmental perspective. |

| Author (Year) | Model | Objective | Sample / Method | Outcome | Findings |
|---|---|---|---|---|---|
| Kato et al. (2016) | No specific model | Understand the role of positive attitudes and emotional expression, and self-rated health in mental health. | 357 old participants (aged 94–109 years) Mean age 100.13 (SD 1.85) Quantitative study | Successful aging as outcome: – Mental Health (depression) | Positive attitudes, affect, and personality characteristics in conjunction with better perceived health status represent psychological determinants, which may positively influence mental health outcomes and subsequently lead to better emotional well-being and successful aging. |
| Kim (2013) | No specific model | Estimate the centenarian rate and elucidate on the influence of social factors on successful aging | Data of 32 OECD countries from World Population Prospects and United Nations database Quantitative study | Centenarian rate as an indicator of longevity, and therefore of successful aging | Three important social factors were implicated in successful aging: – a higher expenditure on health as a percentage of gross domestic product, and as a health expenditure factor related to good physical health; – a higher proportion of the population using fixed-telephone subscriptions, as a factor indicating a high general standard of living and higher social functioning in the elderly; – a higher human development index value, as indicative of social well-being. |

*(cont.)*

Table 27.1 (*cont.*)

| Authors/Year | Conceptualization | Aim(s) | Sample and Method | Operationalization of SA | Conclusions |
|---|---|---|---|---|---|
| Kock et al. (2010) | No specific model | Presents alternative stories of aging that counter the prevailing negative stereotypes of older people by interviewing centenarians about their lives. | 16 centenarians (11 women, 5 men; between 100 and 106; average age of 101.4 years) Qualitative study | Semi-structured interview; example of questions: – What is it like to have lived to 100 years and beyond? – What, in your opinion, is the secret of successful aging? – What matters to you today? | Several broad themes were identified as aspects of successful aging, mostly relating to lifestyle and environment, and the ability to handle stress. |
| Motta et al. (2005) | No specific model | Study of the clinical, psychical, and functional aspects in a centenarian group, verifying the real autonomy, instrumental capacities, and working abilities. | 602 centenarians (79.2% females and 20.8% males) Quantitative study | Domains of SA: – Clinical-anamnestic evaluation; – Cognitive-functional tests by means of the MMSE; – The independence index in activities of daily living (ADL), and instrumental activities of daily living (IADL) | 20.0% of the total centenarians were in good health status; 33.4% were in an intermediate health status; and 46.6% in bad health status. There are centenarians that indeed are free of invalidating chronic diseases, autonomous, and maintain good physical and cognitive capacities; however, they have not maintained any social or productive activities. |

| Study | Model | Aims | Sample | Domains / Outcomes | Findings |
|---|---|---|---|---|---|
| Ozaki et al. (2007) | No specific model | (1) Estimate the functional capacity, cognitive status, and psychosocial status of a sample of centenarians. (2) Clarify the influence of certain correlates on preservation of ADLs, cognitive abilities, and psychosocial status. | 1,907 centenarians (1,341 women and 566 men; mean age 101.1, SD 1.5) Quantitative study | Domains of SA: – Activities of daily living – Cognitive status – Psychosocial Status | 10.4% centenarians were considered to be models of successful aging, since they were autonomous, i.e., had preserved ADL, cognitive status, and psychosocial status. Autonomy in centenarians was associated with better visual acuity, getting regular exercise, spontaneous awakening regularly in the morning, preserved masticatory ability, having no history of drinking, having no history of severe falls after the age of 95, more frequent intake of protein, living at home, and being male. |
| Shimonaka et al. (1996) | No specific model | Analyze if androgyny/femininity and personality characteristics associated are related to successful aging. | 82 centenarians (37 men and 45 women) Quantitative study | Successful aging as outcome: – Self-esteem – Anxiety | Femininity is related to longevity; androgyny may be related to successful aging. Type B behavior is associated with longevity, but its relationship to successful aging differs between men and women. |
| Rosado-Medina et al. (2012) | No specific model | Identify the internal factors of resilience in centenarians. | 23 centenarians (15 men and 8 women) Quantitative and qualitative study | Successful aging as outcome: – Internal Resilience Factors | Internal resilience factors such as emotional stability, optimism, behavioral factor, and behavioral and emotional skills were linked to successfully aging. |

Developmental Adaptation Model, and concluded that integrating the two different models provided a better comprehensive view of centenarians' successful aging, since it allows for valuing the process and developmental perspective.

Due to the high likelihood of having diseases in very advanced age, the study of Araújo et al. (2016b) presented an adaptation of Young et al.'s (2009) Multidimensional Model of successful aging for centenarians, which included four domains: physiological, cognitive, well-being, and social domains. The eighty centenarians considered were grouped into two distinct clusters ($n = 40$ in each other). The one cluster, with better health status, lower comorbidity and functional impairment (i.e., fewer diseases and higher scores in ADL and IADL), better cognitive status (i.e., a higher score in cognitive functioning) and emotional functioning (i.e., a higher score in subjective well-being and a lower score in depression), and a better social engagement (i.e., more time spent with social interactions, more visits, and more activities) was considered to be the "successful" group. Following this trend, another study from this review proposed a new multidimensional model of successful aging for centenarians with four dimensions: physical and functional health, psychological well-being and cognition, social engagement and family support, and economic resources and financial security (Cheung & Lau, 2016). Based on Hong Kong Chinese centenarians, this study demonstrated that although only 5.8 percent of participants attained SA in all four dimensions, 86.7 percent of participants achieved successful aging (SA) on at least one dimension.

## The Use of Distinct Constructs and the Need for Additional Theoretical Work

The remaining eight studies from the present review are not based in a defined model of successful aging. Instead, their main objective was to explore characteristics and factors associated with successful aging in centenarians. Such an approach has been a concern of different researchers as expressed in extensive literature reviews (Depp & Jeste, 2006, 2010). Férnandez-Ballesteros and her team (2011a), for instance, in their study focusing on 458 participants (288 females, mean age: 66.47, range: 55–75) from the Longitudinal Study on Active Ageing (ELEA) found that affective functioning and personality, along with sociodemographic conditions, lifestyle, and other factors, were predictors of successful aging. Specifically on the psychological factors, authors found that a positive emotional balance, extraversion, neuroticism (with negative weight), and self-efficacy were associated with higher probability of being successful. In a further study, based on the participants from the longitudinal 90+ project, Fernández-Ballesteros et al. (2011b) found that regular physical activities, fitness, perceived control, and openness assessed at the baseline differentiate three distinct groups: those who died, those who dropped out the study, and those who continued in the study. According to their findings, 90 percent of those who died were identified at the baseline as "non-successful agers," while more than a half of those who participated and a third of the non-participants were identified as "successful agers." Authors argued that a multidimensional measure of successful aging could differentiate the three groups considered. Explicitly on the centenarian population, Poon et al. (2010) demonstrated that although centenarians display a wide variability among themselves and over time within themselves in terms of cognitive and emotional phenotypes, emotional stability and a capacity to handle negative affect appear to be traits associated with this population.

In the present review, the extent of indicators used to form composite indices of successful aging is wide-ranging. In the study by Kim (2013), for instance, macro factors such as higher expenditure on health, proportion of the population using fixed-telephone, and higher human development index value were associated with good physical health, higher social functioning, and social well-being respectively, and therefore considered important social factors of successful aging. Also, other studies found social and demographic factors, such as sex (i.e., being male) (Ozaki et al., 2007; Araújo et al., 2016b), better income adequacy (Araújo et al., 2016b), living at home (Ozaki et al., 2007), living with family or friends, and having less barriers to social activities (Cheung & Lau, 2016) were important factors of successful aging in centenarians. Despite the recognition of these social factors for positive aging, the way active engagement with life (successful aging's domain) is operationalized appears to be particularly challenging among the oldest-old. In very advanced age, the loss of family and friends can contribute to a reduction in social network, and the sensory and mobility difficulties may lead to a restriction in social participation. Indeed, Motta and colleagues (2005) questioned the conditions for having social participation, since in their study, even if centenarians were free of chronic diseases, autonomous, and maintained good physical and cognitive capacities, they did not maintain any social or productive activities. The importance to overcome negative influence in environmental factors is an open issue for future debate.

As for the set of health-related variables, Ozaki et al. (2007) verified that autonomy in centenarians was associated with getting regular exercise, spontaneous awakening regularly in the morning, having no history of drinking, having no history of severe falls after the age of 95, having more frequent intake of protein, reporting lifestyle and health practices as important factors in preserving ADLs, and good cognitive and psychosocial status after reaching the age of 100. When focusing on the increasing number of nonagenarians and/or centenarians, Berr et al. (2012) reinforced the importance of a healthy diet, having physically and intellectually appropriate activities, and a right use of medical care; these authors also stressed the importance of maintaining a social role and a *raison d'être* in old age as major factors in successful aging.

The search for psychological factors associated to successful aging revealed the importance of hope, optimism (Araújo et al., 2016a; Cheung & Lau, 2016; Rosado-Medina et al., 2012), and personality (Kato et al., 2016; Shimonaka et al., 1996; Rosado-Medina et al., 2012), which were common in three of the studies included in this review. Other factors include positive attitudes, self-efficacy, purpose in life, and perceived good health status (Araújo et al., 2016a; Kato et al., 2016), supporting the presence of psychological resilience in very long-lived adults (Cheung & Lau, 2016). Qualitative studies also support these conclusions: centenarians' lay perspectives of successful aging are related with lifestyle and environment and the ability to handle stress (Kock et al., 2010). As considered by Rosado-Medina et al. (2012), these psychological factors can be the proof that centenarians may be special phenotypes of resilience. As a matter of fact, the study of successful aging in centenarians has been stressing that the most important aspect for the status of "successful agers" is a remarkable resilient capacity to improve in the face of challenge. According to some authors, that capacity would explain how one might move beyond usual aging toward the positive extreme of the aging continuum (Hochhalter et al., 2011).

Considering that maintaining health, high physical and cognitive capacity, and productive engagement in life is more difficult with advancing age, the goal of longer and positive aging is to adapt and to make the best of personal situations, even in the presence of chronic illness and decline. At 100 years old, being successful and resilient is not postponing decline, but instead being prepared for the losses when they occur. Preparing oneself for dying and having a good death is also an important aspect to consider. On this matter, when conducting a thorough review and evaluation of the literature on successful aging, Martin and colleagues (2015) called for the importance of considering perspectives on success in achieving a good death, suggesting the need for integrating the concept of "successful dying" in the discourse on successful aging and calling for additional theoretical work that can encompass disability, death, and dying.

## The Incontrovertible Subjectivity of "Success" in Very Old Age

The importance of subjectivity when assessing successful aging has been receiving increasing attention; likewise, the use of subjective measures has emerged as a valuable aspect that contrasts with the attention traditionally given to the objective, or so-called "researcher-defined" criteria (Pruchno et al., 2010). Studies based on subjective criteria began to widely emerge over the last years and, not surprisingly, when comparing subjective and objective definitions of successful aging, the results tend to demonstrate that more people categorize themselves as successful according to their subjective perceptions (von Faber et al., 2001; Strawbridge et al., 2002; Montross et al., 2006; Pruchno et al., 2010).

The discrepancy of subjective versus objective criteria is of particular relevance when considering the centenarian population, since the goal of staying healthy, autonomous, and productively engaged in life may not be a realistic one. As shown in some of the conducted research included in this review, only 20 percent of the total centenarians were in good health status (Motta et al., 2005), while only 10.4 percent of the centenarians were autonomous, i.e., had preserved ADL, cognitive status, and psychosocial status (Osaki et al., 2017). The Araújo et al. (2016a) and Cho et al. (2012) studies aimed to further explore the differences between subjective versus objective criteria. In both studies (from Portugal and Georgia), subjective measures of successful aging identified a significant proportion of centenarians who did not fulfill the objective criteria, but were considered subjectively successful. Together, both studies point to the importance of integrating older adults' subjective rating of successful aging in order to reach respondents' own feelings and to incorporate conditions that are not objectively considered by researchers. Subjective successful aging may reveal important psychosocial resources and processes that result in older adults maintaining a perception of well-being and life satisfaction, even in the presence of constraints (Romo et al., 2013).

## Conclusions on What Does It Mean to Be Successful in Very Old Age

Research on exceptional longevity has long been of interest to scientists as well as to the general public. Conventionally, old-old age has been viewed as a period of progressive decline in physical, cognitive, and psychosocial functioning; nevertheless, centenarians are still considered to be representative cases of exceptional longevity and, consequently, "cases of success." Their increased representativeness challenges researchers and professionals to understand new life stages that are unique to late life and, in a more social dimension, may contribute to the reduction of ageism and negative stereotyping of older people (Kock et al., 2010).

This chapter focused on how the link between "success" and "centenarians" operates from an empirical point of view, and has reviewed a set of international studies that highlight the importance still given to longevity as *per se*, and the need of more constructs that recognize the role of psychological aspects of adaptation to extreme longevity. Both these findings deserve some thought, as it seems that a number of research teams, particularly from the biological sciences, have focused on longevity research, or more specifically, centenarian research, to precisely define successful aging.

First, it seems that remarkable longevity may not be the ideal phenotype with which to measure successful aging. According to Martin and colleagues (2015), the terms "healthy longevity" or "exceptional longevity" are often used in the literature to emphasize the importance of having lived a long and healthy life, and back in the early 1990s, some researchers even named those in their 100's as "expert survivors" (e.g., Poon et al., 1992). As seen in one of the papers included in this review, about half of all centenarians in the Georgia Centenarian Study could be classified as "successful" only if definitions of subjective health, perceived happiness, and better economic status were used (none would be classified as such according to Rowe and Kahn's criteria). This important finding, present in other studies included in this review, subscribes to the calling for more research focused on the centenarian's subjective and lay perspectives of successful aging (Martin et al., 2015; Jopp et al., 2016). As mentioned in Martin and Poon's (2016) comment on one of the analyzed papers (Araújo et al., 2016a), "success at 100 is easier said than done." Furthermore, successful aging ought to be more about what older adults value, rather than what younger researchers assume and define.

Second, although a few studies have followed specific theoretical models on successful aging, it seems that a movement toward the use of psychosocial models and/or constructs is emerging in the study of this population. One of those constructs regards the concept of resilience (i.e., individuals' psychological capacities and resources as sources of life strengths), which seems to be receiving quite a bit of attention in recent centenarian research (Martin et al., 2010). With advancing age, when very old adults fail to derive basic, conditional, or personal resources to respond to adversity, change is to be expected, and adjustments and adaptation to changing roles and environments is fundamental to resilience functioning. They may also tend to shift their priorities to spiritually meaningful resources and activities. This is one of the assumptions of the Gerotranscendence Theory, developed by Tornstam (2005), and lately presented as a new concept of successful aging in the oldest-old (Gondo, 2012), which seems to be another important psychosocial concept for improving successful aging research.

It is important to mention, within this tendency to incorporate wide-ranging psychological constructs, that although the role of psychological aspects is becoming more visible in scientific discussions, more research with a biopsychosocial focus is still needed. The complex reality of what it means to live to age 100, and the potential individual differences should be investigated (Jopp et al., 2016). The definition of "being socially engaged" at advanced ages, as an expression of success, is to be particularly cautioned. According to Antonini et al. (2008), there are several examples of individuals (artists, scientists, explorers, etc.) who remained active even after reaching 100, suggesting that maintaining work or other socially significant activities is a realistic possibility. Preserving competence and professional attitudes is not in conflict with the reaching of extreme longevity, yet there are no systemic studies on centenarian works or activities. It is timely to (re)think about the concept of participation in very advanced age, considering that age-related constrains lead to less functional capacity and few opportunities of being active.

Centenarians still represent a tiny proportion of the total population but projected figures suggest a substantial increase over the next years. In Europe, the rise in the number of centenarians is a particular feature. As the successful aging literature has grown, so too has the interest in the extent to which very old individuals can age successfully. But enhancing the likelihood of successful aging at very advanced ages urgently needs to make it clearer what is meant by the word "success." The contributions made by the studies mentioned in this chapter offer new insights into the nature of successful aging at very advanced age, but more research on this topic is surely needed. Additional theoretical work should include the way successful aging can encompass disability, death, and dying. Considering that successful or "good aging" is also culture dependent, associated variables to each location (e.g., Western countries versus Eastern countries) should also be further considered.

## References

Antonini, F., Magnolfi, S., Petruzzi, E., et al. (2008). Physical performance and creative activities of centenarians. *Archives of Gerontology and Geriatrics*, 46, 253–61.

Araújo, L., Ribeiro, O., Teixeira, L., et al. (2016a). Successful aging at 100 years: the relevance of subjectivity and psychological resources. *International Psychogeriatrics*, 28, 179–88.

Araújo, L., Ribeiro, O., Teixeira, L., et al. (2016b). Predicting Successful Aging at One Hundred Years of Age. *Research on Aging*, 38, 689–709.

Baltes, P. B. (1997). On the incomplete architecture of human ontogeny. *American Psychologist*, 52, 366–80.

Berkman, L., Seeman, T., Albert, M., et al. (1993). High, usual and impaired functioning in community-dwelling older men and women: Findings from the MacArthur Foundation Research Network on Successful Aging. *Journal of Clinical Epidemiology*, 46, 1129–40.

Berr, C., Balard, F., Blain, H., et al. (2012). How to define old age: successful aging and/or longevity. *Médecine Sciences*, 28 (3), 281–7.A

Bowling, A., Dieppe, P. (2005). What is successful aging and who should defined it? *BMJ*, 331(7531), 1548–51.

Carstensen, L. L., Turk-Charles, S. (1994). The salience of emotion across the adult life spam. *Psychology and Aging*, 9, 259–64.

Carver, L. F., Buchanan, D. (2016). Successful aging: considering non-biomedical constructs. *Clinical Interventions in Aging*, 11, 1623–30.

Cheung, K., Lau, B. (2016). Successful aging among Chinese near-centenarians and centenarians in Hong Kong: a multidimensional and interdisciplinary approach. *Aging & Mental Health*, 20(12), 1314–26.

Cho, J., Martin, P., Poon, L. (2012). The older they are, the less successful they become? Findings from the Georgia Centenarian Study. *Journal of Aging Research*. http://dx.doi.org/10.1155/2012/695854.

(2015). Successful aging and subjective well-being among oldest-old adults. *Gerontologist*, 55, 132–43.

Cosco, T., Prina, A., Perales, J., et al. (2013). Operational definitions of successful aging: a systematic review. *International Psychogeriatrics*, 26(3), 373–81. doi:10.1017/S1041610213002287.

Cosco, T. D., Prina, A. M., Perales, J., et al. (2014). Whose "successful ageing"? Lay- and researcher-driven conceptualizations of ageing well. *European Psychiatry*, 28(2), 124–30.

Crowther, M., Parker, M., Achenbaum, W., et al. (2002). Rowe and Kahn's model of successful aging revisited: positive spirituality—the forgotten factor. *Gerontologist*, 42, 613–20.

Depp, C. A., Jeste, D. V. (2006). Definitions and predictors of successful aging: a comprehensive review of larger quantitative studies. *American Journal of Geriatric Psychiatry*, 14, 6–20.

(2010). Phenotypes of successful aging: historical overview. In C. A. Depp & D. V. Jeste (Eds.), *Successful Cognitive and Emotional Aging* (pp. 1–14). Washington, DC: American Psychiatric Publishing, Inc.

Engberg, H., Oksuzyan, A., Jeune, B., et al. (2009). Centenarians—a useful model for healthy aging? A 29-year follow-up of hospitalizations among 40,000 Danes born in 1905. *Aging Cell*, 8, 270–6.

European Commission (2014). *Super-centenarian societies*. Retrieved in 10 December, 2014, from: https://ec.europa.eu/digital-agenda/futurium/en/content/super-centenarian-societies-0

Férnandez-Ballesteros, R. (2011). Positive ageing: Objective, subjective, and combined outcomes. *Electronic Journal of Applied Psychology*, 7, 22–30.

Fernández-Ballesteros, R., Casinello, M. D., Lopez-Bravo, M. D., et al. (2011a). Successful ageing: criteria and predictors. *Psychology in Spain*, 15, 94–101.

Fernández-Ballesteros, R., Zamarrón, M. D., Dıez-Nicolas, J., et al. (2011b). Mortality and refusal in the longitudinal 90+project. *Archives of Gerontology and Geriatrics*, 53, 203–8.

Gondo, Y. (2012). Longevity and successful ageing: implications from the oldest old and centenarians. *Asian Journal of Gerontology and Geriatrics*, 7, 39–43.

Hank, K. (2011). How "successful" do older Europeans age? Findings from SHARE. *Journal of Gerontology Series B: Psychological Sciences and Social Sciences*, 66(2), 230–6.

Hitt, R., Young-Xu, Y., Silver, M., et al. (1999). Centenarians: the older you get, the healthier you have been. *The Lancet*, 354(21), 652.

Hochhalter, A., Smith, M., Ory, M. (2011). Successful aging and resilience: applications for public health and health care. In B. Resnick, L. Gwyther & K. Roberto (Eds.), *Resilience in Aging: Concepts, Research and Outcomes* (pp. 15–30). New York, NY: Springer.

Jopp, D., Boerner, K. Ribeiro, O., et al. (2016). Life at Age 100: An International Research Agenda for Centenarian Studies. *Journal of Aging & Social Policy*, 28, 133–47.

Jeste, D. V., Depp, C. A., Vahia, I. V. (2010). Successful cognitive and emotional aging. *World Psychiatry*, 9, 78–84.

Jeste, D. V, Savla, G. N., Thompson, W. K., et al. (2013). Older age is associated with more successful ageing: role of resilience and depression. *American Journal of Psychiatry*, 170(2), 188–96.

Kato, K., Zweig, R., Schechter, C., et al. (2016). Positive attitude toward life, emotional expression, self-rated health, and depressive symptoms among centenarians and near-centenarians. *Aging Mental Health*, 20, 930–9.

Kim, J. (2013). Social factors associated with centenarian rate (CR) in 32 OECD countries. *BMC International Health and Human Rights*, 13. DOI: 10.1186/1472-698X-13-16.

Kock, T., Turner, R., Smith, P., et al. (2010). Storytelling reveals the active, positive lives of centenarians. *Nursing Older People*, 22, 31–6.

Lee, P., Lan, W., Yen, T. (2011). Aging successfully: a four-factor model. *Educational Gerontology*, 37(3), 210–27.

Osaki, A., Uchiyama, M., Tagaya, H., et al. (2017). The Japanese centenarian study: Autonomy was associated with health practices as well as physical status. *Journal of the American Geriatric Society*, 55(1), 95–101.

Pruchno, R., Wilson-Genderson, M., Cartwright, F. (2010). A two-factor model of successful aging. *Journal of Gerontology Series B: Psych ological Sciences and Social Sciences*, 65B, 671–9.

Martin, D., Gillen, L. (2014). Revisiting Gerontology's Scrapbook: From Metchnikoff to the Spectrum Model of Aging. *The Gerontologist*, 54(1), 51–8.

Martin, P., MacDonald, M., Margrett, J. et al. (2010). Resilience and longevity: expert survivorship of centenarians. In P. S. Fry & C. L. M. Keyes (Eds.), *New Frontiers in Resilient Aging: Life-Strenghts and Well-Being in Late Life* (pp. 213–238). New York: Cambridge University Press.

Martin, P., Martin, M. (2002). Proximal and distal influences on development: The model of developmental adaptation. *Developmental Review*, 22, 78–96.

Martin, P., Poon, L. (2016). Success at 100 is easier said than done–comments on Araújo et al: successful aging at 100 years. *International Psychogeriatrics*, 28, 177–8.

Martin, P., Kelly, N., Kahana, B., et al. (2015). Defining successful aging: a tangible or elusive concept? *The Gerontologist*, 55(1), 14–25.

McLaughlin, S., Connell, C., Heeringa, S., et al. (2010). Successful aging in the United States: prevalence estimates from a national sample of older adults. *Journal of Gerontology Series B: Psychological Sciences and Social Sciences*, 65B, 216–26.

Molton, I. R., Yorkston, K. M. (2016). Growing older with a physical disability: a special application of the successful aging paradigm. *Journal of Gerontology Series B: Psychological Sciences and Social Sciences*. DOI:10.1093/geronb/gbw122.

Montross, L. P., Depp, C., Daly, J., et al. (2006). Correlates of self-rated successful aging among community-dwelling older adults. *American Journal of Geriatric Psychiatry*, 14, 43–51.

Motta, M., Bennati, E., Ferlito, L., et al., Italian Multicenter Study on Centenarians (IMUSCE). (2005). Successful aging in centenarians: myths and reality. *Archives of Gerontology and Geriatrics*, 40(3), 241–51.

Poon, L. W., Clayton, G. M., Martin, P., et al. (1992). The Georgia centenarian study. *International Journal of Aging and Human Development*, 34, 1–17.

Poon, L. W., Martin, P., Margrett, J. (2010). Cognition and emotion in centenarians. In C. A. Depp & D. V. Jeste (Eds.), *Successful Cognitive and Emotional Aging* (pp. 115–33). Washington DC: American Psychiatric Publishing, Inc.

Rosado-Medina, J., Rodríguez-Gómez, J., Ramirez, G. (2012). Study on resilience internal factors in a sample of Puerto Rican centenarians. *Boletín de la Asociación Médica de Puerto Rico*, 104, 17–25.

Rowe, J. W., Kahn, R. L. (1987). Human aging: usual and successful. *Science*, 237, 143–9.

(1997). Successful aging. *The Gerontologist*, 37, 433–40.

(2015). Successful aging 2.0: conceptual expansions for the 21st century. *Journal of Gerontology Series B: Psychological Sciences and Social Sciences*, 70(4), 593–6.

Romo, R., Wallhagen, M. I., Yourman, L., et al. (2013). Perceptions of successful aging among diverse elders with late-life disability. *Gerontologist*, 53(6),939–49.

Shimonaka, Y., Nakazato, K., Homma, A. (1996). Personality, longevity, and successful aging among Tokyo metropolitan centenarians. *International Journal of Aging and Human Development*, 42, 173–87.

Strawbridge, W., Wallhagen, M., Cohen, R. (2002). Successful aging and well-being: self-rated compared with Rowe and Kahn. *The Gerontologist*, 42, 727–33.

Tornstam, L. (2005). *Gerotranscendence: A Developmental Theory of Positive Ageing*. New York: Springer.

United Nations, Department of Economic and Social Affairs, Population Division (2015). *World Populations Prospects: 2015 Revision, Key Findings and Advance Tables*. Working Paper No. ESA/P/WP.241. Retrieved in 10 july, 2016, from: https://esa.un.org/unpd/wpp/

Von Faber, M., Bootsma-van der Wiel, A., van Exel, E., et al. (2001). Successful aging in the oldest old: who can be characterized as successfully aged? *Archives of Internal Medicine*, 161, 2694–700.

Young, Y., Frick, K. D., Phelan, E. A. (2009). Can successful aging and chronic illness coexist in the same individual? A multidimensional concept of successful aging. *American Medical Directors Association*, 10, 87–92.

Zeng, Y., Shen, K. (2010). Resilience significantly contributes to exceptional longevity. *Current Gerontology and Geriatrics Research*. doi:10.1155/2010/525693

# 28 Promoting Successful Aging

A Psychosocial Perspective

## Maríagiovanna Caprara and
## Neyda Ma. Mendoza-Ruvalcaba

## Introduction

Aging in the twenty-first century is a challenge at the political, social, economic, and health levels. Indeed, aging is not only a demographic phenomenon, but also an individual and collective experience. Therefore, the scientific community dealing with the study of aging should identify and implement strategies for improving health and well-being during the aging process at several levels of analysis, and for engaging multiple disciplines. The knowledge that has been acquired in recent decades has enabled the development of programs specifically designed to prolong a life that is worth living and to postpone a variety of disabilities commonly associated with old age.

The notion of successful aging, in particular, has been crucial to promote a new paradigm that acknowledges the value of aging well and counteracts a vision of loss and deficit spread out through negative stereotypes and prejudices against aging. In particular, the notion of successful aging must overcome the undesirable connotations of adjectives associated with old age, such as weak, frail, and decrepit, as well as the negative view of aging that has long prevailed in many sectors of society, and even among health professionals. Instead, a new focus on successful aging should be encouraged, as it is largely dependent on how people prepare, based on the opportunities and capacities they have to make the best use of their potential.

In this chapter, we will point to major theoretical changes that have occurred over the last decades and to major contributions that have laid the groundwork for the development of interventions designed to promote successful aging. The goal of this contribution is to present a review of psychosocial intervention programs designed to promote successful aging.

## Some Theories of Aging Well

Although the notion of successful aging can be found in earlier literature, the concept gained salience in the last decades of the twentieth century, in accordance with findings from longitudinal, cross-sectional, experimental, and quasi-experimental studies. These studies pointed to the manifold bio-psycho-social factors that affect aging, the great plasticity of the human brain, and the potential of the human mind. In addition, research in this field has provided growing evidence that aging is not associated solely with physical and psychological decline. In reality, psychosocial conditions may contribute to value experience and to sustain further development (Baltes & Baltes, 1990; Fernández-Ballesteros, 2008).

Scholars like Havighurst (1961, 1963), Fries & Crapo (1981), Baltes & Baltes (1990), Atchley (1989), Ryff (1982, 1989), Rowe & Khan (1998), and Fernandez-Ballesteros (2002a) have provided new approaches to aging that acknowledge the important contributions that old people may offer to society. This perspective has led to the need for policies and programs designed to prolong and sustain old people's positive engagement in their communities. This new approach, along with the financial support of enlightened funding agencies, like the MacArthur Foundation in the 1980s, brought about a 180-degree turn in the typical view of the aging process.

Rowe and Kahn (1997, 1998) provided both an empirical definition and a set of criteria to assess and promote successful aging: (a) a low probability of disease and disease-related disability, (b) a high cognitive and physical functional capacity, and (c) an active engagement with life. Following this model, specific programs were designed in order to prevent illness and its associated disability, to optimize psychological (especially cognitive) and physical function, and to maximize commitment to life.

While acknowledging the unavoidable losses carried by aging in the physical and psychosocial domains, Baltes and Baltes (1990) pointed to the assets old people may still have and outlined strategies conducive to people's optimal use of their strengths and resources. While changes have to be carefully examined under scientific scrutiny, a comprehensive understanding of the aging process requires a focus on strength and potential, and not simply on losses and decline. To this end, Baltes and Baltes's Selection, Optimization, and Compensation (SOC) model advances a broad definition of successful aging that rests on both objective and subjective criteria, and acknowledges the importance of individual cultural variations. According to the model, aging well reflects people's capacity to make the best of their lives by selecting activities, encounters, and situations that most suit their psychological and physical resources. Individuals may compensate for the unavoidable decline and weakness associated with aging by using the abilities and strategies that derive from their life experiences. To this end, the social and cultural context may exert a crucial role in providing opportunities, reducing obstacles, making available models and incentives, and sustaining efforts to achieve optimal outcomes.

Fernández-Ballesteros (2008) has made clear that promoting successful aging requires situating the aging person in her/his historical social context and addressing its manifold expressions at both the social and individual levels. Aging in fact is a multidimensional process whose manifestations and development reflect biological, psychological, and sociocultural determinants that operate in various combinations at different ages, in different contexts, and across time. Because human beings are plastic organisms, with broad adaptation and learning capacities, aging well largely depends upon learning to adjust and to respond properly to biological and social changes (Baltes et al., 2005; Fernández-Ballesteros & Calero, 1995; Kliegl et al., 1989). Fernández-Ballesteros and her group tested a four domains model (similar to the Rowe and Khan model) through multiple samples and multiple methods: (1) health, (2) physical and cognitive fitness, (3) affect and control, and (4) social participation. They also examined the most important predictors such as socioeconomic conditions (i.e., age, gender, income, and education), lifestyles and psychological conditions (Fernández-Ballesteros et al., 2010).

The discovery of the great potential of the nature-nurture for culture interplay and of the great plasticity of brain function has led to increased appreciation of the notable contributions of socio-environmental conditions and habitual behaviors for extending longevity (Fernández-Ballesteros et al., 2012a; González-Pardo & Pérez-Álvarez, 2013; Kirkwood, 2005; Staehelin, 2005). Thus, society and the socio-political context are important actors in the process by which a population ages well, or actively. It is likely that social and individual factors operate in concert in predisposing people to lifestyles that may amplify or mitigate the difficulties of old age. Thus, effective interventions require changes in norms, attitude and habits. Individuals can be responsible for their own aging process, to the extent that the social and cultural environments allow a large degree of freedom in charting their own life course.

Enabling people to improve their lifestyles through self-management procedure is crucial to extending their healthy survival to even older ages. Extensive evidence shows that disuse of one's abilities, lack of activity, overdependence, and withdrawal account for decline, deficits, and impairment in cognitive and physical fitness (Schaie, 2005). Thus, aging well can be achieved through activities and relationships that effectively allocate one's personal resources and take the greatest possible advantage of environmental opportunities. This implies both the ability to select the activities that enable individuals to optimize their assets and the ability to compensate for losses and impairments due to obsolescence and disuse through knowledge, activity, and training (Baltes & Baltes, 1990; Schaie, 2005).

## Pursuing Aging Well through Healthy Habits, Physical and Cognitive Fitness, Positive Affect and Control, and Social Engagement

Successful aging can be assessed by the degree of occurrence of four major conditions: health and independence, high physical and cognitive functioning, positive affect and control, and social participation and engagement (e.g., Bowling & Iliffe, 2006; Fernández-Ballesteros, 2002b, 2008; Hank, 2011). Improving health, and preventing and/or delaying disability and disease, can be achieved by promoting lifestyles that avoid risky habits, like smoking, and including activities that preserve physical fitness (Aldwin et al., 2006; Hartman-Stein & Potkanowicz, 2003). Elders with healthy behavioral lifestyles show four times less disability than those who smoke, drink too much, do not exercise, and are obese (Fries, 2002). Thus, promoting successful aging requires making people acknowledge the harmful effects of unhealthy habits such as smoking, poor nutrition, and lack of physical exercise, and enabling them to abandon old habits and adopt new ones. Positive changes rest upon the individual's sense of purpose, efforts, and capacity to align his or her daily behaviors with new, healthy goals.

Optimal cognitive function can be achieved through lifelong learning and by engaging in activities that exercise and enhance memory, judgment, and problem-solving abilities (Hertzog et al., 2009). Exercise and practice allow older adults to moderate the decline that is usually associated with aging by sustaining their access to new sources of knowledge, and by enabling them to value previous learning and experiences. Cognitive training has shown beneficial effects on improving cognitive skills (Calero, 2003), cognitive reserve, and general cognitive function. Cognitive training in particular can play a significant role in maintaining and enhancing the cognitive reserve that is necessary for normal functioning as well as for situations of brain damage. Cognitive reserve is considered a good measure of individual's cognitive modifiability, and a good moderator of the cognitive impairment in old age (Fernández-Ballesteros et al., 2007). It has been reported that people with low cognitive reserves show steeper decline early in the process of deterioration, compared to those with high levels of reserves, in whom this marked deterioration appears at the end of the process due to the protective role of their cognitive reserves (Lojo-Seoana et al., 2012).

In addition to cognitive factors, a growing body of research concerning aging and health has focused on individual differences in personality as the self-regulating system accounting for the manifold ways in which people manage themselves and interact with the outside world. This has led to a focus on the traits, self-beliefs, attitudes, and habits that foster better adaptation to aging.

Researchers have identified a variety of self-referent constructs like self-esteem, life satisfaction, and optimism as crucial to sustaining healthy habits and promoting successful aging (e.g., Diener & Chan, 2011; Hertzog et al., 2009; Warner et al., 2012). People's judgments of their own lives and expectations for the future affect their habits, their interpersonal relationships, and the ways they acknowledge and manage the changes that occur in their physical and psychological functioning during the course of their lives (Warner et al., 2012). Several findings corroborate social-cognitive approaches that point to self-regulation, self-reflection, and perceived self-efficacy as core personal determinants of optimal aging (Baltes & Baltes, 1990; Keyes, 2007; Rowe & Khan, 1998). Likewise, findings suggest that nurturing positive emotions like joy and pride may serve to balance negative emotions such as anxiety or depression, and contribute to promoting elderly people's well-being (Frederickson & Losada, 2005; Lyubomirsky et al., 2005). Finally, many models of aging agree on the importance of social relations, social competence, and social engagement (Baltes & Baltes, 1990; Rowe & Khan, 1998; WHO, 2002). Studies have shown a strong and robust cross-sectional association between social engagement and disability, with socially active persons reporting lower levels of disability than their less active counterparts (Mendes de Leon et al., 2003). Empirical evidence attests to the positive link between social activity and participation and cognitive functioning (Park et al., 2007), although the protective effects of social engagement tend to diminish over time (Zunzunegui et al., 2005). Findings support the effectiveness of interventions aimed at widening older individuals' social networks and at encouraging their social engagement in activities like volunteerism, lifelong education, arts, and culture. Encouraging social relationships and pro-social behaviors may serve to improve social competence and to preserve a high sense of self-confidence and autonomy (Caprara et al., 2003; Midlarsky & Kahana, 2007).

In summary, raising old people's awareness of, and responsibility for, their health is the key to enabling them to avoid risky behaviors and to pursue healthy lifestyles. Knowledge of healthy habits, however, must be accompanied by the capacity and will to align one's behavior with this knowledge. This requires self-efficacy, coping skills, and effort, which, in combination with a positive orientation toward life, are conducive to the adoption of protective lifestyles and to the prevention of risk factors. Thus, the transmission of knowledge on the importance of physical activity, cognitive exercise, and social engagement should be combined with learning experiences that directly attest to their benefits. Ultimately, it is a sense of personal mastery in managing their aging that enables people to cope effectively with frailties, loss, and adversity.

## The Development of Psychosocial Programs Promoting Successful Aging

A large variety of programs have been developed across the world to meet the needs of societies to encourage seniors to pursue healthy lifestyles and to preserve a satisfactory quality of life across life span (Chi & Lubben, 1994; Mnich et al., 2013; Tang et al., 2009). Yet, the fact that most of these programs are community-based and rarely include systematic evaluations of outcomes represents a serious limitation that makes it difficult to achieve adequate comparisons of their effectiveness and generalizability. A further limitation concerns the clarity of the theories that form the basis of various interventions.

In reality, a comprehensive theory of successful aging should account for both individuals' development and functioning, and for how society and culture impinge on peoples' psychological and physical well-being. Thus, it is not surprising that significant progress has been made by psychosocial programs that have addressed aging as an individual experience that engages the whole person and her/his social world, namely her/his body, mind, habits, and social relations.

While individuals' feelings, thoughts, and actions are reciprocally determined and culturally and historically situated, aging well rests upon individuals' resources and efforts no less than upon others' expectations and reactions. Psychosocial programs can be delivered in group or individual sessions, with tailored or pre-designed contents, through self-help manuals and webpages, all aimed at transferring the knowledge and sustaining the motivation needed to anticipate and combat the various frailties and diseases associated with aging. An example of a program of this type is "Vital Aging" by Fernández-Ballesteros (2002b).

In the following section we will present an overview of psychosocial strategies aimed to promote successful aging and underlie the multidisciplinary focus that is required to properly address the complexity of aging.

## Reviewing Psychosocial Programs to Promote Successful Aging

In order to identify published descriptions of psychosocial programs designed to promote successful aging, we conducted a literature search. The keywords selected were "intervention program," "successful aging," "active aging," "healthy aging," "aging well," "optimal aging," "positive aging," and "health promotion." The search was conducted on MEDLINE, Web of Science, PsycINFO, EBSCO, Proquest Central, CINAHL, and AgeLine between May 15, 2016 and November 15, 2016, with no language restriction. Articles were included in the review if they met the following criteria: (1) the article referred to an intervention program; (2) the program had a psychosocial perspective; (3) the objectives included promoting successful aging (e.g., active, healthy, aging well, optimal, positive); (4) the characteristics of the intervention program were reported in detail; and (5) the effectiveness of the program was assessed.

The first screening of the records was guided by the title, then by the abstract, and finally by reading the full-text. This first screening produced 43 eligible studies. Nineteen records were excluded after a deeper screening, when it was deemed that the inclusion criteria were not fulfilled, and one additional record was excluded because it only included an intervention proposal. The final sample thus included 24 full-text records (22 articles and 1 doctoral thesis). Some intervention programs produced more than one record (e.g., one program produced four records), but were counted as only one intervention program (see Figure 28.1). Finally, 19 intervention programs were included in the review, involving a total of 2,959 participants (see Table 28.1).

Once the records were identified, the data were extracted and introduced into a review matrix for analysis; the data collected included bibliometrics, theoretical background (i.e., concept or terminology used to refer to successful aging, disciplinary focus), methodology of the study (i.e., methodological approach, design, objective, participants, variables, and outcomes), and intervention

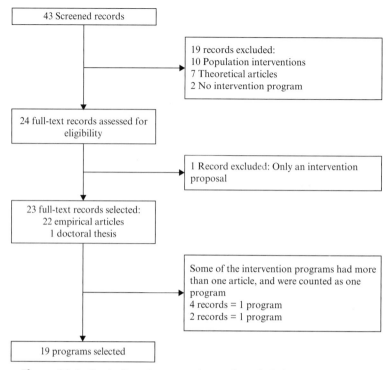

**Figure 28.1.** *Study flow diagram of records included in the review*

characteristics (i.e., name of the program, targeted audience, format, setting, domains involved, and strategies for implementation).

## Bibliometric Results

The interventions for promoting successful aging included in this review were published between 2002 and 2016. The first intervention program identified was the "Vital Aging Program" (1), which has been applied successfully in several editions in Spain (Caprara et al., 2015; Fernández-Ballesteros, 2005; Fernández-Ballesteros et al., 2004, 2005a), and recently in Mexico (Mendoza Ruvalcaba & Fernández-Ballesteros, 2016). One study was reported in each of the following years: 2006 (2), 2007 (3), 2010 (4), and 2012 (5); three intervention programs were reported in 2013 (6–8) and 2014 (9–11), five in 2015 (12–16), and four in 2016 (1, 17–19). Most of the studies were published in the English language.

In terms of the countries where the interventions were carried out, the results are diverse. Spain had the highest number of applied programs with four (1, 8, 13, 17). One program was carried out in the Netherlands (3) and one in England (4). Six programs were developed in Latin America, including one in Brazil

Table 28.1 *Studies included in the review*

| Program No. | Year | Program/Reference |
|---|---|---|
| 1 | | *"Vital Aging"* |
| | 2002 | Fernández-Ballesteros, R. (2002b). *Vivir con Vitalidad*. Madrid: Pirámide. |
| | 2004 | Fernández-Ballesteros, R., Caprara, M. G., & García, L. F. (2004). Vivir con Vitalidad-M: Un programa europeo multimedia [Vital Aging-M: A European multimedia program]. *Intervención Social, 13*, 63–85. |
| | 2005 | Fernández-Ballesteros, R., Caprara, M. G., Iñiguez, J., & García, L. F. (2005b). Promoción del envejecimiento activo: Efectos del programa Vivir con Vitalidad. *Revista Española de Geriatría y Gerontología, 40*(2), 92–102. |
| | 2013 | Caprara, M. G., Molina, M. A., Schettini, R., et al. (2013). Active aging promotion: Results from the vital aging program. *Current Gerontology and Geriatrics Research, 2013*, 1–14. doi: http://dx.doi.org/10.1155/2013/817813. |
| | 2015 | Caprara, M. G., Fernández-Ballesteros, R., Alessandri, G. (2015). Promoting aging well: Evaluation of Vital-Aging-Multimedia Program in Madrid, Spain. *Health Promotion International, 31*(3), 515–522. |
| | 2016 | Mendoza Ruvalcaba, N. M. &Fernández-Ballesteros, R. (2016). Effectiveness of the Vital Aging program to promote active aging in Mexican older adults. *Clinical Interventions in Aging, 10*, 829–837. |
| 2 | 2006 | *"Optimal Aging Program"* <br> Sikora, S. (2008). The University of Arizona College of Medicine Optimal Aging Program. *Gerontology & Geriatrics Education, 27*(2), 59–67. |
| 3 | 2007 | Bode, C., De Ridder, D. T., Kuijer, R. G., &Bensing, J. M. (2007). Effects of an intervention promoting proactive coping competencies in middle and late adulthood. *The Gerontologist, 47*(1), 42–51. |
| 4 | 2010 | *"Mental Fitness for Life"* <br> Cusack, S. A. (2003). Mental fitness for life: Assessing the impact of an 8-week mental fitness program on healthy aging. *Educational Gerontology, 29*(5), 393–403. |
| 5 | 2012 | Correa-Bautista, J. E., Sandoval-Cuellar, C., Alfonso Mara, M. L., & Rodríguez-Daza, K. D. (2012). Cambios en la aptitud física en un grupo de mujeres adultas mayores bajo el modelo de envejecimiento activo. *Revista de la Facultad de Medicina, 60*(1), 21–30. |
| 6 | 2013 | Boyes, M. (2013). Outdoor adventure and successful aging. *Aging and Society, 33*(4), 644–665. |
| 7 | 2013 | Foy, C. G., Vitolins, M. Z., Case, L. D., Harris, S. J., Massa-Fanale, C., Hopley, R. J., & Goff, D. C. (2013). Incorporating prosocial behavior to promote physical activity in older adults: Rationale and design of the Program for Active Aging and Community Engagement (PACE). *Contemporary Clinical Trials, 36*(2013), 284–297. |
| 8 | 2013 | *"Gero-Health"* <br> Lorenzo, T., Millan-Calenti, J. C., Lorenzo López, L., &Maseda, A. (2013). Efectos del programa educativo Gero-Health sobre el nivel de interiorización de conocimientos de prevención y promoción de la salud en personas mayores. *Revista de Investigación Educativa, 31*(2), 502–515. |

*(cont.)*

Table 28.1 (*cont.*)

| Program No. | Year | Program/Reference |
|---|---|---|
| 9 | 2014 | Estebsari, F., Hossein, M., Foroushani, A. R., Ardebili, H. E., & Shojaeizadeh, V. (2014). An educational program based on the successful aging approach on health-promoting behaviours in the elderly: A clinical trial study. *Iranian Red Crescent Medical Journal, 16*(4), e16314. |
| 10 | 2014 | Mastropietro, E. (2014). Clubes de memoria. Programas de Intervención Comunitaria en Salud para Adultos Mayores. *Revista Psicología, 33*(1), 15–32. |
| 11 | 2014 | *"Integrated Health Management Program"*<br>Ahn, O., Gyeong, H., Chang, S. J., Cho, H., & Kim, H. S. (2014). Effect of an integrated health management program based on successful aging in Korean women. *Public Health Nursing, 32*(4), 307–315. |
| 12 | 2015 | Canseco, M. (2015). Programa de intervención para envejecer con éxito dirigido a personas mayores de la ciudad de México. Retrieved from: www.tesisenred.net/handle/10803/310381 |
| 13 | 2015 | Latorre, J. M. et al. (2015). Life review based on remembering specific positive events in active aging. *Journal of Aging and Health, 27*(1), 140–157. |
| 14 | 2015 | *"I Am Active"*<br>Mendoza-Ruvalcaba, N. M., & Arias Merino, E. D. (2015). "I Am Active": Effects of a program to promote active aging. *Clinical Interventions in Aging, 2015*(10), 829–837. |
| 15 | 2015 | Santos, L. C. et al. (2015). Calidad de vida de los mayores que participanen el grupo de promoción de la salud. Enfermería Global, 1–11. |
| 16 | 2015 | *"Healthy Aging Mind Body Intervention"*<br>Scult, M., Haime, V., Jacquart, J., Takahashi, J., Moscowitz, B., Webster, A., Denninger, J. W., & Mehta, D. (2015). A healthy aging program for older adults: Effects on self-efficacy and morale. *Advances in Mind Body Medicine, 29*(1), 26–33. |
| 17 | 2016 | Jiménez, M. G., Izal, M., & Montorio, I. (2016). Programa para la mejora del bienestar de las personas mayores. Estudio piloto basado en la psicología positiva. *Suma Psicológica, 23*(1), 51–59. |
| 18 | 2016 | *"Islamic Spiritual Program"*<br>Moeini, M., Sharifi, S., & Zandiyeh, Z. (2016). Does Islamic spiritual program lead to successful aging? A randomized clinical trial. *Journal of Education and Health Promotion, 5*, 1–7. |
| 19 | 2016 | Newman, A. B., Dodson, J. A., Church, T. S., Buford, T. W., Fielding, R. A., et al. Cardiovascular events in a physical activity intervention compared with a successful aging intervention. The LIFE study randomized trial. *Journal of the American Medical Association Cardiology, 1*(5), 568–674. |

Table 28.2 *Terminology and discipline used in the programs for promoting successful aging*

| Variable | | $n =$ | Program n° |
|---|---|---|---|
| Terminology | Successful | 9 | 2, 3, 6, 9, 11, 12, 17–19 |
| | Active | 7 | 1, 2, 5, 7, 8, 10, 14 |
| | Healthy | 5 | 4, 7, 10, 15, 16 |
| | Optimal | 1 | 2 |
| Discipline | Psychology | 11 | 1, 3, 4, 6, 10, 12–14, 16, 178 |
| | Medicine | 5 | 2, 5, 7, 9, 19 |
| | Gerontology | 1 | 8 |
| | Nursing | 1 | 15 |
| | Public Health | 1 | 11 |

(15), one in Colombia (5), one in Venezuela (10), and three different programs in Mexico (1, 12, 14), including an adaptation of the "Vital Aging" program (Mendoza Ruvalcaba & Fernández-Ballesteros, 2016). Four programs were implemented in the United States (2, 7, 16, 19), two in Iran (9, 18), one in New Zealand (6), and one in Korea (11).

## Theoretical Background

The most used term to name the intervention programs was *successful* aging, followed by *active healthy*, and *optimal* aging. Two programs used more than one term: the "Memory Club" (10) used two, and the "Optimal Aging Program" (2) used optimal, active, and successful as synonyms (see Table 28.2).

Although all the intervention programs showed a psychosocial perspective, and most of them were delivered from a psychological perspective (11 out of 19 programs), some programs were delivered from another disciplinary perspective: five from medicine, one from gerontology, one from nursing, and one from a public health perspective (see Table 28.2).

## Methodological Characteristics

Regarding the methodological characteristics of the programs (See Table 28.3), 17 out of 19 intervention programs used quantitative methods, one used qualitative methods (2), and one used both qualitative and quantitative (mixed) methods (6).

To classify the design of the studies, we referred to the classification proposed by Campbell and Stanley (1995). The randomized controlled trial used in nine studies (3, 7, 9, 12–14, 17–19) was the most common design; three of

Table 28.3 *Method and design implemented in the programs for promoting successful aging*

| Variable | | $n =$ | Program n° |
|---|---|---|---|
| Methods | Quantitative | 17 | 1, 3, 4, 5, 7–10, 12–19 |
| | Qualitative | 1 | 2 |
| | Mixed | 1 | 6 |
| Design | RCT | 9 | 3, 7, 9 ,12–14, 17–19 |
| | Quasi-experimental | 1 | 1 |
| | Pre-experimental | | | |
| |   Pre-post | 6 | 4, 5, 8, 10, 11, 16 |
| |   Post | 3 | 2, 6, 15 |

RCT = Randomized controlled trial.

these studies included a follow-up at 3 (3), 6 (14), or 12 months (7). One study adopted a quasi-experimental design (1), and although randomization was not present, pre-posttests were conducted in experimental and control groups. Six studies included pre-posttest comparison (4, 5, 8, 10, 11, 16), and three studies included only posttest measurement in one experimental group (2, 6, 15).

Sample size varied among the studies, ranging from $n = 17$ to $n = 817$ participants, and all the studies and interventions were in accordance with common ethical standards and involved an informed consent.

## Intervention Characteristics

The target population in all of the studies was community-dwelling older adults (60 or 65 years and over), except in the "Optimal Aging Program" (2), where college students were also participants in an intergenerational experience. The settings of the interventions were mainly senior centers or health houses. Professionals from diverse disciplines, mainly psychologists, gerontologists, geriatricians, or nurses, delivered the interventions. The group session was the most common format of intervention, adopted by 16 out of 19 studies; only one program was individually implemented (4), and two interventions mixed group and individual formats (2, 12).

For analytical purposes, the programs were categorized, considering first the strategy used to promote successful aging, then the outcome variables and their specific indicators. Strategies and outcomes were analyzed according to the four domains of successful aging listed above. Table 28.4 reports the strategies used to promote successful aging. The program was considered to be "unidimensional" or "multidimensional," depending on whether one or more domains of successful aging were addressed.

Table 28.4 *Intervention strategies implemented by unidimensional and multidimensional intervention programs to promote successful aging (program number in parentheses)*

| Dimension | Unidimensional programs ($n = 12$) | Multidimensional programs ($n = 7$) |
|---|---|---|
| Healthy lifestyles | Physical activity (5) <br> Outdoor activity involvement: biking, camping (6) | Physical activity (1, 7, 9, 11, 12, 14) <br> Nutrition habits (1, 9, 11, 12, 14) <br> Health promotion (1) <br> Responsibility for health (9) <br> Health education (11) |
| Psychological | Cognitive training (4, 10) <br> Behavioral change: promoting proactive coping competencies (3) <br> Life review techniques (13) <br> Education on prevention and health promotion (8, 19) <br> Psychological well-being promotion (17) <br> Spiritual skills training: Islamic (18) <br> Cognitive behavioral therapy (16) | Cognitive training (1, 11, 12, 14) <br> Behavioral change (9, 7, 14) <br> Affect and control (1, 11) <br> Pro-social behavior (7) <br> Education methods (9) |
| Social | Performing activities: leisure and artistic (15) <br> Intergenerational experiences (2) | Social participation (1, 12) <br> Social interaction (9) <br> Volunteerism (7) <br> Social support (11) |

Following a unidimensional strategy targeting physical activity, Correa-Bautista, Sandoval-Cuellar, Alfonso Mara & Rodríguez-Daza (2012) implemented an exercise program over 12 weeks (hour-long daily sessions) designed to improve physical performance and functional status.

Among unidimensional strategies targeting cognitive functioning, Mastropietro (2014) trained older adults in the use of mnemonics, cognitive stimulation, Sudoku, and tangrams in "Memory Club." Cusack (2003) designed an 8-week mental fitness program to promote healthy aging. Latorre, Serrano, Ricarte, Bonete, Ros & Sitges (2015) implemented life review techniques for remembering positive events in non-depressed older adults; the six-session program was designed for enhancing emotional well-being, and thus, active aging. The GERO-HEALTH program focused on knowledge and learning about active aging (Lorenzo et al., 2013). Other programs focused on coping capacities (Bode et al., 2007), taking advantage of experiences, and practices from positive psychology (Jiménez et al., 2016), from psychotherapy and cognitive behavioral treatments (Scult et al., 2015), and even from training in spiritual skills (Moeini et al., 2016).

Other programs focused on strategies related to social functioning and participation. In Sikora (2008), the "Optimal Aging Program" aimed to expand the concept of aging to include the reality of healthy, active older adulthood, and to provide the opportunity for sharing experiences. Santos et al. (2015) centered their program on artistic and leisure activities for promoting quality of life, leading to healthy and active aging.

Among multidimensional programs addressing various domains of aging well, the validity of the Vital Aging program (Fernández-Ballesteros, 2002b) is well established (Caprara et al., 2013). Initially developed in 1996 as a face-to-face course at the Autonomous University of Madrid, the objective of the program is to promote active aging using a variety of strategies. The program teaches basic knowledge about aging and promotes healthy lifestyle choices (e.g., physical exercise, nutrition). It trains individuals in strategies for optimizing cognitive function and compensating for potential cognitive declines. It also teaches older adults to optimize positive affect, emotion, and control. Finally, the program promotes social relationships and social engagement throughout the life course by using new technologies. Using a variety of delivery versions (e.g., Face-to-Face, Multimedia, e-Learning, Open Course Ware, and the Internet) and through several iterations, the program has proved to be an effective tool for promoting active aging across cultural contexts (Mendoza Ruvalcaba & Fernández Ballesteros, 2016).

Among other multidimensional programs ($n = 7$), physical exercise and activity form the core of strategies that are recommended to promote successful aging due to their established and pervasive effects on mood, health, and social inclusion (Ahn et al., 2014). Cognitive and social strategies are also frequently included. For instance, the PACE program includes cognitive-behavioral counseling, pro-social behavior, and volunteering (Foy et al., 2013). Estebsari et al. (2014) include social interactions, nutrition, and leisure activities, as well as physical, mental, and spiritual growth. Canseco (2015) includes nutrition techniques, cognitive training, and social participation.

Table 28.5 shows the outcome variables and indicators taken into account by the intervention programs included in this review. On the healthy lifestyles dimension, the most common outcome variable was physical activity, considered by 9 out of 19 programs. However, outcome indicators were diverse, with measures of frequency of exercise, strength, flexibility, and balance being the most commonly used. Nutritional outcomes were considered in 8 out of 19 programs, mainly by anthropometric measures. Health status was also included as an outcome variable.

Outcomes in the domain of cognitive activity and training were measured by changes in cognitive function, including improvements in memory, executive function, processing speed, and other specific cognitive functions. For outcomes in the personality dimension, most interventions pursued positive changes in affect, mood, and emotional regulation; others targeted self-efficacy and control, coping skills, and disposition (optimism). Awareness and knowledge of the aging process were also considered among the relevant outcomes of programs

Table 28.5 *Outcome variables and indicators of successful aging included in the interventions of successful aging*

| Dimension | Outcome | Frequency (out of 19 studies) | Indicators (program number) |
|---|---|---|---|
| Behavioral Lifestyles | Physical activity | 9 | Frequency of exercise (1, 7, 9, 12)<br>Strength (5, 6, 7, 11, 14)<br>Flexibility (5, 6, 11, 14)<br>Balance (6, 12, 11, 14)<br>Intensity and duration of exercise (7, 12)<br>Physical performance (7, 6)<br>Cardiovascular endurance (5)<br>Exercise motivation (7)<br>Disability (7)<br>Physically active (6)<br>Physical agility (5)<br>Endurance, energy level, coordination (6)<br>Systolic blood pressure (11, 17)<br>Blood glucose (11) |
| | Nutrition | 8 | Anthropometric measures: weight, waist circumference, BMI (5–7, 11, 12, 14)<br>Nutritional habits (1, 9, 12)<br>Nutritional status (12, 14) |
| | Health | 8 | General health status (1, 6, 12, 18)<br>Possibility of falls (6, 14)<br>Subjective health (1)Use of medication (7)<br>Health responsibility (9)<br>Quality of sleep (6, 12)<br>Healthy lifestyle promotion behaviors (9, 16)<br>Cardiovascular disease: stroke, angina (19) |
| Cognitive Activity and Training | Cognitive function | 8 | Memory (1, 4, 7, 12, 13, 14)<br>General cognitive function (6, 7, 10, 12)<br>Subjective memory/complaints (1, 10, 12)<br>Executive functions (10, 12)<br>Processing speed (12, 14)<br>Level of mental fitness (4)<br>Visuospatial skills (10) |
| | Cognitive skills | 4 | Use of mnemonic strategies (1)<br>Confidence in mental abilities (4)<br>Knowledge and interiorization (8)<br>Frequency of intellectual activities (1)<br>Learn new things (6)<br>Ability to do new things (4) |

*(cont.)*

Table 28.5  (*cont.*)

| Dimension | Outcome | Frequency (out of 19 studies) | Indicators (program number) |
|---|---|---|---|
| Affect and Personality | Affect | 11 | Depression (4, 7, 10–13)<br>Negative/positive emotions (1, 3, 6, 17)<br>Happiness/life satisfaction (1, 13, 17, 18)<br>Subjective well-being (3, 6)<br>Self-esteem (4)<br>Affective balance (17)<br>Hedonic balance (1) |
| | Control | 9 | Self-efficacy beliefs (1, 3, 7, 14, 16)<br>Self-efficacy for exercise (7, 14)<br>Self-efficacy for nutrition (14)<br>Self-efficacy for improving memory (14) Stress perception and management (6, 7, 9)<br>Level of worry (3, 17)<br>Use of feedback (3)<br>Realistic goal setting (3, 4)<br>Proactive orientation (3)<br>Adjustment (12) |
| | Personality | 5 | Optimism (4, 12, 17)<br>Creativity (4)<br>Mental flexibility (4)<br>Spiritual growth (9)<br>Willingness to take risks (4)<br>Morale (16) |
| | Awareness of aging process | 2 | Knowledge of aging process (1, 9)<br>Perceptions on aging (1)<br>False beliefs on aging (9) |
| Social Functioning and Participation | Social participation | 7 | Frequency and satisfaction of social relationships (1, 9, 12)<br>Volunteerism (7, 12)<br>Feel safe and supported (6, 12)<br>Intergenerational relationships (2)<br>Leisure activities (1)<br>Involvement in social activities (6)<br>Loneliness/social networks (6)<br>Pro-social behavior (7)<br>Social support (11) |
| Quality of Life (QoL) | Quality of life | 3 | Health-related QoL (7, 14, 15)<br>General (14, 15)<br>Psychological/Spiritual (14, 15)<br>Socioeconomic/Family (14)<br>Environmental (15) |

geared toward promoting successful aging, given the programs' role in combating inaccurate perceptions, prejudices, stereotypes, and false beliefs. While social functioning and participation were adopted as outcome variables in 7 out of 19 programs, frequency of – and satisfaction with – social relationships emerged as the main indicator of successful aging. Finally, only three programs considered quality of life as an outcome variable.

## Conclusions and Future Perspectives

The active involvement of citizens in safeguarding their own health is of paramount importance to meeting the challenges associated with the extension of healthy life expectancy. This is required both by growing concern for social welfare and well-being, and by the increasing cost to individuals and societies of prolonged aging. Extended aging can be better addressed by enabling people to better manage the inevitable decline associated with aging and by avoiding prejudices that may lead to addressing aging in an inappropriate manner. This requires acknowledging the assets that allow individuals to continue to function in good health and to identify the policies and interventions capable of attenuating and moderating the losses and impairments most commonly associated with old age. Above, we have given an account of research and interventions showing that aging people have assets that should be valued and that the negative sides of aging can be effectively compensated or postponed.

Interventions designed to promote successful aging differ in theoretical background (conceptual and disciplinary), methods (design, goals, and targets), focus, and priorities. Clarity in their terms and aims, however, are pre-conditions to bringing theories and practices to convergence, and to creating the synergies among disciplines that are required to address the complexity of the phenomena under investigation. In this regard, much remains to be done.

Close examination of the methods used by the studies reviewed here revealed that more randomized controlled trials are needed to improve the confidence that observed changes are caused by the intervention program. In addition, greater follow-up is needed, as only three studies in the analysis were followed. It was found that pre-experimental design (which was used in many interventions, specifically the pre-post one group design) has the lowest level of scientific quality and provides the least confidence that any observed changes were caused by the intervention. Because pre-experimental design does not involve a control group, this type of study provides limited evidence that the observed changes were due to the intervention and not due to other influences.

The majority of programs reviewed here were unidimensional, focusing on a single dimension of successful aging, and centered on one strategy, most commonly psychological. However, some programs were more comprehensive and complex, involving multiple dimensions (e.g., physical activity, cognitive training, nutrition, and social participation). Again, the results of the lack of theoretical consensus in the field are a great variety of applied strategies, all of them claiming to effectively promote successful aging. In this sense, the debate on what successful aging is, how to measure it, and how to develop interventions to promote it is still open (Pruchno, 2015).

The outcome variables adopted in order to assess successful aging were also very diverse among the studies reviewed here. Physical activity was a very common target across programs; however, it was operationalized by 14 different indicators (i.e., frequency of exercise, flexibility, balance, disability index, endurance, etc.).

Despite the wide variation of strategies used and indicators of success adopted, the analyzed programs focused, in one way or another, on domains of experience commonly associated with aging well: (a) health and healthy habits, (b) cognitive function, (c) development of affectivity and control, and (d) social participation (Fernández-Ballesteros, 2002b, 2005; Fernández-Ballesteros et al., 2010, 2013).

In the first domain, most programs addressed promotion of health, physical fitness, and prevention of physical disability as key strategies, and their outcome variables were related to these. A group of programs focused on improving health status, physical performance, and functional status, controlling physical exercise and fitness, functional adequacy, and nutritional habits. According to WHO (2016), the extent to which individuals and society can benefit from extra years during aging depends heavily on health. A longer life brings great opportunities, but only if strategies for enhancing health are implemented.

In the domain of cognitive function, the programs focused on cognitive optimization and compensation for the decline associated with age. Cognitive function is an essential component of health and well-being across the life span, and understanding the relationship of aging to cognitive function is an increasingly high priority for societies, not only because of the realities of population aging, but also because of the cognitive function's intrinsic relevance to the lives of older adults (Hoffer & Alwin, 2008). Thus, efforts to improve general cognitive function, memory, attention, processing speed, and executive function, as well as training in the use of mnemonic strategies, are needed to improve health and successful aging.

Another common domain which programs focused on was the regulation of affect and personality. The promotion of positive emotions and the proper management of despondent feelings are crucial in order to cope with stress and avoid depression. To this end, sustaining and fostering self-efficacy beliefs across domains of functioning appears crucial to promote successful aging. Self-efficacy beliefs, in fact, influence people's thoughts, the course of action they choose to pursue, their challenges and goals, their commitment to action and the amount of effort invested. Likewise, they affect the outcomes people expect to achieve, their efforts, and perseverance in the face of obstacles, their resilience in the face of adversities and setbacks, the levels of stress and depression they might experience when faced with a demanding and/or inhospitable environment, and, ultimately, the achievements they attain (Bandura, 1997).

The maximization of social involvement was the fourth domain in which the programs coincided; the strategies used were the improvement of social relationships with family and friends, volunteerism, and social participation in general. Social relations exist within the context of the individual, the family, and societal development and change, and have both a main and a buffering effect on well-being (Antonucci, 1991).

Despite their differences in methods, dimensions and outcomes, the common thread running throughout the psychosocial programs reviewed here is the recognition of the importance of effective self-management, and thus, the need to develop and implement strategies for enabling older adults to pursue a life worth living long. According to WHO (2016), the implementation of these strategies should be underpinned by the following principles: human rights, equity, equality and non-discrimination (particularly on the basis of age), and intergenerational solidarity.

Finally, it should be emphasized that promoting successful aging faces numerous challenges: (1) political and public organizations should eliminate potential barriers and enhance community resources to strengthen health education programs that promote successful aging; (2) scientists and practitioners should have the resources they need to investigate and design suitable projects to promote successful aging across contexts and times; (3) older adults should be aware of their responsibility in aging well; and finally (4) society must take into consideration that older adults are an important capital and worth the investment.

## References

Ahn, O., Gyeong, H., Chang, S. J., et al. (2014). Effect of an integrated health management program based on successful aging in Korean women. *Public Health Nursing*, 32(4), 307–15. doi: 10.1111/phn.12177.

Antonucci, T. C. (1991). Social relationships and aging well. *Journal of the American Society on Aging*, 15(1), 39–44.

Aldwin, C. M., Spiro, A., Park, C. L. (2006). Health, behavior, and optimal aging: a life span developmental perspective. In J. E. Birren & K. W. Schaie (Eds.), *Handbook of the Psychology of Aging* (6th edn., pp. 85–104). Burlington, USA: Elsevier Academic Press.

Atchley, R. C. (1989). A continuity theory of normal aging. *The Gerontologist*, 29(2), 183–90. doi: https://doi.org/10.1093/geront/29.2.183.

Baltes, P. B., Baltes, M. M. (1990). Psychological perspectives on successful aging: The model of selective optimization with compensation. In P. B. Baltes & M. M. Baltes (Eds.), *Successful Aging: Perspectives from the Behavioral Sciences* (pp. 1–34). New York, USA: Cambridge University Press.

Baltes, P. B., Freund, A. M., Li, S. C. (2005). The psychological science of human aging. In M. L. Johnson, V. L. Bengston, P.G. Coleman & R. B. L. Kirkwood (Eds.), *The Cambridge Handbook of Age and Ageing*. Cambridge, UK: University Press.

Bandura, A. (1977). Self-efficacy: toward a unifying theory of behavioral change. *Psychological Review*, 84(2), 191–215.

Bode, C., De Ridder, D. T., Kuijer, R. G., et al. (2007). Effects of an intervention promoting proactive coping competencies in middle and late adulthood. *The Gerontologist*, 47(1), 42–51. doi: https://doi.org/10.1093/geront/47.1.42.

Boyes, M. (2013). Outdoor adventure and successful aging. *Aging and Society*, 33(4), 644–65. doi: https://doi.org/10.1017/S0144686X12000165.

Bowling, A., Iliffe, S. (2006). Which model of successful ageing should be used? Baseline findings from a British longitudinal survey of ageing. *Age and Ageing*, 35(6), 607–14. doi: https://doi.org/10.1093/ageing/afl100.

Calero, M. D. (2003). La utilidad de los programas de intervención cognitiva en personas mayores. *Revista Española de Geriatría y Gerontología*. 38(3), 305–7. doi: 10.1016/S0211-139X(03)74905-1.

Canseco, M. (2015). *Programa de intervención para envejecer con éxito dirigido a personas mayores de la ciudad de México (Doctoral Thesis)*. Universidad de Santiago de Compostela, España.

Campbell, D. T., Stanley, J. C. (1995). *Diseños experimentales y cuasiexperimentales en la investigación social*. Argentina: Amorrortu Editores.

Caprara, G. V., Caprara, M., Steca, P. (2003). Personality's correlates of adult development and aging. *European Psychologist*, 8(3), 131–47. doi: http://dx.doi.org/10.1027//1016-9040.8.3.131.

Caprara, M. G., Molina, M. A., Schettini, R., et al. (2013). Active aging promotion: Results from the Vital Aging Program. *Current Gerontology and Geriatrics Research*, 2013, 1–14. doi: http://dx.doi.org/10.1155/2013/817813.

Caprara, M. G., Fernández-Ballesteros, R., Alessandri, G. (2015). Promoting aging well: evaluation of Vital-Aging-Multimedia Program in Madrid, Spain. *Health Promotion International*, 31(3), 515–22. doi: https://doi.org/10.1093/heapro/dav014.

Chi, I., Lubben, J. (1994). The California preventive health care for the aging program: differences between the younger old and the oldest old. *Health Promotion International*, 9(3), 169–76. doi: https://doi.org/10.1093/heapro/9.3.169.

Correa-Bautista, J. E., Sandoval-Cuellar, C., Alfonso Mara, M. L., Rodríguez-Daza, K. M. (2012). Cambios en la aptitud física en un grupo de mujeres adultas mayores bajo el modelo de envejecimiento activo. *Revista de la Facultad de Medicina*, 60(1), 21–30.

Cusack, S. A. (2003). Mental fitness for life: Assessing the impact of an 8-week mental fitness program on healthy aging. *Educational Gerontology*, 29(5), 393–403.

Diener, E., Chan, M. Y. (2011). Happy people live longer: subjective well-being contributes to health and longevity. *Applied Psychology Health and Well-Being*, 3(1), 1–43. doi: 10.1111/j.1758-0854.2010.01045.x

Estebsari, F., Hossein, M., Foroushani, A. R., et al. (2014). An educational program based on the successful aging approach on health-promoting behaviours in the elderly: a clinical trial study. *Iranian Red Crescent Medical Journal*, 16(4), e16314.

Fernández-Ballesteros, R. (2002a). Envejecimiento satisfactorio. In J. M. Martínez Lage (Ed.), *Corazón y cerebro, ecuación crucial de envejecimiento*. Madrid, España: Pfeizer.

      (2002b). *Vivir con vitalidad*. Madrid, Spain: Pirámide.

      (2005). Evaluation of "Vital Aging-M": a psychological program for promoting optimal aging. *European Psychologist*, 10(2), 146–56.

      (2008). *Active Ageing. The Contribution of Psychology*. Göttingen, Germany: Hogrefe & Huber Publishers.

Fernández-Ballesteros, R., Calero, M. D. (1995). Training effects on intelligence of older persons. *Archives of Gerontology and Geriatrics*, 26, 185–98.

Fernández-Ballesteros, R., Caprara, M. G., García, L. F. (2004). Vivir con Vitalidad-M: un programa europeo multimedia. *Psychosocial Intervention*, 13(1), 63–84.

Fernández-Ballesteros, R., Caprara, M. G., Iñiguez, J, et al. (2005a). Vital Aging-M: an European multimedia programme. *Psychology in Spain*, 9(1), 1–12.

Fernández-Ballesteros, R., Caprara, M. G., Iñiguez, J., et al. (2005b). Promocion del envejecimiento activo: Efectos del programa Vivir con Vitalidad. *Revista Española de Geriatría y Gerontología*, 40(2), 92–102.

Fernández-Ballesteros, R., Zamarrón, M. D., Calero, M. D, et al. (2007). Cognitive Plasticity and cognitive impairment. In R. Fernández-Ballesteros (Ed.), *Geropsychology: European perspectives for an aging world* (pp. 145–64). Göttingen, Germany: Hogrefe & Huber Publishers.

Fernández-Ballesteros, R., Zamarrón, M. D., Molina, M. A., et al. (2010). Successful ageing: criteria and predictors. *Psicothema*, 22(4), 641–7.

Fernández-Ballesteros, R., Botella, J., Zamarrón, M. D., et al. (2012a).Cognitive plasticity in normal and pathological aging. *Clinical Interventions in Aging*, 7, 15–25. doi: http://dx.doi.org/10.2147/CIA.S27008

Fernández-Ballesteros, R., Molina, M. A., Schettini, R., Santacreu, M. (2013). *The semantic network of aging well*. In J. M. Robine, C. Jagger, & E. M. Crimmins (Eds.), Healthy Longevity: Annual Review of Gerontology and Geriatrics (p. 33). New York, NY: Springer.

Foy, C. G., Vitolins, M. Z., Case, L. D., et al. (2013). Incorporating prosocial behavior to promote physical activity in older adults: Rationale and design of the Program for Active Aging and Community Engagement (PACE). *Contemporary Clinical Trials*, 36(1), 284–97. doi: 10.1016/j.cct.2013.07.004.

Frederickson, B. L., Losada, M. F. (2005). Positive affect and the complex dynamics of human flourishing. *American Psychologist*, 60(7), 678–86. doi: 10.1037/0003-066X.60.7.678.

Fries, J. F. (2002). Reducing disability in older age. *Journal of the American Medical Association*, 288(24), 3164–6. doi: doi:10.1001/jama.288.24.3164.

Fries, J. F., Crapo, L. M. (1981). *Vitality and Aging*. New York, USA: Freeman.

González-Pardo, H., Pérez-Álvarez, M. (2013).Epigenetics and its implications for psychology. *Psicothema*, 25(1), 3–12.

Hank, K. (2011). How successful in aging do older Europeans age? Finding from SHARE. *Journal of Gerontology. Series B, Psychological Sciences and Social Sciences*, 66(2), 230–6. doi: 10.1093/geronb/gbq089.

Hartman-Stein, P., Potkanowicz, E. S. (2003). Behavioral determinants of healthyaging: good news for the baby boomer generation. *Online Journal of Issues in Nursing*, 8. Retrieved from www.nursingworld.org/MainMenuCategories/ANAMarketplace/ANAPeriodicals/OJIN/TableofContents/Volume82003/No2May2003/BehaviorandHealthyAging.aspx (last accessed 01/25/2017).

Havighurst, R. J. (1961). Successful aging. *The Gerontologist*, 1(1), 8–13. doi: https://doi.org/10.1093/geront/1.1.8.

Havighurst, R. (1963). Successful aging. In R. H. Williams, C. Tibbitts & W. Donahue (Eds.), *Processes of Aging* (Vol. 1, pp. 299–320). New York, USA: Atherton.

Hertzog, C., Kramer, A. F., Wilson, R. S. et al. (2009). Enrichment effects on adult cognitive development. *Psychological Science in the Public Interest*, 9 (1), 1–65. doi: 10.1111/j.1539-6053.2009.01034.x.

Hoffer, S. M., Alwin, D. F. (2008). *Handbook of cognitive aging. Interdisciplinary perspectives*. Thousand Oaks, USA: Sage Publications Inc.

Jiménez, M. G., Izal, M., Montorio, I. (2016). Programa para la mejora del bienestar de las personas mayores. Estudio piloto basado en la psicología positiva. *Suma Psicológica*, 23(1), 51–9.

Keyes, C. L. (2007). Psychological Well-Being. In J. E. Birren (Ed.), *Encyclopedia of Gerontology*, 2nd Ed. Elsevier Academic Press.

Kirkwood T. B. L. (2005). The Biological Science of Human Aging. In M. L. Johnson (Ed.), *Age and Ageing* (pp. 72–84). Cambridge, UK: Cambridge University Press.

Kliegl, R., Smith, J., Baltes P. B. (1989). Testing-the limits and the study of adult age differences in cognitive plasticity of a mnemonic skill. *Developmental Psychology*, 25(2), 247–56.

Latorre, J. M., Serrano, J. P., Ricarte, J., Bonete, B., Ros, L., Sitges, E. (2015). Life review based on remembering specific positive events in active aging. *Journal of Aging and Health*, 27(1), 140–57. doi: 10.1177/0898264314541699.

Lojo-Seoane, C., Facal, D., Juncos-Rabadán, O. (2012). ¿Previene la actividad intelectual el deterioro cognitivo? Relaciones entre reserva cognitiva y deterioro cognitivo ligero. *Revista Española de Geriatría y Gerontología*, 47(6), 270–8. doi: 10.1016/j.regg.2012.02.006.

Lorenzo, T., Millan-Calenti, J. C., Lorenzo López, L., et al. (2013). Efectos del programa educativo Gero- Health sobre el nivel de interiorización de conocimientos de prevención y promoción de la salud en personas mayores. *Revista de Investigación Educativa*, 31(2), 502–15. doi: http://dx.doi.org/10.6018/rie.31.2.163391

Lyubomirsky, S., King, L. A., Diener, E. (2005). The benefits of frequent positive affect: Does happiness lead to success? *Psychological Bulletin*, 131(6), 803–55. doi: 10.1037/0033-2909.131.6.803.

Mastropietro, E. (2014). Clubes de memoria. Programas de Intervención Comunitaria en Salud para Adultos Mayores. *Revista Psicología*, 33(1), 15–32.

Mendes de Leon, C. F., Glass, T. A., Berkman, L. F. (2003). Social engagement and disability in a community population of older adults: the New Haven EPESE. *American Journal of Epidemiology*, 157(7), 633–42.

Mendoza Ruvalcaba, N. M., Arias Merino, E. D. (2015). "I am active": effects of a program to promote active aging. *Clinical Interventions in Aging*, 2015(10), 829–37. doi: 10.2147/CIA.S79511.

Mendoza Ruvalcaba, N. M., Fernández Ballesteros, R. (2016). Effectiveness of the Vital Aging program to promote active aging in Mexican older adults. *Clinical Interventions in Aging*, 11, 1631–44. doi: 10.2147/CIA.S102930.

Midlarsky, E., Kahana E. (2007). Altruism, well-being, and mental health in late life. In Post S. G. (Ed.), *Altruism and health: Perspectives from empirical research* (pp. 56–69). New York, USA: Oxford University Press.

Mnich, E., Hofreuter-Gätgens, K., Salomon, T., et al. (2013). Outcome evaluation of a health promotion among the elderly. *Gesundheitswesen*, 75(2), 5–10. doi: 10.1055/s-0032-1311617.

Moeini, M., Sharifi, S., Zandiyeh, Z. (2016). Does Islamic spiritual program lead to successful aging? A randomized clinical trial. *Journal of Education and Health Promotion*, 5(2), 1–7. doi: 10.4103/2277-9531.184561.

Newman, A. B., Dodson, J. A., Church, T. S., et al., LIFE study group. (2016). Cardiovascular events in a physical activity intervention compared with a successful aging intervention. The LIFE study randomized trial. *Journal of the American Medical Association Cardiology*, 1(5), 568–74. doi: 10.1001/jamacardio.2016.1324.

Park, D. C., Gutchess, A. H. Meade, M. L., et al. (2007). Improving cognitive function in older adults: nontraditional approaches. *The Journals of Gerontology B Psychological Sciences Social Sciences*, 62(s1), 45–52.

Pruchno, R. (2015). Successful aging: contentious past, productive future. *The Gerontologist*, 55(1), 1–4. doi: https://doi.org/10.1093/geront/gnv002.

Rowe, J. W., Kahn, R. L. (1997). Successful aging. *The Gerontologist*, 37(4), 433–40. doi: https://doi.org/10.1093/geront/37.4.433.

(1998). *Successful Aging*. New York, USA: Pantheon.

Ryff, C. D. (1982). Successful aging: a developmental approach. *The Gerontologist*, 22(2), 209–14. doi: https://doi.org/10.1093/geront/22.2.209.

(1989). Beyond Ponce de Leon and life satisfaction: New directions in quest of successful aging. *International Journal of Behavioral Development*, 12(1), 35–55.

Santos, L. C., Oliveira, L. M. A., Alves Barbosa, M., et al. (2015). Calidad de vida de los mayores que participan en el grupo de promoción de la salud. *Enfermería Global*, 14(4), 1–11.

Scult, M., Haime, V., Jacquart, J., et al. (2015). A healthy aging program for older adults: effects on self-efficacy and morale. *Advances in Mind Body Medicine*, 29(1), 26–33.

Schaie K. W. (2005). *Developmental Influences on Adult Intelligence: The Seattle Longitudinal Study*. New York, USA: Oxford University Press.

Sikora, S. (2008).The University of Arizona College of Medicine Optimal Aging Program. *Gerontology & Geriatrics Education*, 27(2), 59–67. doi: http://dx.doi.org/10.1300/J021v27n02_07.

Staehelin, H. R. (2005). Promoting health and well-being in later life. In M. L. Johnson (Ed.), *Age and Ageing* (pp. 165–77). Cambridge, UK: Cambridge University Press.

Tang, K. C., Nutbeam, D., Aldinger, C., et al. (2009). Schools for health, education and development: a call for action. *Health Promotion International*, 24(1), 68–77. doi: https://doi.org/10.1093/heapro/dan037.

Warner, L. M., Schwarzer, R., Schüz, B., et al. (2012). Health-specific optimism mediates between objective and perceived physical functioning in older adults. *Journal of Behavioral Medicine*, 35(4), 400–6. doi:10.1007/s10865-011-9368-y.

World Health Organization WHO. (2002). *Active Aging. A Policy Framework*. Geneva, Switzerland: World Health Organization.

World Health Organization WHO. (2016). *Global Strategy and Action Plan on Aging and Health (2016-2010)*. Geneva, Switzerland: World Health Organization.

Zunzunegui, M. V., Rodriguez-Laso, A., Otero, A., et al. (2005). Disability and social ties: comparative findings of the CLESA study. *European Journal of Ageing*, 2(1), 40–7. doi: 10.1007/s10433-005-0021-x.

# 29 Promoting Successful Aging in the Community

Víctor Manuel Mendoza-Núñez and María de la Luz Martínez-Maldonado

## Introduction

Population aging represents major challenges for all societies, and it has profound consequences for individual and community life, as well as repercussions in the various spheres of human existence such as the social, economic, political, cultural, and psychological spheres.

In Mexico, 10.4 percent of the total population (12.4 million) is older (≥60 years), and the average life expectancy at age 60 is 22 years (INEGI, 2016). This demographic situation has legal, social, and economic implications and, above all, health risks. However, more than half of all older adults between 60 and 74 years maintain their health and are functional in the basic and instrumental activities of daily life, and their cognitive function is conserved, which represents an opportunity to strengthen the actions for maintaining and extending functionality. Additionally, there is a high prevalence of chronic-degenerative diseases linked to disability and poverty, which affects the quality of life of the elderly and their families. For this reason, it is necessary to propose and develop programs for promoting successful aging in the community based on scientific knowledge and the sociocultural context of each country.

From an individual perspective, in 1997 Rowe and Kahn defined successful aging as a "low probability of disease and disease-related disability, high cognitive and physical functional capacity, and active engagement with life. All three terms are relative and the relationship among them is to some extent hierarchical" (Rowe & Kahn, 1997). This concept has been tested through several longitudinal and cross-sectional studies (e.g., McArthur Foundation Longitudinal study, Karlamangla et al., 2002; SHARE study, Hank, 2011; MHAS Cohort, Wong et al., 2015; ELEA Study, Fernandez-Ballesteros et al., 2010).

On the other hand, the World Health Organization (WHO) proposed the concept of Active Aging (AA), which is defined as "the process of optimizing opportunities for health, participation and security in order to enhance the quality of life as people age" (WHO, 2002). This paradigm raises an alternative approach for looking at work strategies and community interventions around the older people group. Active Aging emphasizes the importance of activities related to the continued participation of older adults in social, economic, cultural, spiritual, and civic issues. In recent years, several studies and international organisms have been developing indicators to clarify the concept of AA. In this sense, although there is no consensus on the components and indicators that allow objective measurements of active aging, the common element of the different proposals is "social participation" (Walker, 2006; Fernández-Ballesteros, 2008; Bélanger et al., 2015; UNECE, 2015).

Healthy aging is another concept considered in the focus of our Model of Community Gerontology. In this regard, in the World Report on Ageing and Health (2015), healthy aging was defined as "the process of developing and maintaining the functional ability that enables well-being in older age" (WHO, 2015), stating that:

- "**Functional ability** comprises the health related attributes that enable people to be and to do what they have reason to value. It is made up of the **intrinsic capacity** of the individual, relevant **environmental characteristics**, and the interactions between the individual and these characteristics."
- "**Intrinsic capacity** is the composite of all the physical and mental capacities of an individual."
- "**Environments** comprise all the factors in the extrinsic world that form the context of an individual's life. These include – from the micro level to the macro-level – home, communities, and the broader society. Within these environments are a range of factors, including the built environment, people, and their relationships, attitudes and values, health and social policies, the systems that support them, and the services that they implement."
- "**Well-being** is considered in the broadest sense and includes domains such as happiness, satisfaction, and fulfillment."
- "**Healthy Aging** starts at birth with our genetic inheritance. The expression of these genes can be influenced by experiences in the womb, and by subsequent environmental exposures and behaviors."
- "**Personal characteristics** include those that are usually fixed, such as our sex and ethnicity, as well as those that have some mobility or reflect social norms, such as our occupation, educational attainment, gender, or wealth."
- "An individual may have **reserves of functional ability** that they are not drawing on. These reserves contribute to an older person's resilience."
- "Healthy Aging model conceptualizes **resilience** as the ability to maintain or improve a level of functional ability in the face of adversity (either through resistance, recovery, or adaptation).

Our working group, from a pragmatic point of view, frames active and successful aging and then proposes conceptualizing healthy aging as the process by which the elderly adopt or strengthen healthy lifestyles through self-care strategies, mutual assistance, and self-management. As a result, they can make optimal use of networks of formal and informal social support to maintain, extend, and restore physical, mental, and social functioning, and can achieve maximum wellness, health, and quality of life in the sociocultural context (Mendoza-Núñez, 2013).

In this framework, the National Autonomous University of Mexico (FES Zaragoza, UNAM) developed a Multidisciplinary Model of Community Gerontology for Community-Dwelling Older Adults with the aim of training the elderly in self-care, mutual-help, and self-promotion, all related to preventing and controlling chronic diseases that have a high prevalence in old age, which in turn, maintains the functionality and well-being of the elderly (Mendoza-Núñez et al., 1996, 2009a; Martínez-Maldonado et al., 2007).

Our research group has evaluated the effect of training older adults on basic gerontology topics that can help them adopt healthy lifestyles to prevent and control of chronic diseases. We also aimed to determine the relationship between oxidative stress (OxS) and the health and disease status in an older Mexican urban-dwelling population. This chapter presents some findings from our studies. We begin with the conceptual framework that we used to develop our research, which is followed by a presentation of the most relevant results.

## Conceptual Framework

### Human Aging and Old Age

Humans are complex beings with diverse biological, psychological, and social elements. These are interdependent, while also combining together and complementing each other. Therefore, human aging is different from cellular, organ, or system aging. In addition, as noted by Leonard Hayflick (1996), "it is not the mere passage of time; but the manifestation of biological events that occur during a period of time, which defines aging"; hence, "aging occurs over time, but not because of the passage of time." In this sense, most of the cells that are present in our body now did not exist 5 or 10 years ago, or even 2 days ago; this phenomenon occurs in all stages of life (i.e., in children, adults, and the elderly). Therefore, the cells that are renewed and replaced by new ones in the past decade are younger in all age groups, including the elderly.

In this context, we define human aging as "a gradual and adaptive process, characterized by a relative decrease in the biological reserve and response to demands to maintain or restore homeostasis, due to morphological, physiological, biochemical, psychological, and social changes, prompted by genetic load and accumulated wear, and the challenges that a person faces throughout their life in a given environment" (Mendoza-Núñez et al., 2016a).

There is no consensus in the gerontological field about the age at which aging begins; however, some authors, based on a time-limited approach, have established that aging begins at birth or conception (Gutierrez-Robledo, 1999). We assume that human aging starts from the fifth decade of life, at approximately 45 years of age, based on biological, physical, psychological, and social changes that are evident and related to the aging process in most of the population at this stage of life (Jones et al., 2002; Troen, 2003). This does not mean that we will ignore that human aging is a complex, multidimensional, and multifactorial process, which is individualized; however, a starting point of aging should be assumed for implementing social and community programs aimed at this section of the population (Mendoza-Núñez et al., 2016a).

By contrast, chronological age is usually considered a parameter to indicate the point of time at which a person becomes old. In this sense, it has been established that old age begins at 60 years of age in developing countries and at 65 years in developed countries (Naciones Unidas, 1979). Old age is a social condition with specific qualities that are manifested in different ways, depending on the historical and social characteristics of each person. We should consider the age of onset of aging proposed for community intervention (approximately 45 years), which does not coincide with the onset of old age ($\geq$60 years). Therefore, to implement community intervention programs aimed at people who are in process of aging, the programs should include the population of people aged 45 years and older.

## Homeostasis, Oxidative Stress, and Chronic Diseases

The main biological mechanisms linked to aging and health in older community-dwelling individuals include homeostasis, allostasis, allostatic load, hormesis, inflamm-aging, and OxS (Seeman et al., 2001; Rattan, 2001; McEwen, 2002; Radak et al., 2005; Davies, 2016). These mechanisms influence the endocrine, immune, cardiovascular, musculoskeletal, and nervous systems, affecting health as well as physical, psychological, and social functionality.

**Homeostasis** is defined as the dynamic equilibrium of a multisystem that allows the maintenance of adequate physiological function in response to the endogenous and exogenous demands to which an individual is constantly exposed. In this regard, Kelvin Davies (2016) recently modified the concept as "adaptive homeostasis," which is defined as "the transient expansion or contraction of the homeostatic range in response to exposure to sub-toxic, non-damaging, signaling molecules or events, or the removal or cessation of such molecules or events." Homeostatic reserves gradually decrease with aging; however, the adaptive capacity is maintained on an individual basis, considering the genetics, lifestyle, environment, and life history of the individual.

**Allostasis** is an adaptive response of the body to maintain homeostasis in response to the endogenous and exogenous requirements determined by the state of health, lifestyle, and psychological and environmental factors. This mechanism of the adaptive response has a biological cost. Therefore, when it is required repetitively or the process is inefficient due to continuous exposure to factors that generate biological stress, it promotes an *allostatic load*, resulting in a less efficient allostatic process and increasing vulnerability to the onset of acute and chronic diseases during aging (Seeman et al., 2001; McEwen, 2002).

**Hormesis** is another biological mechanism related to longevity and successful aging. It is defined as a secondary adaptive process in response to gradual exposure, continuous and safe dosages, and chemical, physical, psychological, and social changes that strengthen homeostasis and increase longevity. In high doses, these exposures are harmful, such as alcohol intake, exercise, and radiation and psychosocial stress (Rattan, 2001; Radak et al., 2005). For example, it has been shown that the daily intake of two glasses of red wine has a beneficial effect on health; however, when these doses are exceeded, the effect is harmful. Additionally, moderate physical exercise after which the person does not feel fatigued (40 to 60 minutes, five days/week, which is less intense than exhaustive exercise) has a positive effect on health, but if exercise is performed exhaustively, there is greater OxS and a higher chronic disease risk.

Inflammation related to aging, or "inflamm-aging," is characterized by an inflammatory process that is low grade, controlled, asymptomatic, chronic, and systemic, and favors an increase in the production of pro-inflammatory factors, such as interleukins 1 and 6 (IL 1 and 6) and tumor necrosis factor-alpha (TNF) (Franceschi et al., 2000). In addition, the oxidative damage generated by free radicals related to aging potentiates the inflammatory process through inflammasomes, thereby increasing the risk of chronic disease and its complications (Cannizzo et al., 2011; Salminen et al., 2012).

However, it has been observed that centenarians and elderly individuals, who present with successful aging, develop a parallel mechanism to inflamm-aging, termed "anti-inflammaging," which is associated with the increased production of interleukin 10 and cortisol (Franceschi et al., 2007).

**Oxidative stress** is a biochemical alteration characterized by an imbalance between the generation of free radicals (FR) and antioxidants, which is in favor of FR, leading to oxidative damage of macromolecules (proteins, carbohydrates, lipids, and DNA). OxS has been linked to the aging process (Oliveira et al., 2010; Semba et al., 2010; Pandey & Rizvi, 2010), with Harman (1956) being the first to note that aging occurs because of OxS.

## Model of Community Gerontology

Our working group developed a Model of Community Gerontology for Community-Dwelling Older Adults for healthy aging at the community level, which is framed in active aging and considers key strategies for self-care, mutual-help, and self-promotion by establishing the adoption and maintenance of healthy lifestyles (Figure 29.1). These include physical exercise, adequate diet, sleep hygiene, and self-esteem to maintain, extend, and restore physical, mental, and social functioning at the community level (Martínez-Maldonado et al., 2007; Mendoza-Núñez et al., 2009a). In this sense, the aim of this model is to train older people on the basic knowledge of gerontology for self-care, mutual-help, and self-promotion related to preventing and controlling chronic diseases that have a high prevalence in older age. As a result, individuals can better maintain their functionality and well-being.

This model considers empowerment, active participation, solidarity, and reciprocity to be key elements for development of successful aging in the community through the optimal use of formal and informal social-support networks for participants. These can help train older people in self-care, mutual-help, and self-promotion related to the prevention and control of chronic diseases that have a high prevalence in old age, thereby maintaining their functionality and well-being.

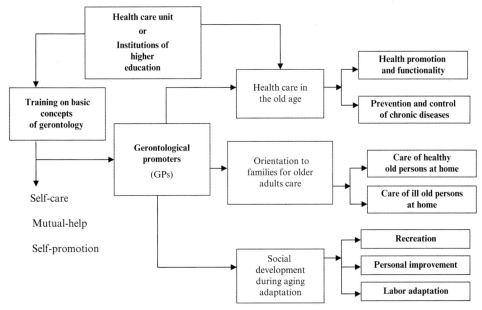

**Figure 29.1.** *Model of community gerontology for community-dwelling older adults*

Primary Gerontological Health Care Unit or Institutions of Higher Education in Gerontology are responsible of the design and implementation of educational programs and guides the training of the gerontological promoters for the development of mutual-help groups. These groups are integrated by ten to fifteen older adults of nearby communities with similar interests. They are mainly involved in promoting successful aging in the community through of self-care, mutual help, and self-promotion guidelines established by the program. The model is addressed toward the following objectives: (i) the supervision of the gerontological health status of participants in the program; (ii) the training of qualified gerontological healthcare promoters; (iii) to provide orientation and guidance to families with regard to basic care practices with both healthy and sick older adults; and (iv) to promote the social and gerontological development of the older populations.

With this approach, we have proposed community gerontology as a strategy for the implementation of healthy aging programs that are framed in terms of active aging in the theoretical approach of collective health. Therefore, the participation of older adults in the organization and development of gerontological programs is a key element because older individuals should be recognized as a social capital for their own development (Mendoza-Núñez et al., 2013).

As a key element, the model establishes the training of gerontological promoters (GPs) from among the older adults themselves. The GPs function as mutual-help group coordinators and establish self-care and self-promotion actions for elderly well-being and social development (Mendoza-Núñez et al., 2009a).

Self-care at the gerontological level refers to the reasoned and theoretically based behavior of the individual that allows an elderly adult to decide and act on the prevention, diagnosis, and treatment of his/her disease. At the same time, the individual can maintain health and maximal enjoyment of the quality of life (QoL) according to his/her sociocultural context, utilizing formal and informal social networks in an optimal fashion during aging. Similarly, mutual-help

Table 29.1 *Basic topics of gerontology for the training of gerontological promoters*

| | |
|---|---|
| Aging and old age | Depression |
| Age-related biological, psychological, and social changes | Prevention of falls in the elderly |
| Ageism | Nutrition in the aging |
| Active aging and empowerment | Physical exercise in the aging |
| Social support networks | Skin, nails, and foot care in the elderly |
| Healthy aging and functionality | Mouth and teeth care in the elderly |
| Self-care, mutual-help, and self-promotion | Sexuality in older adults |
| Self-esteem and aging | Elder abuse |
| Diabetes mellitus and arterial hypertension | Thanatology |
| Mild cognitive impairment and memory training | Quality of life and aging |

includes reasoned solidarity-oriented behavior that is adopted by a group of elderly individuals who share similar problems, and whose members are aware of the advantages and commitments with voluntarily participating in a group. Self-promotion involves the actions that an older adult or a self-help group autonomously perform in optimal form, while considering elements and mechanisms of formal and informal social support networks.

The model considers a healthcare unit or institution of higher education whose purpose is to coordinate the big-network of mutual-help groups for elderly adults in which self-care is a daily practice for chronic disease prevention and control, as well as for achieving maximal well-being and QoL in old age (Figure 29.1).

The healthcare unit or institution of higher education will be responsible for training gerontological promoters (GPs) according to the formal academic structure of a workshop (Table 29.1), with consideration given to the following principles in teaching older adults (García et al., 2002): (1) older adults only learn what they want to learn; (2) older adults only learn what they are capable of learning; (3) older adults mainly learn what they teach themselves; and (4) older adults mainly learn in terms of their experience.

The requirements for participating in the training courses for GPs are as follows: (1) interest in participating in an intensive training program focused on holistic gerontological development; (2) between 60 and 74 years of age; (3) literate; (4) absence of handicapping illnesses or serious visual or auditory disabilities; and (5) leadership attributes and the ability to coordinate small groups.

We implemented a 60-hour workshop that integrated both theoretical and practical aspects (14 weekly sessions). An introductory textbook, titled: "Envejecimiento Activo y Saludable. Fundamentos y Estrategias desde la Gerontología Comunitaria," was specifically designed for this aim (Mendoza-Núñez et al., 2013).

The topics for the workshop were selected and approved by a panel of four gerontologists who took into consideration basic knowledge on Community Gerontology and age-related changes in the following categories: (a) biological, psychological, and social aspects; (b) prevention of chronic diseases; (c) healthy lifestyle in the aging period; (d) empowerment; and (e) social networks according to the active aging paradigm.

The pillars of the model are as follows: (1) Health Care in Old Age, (2) Orientation to Families for Older Adults Care, and (3) Social Development during Aging

## Healthcare in Old Age (HC-Old Age)

The fundamental objective of HC-old age is to prevent and detect the diseases that have the greatest prevalence in the elderly (e.g., high blood pressure, diabetes mellitus, depression, osteoarthrosis, cognitive deterioration, and osteoporosis), and to establish healthy aging actions for the maintenance, prolongation, and recuperation of physical, mental, and social functionality (Figure 29.1). The active aging program also seeks to improve the self-perception of psychosocial well-being, while considering the elderly adult's physical condition and sociocultural environment. Control programs should be implemented for healthy and ill older adults that include pre-established evaluation, surveillance, and primary healthcare actions. These actions should be performed by previously trained older adults in coordination with GPs, who are in turn supported and supervised by the healthcare unit or institution of higher education.

## Orientation to Families for Older Adult Care

Gerontological promoters should possess sufficient knowledge for orienting and training family members to provide basic care for the healthy and ill elderly adults in their homes, with the purpose of preventing diseases and/or their complications in addition to promoting healthy lifestyles for the maintenance, prolongation, and recuperation of physical, mental, and social functionality.

## Gerontological Social Development

Among its goals, the model contemplates maximum enjoyment by older adults of their situation of being old. Therefore, implementing programs for recreation, adaptation, and psychosocial and occupational improvement within an anthropological focus is recommended according to the elderly individual's interests, age, education level, gender, health state, and socioeconomic situation.

The model established flexible general guidelines that were framed within an active aging paradigm. Therefore, actions for Gerontological Social Development (GSD) should be adopted by the population in which the model is implemented (rural or urban), as well as by older adult groups with different sociocultural and economic conditions.

## Factors Linked to Empowerment and Active Aging of Older Adults

Education is one of the key elements in the promotion of successful aging in a community with a thorough paradigm for active aging (WHO, 2002). Similarly, the importance of social support networks to achieve healthy aging has been recognized (Uchino, 2006). In this sense, our research group proposed the aforementioned model with the aim of training older adults on basic gerontology topics for adopting healthy lifestyles to prevent and control chronic diseases, while optimally using social support networks (Mendoza-Núñez et al., 1996). In this framework, a study was conducted in a rural Mexican community (Valle del Mezquital) based on an action-research paradigm. The aim of this study is to analyze the factors that contribute to the empowerment of older adults in a rural Mexican community, which in turn, promotes active aging. The 155 elderly subjects, with elementary school education, participated in a formal training program promoting gerontological development and health education. The participants then became coordinators of mutual-help groups (gerontological nucleus) in Mexico. In-depth interviews were performed to assess the empowerment after training for active aging. There was an increasing feeling of empowerment, creativity, and self-fulfillment among participants. Among the main factors that positively influenced training of the elderly in active aging was the teaching of gerontology topics themselves, as were their motivation, self-esteem, increased undertaking of responsibility, feeling of belonging to the group, and sharing of information based on personal experience and gerontological knowledge. We found that the main factors that contribute to the empowerment of older adults in a rural Mexican community, who participate in active aging programs, are the training and teaching of gerontology topics themselves, as well as their interest, experience, and involvement (Martínez-Maldonado et al., 2007).

## Social Support Networks and Diabetes Control

In Mexico, the National Health and Nutrition Examination Survey reported that the prevalence of type 2 diabetes mellitus (DM2) in people over 60 years of age is more than 20 percent. The highest rates of DM2 are seen in men aged 60–69 years (24.1 percent) and women aged 70–79 years (27.4 percent) (Gutiérrez et al., 2013). Additionally, it has been reported that only 30 percent of diagnosed adult diabetics in Mexico have adequate control; hence, it is estimated that 2 of every 3 diabetics are uncontrolled (Hernández-Romieu et al., 2011). Additionally, it has been noted that social support networks are a key determinant of several diseases and therapeutic adherence for diabetes control (Uchino, 2006; Miller & Dimatteo, 2013). Therefore, it is of interest to determine the relationship and mechanisms that explain the effect of social support networks on diabetes mellitus control. For this reason, a cross-sectional study was performed on a convenience sample of 182 older diabetic people who were active participants in community self-care and mutual help groups in Mexico City for more than 1 year. All were independents and had medical diagnostics, demonstrating that they had diabetes without complications for 1 or more years. We measured the biochemical and anthropometric parameters, social support networks for older people (SSN-Older), and then determined their perceived quality of life. Patients with uncontrolled diabetes mellitus had an HbA1c (%) $\geq$ 8. It was found that 65 percent (118/182) of the elderly diabetics in the study were controlled. We observed a significantly higher average score in the SSN-Older scale on the extra-familial support subscale in the controlled diabetic group compared with the uncontrolled group (57 $\pm$ 25 vs. 49 $\pm$ 30, $p < 0.05$). Additionally, the average satisfaction score, as observed from SSN-Older scale data, was significantly higher in the controlled diabetics group compared with the uncontrolled group (51 $\pm$ 21 vs. 42 $\pm$ 22, $p = 0.01$). Similarly, in the quality of life analysis, we observed that 81 percent of the controlled diabetics perceived a high quality of life compared with 19 percent of the uncontrolled group ($p < 0.001$). Our findings suggest that social support networks, especially community self-help groups, determine the social capital for the control of diabetes mellitus in older people in the community (Mendoza-Núñez et al., 2016b). It would be necessary to continue this line of research with longitudinal studies to confirm our findings.

## Effects of a Model of Community Gerontology on Oxidative Stress and Cognitive Function

It has been shown that some self-care-associated lifestyles, such as physical exercise, adequate nutrition, sleep, and social interaction, can improve the efficiency of antioxidant activity, preventing and/or controlling age-related chronic disease (Sakano et al., 2009). Likewise, we have demonstrated that efficient antioxidant activity in elderly Mexicans is linked with their lifestyle (Sánchez-Rodríguez et al., 2005). For this reason, we performed a longitudinal and pre-experimental study in a sample of 79 older healthy, urban-dwelling individuals residing in Mexico City (62 females and 17 males); 71 (59 women and 12 males) complied with the entire self-care program of the Model of Community Gerontology proposed by our research group. The objective was to determine the effect of a self-care program on OxS and cognitive function in an older, Mexican, urban-dwelling population. The participants' OxS, cognitive function, Nagi Disability Scale of physical task functioning, and Instrumental Activities of Daily Living (IADL) were measured prior to and 2 years after intervention with an active aging program. We observed that all older individuals adopted

Table 29.2 *Oxidative stress biomarkers and cognitive function*

|  | Basal | After 2 years |
| --- | --- | --- |
| TBARS (µmol/L) | $0.304 \pm 0.11$ | $0.261 \pm 0.09^*$ |
| Glutathione peroxidase (U/g Hb) | $43.1 \pm 18.6$ | $49 \pm 16.9^\dagger$ |
| Superoxide dismutase (U/g Hb) | $1.13 \pm 0.12$ | $1.16 \pm 0.12^\dagger$ |
| Total antioxidant status (µmol/L) | $1,007 \pm 207$ | $965 \pm 209$ |
| DNA migration (µm) | $38.6 \pm 20.1$ | $35.7 \pm 18.3$ |
| SOD/GPx ratio | $0.032 \pm 0.010$ | $0.027 \pm 0.009^*$ |
| MMSE score | $27.8 \pm 2.3$ | $26.3 \pm 3.0^\dagger$ |

TBARS, Plasma Thiobarbituric Acid Reacting Substances, MMSE, Mini Mental State Examination.
Mean value $\pm$ SD (standard deviation). Paired t-test, $^*p < 0.01$, $^\dagger p < 0.05$.

healthy, self-care-based lifestyles according to the active aging program in which they were trained, which was associated with a statistically significant improvement in the OxS and cognitive function markers on comparing pre- and post-community intervention data (Table 29.2). Our findings suggest that self-care-based healthy lifestyles programs can improve OxS and cognitive function in an urban-dwelling elderly population (Sánchez-Rodríguez et al., 2009).

The effectiveness of the implementation of self-care models for older adults at the community level has recently been reported by other research groups (Pérez-Cuevas et al., 2015; Mendoza-Ruvalcaba & Fernández-Ballesteros, 2016). For this reason, it would be desirable for state public health programs to consider developing self-care models as a priority for achieving healthy aging.

## Aging, Residence, and Mild Cognitive Impairment and Oxidative Stress

As stated above, Harman, in 1956, first noted the relationship between OxS and aging; however, most studies have been performed on animal models. For this reason, our research group performed a comparative cross-sectional study in a sample of 249 healthy subjects: (i) 25–29 years ($n=22$); (ii) 30–39 years ($n=24$); 40–49 years ($n=30$); 50–59 years ($n=48$); 60–69 years ($n=60$); and $\geq 70$ years ($n=65$). The aim was to measure the relationship between the concentration of OxS markers and increase in age. We observed a significant increase in lipid peroxides with increasing age in the adult population coupled with a decrease in antioxidant enzymes, superoxide dismutase (SOD), and glutathione peroxidase (GPx), as well as total antioxidant capacity (Table 29.3) (Mendoza-Núñez et al., 2007).

On the other hand, psychological stress and environmental pollution are frequently associated with the urban environment and OxS. Likewise, OxS is a risk

Table 29.3 *Biological markers of oxidative stress by age groups*

| | Age groups (years) | | | | | |
|---|---|---|---|---|---|---|
| | 25–29 | 30–39 | 40–49 | 50–59 | 60–69 | ≥70 |
| Lipoperoxides (LPO μmol/L) | 0.22 ± 0.11 | 0.28 ± 0.11 | 0.31 ± 0.12 | 0.31 ± 0.1 | 0.38 ± 0.18 | 0.42 ± 0.19[b] |
| Total antioxidant status (TAS mmol/L) | 1.4 ± 0.31 | 1.3 ± 0.26 | 1.2 ± 0.28 | 1.2 ± 0.25 | 1.1 ± 0.21[c] | 1.1 ± 0.22[d] |
| Glutathione peroxidase (GPx UI/L) | 1.4 ± 0.31 | 7,660 ± 2,316 | 7,827 ± 1,637 | 6,981 ± 2,226 | 6,193 ± 2,235 | 6,547 ± 2,307[f] |
| Superoxide dismutase (SOD UI/L) | 178 ± 14 | 173 ± 12 | 174 ± 8 | 172 ± 12 | 173 ± 15 | 172 ± 20 |

Data are mean values ± SE (standard error); ANOVA with Tukey test.
**LPO**: [a]25–29 versus 60–69 years, $p < 0.01$; [b]25–29 versus ≥70 years, $p < 0.001$. **TAS**: [c]25–29 versus 60–69 years, $p < 0.05$; [d]25–29 versus ≥70 years, $p < 0.05$. **GPx**: [e]25–29 versus 60–60 years, $p < 0.001$; [f]25–29 versus ≥70 years, $p < 0.001$.

factor for cognitive impairment (CI) in the elderly. Therefore, we hypothesized that the prevalence of CI in subjects in the urban area could be higher than in a rural area and that this difference was linked to higher OxS. We conducted a cross-sectional comparative study of free-living subjects from Mexico who resided in urban or rural areas for 10 or more years and who had 3 or more years of elementary school education. Subjects included 104 elderly individuals with an age ≥60 years (mean 66.8 ± 6.4 years) from urban Mexico City (altitude 2,260 m above sea level) and 85 elderly individuals with an age ≥60 years (mean 70.8 ± 8.4 years) from a rural area (Actopan, Hidalgo State, Mexico, to 130 km away from Mexico City and 2,069 m above sea level). We observed that the elderly living in urban areas had higher OxS than rural elderly, which was linked to an increased risk of mild cognitive impairment (MCI) (Sánchez-Rodríguez et al., 2006). The relationship among OxS, aging, and the increase in the incidence of chronic diseases related to old age is accepted (Chandrasekaran et al., 2016). Although we know that aging *per se* does not increase OxS markers, OxS is not the only causal factor for aging (Mendoza-Núñez et al., 2007).

## Diabetes Mellitus, Aging, and Oxidative Stress

More than 100 chronic diseases have been linked to OxS and aging, such as diabetes mellitus (Knight, 1999). In this sense, our research group has found a statistically significant relationship between the OxS grade and presence of diabetes mellitus, hypertension, osteoporosis, depression, and cognitive impairment in older community-dwelling adults (Sánchez-Rodríguez et al., 2006, 2013; Mendoza-Núñez et al., 2009b, 2011).

Table 29.4  *Diabetes mellitus and age as risk factors for oxidative stress*

|  | OR | CI | $p$ value |
|---|---|---|---|
| Diabetes mellitus | 2.1 | 1.2–3.8 | 0.015 |
| Age (≥60 years) | 1.6 | 1.1–3.3 | 0.020 |
| Interaction (diabetes mellitus by age) | 3.1 | 1.3–7.5 | 0.014 |

OR, odds ratio; CI, 95 percent confidence interval.

With respect to diabetes mellitus, we conducted a cross-sectional comparative study in a sample of 228 subjects in the following groups: (i) 56 healthy adults (mean age: 47 ± 7 years); (ii) 60 diabetic adults (mean age: 52 ± 6 years); (iii) 40 healthy elderly adults (mean age: 67 ± 7 years); and (iv) 72 diabetic elderly adults (mean age: 68 ± 7 years). The aim was to determine the effect of aging linked to diabetes mellitus on OxS. We observed that diabetes mellitus is an independent risk factor for OxS and a stronger factor in older subjects. These findings suggest that aging, in concert with diabetes, exerts an additive effect on OxS (Table 29.4) (Mendoza-Núñez et al., 2011). In this sense, it has been demonstrated that aging is an independent factor for reduced glucose tolerance and increased insulin resistance beyond increasing OxS (Salmon, 2012). Therefore, aging *per se* is a risk factor for type 2 diabetes mellitus.

## Oxidative Stress and Osteoporosis

Recent studies have suggested that there is an association between bone mineral density (BMD) and OxS. In this regard, it has been demonstrated that high hydrogen peroxide levels favor differentiation of osteoclastic cells from osteoclasts and inhibit differentiation of osteoblastic cells from osteoblasts, propitiating an accentuated diminution in OxS-related BMD (Maggio et al., 2003; Bai et al., 2004). Therefore, we determined the relationship between the total antioxidant status (TAS), plasma lipid peroxides, antioxidant activity of SOD, and GPx, with BMD in 94 subjects, ≥60 years of age (50 healthy subjects and 44 subjects with osteoporosis). The aim of our study was to determine the relationship between OxS as an independent risk factor for osteoporosis in a population of elderly adults. We found that the GPx antioxidant activity was significantly lower in the group of subjects with osteoporosis compared with the group of healthy subjects ($p < 0.01$). In logistic regression analysis, OxS was found to be an independent risk factor for osteoporosis (odds ratio [OR] = 2.79; 95% confidence interval [95% CI] = 1.08–7.23; $p = 0.034$) (Table 29.5) (Sánchez-Rodríguez et al., 2007). These findings suggest that OxS is an independent risk factor for osteoporosis. In the other study, we determined the effect of ascorbic acid and alpha-tocopherol on OxS and BMD in elderly people.

Table 29.5 *Risk factors for osteoporosis in older community-dwelling*

| | OR | $CI_{95\%}$ | $p$ value |
|---|---|---|---|
| Sex (female) | 4.47 | 1.25–16.02 | 0.022 |
| Age (≥70 years) | 3.45 | 1.21–9.81 | 0.020 |
| Oxidative stress | 2.79 | 1.08–7.23 | 0.034 |
| Smoke | 3.18 | 0.62–16.29 | 0.165 |
| Alcohol ingestion (≥2 cups/day) | 2.16 | 0.77–6.00 | 0.140 |
| Overweight (BMI≥27) | 0.36 | 0.14–0.93 | 0.035 |

*Logistic regression $R^2 = 0.255$; OR = odds ratio; CI = confidence interval.

On the other hand, we also determined the effect of ascorbic acid and alpha-tocopherol on the OxS and BMD in elderly people. A double-blind controlled clinical assay was performed in a sample of 90 elderly subjects divided into three age-paired random groups with 30 subjects in each group. Group Tx0 received placebo, group Tx1 received 500 mg of ascorbic acid and 400 IU of alpha-tocopherol, and group Tx2 received 1,000 mg of ascorbic acid and 400 IU of alpha-tocopherol for a 12-month period. We measured the thiobarbituric acid reactive substances (TBARS), TAS, SOD, and GPx. The BMD was obtained on the DXA of the hip and spine before and after the 12-month treatment period with supplementation of vitamins C and E. We found a positive correlation between the hip-BMD and both the SOD ($r = 0.298$, $p < 0.05$) and GPx ($r = 0.214$, $p < 0.05$). Additionally, a significantly lower decrease in the LPO ($p < 0.05$) was observed, which was linked with hip bone loss in the Tx2 group compared to the Tx0 group. These findings suggest that the administration of 1,000 mg of ascorbic acid together with 400 IU of alpha-tocopherol could be useful in preventing or aiding in the treatment of age-related osteoporosis (Ruiz-Ramos et al., 2010). In this sense, the usefulness of the administration of antioxidant vitamins and repair of bone tissue after surgery has also been demonstrated (Sandukji et al., 2011). However, it is necessary to continue this line of research to recommend the use of antioxidant vitamins as an adjuvant for preventing and treating osteoporosis.

## Healthy Lifestyles and Oxidative Stress

The relationship between healthy lifestyles and OxS has been widely demonstrated (Dato et al., 2013). In this sense, our research group conducted some studies that have shown the effect of adequate diet, moderate exercise, and participation in programs of health education on the health and functionality of older community-dwelling adults (Mendoza-Núñez et al., 2005; Rosado-Pérez et al., 2011, 2012, 2013).

## Caloric Restriction and DNA Damage

We have examined whether undernutrition without malnutrition (Caloric Restriction, CR) was a protective factor for DNA damage in the elderly. The sample included a total of 260 older subjects, including 96 well-nourished subjects, 52 subjects with undernutrition, but without malnutrition (CR 10–20 percent), and 112 overweight subjects, all of whom were diagnosed as clinically healthy. DNA damage in peripheral blood lymphocytes was assessed through an alkaline unicellular electrophoresis procedure (comet assay). Fifty-six percent of the well-nourished subjects, 38 percent of the CR, and 44 percent of the overweight had DNA damage, and men had more DNA damage than women did (Table 29.4). These findings suggest that a 10 to 20 percent CR is a protective factor for DNA damage in elderly people and that CR has better effects on women and on subjects aged 60 and 69 years (Mendoza-Núñez et al., 2005).

## Effects of Physical Activity on Oxidative Stress and Inflammatory Markers

We performed a cross-sectional, comparative study in a sample of 56 healthy elderly people as follows: (i) sedentary subjects ($\leq 2$ metabolic equivalent tasks [METS]) in 30 subjects aged $68 \pm 7$ years, and (ii) moderate physical activity (3–6 METS) in 26 subjects aged $63 \pm 8$ years. The aim was to determine the effect of moderate physical activity on OxS and chronic inflammation markers in elderly Mexicans. We measured the plasma lipoperoxides, SOD, GPx, and TAS. Additionally, the inflammatory markers interleukin 6 (IL-6) and tumor necrosis factor alpha (TNF-$\alpha$) were measured. We found a statistically significant negative correlation between the METS in subjects with moderate physical activity ($r = -0.369$; $p < 0.05$) linked to a positive correlation between the METS and IL-6 ($r = 0.773$; $p < 0.05$) (Rosado-Pérez et al., 2011). Our findings suggest that moderate physical activity diminishes OxS and the inflammatory process in the elderly.

## Thai Chi and Oxidative Stress

Several studies have demonstrated the positive effect of tai chi practice on health status, especially in older adults (Li et al., 2001; Hong, 2008). In contrast, Goon et al. (2009) demonstrated that tai chi practice decreased DNA damage and increased antioxidant levels in middle-aged adults. For this reason, our research group performed a quasi-experimental study with a sample of 55 healthy subjects who were randomly divided into two age-matched groups: (i) a control group with 23 subjects, and (ii) an experimental group with 32 subjects. The aim was to determine the effect of tai chi on OxS in a population of elderly Mexican subjects. The experimental group received daily training in tai chi for 50 minutes. The following was measured before and after a 6-month exercise period: TBARS, TAS, SOD, and GPx. The experimental group exhibited a statistically

Table 29.6 *Oxidative stress markers at baseline and post-intervention*

| Parameter | Control group n=23 | | Tai Chi group n=32 | |
|---|---|---|---|---|
| | Baseline | 6 months | Baseline | 6 months |
| LPO (µmol/L) | 0.28 ± 0.07 | 0.3 ± 0.10 | 0.289 ± 0.1 | 0.257 ± 0.09* |
| SOD (U/mL) | 171 ± 14 | 170 ± 8 | 169 ± 7 | 178 ± 9* |
| GPx (U/L) | 8,123 ± 4,297 | 8,153 ± 4,380 | 7,658 ± 8,175 | 8,427 ± 4,016 |
| SOD/GPx ratio | 25 ±11 | 32 ± 24 | 32 ± 19 | 36 ± 47 |
| TAS (mmol/L) | 1.11 ± 0.27 | 1.02 ± 0.019 | 0.75 ± 0.32 | 1.04 ± 0.16* |
| OxS-score | 1.13 ± 1.01 | 2.0 ± 0.95* | 2.62 ± 1.09 | 0.97 ± 0.82* |

LPO, Lipoperoxides; SOD, superoxide dismutase; GPx, glutathione peroxidase; SOD/GPx ratio; TAS, total antioxidant status; OxS-score, oxidative stress score. Data are displayed as mean ± standard deviation. Paired T test, baseline vs. post intervention, *$p < 0.001$. Wilcoxon test was calculated for OxS-score, baseline vs. post intervention, *$p < 0.001$.

significant decrease in glucose levels, total cholesterol, low-density lipoprotein cholesterol (LDLC), and systolic blood pressure, and an increase in the SOD and GPx activity and TAS, compared with the control group ($p < 0.05$) (Table 29.6). Our findings suggest that the daily practice of tai chi is useful for reducing OxS in healthy older adults (Rosado-Pérez et al., 2012).

Additionally, we performed a quasi-experimental study with 106 older adults between 60 and 74 years of age who were clinically healthy and divided into the following groups: (i) control group ($n = 23$), (ii) walking group ($n = 43$), and (iii) tai chi group ($n = 31$). The objective of this study was to evaluate the effect of the practice of tai chi versus walking on markers for OxS. We measured the levels of lipoperoxides (LPO), antioxidant enzymes SOD, and GPx, as well as the TAS pre- and post-intervention in all subjects. The data were subjected to a covariant analysis. We found lower levels of LPO in the tai chi group compared with the walking group (tai chi, 0.261 ± 0.02; walking, 0.331 ± 0.02; control, 0.304 ± 0.023 µmol/L; $p < 0.05$). Similarly, we observed significantly higher SOD activity and a lower OxS-score in the tai chi group ($p < 0.05$). Our findings suggest that the practice of tai chi produces a more effective antioxidant effect than walking does (Rosado-Pérez et al., 2013).

## Conclusions and Futures Perspectives

Although a high percentage of older people have chronic health problems at the end of life, the current statistical data indicate that the percentage of frail, unhealthy older persons is lower than 15 percent of those over 65 years, contradicting the medicalized perspective on aging (Rodriguez-Mañas & Fried,

2015). Accordingly, it is important to promote inclusive initiatives based on the strengths inherent in the remaining percentage of older people (over 80 percent), who may continue to contribute significantly to the development of their communities (Mendoza-Núñez et al., 2009a; Chatterji et al., 2015). Currently, the average life expectancy at 60 years in the world is up to 26.9 years for women and 22.7 years for men. A high percentage of over-60-year-olds do not have any physical limitations for performing their daily lives (Chatterji et al., 2015).

Therefore, the implementation of healthy aging programs should not be limited to the healthy elderly, considering that healthy lifestyles have a beneficial effect for older adults with successful aging, those with chronic diseases, and the frail elderly (dependent). As a result, we should establish public policies and public health programs with this approach (Mendoza-Núñez, 2013).

One of the fundamental purposes of the model is to achieve the emancipation, independence, and autonomy of the groups of older people, so they can make decisions and optimally use their social support networks. The Model of Community Gerontology proposed considering the optimization of physical and financial resources, potential of people in the process of aging, participation of older adults for their own development, and incorporation of formal and non-formal education to achieve healthy aging. In this regard, we have demonstrated a positive effect of the model on the health status, well-being, quality life, and OxS in the older community-dwelling. However, it is necessary to continue cohort studies in different sociocultural contexts linked to state health promotion programs, so the community care model is considered an option to achieve successful or healthy aging in the community, thereby recognizing and boosting the active participation of older adults.

## References

Bai, X. C., Lu, D., Bai, J., et al. (2004). Oxidative stress inhibits osteoblastic differentiation of bone cells by ERK and NF-kappaB. *Biochemical and Biophysical Research Communications*, 314, 197–207.

Bélanger, E., Ahmed, T., Filiatrault, J., et al. (2015). An empirical comparison of different models of active aging in Canada: The International Mobility in Aging Study. *Gerontologist*. DOI: 10.1093/geront/gnv126.

Cannizzo, E. S., Clement, C. C., Sahu, R., et al. (2011). Oxidative stress, inflamm-aging and immunosenescence. *Journal of Proteomics*, 74, 2313–23.

Chandrasekaran, A., Idelchik, M. D., Melendez, J. A. (2016). Redox control of senescence and age-related disease. *Redox Biology*, 11, 91–102. DOI: 10.1016/j.redox.2016.11.005.

Chatterji, S., Byles, J., Cutler, D. (2015). Health, functioning, and disability in older adults—present status and future implications. *Lancet*, 385(9967), 563–75.

Dato, S., Crocco, P., D'Aquila, P., et al. (2013). Exploring the role of genetic variability and lifestyle in oxidative stress response for healthy aging and longevity. *International Journal of Molecular Sciences*, 14(8), 16443–72. DOI: 10.3390/ijms140816443.

Davies, K. J. (2016). Adaptive homeostasis. *Molecular Aspects of Medicine*, 49, 1–7. DOI: 10.1016/j.mam.2016.04.007. Available from: http://doi.org/10.1016/j.mam.2016.04.007

Fernández-Ballesteros, R. (2008). *Active Aging: The Contribution of Psychology*. Toronto: Hogrefe Publishing.

Fernández-Ballesteros, R., Zamarrón Casinello, M. D., López Bravo, M. D., et al. (2010). Envejecimiento con éxito: criterios y predictores. *Psicothema*, 22(4), 641–7.

Franceschi, C., Bonafè, M., Valensin, S., et al. (2000). Inflamm-aging. An evolutionary perspective on immunosenescence. *Annals of the New York Academy of Sciences*, 908, 244–54.

Franceschi, C., Capri, M., Monti, D., et al. (2007). Inflammaging and anti-inflammaging: a systemic perspective on aging and longevity emerged from studies in humans. *Mechanisms of Ageing and Development*, 128(1), 92–105.

García, M. A., Martínez-Artero, R., Sánchez, L. A., et al. (2002). *Las personas mayores desde la perspectiva educativa para la salud*. Murcia: Universidad de Murcia.

Goon, J. A., Aini, A. H., Musalmah, M., et al. (2009). Effect of Tai Chi exercise on DNA damage, antioxidant enzymes, and oxidative stress in middle-age adults. *Journal of Physical Activity and Health*, 6, 43–54.

Gutiérrez Robledo, L. M. (1999). El proceso de envejecimiento humano: algunas implicaciones asistenciales y para la prevención. *Papeles de Población*, 5(19), 125–47.

Gutiérrez, J. P., Rivera-Dommarco, J., Shamah-Levy, et al. (2013). Encuesta Nacional de Salud y Nutrición 2012. *Resultados Nacionales*. Cuernavaca, México: Instituto Nacional de Salud Pública(MX).

Hank, K. (2011). How "successful" do older europeans age? findings from share. *Journal of Gerontology: Social Sciences*, 66B(2), 230–6, DOI: 10.1093/geronb/gbq089.

Harman, D. (1956). Aging: a theory based on free radical and radiation chemistry. *Journal of Gerontology*, 11(3), 298–300.

Hayflick, L. (1996). *How and Why We Age*. New York: Ballantine Books, 49–57.

Hernández-Romieu, A. C., Elnecavé-Olaiz, A., Huerta-Uribe, N., et al. (2011). Análisis de una encuesta poblacional para determinar los factores asociados al control de la diabetes mellitus en México. *Salud Pública de México*, 53, 34–39.

Hong, Y. (2008). Tai Chi Chuan. State of the art in international research. *Hong Kong Medicine and Sport Science*, Basel: Karger. DOI:10.1159/isbn.978-3-8055-8490-6.

Instituto Nacional de Estadística y Geografía (2016). *Estadísticas a propósito del día internacional de las personas de edad (1 de octubre)*. México: INEGI. Available from: www.inegi.org.mx/saladeprensa/aproposito/2014/adultos0.pdf

Jones, D. P., Mody, V. C. Jr., Carlson, J. L., et al. (2002). Redox analysis of human plasma allows separation of pro-oxidant events of aging from decline in antioxidant defenses. *Free Radical Biology and Medicine*, 33, 1290–300.

Karlamangla, A. S., Singer, B. H., McEwen, B. S., et al. (2002). Allostatic load as a predictor of functional decline. MacArthur studies of successful aging. *Journal of Clinical Epidemiology*, 55, 696–710.

Knight, J. A. (1999). *Free radicals, antioxidants, aging, and disease*. Washington, DC: AACC Press, 75–329.

Li, J. X., Hong, Y., Chan, K. M. (2001). Tai chi: physiological characteristics and beneficial effects on health. *British Journal of Sports Medicine*, 35(3), 148–56.

Maggio, D., Barabani, M., Pierandrei, M., et al. (2003). Marked decrease in plasma antioxidants in aged osteoporotic women: results of a cross-sectional study. *Journal of Clinical Endocrinology and Metabolism*, 88, 1523–7.

Martínez-Maldonado, M. L., Correa-Muñoz, E., Mendoza-Núñez, V. M. (2007). Program of active aging in a rural Mexican community: a qualitative approach. *BMC Public Health*, 7, 276. Available from: http://bmcpublichealth.biomedcentral.com/articles/10.1186/1471-2458-7-276

McEwen, B. S. (2002). Sex, stress and hippocampus: allostasis, allostatic load and the aging process. *Neurobiology of Aging*, 23, 921–39.

Mendoza-Núñez, V. M. (2013). Envejecimiento saludable (Libro 4). En: López Barcena J (Ed.). *PAC Medicina General 5 Tomo I*. México: Intersistemas Editores, 162–229.

Mendoza-Ruvalcaba, N. M., Fernánde-Ballesteros, R. (2016). Effectiveness of the Vital Aging program to promote active aging in Mexican older adults. *Clinical Interventions in Aging*, 11, 1631–44.

Mendoza-Núñez, V. M., Correa-Muñoz, E., Sánchez-Rodríguez, M., et al. (1996). Modelo de atención de núcleos gerontológicos. *GERIATRIKA. Revista Iberoamericana de Geriatría y Gerontología*, 12(10), 15–21.

Mendoza-Núñez, V. M., Sánchez-Rodríguez, M, Retana-Ugalde, R., et al. (2005). Undernutrition without malnutrition as a risk factor for DNA damage. *Nutrition Research*. 25, 271–80.

Mendoza-Núñez, V. M., Ruiz-Ramos, M., Sánchez-Rodríguez, M., et al. (2007). Aging-related oxidative stress in healthy humans. *Tohoku Journal of Experimental Medicine*, 213, 261–8.

Mendoza-Núñez, V. M., Martínez-Maldonado, M. L., Correa-Muñoz, E. (2009a). Implementation of an active aging model in Mexico for prevention and control of chronic diseases in the elderly. *BMC Geriatrics*, 9, 40. Available from: http://bmcgeriatr.biomedcentral.com/articles/10.1186/1471-2318-9-40

Mendoza-Núñez, V. M., Sánchez-Rodríguez, M. A., Correa-Muñoz, E. (2009b). Undernutrition and oxidative stress as risk factors for high blood pressure in older Mexican adults. *Annals of Nutrition and Metabolism*, 54, 119–23.

Mendoza-Núñez, V. M., Rosado-Pérez, J., Santiago-Osorio, E., et al. (2011). Aging linked to type 2 diabetes increases oxidative stress and chronic inflammation. *Rejuvenation Research*, 14, 25–31.

Mendoza-Núñez, V. M., Martínez-Maldonado, M. L., Vargas-Guadarrama, L. A. (2013). *Envejecimiento Activo y Saludable. Fundamentos y Estrategias desde la Gerontología Comunitaria*. México: FES "ZARAGOZA," UNAM.

Mendoza-Núñez, V. M., Martínez-Maldonado, M. L., Vivaldo-Martínez, M. (2016a). What is the onset age of human aging and old age?. *International Journal of Gerontology*, 10, 56. Available from: www.ijge-online.com/article/S1873-9598(16)00006-5/abstract

Mendoza-Núñez, V. M., Flores-Bello, C., Correa-Muñoz, E., et al. (2016b). Relationship between social support networks and diabetes control and its impact on the quality of life in older community-dwelling Mexicans. *Nutrición Hospitalaria*, 33, 1312–16.

Miller, T. A., Dimatteo, M. R. (2013). Importance of family/social support and impact on adherence to diabetic therapy. *Diabetes, Metabolic Syndrome and Obesity*, 6, 421–6.

Oliveira, B. F., Nogueira-Machado, J. A., Chaves, M. M. (2010). The role of oxidative stress in the aging process. *Scientific World Journal*, 10, 1121–8.

Organización de Naciones Unidas (1979). *Reunión sobre envejecimiento*. Kiev, URSS: ONU.

Pandey, K. B., Rizvi, S. I. (2010). Markers of oxidative stress in erythrocytes and plasma during aging in humans. *Oxidative Medicine and Cellular Longevity*, 3, 2–12. DOI: 10.4161/oxim.3.1.10476. Available from: www.hindawi.com/journals/oximed/2010/565920/abs/

Pérez-Cuevas, R., Doubova, S. V., Bazaldúa-Merino, L. A., et al. (2015). A social health services model to promote active ageing in Mexico: design and evaluation of a pilot programme. *Ageing and Society*, 35, 1457–80.

Radak, Z., Chung, H. Y., Goto, S. (2005). Exercise and hormesis: oxidative stress-related adaptation for successful aging. *Biogerontology*, 6, 71–5.

Rattan, S. (2001). Applying hormesis in aging research and therapy. *Human and Experimental Toxicology*, 20, 281–5.

Rodriguez-Mañas, L., Fried, L. P. (2015). Frailty in the clinical scenario. *Lancet*, 385 (9968), e7–e8. DOI: 10.1016/S0140-6736(14)61595-6.

Rosado-Pérez, J., Santiago-Osorio, E., Ortiz, R., et al. (2011). Moderate physical activity diminishes oxidative stress and the inflammatory process in elderly. *Health Med*. 5(1), 173–9.

Rosado-Pérez, J., Santiago-Osorio, E., Ortiz, R., et al. (2012). Tai Chi improves oxidative stress in Mexican older adults. *Journal of Nutrition, Health and Aging*, 16, 642–6.

Rosado-Pérez, J., Rocío Ortiz, R., Santiago-Osorio, E., et al. (2013). Effect of Tai Chi versus walking on oxidative stress in Mexican older adults. *Oxidative Medicine and Cellular Longevity*, 298590. DOI: 10.1155/2013/298590.

Rowe, J. W., Kahn, R. L. (1997). Successful aging. *The Cerontologist*, 37, 433–40.

Ruiz-Ramos, M., Vargas, L. A., Fortoul Van Der Goes, T. I., et al. (2010). Supplementation of ascorbic acid and alpha-tocopherol is useful to preventing bone loss linked to oxidative stress in elderly. *Journal of Nutrition, Health and Aging*, 14, 467–72.

Sakano, N., Wang, D. H., Takahashi, N., et al. (2009). Oxidative stress biomarkers and lifestyles in Japanese healthy people. *Journal of Clinical Biochemistry and Nutrition*, 44, 185–95.

Salminen, A., Kaarniranta, K., Kauppinen, A. (2012). Inflammaging: disturbed interplay between autophagy and inflammasomes. *Aging (Albany NY)*, 4(3), 166–75.

Salmon, A. B. (2012). Oxidative stress in the etiology of age-associated decline in glucose metabolism.*Longevity and Healthspan*, 1, 7. DOI: 10.1186/2046-2395-1-7

Sánchez-Rodríguez, M. A., Retana-Ugalde, R., Ruiz-Ramos, M., et al. (2005). Efficient antioxidant capacity against lipid peroxide levels in healthy elderly of Mexico City. *Environmental Research*, 97, 322–9.

Sánchez-Rodríguez, M. A., Santiago, E., Arronte-Rosales, A., et al. (2006). Relationship between oxidative stress and cognitive impairment in the elderly of rural vs. urban communities.*Life Sciences*, 78, 1682–7.

Sánchez-Rodríguez, M. A., Ruiz-Ramos, M., Correa-Muñoz, E., et al. (2007). Oxidative stress as a risk factor for osteoporosis in elderly Mexican as characterized by antioxidant enzymes. *BMC Musculoskeletal Disorders*, 8, 124. Available from: http://bmcmusculoskeletdisord.biomedcentral.com/articles/10.1186/1471-2474-8-124

Sánchez-Rodríguez, M. A., Arronte-Rosales, A., Mendoza-Núñez, V. M. (2009). Effect of a self-care program on oxidative stress and cognitive function in an older Mexican urban-dwelling population. *Journal of Nutrition, Health and Aging*, 13, 791–6.

Sánchez-Rodríguez, M. A., Garduño-Espinosa. J., Arronte-Rosales, A., et al. (2013). Relationship between depressive personality and DNA damage in Mexican Community-Dwelling Elderly Adults. *HealthMed*, 7(10), 2720–7.

Sandukji, A., Al-Sawaf, H., Mohamadin, A., et al. (2011). Oxidative stress and bone markers in plasma of patients with long-bone fixative surgery: Role of antioxidants.*Human and Experimental Toxicology*, 30(6), 435–42.

Seeman, T. E., McEwen, B. S., Rowe, J. W., et al. (2001). Allostatic load as a marker of cumulative biological risk: MacArthur studies of successful aging. *Proceedings of the National Academy of Sciences of the United States of America*, 98, 4770–5.

Semba, R. D., Nicklett, E. J., Ferrucci, L. (2010). Does accumulation of advanced glycation end products contribute to the aging phenotype?. *Journal of Gerontology Series A Biological Sciences and Medical Sciences*, 65, 963–75.

Troen, B. R. (2003). The biology of aging. *Mount Sinai Journal of Medicine*, 70, 3–22.

Uchino, B. N. (2006). Social support and health: a review of physiological processes potentially underlying links to disease outcomes. *Journal of Behavioral Medicine*, 29(4), 377–87.

UNECE/ European Commission. (2015). "Active Ageing Index 2014: Analytical Report," Report prepared by Asghar Zaidi of Centre for Research on Ageing, University of Southampton and David Stanton, under contract with United Nations Economic Commission for Europe (Geneva), co-funded by European Commission's Directorate General for Employment, Social Affairs and Inclusion (Brussels). Available from: www.age-platform.eu/images/stories/Publications/AAI_2014_Report.pdf

Walker, A. (2006). Active ageing in employment: Its meaning and potential. *Asia-Pacific Review*, 13(1), 78–93.

Wong, R., Michaels-Obregon, A., Palloni, A. (2015). Cohort Profile: The Mexican Health and Aging Study (MHAS). *International Journal of Epidemiology*, 1–10. DOI: 10.1093/ije/dyu263

World Health Organization. (2002). *Active ageing. A policy framework*. Geneva: WHO.
      (2015). Healthy ageing. In *World report on ageing and health*. Geneva: WHO, pp. 25–39.

# PART III

# Socio-Demographic Issues

# 30 The Promise of Active Aging

Alan Walker

Active aging has for two decades been established as the leading global policy strategy in response to population aging. This preeminence was the result of its promotion by international governmental organizations (IGOs), such as the UN, WHO, and OECD. In practice, however, the meaning of "active aging" often lies in the eye of the beholder, and therefore, a range of contrasting policy discourses and initiatives concerning aging and demographic change appear under its label. This chapter argues that this lack of clarity, some of which is intended, undermines the potential of the concept to drive an effective global response to the huge challenges of demographic change. Other barriers are also considered. Then an outline of the steps necessary to achieve the full potential of active aging is provided. Before that, however, it is necessary to establish precisely what active aging promises, and to delineate it from other cognate concepts, especially successful aging. In sum this chapter focuses on the meaning, potential, blockages to, and ways to achieve active aging.

## Why Is Active Aging Important?

In this century, advanced aging is becoming a global phenomenon. In the twentieth century, it was the Global North that saw the most rapid aging, whereas now, it is the turn of the Southern Hemisphere. The main factors behind this unique historical transformation are declining fertility, and improved health and longevity. Soon people aged 65 and over will outnumber children under the age of 15 for the first time in human history. Within this aging trend, the numbers of people aged 80 and over, the "oldest-old," are rising particularly rapidly: 230 percent by 2040, compared with 160 percent for the population aged 65 and over, and 33 percent for the total population of all ages (Kinsella & He, 2009). This demographic transition is currently in overdrive as a result of the high fertility levels after the Second World War (the "baby boomers") and the reduced death rates at older ages.

Aging is a function of economic and social development, which is why it has, for a century, been associated mainly with the industrialized countries of Europe and North America, as well as Japan in Asia. As economic growth, education, and incomes rise in the hitherto less developed countries, fertility declines and longevity increases. Three-fifths of the world's population aged 65 and over now live in less developed countries (62 percent or 313 million people, in 2008). By 2040 this share is expected to be more than three-quarters, or over one billion people.

Two specific features of aging in the Global South require mention. First, the less developed countries are aging much more rapidly than their northern counterparts. For example, it took France more than 100 years to grow its older population from 7 to 14 percent; it took the United States 69 years, Canada 65 years, and the United Kingdom 45 years. In contrast this transition, in UN terms from an aging to an aged society, will take around 20 years in many less developed countries: it is approximated that it will take China 26 years, Brazil 21 years, and South Korea 18 years (Kinsella & He, 2009, p.14). This means that the time available to adjust policy and practice regimes to respond to population aging is much shorter in the global south than was available to the north. Second, the countries of the south are undergoing aging and development simultaneously whereas, generally, in the north the former followed the latter. Thus, the resources available to respond to aging will be constrained by the economic growth priority.

Western Europe is the world's oldest region and, in global comparative terms, it is only Japan that matches its aging profile. Both also have the most prominent demographic aging trends over the next 20 years. The aging of the post-war baby boomer generation started to boost this aging process in Europe from 2005. While this sketch of the quiet demographic revolution is familiar to many, other dimensions of it are less well-known. For example, in many of the world's advanced industrial countries (Australia, Ireland, Japan, The Netherlands, New Zealand, Norway, Sweden, and Switzerland) a linear increase has been observed since 1840! This means that there is no reason to expect that the rise in life expectancy will level off in the foreseeable future (Oeppen & Vaupel, 2002). The remarkable persistence of life expectancy increases – 2.4 years on average each decade for women and 2.2 years for men – has not been understood until very recently and this helps to explain why earlier population forecasts were prone to error. Moreover, the sheer scale of the demographic changes still taking place, and their far-reaching social policy implications, have not been grasped by the policy community let alone more widely.

In response to these unprecedented demographic changes and, in particular, the continuing increase in longevity, policymakers have searched for viable solutions. These endeavors have often been framed within a deficit model of aging or a despairing demography: the "problem" is too many older people creating demands on social protection systems. The solutions flowing from this perspective have been similarly limited: making people work longer and reducing their pension entitlements, for example. The policy of active aging marked a distinct break with the dominant deficit perspective. Instead it proffered a positive vision of later life, emphasizing the health, independence, and productivity of older people. Crucially too, rather than concentrating only on old age, the whole of the life course was brought into consideration. Thus, as defined by WHO (2002,

p. 12), active aging is "the process of optimizing opportunities for health, participation and security in order to enhance quality of life as people age."

The critical importance of the life course emphasis lies in the fact that human aging is the result of lifetime cumulative wear and tear. In this process, environmental (extrinsic) determinants are far more influential than genetic (intrinsic) ones, by a factor of 4 or 5 to 1 (Gems & Partridge, 2013). For example, in studies of monozygous twins, only 20 percent of variance in longevity has been attributed to inherited genes (Steves et al., 2012). This much is a matter of biogerontological consensus, although further research is required to fully understand the gene/environment interactions that cause wear and tear (López-Otin et al., 2013). The consensuses also rejects the notion of an "aging gene," that human beings are programmed to live for a fixed period of time or to age in a certain way (Kirkwood, 2005, 2008). The key environmental risk factors include both political-economic items such as deprivation, low socioeconomic status, air pollution, unhealthy food production, and occupational stress, and behavioral risk factors such as smoking, lack of exercise, and poor diet (Kirkwood & Austad, 2000). For example, longitudinal data analyses, as part of the United Kingdom New Dynamics of Ageing Programme (*newdynamics.group.shef.ac.uk*), have revealed clear associations between low socioeconomic status and area deprivation in childhood and lowered levels of functioning in old age. Similar associations were found between living in deprived areas in mid-life and lower later life functional capacity, and between childhood education and cognition in old age (Kuh et al., 2014).

The preeminence of "environmental" over genetic factors in human aging underpins the massive promise of active aging. The risk factors that inflict damage on the human body and mind, and often result in the chronic conditions associated with loss of function in later life, i.e., biological aging, can be moderated or prevented entirely. The chronic conditions, sometimes referred to as the "geriatric giants" – coronary heart disease, stroke, type 2 diabetes, and so on – may truncate lives prematurely or result in disabilities that reduce functioning and quality of life, and require treatment or care. But, adopting a life course approach to the etiology of these noncommunicable diseases suggests the potential to reduce and postpone the onset of the individual and social costs associated with them. This is the primary aim of the active aging approach, and why its success is so important for aging societies.

This aim may be illustrated with reference to a typical life course in functional terms (Figure 30.1). Physical capacity peaks in early adult life and then declines during middle and later life, but at different rates, due mainly to variable exposure to the risk factors mentioned above. The cumulative impact of physical and mental deterioration is chronic conditions, which may entail traumatic events such as a stroke. The result is a breach of the disability threshold. Active aging aims to prevent the decline in functional capacity, both physical and mental, and thereby extend disability-free health expectancy for as long as possible.

The evidence behind the idea of active aging is strong and mounting rapidly, and is certainly more robust than when it was first advanced by WHO.

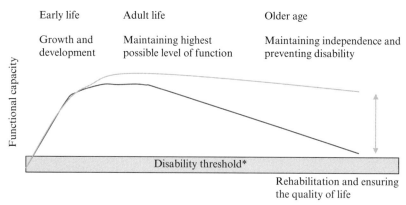

**Figure 30.1.** *Functional capacity and age*
*Source:* Kalache and Kickbush (1997)

Space precludes a full review (see Ballesteros et al., 2013; www.mopact.group
.shef.ac.uk), but key examples include the beneficial effects of physical exercise:
(1) the active have 33–50 percent lower risk of developing type 2 diabetes than
the inactive; and (2) the moderately active have a 20 percent lower risk of stroke
incidence than the inactive (Chief Medical Officer, 2014; Kuh et al., 2014).
With respect to diet, the association between fruit and vegetable intake and the
reduced risk of cardiovascular disease and cancer is clear: reductions in the risk
of cardiovascular disease and all-cause mortality are observed on an intake of
800 g/day of fruit and vegetables, and for total cancer, an intake of 600 g/day
(Aune et al., 2017). Another example is the beneficial effects of long-term calorie restriction, with adequate intake of nutrients, which decreases the risk of
developing type 2 diabetes, hypertension, cardiovascular diseases, and cancer
(Fontana & Partridge, 2015). Thus, as these examples indicate, it is not scientific evidence that is lacking, but the purposeful translation of the evidence into
practical policy strategies. This is the issue that concerns the rest of this chapter,
starting with the relationship between successful and active aging.

## Successful and Active Aging

Although the term "active aging" is of relatively recent origin, its roots
stretch back to the 1950s and 1960s when the activity perspective in gerontology was developed. This perspective was derived from the empirical observation
of the connection between different forms of physical activity and well-being
(Blau, 1973). This positive approach to aging was a reaction to the first major
theory of social gerontology, "disengagement," which argued that old age is an
inevitable mutual period of withdrawal from roles and relationships (Cumming
& Henry, 1961). From a much sounder empirical vantage point, the activity
perspective argued that the key to "successful aging" (Pfeiffer, 1974; Rowe &
Kahn, 1987) was the maintenance in old age of the activity patterns and values

typical of middle age (Havighurst & Albrecht, 1953; Havighurst, 1954, 1963). In short, successful aging was to be achieved by denying the onset of old age and by replacing those relationships, activities, and roles of middle age that are lost, with new ones in order to maintain life satisfaction and well-being.

Later Rowe and Kahn elaborated on their initial model of successful aging to focus on three main components: low probability of disease and disease-related disability, high cognitive and physical functional capacity, and active engagement with life. In the United States this idea became a reference point for public and political discourses on aging and made an important contribution to the case for rejecting the negative notion that older age is an inevitable succession of losses (Boudiny, 2013). It also attracted scientific interest to research the factors that determine aging well and clinical practitioner interest to develop preventative measures (Villar, 2012). In essence, there was a subtle shift in the research and practice focus from those "doing poorly to those doing well" (Strawbridge et al., 2002).

While successful aging derived from the broad activity perspective, the adjective "successful" brought a normative judgment to the concept that has proved to be its major weakness (Foster & Walker, 2013). For one thing, it placed an unrealistic expectation on aging individuals themselves to maintain levels of activity and to defeat the causes of disease. Overlooked were not only the biological or anatomical limitations but also the economic and social structures that frequently inhibit or prevent people from remaining active – enforced retirement and age discrimination being obvious examples (Walker, 1980, 1981). In moral terms, the adjective "successful" implies that there are necessarily winners and losers in the aging process. Of course this is true, because aging is unequal everywhere (Cann & Dean, 2009), but the fault is less often with individuals than with society. Moreover, it is stigmatizing to label someone "unsuccessful" because they have a disease or disability. Finally, even if a person suffers from such limitations, they may still engage in a range of activities and experience a relatively high quality of life (Tate et al., 2003; Bowling, 2005). Despite its continuing currency then, the idea of successful aging tends to be exclusionary and discriminatory, and lacks a clear single definition.

Partly in reaction to the deficiencies of successful aging (from the same intellectual source), the concept of active aging began to emerge in the 1990s, under the influence of the WHO, which, not surprisingly, emphasized the vital connection between activity and health (Butler et al., 1990, p. 201), and the importance of healthy aging (WHO, 1994; see also WHO, 2001b). Given the link with health and the influence of the European Union on its development, this approach to active aging has focused on a broader range of activities than those normally associated with production and the labor market, and has emphasized health and the participation and inclusion of older people as full citizens (see for example, Walker, 1993, 1994). The thinking behind this approach is expressed perfectly in the WHO dictum: "years have been added to life now we must add life to years." This suggests a general strategy for the preservation of physical and mental health as people age, rather than just trying to make them work longer.

Thus the essence of the modern concept of active aging is a combination of the core elements of successful aging, but with a stronger emphasis on the whole life course and on quality of life and mental and physical well-being (European Commission, 1999; WHO, 2001b, 2001c).

## Barriers to Active Aging

Despite the radical promise of the WHO formulation of active aging and its rhetorical prominence across the globe, the actual realization of this promise, in terms of fully formulated and implemented strategies, is incredibly limited. Any radical policy proposal faces barriers to acceptance and take-up, because institutions and professions are inherently conservative and through their bureaucratic rules, training, and supervision processes tend to reproduce this conservatism. But, in the case of active aging, while the concept is at least superficially appealing to policymakers, there are additional barriers that blocked thorough acceptance and implementation. Five sets of barriers are identified here.

First, and perhaps foremost, there is a set of political barriers. On the one hand, there is a simple confusion about aims and purposes while, on the other, there is a purposeful and sometimes cynical hijack of the concept, which betrays its original intentions.

The confusion arises out of the array of cognate terms that are employed simultaneously to describe aging well: successful aging, healthy aging, and so on. Of course there is always a risk attached to the transfer of scientific terms into policy and popular discourses – that their original meanings and intentions will be forgotten purposely or otherwise. However, scientists must take some of the blame here for both using terms as synonyms and for failing to try to correct incorrect usage in the policy domain. As indicated in the previous section, successful aging and active aging are two fundamentally different concepts and should be recognized as such. The continuing tendency for US academics to favor the terms "successful aging" or "productive aging" means that they are essentially speaking a different language to their European counterparts, who tend to favor active aging. In policy terms the implications of these two formulations are very different. Similarly, with the now commonly conjoined terms active aging and healthy aging. The latter is an important idea and goal, but it is not the same as active aging. Briefly, healthy aging concerns health and health interventions and, therefore, is mono-dimensional; it tends to be institutional in focus (health services), and thereby top-down, it privileges professional perspectives. This confusion has been confounded by the recent prioritization of healthy aging by the WHO. In contrast active aging is multi-dimensional and demands a joined-up approach, which includes health; it favors wide stakeholder engagement and, therefore, is inclusive rather than exclusive. In practice, healthy aging should be treated as an important subset of active aging, but this is rarely the case. The EU, for example, frequently employs the couplet "active and healthy aging" and its strategic framework for research and innovation includes a major initiative on active and healthy aging (European Commission, 2010; Walker & Maltby, 2012).

The other political barrier is ideological, and hence, much more fundamental than the issue of nomenclature. Under the influence of neoliberalism, promoted by IGOs such as the OECD, policymakers have come to see the concept of active aging as a narrowly productivist one. Thus, an idea that is intended to embrace the whole life course, with a focus on human development, has become a policy instrument almost exclusively concerned with encouraging, enabling, and even forcing older people to work longer. This tendency is particularly marked in Europe and its evolution has been discussed elsewhere (Walker, 2009a; Walker & Maltby, 2012). The working longer priority is dominant at national level in the EU and also, at European level, it has had high political prominence (Walker, 2009a; Zaidi & Zolyami, 2011).

It would be wrong to suggest, however, that the narrow productivist interpretation of active aging as working longer is so dominant that it excludes other interpretations, and clearly there are competing ones within the European Commission (EC) itself (European Commission, 2006, 2010).

Faced with, at best, policymakers' ambivalence and, at worst, the constraints imposed by neoliberal ideology, it is not difficult to see why Europe has not succeeded in developing a concerted strategy for active aging that joins up all of the potentially influential policy domains. In its absence, the neoliberal reduction of active aging to working longer remains the main policy goal.

The second set of barriers to active aging is cultural, and of highest importance, here, are the misleading and often damaging stereotypes. The most common active aging stereotype is of a super-fit pensioner, who does extraordinary feats of gymnastics or athletics. Such stereotypes severely distort the meaning of active aging by transforming it from a mass pursuit to an exclusive minority one. Although there is no evidence to support this contention, these misleading stereotypes are likely to deter anyone other than the very fit young-old from believing that active aging has any relevance to their lives. Moreover, they always emphasize physical prowess and rarely focus on mental capacity.

The third set of barriers is bureaucratic. As indicated, active aging requires a holistic approach, but governments, local and national, are not geared to respond to such strategic needs. Instead, everywhere (even in socialist China) responsibilities are strictly divided between ministries and departments. This division of labor encourages silo thinking and militates against the implementation of an effective active aging approach. In the same vein, this division supports the reduction of the strategic potential of active aging to older workers or older people, rather than emphasizing the full life course. Thus, in governments everywhere, ministries or departments usually represent older people and children, but no official body is responsible for aging (Walker, 2018).

The fourth set of barriers is societal. This includes the age segmentation that predominates in political and popular thought and practice. As illustrated in Figure 30.2, the traditional paradigm segments the life course into three major stages. Although the life course and working life have been transformed over

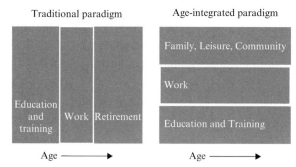

Traditional paradigm          Age-integrated paradigm

Family, Leisure, Community

Work

Education and Training

Education and training    Work    Retirement

Age ⟶              Age ⟶

**Figure 30.2.** *Life course segmentation*
*Source:* Walker and Maltby (2012)

recent decades – the former, for example, by increased longevity, and the latter, by the replacement of careers for large sections of the working population with discontinuous employment – social institutions and popular discourses still operate as if the traditional model is the dominant one. This embeddedness encourages silo thinking in policy and practice: active aging is only for the retired and so on. In contrast, the age-integrated paradigm opens the door to a life course active aging approach.

Equally important are the societal barriers created by age discrimination or ageism. These can include direct discrimination, when older workers are excluded from jobs, or vulnerable older patients are abused; but it also encompasses less direct, more insidious, stereotyping, for example, when older people are described as a "burden" or accused of robbing resources from the young. Discrimination has two unfortunate effects. On the one hand, it excludes and stigmatizes older people, particularly frail older people and, on the other, it encourages younger people to ignore later life, to push it to the back of their minds. Both effects limit the potential of active aging policies. For example, among older people there is often a resigned stoicism – "at my age what can you expect?" – that militates against active engagement.

The fifth set of barriers may be labeled unequal aging – the deep-seated inequalities that exist both between older people and over the life course. Within countries there are inequalities between different groups of older people, for example, based on social class, gender, and race, which segment the experience of later life. These inequalities are usually created not in old age but at earlier stages of the life cycle (Walker, 2009b). Then there are the major inequalities in aging and later life between countries at similar levels of development. In the EU, for example, there are substantial differences between member states in healthy life expectancy – 10 years between Denmark and Estonia (Jagger et al., 2009). Then there are the huge disparities between rich and poor countries – the Global North and South. These three aspects of unequal aging make the task of implementing an active aging strategy more difficult than it already is, because they require flexibility in the design and implementation of such a strategy when the preference of policymakers is invariably closer to "one size fits all."

As indicated, these five sets of barriers help to account for the fact that active aging is not yet reaching its full potential in policy terms. So, what steps are necessary to confront these barriers and enable the comprehensive approach that is called for by the aging challenges? The final main section considers this question.

## Realizing the Promise of Active Aging

As indicated in the previous section, there are formidable barriers confronting a comprehensive active aging approach of the kind espoused by WHO. Some of these stem directly from ideology and must be considered beyond the scope of this chapter. Here, the concern is with the nature of the active aging strategy itself, adopting science's public role to ensure that policymakers and wider society are adequately equipped with knowledge to pursue specific goals. Thus, it is essential to start by clarifying what an active aging strategy should look like, including the principles upon which it should be based.

Seven key principles have been proposed, as the basis for a strategy on active aging, to ensure that it is both comprehensive and consistent (Walker, 2002).

First of all, "activity" should consist of all meaningful pursuits that contribute to the well-being of the individual concerned, his or her family, the local community, or society at large, and should not be concerned only with paid employment or production. Thus, in terms of active aging, volunteering should be as highly valued as paid employment. Secondly, it should be primarily a preventative concept. This means involving all age groups in the process of aging actively across the whole of the life course. Thirdly, active aging should encompass *all* older people, even those who are, to some extent, frail and dependent. This is because of the danger that a focus only on the "young-old" will exclude the "old-old," and the fact that the link between activity and health (including mental stimulation) holds good into advanced old age (WHO, 2001a). There is also an important gender aspect to this principle in that most of the very old are women. Thus, this strategy is framed to be gender-sensitive not gender neutral (Foster & Walker, 2013). Fourthly, the maintenance of intergenerational solidarity should be an important feature of active aging. This means fairness between generations, as well as the opportunity to develop activities that span the generations. Fifthly, the concept should embody both rights and obligations. Thus, the rights to social protection, lifelong education and training, and so on should be accompanied by obligations to take advantage of education and training opportunities and to remain active in other ways. Again, from a gender perspective, this requires support to enable women to participate. Sixthly, a strategy for active aging should be participative and empowering. In other words, there must be a combination of top-down policy action to enable and motivate activity, but also, opportunities for citizens to take action, from the bottom up, for example, in developing their own forms of activity. Seventhly, active aging has to respect national and cultural diversity. For example, there are differences in the forms of participation undertaken between the North and the South of Europe; therefore, value judgments about what sort of activity is "best" are likely to be problematic (European Commission, 2000). Within some EU countries, such as Belgium, there are major cultural variations that require a flexible approach to the implementation of an active aging strategy. Indeed, this cultural diversity and the unequal aging discussed in the previous section suggest that "flexibility" should be an eighth principle (Foster & Walker, 2015).

These principles indicate that an effective strategy on active aging will be based on a *partnership* between the citizen and society. In this partnership, the role of the state is to enable, facilitate, and motivate citizens and, where necessary, to provide high quality social protection for as long as possible. This will require interrelated individual and societal strategies. As far as individuals are concerned, they have a duty to take advantage of lifelong learning and continuous training opportunities, and to promote their own health and well-being throughout the life course. As far as society is concerned, the policy challenge is to recognize the thread that links together all of the relevant policy areas: employment, health, social protection, social inclusion, transport, education, and so on. A comprehensive active aging strategy demands that all of the individual pieces be "joined up" and become mutually supportive. The primary discourse behind this strategic vision of active aging aligns with the UN's society for all ages (www.un.org/esa/socdev/iyop/iyopcfo.htm).

With regard to the scope of the actions necessary to achieve such a comprehensive strategy WHO has highlighted eight main determinants of active aging: culture and gender (both of which are cross-cutting), education level, health and social service, behavioral, the physical environment, the social environment, and economic determinants, and those related to the person concerned (such as biology, genetics, and psychology) (WHO, 2002). In EU policy terms, this would mean linkage between policy domains that have hitherto been separated: employment, health, social protection, pensions, social inclusion, technology, economic policy, and research. At the same time, in line with WHO's call, there is a need to mobilize all stakeholders to "popularize ... active aging through dialogue, discussion, and debate in the political arena, the education sector, public for a [forum] and media" (WHO, 2002, p. 55). The basis for such a comprehensive approach exists already in many developed countries but appears to be stymied by the huge challenge of transcending traditional departmental boundaries and changing deeply entrenched reactive approaches into preventative ones. A case in point is the United Kingdom, which has had a comprehensive strategy on active aging since 2005 that has yet to be thoroughly implemented (Department for Work and Pensions, 2005).

Of course the key stakeholders are not dormant while they wait for the perfect strategic framework to be assembled. Thus, there are countless examples of local community and grass roots level initiatives by older people, NGOs, and municipalities aimed at raising the participation and well-being of this group (Walker & Naegele, 1999). In some countries there are national programs to encourage healthy aging such as "FinnWell" in Finland. There is plenty of evidence too that some employers, albeit a minority, have developed a variety of age management measures designed to retain, recruit, and maximize the potential of an aging workforce (Walker, 1999; Naegele & Walker, 2006). What is lacking at present, however, is a comprehensive strategy on active aging that includes the sharing of the many examples of good practices between countries.

Research and development have a critical role to play in advancing the active aging agenda and, especially, in providing the evidence base for policy. European research, under Framework Programmes 5, 6, and 7, has already added considerably to this knowledge base, and the future research priorities have been mapped, for example, by the ETAN initiative, and coordinated actions like FORUM and ERA-AGE (http://era-age.group.shef.ac.uk/), as well as the Road Map project (FUTURAGE, 2011).

## Conclusion

This chapter has subjected the idea of active aging to close scrutiny, and explained why it is promising as the inspiration for a strategy designed to prevent the course of what has become widely known in gerontological circles as "normal aging." In fact, the acceptance of functional limitation as "normal" may act as an additional barrier to the development of active aging or other related preventative approaches. This acceptance is implicit in the overwhelming priority given in the health systems of more developed countries to curative and palliative medicine, rather than public health measures aimed at prevention. Having considered the barriers to active aging policies, a more proactive approach was taken, in the form of some key principles by which active aging might be implemented, with prevention across the life course at their core. These principles indicate that active aging should engage all of the key actors – from citizens to policymakers.

Thus, taking the WHO definition a stage further, active aging might be defined in policy terms as: a comprehensive strategy to maximize participation and well-being as people age. It should operate simultaneously at the individual, organizational, and societal levels, and at all stages of the life course (Walker, 2009a, p. 80).

## References

Aune, D., et al. (2017) Fruit and vegetable intake and the risk of cardiovascular disease, total cancer and all-cause mortality – a systematic review and dose-response meta-analysis of prospective studies, *International Journal of Epidemiology*, 1–28. doc: 10. 1093/ije/dyw319.

Blau, Z. S. (1973). *Old Age in a Changing Society*. New York: New Viewpoints.

Boudiny, K. (2013). 'Active ageing': From empty rhetoric to effective policy tool. *Ageing and Society*, 33(6), 1077–98. doi:10.1017/S0144686X1200030X

Bowling, A. (2005). *Ageing Well: Quality of Life in Old Age*. Maidenhead: Open University Press.

Butler, R., Oberlink, M., Schecter, M. (Eds.) (1990). *The Promise of Productive Aging*. New York: Springer.

Cann, P., Dean, M. (2009). *Unequal Ageing*. Bristol: Policy Press.

Chief Medical Officer (2014) Report to the Chief Medical Officer, London, Department of Health.

Cumming, E., Henry, W. (1961). *Growing Old – The Process of Disengagement*. New York: Basic Books.

Department for Work and Pensions (DWP). (2005). *Opportunity Age*. London: DWP.

European Commission. (1999). *Towards a Europe for All Ages*. COM (1999) 221, Brussels: European Commission.

  (2000). *Social Agenda 2000-2005*. Brussels: European Commission.

  (2006). *The Demographic Future of Europe – From Challenge to Opportunity*. Brussels: European Commission.

  (2010). *2012 to be the European Year for Active Ageing*. DG Employment, Social Affairs and Inclusion website: http://ec.europa.eu/social/main.jsp?langId=en&catId=89&newsId=860

Fernandez Ballesteros, R., Robine, J. M., Walker, A., et al. (Eds.) (2013). *Active Aging: A Global Goal*, 2013.

Fontana, L., Partridge, L. (2015). "Promoting Health and Longevity Through Diet – From Model Organisations to Humans," *Cell*, 161, 106–18.

Foster, L., Walker, A. (2013). Gender and active ageing in Europe. *European Journal of Ageing*, 10(1), 3–10.

  (2015). Active and successful ageing: a European policy perspective. *The Gerontologist*, 55(1), 83–90.

Futurage. (2011). *A Road Map for European Ageing Research*: www.futurage.group.shef.ac.uk/roadmap.html.

Gems, D., Partridge, L. (2013) Genetics of longevity in model organisms: debate and paradigm shifts, *Annual Review of Physiology*, 75, 621–44.

Havighurst, R. (1954). Flexibility and the social roles of the retired. *American Journal of Sociology*, 59, 309–11.

  (1963). Successful aging. In R. Williams, C. Tibbitts, & W. Donahue (Eds.), *Process of Aging* (1, 299–320). New York: Atherton.

Havighurst, R., Albrecht, R. (1953). *Older People*. London: Longmans.

Jagger, C., Gillies, C., Moscone, F., et al. the EHLEIS team (2009). Inequalities in healthy life years in the 25 countries of the European Union in 2005: a cross-national meta-regression analysis. *Lancet*, 372, 2124–31.

Kinsella, K., He, W. (2009) *An Aging World: 2008*. Washington, DC: US Department of Commerce.

Kirkwood, T. (2005). Understanding the odd science of aging, *Cell*, 120, 437–47.

  (2008). A systematic look at an old problem, *Nature*, 451, 644–647.

Kirkwood, T., Austad, S. (2000). Why do we age?, *Nature*, 408, 233–8.

Kuh, D., Cooper, R., Hardy, R., et al. (Eds.) (2014). *A Life-course Approach to Healthy Ageing*, Oxford: Oxford University Press.

López-Otin, C., Blasco, M., Partridge, L., et al. (2013). The hallmarks of aging, *Cell*, 153, 1194–217.

Naegele, G., Walker, A. (2006). *A Guide to Good Practice in Age Management*. Dublin: European Foundation for the Improvement of Living and Working Conditions.

Oeppen, I., Vaupel, J. (2002). Broken limits to life expectancy. *Science*, 296, 1029–31.

Pfeiffer, E. (Ed.) (1974). *Successful Aging: A Conference Report*. Durham, NC: Duke University.

Rowe, J., Kahn, R. (1987). Human aging: usual and successful. *Science*, 237, 143–9.

Strawbridge, W. J., Wallhagen, M. I., Cohen, R. D. (2002). Successful aging and well-being self-rated compared with Rowe and Kahn. *The Gerontologist*, 42(6), 727–33.

Steves, C., Spector, T., Jackson, S. (2012). Ageing, genes, environment and epigenetics: what twin studies tell us now, and in the future, *Age and Ageing*, 41, 581–6.

Tate, R., Leedine, L., Cuddy, T. (2003). Definition of successful aging by elderly Canadian males: The Manitoba follow-up study. *The Gerontologist*, 43, 735–44. doi:10.1093/geront/43.5.735.

Villar, F. (2012). Successful ageing and development: The contribution of generativity in older age. *Ageing and Society*, 32, 1087–105. doi: 10.1017/S0144686X11000973.

Walker, A. (1980). The social creation of poverty and dependency in old age. *Journal of Social Policy*, 9(1), 49–75.

(1981). Towards a political economy of old age. *Ageing and Society*, 1(1), 73–94.

(1993). *Age and Attitudes*. Brussels: EC.

(1994). Work and income in the third age – an EU perspective. *The Geneva Papers on Risk and Insurance*, 19(73), 397–407.

(1999). *Managing an Ageing Workforce: A Guide to Good Practice*. Dublin: European Foundation for the Improvement of Living and Working Conditions.

(2002). A strategy for active ageing. *International Social Security Review*, 55 (1), 121–40.

(2009a). The emergence and application of active ageing in Europe. *Journal of Ageing and Social Policy*, 21, 75–93.

(2009b). Why is ageing so unequal? In P. Cann, M. Dean (Eds.), *Unequal Ageing* (pp. 141–58). Bristol: Policy Press.

(2018). Why the UK needs a social policy on ageing. *Journal of Social Policy*, 47(2), 253–73.

Walker, A., Naegele, G. (1999). *The Politics of Old Age in Europe*. Open University Press.

Walker, A., Maltby, T. (2012). Active ageing: a strategic policy solution to demographic ageing in the European Union. *International Journal of Social Welfare*, 21(s1), S117–30.

WHO (1994). *Health for All: Updated Targets*. Copenhagen: World Health Organisation.

(2001a). *Active Ageing: From Evidence to Action*. Geneva: World Health Organisation.

(2001b). *Health and Ageing: A Discussion Paper*. Geneva: World Health Organisation.

(2001c). *Active Ageing: From Evidence to Action*. Geneva: World Health Organisation.

(2002). *Active Ageing: A Policy Framework*. Geneva: World Health Organisation.

Zaidi, A., Zolyami, E. (2011). *Active Ageing Research Note 7/2011*. Produced by the Social Situation Observatory, for the European Commission, Directorate-General for Employment, Social Affairs and Inclusion, Brussels.

# 31 Linking the Socio-Physical Environment to Successful Aging

From Basic Research to Intervention to Implementation Science Considerations

Hans-Werner Wahl and Laura N. Gitlin

## Introduction

Where is the environment in models of successful aging? Does the environment matter when it comes to aging successfully; and if so, in what way? These are the central questions posed in this chapter. We argue that models of successful aging have remained primarily at the individual level of aging and continue to lack an environmental perspective, to the detriment of the field theoretically and practically. We suggest that environmental perspectives have the potential to enrich models of successful aging and contribute to a better understanding of successful aging, and more effective strategies and policies. We illustrate respective avenues for integrating environmental perspectives, intervention, and implementation research endeavors in fundamental ways.

Our reasoning is grounded in the field of environmental gerontology (Wahl & Gitlin, 2007; Wahl et al., 2012), which strives to understand the role of environments in the maintenance and improvement of autonomy and well-being, and specifically, the relationship of aging individuals to their environments, as well as its utilization and optimization to effectively support individuals/families with varying conditions, capabilities, and needs. While environmental gerontology primarily considers the relevance of the full range of physical components (e.g., wayfinding or ambulating from one place to another in one's home, stimulation, accessibility, safety/hazards considerations) for aging processes, the social dimension is also acknowledged as having an equally important role. Indeed, both environmental dimensions, the physical and the social, can hardly be separated, prompting us to use the term socio-physical environment throughout this chapter. For example, the home environment is not only a physical structure, but also a place punctuated by pronounced intimacy with one's partner, social interactions, activity engagement, and the symbolization of attachment, normalcy, connectedness, personhood, comfort, security, and loss. Similarly, communities that enable continued physical activity and social engagement opportunities are critical to being age-friendly and contributing to successful aging (Scharlack & Lehning, 2015). Thus, when referring to the socio-physical environment, we do so with sensitivity to and recognition of its social and cultural accouterments and implications. Nevertheless, in this chapter, we do not directly consider the role of social and cultural aspects of environments such as family relations and their dynamics, social capital, resources of communities, and social networking for aging processes and outcomes (see other chapters of the Handbook for these perspectives).

Environmental gerontology is founded in the basic principle that old age is a critical phase in the life course that is profoundly influenced by the socio-physical environment. In fact, as people age, the socio-physical environment appears to matter more than in other life phases. Additionally, it matters differentially based on a person's sociocultural background, financial and social resources, somatic and psychic health, and cognitive and physical functional abilities. Thus, a socio-physical environmental perspective is essential to the consideration of successful aging; in other words, successful aging cannot and must not be considered independently of an understanding of the environments in which aging occurs.

The socio-physical environment can have a wide range of important roles in successful aging, making its relationship complex and multi-faceted. For example, roles may include: (a) as a cause of behavioral or psychological outcomes of interest, (b) as a moderator of a desired outcome(s), (c) as a mediator of a desired outcome(s), (d) as an outcome itself, or (e) as an overall context in which behavioral, cognitive, and affective processes occur or are shaped.

As a causal factor, consider a home with hazards such as torn carpets or uneven stairs. Such conditions may directly cause a fall or undermine the autonomy of an individual with mobility impairment. As a moderating effect, comparing individuals with and without mobility impairments along the number and type of their home hazards, may reveal that falls more frequently occur in home environments with more hazards for those aging with mobility impairments. Alternately, the association between mobility impairment and depressive mood may be lower or even disappear in housing environments without such hazards and with compensatory features (e.g., grab bars, easy-to-access spaces) that optimize environmental support, suggesting a mediation role for the environment. Further, one consideration may be identifying factors that motivate older adults to invest in housing modifications, and possibly the installation of technology support; in this case, a better supportive environment would be the relevant endpoint or outcome of interest. We may also generally assume that the environment serves as the backdrop or framework for any model of aging including social and cognitive development and physical and emotional well-being. Similarly, it may serve as the context in which a novel intervention, program, service, or strategy is implemented to support successful aging. In this case, dimensions of the service environment may serve as barriers to or facilitators of effective implementation of interventions for successful aging (Gitlin & Czaja, 2016).

In addition to these distinct roles, the socio-physical environment can be conceptualized as being immediate or micro (home), proximal or meso (neighborhood or community), and/or distal (social policy). Each of these environmental layers intersects and influences the other and in turn successful aging. For example, the emergence of age-friendly communities to enable successful aging and the social policies to support these efforts reflects the confluence and intersection of policy and community level factors. While we recognize the interconnectedness of each of these environmental layers and their associated factors, we concentrate predominantly on the micro to meso level, leaving social policy to another chapter of this Handbook.

That said, we begin with an overview of established theories/models emanating mainly in environmental gerontology that focus on the person interacting within socio-physical environments (P-E). We consider how P-E transactions are operationalized in practice, echoed, for example, in home-based interventions to improve functionality or newly designed housing and living arrangements for persons with dementia or other impairments. Next, we examine in detail the needed bridge building among theories/models of P-E transaction and successful aging. Following this theoretical grounding, we move on to examine the intervention level and ways the *plasticity* of the P-E system may systematically (and professionally) be used therapeutically to promote successful aging. This also brings us to a discussion of the challenges of *implementing* and sustaining proven interventions directed at enhancing successful aging in daily ecologies and specific environmental factors of relevance to implementation. The environment as the context for implementation of an intervention has not traditionally been considered in environmental gerontology and thus extends its utility to implementation science. We argue that implementation theories implicitly or explicitly draw upon an environmental perspective and that a concern for advancing successful aging must consider interventions and their implementation in different environmental contexts.

## Role of P-E Transactions as People Age – Overview of Conceptualizations

The integration of an environmental perspective with successful aging models must be grounded in a theoretical base. Table 31.1 presents the main elements of key theories/models, which address life span and aging related changes in the P-E system.

Initial P-E models, although still of high relevance, predominantly emphasized the role of the objective physical environment. In particular, the *Competence-Environmental Press Model* (Lawton & Nahemow, 1973) provides a broad, overarching framework allowing different types and levels of competence such as sensory loss, physical mobility loss, or cognitive decline and environmental factors including housing standards, neighborhood conditions, or public transport to be considered. Perhaps the most important element of the model is its fundamental assumption that for each aging person there is an optimal combination of (still) available competence and environmental circumstances leading to the highest possible behavioral and emotional functioning for that person. A term

Table 31.1 *Overview of models/theories addressing person–environment (P-E) dynamics in aging*

| Model/theoretical approach | Fundamental understanding of P-E transaction | Primary role of environment | Key assumptions |
|---|---|---|---|
| | **Focus on Role of Objective E** | | |
| Competence-environmental press model (e.g., Lawton & Nahemow, 1973); person–environment accessibility model (e.g., Iwarsson, 2004). | Objective E (e.g., distance to public transport) interacts with objectively measured P characteristics (e.g., vision impairment), leading to different magnitudes of P-E fit (accessibility). | Predictor, moderator, or mediator of outcomes. | As P competence decreases during aging, E constellations increasingly influence outcomes (e.g., autonomy, well-being, coping with disabilities in daily life). |
| | **Focus on Role of Perceived/Experiential E** | | |
| Place attachment and P-E insideness processes (Rowles, 1983; Rubinstein, 1989) | Perceived and experiential E plays a major role in terms of meaning making late in life. | Predictor, moderator, or mediator of outcomes. | Cognitive and affective ties with E explain major elements of the aging experience such as well-being and identity-related outcomes. |
| | **Focus on Role of Objective and Perceived/Experiential E** | | |
| Agency-belonging model (e.g., Wahl & Oswald, 2016) | Both the objective and perceived E must be considered simultaneously. | Predictor, moderator, or mediator of outcomes. | P-E belonging encompasses all processes of E oriented meaning making; P-E agency encompasses all processes of E oriented shaping and change. Autonomy, identity, and well-being considered as major outcomes. |
| Health integration model (Stineman et al., 2011) | E as important for health and health behaviors. | Predictor, moderator, or mediator of outcomes. | Health and disability always must be seen as the product not only of P conditions, but also E characteristics, facilitating or hindering desired health and disability related outcomes. |

(cont.)

Table 31.1 (cont.)

| Model/theoretical approach | Fundamental understanding of P-E transaction | Primary role of environment | Key assumptions |
|---|---|---|---|
| Residential normalcy model (Golant, 2015) | Residential decision-making and outcomes as interaction of P characteristics, with perceived and objective E characteristics. | E as outcome. | Experienced congruence or incongruence due to interplay of experiencing P-E comfort and P-E mastery. |
| Environments as General Frame of Development and Aging | | | |
| Bio-ecological systems theory (Bronfenbrenner, 1999) | E, both objective and perceived. Developmental goal regulation always operates in certain E. | Making use of E opportunities as key element of development. | Consideration of different levels of P-E trans-actions all assumed of importance for devel-opment (e.g., micro-, meso-, macro-level). |
| Motivational theory of life span development (Heckhausen et al., 2010) | | Making use of E opportunities as key element of development. | Aging as adapting to the challenges of environ-mental opportunities and constraining fac-tors; primary control over E as key human motivation behind goal regulation processes aimed to maintain well-being. |

*Note:* E = socio-physical environment; P-E transaction = person-environment transaction.

frequently used for this in environmental gerontology is *person–environment fit* (Iwarsson, 2004). The model also suggests that it is at the lower levels of competence that older people become the most susceptible to their environment, such that low competence in conjunction with high "environmental press" negatively impacts autonomy, affect, and well-being. A related point is that as competencies decline, the zone of adaptation narrows, such that environmental choices that can promote well-being become increasingly more limited, although there is always an option. The competence-environmental press framework continues to provide the basic mechanism of person–environment relations as people age and has been supported by a considerable body of empirical research. For example, Wahl et al. (2009a) have shown in their systematic review that poor housing quality is related to higher disability. In addition, the ENABLE-AGE project (e.g., Oswald et al., 2007), a large study of European old age samples capturing in-depth P-E transactions, has shown that better P-E fit is associated with more positive outcomes associated with successful aging, including functional independence and reduced depression (Wahl et al., 2009b). Other studies similarly show that providing supportive home environmental features can improve quality of life for persons with physical impairments (Gitlin et al., 2006, 2015; Cho et al., 2016; Szanton et al., 2016), as well as for those with cognitive decline (Gitlin et al., 2016). For individuals with dementia, complex and difficult to navigate environments are associated with behavioral symptoms, withdrawal, disengagement, and poor physical function (Gitlin et al., 2014). Furthermore, the Competence-Environmental Press Model has become a major driver in the practical world of designing and optimizing environments for older people (Scharlach & Lehning, 2015; Golant, 2015).

In parallel to models emphasizing the role of the objective socio-physical environment, the perceived environment has also found much attention since the inception of environmental gerontology. A key theme is that as people age, they build strong affective, cognitive, behavioral, and social bonds in their living environment, thereby transforming "space" into "place," and thus developing intensive forms of place attachment (Rowles, 1983; Rubinstein, 1989; Rowles & Watkins, 2003). Furthermore, concepts on the meaning of home are directly related to place attachment, as they address the most frequent manifestation of attachment processes. Since older adults often live in the same residence for a long period of time, cognitive and emotional aspects of the meaning of home are often strongly linked to their biographies and self-identity, as well as their perceptions of what it means to age successfully. Rowles (1983) argues that processes of place attachment and the allocation of meaning of place reflect different patterns of physical, autobiographical, and social insideness as a result of the long duration of living in the same place: "place becomes a landscape of memories, providing a sense of identity" (see Rowles, 1983, p. 114; see also Rowles & Watkins, 2003), and maintaining this sense of identity informs subjective perceptions of what it means to age well. This iterative, dynamical relationship lies at the heart of successful aging in place.

A number of models also point to the need to integrate both objective as well as the perceived/experiential environmental perspectives. At the core of the framework suggested by Wahl and Oswald (2016) is the assumption that two fundamental processes, experience-driven P-E belonging and behavior-driven P-E agency, are key to or underlie P-E transactions. *P-E belonging processes* account for the full range of subjective evaluations and interpretations of place, and include a mixture of emotional and cognitive elements related to the socio-physical environment. Thus, belonging incorporates all non-goal-oriented experiential aspects that make a space a place. In contrast, *processes of P-E agency* include the full range of goal-directed behaviors such as reactive and proactive aspects of using, compensating, adapting, retrofitting, creating, and sustaining places. Emerging empirical evidence supporting the need to consider both the objective as well as the perceived environment comes from the ENABLE-AGE project; specifically, very old individuals living in more accessible housing, who perceived their home as useful and valuable (belonging), and who thought that they themselves were responsible for their housing situation (agency), were more independent in daily activities, had a better sense of well-being, and had fewer depressive symptoms.

The *Health Environmental Integration model*, an extension of the "environmental press" framework and previous disablement models (Stineman et al., 2011), suggests that intra-individual (combined effects of cognitive, physical, emotional conditions) determinants interact with extra-individual (environmental, social resources, and networks) determinants that serve as barriers or facilitators of performance. The model posits a dynamic system of persons and living environments, such that the understanding of individual factors depends upon characterizing the person within their living environment.

Golant's *model of Residential Normalcy* has found much resonance in environmental gerontology and beyond. The model emphasizes residential decision-making processes in later life from an individual perspective. It highlights subjective environmental experiences of residential comfort and mastery, as well as related adaptive coping strategies to maintain or achieve residential normalcy (Golant, 2015). According to Golant's model, if older people feel comfortable and in control of their environment at home, they achieve residential normalcy such that they might not be motivated or perceive the need to relocate or make environmental adaptations. However, if there is a perceived incongruence on the behavioral or experiential level, they may perceive themselves as being outside of their zone of mastery and/or comfort, and then they may be more motivated or ready to make a change. Consequently, older adults strive to achieve residential normalcy by adopting assimilative or accommodative coping strategies (Brandtstädter & Greve, 1994) within their immediate home environment. The model has been used to examine real-life relocation decision-making in Europe (Granbom et al., 2014).

Finally, the environment has also been considered as a general frame of development. The Bioecological Systems Theory expands on the concept of environment to include different environmental levels, such as microsystems (activities and interaction patterns in immediate surroundings), mesosystems (connections among microsystems), macrosystems (broader systems of culture, values, laws, customs), and chronosystems (life transitions). The bioecological systems theory focuses on the changing interrelationship among these layers of context in individuals over time (Bronfenbrenner, 1999).

The Motivational Theory of Life-span Development provides additional insights as to the psychosocial consequences of person–environment dynamics. It suggests that threats to or losses in a person's ability to control important aspects in his/her life (e.g., performing self-care) may motivate the use of new strategies to buffer these threats and losses. Maintaining function and engagement in daily activities is a highly desired goal that can be threatened by chronic conditions and functional limitations. To the extent that people use positive strategies (e.g., assistive devices, social support) to meet personal and daily performance goals, they minimize threats to or actual losses of control and may achieve positive well-being. However, older adults may need exposure to, training in, and support to use various effective control strategies such as energy conservation techniques, assistive technologies, cognitive reframing, or problem solving. Studies testing this theory show that using strategies minimizing intrinsic/extrinsic demands have psychosocial and physical benefits (Gitlin et al., 2007; Heckhausen et al., 2010). Thus, Bronfenbrenner's Bioecological Systems Theory and the Motivational Theory of Life-span Development suggest that the environment deserves careful consideration in any model of life span development and aging.

In conclusion, an extensive body of theories/models accompanied by considerable empirical evidence supports the need to consider P-E transactions as an important element of life span development and aging related processes and outcomes, including successful aging. Both the objective and perceived environment are critical components of P-E transactions, and outcomes of such transactions include autonomy, identity, and well-being related outcomes. Also, these models suggest that aging individuals are proactive shapers of their environments, exerting considerable agency, and thus, should not be seen as passive or pawns of existing P-E constellations.

## Successful Aging and the Socio-Physical Environment: A Needed Connection

In a now classic essay by M. Powell Lawton (1983) titled, "Environment and Other Determinants of Well-being in Older People," the environment found a prominent role in contributing to what Lawton called the "good life in old age," – a vision close to what the term "successful aging" means (see also Fernandez-Ballesteros, 2008). In this model, the objective environment is identified as one of four highly interactive quadrants (other quadrants include: behavioral competence, psychological well-being, and perceived quality of life) composing the "good life."

Although the term successful aging has a long history in gerontology, dating back to the late 1950s and early 1960s (Havighurst, 1961), its widespread use in gerontology only started with Rowe and Kahn's (1987) *Science* article on "Human Aging: Usual and Successful." Rowe and Kahn's conception, elaborated since this re-inauguration of the term "successful aging" in a series of additional work (e.g., Rowe & Kahn, 2015), has remained the most influential view of the topic until present. Therefore, in this section, we concentrate on linking the environment with successful aging in terms of their view.

The Rowe-Kahn conception of successful aging is based on three components, i.e., (1) low probability of disease and related disability; (2) high cognitive and physical functioning; and (3) active engagement with life. In contrast to "normal aging," successful aging addresses what would be possible if latent reserve capacities and healthy lifestyles come to an optimal unfolding. This visionary view of aging certainly is a major aspect of Rowe and Kahn's conceptualization of successful aging and thus has similarity with Lawton's (1983) "good life" in old age; both suggest that quality life in the later years is achievable under the best circumstances possible, which includes health, economic, and environmental considerations. However, to our knowledge, a systematic analysis of the role of the environment for successful aging has so far not been undertaken, except again, for the conceptualization of the good life, which explicitly identified the environment as one of four influences on life quality. In what follows, we attempt to close this gap based on two primary arguments: (1) the role of environment for unfolding latent reserves in life span development and aging at large; and (2) the role of environment for aging with cognitive and functional limitations.

## Role of Socio-Physical Environment for Unfolding Latent Reserves in Life Span Development and Aging

A major argument in the successful aging debate, including Rowe and Kahn's conception, has been that positive outcomes late in life strongly depend on early lifestyle factors, decisions, and preventive action. Besides the important role of early education, healthy lifestyles such as sufficient physical activity, and *engagement* processes at large (Hertzog et al., 2009), as well as concomitant delay or avoidance of disease, functional impairment, and disablement processes (Verbrugge & Jette, 1994) all have significant environmental components. For example, macrosystem and mesosystem based messaging, to refer again to Bronfenbrenner's (1999) bio-ecological approach, which foster and encourage physical activity, are of key importance for stimulating and maintaining physical activity involvements in daily ecologies. Think of neighborhood factors impacting health behavior choices, the health system, community policy, and labor force related motivational efforts that have revealed as important factors toward sustainable "active" lifestyles (Beard et al., 2015). The worldwide trend toward "age friendly" communities including the dementia friendly community movement as well as universal design movements at the community level all draw from the fundamental principle that environmental improvements (e.g., public transport, way-finding, and orientation, safe green areas, safe walking areas) are a key prerequisite for securing public health and prevention at large, as well as aging successfully throughout the life course.

In addition, the environment can either distil or promulgate negative stereotypes of aging. Stigma affects individuals in profound ways and individuals often incorporate age stereotypes into their personal self-system, which in turn can affect individual development and how one chooses to age (Miche et al., 2015). As it seems, midlife is a particularly important life stage with high sensitivity for incorporating positive or negative views on aging that are indirectly and directly communicated by the environment including mass media, employment environments, and commonly occurring age segregated activities. This is so, because in this period of life span development, (chronic) disease and disability-related occurrences begin to emerge as well as the experience of transitioning to old age (still frequently connected with passing the age of 65 years) and post-retirement life becomes a "real" and near possibility in one's future life. In such a situation, individuals intensively search for interpretations of observed and anticipated life changes. Views of aging offered by the environment are important drivers of development and decision-making processes connected with one's own life. Simply put, determining where and how one wants to live becomes a core feature of decision-making in and management of this stage.

That said, it becomes apparent that planning and action processes at the micro level of P-E transactional regulation are always embedded in mesosystem and macrosystem influences (see above for definitions of these concepts). The chronosystem is also of importance, as ideas on the meaning of a "good life" are subject to historical and cohort related influences, particularly in mid and late life. For example, the emerging trend to "quantify" daily life using activity sensor systems provides a new form of environmental feedback that may have an impact on physical activity, health choices, and disability status (e.g., Dasenbrock et al., 2016).

Viewed in a broader perspective, technology is becoming a new environment in mid and old age, which is having a significant impact on a number of levels (Schulz et al., 2015). For example, aging individuals now use the Internet as a major source for obtaining information and evaluating their health and functioning (Czaja, 2015). The Internet also affords access to cognitive training platforms, different applications for addressing life stressors, and facilitating connectedness with others to overcome isolation (Czaja et al., 2013, 2015). Understanding, examining, and identifying the planning and action processes aimed to maintain high P-E fit in living arrangements are critical to a life span view of successful aging. For example, early anticipation and preparation of transitions to new housing arrangements may help to avoid hasty and ill-informed residential decision-making late in life. Also, early home modification is an important means of fall prevention and maintaining independence in activities of daily living (Iwarsson et al., 2009). Newly designed housing solutions may elicit novel approaches to prevent functional decline and improve and sustain social engagement for subpopulations of aging individuals. Retirement community environments as well as new community housing solutions, including assisted living and multi-generation housing in addition to age-friendly and dementia-friendly communities, may allow new supportive approaches to supporting successful aging in place by promoting solidarity, volunteering, and social engagement opportunities, and enriching a positive culture toward aging. In other words, a diversity of living arrangements and housing solutions may provide important answers toward addressing the extreme diversity and individuation of life span development, differential needs, and aging at large.

Moreover, viewed from the vantage point of the Motivational Theory of Lifespan Development (Heckhausen et al., 2010), successful aging may be understood as goal-directed behaviors to enable continued engagement in daily living activities that include actions upon the environment as the primary mechanism for exerting primary and secondary control-oriented strategies. On the one hand, selecting environments that are congruent with personal needs, preferences, and capabilities, is a key process of successful life span development. However, this is not well understood or communicated to older adults themselves such that there is purposeful planning early on in the aging process concerning the just right fit with a living environment. On the other hand, the environment plays a significant role as a compensatory mechanism, such that it may offset functional challenges when goal attainment is blocked (e.g., due to age-related functional losses). The environment can also support new ways of achieving important life goals to enable older adults to stay in place.

Finally, multi-directionality in the interplay of P-E belonging and P-E agency processes along the adult life course deserves attention (see above for definitions of these concepts). Processes of P-E belonging tend to gain in importance as people age, and particularly in advanced old age, while the relevance of P-E agency tends to decrease (Wahl & Lang, 2004). In other words, changing one's socio-physical environment becomes less personally relevant, whereas cognitive-affective ties to the socio-physical environment become central to quality of life. This also may explain why many older adults are hesitant to relocate, show high stability, and regularity in their out-of-home-related activities (e.g., preferred places and travel patterns), and value their familiar home and neighborhood environment, even when they present inherent safety and other risks (Oswald & Rowles, 2007). At the same time, such strong P-E belonging oriented striving may also prevent older adults from making effective residential decisions at different points in their later life. Seen through the perspective posed by Golant's (2015) model, aging individuals may stay too long in their P-E comfort zone and not take needed proactive (assimilative) efforts to change their P-E, before environmental stress experiences interfere with daily functioning and require quick solutions. Thus, focusing on the role of P-E transactions also highlights a key dilemma in successful aging – successful adaptational P-E strategies, which may become an obstacle for effective aging in place at a later point of personal development. As such, P-E transactions in successful aging are dynamic and have multiple roles and outcomes that change as people age. This transactional dynamic is integral to successful aging and thus must be recognized and understood.

## Role of Socio-Physical Environment for Aging with Disabilities

Most definitions, including that of Rowe and Kahn, exclude disability and physical impairment from successful aging (Depp & Jeste, 2006; Cosco et al., 2014). This neglect and purposeful exclusion of age-related disability is a major limitation of current models of successful aging (Tesch-Römer & Wahl, 2017). We would argue that understanding successful aging for any older adult and, in particular, those with disability, requires careful and purposeful consideration of the environment – from the micro to societal levels.

Generally speaking, the discourse concerning the International Classification of Functioning, Disability, and Health (ICF; WHO, 2001) is of high importance in the context of disability. Based on the consideration of health conditions, functional impairments and disability, the ICF focuses on those individual and environmental factors that enable individuals to take part in meaningful activities and societal participation. The ICF recognizes the experience of disability as a universal human experience and seeks to analyze not only individual impairments, but also opportunities and barriers in the environment that support (or hinder) participation. Also, according to the competence-environmental press model and P-E fit perspectives, older individuals with disabilities need to react to environmental pressure in order to maintain independence and well-being. In this regard, an important implication is that environmental optimization and respective interventions are critical for older adults with disabilities (Wahl & Gitlin, 2007; Wahl et al., 2009a; see also section below on intervention). The recent report on aging and health from the World Health Organization (Beard et al., 2015) also explicitly recognizes function as a primary factor shaping the aging experience. Addressing disablement as a consequence of changes in function is identified as a worldwide imperative for achieving successful aging.

Empirical research also suggests that environmental characteristics are significantly linked to everyday competence; accessibility problems resulting from the interaction of functional limitations and environmental barriers are significantly related to dependence in daily activities (Wahl et al., 2009a). Severe vision loss is significantly influenced by P-E mismatching, suggesting an important role for P-E agency toward proactively shaping one's environment as an older person with disability (Wahl et al., 1999). Similarly, P-E mismatches may result in negative behavioral and psychological symptoms of persons with dementia (Gitlin et al., 2012). A number of interventions to align P-E transactions are discussed more below. However, it is likely that technology solutions such as robotics and sensor-based orientation systems that can compensate for physical and/or cognitive frailness will have a major role in supporting primary control (Heckhausen et al., 2010) for individuals aging with a range of physical and cognitive challenges in the near future (Schulz et al., 2015).

Also, Wahl and Oswald's (2016) concept of P-E belonging may become of particular importance among older adults with significant functional impairment. For instance, Oswald and Wahl (2005) compared older adults who were blind with mobility impaired older adults, and older adults without functional impairment. Adults who were blind experienced their home environments much less as a function of its physical features and more as a behavioral action space (agency) than did those with mobility impairments and those who were unimpaired. In contrast, older adults with vision loss and those with mobility impairment experienced the meaning of familiarity of the home environment (belonging) much more than did the group without functional impairment.

In conclusion, a P-E transactional perspective is important for the better understanding of all three components of Rowe and Kahn's model, i.e., lowering the probability of disease and related disability processes, increasing high cognitive and physical functioning, and supporting active engagement with life. Placing an emphasis on the environment is of particular importance for models of successful aging, as it considers the interplay of successful aging under the conditions of physical and mental impairments, which typify the aging experience for most individuals. Hence, focusing on the role of the environment counteracts the common but unrealistic understanding of successful aging as the "atomistic" struggle for remaining independent as long as possible. It provides a more complex, nuanced, and realistic understanding of successful aging for all individuals as they age with a very wide range of conditions and impairments. Importantly, it places successful aging within the contexts in which aging occurs, suggesting that integral to being successful in aging is one's living environment. Finally, it also suggests that successful aging can be achieved by individuals with different disabilities, preferences, considerations, and resources. It further suggests that what constitutes "successful aging" is highly individuated, reflecting the confluence of multiple factors including personal preferences and life space characteristics.

## Successful Aging and Interventions Involving the Socio-Physical Environment

Throughout we have implied that environmental factors may be malleable, such that P-E transactions can be improved through direct/indirect manipulations to achieve "successful" aging. Using the environment proactively to shape aging processes brings us to considerations related to intervention research. In interventions designed to enhance successful aging, the environment serves in several capacities: as the context in which an intervention occurs, as the backdrop for understanding behavioral outcomes such as mood disorders from which to develop a targeted treatment or intervention plan, as a mediator of desired outcomes such as the use of home modifications and assistive devices to improve daily function, and/or as an outcome itself when, for example, improving home safety or safe way finding is the desired endpoint. For each of these purposes, we consider the fundamental question: when is the socio-physical environment critical in intervention research, and when is it not?

With regard to context, perhaps it goes without saying that all interventions occur within a particular setting or socio-physical environment. Nevertheless, the environmental context in which interventions occur is rarely recognized as supporting or impeding intervention implementation, processes, and outcomes. To understand the environmental context in which interventions occur, we draw upon Gitlin and Czaja's (2016) socio-ecological systems oriented approach. This framework conceptualizes interventions as being embedded within a complex environmental ecosystem involving multiple and interacting components or levels of influence that may change over time and which include: the personal or individual level (e.g., end user of an intervention), the immediate physical environment or setting in which an intervention occurs, the formal and informal social network delivering or supporting the intervention, the community, neighborhood, and organization in which the intervention may be embedded, and policy environments. Take for example home care services, in which a nurse examines an older adult's vital signs, medication profile, and provides wound care, and/or physical and occupational therapists provide rehabilitative strategies and exercises to improve strength, balance, and self-care – all essential approaches to helping older adults with acute or chronic health and functional issues stay at home. The conduct of any of these care interventions in the home may be impacted by the social and policy level (e.g., Is there an adequate payment model to cover the needed care provision?), the neighborhood (e.g., Can health providers access the home safely?), the physical layout of the home (e.g., Can medical and adaptive equipment fit? Is there adequate electrical power for use of specialized equipment such as oxygen?), the contamination level (e.g., Is the home infested? Are there pets? What is the level of cleanliness for prevention of infections?), and the social level (e.g., Is there a family member or caregiver who can help to oversee medication taking or exercising?). As such, each environmental level has varying and dynamic characteristics and the interactions among the levels in turn can have a significant influence on the degree to which the goals and objectives of the intervention for successful aging can be achieved and what its delivery characteristics ought to be to maximize benefits. Using our example, if a neighborhood is unsafe and there is not a parking space close to the home of an older adult, that may deter or prevent home care visits; alternately, the home care agency may need to deploy two health professionals for a single visit, increasing cost. Knowledge of the characteristics of these levels can directly inform construction of an affective intervention. Thus, in the design and execution of approaches to strengthen P-E transactions to achieve successful aging, interventions must be understood as occurring within a context that includes the setting in which the intervention will be delivered (e.g., home, clinic, neighborhood, workplace), formal and informal networks, and social support systems, the community, and policy. All of these aspects involve social, cultural, and physical components of the environment.

Delivery characteristics of an intervention may be shaped by influences at each of these levels and interventions may be more successful and sustainable if the characteristics of each level and their interactions are considered. This is to say that interventions to support/modify/manage P-E transactions cannot be designed and delivered in isolation or in a vacuum and solely focused on individual level determinants of health and behaviors, which is typical practice.

Rather, interventions must consider the independent and joint influences of determinants at all of the specified environmental levels. We conclude that with respect to any type of intervention geared to obtaining or supporting successful aging, the environment as context is always an essential ingredient and in need of consideration.

The environment also serves as a backdrop to certain behaviors, moods, and functional outcomes. This is clearly seen in older adults with dementia, where the socio-physical environment becomes progressively more impactful with disease progression. For example, behavioral and psychological symptoms of dementia (e.g., agitation, aggression, irritability, rejection of care) have been conceptualized as a consequence of increased vulnerability to physical and social environmental factors (Kales et al., 2015), due to decrements in executive functioning and information processing (Gitlin et al., 2016), and reduced abilities to understand and interpret environmental cues (Hall & Buckwalter, 1987).

Similarly, for individuals with visual impairments, difficulties with the functional consequences of vision loss (e.g., navigating or wayfinding in a home environment) have been shown to be associated with depressive symptomatology over and above the level of vision impairment itself (Rovner et al., 1996). Likewise, environmental hazards also appear to contribute to falls in individuals with vision impairments (Swenor et al., 2016).

Unclear however is which behaviors are directly connected (or not) to environmental factors. For example, psychosis and hallucinations in persons with dementia may not be related to environmental factors whereas agitation, aggression, irritability, or rejection of care may be caused at least in part by external environmental determinants (Gitlin et al., 2012)

Interventions involving home modifications to reduce falls, assistive devices to improve daily function, de-cluttering to improve navigation in dementia, are exemplars of ways in which the environment can be actively manipulated to yield a particular outcome (e.g., positive mood, better function, reduction in falls, improved well-being). In this regard, the environment serves as a mediator of or the mechanism by which desired outcomes can be achieved. There is ample evidence to support that environmental adjustments are associated with a wide range of improvements for older adults and such improvements are critical to successful aging (Gitlin et al., 2009; Szanton et al., 2016). However, it is also clear that outcomes are optimized when environmental adjustments are combined with other intervention strategies such as behaviorally-oriented strategies or caregiver supportive approaches (e.g., behavioral activation, problem-solving, cognitive reframing). In this respect, any one environmental adjustment, such as a relocation to a supportive environment, or an environmental modification, such as installing grab bars, may be more effective if accompanied by other social and behavioral changes to achieve desired outcomes, such as enabling social engagement and instructing in safe transfer techniques. As per the conceptual frameworks described earlier, it may be that involving the environment becomes more essential for those most vulnerable to their environments such as individuals with a major physical or cognitive disability.

Finally, the environment can be considered as an outcome in its own right. This is the case for interventions that seek, as their main endpoint, to reduce the number of home hazards or to improve wayfinding. Here the challenge is measurement with only a few tools available to capture and quantify changes in levels of safety, wayfinding, and so forth (see Iwarsson, 2004; Housing Enabler Instrument; Gitlin et al., 2002, Home Environmental Assessment Protocol for Dementia; or Swenor et al., 2016, Home Environment Assessment for the Visually Impaired [HEAVI]). Although the environment as an outcome of an intervention may be important, it is typically considered an immediate or proximal outcome as ultimately the goal is to improve a behavior, well-being or optimize successful aging of an older adult. Thus, in this respect, the socio-physical environment as outcome may serve as an intermediate step, and in this regard, as a mediator, to achieve a slightly more distal and impactful outcome – e.g., successful aging in an individual.

## Naturally Occurring Interventions Supporting Successful Aging: International Trends in Housing and Community Life

P-E transactional models and outcomes find their expression all over the world in daily ecologies of aging, both as naturally occurring P-E adaptations as well as newly and purposively designed solutions. The World Health Organization's 2015 report on aging and health (Beard et al., 2015) highlighted functional ability as key to aging successfully and recommended public health attention to the contributions of intrinsic (individual characteristics) and extrinsic (environmental) factors and their interactions (e.g., P-E fit), to assure positive outcomes as individuals age.

Despite cultural nuances or differences, the overarching trend worldwide is for older adults (and their families) to want to "age in place." P-E transactional models with emphases on the role of place attachment and meaning of home processes in later life (see previous section) likely best explain this strong and practically universal goal. However, changes in objective housing conditions may become quite important to support the need of most older adults who seek to stay put. This has led to a growing trend in many countries and respective health and care systems to invest in home modification programs. The overarching aim of such programs is to improve P-E fit in order to impact autonomy, residential satisfaction, and well-being (Wahl et al., 2009a). Experimental approaches have clearly shown that providing compensatory strategies and home environmental modifications to support the personal functional goals of older adults positively impacts health and well-being, even reducing mortality risk (Gitlin et al., 2009; Szanton & Gitlin, 2016).

There is also hope that such programs may have the potential to prevent re-hospitalizations and delay relocation to long-term care institutions, but the empirical evidence in this regard is still limited. Home modification is also an important preventive approach; it may, for example, prevent fall occurrences in individuals with significant gait, but also sensory and cognitive impairments. The downward trend in disability rates may be explained, in part, by environmental modifications (Freedman et al., 2006, 2013). Technology-oriented solutions such as sensor-based surveillance and alarm systems are gaining importance as part of the repertoire of home modification considerations. Such solutions may be of particular importance for older adults living alone or far from family members, or for those aging with dementia-related disorders as well as for family caregivers. Additionally, the aging in place trend has yielded a wide variety of solutions for care arrangements. For example, there has been a trend in Germany to incorporate informal caregivers from other countries (Poland, in particular) in one's own household to secure aging in place as long as possible, even in situations of significant care needs (Lutz & Palenga-Möllenbeck, 2010). Frequently, such solutions operate in close cooperation with professional home healthcare services.

Going further, a range of old and new living environmental arrangements for older adults with a diversity of needs and competence levels beyond the traditional private household do exist and are proliferating. In the United States, assisted housing solutions offer a maximum of independence for frail older adults in a new place, enriched with various forms of services and social and environmental support possibilities. Similar solutions have been designed all over Europe with countries such as Sweden, Denmark, or the Netherlands being particularly innovative (e.g., Regnier, 1993). The overall goal is to create environments that afford the highest possible level of home-like features and similarity with private households, yet simultaneously offer "unobtrusive" and efficient support systems that compensate for existing functional or cognitive limitations.

New housing solutions have also been proposed for older adults with dementia-related disorders. For example, various European countries have established private housing arrangements with 6 to 8 older adults with dementia served and supported by a network of professional care (van Hoof et al., 2009). Noteworthy, for example, is Hogeway, a novel facility outside of Amsterdam created specifically for persons with dementia. It looks and feels like a real small town with its own town square, theater, garden, stores, and so forth. Residents move freely, but are closely monitored, while professional staff work in the stores, helping residents negotiate daily tasks such as their food purchases. The results so far have been outstanding (Planos, 2014). Housing arrangements installed in Germany include new communities composed of a number of older individuals who also become the owners of larger housing stock (Wahl & Steiner, 2014); the idea is to help each other in daily tasks, as well as to hire professional help based on shared financial resources when needed. However, such housing arrangements remain mostly for "normal" aging, and as they are just emerging, their efficacy and financial viability is yet unknown.

In the United States, but also now in countries such as Great Britain, retirement communities that build on the concept of the segregation of older adults, are available, but seem to fit best with the preferences and needs of subpopulations with sufficient economic means (Joint Center for Housing Studies of Harvard University, 2014). Taking all things together, traditional long-term care institutions remain of importance for older adults with complex and severe care needs, but these settings are being redesigned to better emulate home-like features and support environment-related meaning-making processes. Public housing options for older adults with limited resources are less available in the United States.

Also noteworthy, is the international trend to better serve older adults with dementia within communities. For example, there is a worldwide trend toward dementia friendly communities, including not only housing but also the design of public places and public transport (reference) and training of service providers in dementia. Another example is the village concept designed for demented older adults as discussed above in the Netherlands.

## Implementing Successful Aging Solutions in Socio-Physical Environments

The environment also takes front and center stage in the consideration of how to move a proven intervention/strategy/program/approach to real world ecologies. Here we move away from the direct examination of P-E transactions to consider the broader viewpoint of intervention and implementation of evidence to support P-E. This consideration brings us to implementation science, which seeks to understand the methodologies or strategies for introducing, implementing, and sustaining evidence-based practices; in implementation science, the context – or the environment – prevails and dominates in theories and practices and has been implicated as either supporting or deterring implementation and sustainability of a proven approach.

Hodgson and Gitlin (2016) indicate that there are over 61 implementation theories or models with most incorporating environmental features as facilitators or deterrents of knowledge transfer activities. As suggested by theoretical models and supported by empirical studies, a key challenge when introducing a new approach or intervention in a given setting, is the characteristics of that setting. Environmental characteristics, for example, that may impede implementation, concern meso level factors such as the availability of a viable workforce and their level of preparation, beliefs, practices, routines and work-flow, organizational readiness, and payment and delivery structures, to name a few key elements.

Although the socio-physical environment, or what implementation science refers to as *context*, is widely acknowledged as important, the term itself does not have a clear conceptual and operational definition or measurement approach. That is, although there is much discussion of context, it is unclear what is specifically meant by this term and how it should be measured. Most agree however that context is a multifaceted construct with different factors impacting interventions depending upon intervention characteristics (Gitlin & Leff, 2016). One emerging construct is that of "contextual fit," which parallels in some respects our earlier reference to and discussion of P-E fit. Here however, contextual fit refers to the match between strategies, procedures, or elements of an intervention and the values, needs, skills, and resources of a setting or health and human service organization (Horner & Blitz, 2014). Horner and Blitz (2014) suggest eight key factors influencing contextual fit: (1) the "need" or extent to which an intervention addresses a perceived need by stakeholders of a setting; (2) the "precision" or extent to which intervention characteristics and delivery approach for an intervention are clear and replicable; (3) the "evidence-base" or whether the intervention has demonstrated efficacy/effectiveness for a targeted population; (4) the "efficiency" or the extent to which the intervention is practical; (5) the "skills/competencies," which refer to the skills needed by implementers and how they are acquired and sustained; (6) the "cultural relevance" or the fit of the intervention with the values and preferences of implementers, administrators, and those who may benefit; (7) the "resources" or the time, funding, and materials needed for adoption and maintenance; and (8) the "administrative and organizational support" or extent to which adoption is supported by key leaders and if fidelity can be maintained. While these considerations of contextual fit reflect the perspective of an agency, healthcare organization, or practice setting, and may appear distal from individuals seeking successful aging, they remain important elements to the implementation and scaling up of interventions that are effective. Thus, when considering successful aging, we must also recognize and attend to broad contextual influences on the strategies we seek to implement to improve an older adult's well-being according to the social-ecological model of Gitlin and Czaja (2016). As such, an environmental gerontological perspective is implicit in, and can extend, implementation science.

## Resume and Outlook

In this chapter we have argued that the environment is a core feature of successful aging; yet it has been neglected and sorely overlooked in traditional theories and in the consideration of aging well. The environment has a complex and multifaceted role in successful aging, serving as cause, moderator, mediator, outcome, and backdrop or context, depending upon the research question posed and/or the practical considerations in supporting older adults as they age.

The avoidance of tackling the complexity of the socio-physical environment as an essential ingredient in successful aging considerations has led to a dearth of measurement development and refinement of environmental impacts on aging, as well as a bifurcation of fields; with environmental gerontology and its associated constructs and measures remaining separate from successful aging research and its associated constructs and measures, to the detriment of both bodies of knowledge. We have argued here that from a practical, real life perspective, this division is illusionary and impairs adequate conceptualizations, intervention development, and measurement as well as the implementation of effective strategies to assure successful aging.

Unfortunately, we still need to justify that an environmental perspective is integral to an understanding of successful aging; however, we believe this justification is easy to make and  is demonstrated in part by this chapter. As we have shown, there are well-developed theories/models/frameworks for adequate integration of an environmental perspective with successful aging constructs, as well as strong empirical support at every level (from micro to macro).

## References

Beard, J., Officer, A., Cassels, A. (2015). *World Report on Ageing and Health*. Geneva: World Health Organization. www.who.int/ageing/publications/world-report-2015/en/ (accessed September 10, 2016).

Brandtstädter, J., Greve, W. (1994). The aging self: Stabilizing and protective processes. *Developmental Review*, 14, 52–80. https://doi.org/10.1006/drev.1994.1003

Bronfenbrenner, U. (1999). Environments in developmental perspective: Theoretical and operational models. In S. L. Friedman & T. D. Wachs (Eds.), *Measuring Environment across the Life Span* (pp. 3–28). Washington, DC: American Psychological Association.

Cho, H. Y., MacLachlan, M., Clarke, M., et al. (2016). Accessible home environments for people with functional limitations: A systematic review. *Int. J. Environ. Res. Public Health*, 13, 826; doi:10.3390/ijerph13080826

Cosco, T. D., Prina, A. M., Perales, J., et al. (2014). Operational definitions of successful aging: A systematic review. *International Psychogeriatrics*, 26, 373–81; doi:10.1017/S1041610213002287

Czaja, S. J. (2015) Can technology empower older adults to manage their health? *Generations*, 39(1), 46–51. doi:10.1080/03601277.2012.734266

Czaja, S. J., Loewenstein, D., Schulz, R., et al. (2013). A videophone psychosocial intervention for dementia caregivers. *The American Journal of Geriatric Psychiatry*, 21, 1071–81. doi:10.1016/j.jagp.2013.02.019

Czaja, S. J., Boot, W. R., Charness, N., et al. (2015).The personalized reminder information and social management system (PRISM) trials: rationale, methods, and baseline characteristics. *Contemporary Clinical Trials*, 40, 35–46. doi:10.1016/j.cct.2014.11.004

Dasenbrock, L., Heinks, A., Schwenk, M. et al. (2016). Technology-based measurements for screening, monitoring and preventing frailty. *Zeitschrift für Gerontologie und Geriatrie*. Online published. DOI10.1007/s00391-016-1129-7

Depp, C. A., Jeste, D. V. (2006). Definitions and predictors of successful aging: a comprehensive review of larger quantitative studies. *American Journal of Geriatric Psychiatry*, 14, 6–20. doi: 10.1097/01.JGP.0000192501.03069.bc

Fernandez-Ballesteros, R. (2008). *Active Aging. The Contribution of Psychology*. Göttingen: Hogrefe.

Freedman, V. A., Agree, E., Martin, L. G., et al. (2006). Trends in the use of assistive technology and personal care for late-life disability, 1992–2001. *The Gerontologist*, 46(1), 124–7.

Freedman, V. A., Spillman, B. C., Andreski, P. M., et al. (2013). Trends in late-life activity limitations in the United States: an update from five national surveys. *Demography*, 50(2), 661–71. doi:10.1007/s13524-012-0167-z

Gitlin, L. N., Czaja, S. J. (2016). *Behavioral Intervention Research: Designing, Evaluating and Implementing*. Springer Publishing Company.

Gitlin, L. N., Leff, B. (2016). Lessons learned from implementing proven interventions into real-world contexts. In L. N. Gitlin, S. J. Czaja, *Behavioral Intervention*

*Research: Designing, Evaluating and Implementing* (pp. 379–98), New York: Springer Publ.

Gitlin, L. N., Schinfeld, S., Winter, L., et al. (2002). Evaluating home environments of person with dementia: Interrater reliability and validity of the home environmental assessment protocol (HEAP). *Disability and Rehabilitation*, 24, 59–71. doi:10.1080/09638280110066325

Gitlin, L. N., Winter, L., Dennis, M. P., et al. (2006). A randomized trial of a multi-component home intervention to reduce functional difficulties in older adults. *Journal of the American Geriatrics Society*, 54(5), 809–16. doi:10.1111/j.1532-5415.2006.00703.x

Gitlin, L. N., Winter, L., Dennis, M. P., et al. (2007). A non-pharmacological intervention to manage behavioral and psychological symptoms of dementia and reduce caregiver distress: design and methods of Project ACT. *Clinical Interventions in Aging*, 2(4), 695–703. doi: 10.2147/CIA.S1337

Gitlin, L. N., Hauck, W. W., Dennis, M. P., et al. (2009). Long-term effect on mortality of a home intervention that reduces functional difficulties in older adults: Results from a randomized trial. *Journal of the American Geriatrics Society*, 57(3), 476–81. doi:10.1111/j.1532-5415.2008.02147.x

Gitlin, L. N., Kales, H. C., Lyketsos, C. G. (2012). Nonpharmacologic management of behavioral symptoms in dementia. *JAMA,* 308(19), 2020–9. doi:10.1001/jama.2012.36918

Gitlin, L. N., Hodgson, N., Piersol, C. V., et al. (2014). Correlates of quality of life for individuals with dementia living at home: The role of home environment, caregiver and patient-related characteristics. *American Journal of Geriatric Psychiatry*, 22, 587. doi:10.1016/j.jagp.2012.11.005

Gitlin, L. N., Winter, L., Stanley, I. H. (2015). Compensatory strategies: prevalence of use and relationship to physical function and well-being. *Journal of Applied Gerontology*, 1–20. doi: 10.1177/0733464815581479

Gitlin, L. N., Hodgson, N., Choi, S. (2016). Home-based interventions targeting persons with dementia: What is the evidence and where do we go from here? In M. Boltz & J. Galvin (Eds.), *Dementia Care: An Evidence-based Approach* (pp. 167–88). Switzerland: Springer International Publishing. DOI 10.1007/978-3-319-18377-0_11

Gitlin, L., N., Piersol, C. V., Hodgson, N., et al. (2016). Reducing neuropsychiatric symptoms in persons with dementia and associated burden in family caregivers using tailored activities: Design and methods of a randomized clinical trial. *Contemporary Clinical Trials*, 49, 92–102. doi:S1551-7144(16)30086-6 [pii]

Golant, S. M. (2015). *Aging in the Right Place*. Baltimore, MD: Health Professions Press.

Granbom, M., Himmelsbach, I., Haak, M., et al. (2014). Residential normalcy and environmental experiences of very old people: Changes in residential reasoning over time. *Journal of Aging Studies*, 29, 9–19. doi:10.1016/j.jaging.2013.12.005

Hall, G. R., Buckwalter, K. C. (1987). Progressively lowered stress threshold: A conceptual model for care of adults with Alzheimer's disease. *Arch Psychiatr Nurs.*, 1(6), 399–406. doi:10.1016/j.jad.2009.12.015

Havighurst, R. J. (1961). Successful aging. *The Gerontologist*, 1, 8–13. http://dx.doi.org/10.1093/geront/1.1.8

Heckhausen, J., Wrosch, C., Schulz, R. (2010). *A motivational theory of life-span development. Psychological Review*, 117(1), 32–60. doi: 10.1037/a0017668

Hertzog, C., Kramer, A. F., Wilson, R. S., et al. (2009). Enrichment effects on adult cognitive development: Can the functional capacity of older adults be preserved and enhanced? *Psychological Science in the Public Interest*, 9(1), 1–65. doi: 10.1111/j.1539-6053.2009.01034.x

Hodgson, N. A., Gitlin, L. N. (2016). The role of implementation science in behavioral intervention research. In Gitlin, L. N., Czaja, S. J. *Behavioral Intervention Research: Designing, Evaluating and Implementing* (pp. 361–76). New York: Springer Publ.

Hoof, van J., Kort, H. S. M., Waarde, H. van (2009). Housing and care for older adults with dementia: a European perspective. *Journal of Housing and the Built Environment*, 24, 369–90.

Horner, R., Blitz, C. (2014, September). *The Importance of Contextual Fit When Implementing Evidence-based Interventions* (ASPE Issue Brief). Washington, DC: U.S. Department of Health and Human Services. Office of Human Services Policy. Office of the Assistant Secretary for Planning and Evaluation.

Iwarsson, S. (2004). Assessing the fit between older people and their home environments – An occupational therapy research perspective. In H.-W. Wahl, R. Scheidt, & P. Windley (Eds.), *Annual Review of Gerontology and Geriatrics, 23 (Aging in Context: Socio-Physical Environments*, pp. 85–109). New York: Springer Publ.

Iwarsson, S., Horstmann, V., Carlsson, G., et al. (2009). Person–environment fit predicts falls in older adults better than the consideration of environmental hazards only. *Clinical Rehabilitation*, 23, 558–67. doi: 10.1177/0269215508101740

Joint Center for Housing Studies of Harvard University. (2014). *Housing America's Older Adults: Meeting the Needs of an Aging Population*. Cambridge: Joint Center for Housing Studies of Harvard University. Retrieved from www.jchs.harvard.edu/sites/jchs.harvard.edu/files/jchs-housing_americas_older_adults_2014.pdf

Kales, H. C., Gitlin, L. N., Lyketsos, C. G. (2015). Assessment and management of behavioral and psychological symptoms of dementia. *BMJ (Clinical Research Ed.)*, 350, h369. doi: 10.1136/bmj.h369. PMCID: PMC4707529.

Lawton, M. P. (1983). Environment and other determinants of well-being in older people. *The Gerontologist*, 23(4), 349–57. doi: 10.1093/geront/23.4.349

Lawton, M. P., Nahemow, L. (1973). Ecology and the aging process. In C. Eisdorfer & M. P. Lawton (Eds.), *Psychology of Adult Development and Aging* (pp. 619–74). Washington, DC: American Psychological Association.

Lutz, H., Palenga-Möllenbeck, E. (2010). Care work migration in Germany: Semi-compliance and complicity. *Social Policy & Society*, 9, 419–30. https://doi.org/10.1017/S1474746410000138

Miche, M., Brothers, A., Diehl, M., et al. (2015). The role of subjective aging within the changing ecologies of aging: Perspectives for research and practice. In M. Diehl & H.-W. Wahl (Eds.), *Research on Subjective Aging: New Developments and Future Directions. Annual Review of Gerontology and Geriatrics* (Volume 35, pp. 211–46). New York: Springer Publ.

Oswald, F., Rowles, G. D. (2007). Beyond the relocation trauma in old age: New trends in today's elders' residential decisions. In H.-W. Wahl, C. Tesch-Römer, A. Hoff (Eds.), *New Dynamics in Old Age: Environmental and Societal Perspectives* (pp. 127–52). Amityville, New York: Baywood Publ.

Oswald, F., Wahl, H.-W. (2005). Dimensions of the meaning of home in later life. In G. D. Rowles & H. Chaudhury (Eds.), *Home and Identity in Later Life. International Perspectives* (pp. 21–46). New York: Springer Publ.

Oswald, F., Wahl, H.-W., Schilling, O., et al. (2007). Relationships between housing and healthy aging in very old age. *The Gerontologist,* 47(1), 96–107, doi: 10.1093/geront/47.1.96

Planos, J. (2014). The Dutch village where everyone has dementia. *The Atlantic*, pp. 1–6. Retrieved from www.theatlantic.com/health/archive/2014/11/the-dutch-village-where-everyone-has-dementia/382195/

Regnier, V. (1993). *Assisted Living Housing for the Elderly: Design Innovations from the United States and Europe.* New York: Wiley.

Rovner, B. W., Zisselman, P. M, Shmuely-dulitzki (1996). Depression and disability in older people with impaired vision: A follow-up study. *Journal of the American Geriatrics Society,* 44, 181–4. doi:10.1097/OPX.0b013e318157a6b1

Rowe, J. W., Kahn, R. L. (1987). Human aging: usual and successful. *Science,* 237, 143–9. doi: 10.1126/science.3299702

Rowe, J. W., Kahn, R. L. (2015). Successful Aging 2.0: Conceptual Expansions for the 21st Century. *The Journals of Gerontology Series B: Psychological Sciences and Social Sciences,* 70(4), 593–6. doi: 10.1093/geronb/gbv025

Rowles, G. D. (1983). Geographical dimensions of social support in rural Appalachia. In G. D. Rowles & R. J. Ohta (Eds.), *Aging and Milieu. Environmental Perspectives on Growing Old* (pp. 111–30). New York: Academic Press.

Rowles, G. D., Watkins, J. F. (2003). History, habit, heart and hearth: On making spaces into places. In K. W. Schaie, H.-W. Wahl, H. Mollenkopf & F. Oswald (Eds.), *Aging Independently: Living Arrangements and Mobility* (pp. 77–96). New York: Springer Publishing Company.

Rubinstein, R. L. (1989). The home environments of older people: A description of the psychosocial processes linking person to place. *Journal of Gerontology: Social Sciences,* 44(2), S45–53. doi: 10.1093/geronj/44.2.S45

Scharlach, A., Lehning, A. (2015). Creating aging-friendly communities. Oxford University Press. Schulz, R., Wahl, H.-W., Matthews, J. T., de Vito Dabbs, A., Beach, S. R., Czaja, S. J. (2015). *Advancing the Aging and Technology Agenda in Gerontology. The Gerontologist,* 55, 724–34. doi: 10.1093/geront/gnu07

Stineman, M. G., Strumpf, N., Kurichi, J. E., et al. (2011). Attempts to reach the oldest and frailest: Recruitment, adherence, and retention of urban elderly persons to a falls reduction exercise program. *Gerontologist,* 51(Suppl 1), S59–72. doi: 10.1093/geront/gnr012

Swenor, B. K., Yonge, A. V., Goldhammer, V., et al. (2016). Evaluation of the Home Environment Assessment for the Visually Impaired (HEAVI): an instrument designed to quantify fall-related hazards in the visually impaired. *BMC Geriatrics,* 16, 214–21. doi:10.1186/s12877-016-0391-2

Szanton, S. L., Gitlin, L. N. (2016). Meeting the health care financing imperative through focusing on function: the CAPABLE Studies. *Public Policy & Aging Report,* 26(3), 106–10. doi: 10.1093/ppar/prw014

Szanton, S. L., Leff, B., Wolff, J. L., et al. (2016). Home-based care program reduces disability and promotes aging in place. *Health Affairs,* 35(9), 1558–63. doi: 10.1377/hlthaff.2016.0140

Tesch-Römer, C. & Wahl, H.-W. (2017). Successful aging and aging with care needs: Arguments for a comprehensive concept of successful aging. *Journal of Gerontology: Social Sciences,* 72, 310–18. doi: 10.1093/geronb/gbw162

Verbrugge, L. M., Jette, A. M. (1994). The Disablement Process. *Social Science and Medicine,* 38(1), 1–14. doi: 10.1016/0277-9536(94)90294-1

Wahl, H.-W., Lang, F. (2004). Aging in context across the adult life course: Integrating physical and social environmental research perspectives. In H.-W. Wahl, R. Scheidt, & P. Windley (Eds.), *Annual Review of Gerontology and Geriatrics*, 23 ("Aging in context: Socio-physical environments," pp. 1–33). New York: Springer.

Wahl, H.-W., Gitlin, L. N. (2007). Environmental gerontology. In J. E. Birren (Ed.), *Encyclopedia of Gerontology: Age, Aging, and the Aged* (2nd edn., pp. 494–501). Oxford: Elsevier.

Wahl, H.-W., Steiner, B. (2014). Innovative Wohnformen [Innovative living arrangements]. In J. Pantel, J. Schröder, C. Sieber, C. Bollheimer, & A. Kruse (Eds.), *Praxishandbuch der Altersmedizin. Geriatrie–Gerontopsychiatrie–Gerontologie [Handbook of Geriatric Medicine–Geropsychiatry–Gerontology]* (pp. 701–7). Stuttgart: Kohlhammer Verlag.

Wahl, H.-W., Fänge, A., Oswald, F., et al. (2009a). The home environment and disability-related outcomes in aging individuals: What is the empirical evidence? *The Gerontologist*, 49, 355–67. doi:10.1093/geront/gnp056

Wahl, H.-W., Oswald, F., Schilling, O., et al. (2009b). The home environment and quality of life related outcomes in advanced old age: Findings of the ENABLE-AGE Project. *European Journal of Ageing*, 6(2), 101–11. doi:10.1007/s10433-009-0114-z

Wahl, H.-W., Iwarsson, S., Oswald, F. (2012). Aging well and the environment: Toward an integrative model and research agenda for the future. *The Gerontologist*, 52(3), 306–16. doi:10.1093/geront/gnr154

Wahl, H.-W. & Oswald, F. (2016). Theories of environmental gerontology: Old and new avenues for ecological views of aging. In V. L. Bengtson & R. Settersten, R. A. (Eds.), *Handbook of Theories of Aging* (3rd edn., pp. 621–41). New York: Springer Publ.

Wahl, H.-W., Oswald, F., Zimprich, D. (1999). Everyday competence in visually impaired older adults: A case for person–environment perspectives. *The Gerontologist*, 39, 140–9. doi:10.1093/geront/39.2.140

WHO (2001). *International Classification of Functioning, Disability and Health (ICF)*. Geneva: World Health Organization.

# 32 The Active Aging Index

Measuring Successful Aging at Population Level

Asghar Zaidi and Marge Unt

## Introduction

An active and healthy life has remained one of the most important aspirations for people, young and old. This ambition has become a genuine possibility for many due to a rising life expectancy among people of diverse attributes across the world. While celebrating longer life, and with more financial security in later life than ever before, we need to challenge how these aspirations can be sustained, through our own behavioral responses and through public policy, institutional reforms, and innovations. The challenge is to identify, recommend, and promote strategies that stimulate and sustain the activity, independence, and health of people of all ages, especially older people and, in the process, promote the well-being and quality of life of people and make public welfare systems more sustainable.

Rowe and Kahn's (1987, 1997) notion of successful aging has influenced particularly this sub-discipline of modern gerontology, by making observations of experiences of those with better-than-usual experiences of aging in old age (see Rowe & Kahn, 2015). It relates not only to what older people are capable of doing but also to what they actually do, by referring to extraordinary experiences of their low risk of disease and disease-related disability, high maintenance of mental and physical functioning, and a continued engagement with life through relations with others and productive activities.

In the 1990s, the concept of active aging started to develop, underlining in particular, the active role of the elderly in society. However, different from the concept of successful aging, active aging emphasized the need to account for optimization of opportunity structures and the enabling environment (Riley & Riley, 1994). In the European context, the active aging concept was strengthened particularly by Walker (2002, 2009), emphasizing a multi-layered policy-oriented model in which active aging at all stages of the life course is emphasized with well-being of older people at its core.

The active aging strategy is predicated on the insight that, in tackling issues associated with population aging, successful measures are those which empower older people to increase their participation in the labor market, and in social and family engagement; it also recognizes that independent, self-reliant, secure, and healthy living are an important prerequisites. The multifaceted design of the active aging policy discourse allows the setting of policy goals to maintain well-being and social cohesion, and improve financial sustainability of public welfare systems (Walker & Zaidi, 2016; Zaidi et al., 2017).

What has also become clear is the necessity for a high-quality and independent evidence base, to demonstrate how aging experience at the individual level can be combined with higher levels of activity – both paid and unpaid, improved health status – both physical and mental, and a greater degree of autonomy and self-reliance, and not just in old age but during earlier phases of life.

This chapter's contribution lies in highlighting the operationalization of these concepts using the Active Ageing Index (AAI) (Zaidi et al., 2013; Zaidi & Stanton, 2015; Zaidi et al., 2017). The work of the AAI draws its inspiration from the following philosophy, "when you cannot express it in numbers, your knowledge is of a meager and unsatisfactory kind" (quote attributed to Lord Kelvin, who was a mathematician, physicist, and engineer, 1824–1907). Using the micro-data of the European Union Survey of Income and Living Conditions, the European Quality of Life Survey, the Labour Force Survey, the European Social Survey (ESS), and statistics provided by European Health and Life Expectancy Information System and by Eurostat on survey of Information and Communication Technology (ICT) usage, this chapter analyzes all AAI indicators and their aggregation into a composite measure.

By drawing special attention to results of the AAI between and within EU countries, AAI research broadens the perspective of different dimensions of contributions and potential of older people of varying attributes. The findings encourage setting goals for a higher, more balanced, and more equal form of active aging in European countries.

## The Active Ageing Index Project

In 2012, the EU celebrated the European Year for Active Ageing and Solidarity between Generations (EY2012). The EY2012 renewed the focus on the potential of active aging as a policy strategy (Council of the European Union, 2012). To mark this occasion, the United Nations Economic Commission for Europe (UNECE), the European Commission's Directorate General for Employment, Social Affairs and Inclusion, and the European Centre for Social Welfare Policy and Research, Vienna, jointly undertook a major research project to construct a composite measure, called the Active Ageing Index (AAI), for 27 EU countries (for further details, see Zaidi et al., 2013).

The AAI is a new analytical tool for policymakers to enable them to devise evidence-based strategies in dealing with the challenges of population aging. The AAI toolkit consists of the overall index, as well as gender and domain-specific indices and their constituting individual indicators. In its design, the AAI draws on the definition offered by the World Health Organization during the Second World Assembly on Ageing (WHO, 2002). The main attributes of this landmark definition are:

> Active ageing is the process of optimizing opportunities for health, participation and security in order to enhance quality of life as people age. It applies to both individuals and population groups.
>
> Active ageing allows people to realize their potential for physical, social, and mental well-being throughout the life course and to participate in society, while providing them with adequate protection, security, and care when they need.
>
> The word "active" refers to continuing participation in social, economic, cultural, spiritual and civic affairs, not just the ability to be physically active or to participate in the labour force. Older people who retire from work and those who are ill or live with disabilities can remain active contributors to their families, peers, communities and nations. Active ageing aims to extend healthy life expectancy and quality of life for all people as they age, including those who are frail, disabled and in need of care.
>
> 'Health' refers to physical, mental, and social well-being. Maintaining health, as well as autonomy and independence, for the older people is a key goal of the policy framework for active ageing.
>
> Ageing takes place within the context of friends, work associates, neighbours and family members. This is why interdependence as well as intergenerational solidarity are important tenets of active ageing.
> (Source: www.who.int/ageing/active_ageing/en/)

The AAI is based on the strands of the EY2012 and uses a methodology similar to the Human Development Index (HDI) of the UNDP. One of the major benefits is that AAI enables credible comparisons between EU countries by quantifying the differential extent to which older people have realized and can further realize their potential in distinct domains that determine their active aging experiences. The AAI also offers a breakdown by gender, thereby highlighting the specific public policy goals of reducing gender disparity in the positive experiences of aging.

On the basis of an extensive review of international studies on this topic and also in consultations with the European Commission, UNECE, and the AAI Expert Group, a conceptual and empirical framework was developed to aid the selection and organization of active aging indicators into specific domains. Active aging was defined as the situation where people continue to participate in the formal labor market as well as engage in other unpaid productive activities (e.g., care provision to family members and volunteering) and live healthy, independent, and secure lives as they age. Framed by this definition, the four domains detailed in Figure 32.1 are used in the AAI. The inclusion of the fourth domain is a particular novelty of the AAI, as it goes beyond assessing how countries and subgroups fare in terms of actual experiences of active aging and takes stock of the health and human capital of older people that can be tapped to improve their quality of life and to make public welfare systems more sustainable. The focus of the AAI is on the current generation of "older" population, thereby providing a snapshot of the aging experience on the basis of the latest

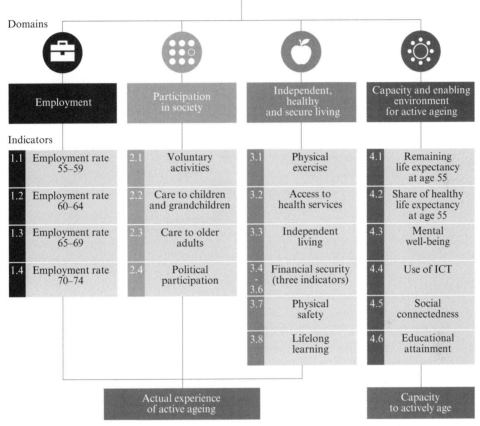

**Figure 32.1.** *Measuring active aging outcomes on AAI-2012: 22 indicators, 4 domains*

data available. It does not provide a life course specific picture, but this is not a denial of the importance of life course experiences in determining active aging outcomes in later life.

## Findings Based on the Latest 2014 AAI

The AAI 2014 results reflect the degree to which healthy and active life during old age has become a reality for the current generation of older Europeans.

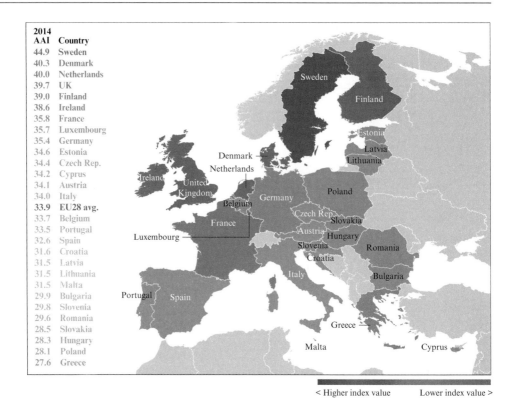

| 2014 AAI | Country |
|---|---|
| 44.9 | Sweden |
| 40.3 | Denmark |
| 40.0 | Netherlands |
| 39.7 | UK |
| 39.0 | Finland |
| 38.6 | Ireland |
| 35.8 | France |
| 35.7 | Luxembourg |
| 35.4 | Germany |
| 34.6 | Estonia |
| 34.4 | Czech Rep. |
| 34.2 | Cyprus |
| 34.1 | Austria |
| 34.0 | Italy |
| **33.9** | **EU28 avg.** |
| 33.7 | Belgium |
| 33.5 | Portugal |
| 32.6 | Spain |
| 31.6 | Croatia |
| 31.5 | Latvia |
| 31.5 | Lithuania |
| 31.5 | Malta |
| 29.9 | Bulgaria |
| 29.8 | Slovenia |
| 29.6 | Romania |
| 28.5 | Slovakia |
| 28.3 | Hungary |
| 28.1 | Poland |
| 27.6 | Greece |

< Higher index value        Lower index value >

**Figure 32.2.** *Ranking of 28 EU Member States based on the 2014 overall AAI*

Figure 32.2 illustrates the position of 28 European Union (EU) Member States using the latest data available (for details, Zaidi & Stanton, 2015).

Sweden is at the top of the ranking across the 28 EU Member States, followed closely by Denmark, the Netherlands, Finland, the United Kingdom, and Ireland. Four Southern European countries (Italy, Portugal, Spain, and Malta) are middle-ranked countries together with most other Western European countries. Greece and the majority of the Central and Eastern European countries are at the bottom of the ranking.

The top position of Nordic and Western European countries is in large part because of their policies that sustain employment levels among older workers who are reaching retirement, and providing income security and access to healthcare to their retired population. The AAI data shows that even in these countries there is scope for improvement in some individual dimensions of active and healthy aging.

The AAI data shows that active aging also has an important non-financial component. There are examples that show this: the United Kingdom and Denmark are respectively seventh and tenth in the ranking for social participation and they can learn from the examples of Ireland and Italy, which have much higher scores in this respect.

Conversely, lower income Central and Eastern European countries as well as Greece face a greater challenge and need to address how they can make their policies supportive and sustainable. Within the low scores for overall AAI, some countries nevertheless achieved employment scores above the EU-28 average (Portugal with 33 points and Latvia with 32 points). In contrast, Greece (20), Spain (23), and Hungary (19) are all much lower than the EU-28 average of 28 points.

Countries at the top of the AAI score have done consistently well across all four domains; this is an indication that active aging is a coherent policy area, where a balanced and well-founded approach could lead to achievements that leave nobody behind. Very few countries, however, score consistently at the very top in each individual indicator of active aging, indicating that there might be trade-offs and different priorities across these countries in achieving progress with respect to active aging (Table 32.1).

Unexpected AAI scores provide some interesting policy lessons. For example, Estonia achieves a very high employment score despite having a relatively low GDP per capita; its employment score for women (40 points) is of special note. Malta scores well across most domains, especially for men, but its overall score is pulled down because it has the lowest score for women's employment (8.5 points only). Understanding why this is so, and why other countries achieve far higher levels of employment among older women, may help Malta formulate policies to achieve a higher overall score.

An analysis of the relationship between the AAI and life satisfaction implies that a higher AAI is correlated with a higher quality of life of older people (see Zaidi & Stanton, 2015). Likewise, a positive relationship is observed between the AAI and GDP per capita. These correlations imply that a push toward active aging does not imply a worsening of older people's quality of life, and it brings real benefits to the economy. There is a weak inverse relationship between the AAI and each EU Member State's income inequality (as measured by the Gini coefficient).

## Gender Inequalities

Women score lower than men in almost all countries, particularly in Malta and Cyprus, but also in Luxembourg and the Netherlands. Only three EU Member States, Estonia, Latvia and Finland have better overall AAI results for women than for men (Figure 32.3; Zaidi & Stanton, 2015).

However, there are some indicators where women tend to do better than men; for instance, their life expectancy is higher and they more often provide informal care. Results included in Figure 32.3 show that the gender disparity is observed across all domains of the AAI, although it is most notable in the first (Employment) and the third (Independent Living) domain where the gender gap in financial security is considerable in most EU countries. This disparity to a large extent arises from the unequal experiences of employment during the

Table 32.1 *Ranking of EU-28 countries on the basis of the overall 2014 Active Ageing Index and its domain-specific scores*

| Rank | Overall | | Employment | | Participation in society | | Independent living | | Capacity for active aging | |
|---|---|---|---|---|---|---|---|---|---|---|
| 1 | Sweden | 44.9 | Sweden | 43.4 | Ireland | 24.1 | Denmark | 79.0 | Sweden | 69.2 |
| 2 | Denmark | 40.3 | Estonia | 39.7 | Italy | 24.1 | Finland | 79.0 | Denmark | 65.1 |
| 3 | Netherlands | 40.0 | Denmark | 35.8 | Sweden | 22.9 | Netherlands | 78.9 | Luxembourg | 63.6 |
| 4 | UK | 39.7 | UK | 35.8 | France | 22.8 | Sweden | 78.6 | Netherlands | 61.8 |
| 5 | Finland | 39.0 | Germany | 34.4 | Netherlands | 22.4 | Luxembourg | 76.7 | UK | 61.3 |
| 6 | Ireland | 38.6 | Netherlands | 33.9 | Luxembourg | 22.2 | France | 75.9 | Finland | 60.5 |
| 7 | France | 35.8 | Finland | 33.7 | UK | 21.6 | Ireland | 74.9 | Belgium | 60.3 |
| 8 | Luxembourg | 35.7 | Portugal | 32.6 | Finland | 20.5 | Germany | 74.4 | Ireland | 60.0 |
| 9 | Germany | 35.4 | Latvia | 32.0 | Belgium | 20.2 | Slovenia | 74.2 | France | 59.1 |
| 10 | Estonia | 34.6 | Cyprus | 31.4 | Denmark | 19.6 | Austria | 73.8 | Austria | 58.2 |
| 11 | Czech Rep | 34.4 | Romania | 31.0 | Czech Rep | 18.8 | UK | 73.7 | Malta | 57.1 |
| 12 | Cyprus | 34.2 | Ireland | 30.6 | Croatia | 18.7 | Belgium | 72.5 | Spain | 56.3 |
| 13 | Austria | 34.1 | Lithuania | 30.5 | Austria | 18.3 | Czech Rep. | 71.2 | Germany | 55.8 |
| 14 | Italy | 34.0 | Czech Rep. | 28.0 | Cyprus | 18.0 | Malta | 70.1 | Czech Rep. | 54.3 |
| 15 | Belgium | 33.7 | Bulgaria | 25.1 | Spain | 17.8 | Spain | 69.8 | Italy | 53.4 |
| 16 | Portugal | 33.5 | Austria | 24.7 | Malta | 17.3 | Croatia | 69.5 | Croatia | 52.8 |
| 17 | Spain | 32.6 | France | 24.1 | Slovenia | 16.3 | Italy | 69.0 | Bulgaria | 52.2 |

| # | | | | | | | | | | |
|---|---|---|---|---|---|---|---|---|---|---|
| 18 | Croatia | 31.6 | Spain | 23.3 | Hungary | 15.4 | Hungary | 68.0 | Portugal | 52.1 |
| 19 | Latvia | 31.5 | Italy | 23.0 | Lithuania | 14.7 | Cyprus | 68.0 | Cyprus | 50.4 |
| 20 | Lithuania | 31.5 | Poland | 22.4 | Portugal | 14.1 | Estonia | 67.3 | Slovenia | 50.0 |
| 21 | Malta | 31.5 | Slovakia | 21.9 | Latvia | 13.8 | Portugal | 67.3 | Latvia | 48.2 |
| 22 | Bulgaria | 29.9 | Luxembourg | 21.9 | Slovakia | 13.7 | Lithuania | 66,2 | Poland | 47.9 |
| 23 | Slovenia | 29.8 | Croatia | 21.7 | Greece | 13.7 | Slovakia | 65.8 | Estonia | 47.5 |
| 24 | Romania | 29.6 | Belgium | 21.0 | Germany | 13.6 | Poland | 64.9 | Slovakia | 47.1 |
| 25 | Slovakia | 28.5 | Greece | 20.4 | Estonia | 12.8 | Greece | 64.9 | Hungary | 46.9 |
| 26 | Hungary | 28.3 | Malta | 20.1 | Romania | 12.7 | Bulgaria | 62.7 | Greece | 45.8 |
| 27 | Poland | 28.1 | Hungary | 19.3 | Bulgaria | 12.5 | Romania | 61.8 | Lithuania | 45.3 |
| 28 | Greece | 27.6 | Slovenia | 19.1 | Poland | 12.1 | Latvia | 58.7 | Romania | 40.9 |
| EU28 avg. | | 33.9 | | 27.8 | | 17.7 | | 70.6 | | 54.1 |
| | The goalpost 57.5 | | The goalpost 54.2 | | The goalpost 40.6 | | The goalpost 87.7 | | The goalpost 77.7 | |

| Gender gap 2014<br>Rank 2014-AAI | Employment + men | Employment women + | Participation in society + men | Participation in society women + | Independent living + men | Independent living women + | Capacity for active ageing + men | Capacity for active ageing women + |
|---|---|---|---|---|---|---|---|---|
| 1 Sweden | 7.1 | | | 0.8 | 1.9 | | 0.7 | |
| 2 Denmark | 9.1 | | 2.6 | | 0.2 | | | 0.5 |
| 3 Netherlands | 13.8 | | 1.9 | | 2.4 | | 2.1 | |
| 4 UK | 10.6 | | | 1.7 | 1.5 | | 1.5 | |
| 5 Finland | 1.5 | | | 3.4 | 2.2 | | | 2.8 |
| 6 Ireland | 12.3 | | | 3.8 | 3.4 | | 0.3 | |
| 7 France | 3.8 | | 2.1 | | 4.0 | | | 1.8 |
| 8 Luxembourg | 7.6 | | 8.9 | | 2.8 | | 3.0 | |
| 9 Germany | 9.3 | | 1.9 | | 3.3 | | 0.5 | |
| 10 Estonia | | 0.8 | | 1.8 | 3.0 | | | 6.1 |
| 11 Czech Rep | 12.4 | | 4.1 | | 1.7 | | | 1.9 |
| 12 Cyprus | 18.1 | | | 1.0 | 2.8 | | 6.1 | |
| 13 Austria | 11.0 | | 2.1 | | 0.9 | | 1.8 | |
| 14 Italy | 13.1 | | | 0.5 | 2.7 | | 2.6 | |
| EU28 avg | 9.5 | | 0.1 | | 2.8 | | 0.5 | |
| 15 Belgium | 7.6 | | 3.0 | | 3.9 | | | 1.3 |
| 16 Portugal | 11.2 | | 0.0 | | 2.5 | | 2.8 | |
| 17 Spain | 8.5 | | | 2.2 | 2.8 | | 1.4 | |
| 18 Croatia | 11.6 | | 1.5 | | 4.5 | | 2.1 | |
| 19 Latvia | 2.4 | | | 6.3 | 3.8 | | | 1.2 |
| 20 Lithuania | 5.3 | | 2.0 | | 1.9 | | | 2.6 |
| 21 Malta | 22.9 | | 1.1 | | | 1.2 | 1.5 | |
| 22 Bulgaria | 6.0 | | | 0.4 | 7.5 | | 0.5 | |
| 23 Slovenia | 9.2 | | 1.7 | | 2.5 | | | 0.3 |
| 24 Romania | 10.5 | | | 1.6 | 4.0 | | 2.9 | |
| 25 Slovakia | 10.6 | | | 1.3 | 2.7 | | 1.1 | |
| 26 Hungary | 6.0 | | 0.6 | | 2.9 | | 1.3 | |
| 27 Poland | 12.5 | | | 2.3 | 3.2 | | | 2.0 |
| 28 Greece | 13.1 | | | 3.7 | 3.4 | | 3.2 | |

**Figure 32.3.** *Gender differences in the experiences of active aging, in 28 EU Member States based on the 2014 overall AAI and its four domains*

life course, a legacy which impacts severely on the income situation of current generations of older women.

The *employment gap* between men and women remains high, despite considerable improvements of women's labor force participation in the EU in recent decades.

There are also some notable exceptions when women's employment rates are higher than men's: Finland and Estonia, as well as Latvia and Bulgaria, in the age group 55–59.

The gender disparity in employment is particularly large in the two Mediterranean countries, Malta and Cyprus, but also in the Netherlands, Greece, and Italy. In 14 EU Member States, the gender differential in employment exceeds 10 points.

In the *Social Participation domain*, women score worse than men particularly in Luxembourg, and also in Denmark, Austria, the Czech Republic, Belgium, Lithuania, France, Germany, and the Netherlands, where higher men's involvement in voluntary and political activities outweighs women's prevalence in care provision. In contrast, Latvia, Greece, Poland, Ireland, Finland, and Spain are the countries that exhibit higher AAI in this domain for women than for men.

In the third domain, *Independent, healthy, and secure living,* the AAI for women is lower than the AAI for men in almost all countries as the underlying financial and physical security indicators are notably worse for women. An exception is observed for Malta, where the AAI for women is slightly higher than the AAI for men in this domain.

In the fourth domain, capacity for active aging, women score worse than men, particularly in Cyprus, but also in Greece and Luxembourg. The opposite is observed for Estonia, where the AAI is notably higher for women than for men. Older Estonian women do better than their male counterparts in almost all individual indicators, but noticeably better in the remaining life expectancy and social connectedness. Also, the gender gap in mental well-being is second from the top for Estonia (only after Slovenia), and women fare the best in comparison to men in Estonia regarding use of ICT – in fact, it is the only country where men trail women with regard to ICT use.

## Educational Inequalities

There is a clear educational gradient in almost all countries as highly educated are more advantaged, particularly in the *Employment domain* (See Appendix A). The employment gap between people with different educational resources is high and the inequalities deepen while people age, especially between those having tertiary education or not. Also, previous research has shown that people with higher qualifications have more opportunities to work longer, but also plan to work longer due to higher job attachment (examples for Germany, Hofäcker & Naumann, 2015; for Estonia, Lindemann, & Unt, 2016). Those with low education participate in the labor market less than those with secondary education. However, there are some exceptions from Southern Europe, like Greece, Cyprus, and also Romania, Slovenia, and Croatia, were low educated are less active in age group 55–59, but the differences vanish or they are even more active in older age groups. This might not always be a voluntary choice, but may suggest that in some cases people may stay employed due to financial constraints.

In addition or apart from participation in paid work, older people also remain active in other spheres like voluntary work, political engagement, or taking care of their frail family members or grandchildren. In the *Social Participation domain*, people with less educational resources are less likely to be engaged in voluntary work and political participation. Still, the biggest gap is between highly educated and people with secondary education, as the low educated and people with secondary education differ less. There is no clear pattern by educational attainment in the care provision activities of the elderly.

In the third domain, *Independent, healthy, and secure living*, the more educated are generally more active in physical exercise, but differences between countries are bigger than the differences across subgroups of low and high education within countries. The highly educated are better shielded against the poverty risk and material deprivation. Still, the main difference in material deprivation relates to the general affluence level, and educational inequalities are more evident in countries where there is in general higher risk of material deprivation (e.g., in Bulgaria or Romania).

## Monitoring Trends in the AAI for 28 EU Countries

In its current stage, with results for three data points, the Active Ageing Index has started to allow the benchmarking of country performances. It can therefore be hoped that AAI data will encourage European countries to look at policies and programs that other countries have adopted, and learn from those experiences – both positive and otherwise.

Looking at trends between the 2010 AAI (year: 2008) and the 2014 AAI (year: 2012), an increase of 2 points is recorded on average across EU28 countries. An increase by three points or more is observed in nine EU countries during this period (see Figure 32.4). This improvement is quite remarkable, given the financial and economic crisis, and the fiscal austerity measures observed during this period. It is also reassuring, and in favor of active aging strategies, that policies to phase out early retirement and to raise the age of retirement were not reversed during the crisis. Further, progress can be expected once economic and budgetary conditions have returned to normal.

The highest increase observed is in the Social Participation domain, about 3 points, with two other domains increasing by about 2 points each, i.e., independent living and capacity for active aging. For the Employment domain, the change is marginal (0.6 point). Significantly, all four domains registered increases. For most countries, the changes in the overall index for men and for

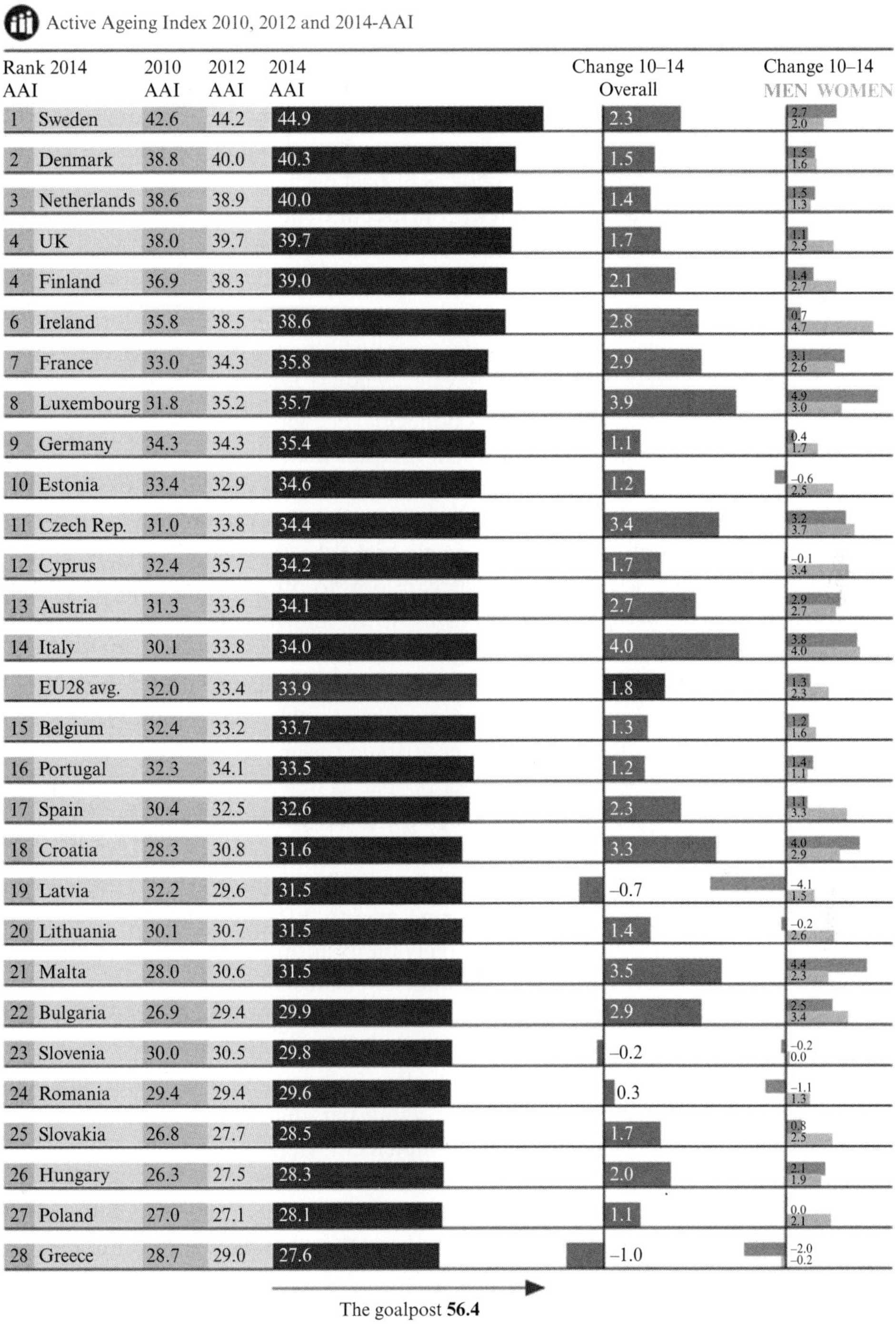

Active Ageing Index 2010, 2012 and 2014-AAI

| Rank 2014 AAI | 2010 AAI | 2012 AAI | 2014 AAI | Change 10–14 Overall | Change 10–14 MEN / WOMEN |
|---|---|---|---|---|---|
| 1 Sweden | 42.6 | 44.2 | 44.9 | 2.3 | 2.7 / 2.0 |
| 2 Denmark | 38.8 | 40.0 | 40.3 | 1.5 | 1.5 / 1.6 |
| 3 Netherlands | 38.6 | 38.9 | 40.0 | 1.4 | 1.5 / 1.3 |
| 4 UK | 38.0 | 39.7 | 39.7 | 1.7 | 1.1 / 2.5 |
| 4 Finland | 36.9 | 38.3 | 39.0 | 2.1 | 1.4 / 2.7 |
| 6 Ireland | 35.8 | 38.5 | 38.6 | 2.8 | 0.7 / 4.7 |
| 7 France | 33.0 | 34.3 | 35.8 | 2.9 | 3.1 / 2.6 |
| 8 Luxembourg | 31.8 | 35.2 | 35.7 | 3.9 | 4.9 / 3.0 |
| 9 Germany | 34.3 | 34.3 | 35.4 | 1.1 | 0.4 / 1.7 |
| 10 Estonia | 33.4 | 32.9 | 34.6 | 1.2 | −0.6 / 2.5 |
| 11 Czech Rep. | 31.0 | 33.8 | 34.4 | 3.4 | 3.2 / 3.7 |
| 12 Cyprus | 32.4 | 35.7 | 34.2 | 1.7 | −0.1 / 3.4 |
| 13 Austria | 31.3 | 33.6 | 34.1 | 2.7 | 2.9 / 2.7 |
| 14 Italy | 30.1 | 33.8 | 34.0 | 4.0 | 3.8 / 4.0 |
| EU28 avg. | 32.0 | 33.4 | 33.9 | 1.8 | 1.3 / 2.3 |
| 15 Belgium | 32.4 | 33.2 | 33.7 | 1.3 | 1.2 / 1.6 |
| 16 Portugal | 32.3 | 34.1 | 33.5 | 1.2 | 1.4 / 1.1 |
| 17 Spain | 30.4 | 32.5 | 32.6 | 2.3 | 1.1 / 3.3 |
| 18 Croatia | 28.3 | 30.8 | 31.6 | 3.3 | 4.0 / 2.9 |
| 19 Latvia | 32.2 | 29.6 | 31.5 | −0.7 | −4.1 / 1.5 |
| 20 Lithuania | 30.1 | 30.7 | 31.5 | 1.4 | −0.2 / 2.6 |
| 21 Malta | 28.0 | 30.6 | 31.5 | 3.5 | 4.4 / 2.3 |
| 22 Bulgaria | 26.9 | 29.4 | 29.9 | 2.9 | 2.5 / 3.4 |
| 23 Slovenia | 30.0 | 30.5 | 29.8 | −0.2 | −0.2 / 0.0 |
| 24 Romania | 29.4 | 29.4 | 29.6 | 0.3 | −1.1 / 1.3 |
| 25 Slovakia | 26.8 | 27.7 | 28.5 | 1.7 | 0.8 / 2.5 |
| 26 Hungary | 26.3 | 27.5 | 28.3 | 2.0 | 2.1 / 1.9 |
| 27 Poland | 27.0 | 27.1 | 28.1 | 1.1 | 0.0 / 2.1 |
| 28 Greece | 28.7 | 29.0 | 27.6 | −1.0 | −2.0 / −0.2 |

The goalpost **56.4**

**Figure 32.4.** *Changes in the overall AAI, between 2010, 2012, and 2014*

women also showed improvement, although still with a significant gender gap in almost all countries.

Overall, it is safe to say that some progress has been made with regard to active aging in EU countries over this period. It is unclear though how much of this progress is attributable to policy changes, how much is the result of cohort effects (which may reflect policy choices of past decades), and how much is simply the result of data inconsistencies. Further in-depth analysis may be required to draw further policy insights from these results.

## Synthesizing Discussion

The AAI framework offers policymakers with evidence in key areas of active and healthy aging to enable them to assess their country's relative position as of 2012. Each country's position highlights where policy areas for older people are already effective and where they need further development.

Comparisons with other countries help highlight, for each country, where the biggest potentials lie and where they can look to others' achievements in policy design. These comparisons and assessments inform policymakers and allow them to set targets and monitor progress toward them.

Most importantly, active aging strategies move policy thinking away from a one-sided concern about affordability – where older people are viewed as a burden. Data presented in the AAI contribute toward raising awareness of the challenges and opportunities for older people, as well as to seek ways to develop their full potential, not just to enhance their own well-being, but also to enhance the prosperity of societies in which they live.

Many aspects of active aging are influenced by policies at the regional and local level. The effectiveness of the AAI as a tool for fostering better policies for active aging therefore depends largely on its adoption by local and regional policymakers and stakeholders. An important next step is to use the AAI framework for comparing individual regions within countries (as in Poland, Spain, and Italy).

A final point to make concerns the often-expressed idea that adopting and implementing a comprehensive active aging paradigm will be expensive, and too expensive for poorer countries to implement. In fact, this is not the case, as people making these remarks rarely do the math correctly. Active aging strategies based on social investment principles prevent the loss of valuable expertise, preserve the potential of older people, and strengthen society's human and structural resilience. The cost for managing aging actively is much cheaper than the passive management of older people left marginalized and fully dependent on the state and family.

# Appendix A

Appendix 32.A1 *Domain specific scores by educational attainment in 28 EU Member States*

| Nr. | Country | Employment | | | Participation | | | Independent living | | |
|---|---|---|---|---|---|---|---|---|---|---|
| | | Low | Secondary | Tertiary | Low | Secondary | Tertiary | Low | Secondary | Tertiary |
| 1 | Belgium | 18.4 | 29.7 | 39.6 | 12.3 | 20.9 | 30.7 | 76.4 | 82.1 | 83.3 |
| 2 | Bulgaria | 21.4 | 33.4 | 45.0 | 5.1 | 16.0 | 19.9 | 59.9 | 62.3 | 67.0 |
| 3 | Czech Republic | 18.7 | 35.4 | 57.9 | 18.8 | 21.0 | 22.5 | 75.7 | 77.6 | 82.7 |
| 4 | Denmark | 34.8 | 47.4 | 55.5 | 17.4 | 20.0 | 27.5 | 82.0 | 85.9 | 87.8 |
| 5 | Germany | 31.8 | 42.5 | 55.6 | 14.4 | 15.7 | 22.7 | 75.5 | 80.3 | 84.6 |
| 6 | Estonia | 29.8 | 45.5 | 62.2 | 5.5 | 17.0 | 19.1 | 70.3 | 72.9 | 75.5 |
| 7 | Ireland | 30.3 | 42.7 | 46.3 | 21.7 | 29.1 | 30.7 | 80.3 | 83.4 | 85.6 |
| 8 | Greece | 25.0 | 22.4 | 37.3 | 13.8 | 18.9 | 22.2 | 67.8 | 68.5 | 76.6 |
| 9 | Spain | 24.8 | 36.0 | 47.1 | 18.0 | 22.0 | 25.3 | 73.2 | 77.2 | 79.1 |
| 10 | France | 26.4 | 31.0 | 43.6 | 16.4 | 27.1 | 32.9 | 79.6 | 83.1 | 85.5 |
| 11 | Italy | 21.7 | 35.7 | 53.1 | 18.5 | 25.4 | 26.5 | 72.8 | 77.4 | 77.7 |
| 12 | Cyprus | 33.5 | 37.6 | 48.8 | 15.2 | 21.3 | 21.3 | 73.0 | 77.1 | 77.5 |
| 13 | Latvia | 25.7 | 37.2 | 58.8 | 0.0 | 16.7 | 26.2 | 59.9 | 62.2 | 69.2 |
| 14 | Lithuania | 0.0 | 35.6 | 57.7 | 7.6 | 19.3 | 25.6 | 68.6 | 72.4 | 74.3 |
| 15 | Luxembourg | 18.6 | 23.3 | 46.5 | 16.2 | 25.7 | 27.8 | 78.6 | 83.0 | 86.2 |
| 16 | Hungary | 13.7 | 25.9 | 40.1 | 13.2 | 17.4 | 21.7 | 70.8 | 74.7 | 80.1 |

*(cont.)*

Appendix 32.A1 (*cont.*)

| Nr. | Country | Employment | | | Participation | | | Independent living | | |
|---|---|---|---|---|---|---|---|---|---|---|
| | | Low | Secondary | Tertiary | Low | Secondary | Tertiary | Low | Secondary | Tertiary |
| 17 | Malta | 21.8 | 29.2 | 49.5 | 15.7 | 21.0 | 19.3 | 77.1 | 79.5 | 77.8 |
| 18 | Netherlands | 34.7 | 43.8 | 55.4 | 15.7 | 23.7 | 28.6 | 84.9 | 86.3 | 88.5 |
| 19 | Austria | 22.3 | 30.0 | 48.5 | 10.5 | 21.6 | 30.6 | 74.1 | 83.9 | 85.4 |
| 20 | Poland | 18.8 | 27.0 | 48.7 | 11.0 | 16.5 | 23.9 | 67.1 | 72.2 | 77.4 |
| 21 | Portugal | 36.9 | 32.0 | 44.5 | 15.9 | 19.9 | 23.0 | 72.3 | 80.9 | 79.4 |
| 22 | Romania | 37.7 | 28.0 | 36.7 | 10.2 | 17.7 | 20.0 | 63.7 | 68.3 | 75.4 |
| 23 | Slovenia | 19.7 | 20.7 | 37.7 | 5.3 | 17.7 | 25.2 | 73.0 | 77.5 | 81.2 |
| 24 | Slovakia | 13.7 | 28.4 | 46.0 | 13.2 | 16.7 | 18.6 | 72.2 | 78.4 | 83.6 |
| 25 | Finland | 33.9 | 42.6 | 52.4 | 10.0 | 23.7 | 30.3 | 83.2 | 85.8 | 90.4 |
| 26 | Sweden | 46.1 | 55.8 | 63.7 | 14.9 | 23.2 | 29.5 | 82.8 | 84.7 | 88.3 |
| 27 | United Kingdom | 34.1 | 49.3 | 51.0 | 18.6 | 21.6 | 29.0 | 77.9 | 81.8 | 85.1 |
| 28 | Croatia | 20.7 | 24.2 | 44.3 | 15.7 | 21.5 | 24.9 | 69.9 | 78.5 | 80.8 |

## References

Council of the European Union. (2012) Council Declaration on the European Year for Active Ageing and Solidarity between Generations: The Way Forward, 17468/12, SOC 992, SAN 322. http://europa.eu/ey2012/BlobServlet?docId= 9231&langId=en.

Hofäcker, D., Naumann, E. (2015). The emerging trend of work beyond retirement age in Germany. *Zeitschrift für Gerontologie and Geriatrie*, 48(5), 1–7.

Lindemann, K., Unt, M. (2016). Trapped in "involuntary" work in the late career? Retirement expectations versus "desire to retire" in Estonia. *Studies of Transition States and Societies*, 8(2), 60–77.

Riley, M. W., Riley, J. W., Jr. (1994). Structural lag: Past and future. In M. W. Riley, R. L. Kahn, & A. Foner (Eds.), *Age and structural lag: Society's failure to provide meaningful opportunities in work, family and leisure* (pp. 15–36). New York: Wiley.

Rowe, J. W., Kahn, R. L. (1987). Human aging: usual and successful. *Science*, 237(4811), 143–9.

   (1997). Successful aging. *The Gerontologist*, 37(4), 433–40. DOI: 10.1093/ geront/37.4.433.

   (2015). Editorial: successful aging 2.0: conceptual expansions for the twenty-first century. *The Gerontologist*, 55, 1–4.

Walker, A. (2002). A strategy for active ageing. *International Social Security Review*, 55(1), 121–40

Walker, A. (2009). The emergence of active ageing in Europe. *Journal of Ageing and Social Policy*, 21(1), 75–93.

Walker, A., Zaidi, A. (2016). New evidence on active ageing in Europe. *Intereconomics*, May, 51(3), 139–44.

World Health Organization (WHO). (2002). *Active aging. Geneva: A Policy Framework*. World Health Organization.

Zaidi, A., Stanton, D. (2015). Active ageing index 2014: analytical report, report produced at the Centre for Research on ageing, University of Southampton, under contract with UNECE (Geneva), co-funded by European Commission, Brussels. www .southampton.ac.uk/assets/sharepoint/groupsite/Administration/SitePublisher-document-store/Documents/aai_report.pdf.

Zaidi, A., Gasior, K., Hofmarcher, M. M., et al. (2013) Active Ageing Index 2012. Concept, Methodology, and Final Results, Research Memorandum, Methodology Report, European Centre Vienna. www.euro.centre.org/data/ aai/1253897823_70974.pdf

Zaidi, A., Gasior, K., Zólyomi, E., et al. (2017). Measuring active and healthy ageing in Europe. *Journal of European Social Policy*. 27(2), 138–57. DOI: 10.1177/0958928716676550

# 33 Aging and Capabilities

Catherine Le Galès

## Introduction

From the beginning of the twentieth century, and largely encouraged by medical discourse, the prevailing perception of aging was one of loss (Bourdelais, 1993). This loss, or more precisely, these losses, are described as affecting – with varying rhythms and intensities, synergistically or in complementary fashion – aging people's abilities, performance, physical and cognitive functioning, and social relationships and participation. The development of gerontology as a multidisciplinary field of study and the establishment of geriatrics as a medical specialty opened up a new era several decades later (Ballenger, 2006). Geriatricians and social gerontologists suggested a more optimistic image of aging, especially work by Havighurst (1961) and the Rowe–Kahn model of successful aging (Rowe & Kahn, 1987), which rejects the paradigm of the deterioration of life with aging. In this approach, two trajectories of aging are possible, one of which is called *successful aging*. In addition, the model encourages redirecting attention – up to now almost exclusively focused on loss – toward the prevention of illnesses and deficiencies, the maintenance of good physical and mental functioning as well as social commitment.

Today, hundreds of articles suggest applications or variations of the original model. Successful aging is regularly the subject of special issues of major gerontology journals (such as the special issue of *The Gerontologist* in 2015). However, numerous criticisms have also been directed at the model (for a recent overview see Martinson & Berridge, 2015). Among these, a first subgroup underlines the incompleteness of the model, whereas a second body of criticism accuses the successful aging model of being overly reductionist, because it implies a binary concept of aging – *successful or usual* (Tesch-Römer & Wahl, 2017), or of being too individualistic, because the path of successful aging depends essentially on the responsibility of the individual (Katz & Calasanti, 2014).

The general objective of this chapter is to show how the capability approach can provide answers to some of these criticisms. Initially developed by the economist Amartya Sen (Sen, 1985, 1999a, 2009) – who is one of its most influential authors, along with the philosopher Martha Nussbaum (Nussbaum & Sen, 1993; Nussbaum, 2000, 2011) – the capability approach is a general method of evaluation and comparison of people's situations. We wish to show that the capability approach provides a theoretical and methodological framework for evaluating successful aging that enables developing the multidimensionality of the concept. This makes it possible to go beyond the dichotomization (*successful/usual aging*) of trajectories of aging used in the initial model, to identify the determinants of these trajectories, to evaluate courses of action taken, and to guide policy decisions. The capability approach thus offers a framework that transcends the reductionism and individualism criticized in the Rowe and Kahn (1987) model.

In the first section, this chapter briefly describes the concept of successful aging and summarizes criticisms made of it. In the next section, the capability approach is introduced. The importance of this approach is then illustrated using several examples of published or on-going research on (successful) aging. The first example shows how the capability approach can help develop a methodological framework that enriches the definition and the operational implementation of the successful aging model, while remaining within the spirit of the initial model. The examples that follow illustrate the advantage of using the capability approach as a theoretical framework.

## The Model of Successful Aging

### Presentation of the Model

The model published by Rowe and Kahn (1987) is commonly accepted as the first model of successful aging even though work by Havighurst (1961) came out prior to their publication. It was in their 1987 article that the distinction between an ordinary trajectory of aging and a trajectory of successful aging was first made. This model was the product of multidisciplinary work, the objective of which was to build the foundations of a new gerontology. One of its especially appealing aspects is its positive portrayal of the process of aging, which constitutes a clear break with the dominant paradigm of loss (Katz & Calasanti, 2014).

In a first version, successful aging was the absence or avoidance of illness, but it was rapidly expanded and now includes three elements: a high level of physical and cognitive functioning, a low risk of illness, and the maintenance of social participation. The model can be used as a classifying tool for distinguishing among elderly persons, for identifying persons likely to follow a more favorable aging trajectory and interventions liable to facilitate this, or even more recently, for reflecting on the characteristics of a successfully aging society (Rowe & Kahn, 2015).

### Critical Analysis

However, the model is also subject to criticism. A comprehensive analysis of these criticisms was published by Martinson and Berridge (2015) and shows that most attempt to improve the model whereas, less frequently, others question its pertinence or its theoretical foundations.

In the first group of criticisms, the most frequent one is that the model includes only a limited number of dimensions (3) for describing the aging process; in addition, for each one dimension, there are many indicators that may be used for empirical evaluation. From an operational perspective, the incomplete specification of the model leads to heterogeneous empirical research, and results are thus impossible to compare. This is well illustrated in a recent review by Cosco et al. (2014), who list more than 100 published operational definitions of the Rowe and Kahn (1987) model, many of which suggest retaining other dimensions in addition to those of the initial model. Nearly all the definitions listed included physiological components (i.e., physical or cognitive functions, health status, presence of illnesses or disease), and close to half had factors related to social participation (i.e., active life, involvement in voluntary work) and life satisfaction. Slightly more than a quarter also included psychological behaviors and attitudes such as resilience, coping, independence, and autonomy. A small number of operational definitions of successful aging also included environment, finances, etc. The automatic result of this is that, depending on the definition used, the prevalence of persons whose aging is considered as successful is extremely variable, from a few percent to nearly the entire population studied.

Another very frequent criticism is that the subjective representations of aging persons are not taken into account; in other words, what does successful aging mean from the perspective of those directly involved? Qualitative research on these representations shows much richer concepts of aging than those found in the model, which is seen as highly biomedical (Cosco et al., 2013). Among the elements highlighted in this research are those of commitment, well-being, and/or behavioral attitudes already found in several operational definitions. However, a great many people interviewed emphasized the importance of the environment – financial, relational, or residential – something rarely taken into consideration in operational definitions of the model. These results help explain why there is always a certain discrepancy between the subjective evaluation of successful aging and its evaluation using objective indicators for the same group of people.

The model of successful aging has also been the focus of more fundamental criticisms for being based on a dichotomous vision – usual versus successful – which is too reductionist of the diversity of observed aging trajectories. This dichotomy favors the hypothesis of a compression of morbidity on a population level according to which the increase in life expectancy is in the form of years of life in good health and not in a state of disability (Tesch-Römer & Wahl, 2017). However, comparative demographic research shows that an increase in life expectancy is in fact associated with an increase in the number of years with disability, even if this increase is very different depending on people's characteristics (in terms of deficits, age, gender) and their economic, social, and political environment (Cambois & Robine, 2017). Thus, the number of years that older people live with limitations in their daily activities – and therefore in various situations of aging with equally variable care needs – increases, as do the number of persons affected. Whereas, by definition, these people are excluded from a trajectory of successful aging, though this fact does not prevent many of them from aging well.

The model of successful aging is also criticized for promoting an individualistic concept of life trajectories and placing responsibility for successful aging solely on individuals: "To succeed means having desired it, planned it, worked for it" (Rowe & Kahn, 1998; Katz & Calasanti, 2014). But individuals' lives are the products of differential opportunities, of structural environmental factors of an economic, social, and political nature, and of social inequalities in a society afflicted by ageism (Calasanti, 2015). In the field of health, this assessment has led to the development and adoption, both scientific and political, of the model of the social determinants of health (World Health Organization, 2014), but this approach is not integrated into the model of successful aging.

While successful aging thus enables taking distance from the paradigm of aging as irremediable loss, critical work on it suggests considering aging – and therefore ultimately human life – as multidimensional and adaptable, but never as capital lost in advance whose value would be (collectively) negligible (Butler, 2012).

## The Capability Approach

The capability approach[1] was developed to assess physical, social, or economic disadvantages that affect some people (Robeyns, 2006), to understand conditions that bring about these disadvantages, and in the case of those considered unjust, look for ways to correct and even prevent them, with the goal of making society less unjust (Sen, 2009).

### Agency and the Diversity of Human Beings

Sen's perspective promotes a moral view of human motivation, that of living a satisfying human life, of acceding to a life course to which we attach value, that we consider is in keeping with our wishes, and more broadly, with our values. This concept is expressed by the notion of the agency of the person. Agency includes all the goals individuals set for themselves, taking into account general conditions of a political, economic, or social nature that may limit and influence them. One of the goals may concern the individuals' well-being, but nothing requires this to be the only one. Agency can also include general values and

---

1 This presentation is based on other presentations of the capability approach by the author, especially Le Galès et al. (2015). *Alzheimer : Préserver ce qui importe. Les capabilités dans l'accompagnement à domicile de la maladie d'Alzheimer*. Rennes, France, Presses Universitaires de Rennes, Le Galès, C. and M. Bungener (2016). "The family accompaniment of persons with dementia seen through the lens of the capability approach." *Dementia* **7**: 1471301216657476, Le Galès, C., and M. Bungener (2017). "Poursuivre, avec une maladie d'Alzheimer, une vie qui a de la valeur : la valeur de la vie dans l'approche par les capabilités." *Revue française d'Ethique Appliquée* **3**(1): 43–56.

objectives, including sympathy, commitment, or respect for existing social or ethical norms (rules of conduct) (Sen 1999b).

A central element in the capability approach is recognizing the diversity of human beings as agents who think and act, the plurality of their values, and thus their aspirations and reasons for acting, and ultimately, their social identities (Sen, 2004). Therefore, along with agency, the approach asserts that the diversity of people is a central characteristic of life situations to be evaluated.

## Capabilities and Functionings

Sen proposes to evaluate real situations and the freedoms individuals have to choose between various ways of living to which they attach value, in other words, their functionings and their capabilities.

While capabilities are the possibilities of functionings that people value and *can* achieve, whether they choose to do so or not, functionings are the valued things and states that individuals "do" or "are." Functionings describe achievements or accomplishments in various dimensions of life, whereas capabilities express individuals' freedom to choose between different functionings, and ultimately, between different valued life courses. Functionings can also be described as valued comprehensive outcomes "that include the actions undertaken, the identities of those involved, the procedures put in place, etc." (Sen, 2009), which result from a choice based on sustainable reasons, or reasons "that we can reflectively sustain if we subject them to critical scrutiny" (Sen, 2009). It is not necessary that this reasoning always be explicit and carried out beforehand. There can be sound reasoning even when explicit procedures are not always followed. However, the capability approach does not assert that individuals invariably have sufficient reasons for acting.

## Resources and Conversion

Unlike other methods of economic evaluation, rights and the human, material, and financial resources available to each person are not at the heart of the evaluation, but the capability approach acknowledges they shape people's lives. However, evaluating a person's formal rights and resources does not enable gaining an accurate description of his or her freedoms. The example usually given for illustrating the importance of not concentrating evaluation solely on people's resources is that of the bicycle. To own a bicycle provides no information on the quality of the person's life, if road infrastructure and social norms prevent a person from using it, or if the person lacks a sense of balance. In other words, it is not enough that rights or resources be available to people in order for them to be able to transform them into opportunities or freedoms. The concept of conversion refers back to the operation of transforming resources and rights into capabilities or freedoms, and enables the evaluation to take into account that the possibilities of effectively converting these means into a valued life course vary according to individuals.

Four categories of factors are at the origins of the observed variations:

- Personal differences: characteristics of individuals, linked to age, sex, illnesses, and deficits that
- greatly diversify their capacities and needs;
- The physical environment;
- The variety of social and political conditions, and relationships; and
- The behavioral norms of a society.

The following diagram (Figure 33.1) – progressively developed by Ingrid Robeyns, reworked by Nicolas Farvaque (Farvaque, 2005; Robeyns, 2005a), and modified by us – gives a global presentation of the key ideas in the capability approach and the relationships (of conversion and choice) that exist between resources, capabilities, and functionings.

## List of Dimensions

The capability approach retains a multidimensional concept of "the good life." For Sen, the identification of these dimensions is part of the evaluation (Sen, 2009), unless the list of pertinent dimensions already garners sufficient consensus. If this is not the case, the identification of the dimensions is the first step of the evaluation in order to be aware of the context, the group of people involved, and the type of evaluation performed (Robeyns, 2005b). However, Sen's position is not shared by all. In contrast, Nussbaum makes a case for a fixed list grounded in an argument for the existence of universal human values (Nussbaum, 2000, 2011). This list is a subject of contention in the capabilities literature.

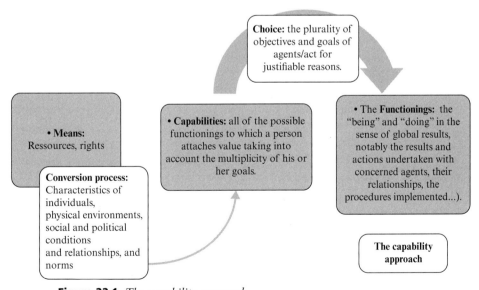

**Figure 33.1.** *The capability approach*

## Adaptation

Regardless of the position taken on the list of dimensions, universal or ad hoc, in the end, the definition of what constitutes a good life is neither unchanging over time nor unaffected by negotiations among its different dimensions. For example, the approach argues that a person may prefer a life limited along certain dimensions rather than along others, but provided that it is the result of his or her choice among different possibilities. This is an important point for taking into account a potential phenomenon of adaptation.

This refers back to the fact that the evaluation a person makes of his or her situation and possibilities for change is influenced by past experience (like the fox faced with the inaccessible grapes in the fable by La Fontaine), as well as the social, political, and relational context. Adaptation can lead disadvantaged persons to accept chronic privation, and thus, to no longer pay attention to it; but in so doing, it creates a distortion in the hierarchy of their goals and opportunities. By focusing evaluation on capabilities and functionings, the approach draws attention to two distinct aspects of freedom: that which is offered by what is possible (freedom of opportunity) and that which is linked to the very process of choosing itself.

## Individual Responsibility and Collective Responsibility

The capability approach may be understood as embracing ethical individualism, in the sense that the approach considers that what is important in the end is people's agency (Robeyns, 2005a). Functionings and capabilities are attributes of individuals. However, by expressing concern for the opportunities available to people to live the kind of life to which they attach value, Sen gives a role to social, cultural, political, and economic influences in defining what is recognized as having value. He gives importance to the diversity of behaviors and incorporates social interactions, as well as social, economic, political, and cultural conditions, in the creation of those life possibilities.

For Sen, public action is essential for increasing people's freedoms and in enabling people to exercise their choice among several possibilities to which they attach importance. Even so, the objective of public action is not so that everyone must have the same set of freedoms in all areas of their life. But comparing people in terms of both capabilities and functionings leads to identifying those whose situation is more disadvantaged than that of others (the evaluation is based on an indicator that combines all the dimensions) or who are more disadvantaged in one or several specific areas. Correcting these disadvantages may be the responsibility of the individual but is also a collective responsibility to act in favor of disadvantaged persons. It is this objective of reducing inequalities that should guide the identification of public interventions, as well as the evaluation of their efficacy.

## The Capability Approach in Practice: The Case of Aging

The capability approach is a theoretical framework that offers an extensive definition of quality of life in terms of opportunities and choices that people have available in order to lead valued lives. It proposes a major transformation in the evaluation of quality of life, compared with evaluation methods interested solely in people's resources and means.

Initially viewed as an approach to poverty, and therefore to economically less developed countries, the areas of application of the capability approach became rapidly diversified. Much empirical research based on the capability approach has since been published in several fields (see https://hd-ca.org/publication-and-resources/ca-bibliograhy for a comprehensive listing). The capability approach is now giving rise to renewed reflection in areas related to aging. Several projects show how the capability approach renews the way health is conceptualized (Anand et al., 2004; Anand & Dolan, 2005; Ruger, 2006; Venkatapuram, 2011; Burchardt & Vizard, 2014), by ensuring a much more extensive evaluation of the quality of life than the psychometric scales that measure health-related quality of life. The field of disability is another area where empirical and theoretical work based on the capability approach is rapidly developing (Zaidi & Burchardt, 2003; Kuklys & Robeyns, 2004; Kuklys, 2005; Mitra, 2006; Trani et al., 2011; Mitra, 2014, 2018).

Capability indices for assessing the well-being of older people (ICECAP-O) have been developed by the ICECAP group (Coast et al., 2008; Flynn et al., 2011). The ICECAP-O has been used to investigate the quality of life of nursing home residents with dementia (Makai et al., 2012, 2014) and that of their caregivers (Jones et al., 2014). The perspective of the capability approach is also at the center of ASCOT – an equivalent to the quality-adjusted life years measure (QALY) for social care interventions (Netten et al., 2012). In the United Kingdom, public decision-makers decided that ASCOT instruments may be used as measures of social care quality of life and ICECAP instruments may be used to measure capability (www.nice.org.uk/process/pmg10/chapter/incorporating-economic-evaluation).

More recently, Le Galès and colleagues (Le Galès et al., 2015; Le Galès & Bungener, 2016) used the capability approach – in a methodology combining quantitative and qualitative procedures – to analyze the family accompaniment of persons with dementia.

More specifically, Olivera and Tournier (2016) used the capability approach to strengthen the operational implementation of the Successful aging model. Other authors (Tellez et al., 2016; Mitra et al., 2017) illustrate how the capability approach can define successful aging in terms of capabilities and identify groups of persons with different aging circumstances and the factors that influence them, especially those factors that may be modified by individual or collective action.

## The Capability Approach: A Methodological Framework for Taking into Account the Diversity of the Situations of Aging

In their review of the literature, Deep and Jeste (2006) concluded that the most significant predictors of successful aging were age, income, educational level, gender, the level of cognitive and physical performance, lifestyle (e.g., tobacco and alcohol use, physical activity), and the perceived state of health. This review also emphasized that most research on measuring successful aging and its determinants has been done on populations of elderly individuals living in industrialized countries. The article by Olivera and Tournier (2016) contributes to compensating for this deficit, since it is especially concerned with elderly and poor individuals living in a developing country, i.e., Peru. Its objective was also to develop a methodology that goes beyond the dichotomous approach of successful aging by suggesting more flexible rules for categorizing certain groups within the elderly population.

To reach this dual objective, the authors combined the model of successful aging with the multidimensional approach to poverty and well-being developed by Alkire and Foster (2011) in reference to the capability approach. The data used were those from a study carried out in 2012 on socioeconomic conditions, subjective well-being, expectations, beliefs, and several self-reported subjective and objective health measures in a large sample (4,151) of people 65 to 85 years old living in Peru in households considered as poor by Peruvian public authorities.

Successful aging was defined according to five dimensions: physical health, limitations in daily activities, cognition, emotional health, and life satisfaction. For each dimension, 1 to 4 indicators were recorded. Following Alkire and Foster (2011), different rules of classification were constructed using scores defined for each indicator and each dimension, considering each indicator as a functioning. Once a so-called success threshold had been chosen for each indicator, a binary score was attributed to each respondent depending on whether or not his or her functioning was above this threshold. An aggregate score was then constructed for each of the five dimensions, and finally all dimensions were combined. For a more in-depth description of the method, its use, and contribution, see for example Alkire and Foster (2011) and Alkire et al. (2015). This practical methodology thus enables the construction of different classification rules by varying the thresholds, the functionings, and the dimensions used. For each classification rule, at the aggregate level, by dimension or by indicator, a distribution for the study population was calculated. It makes it possible to identify the functionings and/or the dimensions that are the most discriminating, and to study the effect of the choice of thresholds on the segment of the population considered as having/not having successful aging.

The second methodological aspect borrowed from Alkire and Foster (2011a) concerns the choice and the mode of analysis of the determinants of the successful aging score. For each rule of classification, several predictive variables were tested, and the strength of their relationship with the score was estimated. There are three types of predictive variables: (1) socio-demographic (e.g., gender, age, marital status, education, working status, retiree condition, health insurance, total annual household income, household size, ethnicity, area of living, and food insecurity index), (2) physical (e.g., anemia, nutritional status, type of physical disability, past or present smoking behavior, and present habitual alcohol consumption), and (3) psychological (e.g., empowerment, self-esteem, cognitive-related disabilities, and social support network size). Finally, unobservable characteristics at the local level, such as labor market conditions, community deprivation of health and basic services, healthy environments – the economic environment broadly speaking – are accounted for by the area of residence. Here we find the four categories of factors at the origin of the heterogeneity in the conversion of resources into capabilities, and ultimately into functionings. The authors thus estimated the relationship between the means available to people and their functionings, in a way aggregating the processes of conversion and choice into a single process.

Unsurprisingly, the empirical results showed that the sensitivity of the prevalence of successful aging depends on what classification rule is adopted: this is less than 15 percent of the population surveyed if only those considered to have successful aging are those judged successful on all indicators, in conformity with the approach of Rowe and Kahn (1987). But as pointed out by Olivera and Tournier (2016), "in our counting approach we do not simply intend to establish these two groups. Instead, we look at the variance in the contribution of each indicator. For example, 18 percent of the sample satisfied a maximum of three indicators with success, and 29.2 percent satisfied eight or nine indicators." While several predictive variables are common to other studies (e.g., work, education, higher food security, male, younger and lack of health insurance registration) as Depp and Jeste (2006) surmise, "results (also) account for the concentration of some individuals in specific, more economically deprived, geographical areas and the importance of dealing with unobservable factors at the community level." Olivera and Tournier (2016) thus emphasize the importance of not considering successful aging as an outcome that depends solely on the responsibility of the individuals. Finally, these results have policy implications. Depending on the rule of classification chosen, the number and characteristics of persons liable to be considered as disadvantaged in terms of aging are very different. Once these differences are identified by varying the technical hypotheses used for constructing the rule, the choice of the classification rule is not of a technical nature, but rather a policy choice. It makes it possible to translate into practical terms what is collectively judged to be an unjust level of disadvantage. The second policy implication of these results is that they also enable the identification of the predictive factors on which it is possible to act in order to correct disadvantages considered unjust. In this particular case, nutritional status, food security, and self-esteem should be three areas for priority action so that persons 65–85 years old living in Peru can achieve a valued life course.

## The Capability Approach: A Different Theoretical Framework for Successful Aging

The point of departure of research by Mitra et al. (2017) is the refusal to exclude – as a priori reason – anyone with a disability or an illness from the successful aging trajectory, like the Rowe–Kahn model (Rowe & Kahn, 1987, 2015). Drawing on the human development model of disability developed by

Mitra (2018), the authors not only use the method of Alkire and Foster (2011b) to break with a dichotomous model, as in the preceding example, but also to construct a definition of successful aging based more directly on the capability approach. Successful aging is redefined as well-being, the good life, the life to which one attaches value when aging. Unlike ICECAP whose dimensions were developed following work involving only the elderly (Grewal et al., 2006), the authors prefer to refer to dimensions developed following a broad consultation (Stiglitz et al., 2009).

This theoretical proposal of successful aging based on the capability approach is operationalized using data from an American study, the US Panel Study of Income Dynamics (PSID) 2013 Supplement on Disability and Time Use (DUST), although it only enables documenting five of the eight dimensions of Stiglitz et al. (2009), namely material well-being, health, personal activities, social connectedness, and insecurity. For each dimension, 1 to 4 indicators are defined, or 13 in all. As with Olivera and Tournier (2016), a score of success is defined for each indicator. The five dimensions are equally weighted and when more than one indicator is used within a dimension, indicators are equally weighted within the dimension. An individual is aging successfully if he or she achieves a combination of indicators whose weighted sum equals or exceeds 80 percent. This threshold is varied to assess how the successful aging rate varies as the threshold increases or decreases. However, individuals who are deprived in 20 percent of all dimensions were always excluded from those considered to age successfully.

At the threshold level of 80 percent, 33 percent of adults aged 60 and older in the United States are aging successfully. However, as in the preceding example, the percentage varies considerably according to the indicators and the rate used. If the threshold is 90 percent, the percentage falls from 33 to 11. This percentage of successfully aging people is also lower (between 4 and 18 percent) when it is calculated solely for persons with limitations or health conditions. Thus, persons with limitations or health conditions age well, but there are fewer of them in this situation than the others and, above all, these persons form a homogenous group. Depending on the type of limitation, the percentage of those with successful aging varies significantly.

Data from the PSID also allow an understanding of how means and resources are converted into successful aging by all the people studied and by particular sub-groups, notably those with health conditions or functional limitations. The statistical assessment of the relationship between resources, means, and successful aging also underlines an important diversity in the ability of persons to convert resources and means into successful aging, in relation to their limitations or health conditions. As for Depp and Jeste (2006), being female, Caucasian, married, and years of education are important characteristics for the whole population, but also having the feeling of some level of control over one's life (and thus the feeling of being the agent of one's life, to have freedom of opportunity and choice). On the other hand, the intensity of relationships differs according to the sub-populations of persons with limitations or health conditions, as well as the importance of deleterious situations (e.g., unemployment, poverty, absence of health insurance), which may have left their mark on life courses prior to the study.

Thus, the results of Mitra et al. (2017) confirm that people with a disability or illness can successfully age and that there are no sustainable reasons (in the sense of the capability approach) to exclude them a priori. They also emphasize the need for policy and program interventions in several areas, not only in the area of health, and of programs that, from the outset, recognize people's diversity. Finally, they call for actions that target more than individual prevention; aging is also the product of past events that depend only partly on individual responsibility, and even less on individuals' simply subscribing to a healthy lifestyle.

This is also the conclusion of Tellez et al. (2016) who used the capability approach to assess the capabilities of people over 60 years old living at home in France and compared them to the capabilities of people suffering from dementia. This example thus provides an illustration of work that focuses not just on functionings, as in the two preceding research projects, but on capabilities and notably on the freedoms of opportunities available to people.

The research targeted two specific capabilities: freedom to perform self-care and freedom to participate in household life. The reasons for this choice are manifold. Firstly, personal care and household tasks occupy a predominant place in the evaluation criteria in France for providing public financial assistance to older people, and especially those with dementia. Secondly, while studies have demonstrated that the ability of persons with dementia to perform daily life activities deteriorates differently for different activities, the extent to which this deterioration impacts (health-related) quality of life remains unclear (Giebel et al., 2014, 2015). Finally, freedom to perform self-care and freedom to participate in household life are two capabilities considered significant in other empirical work on health or disability using the capability approach (Trani & Bakhshi, 2008). They can also be considered basic capabilities (Ruger, 2009) since, in their absence, most other capabilities are unattainable.

The empirical work was based on the secondary analysis of the study "Disability and Health Household Survey" (HSM survey) conducted by the French National Institute of Statistics and Economic Studies (INSEE) in 2008 on a representative sample of France's population living at home. The sample consists of 8,841 individuals above 60 years of age.

The authors postulated that freedoms are unobservable (latent) concepts which partially manifest themselves through observed functionings, and that they are influenced by individual and external factors. They therefore used a model "with a latent variable having multiple indicators and causes" (Kuklys, 2005; Di Tommaso, 2007; Krishnakumar & Ballon, 2008; Di Tommaso et al., 2009). Latent variables are representations of concepts that cannot be directly observed but whose manifestations can be observed and quantified, in this case the functionings. In this model, the statistical linking of the latent variables (capabilities) and their measurable manifestations (the functionings), also called the measurement equation, is the choice procedure. This is done at the same time as the structural equation that formalizes the causal relationships between external variables and latent variables. The structural equation thus models the relationship of the conversion of resources and rights available to people into capabilities, taking into account individual and environmental factors.

Results showed that the older people are, the lower their capability levels. A gender effect is found for both capabilities, but to a much lesser degree for self-care. Men have fewer "capabilities" than women when it comes to self-care, but more where participation in household life is concerned. Income level and property tenure have a positive but weak influence. "Having living children" and "living as a couple" are associated with an increase in the capabilities of older persons. The high and significant coefficients of health variables in both structural equations demonstrate the important role limitations – due to health, self-reported health status, and difficulties in learning new things and solving day-to-day problems – play in reducing the freedom to achieve valued functionings.

Results highlighted differences in capabilities depending on whether people can regularly go outside of their homes as well as whether they have easy access to public services and shops. For the first capability, this reflects a positive association between more mobility and higher self-care freedom. Concerning the second, results emphasized the important contribution of the nearby presence of retail stores – and health and public services – in the enhancement of the freedom to perform household tasks. Results also showed that public arrangements and benefits designed for older people who need help in their daily lives seem to reach the target populations.

Dementia has a specific effect on capabilities of persons with dementia. Dementia puts the ill persons at a more serious disadvantage (fewer capabilities) compared to other persons living at home with whom they may share other sources of deprivation such as advanced age, living alone, or poor self-reported health status. However, the analysis also highlights the considerable heterogeneity in the extent of disadvantage that characterizes the lives of persons with dementia. While the majority have fewer freedoms, some could be in a more favorable situation than some without dementia. If these research results are confirmed, this would mean that, for persons with dementia and their family, dementia creates a particular situation of disadvantage compared with those experienced by other elderly persons who are ill, disabled, or losing their autonomy. Thus, it would be inefficient in terms of justice to offer these people programs devised for aging persons in general.

This econometric research shows that resources called upon by people in using capabilities go far beyond just financial resources. As emphasized by Robeyns (2008), the more distant people being evaluated are from the stylized figure of workers in good health, independent, carefree, and who are largely in control of their lives, the more factors beyond income and financial resources take on importance and need to be taken into account to gain a complete understanding of their situation. Of course, material resources are important and have a positive influence on all of their capabilities, but other factors such as the proximity of the family and public, social, and medical services can be at least as important for capabilities, and in the end, people's well-being or agency.

## Conclusion

The empirical use of the capability approach in the field of aging is still rare. The examples given here do not pretend to be an exhaustive list, other publications such as Stephens et al. (2015) and Yeung and Breheny (2016) could also have been reported. The works presented in this chapter were selected to succinctly illustrate what the capability approach can contribute. They show that the approach can provide a methodological framework to enrich the multidimensionality of the concept, go beyond the dichotomy (successful/usual aging) of aging trajectories, identify the determinants of these trajectories, evaluate programs, and guide policies. It can also constitute an appropriate theoretical framework for going beyond the reductionism and individualism criticized in the initial model. It is no doubt important to promote a dialogue that brings together thinking by geriatricians and gerontologists – who care about the good life for aging persons and for their successful aging – as well as practitioners and researchers who use the capability approach in other areas, with the goal of mutual enrichment.

## References

Alkire, S., J. Foster (2011a). "Counting and multidimensional poverty measurement." *Journal of Public Economics*, 95(7): 476–87.

(2011b). "Understandings and misunderstandings of multidimensional poverty measurement." *Journal of Economic Inequality* 9(2): 289–314.

Alkire, S., J. Foster, S. Seth, et al. (2015). *Multidimensional Poverty Measurement and Analysis*. USA: Oxford University Press.

Anand, P., P. Dolan (2005). "Equity, capabilities and health." *Social Science & Medicine* 60(2): 219.

Anand, S., F. Peter, A. K. Sen, Eds. (2004). *Public Health, Ethics, and Equity*. Oxford, New York: Oxford University Press.

Ballenger, J. F. (2006). *Self, Senility, and Alzheimer's Disease in Modern America: A History*. Baltimore, MD: Johns Hopkins University Press.

Bourdelais, P. (1993). *L'âge de la vieillesse*. Paris: Editions Odile Jacob.

Burchardt, T., P. Vizard (2014). Using the capability approach to evaluate health and care for individuals and groups in England. *The Capability Approach*. S. Ibrahim, M. Tiwari, Eds. Palgrave: Macmillan: 148–70.

Butler, J. (2012). Can one lead a good life in a bad life? Adorno Prize Lecture.

Calasanti, T. (2015). "Combating ageism: How successful is successful aging?" *The Gerontologist* 56(6): 1093–101.

Cambois, E., J.-M. Robine (2017). "L'allongement de l'espérance de vie en Europe. Quelles conséquences pour l'état de santé." *Revue européenne des sciences sociales* 55(1): 67.

Coast, J., T. N. Flynn, L. Natarajan, et al. (2008). "Valuing the ICECAP capability index for older people." *Social Science & Medicine* 67(5): 874.

Cosco, T. D., A. M. Prina, J. Perales, et al. (2013). "Lay perspectives of successful ageing: a systematic review and meta-ethnography." *BMJ Open* 3: e002710. doi: 10.1136/bmjopen-2013-002710

Cosco, T. D., A. M. Prina, J. Perales, et al. (2014). "Operational definitions of successful aging: a systematic review." *Int Psychogeriatr* 26(3): 373–81.

Depp, C. A., D. V. Jeste (2006). "Definitions and predictors of successful aging: a comprehensive review of larger quantitative studies." *The American Journal of Geriatric Psychiatry* 14(1): 6–20.

Di Tommaso, M. L. (2007). "Children capabilities: A structural equation model for India." *Journal of Socio-Economics* 36(3): 436–50.

Di Tommaso, M. L., I. Shima, S. Strom et al. (2009). "As bad as it gets: Well-being deprivation of sexually exploited trafficked women." *European Journal of Political Economy* 25(2): 143.

Farvaque, N. (2005). Action publique et approche par les capacités: une analyse des dispositifs et trajectoires d'insertion. Doctorat Sciences Economiques Doctorat en Sciences économiques, Polytechnicum Marne-la-vallée.

Flynn, T. N., P. Chan, J. Coast et al. (2011). "Assessing quality of life among British older people using the ICEPOP CAPability (ICECAP-O) measure." *Applied Health Economics and Health Policy* 9(5): 317–29.

Giebel, C. M., C. Sutcliffe, M. Stolt, et al. (2014). "Deterioration of basic activities of daily living and their impact on quality of life across different cognitive stages of dementia: a European study." *International Psychogeriatrics* 26: 1283–93.

Giebel, C. M., C. Sutcliffe, D. Challis (2015). "Activities of daily living and quality of life across different stages of dementia: a UK study." *Aging Ment Health* 19(1): 63–71.

Grewal, I., J. Lewis, T. Flynn, et al. (2006). "Developing attributes for a generic quality of life measure for older people: Preferences or capabilities?" *Social Science & Medicine* 62(8): 1891.

Havighurst, R. J. (1961). "Successful Aging." *The Gerontologist* 1(1): 8–13.

Jones, C., R. T. Edwards, B. Hounsome (2014). "Qualitative Exploration of the Suitability of Capability Based Instruments to Measure Quality of Life in Family Carers of People with Dementia." *ISRN Family Medicine 2014*: 9.

Katz, S., T. Calasanti (2014). "Critical perspectives on successful aging: Does it "appeal more than it illuminates"?" *The Gerontologist* 55(1): 26–33.

Krishnakumar, J., P. Ballon (2008). "Estimating Basic Capabilities: A Structural Equation Model Applied to Bolivia." *World Development* 36(6): 992–1010.

Kuklys, W. (2005). *Amartya Sen's Capability Approach: Theoretical Insights and Empirical Applications*. Berlin, New York: Springer.

Kuklys, W., I. Robeyns (2004). Sen's Capability Approach to Welfare Economics. CWPE0415, University of Cambridge and Max Planck Institute for Research Into Economic Systems: 42.

Le Galès, C., M. Bungener (2016). "The family accompaniment of persons with dementia seen through the lens of the capability approach." *Dementia* 7: 1471301216657476.

Le Galès, C., M. Bungener, le groupe Capabilités (2015). *Alzheimer : Préserver ce qui importe. Les capabilités dans l'accompagnement à domicile de la maladie d'Alzheimer*. Rennes, France: Presses Universitaires de Rennes.

Makai, P., W. B. Brouwer, M. A. Koopmanschap, et al. (2012). "Capabilities and quality of life in Dutch psycho-geriatric nursing homes: an exploratory study using a proxy version of the ICECAP-O." *Quality of Life Research* 21(5): 801–12.

Makai, P., W. B. Brouwer, M. A. Koopmanschap, et al. (2014). "Quality of life instruments for economic evaluations in health and social care for older people: A systematic review." *Social Science & Medicine* 102: 83–93.

Martinson, M., C. Berridge (2015). "Successful aging and its discontents: A systematic review of the social gerontology literature." *The Gerontologist* 55(1): 58–69.

Mitra, S. (2006). "The capability approach and disability." *Journal of Disability Policy Studies* 16(4): 236–47.

(2014). "Reconciling the capability approach and the ICF: A response." *ALTER - European Journal of Disability Research/Revue Européenne de Recherche sur le Handicap* 8(1): 24–9.

(2018). *Disability, Health and Human Development*. New York: Springer.

Mitra, S., D. Brucker, K. Jajtner (2017). Successful Aging Through a Capability and Human Development Lens Working Paper. Prepared for the Panel Study of Income Dynamics Life Course Conference June 23. New York: Fordham University.

Netten, A., P. Burge, J. Malley, et al. (2012). "Outcomes of social care for adults: developing a preference weighted measure." *Health Technology Assessment* 16(16): 165.

Nussbaum, M. C. (2000). *Women and Human Development. The Capabilities Approach*. Cambridge, MA: Cambridge University Press.

(2011). *Creating Capabilities. The Human Development Approach*. Cambridge, MA and London: Belknap Press of Harvard University Press.

Nussbaum, M. C., A. K. Sen, Eds. (1993). *The Quality of life*. Oxford (England)–New York: Clarendon Press–Oxford University Press.

Olivera, J., I. Tournier (2016). "Successful ageing and multi-dimensional poverty: the case of Peru." *Ageing & Society* 36(8): 1690–714.

Robeyns, I. (2005a). "The Capability Approach: a theoretical survey." *Journal of Human Development* 6(1): 93–114.

Robeyns, I. (2005b). "Selecting Capabilities for Quality of Life Measurement." *Social Indicators Research* 74(1: Special Issue on the Quality of Life and the Capability Approach, edited by Paul Anand): 191–215.

Robeyns, I. (2006). "The Capability Approach in Practice." *Journal of Political Philosophy* 14(3): 351.

(2008). Sen's capability approach and feminist concerns. *The Capability Approach. Concepts, Measures and Applications*. F. Comim, M. Qizilbash, S. Alkire, Eds. Cambridge: Cambridge University Press: 82–104.

Rowe, J., R. Kahn (1998). *Successful Aging*. New York, NY: Pantheon.

Rowe, J. W., R. L. Kahn (1987). "Human aging: usual and successful." *Science* 237(4811): 143–9.

(2015). "Successful aging 2.0: Conceptual expansions for the 21st century." *The Journals of Gerontology: Series B* 70(4): 593–6.

Ruger, J. P. (2006). "Health, capability, and justice: towards a new paradigm of health ethics, policy and law." *Cornell Journal of Law and Public Policy* 15(2): 103–87.

(2009). *Health and Social Justice*. Oxford, UK: Oxford University Press,.

Sen, A. K. (1985). "Well-being, agency and freedom: the Dewey lectures 1984." *The Journal of Philosophy* 82(4): 169–221.

(1999a). *Development as Freedom*. Oxford, UK: Oxford University Press.

(1999b). *Inequalities Reexamined*. Oxford, UK: Oxford University Press.

(2004). "Social identity." *Revue de philosophie économique*(9): 7–27.

(2009). *The Idea of Justice*. London, UK: Allen Lane.

Stephens, C., M. Breheny, J. Mansvelt (2015). "Healthy ageing from the perspective of older people: A capability approach to resilience." *Psychology & Health* 30(6): 715–31.

Stiglitz, J. E., A. K. Sen, J.-P. Fitoussi (2009). Report of the Commission on the Measurement of Economic Performance and Social Progress. www.stiglitz-sen-fitoussi.fr/documents/rapport_anglais.pdf. Original publication: Richesse des nations et bien-être des individus. Rapport de la Commission sur la mesure des performances économiques et du progrès social. Paris: Odile Jacob.

Tellez, J., J. Krishnakumar, M. Bungener et al. (2016). "Capability deprivation of people with Alzheimer's disease: An empirical analysis using a national survey." *Social Science & Medicine* 151: 56–68.

Tesch-Römer, C., H.-W. Wahl (2017). "Toward a More Comprehensive Concept of Successful Aging: Disability and Care Needs." *The Journals of Gerontology: Series B* 72(2): 310–18.

Trani, J.-F., P. Bakhshi (2008). "Challenges for assessing disability prevalence: The case of Afghanistan." *Alter - European Journal of Disability Research/Revue Européenne de Recherche sur le Handicap* 2(1): 44–64.

Trani, J.-F., P. Bakhshi, N. Bellanca, et al. (2011). "Disabilities through the Capability Approach lens: Implications for public policies." *ALTER – European Journal of Disability Research/Revue Européenne de Recherche sur le Handicap* 5(3): 143–57.

Venkatapuram, S. (2011). *Health Justice: An Argument from the Capabilities Approach.* Cambridge: Polity Press.

World Health Organization (2014). *Social Determinants of Mental Health.* Geneva: World Health Organization.

Yeung, P., M. Breheny (2016). "Using the capability approach to understand the determinants of subjective well-being among community-dwelling older people in New Zealand." *Age and Ageing* 45(2): 292–8.

Zaidi, A., T. Burchardt (2003). Comparing incomes when needs differ: Equivalisation for the extra costs of disability in the UK, Centre for Analysis of Social Exclusion, London School of Economics: 3.

# Index

*Note:* Page numbers followed by "f", "t", and "b" refer to figures, tables, and boxes, respectively.